PUBLIC SPEAKING
The Evolving Art

Second Edition

Stephanie J. Coopman
San José State University

James Lull
San José State University (Emeritus)

WADSWORTH
CENGAGE Learning·

Australia · Brazil · Japan · Korea · Mexico · Singapore · Spain · United Kingdom · United States

WADSWORTH
CENGAGE Learning™

Public Speaking: The Evolving Art, Second Edition

Stephanie J. Coopman, James Lull

Senior Publisher: Lyn Uhl

Executive Editor: Monica Eckman

Senior Development Editor: Greer Lleuad

Assistant Editor: Rebekah Matthews

Editorial Assistant: Colin Solan

Media Editor: Jessica Badiner

Marketing Manager: Amy Whitaker

Marketing Coordinator: Gurpreet Saran

Marketing Communications Manager:
Caitlin Green

Senior Content Project Manager:
Michael Lepera

Art Director: Linda Helcher

Senior Print Buyer: Justin Palmeiro

Rights Acquisition Specialist, Image:
Mandy Groszko

Senior Rights Acquisition Specialist, Text:
Katie Huha

Compositor/Production Service:
MPS Limited, a Macmillan Company

Text Designer: Grannan Graphic Design

Cover Designer: Rokusek Design

Cover Image: ©Image Source/Getty Images

For product information and technology assistance, contact us at
Cengage Learning Customer & Sales Support, 1-800-354-9706
For permission to use material from this text or product,
submit all requests online at **www.cengage.com/permissions.**
Further permissions questions can be emailed to
permissionrequest@cengage.com

Library of Congress Control Number: 2010928364

ISBN-13: 978-0-495-90564-6

ISBN-10: 0-495-90564-X

Wadsworth
20 Channel Center Street
Boston, MA 02210
USA

Cengage Learning is a leading provider of customized learning solutions with office locations around the globe, including Singapore, the United Kingdom, Australia, Mexico, Brazil, and Japan. Locate your local office at **international.cengage.com/region**

Cengage Learning products are represented in Canada by Nelson Education, Ltd.

For your course and learning solutions, visit **www.cengage.com**

Purchase any of our products at your local college store or at our preferred online store **www.cengagebrain.com.**

Printed in the United States of America
1 2 3 4 5 6 7 14 13 12 11 10

Brief Contents

Bonus Chapters

Go to page xvii for information about these bonus custom chapters.

Group Speaking
Mediated Public Speaking

Contents

Part II Developing and Researching Your Speech

Bonus Chapters

Go to page xvii for information about these bonus custom chapters.

Group Speaking

Mediated Public Speaking

▶ Watch it Videos and ▶ Use it Activities

Chapter	WATCH It Videos	USE It Activities
1 The Evolving Art of Public Speaking	1.1: Meeting the Speech Buddies	1.1: What Are Your Public Speaking Goals?
2 Building Your Confidence	2.1: Using Strategies for Managing Speech Anxiety 2.2: Taking a Closer Look at Your Public Speaking Anxiety	2.1: Anxiety Management Trainee 2.2: What, Me Worry?
3 Ethical Speaking and Listening	3.1: Avoiding Plagiarism 3.2: Promoting Dialogue in Q&A	3.1: But Is It Plagiarism? 3.2: You Have the Floor
4 Developing Your Purpose and Topic	4.1: Brainstorming for and Evaluating Topics	4.1: Search and Find Missions
5 Adapting to Your Audience	5.1: Analyzing and Using Audience Data	5.1: According to Our Data
6 Researching Your Topic	6.1: Managing the Research Process	6.1: The Research Detective
7 Supporting Your Ideas	7.1: Selecting the Best Supporting Materials 7.2: Evaluating Media Credibility	7.1: Use Your Support System 7.2: Press Pass
8 Organizing and Outlining Your Speech	8.1: Reviewing Patterns of Organization 8.2: Linking Effectively: Transitions	8.1: Everything in Its Place 8.2: Polite to Point
9 Beginning and Ending Your Speech	9.1: Beginning Effectively: Introductions 9.2: Ending Effectively: Conclusions	9.1: Here We Go 9.2: It's a Wrap
10 Using Language Effectively	10.1: Engaging Your Audience with Language 10.2: Making Language Choices	10.1: You're Engaged! 10.2: Wrong Word, Right Word
11 Integrating Presentation Media	11.1: Using Digital Slides 11.2: Integrating Presentation Media	11.1: PowerPoint Makeover 11.2: Exhibit A
12 Delivering Your Speech	12.1: Reviewing Vocal Delivery 12.2: Reviewing Physical Delivery 12.3: Practicing Your Speech	12.1: Speak Up 12.2: Move with Purpose 12.3: Take It from the Top
13 Informative Speaking	13.1: Speaking to Inform	13.1: Pleased to Inform You
14 Persuasive Speaking	14.1: Speaking to Persuade	14.1: Persuasion Equation
15 Understanding Argument	15.1: Identifying the Elements of Argument	15.1: Convince Me
16 Special Occasion and Group Speaking	16.1: Evaluating Group Presentations	16.1: As a Group

Full-length Sample Speeches for *Public Speaking: The Evolving Art*

Student speeches	Speech type	Location in your textbook resources
Speech of self-introduction, Adam Currier	Self-introduction	Interactive Video Activities, Chapter 1
"Study Abroad," Anna Lubowing	Self-introduction	Interactive Video Activities, Chapter 1
"El Equipo Perfecto (The Perfect Team)," Uriel Plascencia, interpreted by Kelly Bilinski	Self-introduction	Interactive Video Activities, Chapter 1
Speech of self-introduction, Jessica Howard	Self-introduction	Interactive Video Activities, Chapter 2
Handed-down story speech, Dory Schaeffer	Self-introduction	Interactive Video Activities, Chapter 6
"Left on a Doorstep," Cara Langus	Self-introduction	Interactive Video Activities, Chapter 8
Speech of self-introduction, Tiffany Brisco	Self-introduction	Interactive Video Activities, Chapter 12
"How to Become a Successful Business Person," Husam Al-Khirbash	Informative	Interactive Video Activities, Chapter 4
"Meat-free and Me," Tiffany Mindt	Informative	Interactive Video Activities, Chapter 4
"Terrestrial Pulmonate Gastropods," Shaura Neil	Informative	Interactive Video Activities, Chapter 6
"Impressionistic Painting," Chris Lucke	Informative	Interactive Video Activities, Chapter 7
text only: "The Colors of the Filipino Flag"	Informative	End of Chapter 8
"Educational Requirements to Become a Pediatrician," Ganiel Singh	Informative	Interactive Video Activities, Chapter 8
"Why Pi?" Katy Mazz	Informative	Interactive Video Activities, Chapter 9
"U.S. Flag Etiquette," Cindy Gardner	Informative	Interactive Video Activities, Chapter 11
"Is That Kosher?" Katherine	Informative	Interactive Video Activities, Chapter 12
"Sikhism," Ramit Kaur	Informative	Interactive Video Activities, Chapter 12, USE It Activity 12.1
"Wrath," David Manson	Informative	Interactive Video Activities, Chapter 12, USE It Activity 12.2
"The Ilogot Headhunters," Carl	Informative	Interactive Video Activities, Chapter 13
"The Universal Language of Techno Music," Tudor Matei, delivered by Speech Buddy Evan	Informative	End of Chapter 13; Interactive Video Activities, Chapter 13, WATCH It Video 13.1A
"The Kodak Camera: Changing the Way We Communicate," Janeece Pourroy, delivered by Speech Buddy Janine	Informative	Interactive Video Activities, Chapter 13, WATCH It Video 13.1A
"Creationism versus the Big Bang Theory," Cara Buckley-Ott	Invitational	Interactive Video Activities, Chapter 3
"Wear a Ribbon," Loren Rozakos	Persuasive	Interactive Video Activities, Chapter 2
"Anatomy of a Hate Crime," Chuck	Persuasive	Interactive Video Activities, Chapter 3
"Drinking," Matthew Naso	Persuasive	Interactive Video Activities, Chapter 5
"Drinking and Driving," Peter Bodrog	Persuasive	Interactive Video Activities, Chapter 7
text only: First-place speech at the 18th Annual Gardere Martin Luther King Jr. Oratory Competition, 2010, Tamia Gaines	Persuasive	End of Chapter 10
"Feeding Wildlife: Don't Do It!" Brandi Lafferty	Persuasive	Interactive Video Activities, Chapter 10

Student speeches	Speech type	Location in your textbook resources
"Domestic Violence," Amanda	Persuasive	Interactive Video Activities, Chapter 11
"11 Lives a Day: Youth Suicide," Chelsey Penoyer	Persuasive	Interactive Video Activities, Chapter 11, USE It Activity 11.1
"American Overconsumption," Janeece Pourroy	Persuasive	Interactive Video Activities, Chapter 12, USE It Activity 12.1
"Fat Discrimination," Carol Godart	Persuasive	Interactive Video Activities, Chapter 14
"DWY (Driving While Yakking): Why the U.S. Needs to Ban Drivers' Use of Cell Phone," Cedrick McBeth, delivered by Speech Buddy Erin	Persuasive	Interactive Video Activities, Chapter 14, WATCH It Video 14.1
text only: "Turn Off Your TV," Lisa Taylor	Persuasive	End of Chapter 14
"Home Schooling: Superiority and Success," Dixie	Persuasive	Interactive Video Activities, Chapter 15
"Home Schooling: Not the Best Choice," Robert	Persuasive	End of Chapter 15; Interactive Video Activities, Chapter 15
"Fallen Soldiers," Stacey Newman	Special occasion	Interactive Video Activities, Chapter 10
"The Dirty Truth about Antibacterial Products," Jennifer, Megan, Stephanie, and Daniel	Group	Interactive Video Activities, Chapter 16

Professional speeches	Speech type	Location in your textbook resources
text only: "The Other E in e-Learning," Marcela Perez de Alonso, Executive Vice President, Human Resources, Hewlett-Packard	Informative	Speech Communication CourseMate for *Public Speaking: The Evolving Art,* Chapter 13, Speeches for Review and Analysis
"A Whisper of AIDS," address at the 1992 Republican National Convention, Mary Fisher, political activist	Persuasive	Interactive Video Activities, Chapter 9
text only (excerpt): "The World's Tipping Point," Bianca Jagger, Council of Europe Goodwill Ambassador	Persuasive	End of Chapter 16
text only: Speech in London's Trafalgar Square for the campaign to end poverty in the developing world, Nelson Mandela, anti-apartheid activist and former President of South Africa	Persuasive	Speech Communication CourseMate for *Public Speaking: The Evolving Art,* Chapter 16, Speeches for Review and Analysis
text only: Opening statement before the U.S. Senate Judiciary Committee during confirmation hearing, Sonia Sotomayor, U.S. Supreme Court Judge	Special occasion	End of Chapter 9
text only: Eulogy for Rosa Parks, Jennifer Granholm, Michigan governor	Special occasion	Speech Communication CourseMate for *Public Speaking: The Evolving Art,* Chapter 16, Speeches for Review and Analysis
text only: Speech to commemorate the groundbreaking of the Dr. Martin Luther King Jr. monument, Barack Obama, then-U.S. Senator	Special occasion	Speech Communication CourseMate for *Public Speaking: The Evolving Art,* Chapter 16, Speeches for Review and Analysis
Dedication address at the opening of National Museum of the American Indian, Lawrence Small, then-Secretary of the Smithsonian Institution	Special occasion	Interactive Video Activities, Chapter 16

Note to Instructors

Although the foundations of effective public speaking have endured since classical times, the internet and other new media have influenced every aspect of public speaking—from the initial stages of topic selection and research to the final stages of practicing and delivering a speech. Consider these current trends:

- Communicators have unprecedented access to information.
- Digitized content is exceptionally easy to appropriate, making the ethics of public speaking increasingly complex.
- Communication technologies—including cell phones, email, instant messaging, video-sharing websites like YouTube, and social networks like Facebook™—make connecting with others, both locally and globally, faster and easier than ever.
- Digital technologies such as podcasting, webcasting, and presentation software give speakers numerous options for delivering speeches.
- The pervasiveness of the media has made communicators more visually oriented and attuned to pop culture.
- Globalism and increased cultural awareness require that communicators consistently demonstrate a high degree of multicultural and intercultural knowledge.
- Audiences have different expectations, often preferring a friendly, conversational delivery style, presentation media, and messages targeted to their interests.

Taking an applied approach, *Public Speaking: The Evolving Art,* Second Edition, and its unique suite of companion resources address the ways in which digital technology, social transitions, and cultural shifts have affected students and the communication discipline. This text offers a unique combination of time-honored, classic public speaking instruction and specific guidelines for effective public communication in today's evolving world.

If you and your students are fully immersed in digital culture, you'll feel right at home with the package's relevance to your course objectives, and your students will appreciate materials that present useful information in formats they're comfortable using. Conversely, if you and your students only dip into digital culture as needed, you'll find the text to be a reliable guide that understands and respects your selectivity. Regardless of where on the digital-immersion spectrum your students fall, *Public Speaking:*

The Evolving Art is committed to enriching their learning experience, helping them maximize their efficiency and effectiveness, and greatly enhancing the quality and impact of their public communication.

Distinctive Features of *Public Speaking: The Evolving Art*

In addition to comprehensive coverage, *Public Speaking: The Evolving Art,* offers several carefully developed features that set it apart from other introductory public speaking texts and help ensure both your and your students' satisfaction.

Flexibility

This text's table of contents appears fairly traditional at first glance. That's not an accident, as the book covers all the topics instructors and students need in an introductory public speaking course, presented in a logical and familiar order. However, each chapter is freestanding so that instructors may use the chapters in whatever order best suits their needs. The text's Enhanced eBook, single eChapters purchasing options for students, and custom publishing solutions offer additional flexibility and online tools available only with *Public Speaking: The Evolving Art.* (Go to pages xiii, xvi, and xvii for descriptions of these options.)

A Proven Learning Sequence

Without compromising its flexibility, *Public Speaking: The Evolving Art* provides a sound pedagogical approach in sync with how today's students learn: **READ It, WATCH It, USE It, REVIEW It.** Each chapter's material, both in the book and online, engages students with a user-friendly text, content-rich videos, companion interactive activities, and an unparalleled array of study and self-assessment resources. Chapter materials are presented within this framework on the first page of every chapter and consistently reinforced throughout. Students can apply the book's approach in the way that works best for them. For example, some may start with the online videos, which pique their interest, and then read the text for expanded content. Others may start an interactive activity and then refer back to the text and video for additional information. Students today expect flexibility, and they get it with *Public Speaking: The Evolving Art.*

Unique Tools Developed to Appeal to Today's Students

Public Speaking: The Evolving Art features a number of tools designed to complement the learning styles and preferences of today's students.

Read it

- **APPLY It boxes.** New to this edition, these boxes encourages students to apply their new public speaking skills in contexts outside the classroom. Go to the "New to This Edition" section for more about these boxes.

- **Speaking of . . . boxes.** These boxes appear in each chapter and present brief discussions of topics relevant but not central to the focus of the chapters. The Speaking of . . . topics can be assigned for in-class discussion or journal assignments, or they can be used simply for enrichment.

Watch it

- **Speech Buddy videos.** Available online around the clock to guide students through the public speaking process, we developed these peer mentor videos to help keep today's students engaged and motivated. The Speech Buddies are a diverse group of four personable undergraduates who have successfully completed the beginning public speaking course: Janine, Anthony, Erin, and Evan. These students appear in brief, easily accessed and close-captioned videos, usually two to three per chapter, to reinforce key concepts covered in the book, model strategies, and introduce video clips from their own and others' speeches. The Speech Buddies bring the text's instruction and examples to life. Featured in WATCH It Speech Buddy Video boxes within each chapter, these videos address the following topics and much more:
  - Using Strategies for Managing Speech Anxiety
  - Selecting the Best Supporting Materials
  - Avoiding Plagiarism
  - Integrating Presentation Media
  - Reviewing Physical Delivery

Use it

- **Interactive activities.** Each Speech Buddy video concludes with a prompt to an interactive activity, which makes assigning the videos easy. Featured in the USE It Activity boxes in the text, the activities may be completed in or outside class, and many of them can be adapted for use as group activities. Here's a sampling:
  - The Research Detective (using research strategies)
  - Everything in Its Place (identifying organizational patterns in speeches)

- PowerPoint Makeover (evaluating digital slides)
- Take It from the Top (practicing your speech)
- Persuasion Equation (analyzing a persuasive speech)

Review it

- **Study and self-assessment resources.** Each chapter concludes with a chapter summary and a Directory of Study and Review Resources, a map of companion resources available online such as self-assessment quizzes, the student workbook, Speech Studio, Speech Builder Express, InfoTrac College Edition, and Audio Study Tools. Also featured are a list of key terms and Critical Challenges: Questions for Reflection and Discussion.

- **Speeches for Review and Analysis.** Sample student and professional speeches at the ends of Chapters 6, 8, 9, 10, 13, 14, 15, and 16 allow students to consider chapter concepts in the context of real speeches. Each speech is accompanied by a brief overview of the speech's context and questions for discussion. Dozens more speeches are featured on the book's online resources—these speeches include informative and persuasive speeches delivered by the Speech Buddies and other students and professionals. A comprehensive list of the full-length informative, persuasive, special occasion, and group speeches that students can access in the book, through the book's online Interactive Video Activities, and through the Speech Communication CourseMate for *Public Speaking: The Evolving Art* is featured on pages x and xi. (Go to page xv for a full description of the Interactive Video Activities and the CourseMate.)

Public Speaking: The Evolving Art **is also available as an Enhanced eBook.** This version of the book is a web-based, multimedia text in which students are able to read the book's content, launch embedded Speech Buddy videos and videos of speeches by students and public figures, link out to websites, complete interactive activities and homework, and submit self-quizzes. Offering ease of use and maximum flexibility and interactivity for students and other users who truly want to create their own learning experience, the Enhanced eBook for *Public Speaking: The Evolving Art* also includes advanced book tools such as an audio glossary, hypertext index, and bookmarking, streamlined note-taking and note-storing, easy highlighting, and faster searching. The note-taking feature allows students to make annotations right on the electronic page. Students get access to the Enhanced eBook with the printed text, or they can just purchase access to the Enhanced eBook stand-alone.

Because public speaking instruction aims to prepare people to willingly and effectively express themselves in any communication context, *Public Speaking: The Evolving Art* was developed to help students gain the practical public speaking skills they need to further shape our society, not just live in it. This text and its companion resources offer today's students a timely means of improving the communication skills essential to productively evolve in their own personal, work, social, and civic worlds.

New to This Edition

- **All-new APPLY It boxes** are introduced and described in Chapter 1, and then featured in each chapter thereafter. These boxes reinforce the book's emphasis on audience-centered speaking, touching on how public speaking can be used in the contexts of community, civility, personal responsibility, service learning, and active learning. Each of the boxes encourages students to apply their new public speaking skills in these contexts so that they recognize the relevance of public speaking in their lives.

- This edition provides an **increased focus on audience-centered speaking,** stressing the importance of relating to and empowering your audience. For example, the book now provides a stronger emphasis on the fact that speakers must concentrate not only on coming up with the "right" message, but also on how their message resonates with audiences.

- **Expanded discussions and explanations of Monroe's motivated sequence** are featured in Chapters 8 (organization and outlining) and 14 (persuasive speaking), showing how this organizational pattern can be applied to both informative and persuasive speaking, and linking it more clearly to audience-centered speaking.

- **Sample speeches are now featured at the ends of select chapters** rather than in an appendix. This edition features **several new student and professional speeches,** including U.S. Supreme Court Justice Sonia Sotomayor's opening statement before the U.S. Senate Judiciary Committee during her confirmation hearing (Chapter 9); fifth-grader Tamia Gaines award-winning speech about Martin Luther King, Jr., (Chapter 10); and college student Tara Flanagan's tribute speech about her grandfather (Chapter 16). Go to the table on page x and xi for a complete list of all the full-length in-text and online speeches that accompany this book.

- Throughout the book, **examples have been updated** to incorporate figures and events that students will recognize and relate to, more examples from historical and contemporary speeches, and more examples about public speaking in particular and communication behavior in general.

- In addition, throughout the book **research has been updated as appropriate and expanded** to focus more on content that reflects communication research.

- **A new "How to Use This Book" section** on page xx provides clearer direction about how to use the book's companion technology and supplements.

- **Chapter 1, "The Evolving Art of Public Speaking,"** has been reorganized and streamlined to provide an even more accessible introduction to the book. In response to reviewer feedback, the discussion of the foundations of public speaking now follows from the introduction of public speaking as an evolving art, the table on the evolving aspects of public speaking has been converted into an engaging narrative, and the discussion of communication models has been streamlined to focus primarily on today's communication environment.

- **Chapter 2, "Building Your Confidence,"** features a new discussion of the sources of public speaking anxiety: temperament (communibiology paradigm) and responses to uncertainty (uncertainty reduction theory). The chapter's discussions of the uncertainties produced in the public speaking context and strategies for building confidence have been refined to complement the new discussion of theory.

- **Chapter 3, "Ethical Speaking and Listening,"** has been heavily revised and expanded, providing a clearer emphasis on the importance of maintaining a communication code of ethics. To help students understand how codes of ethics apply to communication situations, Table 3.1 has been revised to focus solely on public speaking and communication, providing the codes of ethics for the National Communication Association and International Association of Business Communicators. The discussion of plagiarism has been expanded, providing more instruction about what plagiarism is and how to avoid it. This chapter's discussion of ethical listening now features the HURIER listening model, and the discussion of listening effectiveness has been recast to help students better understand the link between listening skills and evaluating a speaker's message.

- In **Chapter 4, "Developing Your Purpose and Topic,"** the discussion of thesis statements has been expanded to clarify the relationship between a thesis statement and a preview statement.

- **Chapter 6, "Researching Your Topic,"** now includes updated search resources, a new table of examples and hints for searching useful online library databases, and a new discussion of real-time web search engines.

- **Chapter 11, "Integrating Presentation Media,"** now features an expanded section of tips for evaluating video clips and showing them during a speech.

- In **Chapter 14, "Persuasive Speaking,"** the definition of persuasion has been expanded to make the distinction between coercion and persuasion. In addition, the discussion of persuading different types of audiences now includes some additional tips for addressing negative and apathetic audiences.

■ **Chapter 16, "Special Occasion and Group Speaking,"** has been expanded to include discussions of additional types of special occasion speeches: speeches of nomination, public testimony, and roasts and toasts.

Companion Resources for Students and Instructors

Accompanying this book is an integrated suite of companion resources to support both you and your students. **Note:** If you want your students to have access to the online resources for *Public Speaking: The Evolving Art*, please be sure to order them for your course—if you do not order them, your students will not have access to them on the first day of class. These resources can be bundled with every new copy of the text or ordered separately. Students whose instructors do not order these resources as a package with the text may purchase them or access to them at **cengagebrain.com.** *Contact your local Wadsworth Cengage Learning sales representative for more details.*

Student Resources

Students have the option of utilizing a rich array of resources to enhance and extend their learning while using *Public Speaking: The Evolving Art.*

■ **Speech Communication CourseMate for *Public Speaking: The Evolving Art.*** This site provides students with easy access to the integrated technology resources that accompany the book. These resources include learning, study, and exam preparation tools such as the interactive eBook, Audio Study Tools, flashcards, chapter notepads, WebLinks, and Critical Challenge questions that support the printed textbook. In addition, CourseMate's Engagement Tracker tracking tools allow you to monitor the progress of the class as a whole or of individual students. Engagement Tracker helps you identify students at risk early in the course, uncover which concepts are most difficult for your class, monitor time on task, and keep your students engaged.

■ **Enhanced eBook.** You'll find a full description of this resource that looks like the book but functions like a website on page xiii.

■ **Interactive Video Activities.** Presented within Wadsworth Cengage Learning's unique interactive user interface, the speech videos help students gain experience evaluating and critiquing introductory, informative, persuasive, and special occasion speeches so that they can more effectively provide feedback to their peers and improve their own speeches and delivery. This highly praised resource includes the following features:

• Transcripts and closed-captioning for all speech videos.

• Complete-sentence outlines, keyword outlines, and note cards for full-length student speech videos so students can recognize the connection between creating an effective speech outline and delivering a speech.

• A "scroll" function that students may choose to turn on or off for full-length speech videos. When the scroll feature is on, synchronized highlighting tracks each speaker's progress through an outline or transcript of the speech as the video of the speaker's delivery plays alongside.

• A "notes" function that lets students insert written comments while watching the video. At a student's command, the program pauses, enters a time-stamp that indicates where the video was paused, and offers students the ability to write their own critiques of the video or choose from a set of pre-written rubrics that teach students how to effectively evaluate speeches.

• Assignable analysis questions with responses written by the text's authors, available when students answer the questions themselves and submit them to their instructor.

■ **Audio Study Tools.** This text's Audio Study Tools provides a fun and easy way for students to download audio files and review chapter content whenever and wherever. For each chapter of the text, students will have access to a chapter review consisting of the learning objectives for the chapter, a brief summary of the main points in the text, audio of a sample student speech, and five to seven critical thinking questions. Students can go to the CourseMate for *Public Speaking: The Evolving Art* to listen to or download the Audio Study Tools.

■ **Student Workbook.** This comprehensive workbook provides tools students can use to review, practice, and develop their communication and public speaking skills, such as chapter goals, chapter outlines, key terms, activities, and self-tests.

■ **Speech Studio™.** With Speech Studio, students can upload video files of practice speeches or final performances, comment on their peer's speeches, and review their grades and instructor feedback. Speech Studio's flexibility lends itself to use in traditional, hybrid, and online courses. It allows instructors to save valuable in-class time by conducting practice sessions and peer review work virtually; combine the ease of a course management tool with a convenient way to capture, grade, and review videos of live, in-class performances; and simulate an in-class experience for online courses.

■ **Speech Builder Express 3.0™.** This interactive web-based tool coaches students through the speech organization and outlining process. By completing interactive sessions, students can prepare and save their outlines, formatted according to the principles presented in the text. Text models of speech elements reinforce students' interactive practice.

- **InfoTrac College Edition with InfoMarks™.** This virtual library's more than 18 million reliable, full-length articles from 5,000 academic and popular periodicals allow students to retrieve results almost instantly. They also have access to InfoMarks—stable URLs that can be linked to articles, journals, and searches to save valuable time when doing research—and to the InfoWrite online resource center, where students can access grammar help, critical-thinking guidelines, guides to writing research papers, and much more.

- **CengageBrain Online Store.** CengageBrain.com is a single destination for more than 15,000 new print textbooks, textbook rentals, eBooks, single eChapters, and print, digital, and audio study tools. CengageBrain.com provides the freedom to purchase Cengage Learning products à-la-carte—exactly what you need, when you need it. Visit **cengagebrain.com** for details.

- *A Guide to the Basic Course for ESL Students.* Written by Esther Yook, Mary Washington College, this guide for non-native speakers includes strategies for accent management and overcoming speech apprehension, in addition to helpful web addresses and answers to frequently asked questions.

Instructor Resources

Instructors who adopt this book may request the following resources to support their teaching.

- **Instructor's Resource Manual.** This useful manual presents its own PREPARE It, TEACH It, ASSESS It, ADAPT It framework to parallel the student text's READ It, WATCH It, USE It, REVIEW It pedagogy. This manual offers guidelines for setting up your course, sample syllabi, chapter-by-chapter outlines of content, suggested topics for lectures and discussion, and a wealth of exercises and assignments for both individuals and groups. It also includes a test bank with questions of diverse types and varying levels of difficulty. The test bank is also available in electronic, highly customizable format within ExamView® on the PowerLecture CD-ROM.

- **Instructor Website.** The password-protected site allows you to view all the assets your students can view, helps you determine what you can assign and encourage your students to use, and includes electronic access to the Instructor's Resource Manual, downloadable versions of the book's Microsoft PowerPoint® presentations, and more. Visit the Instructor Website by accessing **http://login.cengage.com** or by contacting your local sales representative.

- **PowerLecture.** This CD-ROM contains an electronic version of the Instructor's Resource Manual, ExamView computerized testing, and ready-to-use Microsoft PowerPoint presentations. The PowerPoint slides contain text, images, and cued videos of the Speech Buddy and sample speech videos, and they can be used as is or customized to suit your course needs. This all-in-one lecture tool makes it easy for you to assemble, edit, publish, and present custom lectures for your course.

- **Instructor Workbooks:** *Public Speaking: An Online Approach, Public Speaking: A Problem Based Learning Approach,* and *Public Speaking: A Service-Learning Approach for Instructors.* Written by Deanna Sellnow, University of Kentucky, these instructor workbooks include a course-syllabus and icebreakers; public speaking basics such as coping with anxiety, learning cycle and learning styles; outlining; ethics; and informative, persuasive, and ceremonial (special occasion) speeches.

- **Wadsworth Communication Video and DVD Library.** Wadsworth's video and DVD series for Speech Communication includes Student Speeches for Critique and Analysis as well as Communication Scenarios for Critique and Analysis.

- **Videos for Speech Communication 2010: Public Speaking, Human Communication, and Interpersonal Communication.** This DVD provides footage of news stories from BBC and CBS that relate to current topics in communication, such as teamwork and how to interview for jobs, as well as news clips about speaking anxiety and speeches from contemporary public speakers, such as Michelle Obama and Senator Hillary Clinton.

- **ABC News DVD: Speeches by Barack Obama.** This DVD includes nine famous speeches by President Barack Obama, from 2004 to present day, including his speech at the 2004 Democratic National Convention; his 2008 speech on race, "A More Perfect Union"; and his 2009 inaugural address. Speeches are divided into short video segments for easy, time-efficient viewing. This instructor supplement also features critical thinking questions and answers for each speech, designed to spark class discussion.

- *The Teaching Assistant's Guide to the Basic Course.* Written by Katherine G. Hendrix, University of Memphis, this resource was prepared specifically for new instructors. Based on leading communication teacher training programs, this guide discusses some of the general issues that accompany a teaching role and offers specific strategies for managing the first week of classes, leading productive discussions, managing sensitive topics in the classroom, and grading students' written and oral work.

- *Guide to Teaching Public Speaking Online.* Written by Todd Brand of Meridian Community College, this helpful online guide provides instructors who teach public speaking online with tips for establishing "classroom" norms with students, utilizing course management software and other eResources, managing logistics such as delivering and submitting speeches and making up work, discussing how peer feedback is different online, strategies for assessment, and tools such as sample syllabi and critique and evaluation forms tailored to the online course.

- *Service Learning in Communication Studies: A Handbook.* Written by Rick Isaacson and Jeff Saperstein, this is an invaluable resource for students in the basic course that integrates or will soon integrate a service learning component. This handbook provides guidelines for connecting service learning work with classroom concepts and advice for working effectively with agencies and organizations. It also provides model forms and reports and a directory of online resources.

- **CourseCare Training and Support**. Get trained, get connected, and get the support you need for the seamless integration of digital resources into your course. This unparalleled technology service and training program provides robust online resources, peer-to-peer instruction, personalized training, and a customizable program you can count on. Visit **cengage.com/coursecare/** to sign up for online seminars, first days of class services, technical support, or personalized, face-to-face training. Our online and onsite trainings are frequently led by one of our Lead Teachers, faculty members who are experts in using Wadsworth Cengage Learning technology and can provide best practices and teaching tips.

- **Custom Chapters for *Public Speaking: The Evolving Art.*** Customize your chapter coverage with two bonus chapters, Group Speaking and Mediated Public Speaking. You can access these chapters online within the Instructor Website, or you can order print versions of the student text that include the extra chapter of your choice. Contact your local sales representative for ordering details.

- **Flex-Text Customization Program**. With this program you can create a text as unique as your course: quickly, simply, and affordably. As part of our flex-text program, you can add your personal touch to *Public Speaking: The Evolving Art* with a course-specific cover and up to thirty-two pages of your own content—at no additional cost.

These resources are available to qualified adopters, and ordering options for student supplements are flexible. Please consult your local Wadsworth Cengage Learning sales representative for more information, to evaluate examination copies of any of these instructor or student resources, or to request product demonstrations.

Acknowledgments

This project was a team effort, and we appreciate all the work others have contributed to *Public Speaking: The Evolving Art.* Our Wadsworth Cengage Learning team included Lyn Uhl, senior publisher; Monica Eckman, executive editor; Greer Lleuad, senior development editor; Amy Whitaker, senior marketing manager; Rebekah Matthews, assistant editor; Colin Solan, editorial assistant; Jessica Badiner, media editor; Mandy Grozsko and Katie Huha, rights acquisition specialists; Lisa Jelly Smith, photo researcher; Michael Lepera, senior content project manager; Laurene Sorensen, copyeditor; Lindsay Schmonsees, project manager at MPS Content Services; and Linda Helcher, art director.

Many people helped develop the ancillary materials that accompany this text: Kathy Werking, University of Louisville, wrote the Instructors' Resource Manual. Matt McGarrity, University of Washington, created the student workbook. Cameron Basquiat, College of Southern Nevada, wrote the quizzes for the companion website. Lisa Heller Boragine, Cape Cod Community College, created the Audio Study Tools. Amber Finn, Texas Christian University, created the PowerLecture PowerPoint slides. Kim Cowden, North Dakota State University, and Mike Sloat, Roaring Mouse Productions, directed and produced the Speech Buddy videos. Nita George, San José State University, created the USE It activities and prepared the Interactive Video Activities. And Angela Grupas, St. Louis Community College, and Rita Dienst helped prepare the Interactive Video Activities.

Many thanks to the reviewers and survey respondents for this second edition: Richard Armstrong, Wichita State University; Leonard Assante, Volunteer State Community College; Patrick Barton, College of Southern Nevada; Cameron Basquiat, College of Southern Nevada; Jennifer Basquiat, College of Southern Nevada; LeAnn Brazeal, Kansas State University; Rebecca Carlton, Indiana University Southeast; Audrey Deterding, Indiana University Southeast; Robert Dunkerly, College of Southern Nevada; Teddy A. Farias, St. Louis College of Health Careers; Neva Gronert, Arapahoe Community College; Angela Grupas, St. Louis Community College, Meramec; Carla Harrell, Old Dominion University; Teresa Moore, Brevard Community College; Peter J. Nowak, Suffolk University; Kekeli Nuviadenu, Bethune-Cookman University; Sandra Pensoneau-Conway, Wayne State University; Hannah Rockwell, Loyola University Chicago; Kristi Schaller, University of Georgia; Sherry Simkins, North Idaho College; Bonnye Stuart, Winthrop University; Richard Underwood, Kirkwood Community College; Stephanie Webster, University of Florida; Cicely Wilson, Crichton College; and Melinda Womack, Santiago Canyon College.

The authors are especially grateful to the communication studies faculty at San José State University, who voted to adopt the book for the department's basic course. All royalties from the sale of *Public Speaking: The Evolving Art* at SJSU go to a fund to support programs in the department.

Note to Students

Welcome to *Public Speaking: The Evolving Art,* Second Edition!

The basics of public speaking haven't changed much since classical times, but how you go about preparing and delivering a good speech have changed a great deal. This book and the resources that go with it combine proven traditions with the latest innovations to give you the best possible instruction in public speaking.

Each chapter and the companion resource materials for this text integrate a consistent learning approach that makes the book enjoyable and easy to use: READ It, WATCH It, USE It, REVIEW It. This approach allows you to read the text, view peer mentor and sample speech videos, complete interactive activities that apply chapter concepts and help you develop your own speeches, and access an array of study and self-assessment resources to reinforce what you've learned. You may follow the READ It, WATCH It, USE It, REVIEW It sequence described in the How to Use This Book section on page xx, or you may adapt the approach in a way that works best for you. For example, some students watch the Speech Buddy videos first to get a sense of what the chapter is about. They then read the text and go through the review resources. And then they complete the interactive activities. Apply whatever approach works best for you.

Most of the companion resources are free when your instructor orders them, but they're also available for sale to you at **cengagebrain.com.**

Successfully completing a public speaking course will help you develop communication skills you'll use throughout your life in a wide range of settings and for a variety of purposes. We look forward to helping you master those valuable skills.

Stephanie J. Coopman, San José State University

James Lull, San José State University

About the Authors

Stephanie J. Coopman (Ph.D., University of Kentucky) is Professor and Chair of Communication Studies at San José State University and Chair of the SJSU University Council of Chairs and Directors. In addition to teaching public speaking since the start of her career, she has conducted numerous workshops on public speaking and communication pedagogy. Professor Coopman has published her research in a variety of scholarly outlets, including *First Monday, Communication Education, Western Journal of Communication, Communication Yearbook, American Communication Journal, Journal of Business Communication*, and *Management Communication Quarterly*.

James Lull (Ph.D., University of Wisconsin-Madison) is Professor Emeritus of Communication Studies at San José State University. Winner of the National Communication Association's Golden Anniversary Monograph Award, he has taught public speaking for more than twenty-five years. An internationally recognized leader in media studies and cultural analysis, Professor Lull is author or editor of twelve books with translations into many languages. Dr. Lull holds an Honorary Doctorate from the University of Helsinki, Finland, and an Honorary Professorship at Alborg University, Denmark. He regularly gives plenary addresses and seminars at universities in Europe, Mexico, and Latin America.

How to Use This Book

Public Speaking: The Evolving Art provides you with an innovative **READ It**, **WATCH It**, **USE It**, **REVIEW It** sequence that helps you learn about the speech-making process is in a fun, interactive way. You can follow this sequence as described here, or you can complete each element in the sequence in any order that works best for you. Here's how the sequence is presented in each chapter:

▶ Read it

First, READ the chapter.

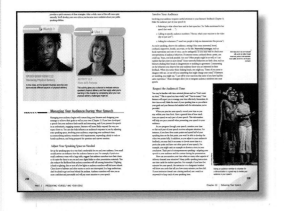

▶ Watch it

Then go to your online resources to WATCH the Speech Buddy videos featured in each chapter. The Speech Buddies are four former public speaking students who will review key concepts covered in the book, give you pointers on how to apply speech-making strategies they used in their own speeches, and introduce video clips from their own and other students' sample speeches.

▶ Use it

USE what you've learned in the book and from the Speech Buddies by completing the interactive activities linked to the videos. These activities will allow you to apply chapter concepts first to hypothetical scenarios and then to your own speech projects.

▶ Review it

Finally, REVIEW what you've learned by accessing the print and electronic resources categorized at the end of each chapter in the book. These resources include sample speech videos, sample outlines and note cards, an online speech organizing and outlining tool, web links, a workbook, and study aids such as glossary flashcards and review quizzes. If your instructor ordered these resources with your textbook, go to **http://login.cengage.com** to access them. If your instructor didn't order them but you'd like to use them, you can purchase them at **www.cengagebrain.com**.

A Brief Guide to Successful Public Speaking

You can use this guide to prepare for your first speech and as a checklist for all the speeches you give in your public speaking class. You can also use the guide as a handy reference for speeches you give after college.

Presenting a speech involves six basic stages:

1. Determining your purpose and topic (Chapter 4)
2. Adapting to your audience (Chapter 5)
3. Researching your topic (Chapter 6)
4. Organizing your ideas (Chapter 8)
5. Practicing your speech (Chapter 12)
6. Presenting your speech (Chapter 12)

These stages blend together—they're integrated parts of a whole, not discrete units. For example,

- As you're analyzing your audience (stage 2), you revise your topic focus (stage 1).
- What you find out about your audience (stage 2) will influence how you research your topic (stage 3).
- When practicing your speech (stage 5), you may decide that the flow of your ideas won't work for your audience (stage 2), so you go back and modify the organization of your ideas (stage 4).

Although public speaking may seem to be all about presenting, most of a successful speaker's work takes place behind the scenes, well before the speaking event. Let's go through each activity in the speechmaking process.

1. Determine Your Purpose and Topic

a. **Decide on your overall goal**, or the general purpose of your speech.

- First speeches in a public speaking class usually aim to inform or enhance listeners' knowledge of a topic. *Example:* In introducing a classmate, you'd want your audience to learn a few key bits of information about the person.
- Some first speeches seek to entertain listeners by sharing anecdotes and using humor. *Example:* In introducing yourself, you might tell your audience a funny story about your summer vacation.
- Speeches to persuade focus on influencing people's behaviors, values, or attitudes. *Example:* Trying to convince audience members to exercise regularly involves persuasion.

b. After you've identified the speech's general purpose, **choose your topic.**

- Sometimes your instructor will assign a topic for your first speech, such as introducing yourself to the class.
- In other cases, your assignment may be more broad, like informing the audience about an important campus issue.
- Pick something of interest to you that you think will appeal to your audience too.

2. Adapt to Your Audience

a. In choosing a topic, **keep your audience in mind** so your speech will interest them.

- In-depth research allows you to design a speech tailored to your audience.
- You probably won't be able to do in-depth research for your first speech, but just looking around the classroom gives you some clues about your audience. Demographic characteristics such as ethnic background, age, sex, and educational level tell you a lot. *Example:* If you wanted to give a speech about affordable housing in your community, you'd probably want to approach the issue from the point of view of renters, not landlords, because your student audience is far more likely to rent than to own their own home.

b. Adapting your speech to your audience means that you **apply the information you've gathered about them** when designing your speech.

- Target your message to *this* particular audience at *this* particular time and place.
- Use audience-centered communication that engages your listeners and helps you achieve your goal for the speech.
- You want your audience to feel as if you're speaking directly to them.

3. Research Your Topic

a. **You have many sources of information** for your speech topics.

- Common sources are books, websites, magazines, newspapers, government publications, and interviews with individuals.
- But begin with yourself and what you already know about the topic.

b. Once you've identified your knowledge base, **seek out additional sources of information.**

- A trip to the library and brief conference with the reference librarian helps locate the information you need.
- All campus libraries include extensive electronic databases that serve as gateways to academic journals, newspapers, legal opinions, trade publications, and numerous other sources.

c. You've probably already searched the internet for information about a wide range of topics. However, finding what you need for a speech is another matter.

- Locating relevant information online requires determining the right key terms associated with your topic. *Example:* If you're introducing a classmate who enjoys surfing, you may want to find out more about this activity. Typing in "surfing" on Google produces about 33 million web pages, ranging from internet surfing, to the surfing lawyer, to mind surfing—not exactly relevant to your speech. However, adding key terms to "surfing," such as "sport," "ocean," and "surfboard," refines your search.

4. Organize Your Ideas

a. Organizing your ideas involves identifying the main points you want to cover in your speech and putting them in a logical order: introduction, body, and conclusion.

b. With your introduction, you **gain your audience's attention and preview your main points**.

- Encourage listeners to focus on your ideas by gaining their attention with startling statistics, engaging quotes, rhetorical questions, brief anecdotes, or vivid visual materials that are relevant to your topic.
- Preview your main points in your thesis statement or in a separate preview statement. *Example:*

"The two campus services I'll cover today are the university credit union and the computer recycling program."

c. Once you've introduced your speech, you've **set the stage for the body of your speech**.

- The body of your speech includes all your main points organized in some logical way. *Example:* If you were describing a stadium, you might begin with the outside, then take the audience through the gates, then into the first level, and on through the arena using a spatial organizational pattern.
- However you organize your ideas, the pattern must be clear to your audience.

d. In your conclusion, you'll **summarize the main points and let your audience know you're finished**.

- *Example:* Signal that you're finishing your speech by saying something like, "Let's review what I've covered today . . ." or "To summarize, the most important aspects of . . ."
- End with a memorable statement. *Example:* "Now you've met Bailey—political science major, entrepreneur, and future mayor of this city."

e. With an outline, you **develop a numbered list of your main points and all the points supporting them**.

- Outlining your speech shows how you've arranged your ideas.
- Successful public speaking requires creating and using three different kinds of outlines for different stages in the development of your speech: working, complete-sentence, and presentation.
- The table "Types of Outlines" provides an overview of each type of outline, including what it's used for (function), what it includes (key features), and in which chapter of this text you'll find it covered.

Types of Outlines

Type of Outline	Functions	Key features	Chapter
Working	Assists in initial topic development; guides research	Includes main points and possible subpoints; revised during research process	4: Developing Your Purpose and Topic
Complete-sentence	Clearly identifies all the pieces of information for the speech; puts ideas in order; forms the basis for developing the presentation outline	Uses complete sentences; lists all sections of speech and all references; revised during preparation process	8: Organizing and Outlining Your Speech
Presentation	Assists you in practicing and giving your speech	Uses keywords; revised as you practice your speech; often transferred to note cards for use during practice and the final presentation	12: Delivering Your Speech

A BRIEF GUIDE TO SUCCESSFUL PUBLIC SPEAKING

5. Practice Your Speech

a. **Begin rehearsing your speech** by running through your outline and editing it as needed.

- Go through your complete-sentence outline, talking out loud, listening for how your ideas flow and fit together.

- Then give your speech aloud again, checking that you're within the time limit.

- Based on how well you meet the time limit and how your ideas work together, edit and revise for clarity and ease of understanding.

b. **Create your presentation outline.**

- Transfer key words from your complete-sentence outline to note cards, including only those words that trigger your memory. What you write on your note cards will become your presentation outline—the outline you'll use when you give your speech to the audience.

- Holding your note cards in one hand, stand up and say your speech, just as you would if your audience were there.

- If you plan to use presentation media like digital slides or posters in your speech, practice incorporating them into your presentation at this point too.

- Because you're using your notes only as a reminder, you'll need to glance at them only briefly and infrequently.

c. Strive to **give an excellent version of your speech rather than a perfect speech.**

- As you're practicing, your speech will sound a little different each time.

- Aim for a conversational presentation that you adapt to your audience as you're speaking.

6. Present Your Speech

a. When you present your speech, **manage your voice and your body.**

- Dress for the setting, audience, and topic.

- It's perfectly normal to feel a little nervous before and during your presentation. Think of any anxiety you feel as energy, then re-channel that energy into enthusiasm for your topic and audience.

- Maintain good eye contact with your audience, glancing at your note cards only to remind you of what you planned to say.

- Speak loudly so your audience can easily hear you.

- Move with purpose and spontaneity, using gestures that appear natural and comfortable.

b. For your first speech, you probably won't have slides, videos, or other presentation media. For longer speeches, **manage your presentation media**, arriving early on the day of your speech and checking the equipment you're going to use.

c. It will help you **manage your audience** as you present your speech if you analyze audience members beforehand.

- What you know about your listeners gives you clues about their possible reactions to your speech.

- Maintaining good eye contact gives you a sense of how they're responding to what you say.

d. **Monitor your time and adjust your speech as needed** if you find you're going to go on too long or fall short of the time limit.

- Effective public speaking means having the flexibility to adjust your presentation as you go along.

- Having a good grasp of the content of your speech will give you the confidence to make whatever adjustments you deem necessary during your presentation.

1 | The Evolving Art of Public Speaking

Cengage Learning

Cengage Learning

Y ou may not realize it, but you use public speaking skills every day, although not usually in the formal way most people associate with speaking in public. You answer questions in class, participate in meetings at work, tell classmates about a concert you attended, or persuade friends to go to a restaurant you like. What you'll learn in your public speaking course builds on experiences like these and helps you improve the communication skills you already have.

Public speaking is one of the most practical classes you'll ever take, and here's why: You often may be required to give presentations in other classes, and this course helps prepare you for that. Effective speaking skills give you a tremendous advantage at work too. Overall, public speaking ability helps you become a more active member of your community, allows you to participate more fully in organizations you belong to, and boosts your self-confidence in both personal and professional contexts. It's no wonder that so many college graduates say public speaking was one of the most beneficial classes they took in school. Here's what one blogger, Naomi, posted on an educational review blog: "Everyone's scared of public speaking, and they still wind up finding out that this is one of the most valuable classes you can take in college. No matter what you do with your life, you're going to need to communicate with others verbally, and this class is one of the best ways to help you get over your fears and learn."[1]

Wadsworth/Cengage Learning

The information-driven world we live in offers many new opportunities for **public speaking** and provides you with an array of options for preparing and delivering speeches. For instance, you can search the internet and online databases when researching a speech topic. When you deliver your speech, you have the option of using presentation software such as PowerPoint and Keynote to enhance your message. In some situations, you may even give a presentation via video conference or webcast. Access to so much information and so many options brings additional responsibilities. For example, speakers must make sure they use only the most reliable sources to support their speeches, and clearly document those sources. The ease of copying digital files can get speakers into trouble when they don't keep track of or acknowledge their sources properly.

Audiences also have many options and responsibilities, so it's as important to learn techniques that help you listen effectively and connect with audiences as it is to learn how to deliver a good speech. Public speaking is **audience centered**, which means speakers must acknowledge their audience's expectations and situations. For instance, today's audiences respond favorably to speakers who take a personal and conversational approach, use stories in their presentations, and include visual materials.[2] In addition, with the technology available today, audience members are not always in the same physical location as the speaker. Audience members can often access a video or transcript of a speech online weeks or even years after it was delivered. Voice-recognition software allows audience members to listen to a speech in a language they don't know as it is simultaneously translated into a language they understand. And just as speakers have easy access to information, so too do audience members. They can go online to check a fact after, or even while, listening to a presentation, or they can text a friend to comment on a speaker's statements. This ease of access to information means that speakers must research their topics more carefully than ever before.

With so much information and so many communication technologies readily available, you might wonder why anyone has to give speeches any more, or why someone might choose to attend a public lecture. Despite all the benefits of our new technologies, face-to-face public speaking remains an essential and necessary form of human communication. Why? Because unmediated public communication will always help fulfill fundamental human needs at the biological, psychological, social, and cultural levels, regardless of the technological resources available.[3]

But as societies change—economically, demographically, technologically, culturally—so do the roles of public speakers and audience members. Throughout history, much has changed for public speakers and their audiences: who has the opportunity, or authority, to speak; what makes an audience see a speaker as credible; the sources of information available to a speaker; the different ways a speaker may deliver a speech; and the expectations audiences have when listening. As a result, some of the skills people associate with effective speaking and listening have also changed. The foundational skills of public speaking, established centuries ago, have a long and successful track record. But successful public speakers today adjust their approach to take advantage of our rapidly changing world. That's why this book refers to public speaking as "the evolving art."

The Evolution of Human Communication

Because speech leaves no fossil trace, it is impossible to know precisely when humans first began to talk. However, some of the conditions that led to the development of modern communication *have* been discovered. For instance, it is certain that our hominid ancestors were physically able to utter sounds more than three million years ago.[4] Moreover, in order to coordinate hunting, care for offspring, and create

A situation in which an individual speaks to a group of people, assuming responsibility for speaking for a defined length of time.

Acknowledging an audience's expectations and situations before, during, and after a speech.

Cicero, a Roman statesman and scholar, addresses a group of men during the classical era. Compared with the political speeches of today, Cicero's speeches weren't heard by very many people. Although many of his speeches were recorded in writing, they probably weren't read by very many people during his lifetime—in ancient Rome, books were very expensive and only a small percentage of the population could read.

communities, the human populations that began to migrate out of Africa more than 50,000 years ago must have already developed a prototype of language.[5] Since then, the ability to use complex language has developed over thousands of years.

Early humans used rudimentary speech to convey their thoughts, experiences, and instructions to others. This behavior forms the foundation of public communication.[6] Gradually, the ability to speak well became a valuable social skill. But as civilizations developed, not everyone was allowed to participate in the public discourse—culture dictated who had the right to speak in public. For example, in Greece during the classical era (500–100 BCE), only well-educated men could speak in public, and the forms of communication available to them were greatly limited. These cultural, social, and technological conditions defined public speaking in Western civilization for centuries, right up through the Middle Ages (1000–1500 CE).

The industrial age (mid-1700s–early 1900s) brought tremendous changes in the way people communicate. In Western countries, a rapidly growing and educated middle class demanded more and more information and entertainment. Newspapers and magazines, and then radio and early films, fed these demands, and black-and-white television wasn't far behind. Other early consumer technologies—the home telephone, the instant camera, and simple audio recording devices—became the precursors of the personal communications devices used today.

In the midst of this technological revolution, public speaking remained a valued form of communication. True, the methods and techniques of public speech were much the same as they had been during the classical era, but over time the opportunities for speaking increased dramatically. Speeches printed in newspapers or broadcast over radio reached people around the world, not just local communities. Moreover, more people were allowed to contribute to the public discourse. Famous examples include women's rights activists Elizabeth Cady Stanton and Susan B. Anthony, who fought for voting rights for women, and abolitionists such as Frederick Douglass, a former African American slave who became a powerful and influential orator.

The information age (1960–present) exploded in the Sixties, a turbulent time whose sweeping technological and cultural changes continue to influence the way we live. In the United States, political battles raged over the Vietnam War, civil rights, gender equality, environmentalism, and "establishment" American values. Freedom of speech was a crucial issue, and college campuses were hotbeds of political debate. Prevailing notions of who could participate in the public discourse, and thus who wielded social power, were challenged constantly. More than at any other time in history, social minorities,

Electronic media invented during the industrial page dramatically changed the nature of public speaking for politicians. During the Great Depression and World War II, President Franklin D. Roosevelt was able to address the entire nation at once, with the goal of encouraging a national identity and active citizenry. These "fireside chats" on AM radio were one of the most popular radio shows in the nation in the 1930s and 1940s.

women, and college and high school students were able to join the public dialogue to protest, advocate, and fight for their rights. In addition, new media like cable television and progressive FM radio were springing up, increasing the opportunities for ordinary people to speak their minds in public forums.

Influences on Public Speaking Today

Now more than ever, communications technology influences all of public life, especially politics. For instance, when the president addresses Congress in the annual State of the Union speech, millions watch the speech on national and international television or the internet. Voters also rely more on communications technology to make their voices heard. In the 2008 presidential election, almost three-quarters of the U.S. voting-age population used the internet to get involved in the political process—an historic first![7]

Effective speakers today understand that Americans are extreme users of media and communications technology. People born in the 1990s and 2000s are especially technologically literate—they use cell phones, computers, television, MP3 players, digital cameras, and other electronic devices in combination more than 11 hours a day.[8] In fact, for these people, communications technology has become so ubiquitous that it defines cultural identity and experience—they expect instant access to information and to other people.

Public speaking has gone global. Today, many speeches are recorded in writing or on video and uploaded to the internet for anyone in the world to read and watch. Speakers can even speak in real time to audiences who are thousands of miles away. Here, NASA Astronaut Commander Sunita Williams speaks to students in India from Houston via a videoconferencing link.

On the other hand, today's speakers must remember that the technological and social advantages most of us take for granted aren't distributed evenly to everyone. In many developing countries, education levels are low and very few people have internet access. Less than 7 percent of the population in Africa, 20 percent in Asia, and 30 percent in China and the Middle East use the internet.[9] Even in the United States, only about 75 percent of the adult population is online.[10] This **digital divide** reveals other differences, too, including disparities based on age, race, education level, and internet connection speed.[11] Therefore, speakers can't assume that everyone in their audience, even here at home, is fully versed in online technology and culture.

Refers to the gap between populations that have a high level of access to and use of digital communications technology, and populations that have a low level of access and use.

As our communication landscape continues to evolve, speakers and audiences will face new challenges. For example, independent blogs and social media like Facebook, LinkedIn, and Twitter have become major parts of everyday life, but how do they fit into speechmaking? Can you trust the authenticity of the digital images you grab off the internet? Can you use a clip from YouTube or Hulu without permission? Is Wikipedia a reliable source of information? These are among the many important questions today's public speakers must consider. This text and its accompanying electronic materials have been designed to provide an up-to-date guide to both the foundations of public speaking and what today's public speakers need to know to be successful.

Foundations of Public Speaking

Beginning with the Sophists (500–300 BCE), the ancient Greeks promoted public communication in the Western tradition. The Sophists were teachers who traveled from place to place, lecturing students on how to communicate well in a democratic society. They considered the manner of presenting ideas—delivery—the hallmark of an eloquent speaker. But effective public speaking is by no means limited to delivery techniques. The philosopher Socrates (c. 470–399 BCE) and his student Plato (428–348 BCE) identified logic and reasoning as the basis of effective public speaking.[12] Aristotle (384–322 BCE), a student of Plato, focused on argument and audiences. Aristotle's ideas about oratory were so influential that he became a key figure in the development of communication as an academic discipline.

Aristotle's term for public speaking.

Aristotle's *Rhetoric*

Aristotle (384–322 BCE) took a systematic approach to studying **rhetoric**, as public speaking was called at the time.[13] In Aristotle's major work, *Rhetoric*, he emphasized the importance of adapting speeches to specific audiences and situations. Today this is called audience-centered communication. Adapting to audiences and building your credibility as a speaker form major parts of the audience-centered approach. If, for example, you're attempting to convince your classmates to get more involved in the local community, you might stress the benefits of listing volunteer work on a résumé. In discussing the same topic with parents of young children, you could shift your focus to how their activities might help make the community a place where their kids can thrive.

The ancient Greek philosopher Aristotle's writing about oratory still influences the teaching of public speaking today.

Another foundation of public speaking is what Aristotle called *proofs*— the various approaches a speaker can use to appeal to a specific audience on a particular occasion. Aristotle identified three types of proofs: logos, pathos, and ethos. *Logos* refers to rational appeals based on logic, facts, and objective analysis. Traditional examples of logos include the deployment of scientific evidence and the kinds of arguments prosecutors and defense attorneys use in courts of law when they attempt to establish the facts of a case. But presenting a detailed set of recommendations at a committee meeting or praising a friend's accomplishments when you nominate him for a leadership position is also an appeal based on logos.

The Print Collector / Alamy

7

The five arts of public speaking come from the Western cultural tradition, but some other cultures also emphasize these core principles. For example, Buddhist preaching in Japan follows similar principles. Established guidelines specify what subjects preachers can discuss (invention), the way in which ideas are organized (arrangement), the type of language used (style), what information requires memorization (memory), and how the voice and body should be used when preaching (delivery). Many of these guidelines are highly detailed, such as those for using a specific organizational pattern for a sermon: recite a verse from a religious text, explain the verse's central theme, tell a relevant fictional story, tell a true story, and make concluding comments. Although not all Buddhist preachers rely on this way of organizing their sermons, many still use this traditional organizational pattern.[18]

Pathos refers to appeals to our emotions. Speakers use pathos to appeal to the audience's feelings, such as when they display poignant photos to convince us to contribute to charitable organizations. Appeals based on *ethos* rest on the speaker's credibility or character. When you speak at a neighborhood meeting or offer comments in class, the audience, even subconsciously, evaluates your trustworthiness and believability—key components of good character and credibility.

A fourth type of appeal to the audience, *mythos*, focuses on the values and beliefs embedded in cultural narratives or stories.[14] Contemporary scholars added this concept to the three original proofs because stories represent important cultural values that can also appeal to an audience. Chapter 15 covers all four types of appeals—logos, pathos, ethos, and mythos—and provides detailed guidance about how to use them to support a speech's message.

Cicero and the Five Arts

The Roman statesman Cicero (106–43 BCE) categorized the elements of public communication into five "arts of public speaking," or canons of rhetoric, that still apply today.[15] Cicero argued that these five arts—invention, arrangement, style, memory, and delivery—constitute the groundwork for learning about public speaking. The five arts provide guidelines for speaking effectively in public.

1. **Invention** focuses on what you have or want to say. As the first art, invention refers to the moment when you find an idea, line of thought, or argument you might use in a speech. Choosing a topic (Chapter 4) and developing good arguments (Chapter 15) are both part of invention.

   Discovering what you want to say in a speech, such as by choosing a topic and developing good arguments.

2. **Arrangement**, the second art, refers to how you organize your ideas. This art accounts for the basic parts of a speech (introduction, body, and conclusion) as well as the order in which points are presented (Chapter 8). Good organization helps maintain the audience's attention and keeps them focused on the ideas the speaker presents.[16] For example, sometimes a speaker tells the end of a story first because the audience will then be curious about how the ending came about. At other times, the speaker tells a story in the order in which events happened because the end will be a surprise.

   The way ideas presented in a speech are organized.

3. The third art, **style**, involves the language you use to bring a speech's content to life (Chapter 10). Consider the differences between saying, "My trip last summer was fun," and "My adventures last summer included a strenuous but thrilling trek through the Rocky Mountains." Both statements reflect the same idea, but the second one grabs the audience's attention so they want to know more about the "thrilling trek."

   The language or words used in a speech.

4. **Memory**, the fourth art, refers to using your memory to give an effective speech. Memory goes beyond simple memorization, referring instead to the importance of practicing public speaking skills (Chapter 12).[17] That is, when you present a speech, you rely on everything you've learned about public speaking, your topic, the audience, and the occasion.

   Using the ability to recall information to give an effective speech.

5. As the fifth art, **delivery** is the moment when a speech goes public—when it is presented to an audience. Delivery involves how you use your voice, gestures, and body movement when giving a speech. Chapter 12 covers how to achieve the natural, conversational delivery style today's audiences expect and prefer.

   The presentation of a speech to an audience.

Storytelling

Most people love to hear stories. Stories not only entertain, but they also help both storytellers and listeners understand the world. In this regard, stories form part of the foundation of public speaking. Effective speakers know that it makes sense to take advantage of the natural attraction humans have to stories. After all, most people have been conditioned since childhood to use narrative thinking to listen to and tell stories. **Narrative** thinking relies on narratives, or stories, to connect the self with the world, envision what could be, apply logic to identify patterns and causal connections, and structure events in a logical order.[19] Because storytelling is so basic to human communication and existence, today's audiences welcome narratives in speeches as much as their ancestors did long ago.

A story used in a speech or other form of communication.

Plato famously said, "Those who tell the stories rule society." It's certainly true that having a platform to speak from allows a speaker to tell a story that creates a favorable version of reality for herself or her cause. However, to influence audiences most effectively, stories must be used in conjunction with other aspects of good speechmaking. Being able to combine the power of storytelling with well-supported arguments, inclusive language, and an ethical consideration of the audience is a skill that will benefit you for the rest of your life.

Public Speaking Is a Life Skill

When you think about public speaking, you probably focus most on the act of delivering a speech. However, a public speaking course gives you a chance to develop many other communication skills, such as critically analyzing a topic, managing nervousness, listening effectively, adapting to an audience, building your credibility, finding and using many different types of information, organizing ideas, and presenting ideas and information.

Developing Transferable Skills

Transferable skills, such as finding information and organizing ideas, can be carried over from one context or occasion to another. So, for example, when you learn to manage anxiety in your public speaking class, you'll be able to apply that skill in other settings, such as a job interview. The skills you learn in your public speaking class will help you in other communication situations as well.

Becoming More Confident and Managing Speech Anxiety Nearly everyone gets nervous when speaking in public. Good speakers learn to cope with that anxiety. Successfully completing a public speaking course will help build your confidence, which will in turn help you manage speech anxiety.[20]

The process of *habituation*—fearing a situation less as it becomes more familiar, or *habit*-like—helps you manage your speech anxiety over time, just as doing almost anything repeatedly makes you more comfortable doing it. For example, you probably experienced some nervousness the first time you attended a college class. After a few class meetings, though, you likely became more comfortable because you had a better idea of what to expect. Repetition alone isn't enough, however; you also need positive experiences. You didn't become more comfortable taking college courses only because you attended a certain number of class sessions. Your comfort level increased because you started to get to know your classmates, you made a comment that your instructor praised, or you successfully completed the first assignment. In other words, you were encouraged to come back and feel more comfortable.

In the same way, positive experiences in a public speaking course can help you get used to speaking outside of a classroom setting. You'll get positive feedback about your speeches, and you'll get constructive suggestions about what you might change so that you give a more effective speech next time. Both kinds of feedback give you direction and remind you that you have the support of your instructor and classmates. The increased confidence and decreased anxiety you experience as your public speaking class progresses will transfer to speaking situations outside of class. When speaking opportunities arise, such as stating your opinion about a political issue at a town hall meeting or explaining an idea to colleagues in a meeting at work, you'll feel more enthusiastic about them. Chapter 2 covers specific strategies for increasing your confidence and managing the common psychological and physiological effects of public speaking anxiety.

Becoming a Better Listener Poor listening skills can cause all sorts of problems—missing a key point during a staff meeting, misunderstanding a doctor's advice, or giving an inappropriate response to a friend's question. A public speaking course sharpens your listening skills.[21]

As you build your communication skills, one goal is learning how to listen reciprocally, meaning that all participants in any social interaction listen to one another with open minds and full attention. Ethical communicators listen openly even when they disagree with someone. Chapter 3 presents specific strategies that will help you become a more effective listener and better at compensating for the poor listening skills of others.

Adapting to Different Audiences and Building Your Credibility Gathering and analyzing information about an audience helps you identify audience members' interests and concerns, what they know about your topic, and how they might respond to what you say. Whether you're telling coworkers about a new software program, running for election to student government, or even just entertaining friends with stories from your travels, knowing your audience is essential to getting your message across well. Chapter 5 explains the best methods for researching and analyzing audiences.

Another related skill is building your credibility as a communicator. Speaker credibility refers to how much an audience views the speaker as competent, friendly, trustworthy, and dynamic. How you establish and maintain your credibility as a speaker varies from audience to audience and topic to topic. As a result, knowing how to communicate your credibility will help you get your ideas across to others no matter what the context. Suppose, for instance, that you'd like to get your college to provide more funding for student organizations on campus. Your message will be much more persuasive if the school's administrators view you as a credible spokesperson. Chapter 5 describes the four components of credibility and explains how they can help you become a more believable and respected speaker.

Finding and Using Reliable Information Knowing how to locate information, evaluate its reliability and usefulness for your purpose, and apply it ethically and effectively can serve you well in all aspects of your life. Finding and assessing information at work is an obvious example. But research skills are essential for your home life as well. A recent study found that 80 percent of internet users in the United States search for health information online, yet very few check the sources of that information.[22] As a result, millions of Americans rely on health information that may or may not be accurate or reliable. Learning how to systematically find, analyze, and evaluate information in your public speaking class will help you avoid poor and discredited information. Chapter 6 covers the research process in depth.

Organizing Ideas and Information Effectively Speakers who force their audiences to try to figure out what they're saying don't get very far. Listeners expect and need to hear information that is clearly organized. One of the best ways for you to provide this clarity is by using familiar patterns of organization such as chronological (how something develops over time), spatial (what physical relationships exist between things), cause-and-effect (how one thing results in another), and problem–solution (which identifies a problem and discusses how to solve it). To further help audiences follow what you're saying, use purposeful transitions to link points together. You can also organize the content of your speech with an outline. An outline keeps you on track and gives you a basic plan for researching, constructing, and delivering what you want to say about your topic.

Public speaking students develop ways to organize their ideas more effectively outside the classroom too.[23] Whether you're giving directions to your home or explaining how to use a new piece of equipment, organizing what you want to say makes it easier for other people to understand you. When you give a speech, organizing your points before you speak can give your ideas greater impact. Chapter 8 covers how to organize and outline your ideas.

Yellow Dog Productions/Getty Images

Public speakers not only develop skills that help them give compelling speeches. They also develop organizational and leadership skills that can be used in all kinds of contexts, such as in this study session taking place in a college dorm.

Presenting Ideas and Information Effectively Effective communication requires *mindfulness*: consciously focusing on a situation and maintaining awareness of what you say and how others respond.[24] A mindful public speaker is an audience-centered speaker. Being mindful in your public speaking course will help you be more mindful as you present ideas and information in your other social interactions too.

Mindfulness also applies to planning, preparing, and using presentation media effectively. Integrating PowerPoint, Keynote, or other digital slide software has become a requirement for many business presentations, but it's not appropriate for every speaking situation. For instance, when you get together with your friends for dinner, you wouldn't use digital slides to tell them about your whitewater kayaking trip in Chile. However, you might put together a digital slide show to share your adventure at a meeting of your kayaking club. Chapter 11 gives you tips and strategies for using all presentation media.

Public speaking skills are *life skills*. That is, you'll use what you learn in your public speaking class in all aspects of your life. **Table 1.1** on page 12 summarizes the transferable skills learned in a public speaking course, how they're developed, and how they benefit people in everyday life.

Chapter 1 : The Evolving Art of Public Speaking

Table 1.1 Transferable Life Skills Gained in a Public Speaking Course

Transferable skill	How public speaking helps you develop the skill	Examples of how the skill might benefit you in everyday life
Being more confident and managing communication anxiety	• Habituation • Using proven strategies	Feeling more comfortable talking with people in unfamiliar social situations
Being a good listener	• Understanding listening • Listening reciprocally	Understanding better what a friend has to say, and the friend understanding you better
Adapting to different audiences and building your credibility	• Knowing how to research and analyze audiences • Increasing competence and dynamism	Being able to confront a friend or coworker about a difficult issue without damaging the relationship
Finding and evaluating information	• Recognizing appropriate and reliable sources • Assessing the accuracy and validity of information	Researching a company you think you would like to work for
Organizing ideas	• Understanding patterns of organization • Understanding how people process information	Explaining to a classmate the advantages and disadvantages of joining a fraternity or sorority
Presenting ideas effectively	• Communicating mindfully • Knowing how to plan and prepare effective presentation materials	Integrating effective presentation resources into a speech about college life at your high school

Speaking Effectively in Common Public Communication Contexts

Even in today's era of more personal forms of communication—text messaging, instant messaging, chatting, blogging, and the like—you take part in many public communication contexts. This section discusses four of those contexts: the college classroom, the workplace, your community, social events, and online.

In Classes At this point in your school career, you've probably already answered instructors' questions, asked questions yourself, given reports, or explained ideas in class. You've probably also told stories, had spontaneous conversations, expressed your views in discussion groups, and collaborated on assignments. These are all informal speaking opportunities in the classroom.

Higher education today requires students to participate more actively in their classroom experiences than ever before. Consequently, communication across the curriculum (CXC) has become commonplace on most campuses.[25] Rather than requiring oral presentations only in communication courses, CXC recommends that speaking assignments be given in all sorts of classes, from biology to dance. If you haven't already, you'll get plenty of opportunities to exercise and refine your public speaking skills in your other classes.

In the Workplace As the basis of our economy continues to shift from manufacturing to information, the ability to communicate well becomes even more essential to professional success.[26] Employers in all types of organizations and industries rank effective oral and written communication skills as the most important skill set for college graduates to have when they enter the workforce (**Figure 1.1**). Notice how communication skills provide the foundation for the development of other important skills, like working well with others and solving problems. All organizations need people who interact with coworkers, supervisors, and the public effectively. Research shows that students who successfully complete a class in public speaking improve their communication skills in the workplace.[27]

You may think, "I'll never do any public speaking in my job." At first, you might be able to avoid public speaking situations at work. However, you'll need excellent communication skills to advance your career in any field. Even in professions such as accounting—usually not associated with public speaking—very good oral communication skills are essential for building business contacts and being promoted.[28] Some companies even hire speech coaches to help employees improve their speaking abilities before considering them for promotion.[29] However, it's far better to arrive at hiring or promotion interviews with those skills already developed.

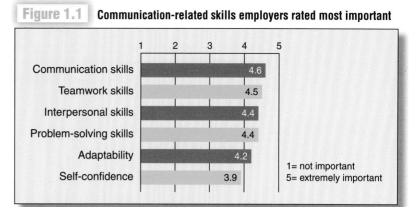

Source: Job Outlook 2010, National Association of Colleges and Employers

In Communities Citizens who are willing to speak in their communities make up the very foundation of a democracy.[30] When you use your public speaking skills to discuss issues with others in your community, you contribute to a more informed society and feel a greater sense of belonging. By communicating publicly, you participate in democracy at its most basic level.[31] The skills you develop in your public speaking class can help you contribute much to the various communities to which you belong.

Consider the example of Mike Sessions, the high school student who won the Hillsdale, Michigan, mayoral campaign in 2005. Just days after turning 18 and registering to vote, Mike filed his intention to run for mayor as a write-in candidate in his south-central Michigan town. Each day after school, Mike went from door to door, telling people who he was and why he was running for mayor. The young candidate spoke at the Kiwanis Club, a record shop, and the local firehouse. In the end, his determination and speaking skills paid off: He won the election, defeating incumbent Don Ingles by two votes.[32]

At Social Events Many social events, such as *quinceañeras*, graduations, wedding receptions, retirement banquets, and family reunions call for public speaking. Casual

Mike Sessions, 18 years old when he was elected mayor of Hillsdale, Michigan, used his public speaking skills to win over voters and unseat the incumbent mayor.

AP Photo/Scott Erskine

get-togethers like birthday celebrations, holiday gatherings, going-away parties, neighborhood barbeques, and dinners with friends often become more meaningful when attendees mark the moment with a few brief comments to the group. Such occasions serve important cultural functions by transmitting values and strengthening the social fabric.

When you celebrate graduating from your college or university, for example, you may be called on to say a few words, even if the event is an informal gathering. Successfully completing a class in public speaking will help you prepare a short speech your audience will remember, and that truly expresses the meaning of the occasion for you. It will probably be captured on video as well, so why not make it memorable in a positive way! Social events offer fairly regular opportunities to demonstrate and further develop your public speaking skills throughout your life.

Online As technology has evolved, so too have the opportunities for public speaking. If you're like most people today, you spend a considerable part of your life online. You go online for school and work; to get caught up on news, entertainment, and sports; and to use social media to connect with friends. But you probably aren't just a consumer of online media—you may create it too. For example, you may post commentaries on YouTube, upload video biographies to job websites, make videos for a web-based dating service, create long-distance business presentations, start up blogs, and provide status updates to your colleagues in online business meetings.

Distance speaking is fast becoming part of the public speaking landscape. **Distance speaking** is the planned and structured presentation of ideas transmitted from one physical location to other locations by means of information and communications technology. You can adapt the skills you learn in your public speaking class to all kinds of online communication. Although the technologies used for distance speaking create their own speaking advantages and challenges, the skills you need for effective public speaking don't change. Online speaking still involves a human speaker sending a message to a human audience, just as face-to-face speaking does. Knowing how to come up with good ideas, research a topic, organize the content, and deliver a speech effectively all transfer smoothly from face-to-face to online speaking.

> The planned and structured presentation of ideas transmitted from one physical location to other locations by means of information and communications technology.

Public Speaking and Human Communication Today

Public speaking shares some characteristics with other types of communication, but also differs in several important ways. Knowing the similarities and differences will help you understand the place of public speaking within the spectrum of human communication and help you see how your speaking skills apply in other contexts.

Contexts for Human Communication

Communication scholars traditionally use the following categories to identify contexts for human communication:

- *Interpersonal communication* occurs between two or more people interacting with each other as unique individuals. You develop personal relationships with friends, family, and coworkers through interpersonal communication.

- *In small-group communication*, three or more people interact to accomplish a task or reach a shared objective. Local theater groups, committees, and collaborative work groups are examples of small groups.

- *Organizational communication* takes place within and among organizations for the purpose of accomplishing common goals, such as creating products and offering services. Organizations often provide the setting for speeches, as when a department manager gives a presentation to senior executives.

- *Mass communication* originates with a media organization such as NBC, *People* magazine, XM Satellite Radio, or *The New York Times* and is transmitted to large, fairly anonymous, and often diverse audiences.

- *Public communication* occurs when an individual speaks to a group of people, assuming primary responsibility for speaking for a limited amount of time.

Models of Human Communication

Models of human communication provide visual representations of the communication process. Early models portrayed human communication as moving in one direction, from a *sender* to a *receiver*, and became known as the transmission or linear models of communication.[33] But communication is not strictly a one-way affair. Over the years, scholars developed increasingly complex models of communication to account for the *feedback* that goes back and forth between individuals as they interact and to describe more fully the *channels* through which they exchange messages.[34] These models, which described communication as an interaction or a transaction, highlighted the active role of listening as well as speaking.

In addition, the later communication models added three additional important elements: noise, context, and environment. *Noise* refers to any interference that prevents messages from being understood. The *context* is the setting for any social interaction, such as a conference room or grocery checkout line. The *environment* includes all the outside forces that might affect communication, such as current events or even the weather.

Any current model of communication must take into account the individual person—*you*. You are right in the middle of everything that's going on. Individualization and personalization have become dominant cultural trends in the information age.[35] And because today's information and communications technologies give you tremendous individual freedom and flexibility to communicate with others, new models must also account for a **pervasive communication environment**. In this environment, information can be accessed and shared in multiple forms from multiple locations in ways that transcend time and space.[36]

The ability to access and share information in multiple forms from multiple locations in ways that transcend time and space.

There are four principal spheres of communication constantly available to us—mass media, information technology, personal communications technology, and face-to-face interaction (**Figure 1.2**, page 13).

- *Mass media.* This is the least interactive sphere of communication. Nonetheless, mainstream media occupy an enormous amount of time in our search for information and entertainment.

- *Information technology.* Computer-based information technologies, including the internet, give us convenient ways to communicate and socialize. The internet forms the heart of the pervasive communication environment, linking various technologies and people together.

- *Personal communications technology.* Mobile phones have become the preferred form of telephonic interaction, giving us the ability to connect with others by voice and text, and to have photographic and video capability at our fingertips.

- *Face-to-face.* This type of communication encompasses unmediated contact with others, including most public speaking situations.

Although each sphere has its own form and function, people tend to use and interact with one or more spheres simultaneously. This process is known as *convergence*. For example, personal communication technology often converges with information technology to facilitate web access, file sharing, and more.

The Elements of Public Speaking Integrating the notions of communication spheres and a pervasive communication environment with the processes represented in the

Figure 1.2   The spheres of communication

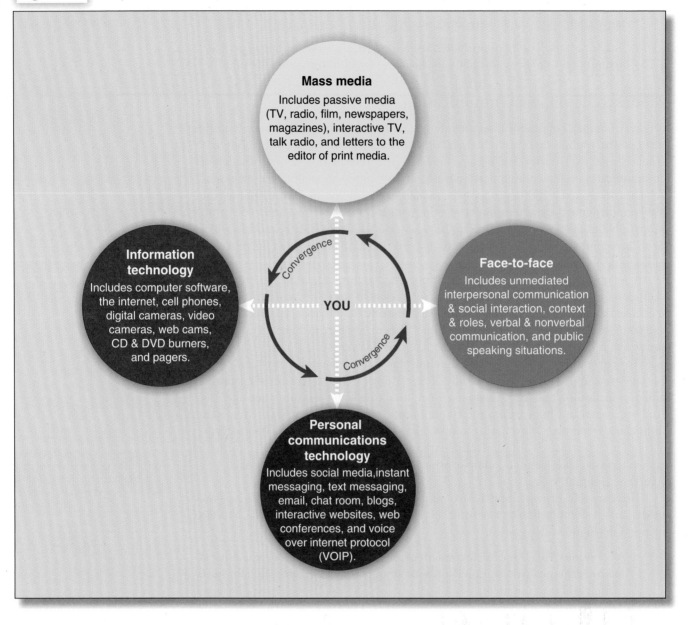

interactional or transactional models of communication creates a more accurate view of the evolving conditions in which public speaking takes place today. **Figure 1.3** shows how the eight elements of public speaking—sender (speaker), message, channel, receiver (audience), noise, feedback, context, and environment—interact.

The source is the individual person—you, a classmate, friend, family member, neighbor, or coworker—anyone who assumes a central role as initiator or participant in a communicative interaction. In public speaking situations, the **speaker** is usually the initiator and has the primary responsibility for talking. Yet audience members also fulfill the speaker role when they ask questions or make comments after a speech.

The **message** includes the words a speaker uses—verbal communication—and how the speaker presents those words—nonverbal communication. When you interpret what someone else says, you pay attention to what they say and how they say it. In public speaking, you listen to the speaker's main points and ideas, and observe how the speaker moves, incorporates gestures, makes eye contact, and uses his or her voice. Notice that Cicero's five arts of public speaking make up the sum total of the message: the speaker's ideas (invention), how the points are organized (arrangement), the specific words the

The person who assumes the primary responsibility for conveying a message in a public communication context.

The words and nonverbal cues a speaker uses to convey ideas, feelings, and thoughts.

Figure 1.3 **A model of public speaking**

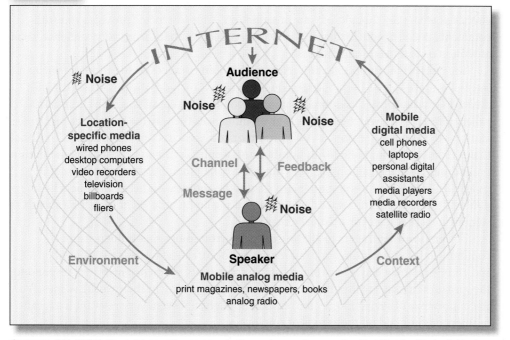

Coopman, T.M. (2009). *Toward a pervasive communication environment perspective.* First Monday 14. *Available at firstmonday.org*

speaker chooses (style), evidence that the speaker knows the topic (memory), and the actual speech presentation (delivery).

Channel refers to the mode or medium of communication—in person, print, or electronic. Public speaking often involves multiple channels. In addition to speaking to an audience, a speaker may use presentation media to display a graph, play a clip from a relevant musical piece, and make available a paper handout with additional information. Many more communication channels are available today than in the past. Speakers make presentations in person but may also give a speech via webcam or videoconferencing and make their digital slides available to the audience. In the business world, digital slides make up a key component of many speeches. Audience members may respond using multiple channels as well, such as text messaging a speaker or emailing a question.

The receiver refers to the intended recipient of the speaker's message. In public speaking, receivers are the **audience** members. In many speaking situations, you speak to an audience in person. However, today your audience may extend far beyond the people you speak with in person. A speech may be digitally recorded for online distribution at a later time, or some audience members may be linked in via webcams. Speakers are listeners, too. When you give a speech, you listen to what you're saying and attend to the audience's responses.

Noise occurs when something interferes with understanding a message. In public speaking, noise may be internal to the listener, as with daydreaming or thinking about something else. Being hungry or tired can also cause internal noise. External noise includes sounds that prevent listeners from easily hearing what the speaker has to say, such as other people talking or a cell phone going off. Poor lighting, blurry overhead transparencies, and cluttered digital slides are also sources of noise. Chapter 3 discusses ways to reduce noise and distractions.

Feedback gives the source a sense of how the message is being interpreted. Public speakers should be especially alert to feedback. Nods and smiles indicate that listeners agree and understand. Shaking heads and frowns suggest that audience members may disagree, feel confused, or not understand the speaker's point. Getting feedback from listeners lets you know how effective you are as a speaker and indicates areas in which

A mode or medium of communication.

The intended recipients of a speaker's message.

Anything that interferes with the understanding of a message.

Audience members' responses to a speech.

you might improve. In your public speaking class, you may gather feedback informally by observing your audience as you speak, listening to their questions, and asking them after class what they thought of your presentation. Your instructor provides you with comments that are more formal and may even collect feedback from your audience, such as written or oral peer evaluations.

The **context** of communication refers to the circumstances or situation in which an interaction takes place. In public speaking the context includes the physical setting for a speech—auditorium, classroom, conference room, the steps of city hall, a museum gallery. The space in which a speech is given influences the way the message is delivered and how the audience responds. A classroom or conference room is generally less formal than a large auditorium filled with hundreds of people. Trying to keep listeners' attention poses different challenges on the steps outside city hall than inside a quiet museum gallery. The occasion for the speech also shapes the context. Audience members have different expectations for a speech commemorating an historic event than for a speech supporting a candidate for political office.

The **environment** refers to all the external surroundings that influence any communicative interaction. For example, events occurring at or near the time when a speech is given may play a key role in listeners' reactions. Audience members respond to the speaker's message within the context of what's happening in their world. A speech on the importance of saving money for retirement might not seem very relevant if a local business has just laid off thousands of employees.

The situation within which a speech is given.

The external surroundings that influence a public speaking event.

Key Issues for Today's Public Speaker

Because communicators can interact with others and access information at nearly any time and in any place, speakers and audiences enjoy new opportunities and face new challenges. Ethics, critical thinking, cultural awareness, and using presentation software appropriately are all issues today's public speaker should be aware of—in every public speaking context.

Ethics

The concept of *ethics* merges the Greek idea of personal character, *ethos*, with the Latin sense of morality, *mores*, and refers to rules or standards within a culture about what is right and wrong.[37] Regardless of the era, ethics are central to public speaking. Computers and digital technology, however, have added layers of ethical issues that speakers and audiences didn't face in the past. For example, with the availability of so much information in digital form, plagiarism has become easier. *Plagiarism* occurs when you take someone else's idea or work and present it as your own. Chapter 3 provides an in-depth discussion of ethics, and Chapter 6 covers the specifics of plagiarism in the context of research as well as a detailed guide to evaluating sources.

Critical Thinking

Now that they have access to so much information in digital formats, public speakers and their audiences must be especially vigilant and use their critical thinking skills consistently. As discussed in Chapter 6, speakers must ask critical questions when evaluating sources that support their main points, such as "Where did this information come from?" and "Is the source of this evidence credible?" Information literacy involves the ability to access, select, evaluate, and use information effectively.[38] Knowing how to sort through less-useful information to get the information you really need is a skill you apply every day throughout your life. Whether you're searching for information about your speech topic or trying to identify the best car for your transportation needs and budget, information literacy skills are a must.

Cultural Awareness

Effective listeners and speakers display sensitivity to others' cultural perspectives. Whether speaking to a relatively homogeneous or a very diverse audience, successful speakers always keep in mind ways of looking at the world that don't match their own views. Today more than ever, for speakers to do well, they must demonstrate they are aware and respectful of other cultures. Chapters 5 and 10 address the specifics of cultural awareness for public speakers.

Using Presentation Software

What's considered good delivery has changed considerably since Aristotle's time. The sophisticated presentation software available today has conditioned audiences to anticipate a certain level of flair in most public speaking situations. Audiences expect creativity, such as integrating relevant video and audio clips into digital slides or showing an image that will provoke discussion. However, overreliance on presentation software, especially digital slides, detracts from your message.[39] Chapter 11 provides concrete guidelines for using presentation software and other presentation media effectively.

Introducing the Speech Buddies

Now that you have a sense of what public speaking is and what the key issues facing today's speakers are, it's time to meet the Speech Buddies. They will be your guides as you work through this book, providing advice and tips for giving better speeches. The Speech Buddies are a crew of college students who are available all day, every day in online videos to serve as peer mentors while you use this text and its various learning

> **Watch** it

SPEECH BUDDY VIDEO 1.1
Meeting the Speech Buddies

In this video, Janine, Anthony, Erin, and Evan briefly introduce themselves and talk about an aspect of the role public speaking plays in their lives. As you watch the video, think about how you've used public speaking skills in the past and how you'll be able to apply what you learn in this course in the future.

> **Use** it

ACTIVITY 1.1
What Are Your Public Speaking Goals?

After watching the video, click on the interactive activity link to put the chapter to use. This activity includes a series of prompts that will help you identify your immediate and long-term public speaking goals.

materials. These students—Janine, Anthony, Erin, and Evan—all completed a public speaking course like the one you're taking now.

Intended to be an essential part of your experience while using this text, the Speech Buddies guide you through the process of preparing and delivering effective speeches by telling you about their own public speaking experiences and introducing video clips that present examples from their speeches and those of others. The Speech Buddies also direct you to the interactive activities that accompany each video and give you a chance to use the principles covered, by applying them first in hypothetical scenarios and then to your own speech. To then apply your new skills to real-world situations, see the APPLY It box in each chapter. These boxes provide advice on speaking at work, in your community, and in other venues outside the classroom.

Summary

As an evolving art, public speaking has changed from the classical era to today's information age in six key areas: who may speak, what makes a speaker credible, where speakers find information, what ethical challenges speakers face, how speakers deliver their speeches, and what audiences expect. Tracing public speaking across the centuries illustrates how public speaking has evolved from a time when only well-educated men could speak, and only to a live audience, to an era in which nearly all members of society have the opportunity to speak and can choose among multiple delivery options.

In the public speaking class you're taking now, you'll acquire many transferable skills. Learning how to successfully present a speech increases self-confidence, improves listening skills, teaches audience adaptation and credibility strategies, expands your ability to locate and evaluate information, and provides techniques for better organizing and presenting your ideas.

Your public speaking class won't be the first time you give a speech—nor will it be the last. Many instructors across a wide variety of disciplines require student participation in discussions, debates, and presentations. Oral communication skills are essential to doing well in the workplace. Engaging in public talk at the community level keeps you informed and more connected with others. Speaking at social events contributes to important societal and cultural rituals. Addressing audiences online is becoming commonplace.

Although new communication technologies have transformed how people communicate, four core ideas provide the foundation for public speaking in any age. First, public speaking requires audience-centered communication in which speakers focus on listeners' needs, knowledge, and interests. Second, public speakers must choose excellent supporting materials that fit the audience, topic, and occasion. Third, public speaking incorporates five arts, or divisions: invention, arrangement, style, memory, and delivery. These categories provide guidance in learning about public speaking and developing a speech. Fourth, public speaking encourages narrative thinking, allowing communicators to use their imaginations, recognize patterns, structure past events, and identify their relationships with each other and with the world.

Models of human communication have evolved from the transmission model that views communication as one-way, to more sophisticated models that incorporate today's complex communication environment. Public speaking has eight elements: speaker, message, channel, audience, noise, feedback, context, and environment. The speaker is the person who has the primary responsibility for presenting information. The speaker's message includes both verbal and nonverbal communication. Public speaking typically involves multiple channels of communication, such as integrating presentation media while speaking in person. The intended recipients of the speaker's message are the audience. Noise can interfere with the audience's ability to understand the message. The audience provides feedback in the form of nonverbal responses, questions and comments, and other communication with the speaker. The context for public speaking includes the physical setting and the occasion.

Key issues for today's public speaker center on ethics, cultural awareness, and the use of presentation software. Increased access to information puts greater ethical responsibilities on speakers to carefully research their speeches and scrupulously document their sources. Speakers must remain especially vigilant against plagiarism. Speaking today also requires applying critical thinking skills to reflect on and evaluate information. In addition, because they have so many opportunities to learn about others' perspectives, speakers must speak with cultural sensitivity. Finally, although presentation software provides an important mechanism for developing visually rich presentations, poor use of digital slides detracts from the speaker's message.

Even in today's information- and technology-driven age, excellent public speaking skills remain central to excelling personally and professionally, and for participating in a democratic society. Your public speaking class provides an important opportunity to learn the fundamentals of speaking in public. So get ready to make your voice heard.

Review it

Directory of Study and Review Resources

IN THE BOOK
Summary
Key Terms
Critical Challenges

MORE STUDY RESOURCES
Quizzes
WebLinks
Peer-reviewed videos

CourseMate

SPEECH Studio

STUDENT WORKBOOK
1.1: Introductory Speech
(Introduce Each Other)
1.2: Introductory Speech (Tell a Story)
1.3: Rating a Speaker in Terms of All Five Arts
1.4: The Role of Presentational Software
1.5: Describing a Speech in Terms of the
Communication Model

SPEECH BUDDY VIDEOS
WATCH It Video
1.1: Meeting the Speech Buddies
USE It Activity
1.1: What Are Your Public Speaking Goals?

SAMPLE SPEECH VIDEOS
Adam, self-introduction speech
Anna, "Study Abroad," impromptu speech

Uriel and Kelly, "El Equipo Perfecto,"
self-introduction speech

SPEECH BUILDER EXPRESS
Outline
Introduction
Conclusion

INFOTRAC
Recommended search terms
Public speaking skills
Public speaking in the workplace
Public speaking at social events
Public speaking in the community
Public speaking and storytelling
Confident public speaking
Managing speech anxiety
Ethical public speaking
Human communication models
Digital divide

AUDIO STUDY TOOLS
"Study Abroad," impromptu speech by Anna
Critical thinking questions
Learning objectives
Chapter summary

Guide to Your Online Resources

CourseMate Your Speech Communication CourseMate for *Public Speaking: The Evolving Art* gives you access to the Speech Buddy video and activity featured in this chapter, additional sample speech videos, Speech Studio, Speech Builder Express, InfoTrac College Edition, and study aids such as glossary flashcards, review quizzes, and the Critical Challenge questions for this chapter, which you can respond to via email. If your instructor so requests. In addition, your CourseMate features live WebLinks relevant to this chapter, including the Pew Internet & American Life Project, which reports on the impact of the internet on families, communities, work and home, daily life, education, health care, and civic and political life in the United States. Links are regularly maintained, and new ones are added periodically.

Key Terms

arrangement 8	distance speaking 14	noise 17
audience 17	environment 18	pervasive communication environment 15
audience centered 4	feedback 17	
channel 17	invention 8	public speaking 4
context 18	memory 8	rhetoric 7
delivery 8	message 16	speaker 16
digital divide 7	narrative 9	style 8

Critical Challenges

Questions for Reflection and Discussion

1. How important is storytelling when you get together with family and friends? Reflect on some of the stories your family or friends tell. What do those stories tell you about the connections between the family members or friends and their world? Can you identify a logical sequence the stories tend to follow? How do the stories spark your imagination?

2. The next time you seek information online—any kind of information— carefully consider the believability of the information. Ask yourself, Who posted this information? Why did they post it? What response do they want from me? Use your critical thinking skills to work on your information literacy skills.

3. Consider the other students in your public speaking class. How can you be culturally sensitive to your classmates' perspectives? What information can you give your classmates so they can be more sensitive to your cultural background?

4. The information age brings with it special challenges for managing your communication environment, especially shutting out sources of noise. What are some strategies you can use as an audience member to combat noise that interferes with the speaker's message? As a speaker, what can you do to help your audience shut out noise?

5. How mindful are you in your communication with others? How much attention do you pay to the way you present your ideas? What can you do to become more mindful in all your interactions with others?

6. Check out Speech Studio to evaluate other students' first in-class speeches. Or record the first speech you work on, upload it to Speech Studio, and ask your peers for their feedback. What feedback could you use to fine-tune your first speech before you give it in class?

SPEECH
✓Studio

2 Building Your Confidence

Read it

Cengage Learning

Watch it

Cengage Learning

Use it

Review it

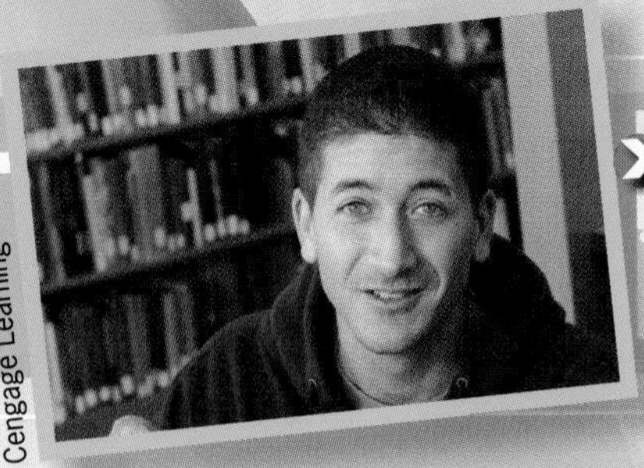

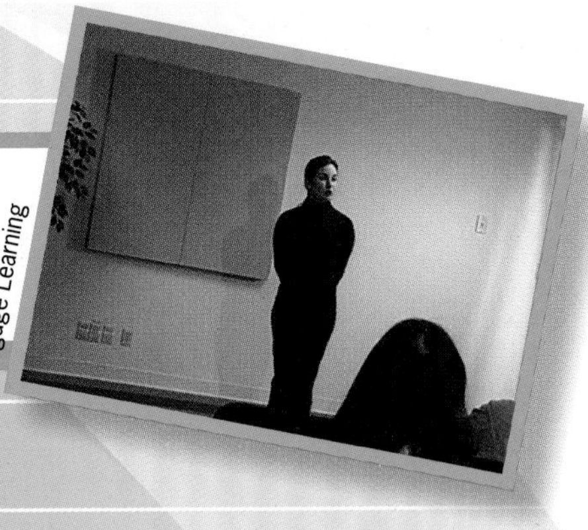

CourseMate SPEECH Studio SPEECH BUILDER EXPRESS

The sixteen women meet on Wednesday afternoons at three o'clock to present their speeches and get feedback from the others in their club. Outside observers report that as the women's public speaking skills improve, their confidence increases—something that's especially important for these women, who are incarcerated at the Decatur Correctional Center in Illinois. In addition, group members develop leadership and interpersonal skills as they become more confident public speakers. Enhancing their communication abilities in this way not only helps the women cope with day-to-day prison life, but also prepares them for the world outside prison.[1]

You may wonder how giving speeches can build confidence. It's true that the vast majority of Americans find public speaking more frightening than natural disasters, cancer, and other life-threatening situations—even death.[2] The fear of public speaking cuts across gender, ethnic background, age, and for students, even grade point average.[3] But learning to present effective speeches—a primary goal of your public speaking class—will raise your confidence and lower your speech anxiety.[4]

In the simplest terms, **speech anxiety** refers to fear of speaking in front of an audience. Before, during, and after giving a speech, speakers experience a wide range of sensations and behaviors that spring from the internal causes of nervousness. These may include quavering voice, shaky hands, changes in body temperature, itchy skin, dry mouth, the mind going blank, increased heart rate, shortness of breath, increased rate of speech, trembling legs, sweaty palms, or cold hands and feet.[5]

Fear of speaking in front of an audience.

Fortunately, speech anxiety is one of the most researched topics in communication.[6] Research has shown you can mitigate many of the causes of speech anxiety, reduce its symptoms, and use your nervous energy in productive ways. You may always feel somewhat nervous when speaking in public. That's natural, normal, and even beneficial. Think of speech anxiety as intelligent fear, an innate reaction that can serve a positive purpose. With intelligent fear, you use the responses associated with fear, such as heightened emotions, increased sensitivity to your surroundings, and greater attention to sensory information, to give a better presentation.[7] In this chapter, you'll learn about why you get nervous in public speaking situations, how you can manage that anxiety, and ways to build your confidence.

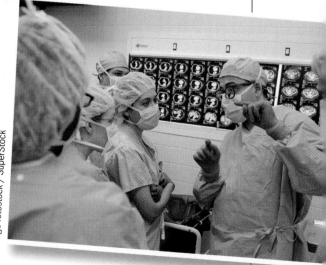
age fotostock / SuperStock

What Causes Speech Anxiety?

Fear of public speaking stems from two sources: your temperament and how you've learned to respond to uncertainty.[8] The communibiology paradigm addresses how speech anxiety is related to temperament. This perspective suggests that a fear response to public speaking is rooted in the basic biological brain activity underlying your personality. That is, your temperament or personality traits directly influence your level of speech anxiety.[9]

According to this perspective, people who are more genetically prone to speech anxiety tend to have personalities that cause them to be uncomfortable in many social situations. For example, they tend to be preoccupied with themselves and their own thoughts, often having a rich imagination and enjoying activities on their own. They also tend to exhibit anxiety, low self-esteem, shyness, guilt, and similar traits. In contrast, people who are less genetically prone to speech anxiety tend to have personality traits that cause them to enjoy social situations more. For example, they focus on their surroundings and the people in them, so they're outgoing and assertive. In addition, they are more calm, self-assured, and easygoing.[10] Few individuals are *totally* shy and anxious or *totally* outgoing and calm. But the more you exhibit personality traits that cause you to be socially uncomfortable, the higher level of speech anxiety you'll experience.

Uncertainty reduction theory addresses the other source of speech anxiety. When individuals face an uncertain or unfamiliar situation, their level of anxiety increases. For most people, speaking in public is not an everyday situation. You communicate with others every day, but probably not in a situation as formal and structured as a speech. The change in context from your regular, everyday interactions with others to an unfamiliar, public interaction naturally makes you nervous.[11] The next section identifies the areas of uncertainty associated with public speaking.

A useful tool that can help you get an idea of your speech anxiety level is the Personal Report of Public Speaking Anxiety (PRPSA).[12] You can access this tool through your CourseMate for *Public Speaking: The Evolving Art.*

> A theory that posits when individuals face an uncertain or unfamiliar situation, their level of anxiety increases.

CourseMate

The Uncertainties of Public Speaking

The public speaking context produces seven different areas of uncertainty: the speaker's role, your speaking abilities, your ideas, the audience's response, the setting, the technology used, and how others will evaluate you. Those sources are summarized in **Table 2.1.**

Table 2.1 Uncertainties and Questions about Public Speaking

Uncertainty about . . .	Question speakers ask themselves
the speaker's role	What should I do?
my speaking abilities	What am I able to do?
my ideas	How well do I know my topic?
the audience's response	How will others react?
the setting	How familiar/unfamiliar is the space?
the technology	Will the technology work?
how others will evaluate me	What impression will I make?

Uncertainty about Your Role as a Speaker

If you're like most people, you're probably much more familiar with listening than with speaking in public. In the speaker role, you may ask yourself, What should I do when I give a speech? Uncertainty about your role as a speaker can begin long before you present a speech—even in the early stages of preparation you might feel your heart rate go up as you think about your speech.[13] The less certain you are about your role as speaker, the more nervous you will feel about presenting a speech.

Uncertainty about Your Speaking Abilities

A second uncertainty associated with public speaking concerns your speaking abilities. You may wonder, What am I able to do as a speaker? You likely haven't had many opportunities to test your skills as a communicator in formal, structured situations. You may lack confidence in your abilities as a public speaker; you may not be sure you have the skills you need to speak effectively. If English is not your first language, you may also feel uncertain about any accent you may have or of your ability to pronounce words correctly.[14] The less confidence you have in your speaking skills, the more apprehension you will feel about public speaking.[15]

Uncertainty about Your Ideas

In everyday conversations, you don't expect people to research thoroughly every topic they talk about. In contrast, your public speaking audience expects you to demonstrate expertise about your subject. As a public speaker, you want to appear knowledgeable in front your audience, especially your peers. You may ask yourself, How well do I know my topic? The less sure you are about your knowledge of your topic, the more nervous you will feel about giving the speech.

Uncertainty about the Audience's Response

When you have a pretty good idea about what will happen in a given situation, you feel fairly comfortable. In public speaking, you don't know exactly how audience members will respond to your message.[17] There's no doubt the audience's response influences the speaker's confidence. If audience members smile and nod their heads, you're more likely to feel confident about your speech and ideas. If audience members avoid eye contact or frown, you're more likely to feel anxious about your speech.[18] So you might ask yourself, How will listeners react to my speech? When you present a speech, you risk having your ideas rejected. The less you believe you can predict a positive response from your audience, the more anxious you will feel.

Uncertainty about the Setting

As a student, you're used to the instructor standing in the front of the room. As a speaker, you're the one up there in

Jeff Greenberg / Alamy

Most people are nervous about being evaluated. But in speaking situations, few audience members will notice small mistakes you make. They're more interested in what you have to say than in whether you say it perfectly.

Speaking of . . .

Information that Increases Anxiety

A study of middle-school children found that when a peer related a negative public speaking experience, the children's anxiety decreased. The reverse was true as well—a peer's positive story about public speaking increased the children's speech anxiety. Why? The researchers believe that the negative information led the children to think public speaking was something they could do—they could certainly do a better job than the peer who told the dismal story. On the other hand, the positive story made effective public speaking seem unattainable because the peer seemed so extraordinarily skilled at it.[16] When you watch the Speech Buddy videos, remember that Evan, Janine, Anthony, and Erin are students just like you—they're not perfect, and they'll tell you about their speaking mishaps as well as their successes.

27

Chapter 2 : Building Your Confidence

front. The room seems very different—and often more intimidating—from this vantage point. While you may be accustomed to public settings as an audience member, you're probably less used to such settings as a speaker.[19] When considering where you'll give your speech, you might ask, How familiar is the speaking space? The more unfamiliar the setting, the more nervous you may feel about your speech.

Uncertainty about Technology

You text family and friends from your cell phone. If the phone's battery goes dead, you may be annoyed and frustrated, but not embarrassed. In contrast, when the laptop you're using for your speech freezes, you panic and your anxiety level soars. When thinking about giving a speech, you'll probably ask, Will the technology work? Lack of familiarity with technical equipment and concerns about it working increase a speaker's nervousness.

Uncertainty about Evaluation

Fear of negative evaluation plays a major role in students' anxiety about public speaking and contributes to physical symptoms such as elevated heart rate and queasiness. Even after you learn how your instructor grades speeches, you may feel nervous about how your classmates will respond. In other public speaking situations, such as giving an oral report at work or nominating someone at a meeting, speakers are also concerned about how the audience will view them.[20] Research shows, however, that the **spotlight effect** leads a speaker to *think* people observe her or him much more carefully than they actually do.[21] Many minor speaking errors, such as stumbling over a word, briefly losing your place, or skipping to the wrong digital slide, are far more noticeable to you than to the audience. Of course, listeners will evaluate your presentation, but the spotlight probably isn't nearly as bright as you might think.

A phenomenon that leads us to think other people observe us much more carefully than they actually do.

Strategies for Building Your Confidence

The remainder of this chapter takes you through the whole itinerary of the public speaking experience, from the weeks before the speech to the hours afterward, to identify what you can do at each stage to effectively manage speech anxiety and build your confidence. These strategies focus on the two root causes of speech anxiety: your temperament and your uncertainties about public speaking. So whether your speech anxiety comes primarily from your personality or those uncertainties—or both—these approaches to addressing anxiety will help.

Visualization, Relabeling, and Relaxation

Visualization, relabeling, and relaxation are three methods you can use to manage speech anxiety, build your confidence, and improve your effectiveness when you speak.

Visualization When you apply **visualization** to public speaking, you think through the sequence of events that will make up the speech with a positive, detailed, concrete, step-by-step approach. Imagine the place, the audience, and yourself successfully presenting your speech. Focus on what will go right, not what will go wrong. But also imagine how the event will unfold in a realistic way.[22] Use all your senses to *feel* what will happen. Visualize yourself

Imagining a successful communication event by thinking through a sequence of events in a positive, concrete, step-by-step way.

- Gathering your notes, standing up, and walking to the front of the room.
- Facing the audience, making eye contact, smiling, and beginning the speech.

- Observing audience members nodding, jotting down a few notes, and listening intently.

- Presenting each main point.

- Incorporating effective presentation media.

- Giving the conclusion and listening to audience members clapping.

- Answering questions readily.

- Thanking the audience, walking back to your seat, and sitting down.

- Congratulating yourself on giving an effective speech.

Psychologists, teachers, athletes, actors, and many others emphasize the importance of controlling your feelings when facing the challenge of a public presentation. You may already have visualized success in challenging situations. When you visualize your speech going well, you will reduce your anxiety, build your confidence, and give a more dynamic presentation.[23]

Relabeling

Relabeling involves assigning positive words or phrases to the physical reactions and feelings associated with speech anxiety. You stop using negative words and phrases like *fearful* and *apprehensive*, and instead use positive words like *thrilled* and *delighted*. When your voice quavers a bit and your hands shake, attribute those sensations to your body and mind gathering the energy they need to prepare for and present the speech. Say to yourself, "I'm really excited about giving this speech!" rather than, "I'm so nervous about this speech." Your anxiety won't magically disappear, but relabeling puts your response to public speaking in a positive light and can increase your ability to manage your anxiety.

Assigning more positive words or phrases to the physical reactions and feelings associated with speech anxiety.

Relaxation Techniques

Relaxation techniques help reduce the physical symptoms of stress, such as increased heart rate and tense muscles. Developing good breathing habits provides the foundation for relaxing. Three exercises that can help you increase breathing efficiency, reduce nervousness, and help you relax are diaphragmatic breathing, meditation breathing, and tension-release breathing.[24]

The first exercise, *diaphragmatic breathing*, relies upon smooth, even breathing using your diaphragm. Sit or stand with your feet flat on the floor, shoulder-width apart. With your hands just below your rib cage, breathe in with an exaggerated yawn while pushing your abdomen out. Exhale slowly and gently, letting your abdomen relax inward.

Speaking of . . .

Can-do Language

How you label things shapes your experiences with them. Do you view difficult times as challenges or as problems? Do you focus on opportunities or on barriers? When you think of public speaking as a chore, you're probably not going to get very excited about your next speech. In contrast, if you think of public speaking as talking about your ideas and getting feedback from an audience, you're more likely to anticipate your next speech with enthusiasm. That enthusiasm can motivate you to thoroughly plan and prepare your presentation.

Table 2.2 Visualization, Relabeling, and Relaxation

Strategy	Brief Definition	Example
Visualization	Imagining successful presentation	Envision audience's positive response to speech introduction.
Relabeling	Assigning positive words to anxious feelings	Use "lively" or "energetic" instead of "nervous."
Relaxation techniques	Reducing physical symptoms of stress	Engage in meditation breathing by focusing on how it feels to breathe.

The second exercise, *meditation breathing*, helps your body relax. Begin by breathing with your diaphragm, but this time focus on every aspect of the breathing process and how it feels. Clear your mind of all thoughts and concentrate on the rhythm of your breathing: in breath, out breath, in breath, out breath.

The last exercise, *tension-release breathing*, combines diaphragmatic breathing with relaxing specific parts of your body. Begin by finding a comfortable position and breathing naturally. While you're breathing, identify tense muscle areas. Then inhale fully, using your diaphragm. As you slowly exhale, relax one tense muscle area. Continue this process until you feel completely relaxed. This exercise can be done systematically by starting at your head and progressing to your toes, or vice versa.[25]

Visualizing a successful presentation, relabeling anxious feelings, and using relaxation techniques are three proven ways to reduce anxiety. **Table 2.2** summarizes these strategies.

Cengage Learning

SPEECH BUDDY VIDEO 2.1
Using Strategies for Managing Speech Anxiety

In this video, Janine reviews and demonstrates the steps used in visualization, relabeling, and relaxing. You may want to watch the segment twice, first to see how each strategy works, and then to take notes to use when you try the techniques yourself.

Cengage Learning

ACTIVITY 2.1
Anxiety Management Trainee

This activity guides you through visualizing, relabeling, and relaxing. After you've tried out each strategy, you'll identify which strategies worked best for you.

30

Building Your Confidence Before the Day of Your Speech

In addition to using visualization, relabeling, and relaxation techniques to build confidence and manage nervousness, effectively completing all the planning and preparation steps in the speechmaking process will reduce many of the uncertainties associated with public speaking. Use the following strategies to manage anxiety as you develop your speeches.

Start Planning and Preparing Your Speech Early

Getting an early start on speech preparation reduces speech anxiety. Schedule plenty of time to work on your speech—and stick with that schedule. Students who procrastinate invariably experience higher levels of speech anxiety than those who get an early start.[26]

Choose a Topic You Care About

If you're highly interested in your topic, you'll focus more on it and less on yourself.[27] Chapter 4 goes into greater detail about how to choose a topic. For now, consider some topics you might want to discuss with an audience. Are you willing to speak out about them, even with people you may not know very well? Will you get *really* nervous talking about them in front of your audience? Some nervousness is okay, but if you think speaking on a particular topic will make your anxiety unmanageable, avoid that topic. Choose topics you feel confident talking about, find compelling, and believe will interest your audience.

Become an Expert on Your Topic

Thoroughly researching your topic, discussed in depth in Chapter 6, will greatly increase your confidence and success as a public speaker.[28] What you present in your speech comprises only a small portion of what you know about the topic. If you *don't* do your research, you *will* be nervous about your speech.

Research Your Audience

Learn all you can about your audience to reduce your uncertainty about who they are, what they know about your topic, how they feel about it, and how they are likely to respond (Chapter 5). Becoming familiar with your audience makes it easier to design your speech for them and increases the likelihood they will respond positively to it.[29]

Practice Your Speech

Rehearse your speech several times before the presentation day (Chapter 11). If possible, practice in a location similar to the one where you'll give your speech—classroom, conference room, auditorium—to reduce your uncertainty about the setting. Practicing in front of others provides you with observers who can give you feedback and lower your anxiety. And research shows that practicing your speech before an audience—especially an audience of four or more people—not only reduces your anxiety but also results in a higher evaluation of your presentation.[30] As you practice, you'll discover what body movements are appropriate for you and your speech. You'll also identify how best to use your notes and integrate presentation media.

People who are more outgoing and assertive may not experience much anxiety when anticipating a public speaking situation. Although low anxiety may seem like an advantage, it can result in little motivation to plan and practice a speech. Failing to

---

Practicing with Audiences in Your Community

Giving the same or similar speech for multiple audiences is one of the best ways to build your confidence and reduce your speech anxiety.[32] As you develop speeches for your public speaking class, consider other groups that might benefit from your ideas, such as middle school students or a local nonprofit organization. Contact a few of those groups and arrange to give your speech. After your presentation, reflect on your performance, your degree of nervousness, and the audience's response. Compare your community experience with your classroom speech.

rehearse a speech, however, will have a negative impact on the presentation and likely result in increased anxiety during the speech.[31] Even the best speakers practice.

Know Your Introduction and Conclusion Well

Successfully presenting the introduction of your speech will boost your confidence, help calm your nerves, and reduce worrisome thoughts that increase anxiety.[33] Knowing that you'll finish with a coherent, smooth, and memorable conclusion will increase your confidence and lessen your nervousness throughout your speech. One useful strategy for knowing your introduction and conclusion well is to write them out word for word. Then read them aloud a few times, listening to how they sound and making any necessary changes. Once you're satisfied with your introduction and conclusion, commit them to memory as best you can. Although generally you don't want to memorize your entire speech, memorizing your introduction and conclusion will help you present them more fluently and lessen your anxiety.

Careful planning and preparation reduce some of the uncertainties public speakers face. Implementing these long-term strategies won't change your personality, but will increase your confidence. The next section explains additional short-term strategies for managing speech anxiety.

In any public speaking situation, rehearsing beforehand can help you develop a polished presentation and increase your confidence that you'll do well.

Thomas Northcut/Jupiter images

Building Your Confidence on the Day of Your Speech

If you have planned, prepared, and practiced your speech, you should feel more confident about your presentation. But still—your hands are shaking, your stomach is queasy, and your mouth is dry. How can you calm these last-minute jitters? The strategies in this section will help you manage your anxiety on the day of your speech.

Before Presenting Your Speech

The following techniques provide ways to boost your confidence the day you give your speech.

- *Dress for the occasion.* Although great clothes can't make up for a poorly prepared speech, if you're dressed appropriately for the setting you'll feel more comfortable and your nervousness will lessen. Not sure what to wear? Think of how a speaker would dress to gain *your* respect. Choose clothes that convey a professional appearance and fit the occasion.

© Digital Vision / Alamy

© Digital Vision / Alamy

Dressing for the speaking occasion will give you confidence and lower your speech anxiety.

- *Keep all your notes and materials organized.* Put all the materials for your speech in a single location where you'll remember to bring them with you. When you arrive, arrange them so you can calmly and confidently walk to the front of the room when it's your turn to speak.

- *Arrive early.* Give yourself plenty of time to get to your speaking location. If you come rushing in at the last minute, or even late, you'll increase your stress level.

- *Take calming breaths.* Taking a few calming breaths before your speech will help you relax. Recall what you learned earlier in the chapter about diaphragmatic and meditation breathing. Exhale completely and then push out the last bit of air. Pause for a second or two, then gently inhale. Pause again, then exhale, this time as you would naturally. Follow this pattern for a minute or so, thinking only about how you're breathing. You should feel calmer as your body gets the oxygen it needs and you clear your mind and focus on what you're going to say.

- *Warm up your voice.* To get ready to give your speech, talk aloud in a private spot without others around or talk with other people at the speaking event. You'll warm up your voice, and chatting with others will help you relax.[34]

- *Make sure all technical aspects of your speech are ready to go.* If you are using a laptop computer and LCD projector that aren't yours, for example, arrange to have them set up in advance. After you arrive, check that the system is functioning properly. If you are using an overhead projector, make sure it works and provides a clear image on the screen. By taking care of these details, you will reduce technological uncertainty (Chapter 10).

- *Concentrate on the other speakers.* Actively listening to what others are saying takes the focus off yourself and can help calm your nerves. You might even gather some information you can weave into your speech so that you'll better adapt your message to your audience (Chapter 5). Writing down speakers' main points and participating in the question-and-answer sessions after their speeches will keep your attention on what others have to say.

Building your confidence and reducing your anxiety before you give your speech will help prepare you to manage the nervousness you'll likely feel during your presentation.

During Your Speech

Even with the most thorough preparation, you'll probably experience some anxiety as you give your speech. You can use the following strategies to manage anxiety during your presentation:

- *Display a confident attitude.* You've chosen a topic in which you're interested, done your research, analyzed your audience, organized your ideas, and practiced your speech. You're dressed for the occasion, and you arrived early at the location of your speech. You're an expert on your topic, and you're happy to have the opportunity to tell your audience about it. So when it's your turn to get up and speak, put into motion the positive scenario you previously visualized:
  - Calmly walk to the front of the room.
  - Face your audience and look at all your listeners.
  - Take a deep breath and smile.
  - Clearly, confidently, and enthusiastically begin your speech.

- *Expect to experience some speech anxiety.* Most speakers become nervous before they speak, with anxiety generally decreasing after they present the introduction,[35] but your anxiety may fluctuate throughout your speech. With more experience, you'll have a better idea of when you'll feel anxious. Remember, you're managing your speech anxiety, not getting rid of it.

- *Turn your anxiety into productive energy.* Relabel speech anxiety as a positive source of body energy. Put that nervousness to work in appropriate gestures, body movement, facial expressions, and tone of voice. For example, use the little energy jolt you feel when facing an audience to increase your voice volume and gesture expressively to highlight key points in your speech.

- *Avoid overanalyzing your anxiety.* Concentrating on your speech anxiety distracts you from what you want to say and makes you more nervous. Acknowledge your anxiety, but don't dwell on it. Later you can reflect on your presentation and how you felt.

- *Never comment on your speech anxiety.* Most people experience the **illusion of transparency**, believing their internal states, such as speech anxiety, are easily observable by others. Studies show that speakers consistently rate themselves as more nervous than audience members do.[36] However, if you point out your

The tendency of individuals to believe that how they feel is much more apparent to others than is really the case.

nervousness, listeners will search for signs of anxiety, distracting them from what you're saying. Also, you'll sense their scrutiny and feel even more anxious.

- *Focus on your audience, not on yourself.* Analyzing your audience (Chapter 5) helps you concentrate on their needs and interests rather than on yourself. Putting your efforts toward effectively presenting your message reduces your self-consciousness and nervousness. Viewing audience members as friends rather than opponents also diminishes anxiety.[37]

- *Pay attention to audience feedback.* When you appear confident, your audience will return that energy with nods, smiles, and eye contact. This doesn't mean that every audience member will agree with your message, but they will find your confidence agreeable. This positive audience feedback reduces uncertainty about your role as a public speaker and lessens your anxiety.

- *Make no apologies or excuses.* If you misstate a point, get your ideas out of order, or mispronounce a word, simply make the correction and go on. For example, if you realize you've missed a major point, finish the point you're discussing, then say something like, "To put this in context ..." and go back to the point you accidentally skipped. Avoid excuses such as, "My computer crashed last night, so I don't have my digital slides," which hurt your credibility. Your audience may respond negatively, heightening your own nervousness.

Nearly all speakers experience some speech anxiety during their presentations. Use that anxiety or energy to your advantage for a more focused and dynamic speech.

After You've Presented Your Speech

You might still feel some anxiety after you've finished your speech—that's not unusual. Here are some ways to manage that anxiety.

- *Listen carefully to audience members' questions.* Give yourself time to formulate your responses. Ask for clarification if you're not sure you understand a question. For example, you might say, "I'm not exactly sure what you mean by that. Would you elaborate on your question?" Attending to audience members' questions with full concentration will keep the focus on your audience and help you manage anxiety. Many speakers find that their feelings of nervousness decrease considerably during the question-and-answer period after the formal speech.

- *Recognize that speech anxiety can occur even after you finish your speech.* Some speakers say that reflecting back on their speeches makes them more nervous than actually giving their speeches. When this happens, think about your overall presentation. Review what you did well and what you could improve next time, but don't blame yourself for any feelings of nervousness that you experience after your speech.

- *Reinforce your confidence.* Congratulate yourself on completing your speech. Reflect on all the work you put into your presentation.

- *Identify useful strategies for managing speech anxiety.* Recall the times during your speech when you felt most comfortable. What strategies worked well in managing your nervousness?

- *Develop a plan for managing anxiety to use in future public speaking situations.* You've learned about ways to manage speech anxiety, but you need to adjust those strategies to fit your personality and speaking style. List ways to manage anxiety that you'll apply in future speeches. Then consider additional strategies that will increase your confidence and decrease your nervousness.

For most speakers, speech anxiety tapers off at the end of the speech. But some speakers still experience anxiety after the formal speech is completed.

Table 2.3 Strategies for Building Your Confidence

Time leading up to speech day	Speech day, before you speak	Speech day, while you're speaking	Speech day, after you speak
• Start speech preparation early. • Choose a topic you care about. • Become an expert on your topic. • Research your audience. • Practice your speech. • Know your introduction and conclusion. • Use visualization. • Use relabeling. • Use relaxation techniques.	• Dress appropriately. • Keep all speech materials organized. • Arrive early. • Take calming breaths. • Warm up your voice. • Check on technical equipment. • Listen to other speakers. • Use visualization. • Use relabeling. • Use relaxation techniques.	• Display a confident attitude. • Expect to feel some anxiety. • Turn anxiety into productive energy. • Avoid overanalyzing your anxiety. • Do not comment on your anxiety to your audience. • Focus on the audience, not yourself. • Attend to audience feedback. • Make no apologies and give no excuses.	• Listen to audience members' questions. • Know that anxiety may occur. • Reinforce your confident attitude. • Identify effective anxiety management strategies. • Develop plans for managing future speech anxiety.

Nearly everyone experiences speech anxiety, and you probably will, too. Speech anxiety won't go away, but you've learned about many ways to manage it. **Table 2.3** summarizes strategies for increasing confidence before, during, and after your speech.

> **Watch it**

SPEECH BUDDY VIDEO 2.2
Taking a Closer Look at Your Public Speaking Anxiety

Anthony and Janine appear in this video. First they describe their dominant fears or sources of public speaking anxiety, and then they briefly discuss how they each manage those fears.

> **Use it**

ACTIVITY 2.2
What, Me Worry?

This activity gives you a chance to identify your own fears associated with public speaking and develop a plan for managing your speech anxiety.

Summary

You'll never be completely free of your fear of public speaking—and that's good. Why? Because those feelings motivate you to prepare for your speech. When you think about the day you're scheduled to speak, you should feel a little jolt and think, "I need to finish my research," "I need to learn more about my audience," or "I need to practice my speech again." Without nervousness to motivate you, you might not prepare thoroughly for your speech, and will likely do poorly as a result.

Visualization, relabeling, and relaxation techniques help you increase your confidence as a speaker, and decrease your nervousness. Still, you need more than the right mental framework to manage your fear of public speaking. Thorough planning, preparation, and practice give you the confidence that you are truly ready for your presentation. All speakers must learn to live with feelings of nervousness. In this chapter, you've learned about many concrete strategies to cope with these feelings. As you develop ways to manage your speech anxiety, you'll become more confident as a speaker. Rather than overwhelming you, the nervousness you feel can help you present a dynamic, engaging, and audience-centered speech.

Review it

Directory of Study and Review Resources

IN THE BOOK
Summary

Key Terms

Critical Challenges

MORE STUDY RESOURCES
Quizzes

WebLinks

Peer-reviewed videos

STUDENT WORKBOOK
2.1: Identifying Confident Behaviors

2.2: Identifying Nervous Behaviors

2.3: Relabeling Your Experience

2.4: In for Five, Hold for Five, Out for Five

2.5: Unique New York

SPEECH BUDDY VIDEOS
WATCH It Video

2.1: Using Strategies for Managing
    Speech Anxiety

2.2: Taking a Closer Look at Your
    Public Speaking Anxiety

USE It Activity

2.1: Anxiety Management Trainee

2.2: What, Me Worry?

SAMPLE SPEECH VIDEOS
Jessica, self-introduction speech

Loren, "Wear a Ribbon," impromptu speech

SPEECH BUILDER EXPRESS
Outline

Introduction

Conclusion

INFOTRAC COLLEGE EDITION
Recommended search terms

Confident speech delivery

Anxiety and speech delivery

Managing speech anxiety

Visualization techniques

Relabeling techniques

Relaxation techniques

AUDIO STUDY TOOLS
Self-introduction speech by Jessica

Critical thinking questions

Learning objectives

Chapter summary

Guide to Your Online Resources

CourseMate Your Speech Communication CourseMate for *Public Speaking: The Evolving Art* give you access to the Speech Buddy video and activity featured in this chapter, additional sample speech videos, Speech Studio, Speech Builder Express, InfoTrac College Edition, and study aids such as glossary flashcards, review quizzes, and the Critical Challenge questions for this chapter, which you can respond to via email if your instructor so requests. In addition, your CourseMate features live web links relevant to this chapter, including sites on measuring your level of speech anxiety and additional relaxation techniques. Links are regularly maintained, and new ones are added periodically.

Key Terms

illusion of transparency 34	speech anxiety 25	uncertainty reduction theory 26
relabeling 29	spotlight effect 28	visualization 28

Critical Challenges

Questions for Reflection and Discussion

1. Review the section on the communibiological paradigm and speech anxiety. Would you describe yourself as generally uncomfortable in social situations, or do you tend to enjoy them? Considering your personality, which strategies for managing speech anxiety work best for you?

2. Speakers who are generally uncomfortable in social situations tend to experience greater levels of speech anxiety. How might that be a positive response to giving a speech? In contrast, speakers who generally enjoy social situations tend to have lower levels of speech anxiety. How might that cause problems for those speakers?

3. One uncertainty speakers face in public speaking is how the audience will respond to their ideas. Reflect on situations in which you think an audience might reject your ideas. How might fear of rejection lead you to avoid possible speech topics? What might be some positive aspects of such avoidance? What might be the drawbacks of avoiding possible speech topics?

4. The spotlight effect suggests that speakers overestimate how much others notice their actions. Consider recent public speaking situations, such as a classroom lecture or a presentation at work, in which you've been an audience member. Describe the speaker's attire and mannerisms, gestures, voice, main ideas, and other speech content. How observant were you? What are the implications of the spotlight effect? Are audience members not observant enough? Or are speakers too worried about themselves and how they appear to others?

3

Ethical Speaking and Listening

Cengage Learning

Cengage Learning

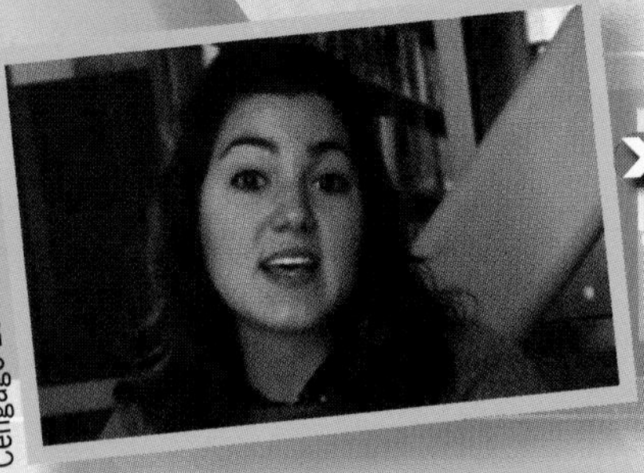

CourseMate

SPEECH Studio

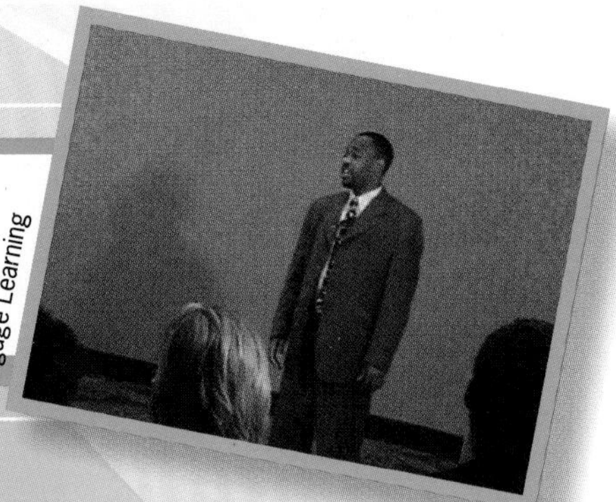

SPEECH BUILDER EXPRESS

Speeches go along with graduation ceremonies—students, administrators, faculty, parents, and alumni often make a few remarks about the graduates' efforts and their future. But in the case of one Illinois high school graduation, both the principal and the valedictorian plagiarized their speeches. That's right—the words they spoke belonged to someone else. The principal copied a former student's speech and the valedictorian downloaded a speech from the internet.[1]

Ethical communication refers to the moral aspects of speaking and listening, such as being truthful, fair, and respectful. In plagiarizing their speeches, the principal and the valedictorian practiced unethical communication, giving presentations taken from other sources.

Digital technology has increased the ethical responsibilities communicators must accept when they interact with others.[2] For instance, you now have access to a wealth of information online. How do speakers apply ethical standards to determine what information to use and what to avoid? You can also easily integrate audio and video files into presentations. What ethical guidelines should speakers apply when using these media? Audience members have digital technology at their disposal that raises ethical dilemmas. Should listeners record a speech without the speaker's knowledge? What are the ethical implications of audience members texting, instant messaging, and using other forms of electronic communication while a speaker is talking? Ethical issues such as these present challenges for public speakers and their audiences.

The moral aspects of our interactions with others, including truthfulness, fairness, responsibility, integrity, and respect.

Colin Hawkins/Taxi/Getty

Codes of Ethics

Many professional organizations have adopted codes of ethics. For example, the National Speakers Association requires members to sign an ethics statement before they join. The National Communication Association established ethical principles to guide members in their teaching, research, service, and professional interactions. The International Association of Business Communicators adopted a code of ethics centered on mutual understanding and cultural sensitivity.[3] Codes of ethics provide a basis for discussing communication practices and suggest the qualities a group or organization expects its members to possess.[4] **Table 3.1** provides abbreviated versions of these organizations' codes of ethics.

Apply it

A Community Code of Ethics

Effective community building requires a sound ethical base, but individuals and groups often don't spend much time talking about ethical behavior and ethical communication. You can help people in your community engage in discussions about ethical communication and practice your public speaking skills at the same time. First, choose a target group you think might be interested in learning about how ethical communication can help build community, such as elementary school children, students in your campus residence halls, or members of a local neighborhood organization or high school student club. Second, gather examples of codes of ethics from various organizations, such as corporations, nonprofits, and schools. Third, facilitate a discussion or a series of discussions in which participants examine the various codes of ethics and create guidelines that will work for their particular group. After the discussion, reflect on what you've learned about ethical communication and community.

Ethical Communication in the Classroom

According to the National Communication Association (NCA), "ethical communication enhances human worth and dignity by fostering truthfulness, fairness, responsibility, personal integrity, and respect for self and other."[5] This short statement offers clear guidance for speakers. For example, ethical speakers present accurate information, consider all sides of an issue, carefully research their topics, and demonstrate respect for themselves and their audiences.

The statement also applies to audience members. Effective listening skills form an important basis for a productive **communication climate**—the psychological and emotional tone that develops as people interact with others.[6] Ethical listeners come to a speaking event prepared to use active listening skills and provide meaningful feedback. Working together, ethical speakers and listeners promote a supportive communication climate in which everyone feels free to express ideas in a respectful manner. In contrast, a defensive communication climate develops when listeners and speakers behave disrespectfully and inhibit the free expression of ideas.

As a speaker and listener in your public speaking class, you can help create an ethical community of communicators in which each person assumes personal and shared responsibility. A public speaking class requires each student to assume a high degree of personal responsibility because so much of the work is undertaken outside of class. To excel in this class, you must make a firm commitment to developing your public speaking skills. A strong sense of community thrives as speakers and listeners collaborate to produce a supportive communication climate.

The psychological and emotional tone that develops as communicators interact with one another.

Table 3.1   Codes of Ethics for Three Professional Organizations

National Speakers Association (NSA) Code of Professional Ethics

Article 1

The NSA member shall accurately represent qualifications and experience in both oral and written communications.

Article 2

The NSA member shall act, operate his/her business, and speak on a high professional level so as to neither offend nor bring discredit to the speaking profession.

Article 3

The NSA member shall exert diligence to understand the client's organization, approaches and goals in advance of the presentation.

Article 4

The NSA member shall avoid using materials, titles and thematic creations originated by others, either orally or in writing, unless approved by the originator.

Article 5

The NSA member shall treat other speakers with professional courtesy, dignity and respect.

Article 6

The NSA member shall maintain and respect the confidentiality of business or personal affairs of clients, agents and other speakers.

Article 7

The NSA member shall protect the public against fraud or unfair practices and shall attempt to eliminate from the speaking profession all practices that bring discredit to the profession.

Article 8

The NSA member shall not be a party to any agreement to unfairly limit or restrain access to the marketplace by any other speaker, client or to the public, based upon economic factors, race, creed, color, sex, age, disability or country of national origin of another speaker.

Source: National Speakers Association

National Communication Association (NCA) General Ethical Principles

1. We advocate truthfulness, accuracy, honesty, and reason as essential to the integrity of communication.
2. We endorse freedom of expression, diversity of perspective, and tolerance of dissent to achieve the informed and responsible decision making fundamental to a civil society.
3. We strive to understand and respect other communicators before evaluating and responding to their messages.
4. We promote access to communication resources and opportunities as necessary to fulfill human potential and contribute to the well-being of families, communities, and society.
5. We promote communication climates of caring and mutual understanding that respect the unique needs and characteristics of individual communicators.
6. We condemn communication that degrades individuals and humanity through distortion, intimidation, coercion, and violence, and through the expression of intolerance and hatred.
7. We are committed to the courageous expression of personal convictions in pursuit of fairness and justice.
8. We advocate sharing information, opinions, and feelings when facing significant choices while also respecting privacy and confidentiality.
9. We accept responsibility for the short- and long-term consequences for our own communication and expect the same of others.

Source: National Communication Association

International Association of Business Communicators (IABC) Code of Ethics

Professional communicators:

1. Uphold the credibility and dignity of their profession by practicing honest, candid, and timely communication.
2. Disseminate accurate information and promptly correct any erroneous communication for which they may be responsible.
3. Understand and support the principles of free speech, freedom of assembly, and access to an open marketplace of ideas and act accordingly.
4. Are sensitive to cultural values and beliefs and engage in fair and balanced communication activities that foster and encourage mutual understanding.
5. Refrain from taking part in any undertaking which the communicator considers to be unethical.
6. Obey laws and public policies governing their professional activities and are sensitive to the spirit of all laws and regulations.
7. Give credit for unique expressions borrowed from others and identify the sources and purposes of all information disseminated to the public.
8. Protect confidential information and, at the same time, comply with all legal requirements for the disclosure of information affecting the welfare of others.
9. Do not use confidential information gained as a result of professional activities for personal benefit.
10. Do not accept undisclosed gifts or payments for professional services from anyone other than a client or employer.
11. Do not guarantee results that are beyond the power of the practitioner to deliver.
12. Are honest not only with others but also, and most importantly, with themselves as individuals.

Source: International Association of Business Communicators

Although there are many perspectives on ethics, *dialogic ethics* provides an especially useful approach to public speaking. Firmly grounded in communication, dialogic ethics promotes **dialogue**, in which communicators are invited to express their ideas with the goal of understanding each other.[7] In contrast, **monologue** occurs when communication is one way and communicators are only concerned with their own individual goals. Creating true dialogue requires a passion for comprehending the speaker and performing well as a listener.[8]

Respect, open-mindedness, and active listening form the basis of dialogic ethics. The principles associated with this approach are discussed in the next section. You can use them as guidelines for facilitating ethical communication in public speaking.

> Occurs when speakers are sensitive to audience needs and listen to audience members' responses, and listeners pay careful attention to speakers' messages so they can respond appropriately and effectively.

> Occurs when communication is one way and communicators are only concerned with their own individual goals.

Facilitate a Supportive Communication Climate

Creating a supportive communication climate gives everyone an equal opportunity to communicate and encourages the open exchange of ideas. As an ethical speaker, you'll deliver speeches that address the needs of specific audience members. For example, you'd deliver a very different speech on emergency preparedness to third graders than you would to college students. As an ethical listener, give each speaker your undivided attention—turn off your cell phone, avoid irrelevant comments and distracting movements, and focus on the speaker's message.

> Words that attack groups such as racial, ethnic, religious, and sexual minorities.

Avoiding the use of derogatory language is also essential to a supportive communication climate.[9] **Hate speech**—words that attack groups such as racial, ethnic, religious, and sexual minorities—is hurtful and degrading. That's why many colleges and universities have adopted policies against hate speech. And research shows that those policies work. Although college students report high levels of tolerance for diverse viewpoints, the same is *not* true for hate speech.[10] Refrain from using hate language in your speeches, and challenge others who use it.

Demonstrate Mutual Respect

Dialogic ethics involves respecting commonalities as well as differences between yourself and others.[11] You show respect for a speaker's ideas by demonstrating your interest—maintaining eye contact, taking notes, and giving relevant feedback. As the speaker is talking, consider the main points presented in light of what you already know about the topic. Also, fully understand the speaker's message before responding. For example, if you disagree with a speaker's position on gun control, you might want to first check for clarification, saying something like, "If I understand you correctly, you support our current laws on gun ownership and want no changes in those laws. Is that a fair interpretation?"

Similarly, as a speaker, listen carefully and respectfully to questions. Try to gather more information from listeners if they object to your ideas. You might say, "In my research, I found strong support for changing our current gun laws. But I know not everyone agrees with that position, including some experts. So I'd like to hear more about your thinking on the issue." In addition, listen to questions without interruption before responding.

Promote Honest Communication

Communication is the fundamental social behavior that links one human being to another. Just as you want to be respected, so do others. You create this respect through truthful, accurate, honest, and logical interaction with others. Truthfulness includes

Speaking of . . .

Hate Speech versus Free Speech

Professor Gerald Uelmen, dean of Santa Clara University's law school and a fellow of the Markkula Center for Applied Ethics, presents arguments both for and against campus hate speech codes. In arguing for such codes, he notes the harm done to individual students and the campus climate when colleges and universities allow hate speech. He also notes that restricting hate speech encourages logical debates, rather than relying on denigration and oppression. In arguing against such codes, Professor Uelmen observes that they run counter to the First Amendment's guarantee of free speech. In addition, students may remain silent, fearful of violating the hate speech code. To learn more about this issue, read Professor Uelmen's comments on the Center's website, scu.edu/ethics.

crediting sources of information. Dishonest communication, such as plagiarizing others' work, can have serious consequences. For example, the valedictorian described in this chapter's opening had to return the award given at graduation and his speech was erased from the videotape of the ceremony. The high school principal lost his job when it was revealed he had given a commencement address using someone else's speech, reciting it word for word and not mentioning the true author.[12]

When taking questions from audience members, you're more likely to encourage dialogue if you listen and respond respectfully to their questions.

Convey Positive Attitude for Learning

When communicators possess a positive attitude for learning, they want to learn all they can about a topic. As a speaker, adhering to this ethical principle means using all the resources available for gathering information as you progress through the speechmaking process. The ethical speaker also participates in public discussions to learn about timely issues and hear diverse opinions, and encourages others to join in. The ethical listener thoughtfully considers and responds to what others say, thereby increasing all participants' access to information.

Ethical communication requires gathering as much information as possible, but *not* at the expense of others' right to privacy and confidentiality. Suppose you email an expert on your topic. Is it all right to use the person's reply without asking for permission? Although legally most email is considered public communication, people generally think of email exchanges between individuals as private communication. In this case, ask the person's permission before including the information in your speech, and then tell your audience the source. Public online communication, such as listservs, chats, newsgroups, and other discussion forums, typically aren't considered private. Still, it's best to check with the group before using any information they provide.

Appreciate Individual Differences

Respecting others' perspectives is one hallmark of the effective listener, which is discussed in greater detail later in this chapter.[13] For example, instead of avoiding speakers whose positions differ from yours, this ethical principle suggests that you listen to them with an open mind in order to better understand viewpoints that differ from your own.

The First Amendment to the U.S. Constitution embodies the basic ideal that freedom, diversity, and tolerance for differing viewpoints are essential to democracy:

> Congress shall make no law respecting an establishment of religion, or prohibiting the free exercise thereof; or abridging the freedom of speech, or of the press; or the right of the people peaceably to assemble, and to petition the Government for a redress of grievances.

For public speaking, this principle gives you the freedom to speak your mind about controversial topics. But with that freedom comes the responsibility to research your topics so that the speeches you give reflect an informed perspective. You may have strong views about contentious subjects such as cloning, the death penalty, and immigration. Informed and responsible public speaking requires that you investigate these topics thoroughly so that you can articulate your position in meaningful ways.

Accept Conflict

Ethical communicators accept conflict as inevitable, recognizing that working through disagreements can produce positive change. Embracing more controversial topics in your speeches demands your audience's attention and engages them in your presentation.

Henry Louis Gates, Jr., chair of the African and African American Studies Department at Harvard University, provides a good example of confronting a contentious topic. In a speech at the Commonwealth Club, he made the following statement:

> The other reason our people are still impoverished… is because we need a revolution in attitude and behavior within the African American community itself. No white racist makes you get pregnant when you're 16 years old. We do not have time for this form of behavior anymore. It is killing our people. No white racist makes you drop out of school. No white racist makes you not do your homework. No white racist makes you equate academic or intellectual success with being white. If George Wallace and Bull Connor and Orval Faubus had sat down, in their wildest drunken bourbon fantasies in 1960, and said, "How can we continue to control them niggras?"—as they would have said—one of them would have said, "You know, we could persuade them to have babies in their teens, do crack cocaine, run drugs, and equate education not with being Thurgood Marshall, Martin Luther King, but with being white. Then we'll have them." Ladies and gentlemen, that's what's happened to our people. We have lost the blackest aspect of the black tradition.[14]

Those are tough words. But Professor Gates chose to speak out about his ideas for regaining what he called "the black tradition," even if those ideas might be controversial for his audience. Choosing to speak about and listen to topics such as disability rights, racial profiling, and child labor shows a genuine commitment to confronting current social issues.

Speaking out about contentious topics is crucial to a democratic society, but be informed when you speak out and listen carefully to all viewpoints.

Provide Effective Feedback

Ethical audience members listen completely to a speaker's message and provide constructive feedback. For instance, during the question-and-answer session that often follows a speech, make relevant comments that demonstrate you listened carefully to the speaker's ideas. The listening section of this chapter suggests ways to listen to speeches more effectively.

In your public speaking class your instructor may ask you to evaluate classmates' speeches. When you give this kind of feedback, identify both what the speaker did well and areas for the speaker to work on. Offer specific examples, such as a particularly good transition, and concrete suggestions for improvement, such as more clearly previewing main points.

As these principles suggest, ethical speakers respect and encourage diverse opinions, do not tolerate communication that degrades and harms others, balance sharing information with respect for privacy, and listen closely before evaluating and critiquing what others have to say. Although this section has discussed ethical communication as it relates to your role as a public speaker or audience member, you can apply the principles to all your communication interactions.

Recognizing and Avoiding Plagiarism

Plagiarism refers to taking someone else's ideas and work, including speeches, papers, and images, and presenting them as your own, whether intentionally or unintentionally. However, plagiarism is not a universal concept. In Aristotle's time, because ideas were considered public property, speakers freely quoted others' work without attribution. The same is true for many cultures today, especially those with a strong oral tradition. Cultures with a print tradition, such as the United States and most of Europe, view ideas and words as commodities owned by individuals or organizations.[15] Therefore, you must credit the authors of materials you use in your speeches.

Presenting someone else's ideas and work, such as speeches, papers, and images, as your own.

In the United States and many other countries, presenting others' work as your own not only violates basic ethical principles, but is also illegal. Article I, Section 8, of the United States Constitution provides the basis for **copyright** or intellectual property laws:

A type of intellectual property law that protects an author's original work (such as a play, book, song, or movie) from being used by others.

> The Congress shall have power…to promote the progress of science and useful arts, by securing for limited times to authors and inventors the exclusive right to their respective writings and discoveries.

Using someone else's original work in a way that does not infringe on the owner's rights, generally for educational purposes, literary criticism, and news reporting.

Copyright laws, including the Digital Millennium Copyright Act of 1998, require you to get permission from authors if you want to use their original published and unpublished works. **Fair use**, however, allows you to use *limited* portions of an author's work *if* you credit the source of the information.

Research shows that about 50 percent of U.S. college students admit they've plagiarized, and over a third report copying information directly from an internet source without providing a reference.[16] Learning about plagiarism will help you understand and avoid it. A recent study found that students who completed a tutorial on academic integrity were much less likely to plagiarize than those who did not.[17]

In his book *Doing Honest Work in College: How to Prepare Citations, Avoid Plagiarism, and Achieve Real Academic Success*, University of Chicago professor Charles Lipson identifies three essential principles for academic integrity:

- When you say you did the work yourself, you actually did it.

- When you rely on someone else's work, you cite it. When you use their words, you quote them openly and accurately, and you cite them, too.

- When you present research materials, you present them fairly and truthfully. That's true whether the research involves data, documents, or the writings of other scholars.[18]

Accurate note taking, paraphrasing, and orally citing sources will help you achieve academic integrity in your speeches.

Taking Accurate Notes

Sometimes plagiarism results from poor note taking. For example, an early version of the University of Texas at San Antonio's honor code contained sections identical to the honor code at Brigham Young University. The plagiarized passages were traced to materials from a conference on academic integrity. As it turned out, the students who attended the conference failed to take accurate notes on the sources for sample honor codes.[19]

As you research your speech, you may jot down notes from various sources without fully recording quotes and citations. But clearly identifying quoted passages and writing out the complete citation will help you give credit where it's due, as shown in the following examples.[20]

■ *Use **boldface** to mark quotations*

Article on individual differences and attitudes toward plagiarism: **We found significant attitudinal differences between high mastery/high performance and low mastery/high performance students, suggesting that there are effects of multiple goals on attitudes towards acts of plagiarism. We also found that performance oriented students were more strict about what they consider to be plagiarism, and males were stricter than females.** (p. 510) *Source*: Koul, R., Clariana, R., Jitgarun, K., & Songsriwittaya, A. (2009). The influence of achievement goal orientation on plagiarism. *Learning & Individual Differences*, *19*(4), 506–512.

■ *Use font color to mark quotations*

Article on a plagiarism tutorial for college students: Our findings suggest that an effective way to reduce unintentional plagiarism is to explicitly teach students how to properly quote and cite sources and to test their understanding of this information. The instructor's clear commitment to academic integrity might also have contributed to the reduction of plagiarism. (p. 260) *Source:* Belter, R., & du Pré, A. (2009). A strategy to reduce plagiarism in an undergraduate course. *Teaching of Psychology*, *36*(4), 257–261.

You can avoid plagiarism by taking careful notes that clearly identify quotes and their sources as you research your topic.

Bob Daemmrich/The Image Works

■ *Use highlighting to mark quotations*

> Article on ways to combat students' justifications for plagiarizing: Our results offer support for two-sided plagiarism messages, whereby students are not only informed why they should not plagiarize but also guided through refutations of arguments for why they should. This inoculation strategy resulted in immediate attitude changes, including changes in accessibility and vested interest, resulting in stronger, healthy attitudes about plagiarism. (p. 114) *Source:* Compton, J., & Pfau, M. (2008). Inoculating against pro-plagiarism justifications: Rational and affective strategies. *Journal of Applied Communication Research, 36*(1), 98–119.

Following a clear and consistent system to identify quotes and their sources as you gather information on your speech topics will help you avoid unintentional plagiarism.

Paraphrasing the Right Way

Paraphrasing involves putting a source's information into your own words. You consider what the author said or wrote and then provide your interpretation, rather than simply altering a few words or phrases. **Table 3.2** on page 50 shows you right and wrong ways to paraphrase.

Your goal when paraphrasing is to capture the essence of what the author said, using language that fits with your way of speaking. If that doesn't work and you find yourself relying on the original quotation too much, then consider using the quote in your speech. Whether paraphrasing or quoting from a source, provide an oral citation in your speech to avoid plagiarism.

Citing Sources in Your Speech

Effective public speakers provide **oral citations**, or brief references to their sources, during their speeches. Citing your sources tells the audience you've done your research on the topic. It also allows your audience to learn more about your topic and check your evidence. Finally, if you're presenting information you believe your audience might view unfavorably, citing your sources lets them know that the ideas did not originate with you.[21] The following examples demonstrate how to integrate an oral citation into your speech:

Brief reference to a source during a speech.

> Disability Rights and Independent Living Movement states on its website, "People with disabilities throughout history have been defined as objects of shame, fear, pity, or ridicule."

> Technology that helps make your everyday life easier can also make it easier for criminals. For example, the GPS system you have in your car helps you—and burglars—find the way to your house. Last week the *Detroit Free Press* reported that thieves stole the GPS systems from victims' automobiles and then used information stored in the GPS to break into victims' homes.

> Owen Hanley Lynch, a communication professor at Southern Methodist University, found in his research that humor in the workplace is more than just fun and games. His article in the November 2009 issue of *Applied Communication Research* reports on the ways in which restaurant chefs use humor to establish their professional identities and manage their workspaces.

In each of these cases, the speaker orally tells the audience who wrote or published a particular piece of information. Chapter 6 provides additional guidelines for integrating oral citations into your speeches, along with instructions on how to include written citations in your speech outline.

Table 3.2 Right and Wrong Ways to Paraphrase

Source	Quote	Wrong paraphrase	Right paraphrase
A question of character. (2009, December 12). *The Economist Technology Quarterly*, p. 8.	Sending a text message is often the most time-consuming and expensive way to transfer data. Yet it remains popular not only in countries that use Latin-based languages, such as America, Britain, and most of Europe, but also in China, Japan, and most of Asia, where written languages often have much larger alphabets.	When you send a text message, it's really the most time-consuming and expensive way to transfer an idea. But it's popular in countries like the United States and England, and in Europe as well as countries in Asia such as China and Japan, where the written languages typically have larger alphabets.	If you're like many people around the world, you send a lot of text messages. And if you send text messages in English, you just have to worry about 26 letters in the alphabet. But for other languages that use characters, such as Japanese and Mandarin Chinese, texting is more complicated.
Young, J. R. (2009, November 27). *Teaching with Twitter: Not for the faint of heart. Chronicle of Higher Education, 56(14)*, pp. A1, A10–11 *(quote on p. A1)*.	Opening up a Twitter-powered channel in class—which several professors at other universities are experimenting with as well—alters classroom power dynamics and signals to students that they're in control. Fans of the approach applaud technology that promises to change professors' role from "sage on the stage" to "guide on the side."	Setting up a Twitter-powered communication channel in class changes the power dynamics in a classroom and lets students know they're in control. Those who agree with the Twitter approach support the technology that likely will change the instructor's role from "sage on the stage" to "guide on the side."	When college instructors use Twitter in the classroom, it changes how students communicate with each other and the instructor. The instructor's role changes, too, from lecturer to facilitator.
Ehrenreich, B. (2001). *Nickel and dimed: On (not) getting by in America.* New York: Metropolitan Books. (p. 208).	What surprised and offended me most about the low-wage workplace (and yes, here all my middle-class privilege is on full display) was the extent to which one is required to surrender one's basic civil rights and—what boils down to the same thing—self-respect. I learned this at the very beginning of my stint as a waitress, when I was warned that my purse could be searched by management at any time.	In the low-wage workplace you have to surrender your basic rights and self-respect. You'll learn this even from a beginning job as a waitress, where you should be warned that your purse could be searched by management at any time.	People who work low-paying jobs often are subjected to humiliating experiences, such as having managers go through their belongings.

Identifying sources also applies to visual and audio materials such as films, songs, and photographs. When you integrate these materials into your speeches, cite your sources just as you do with more traditional forms of information. For example, if you include a brief clip from a movie, tell your audience the film's title. Similarly, name an artist's song either before or after playing the short segment. With images, simply include the source on your digital slide or overhead transparency, as **Figure 3.1** shows.

Keeping careful records of the information you gather for your speech is the first step in avoiding plagiarism. You'll use the notes you take during your research to accurately attribute what you say to the appropriate source. In addition, orally citing your sources lets the audience know you've done your research, and that in turn enhances your credibility.

Figure 3.1 Sample images with sources

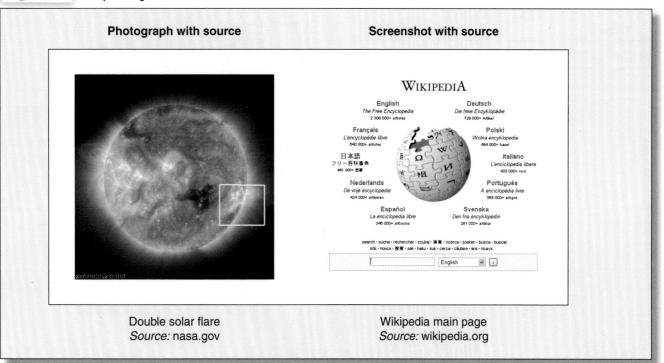

Photograph with source   Screenshot with source

Double solar flare
Source: nasa.gov

Wikipedia main page
Source: wikipedia.org

> **Watch** it

SPEECH BUDDY VIDEO 3.1
Avoiding Plagiarism

In this video, Erin shows examples of how to correctly cite sources in a speech as well as examples of when not citing sources results in plagiarism. You may want to take notes for reference later.

> **Use** it

ACTIVITY 3.1
But Is It Plagiarism?

This activity asks you to evaluate excerpts from sample speeches to determine whether sources have been acknowledged properly.

Ethics and Cultural Diversity

Applying the ethics of communication requires you to respect cultural differences.[22] **Culture** refers to shared values, beliefs, and activities.[23] Cultural commonalities and differences are constructed, reinforced, and revealed through communication. People

Values, beliefs, and activities shared by a group.

51

become socialized into their own cultures directly through communication with their family, friends, and neighbors, for instance, but also indirectly through the media and other social institutions.[24] **Cultural diversity** refers to differences in cultural backgrounds and practices around the globe.

Cultural norms are rules for how members of a culture should behave. Some norms are explicit or stated, such as military codes of conduct. Most norms, however, are implicit or unstated, such as how to act when attending a guest lecture on campus. No one tells you how to behave at a lecture. Instead, you learn by observing what other people do in this and similar situations. Because norms are rules rather than laws, communicators may negotiate changes or modifications in norms. For instance, in the classroom students and instructors might discuss the best way to structure the question-and-answer session after a speech rather than use the same format all the time. In addition, norms generally change over time in response to changes in the environment. For example, when mobile phones were first introduced, communicators didn't have any norms to govern when people made or received calls. Now, especially in public places, there are explicit norms about mobile phone use.

What is appropriate in one culture may not be appropriate in another. When you're speaking publicly, your audience likely will include a range of cultural differences based on age, gender, ethnicity, disabilities, religion, sexual orientation, and socioeconomic level. Effectively analyzing your audience will help you adapt to your audience's cultural norms.

Avoiding Ethnocentrism

Ethnocentrism occurs when individuals think their view of the world is better than anyone else's. Often, rather than explicitly stating, "My perspective is the best," communicators might think, "How can *those people* believe in *that*?" or "People over/under 40 just don't know what's really going on in the world." When you start thinking that anything different from your point of view is inherently wrong, strange, or bad, you're experiencing ethnocentrism.

Ethnocentrism influences how individuals evaluate other communicators' competence and credibility.[25] That is, the more ethnocentric people are, the more likely they are to think individuals who appear different from them are less trustworthy and capable. Ethnocentric listeners, for instance, may respond negatively to a speaker who doesn't share their cultural background.[26] It's okay to disagree with others' perspectives. The problem occurs when you think your way of doing things is always better.

Ethnocentrism can also prevent people from speaking out about difficult issues, especially those associated with race, class, and gender.[27] When communicators think ethnocentrically, they avoid questioning societal and cultural practices that promote discrimination against people based on their ethnic background, religious beliefs, socioeconomic status, sexual orientation, disability, sex, and other demographic categories. Confronting ethnocentrism means confronting accepted ways of doing things that disadvantage particular groups of people.

Stepping out of your own cultural beliefs and values can prove challenging because your cultural worldview is so much a part of your sense of self. All individuals come to accept their perspectives as simply the way things are and should be. But when people believe their way of thinking is superior to other ways, they're practicing ethnocentrism and violating the principles of ethical communication.

Avoiding Sexism

Exhibiting cultural sensitivity also means recognizing the role of gender in public speaking. While *sex* refers to the biological category a person's body fits into (female, male, or intersex), *gender* refers to socially established roles defining what is perceived as masculine and feminine in a given culture.

Differences in cultural backgrounds and practices around the globe.

Prescriptions for how people should interact and what messages should mean in a particular setting.

The belief that your worldview, based on your cultural background, is superior to others' worldviews.

52

At many different times throughout history, public speaking was considered an activity unbecoming to women. In ancient Greece, girls attended school and learned a wide range of subjects, but not public speaking.[28] Women were prohibited from speaking out in public venues. The early history of the United States reflects a similar bias. The first reported speech by a woman occurred in Indiana in 1828. Twenty years later, with the start of the woman suffrage movement, more and more women took to the podium to speak out for women's voting rights to audiences who shouted, heckled, threw rotten vegetables, and spit on them.[29]

Today you expect to hear both women and men giving speeches. Still, because of gender roles, audience members often have different expectations for male and female speakers. As a result, audiences tend to evaluate a speaker's credibility based partly on gender. For example, audiences focus closely on the trustworthiness of a female speaker's sources but are more concerned with how a male speaker organizes his ideas, maintains eye contact, and uses his voice. Even when speakers exhibit similar behaviors, men often are viewed as more persuasive than women.[30]

Sensitivity to gender requires that speakers make conscious language choices. Use gender-neutral or nonsexist language such as *humanity*, *firefighter*, and *flight attendant* rather than gendered language such as *mankind*, *fireman*, and *stewardess*. In addition, frame topics to appeal to all listeners. If you give a speech on the importance of team sports for girls, for instance, make your topic relevant and interesting to everyone in your audience. You might do this by pointing out what girls learn when they play team sports and how those lessons help them function better in society—a benefit for everyone.

Listening and Public Speaking

Especially in a public speaking class, communicators focus their attention on speaking. Yet the public speaking process is not complete without listeners. On speech days, ethical listeners arrive early, prepare themselves to listen carefully, take notes, and respond appropriately to speakers' ideas and perspectives. This section focuses on the components of listening, the types of listening, and how you can improve your listening skills.

Components of Listening

The HURIER model identifies six components that combine to form the listening process: hearing, understanding, remembering, interpreting, evaluating, and responding.[31] The model depicts listening as a dynamic process—an ongoing, ever-changing collaboration between the speaker and the listener.[32]

Hearing is the physical reception of sounds. When you listen, you selectively receive and attend to sounds and other sensory stimuli. At times, you make a conscious decision to listen (or not listen) to what others are saying. At other times, you are not aware of the choices you make. You experience **information overload** when you receive too much information and are unable to interpret it in a meaningful way.[33] Selective listening helps you identify what is important and what is not from all the information you receive every day.

Understanding involves comprehending what you have heard. Effective listening requires your conscious intention to focus on the speaker and strive to understand the meaning of the speaker's message. As a listener, dedicate yourself to listening carefully to each speaker. As a speaker, listen to your audience's responses and questions.

Remembering allows you to think about and recall auditory information. To recall what you've heard and understood, your brain must first commit the information to the immediate memory, or what is happening in the moment. Then the information is passed to the short-term, or working, memory. At this stage of remembering, you need to actively engage with and think about the information so that it is retained in the long-term memory.

When you *interpret*, you assign meaning to the sounds you've received based on your own experiences and knowledge. However, the interpretive element of listening is

> Occurs when individuals receive too much information and are unable to interpret it in a meaningful way.

not a completely individualistic process—your culture and society provide meanings you share with others that help you interpret messages.[34]

Evaluating allows you to critically examine a message, such as when you test a speaker's logic. To effectively evaluate a speech, listeners attend to *all* aspects of a speaker's message. When you listen, you concentrate on what others say and how they say it.[35] Physical settings, gestures, movements, vocal qualities, eye contact, and facial expressions all contribute to how you evaluate a speech.

Finally, listening requires *responding* to what the speaker has said. Appropriate verbal and nonverbal responses let speakers know you're paying attention and reflect your effectiveness as a listener. Smiling, making eye contact, nodding in agreement, and other nonverbal cues show that you're listening.[36] You might also ask questions at the end of a speech.

Your individual listening filters, such as your culture and values, influence each of the components. You routinely apply your imagination, past experiences, and knowledge to what others say. A speaker's words, tone of voice, and body movements also play a role in how you create the meaning of a message. For example, when others talk about their childhood adventures you might associate what they say with your own experiences while growing up.

Figure 3.2 demonstrates how those components work together in the listening process.

Types of Listening

There are different reasons for listening and different ways of listening. In *empathic* listening, you want to know the feelings and emotions the speaker is conveying. When a speaker is giving a eulogy, for instance, you listen with compassion and understanding to the emotional components of the message. In *appreciative* listening, you listen for enjoyment, as when listening to a stand-up comedy routine or an after-dinner speech. When you listen for *content*, you gather information, focusing on the speaker's main ideas, as when an instructor lectures. Finally, *critical* listening requires that you evaluate the speaker's credibility, ideas, and supporting evidence.

Most public speaking situations call for critical listening. For example, when listening to a persuasive speech, you might try to identify the feelings that motivated the

Figure 3.2   **HURIER listening model**

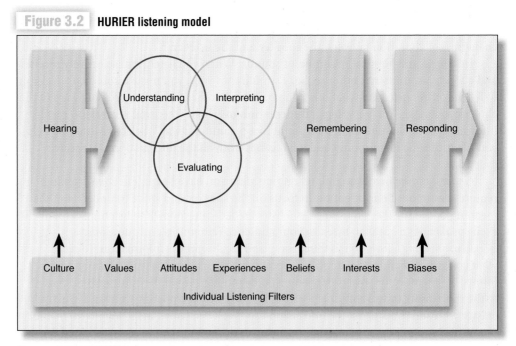

Source: *Brownell (2010)*

speaker to choose her or his topic. You might also laugh at a humorous story and smile as you recall a similar situation. You might want to take a few notes on the main ideas presented. Once you've listened with empathy, with appreciation, and for content, you're ready to evaluate the speech.

Listening Effectively to Speeches

Research shows that immediately after a lecture, listeners recall only about 50 percent of what the speaker said.[37] Setting goals, blocking out distractions, managing listening anxiety, suspending judgment, focusing on main points, taking meaningful notes, using all your senses, and asking good questions are strategies that will help you improve your listening skills and better evaluate the speaker's message.

Set Goals

Different public speaking situations call for different types of listening. Setting goals that correspond with the situation improves your listening skills. For example, after-dinner speeches are generally meant to entertain, so the listener's goal might be to simply enjoy the presentation. When a speaker toasts a newly married couple at a wedding reception, listeners would likely focus on the feelings associated with the occasion. However, in most classroom speaking situations the listener's ultimate goal is to critique speeches. As an audience member in your public speaking class, listen for the speaker's emotions (empathic listening), enjoy the speaker's sense of humor (appreciative listening), and identify the speaker's main ideas (content listening), keeping in mind your final goal of evaluating the speaker's message.

Block Distractions

The human brain processes information about three times faster than speakers can talk.[38] That leaves listeners time to get distracted by internal and external noise. As discussed in Chapter 1, noise occurs when something interferes with your understanding of messages. **Internal noise** includes thoughts, emotions, and physical sensations. Thinking about the movie you watched last night or noticing hunger pangs caused by skipping breakfast can prevent you from turning your full attention to the speaker. **External noise** includes conditions in your environment that interfere with listening. Outside sounds, cramped seating, and an uncomfortable room temperature challenge your active listening skills. By blocking distractions, however, audience members can concentrate on what speakers are saying.

> Thoughts, emotions, and physical sensations that interfere with listening.

> Conditions in the environment that interfere with listening.

Manage Listening Anxiety

Just as speakers experience anxiety when giving a speech, listeners sometimes become anxious. **Listening anxiety** stems from the fear of misunderstanding, not fully comprehending, incorrectly recalling, or being unprepared mentally for information you may hear. Students often experience anxiety when listening to a lengthy lecture they know they'll be tested on.[39] The physical symptoms are similar to those of speech anxiety. Manage listening anxiety by focusing on the speaker, clearing your mind of extraneous thoughts, and maintaining a positive attitude.

> Anxiety produced by the fear of misunderstanding, not fully comprehending, or not being mentally prepared for information you may hear.

Suspend Judgment

Ethical listeners first listen for content and empathy and then evaluate the speaker's message. Controversial topics such as sex education in public schools, capital punishment, welfare policies, and nuclear power can trigger immediate emotional responses. Recognize those responses and then listen carefully to the speaker's ideas, even if they don't correspond with your own. In addition, avoid judging the speaker based on gender, ethnic background, dis/ability, or other demographic attributes.

David Young-Wolff/PhotoEdit

How effective are this speaker's solutions for helping listeners block distractions in this speaking situation? In what other ways could he help the audience better listen to his message?

Instead, concentrate on the information the speaker presents.

Focus on the Speaker's Main Points

Focusing on the speaker's main points is particularly important in content listening and critical listening. To evaluate what the speaker has said, you first need to understand the main ideas being presented. Speakers often call attention to their main points by stating them in the introduction and reviewing them in the conclusion.

Take Effective Notes

Taking effective notes when listening to a speech helps you recall what the speaker said and prepare good questions.[40] Your notes need not be extensive—a few key words will do. Here's a system that promotes effective listening: Divide a piece of paper into three columns. Label the first column "Important Points," the second column "My Response," and the third column "My Questions." As you listen to the speaker, write down your notes in the appropriate column.

Use All Your Senses

To improve your listening, use all your senses, paying attention to how speakers talk as well as what they are saying. While you listen to the speaker's main points, observe nonverbal cues such as gestures and tone of voice. Your senses will give you clues to the speaker's feelings about the topic.

Ask Good Questions

Ethical listeners ask questions that help the speaker clarify or elaborate on the main ideas presented. Even when you disagree with a speaker, focus your questions on gaining more information, not on presenting your point of view. Each question should take just a few seconds to ask. Good questions are

- *Open-ended*—Begin questions with *how, why, what,* or *where.* For example, ask, "How do you think your proposal will affect local residents?" rather than, "Will your proposal affect local residents?"

- *Direct*—Just ask the question, avoiding a long, drawn-out preface. For example, ask, "What do you think will be the impact of these changes over the next 10 years?"

- *On topic*—Stick with the topic. If you think there's a weakness in the speaker's argument, ask about it, but be sure it relates to the speaker's message. For example, ask, "You discussed a few drawbacks associated with this new assessment program in K-12 schools. What have teachers and administrators done to address these issues?" Compare this with, "I know this isn't really related to what you talked about, but I was wondering what you think about the amount of homework teachers assign in their classes."

- *Genuine requests for information*—Ethical listening fosters a supportive communication climate. Conversely, using derogatory language and intentionally distorting the speaker's message produce a defensive communication climate.[41]

As an active listener, ask questions that encourage speakers to provide more information. Compare these questions:

1. "You mentioned some statistics on college students' use of file sharing. What are the sources of those statistics?"

2. "I'm sure you're wrong about those statistics you mentioned on college students and file sharing. What sources are you using? I want to look them up."

In the first question, the listener respectfully asks for the information, giving the speaker a chance to state the sources more precisely. In the second question, the listener attacks the speaker, who will in turn feel compelled to respond defensively. Dialogue evaporates, and a battle ensues over who is "right" and who is "wrong."

With good questions, listeners continue the conversation the speaker began. Listening attentively during speeches and asking good questions that promote the free exchange of ideas are the hallmarks of an ethical listener.

> **Watch** it

SPEECH BUDDY VIDEO 3.2
Promoting Dialogue in Q&A

In this video, Janine provides tips on participating ethically in a dialogue between speaker and audience.

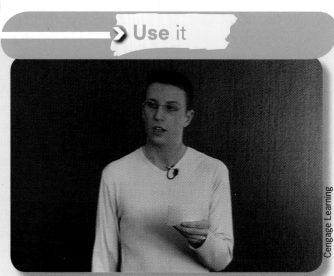

> **Use** it

ACTIVITY 3.2
You Have the Floor

In this activity, you'll develop questions for clips from speeches and suggest comments that audience members might make.

Summary

Ethical communication provides a foundation for effective public speaking and listening. Ethical speakers present accurate and balanced information, carefully researching their topics, using reliable sources, and adhering to copyright laws. Plagiarism is a particularly pressing ethical problem. By recording the sources for your information, referring to those sources in your speech, and listing each source in a written bibliography, you'll avoid plagiarism. Thoroughly preparing for your presentation, using language appropriate to your audience, and giving your speech in a manner that demonstrates respect for the audience help create a productive communication climate.

57

Audience members also have ethical responsibilities. Ethical listeners give speakers undivided attention, respect diverse perspectives, and listen to the entire speech before making a final judgment. In addition, both ethical speakers and listeners demonstrate genuine sensitivity to cultural differences.

Effective listening helps speakers and listeners connect comfortably with each other. Lack of commitment, jumping to conclusions, becoming distracted, poor note taking, and asking inappropriate questions detract from the public speaking experience. When listeners become fully engaged, they create a meaningful conversation between speaker and audience.

Review it

Directory of Study and Review Resources

IN THE BOOK
Summary
Key Terms
Critical Challenges

MORE STUDY RESOURCES
Quizzes
WebLinks
Peer-reviewed videos

STUDENT WORKBOOK
3.1: Quality Questions
3.2: SLANT
3.3: Using Outlines to Take Notes
3.4: Performing Ethical Communication
3.5: Source Citation

SPEECH BUDDY VIDEOS
WATCH It Video
3.1: Avoiding Plagiarism
3.2: Promoting Dialogue in Q&A
USE It Activity
3.1: But Is It Plagiarism?
3.2: You Have the Floor

SAMPLE SPEECH VIDEOS
Chuck, "Anatomy of a Hate Crime," personal significance speech
Cara, "Creationism versus the Big Bang Theory" invitational speech

SPEECH BUILDER EXPRESS
Outline
Supporting materials

INFOTRAC COLLEGE EDITION

Recommended search terms
Ethics and public speaking
Ethical communication
Communication climates
Plagiarism
Fair use and public speaking
Citing sources and speeches
Cultural diversity and communication
Listening and public speaking
Improving listening
Effective listening
Critical listening

AUDIO STUDY TOOLS
"Anatomy of a Hate Crime" by Chuck
Critical thinking questions
Learning objectives
Chapter summary

Guide to Your Online Resources

CourseMate Your Speech Communication CourseMate for *Public Speaking: The Evolving Art* gives you access to the Speech Buddy video and activity featured in this chapter, additional sample speech videos, Speech Studio, Speech Builder Express, InfoTrac College Edition, and study aids such as glossary flashcards, review quizzes, and the Critical Challenge questions for this chapter, which you can respond to via email if your instructor so requests. In addition, your CourseMate features live WebLinks relevant to this chapter, including links to sites about avoiding plagiarism and improving listening. Links are regularly maintained, and new ones are added periodically.

Key Terms

communication climate 42

copyright 47

cultural diversity 52

cultural norms 52

culture 51

dialogue 44

ethical communication 41

ethnocentrism 52

external noise 55

fair use 47

hate speech 44

information overload 53

internal noise 55

listening anxiety 55

monologue 44

oral citations 49

plagiarism 47

Critical Challenges

Questions for Reflection and Discussion

1. Should speakers in college classrooms be able to choose any topic they wish? Or should some topics be off limits? How do you balance free expression, pursuing justice, and promoting a caring communication climate? Think about the public speaking class you're in right now. What topics, if any, do you think students should not be allowed to speak about? Why do you think this way?

2. Review the Speaking Of ... box titled "Hate Speech versus Free Speech". Should there be laws against hate speech? What are the implications of not allowing certain kinds of speech? Does free speech mean you can say anything you want to anyone?

3. Recall a recent experience in which you were a critical listener. How well did you listen with empathy and appreciation? How well did you listen for content? How did you evaluate what the speaker said? What did you learn from listening critically?

4

Developing Your Purpose and Topic

Read it

Cengage Learning

Watch it

Use it

Cengage Learning

Review it

CourseMate ✓Studio SPEECH SPEECH BUILDER EXPRESS

When Lady Gaga spoke at the National Equality March in Washington, D.C., she demanded that the government go beyond promises and take action to support gay rights. Her purpose for speaking was to persuade. In a speech to the general public in Mountain View, California, astrobiologist John Baross described how extreme environments on Earth, like the bottom of the ocean, give clues about possible life elsewhere in the universe. His purpose was to inform. And when former NBC news anchor Tom Brokaw told personal stories about his colleague Tim Russert at Russert's memorial service, Brokaw brought people to tears. His purpose was to soothe family and friends on this sad occasion.

When you talk with other people, you usually have a goal, or purpose, in mind.[1] You may be trying to make them understand an idea you have or appreciate an experience you've had. Perhaps you're trying to influence their opinion about a subject or motivate them to do something. Maybe you're just trying to get a laugh. Having a well-defined purpose is especially important in public speaking. Identifying a clear purpose is essential from the very beginning of your speech preparation. You have to know what is expected of you, what you plan to do in response, and what you can expect to accomplish as a result. Four key steps make up the early part of speech preparation:

- First, you determine your general purpose.
- Second, you evaluate and select your speech topic.
- Third, you combine your general purpose and topic to identify your specific purpose.
- Fourth, you phrase the thesis of your speech as you develop your topic.

zumawireworldphotos/Newscom

Determining Your General Purpose

The speaker's overall objective: to inform, to persuade, or to entertain.

The **general purpose** of your speech refers to your overall goal, and answers the question, "What do I want my speech to do?" The general purpose of your speech typically corresponds to one of the most common types of speeches: informative, persuasive, or entertaining.

Speaking to Inform

The main subject, idea, or theme of a speech.

When you give a speech to inform, your goal is to describe, explain, or demonstrate something. Informative speeches serve to increase listeners' knowledge about a **topic**, or the main subject, idea, or theme of your speech. When the general purpose is to inform, your objective is to help the audience understand and recall information about a topic. In the professional world, informative presentations include employee orientations and project reports. Within communities, they include project proposals and policy updates.

Speaking to Persuade

When you speak to persuade, you attempt to reinforce, modify, or change audience members' beliefs, attitudes, opinions, values, and behaviors. Your objective is to prompt the audience to alter their thinking and possibly take action. You might equate persuasion with advertising and politics. Yet when a student nominates a friend for president of a fraternity, a minister gives a sermon, a community member advocates disaster preparedness, or a university president presents a five-year vision to the faculty, these are persuasive speeches too.

Speaking to Entertain

In an entertaining speech, the speaker seeks to captivate audience members and have them enjoy the speech. Special occasions often provide the context for such speeches. After-dinner speakers, for instance, charm and humor the audience. Entertaining speeches typically include jokes and stories.

Keeping your General Purpose in Mind

For any particular speech, you'll concentrate on a single general purpose: to inform, to persuade, or to entertain. As you develop your speech, always keep your general purpose in mind. Although you might include humor in an informative speech, your ultimate goal is to inform, not to entertain. Similarly, you might offer explanations in a persuasive speech, but your primary objective is to persuade, not to inform. Moreover, you might give your opinions in an entertaining speech, yet in the end you want to entertain, not to persuade, your audience. If you try to entertain *and* persuade, for example, you won't do either one very well.[2] Think about humorous television commercials in which you can recall the joke but not the product advertised. Focusing on one general purpose helps you achieve your overall goal for the speech.

Giving speeches of these types and for these purposes extends the communication skills you already have, because you inform, persuade, and entertain people all the time. In turn, they inform, persuade, and entertain you. Once you know your speech's general purpose, your next step involves coming up with possible speech topics.

Brainstorming for Possible Topics

The free-form generation of ideas, in which individuals think of and record ideas without evaluating them.

A public speaking event gives you an opportunity to speak to an audience, but what will you talk about? Carefully selecting a topic that fits your general purpose will set you on the road to delivering an effective speech. So where do you begin? By **brainstorming**—a free-form way of generating ideas without evaluating them. Brainstorming happens in many ways. As you go about your daily routines, topic ideas may pop into your head, so be ready to record them. A newspaper article, webpage image, radio talk show, or television program may trigger ideas for your speech. Trying out something new may also help you think of alternative topics.[3] Take a new route to a friend's apartment, listen to some new music, or spend some time in a new coffeehouse.

At some point, you'll want to set aside a specific time to generate ideas or expand on the ones you generated previously. Choose a place where you feel relaxed, yet still alert and attentive. The main point of brainstorming is to write down all the topics you might want to talk about without evaluating them. Simply record whatever comes to mind. And be creative. At this stage, you don't want to censor yourself.[4] The rules of brainstorming are few but important (**Figure 4.1**).

Asking yourself key questions can help you focus the brainstorming process. The questions should be broad enough to encourage creativity, but not so broad that you stray far from your original goal. Here are some examples:[5]

- What do I talk or text about with my friends?
- What are my interests and hobbies?
- What unique experiences have I had?
- What am I passionate about?
- What would I like to learn about?

If this strategy doesn't get ideas flowing, check the headlines from a major news source or web portal, or use search engines' pages that list issues, such as dmoz.org. Subjects discussed in blogs and podcasts can also provide topics for brainstorming. When you find an article or post that interests you, write down the topic, as well as any others you associate with it.

Figure 4.1   **Rules for Brainstorming**

Generate as many ideas as possible.
Write down every idea—whatever comes to mind.
Avoid evaluating your ideas.
Be as creative and imaginative as possible.

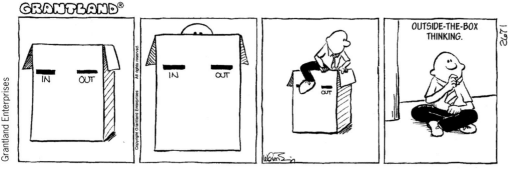

A photo or other image may also give you an idea for a speech topic. For example, news images are widely distributed and recognized. People worldwide see images from the wars and the suicide bombings in the Middle East shortly after they become available. These images could prompt you speak about the history of the region, the reasons for terrorism, or the wisdom of American foreign policy. Images of natural disasters suggest a range of topics, such as volunteer relief efforts, disparities between rich and poor people in affected areas, the use of technology to prepare and issue warnings—the list goes on.

When brainstorming for possible speech topics, think not only in terms of ideas or words that come to mind but also in terms of images that have impressed you. YouTube videos and personal postings on social networking sites like Facebook may provide topic ideas. Start brainstorming for topic ideas well before you're scheduled to present your speech. Research shows that brainstorming works best when done over several sessions.[6] The most useful ideas usually emerge from brainstorming on your own, but asking another knowledgeable person to brainstorm with you can work well too.[7] Trying to brainstorm under the pressure of having to give your speech in a few days will not help you come up with your best ideas, make the best choice, or do justice to the topic you choose.

High-impact images of significant events can help you brainstorm a range of possible speech topics.

Evaluating and Selecting Topic Ideas

Good public speakers always consider the needs and interests of their audiences. However, before you finally select a topic, you also must think about your own interests and knowledge, the availability of resources, and the time and setting for your speech. Evaluating possible topics based on the following considerations can speed up your topic selection process:

- Your own interests
- The audience
- Resource availability
- The time limit and current events
- The setting and event

Consider Your Own Interests

In evaluating your topics, first consider your own interests and what you know. Ask yourself these questions:

- How interested am I in this topic?
- What do I know about this topic?
- How comfortable will I be talking about this topic?

If your answer to the first question is, "not very interested," cross that topic off your list. Your audience will immediately know if you're not enthusiastic about it. However, don't make the mistake of underestimating the originality and appeal of your ideas.[8] A topic you feel passionate about will energize you and produce a more dynamic and interesting speech. Having little knowledge of a topic may also motivate you or give you a chance to learn more about it. But before choosing a topic you don't know much about, be sure you have enough time and resources to research it fully. Finally, consider how comfortable you are talking about a topic. If it's something you don't like discussing with your friends and family, you probably won't want to give a speech about it.[9]

Consider the Audience

Although you'll do more research on your audience after you've chosen your topic, at this point you need to do some preliminary research to get a general idea of audience members' knowledge and interests. Ask yourself these four questions about your audience when evaluating the topics on your list:

- How relevant is this topic to my audience?
- Why do audience members need to know about this topic?
- Will I be able to interest my audience in this topic?
- How much does my audience already know about my topic?

As you evaluate topics, always put yourself in the audience's place. Choose speech topics that are likely to interest and engage them. Some topics may not seem directly relevant to audience members; you may need to provide that link. However, if the topic probably won't pique listeners' interest and you can't think of any reasons why they should know about the topic, cross it off your list. In addition, balance relevance and interest with knowledge level. If a topic is relevant and of interest but audience members already know quite a bit about it, you have to either take an unusual approach to the topic or remove it from your list.

64

Consider Resource Availability

As you narrow down your list of possible topics, think about what resources you can use to develop the content of your speech. Audience members listen for evidence from a variety of credible sources and quickly discern if the information base of your speech is too thin. So, when choosing a topic, be sure you can locate and access relevant and valid resources—books, online articles, news reports, interviews with experts, and the like.

Consider Time

Consider your potential topics in terms of your time limit and the topics' timeliness in light of current events.

Time Limit Successful public speakers stay within their time limits. Examine your list of topics. Would you be able to cover each of the topics you're considering within the allotted time? Speakers sometimes think they won't have enough to say unless they choose a big, comprehensive topic. Then, when they give the speech, they run out of time before covering all the main points. Depending on the time frame, you may need to either narrow or broaden particular speech topics.

Current Events Timely or especially current speeches often appeal to audiences. In choosing a topic, consider how it fits with events in the news and what people are talking about. Select topics that connect current events with the audience's emotions and avoid connections that might reflect poorly on your topic. An upbeat talk about the health of the national economy wouldn't work very well at a time when high unemployment figures have just been released, for instance, but it could work very well if unemployment is decreasing. Similarly, you'd have an easier time convincing your audience to support increasing the budget for the athletic department at your school if the football team is doing well, but less of a chance during a losing season.

Consider the Setting and Speaking Event

The place where you'll present your speech figures in selecting an appropriate topic as well. Are you speaking in a large auditorium, a conference room, or a classroom? Are you speaking to 1000, 100, or 10 people? What might be appropriate for a small

Speaking of . . .

Know Your Audience

Choosing a topic that's not right for your audience can lead to unfavorable responses. Audience members may become bored and distracted. They may feel insulted and even hostile. Thorough audience analysis makes it more likely you'll get the response you want. You won't always make the perfect topic choice. Sometimes, even with the best information about the audience, a topic just doesn't work. But knowing your audience—their interests, needs, knowledge level, values, attitudes, and beliefs—greatly increases the likelihood that you'll choose a topic that is in sync with your audience.

Where you're speaking—a large auditorium, a small conference room, or something in between—will influence your choice of a topic.

classroom may not prove effective in a large auditorium. In the classroom, the setting is more personal; in an auditorium, there's a greater distance between the speaker and the audience.

Place also refers to the type of speaking event. The content of the speech should be appropriate for the event. For example, if you're presenting an after-dinner speech, you don't want to talk about a serious topic such as skin cancer. In addition, consider the event as a whole. Are you the only speaker, or are others presenting as well? Identify who might be speaking before or after you and consider how your topic complements theirs.

Identifying Your Specific Purpose

A concise statement articulating what the speaker will achieve in giving a speech.

The **specific purpose** is what you want to achieve in your speech. In writing your specific purpose, you merge your general purpose, topic, and audience to identify the particular objective you want to accomplish. For example, if the general purpose is to inform and your topic is your campus's student government, your specific purpose might be, "To inform my audience about the two branches of our campus's student government, executive and legislative." This statement integrates your general purpose (to inform) with your topic (student government) and what you want your audience to know about (the two branches of student government).

The specific purpose is a clear, concise statement about your topic that focuses on a single purpose and incorporates the response you want from the audience. For a speech to inform, your specific purpose will begin with something like this:

- to inform my audience about…

- to teach my audience…

- to make my audience aware of…

- to demonstrate to my audience how to…

Each statement begins by placing the audience at the center of attention and refers, directly or indirectly, to the general purpose—in this case, to inform. Then you add in the topic, such as

- to inform my audience about how face recognition systems work

- to teach my audience strategies for time management

- to make my audience aware of the services offered at the campus career center

- to demonstrate to my audience how to take an excellent photograph

Identifying a specific purpose helps you conceptualize your speech from the audience's point of view. It centers your attention on what you want your audience members to know and why they should listen to you. Thinking this way keeps you clearly focused on the reason you're speaking in the first place—to inform the audience.

Speeches to persuade often aim to produce a rational or emotional response or to prompt audience members to take a specific action, such as "exercise daily," "donate blood," or "support legislation." A statement of specific purpose for a persuasive speech might begin with

- to persuade my audience to…

- to convince my audience that…

- to deepen the empathy my audience feels…

- to motivate my audience to…

When merged with a topic, these examples become

- to persuade my audience to support a campus-wide smoking ban
- to convince my audience that genetically modified foods are safe
- to deepen my audience's empathy for people living in poverty
- to motivate my audience to vote

In speeches to entertain, the specific purpose is to engage and amuse the audience. Your statement of specific purpose would begin like this:

- to entertain my audience with…
- to amuse my audience with…
- to delight my audience with…
- to inspire my audience with…

When merged with a topic, these examples become

- to entertain my audience with humorous aspects of working in an office cubicle
- to amuse my audience with the zaniness of family summer vacations
- to delight my audience with unusual inventions of the past
- to inspire my audience with offbeat ways to simplify their lives

Considering the response you want from your audience keeps them uppermost in your mind. Writing down your specific purpose or goal brings together the general purpose, topic, and audience, providing a reference point that will keep you on track.[10] **Table 4.1** provides additional examples of the links among general purpose, topic, and specific purpose.

The specific purpose of your speech guides important decisions in later stages of the speech process, such as researching your topic, deciding on supporting materials, organizing your ideas, making language choices, and integrating presentation resources. As you work on your speech, ask yourself, "Will this quote, statistic, audio clip, or other material help me achieve my specific purpose?"

Table 4.1 Examples of General Purpose, Topic, and Specific Purpose

General Purpose	Topic	Specific Purpose
To inform	Latinos in films	To inform my audience about the history of Latinos in U.S. films
To inform	Wild mushrooms	To teach my audience about the differences between poisonous and edible mushrooms
To inform	Emergency kits	To demonstrate to my audience how to assemble an emergency preparedness kit
To persuade	Zoos	To persuade my audience that zoos serve important purposes for many animals
To persuade	Skateboarding	To convince my audience that campus rules prohibiting skateboarding should be eliminated
To persuade	Poverty	To help my audience feel more empathy for local residents living in poverty
To entertain	Advertisements	To entertain my audience with commercial advertisements that will never be shown on television
To entertain	Nutrition	To amuse my audience with the college student's version of the food pyramid
To entertain	Sports	To inspire my audience with true stories of accomplished athletes in little-known sports

❯ Watch it

SPEECH BUDDY VIDEO 4.1
Brainstorming for and Evaluating Topics

In this video, Anthony and Janine demonstrate the process of brainstorming and evaluating topic ideas.

❯ Use it

ACTIVITY 4.1
Search and Find Missions

In this activity, you have a chance to try brainstorming and evaluating topic ideas.

Phrasing Your Thesis

Your general purpose points you in the direction your speech must take—to inform, persuade, or entertain. Your specific purpose addresses how you want your speech to affect your audience. Your **thesis** summarizes your plan for achieving the specific purpose. A thesis is presented in a single sentence that captures the essence of your speech. (Some people call the thesis the *central idea*.) In that statement, you crystallize your speech in a way that embodies your topic and the main ideas you'll address. Ask yourself, "What is the central idea I want my audience to get from my speech?" That's your thesis.[11]

A well-phrased thesis statement includes a brief summary of your main points. This summary helps make your audience aware of what's coming in your speech and keeps them on track and involved throughout your presentation. Why is this important? Consider that by the time you give your speech, you will have become very familiar with the subject matter you plan to present. However, the members of your audience have little or no clue about what you're going to say. The more you help them organize your presentation in their minds, the better your chances for successfully informing, persuading, or entertaining them. Some speakers prefer to provide a longer summary of main points that is separate from the thesis. This longer summary is often called a *preview statement*, and is similar to the preview of main points provided in your speech introduction (Chapter 9). Stating both a thesis and a preview statement allows you to discuss your main points in a bit more depth before you begin presenting the body of your speech.

The thesis plays a key role in your speech, so be sure to give it sufficient care. Make sure that the language is clear and concise, not vague or wordy. Say it out loud—how does it sound? If it sounds clunky or doesn't give your audience the information they need to listen carefully to your speech, rework it until it sounds right. Your thesis incorporates the topic, flows from the specific purpose, and directly addresses how you will elicit the response you want from your audience. It summarizes the content of your speech, helping you clarify your approach and giving your audience a sense of what

A single declarative sentence that captures the essence or central idea of a speech.

to expect. Formulating a thesis statement well is one of the most important skills an effective public speaker masters.[12] Here are some examples of (1) thesis statements that include a preview of main points and (2) separate thesis and preview statements:

Topic:	Telemedicine
General purpose:	To inform
Specific purpose:	To educate my audience about the role of telemedicine in health care
Thesis:	Telemedicine uses new communication technologies for consultations between doctors, interactions between patients and doctors, and monitoring patients at remote locations.
Thesis plus preview statement:	Telemedicine uses new technologies to improve communication among health care providers and patients. New communication technologies allow doctors to consult with one another more easily, facilitate interactions between patients and doctors, and help health care providers monitor patients at remote locations.
Topic:	Sustainable land development
General purpose:	To persuade
Specific purpose:	To convince my audience that sustainable land development is an essential part of strengthening the local economy
Thesis:	Sustainable land development addresses the community's immediate needs and positions our city as a desirable location for future businesses by protecting our natural environment.
Thesis plus preview statement:	Sustainable land development is an essential part of strengthening the local economy. Not only does sustainable land development address our community's immediate needs, such as providing new housing that makes the most efficient use of our natural resources, but it also positions our city as a desirable location for future businesses by protecting our natural environment.
Topic:	Online dating services
General purpose:	To entertain
Specific purpose:	To amuse my audience with stories about my experience using an online dating service
Thesis:	From setting up my profile to searching through the online personals and finally going on a date, my first experience with an online dating service is one I'll never forget.
Thesis plus preview statement:	My first experience with an online dating service is one I'll never forget. First, setting up my profile was a weeklong process that involved all of my friends "helping" me describe myself in "just the right way." Second, searching through the online personals was sort of like trying on 50 pairs of jeans before finding a pair that fits—you really have to *search* for someone you think you'll be compatible with. And then there was the first date—it was a total comedy of errors, but luckily, my date had a great sense of humor (and is now my husband!).

Each of these thesis statements (or thesis plus preview statements) refines the topic, frames the main points for the speech, and provides guidance for research.

Sometimes you'll determine the thesis as soon as you've written the specific purpose—you have a clear idea of your topic, what you want to accomplish, and how you'll get there. More commonly, the thesis emerges as you begin developing your topic.[13] As you begin thinking about your topic and conducting preliminary research, you'll identify specific points or ideas that will help you achieve your specific purpose. Composing a good thesis statement forces you to clarify exactly what you want to say, which makes developing the rest of your speech much easier.

Building Your Working Outline

Once you know your general purpose, select a topic, and determine the specific purpose of your speech, you're ready to begin putting together your working outline. Chapter 1 introduced the **working outline**, which guides you during the initial stages of topic development, helping to keep you focused on your general purpose and clarify your specific purpose. As your working outline evolves, you'll include the speech topic, general purpose, specific purpose, thesis, and keywords for the main ideas and subpoints you want to address. Later, you'll construct a complete-sentence outline. Then, in the final stages of preparing your speech, you'll create a presentation outline. **Table 4.2** shows where you are in the process of giving a speech based on the type of outline you're creating or using.

Imagine that for an informative speech, you decide to tell your classmates about the most important factors students should consider when choosing a major. Every college student has dealt with this problem, so this subject will be familiar to your audience. Your topic is "Choosing a Major," and your specific purpose is "To make my audience understand how to choose a college major." Let's take a look at how you can apply what you've learned in this chapter to building a working outline for this topic.

An outline that guides you during the initial stages of topic development, helping to keep you focused on your general purpose and clarify your specific purpose.

Table 4.2 Types of Outlines

Type of outline	Functions	Key features	Chapter
Working	Assists in initial topic development; guides research	Includes main points and possible subpoints; revised during research process	Chapter 4: Developing Your Purpose and Topic
Complete-sentence	Clearly identifies all the pieces of information for the speech; puts ideas in order; forms the basis for developing the presentation outline	Uses complete sentences; lists all sections of speech and all references; revised during preparation process	Chapter 8: Organizing and Outlining Your Speech
Presentation	Assists you in practicing and giving your speech	Uses keywords; revised as you practice your speech; often transferred to note cards for use during practice and the final presentation	Chapter 11: Delivering Your Speech

You are here ▶

Brainstorming for Topic Development

The first step in topic development is brainstorming for ideas you may want to include in your speech.[14] Here are some ideas students consider important when choosing a major:

- career goals after college
- the university's reputation in the chosen field
- how long it will take to graduate
- the student's life goals
- majors the student really would not like
- areas of strongest skills
- whether the department is admitting new majors
- potential earnings in jobs related to the major
- quality of instructors
- things the student really likes to do
- job market for students graduating in the major
- requirements for the major
- whether the university offers the major
- department resources to help students

Grouping Ideas to Select Main Points

Once you have a list of ideas for your topic, distill each one down to a single word or short phrase. This will make it easier to identify links among them. Choose accurate and clear terms that capture your ideas, like these:

- career goals after college (career goals)
- the university's reputation in the chosen field (reputation)
- how long it will take to graduate (time needed)
- the student's life goals (personal goals)
- majors the student really would not like (dislikes)
- areas of strongest skills (strengths)
- whether the department is admitting new majors (openings)
- potential earnings in jobs related to the major (money)
- quality of instructors (instructors)
- things the student really likes to do (likes)
- job market for students graduating in the major (job market)
- requirements in the major (requirements)
- whether the university offers the major (curriculum)
- department resources to help students (student support)

Next, group ideas into categories that are more general. You're striving for **internal consistency** in each group of keywords. In terms of your speech, internal consistency

Speaking of . . .

Limit Your Working Outline

Carefully consider each idea you include in your working outline. Including too many points is one of the biggest problems students encounter when learning how to develop a topic. You'll have to make some tough decisions to avoid cluttering your speech with points that may be interesting but don't advance your specific purpose. Learning how to edit your ideas effectively at this stage will save you time and effort as you progress through the speech-making process, and it will greatly improve the flow and impact of your speech.

A logical relationship among the ideas that make up any main heading or subheading in a speech.

Table 4.3 Idea Groupings for "Choosing a Major"

Practical Considerations	Academic Resources	Personal Considerations
Reputation	Openings	Career goals
Time needed	Instructors	Personal goals
Job market	Curriculum	Likes
Money	Student support	Dislikes
Requirements		Strengths

Figure 4.2 Initial Working Outline for "Choosing a Major"

Topic: Choosing a Major
General purpose: To inform
Specific purpose: To inform my audience about how to choose a college major

I. Practical considerations
   A. Reputation
   B. Time to graduation
   C. Job market
   D. Money
   E. Requirements
II. Academic resources
   A. Openings
   B. Instructors
   C. Curriculum
   D. Student support
III. Personal orientations
   A. Career goals
   B. Personal goals
   C. What you enjoy
   D. What you don't like
   E. What you're good at

means that the ideas that make up any main heading or subheading have a logical relationship to one another. For the speech on choosing a major, the ideas fall into three major categories (**Table 4.3**): practical considerations (reputation, time needed, job market, money, and requirements), academic resources (openings, instructors, curriculum, and student support), and personal considerations (career goals, personal goals, likes, dislikes, and strengths).

By identifying and grouping ideas into main themes, you reduce a topic to logical categories. This will help you visualize what the skeleton, or main points, of the speech might look like. The thematically arranged categories provide an initial structure for your main ideas and what you might talk about for each one. For example, in the speech on choosing a major, the "practical considerations" category includes reputation, time needed, job market, money, and requirements. The themes and corresponding ideas provide the basis for your initial working outline (see **Figure 4.2**), which helps you accomplish the following tasks:

- Design your speech so that it connects well with your audience.

- Research your main themes using keyword searches.

- Create the complete-sentence outline you will use as you organize the information you've gathered.

Writing the Thesis

The initial grouping of ideas for the topic of choosing a major suggests the following thesis: "Three factors influence how to choose a major: practical considerations, academic resources, and personal considerations." This sentence sums up the core of the speech, indicates how you intend to fulfill your specific purpose, and can serve as your preliminary thesis statement. Add it to the information at the beginning of your working outline (**Figure 4.3**). This preliminary thesis may change as you analyze your audience and research your speech, but it's a good place to start.

Figure 4.3 Adding the Thesis to the Working Outline for "Choosing a Major"

Topic: Choosing a Major
General purpose: To inform
Specific purpose: To inform my audience about how to choose a college major
Thesis: Three factors influence how to choose a major: practical considerations, academic resources, and personal considerations.

As you analyze your audience and research your topic, refer back to your working outline to keep yourself on track. Although you may make important changes in your outline as you develop your speech, you want to stay focused on your main points. A working outline is a reliable tool that will help you do that.

Apply *it*

Brainstorming at Work

You use brainstorming techniques twice as you develop your speeches—to generate topic ideas and to come up with material for your main points. Brainstorming is a skill you can use in work settings, too. For instance, managers sometimes ask work groups to brainstorm together to come up with ways to solve problems or generate new ideas. However, the best results usually emerge when each person brainstorms independently and then brings the ideas that emerge to the manager or group in person or online.[15]

Summary

Every speech you present has one overall goal or general purpose: to inform, to persuade, or to entertain. The general purpose determines the nature of your speech.

In brainstorming for topics, list all the topic ideas you can think of without evaluating them. Often brainstorming begins long before you finally write down your topic ideas. Nevertheless, setting aside some time to identify and consider all your ideas will help you choose a topic that suits your speaking purpose.

Evaluate possible topics in terms of five basic considerations: yourself, your audience, available resources, time, and setting. Choose a topic that is appropriate for you, the audience, and the situation. Also, make sure you can find enough information to present a well-researched speech.

Your specific purpose—what you want to achieve—brings together your general purpose and topic with the response you seek from your audience. As you work on choosing a topic, you'll determine and frame the specific purpose.

Phrasing the thesis is a crucial step in topic development. Your thesis flows from your specific purpose and indicates how you will achieve the objective of your speech. Written as a single declarative sentence, the thesis captures the essence of your speech by incorporating the main points you plan to address.

Developing the content of your speech starts with brainstorming for ideas associated with your topic. The next step is to identify themes that arise from your brainstorming and group them into categories. These categories become the main points of your speech and suggest the thesis—the essence of what you'll cover.

Your topic, general purpose, specific purpose, thesis, and main points form the basis of your working outline. The working outline provides a tentative plan for your speech that may change as you learn more about your topic and audience. This early work gives you a solid foundation for analyzing your audience, researching your topic, identifying appropriate supporting materials, and determining the best way to organize your ideas.

IN THE BOOK
Summary
Key Terms
Critical Challenges

MORE STUDY RESOURCES
Quizzes
WebLinks
Peer-reviewed videos

CourseMate
Speech Studio

STUDENT WORKBOOK
4.1: Audience Feedback on Topics
4.2: Brainstorming Topics
4.3: Audience-Centered Specific Purpose
4.4: Phrasing Thesis Statements
4.5: Working and Reworking Your
    Working Outline

SPEECH BUDDY VIDEOS
WATCH It Video
4.1: Brainstorming for and Evaluating Topics
USE It Activity
4.1: Search and Find Missions

SAMPLE SPEECH VIDEOS
Tiffany, "Meat-Free and Me," informative
    speech
Husam, "How to Become a Successful
    Business Person," informative speech

SPEECH BUILDER EXPRESS
Goal/purpose
Thesis statement
Outline

INFOTRAC COLLEGE EDITION
Recommended search terms
General purpose and speech
Specific purpose and speech
Thesis statement and speech
Brainstorming
Public speaking topics

AUDIO STUDY TOOLS
"How to Become a Successful
    Business Person," Husam
Critical thinking questions
Learning objectives
Chapter summary

Guide to Your Online Resources

CourseMate Your Speech Communication CourseMate for *Public Speaking: The Evolving Art* gives you access to the Speech Buddy video and activity featured in this chapter, additional sample speech videos, Speech Studio, Speech Builder Express, InfoTrac College Edition, and study aids such as glossary flashcards, review quizzes, and the Critical Challenge questions for this chapter, which you can respond to via email if your instructor so requests. In addition, your CourseMate features live WebLinks relevant to this chapter, including sites that provide ideas for finding speech topics. Links are maintained regularly, and new ones are added periodically.

Key Terms

brainstorming 62

general purpose 62

internal consistency 71

specific purpose 66

thesis 68

topic 62

working outline 70

Critical Challenges

Questions for Reflection and Discussion

1. Being open to new ideas and perspectives helps us exercise our critical thinking skills. How can you brainstorm for topic ideas with an open mind? What are some ways in which you might broaden your perspective on speech topics? How might you apply the strategy of trying out something new to come up with creative topic ideas?

2. Consider events and issues that are currently in the news. How might these serve as a springboard for topic ideas? How will these current events and issues influence your topic choices?

3. As you develop your topic—generating ideas and grouping them together—consider the assumptions you're making about the topic and your audience. Are there alternative ways of approaching the topic and categorizing ideas? How might you group ideas differently? How might you think about the topic in new ways?

4. Check out Speech Studio to evaluate how other students phrased their thesis statements. Or record a speech you're working on, upload it to Speech Studio, and ask your peers for their feedback. What feedback could you use to fine tune your thesis before you give your speech in class?

5

Adapting to Your Audience

Cengage Learning

Watch your Speech Buddy video... ...and what yo... learned i... next spe...

Cengage Learning

CourseMate   SPEECH Studio   SPEECH BUILDER EXPRESS

Successful speakers adapt their messages to appeal to specific audiences. When Microsoft founder Bill Gates goes on his annual fall college tour, he talks about the empowering role of computers at all the schools he visits, but he adjusts his speech for each audience. At the University of Michigan he said, "Microsoft hires about 30 people from the University of Michigan a year, including a lot of our top people. So, let me thank you for that, and hope we can keep up that incredibly strong relationship." He began his speech at the University of Waterloo with, "Well, it's great to be here. As you heard from some of your alums, Waterloo has contributed an amazing amount to Microsoft."[1] Even those brief acknowledgments let audience members know that Gates had prepared his speech with them in mind.

Tailoring a speech to fit your audience requires getting to know the people you'll be addressing—their interests, views, and familiarity with your topic. Your knowledge about the audience begins with **audience analysis**. Analyzing your audience won't guarantee a successful speech, of course, but it's a critical step toward creating a favorable outcome.

Audience analysis and adaptation begins with the first stages of speech preparation and continues through the actual presentation of the speech and beyond.[2] Analyzing your audience means anticipating their needs and interests and designing a strategy to respond to them. As you deliver your speech, audience feedback becomes another key source of information.[3] Are audience members smiling, frowning, making eye contact with you, or looking out the window? Prepare yourself in advance to react appropriately to listeners' nonverbal cues, adapting your speech based on that feedback. If there is a question-and-answer exchange following the presentation of your speech, listen carefully to what the audience has to say and respond appropriately.

Obtaining and evaluating information about your audience in order to anticipate their needs and interests and design a strategy to respond to them.

© Jeff Greenberg/PhotoEdit

REUTERS/Nicholas Roberts/Landov

One way Bill Gates adapts to his audience is by mentioning them at the beginning of his speech.

What Is an Audience?

The term *audience* originally referred to a group of people who share a common interest and physically gather together, usually in a public or semipublic setting such as a public plaza, theater, or stadium. With the arrival of film, movie theaters became another common gathering place for audiences. Radio, television, and the Internet have audiences too, of course, but audiences for these media are physically dispersed. When radio and television were new, it was common for family and friends to listen or watch as a communal audience. Today, you are more than likely to be an audience of one for any type of media. Still, the idea of audience is much the same as it was in Aristotle's time: **Audience** refers to the people the speaker addresses.

The people a speaker addresses.

Appealing to audiences becomes more challenging as new communication technologies allow us to reach a broader range of people. For example, bloggers try to attract readers by encouraging other bloggers to link to their sites. Campus libraries design their websites to serve as public relations tools, reaching out to students, alumni, potential donors, and faculty.[4] Online marketers also attempt to reach specific audiences.[5] For instance, personal profiles associated with users of Yahoo! Mail and Hotmail accounts allow marketers to tailor their advertisements to those audiences. In each case, the speaker, or sender, tries to learn as much as possible about audience members so he or she can design messages that will appeal to their interests, needs, and perspectives.

The Audience–Speaker Connection

Successful speakers view audience members as partners in public speaking, so speakers and listeners work together to create the speech situation.[6] Speakers succeed only to the degree they effectively connect with their audience. Audience members of all kinds have one basic question in mind: "How does what you're saying apply to me and fit with my experiences?" So when you address an audience, you must be able to interest them, intrigue them, or otherwise respond to their needs or appear to advance their interests.[7]

Failure to respect your audience can bring unpleasant results for both the audience and the speaker. Michael Jordan's good-guy image and credibility took a severe hit when he used the occasion of his induction into the Basketball Hall of Fame in 2009 to criticize former coaches, teammates, and opponents by name.[8] Doing so turned the audience off because Jordan acted in a way that served his needs, not the audience's. Jordan even called out LeRoy Smith, the man who was picked ahead of him to play on Jordan's high school team:

> LeRoy Smith was the guy, that when I got cut, he made the team. He's still the same six-foot, seven-inch guy. He's not any bigger, and his game is probably the same. But he started the whole process with me because he made the team and I didn't. I wanted to prove—not just to LeRoy Smith, not just to myself—but to the coach who actually picked LeRoy over me, I wanted to prove, "You made a mistake, dude."

LeRoy Smith was sitting in the audience for the induction speech that day—a special guest of Michael Jordan.

Successful public speaking begins and ends with the audience. Thorough audience analysis is the first step in an **audience-centered** approach to your speech. Understanding how to prepare a speech with the audience firmly in mind applies to every aspect of the speechmaking process. Some speakers make the mistake of focusing too much on preparing the content of their speeches, without sufficiently taking into consideration *who* they're talking to. But analyzing and adapting to specific audiences is crucial for media producers, writers, theater producers, politicians,[9] and all public speakers, including you.

> Describes a speaker who acknowledges the audience by considering and listening to the individual, diverse, and common perspectives of its members before, during, and after the speech.

Classroom Audiences

A college speech class differs from most public speaking situations. As a college student, you have some built-in advantages when you prepare your speeches. You'll share more about yourself than you do in almost any other class. You and your classmates can't avoid getting to know one another. For most students, that's an enjoyable part of the experience. And even though any audience can be challenging to win over, the students you'll speak to this term will want you to succeed.[10]

This unusual access to your audience means that you'll have a basic impression of who they are even before you give your first graded speech. By applying the listening skills presented in Chapter 3, you'll learn even more about your audience as the term progresses. However, becoming familiar with your audience involves more than gaining basic impressions. Adapting your speech to your audience requires determining in advance, as precisely as possible, who will be listening to you and what they know and think about your speech topic.

Adapting to a Diverse Audience

Only if you understand the basic characteristics of your audience and have some idea of their knowledge and feelings about your topic can you tailor your speech to reach them effectively. Politicians and advertisers convince people to vote for them or buy their products by tailoring their messages to their **target audience**—the particular group or subgroup they are trying to reach. For public speakers, the target audience comprises the people the speakers most want to inform, persuade, or entertain. You might, for instance, give a speech at a community center on the need for improved pedestrian safety features on busy streets. Although your audience may be mostly neighborhood residents who agree with your position, your target audience is the city council members in attendance who can actually do something about the problem. Similarly, if you wanted to advocate curriculum changes at your college, you'd target your speech at faculty and administrators—the people with the power to make the changes you seek. Marketing is based on the notion that sellers of goods and ideas must know who their target audiences are and how to connect with them. Just like marketers, public speakers must analyze their target audience in order to determine the best way to present their ideas.

> The particular group or subgroup a speaker most wants to inform, persuade, or entertain.

There is never just one audience in a room, even a public speaking classroom.[11] Particularly in today's media-driven world, students—like all audiences—have a range of personal experiences and easy access to information about a variety of topics. Thus, although the students in your public speaking class will have some history in common, they'll also differ in many ways. Part of your responsibility as a speaker is to recognize the diversity of backgrounds, knowledge, interests, and opinions among the members of your audience and plan your presentation accordingly.

Meeting the Challenges of Audience Diversity

The United States ranks as one of the most diverse countries in the world, with people from a wide variety of cultural, religious, educational, and economic backgrounds. In U.S. colleges, the number of African American, Latino, Native American, and Asian American students nearly doubled in the late twentieth century, from 15 percent of all college students in the mid-1970s to 29 percent nearly thirty years later.[12] This trend will only increase in the future.[13] When you present a speech, more than likely you'll face a diverse audience. Trying to adapt your speech to people with a range of backgrounds, experiences, and interests may seem difficult, but that diversity can work to your advantage and result in a successful experience for you and your audience.[14]

Speaking to a diverse audience can have positive outcomes. When you interact with people whose backgrounds differ from your own, you learn how to

- Promote a supportive communication climate that welcomes differing perspectives on topics and issues.

- Draw from a wide pool of knowledge and information that contributes to a better learning experience for all participants.

- Foster positive intergroup relationships in a cooperative fashion.

- Better articulate your own cultural identity and understand that of others.

- Acknowledge and respect differences while avoiding ethnocentrism.

- Advocate constructive dialogue about contentious topics.

At the same time, diverse audiences pose challenges. For example, most humor relies on cultural context—if members of your audience don't share that context, they likely won't find your attempts at humor very funny. Worse, they may feel uncomfortable and become distracted. Excluding some members of your audience with the language you use or the information you present hinders your ability to achieve the goal of your speech—to affect everyone positively with your ideas.

Techniques for Speaking to Diverse Audiences

Although speakers have many strategies at their disposal for adapting to diverse audiences, research reveals five particularly effective techniques: identify commonalities, establish credibility, include supporting materials relevant to specific audience groups, use appropriate language, and continuously attend to all segments of your audience. Applying these techniques depends on a careful and thorough analysis of your audience.[15] Together, these techniques acknowledge audience diversity yet promote an inclusive communication climate.

First, search for commonalities related to your topic among audience members. If you're giving an informative speech on home schooling to a group with mixed opinions and knowledge of the topic, you might begin by establishing the importance of a good education in general—something all audience members can agree on.

Second, establish your credibility on the topic through enthusiasm, friendliness, and expertise. Regardless of their knowledge, beliefs, and attitudes, audience members are more likely to listen carefully when you give an engaging presentation, appear warm and outgoing, and demonstrate knowledge of the subject.

Third, include supporting materials that resonate especially with one group, yet at the same time leave other audience members with positive or neutral feelings. For example, in an informative speech about women's college basketball, you might mention that women started playing basketball at Smith College in 1892—just one year after the game was invented. Audience members who follow women's basketball will likely find this fact particularly important, while others may simply view it as interesting.

Fourth, use language that appeals to all members of the audience. Choose words audience members find meaningful. This may require defining your terms or avoiding jargon and specialized language that only a few audience members will understand.

Fifth, continuously attend to all segments of your audience. Acknowledge the variety of their experiences throughout your presentation, rather than addressing each group in separate sections of your speech. For example, in a persuasive speech encouraging listeners to become better-informed voters, integrate appeals to the full range of audience members, from completely uninformed to highly informed, in all parts of the speech instead of dedicating a specific section to each group.

Implementing these techniques requires knowing your audience as thoroughly as possible. In the next section, you'll learn how you can begin to analyze your audience by examining basic audience characteristics.

John Giustina/Getty Images

Even if you are very different from the members of your audience, adapting to them by identifying commonalities, establishing credibility, providing relevant supporting materials, using appropriate language, and continuously attending to them can help you connect with the group.

Using Demographic Information

In any speaking situation, successful speakers assess the size of the audience and their demographic characteristics. **Demographics** are key characteristics of populations. These characteristics are often used to divide a population into subgroups. Important demographic categories include age, sex, race and ethnicity, educational level, income level or social class, sexual orientation, urban or rural residence, dis/ability, religious affiliation (if any), relationship status, and parental or guardian responsibilities.

Effective communicators use demographics to identify their target audiences. Demographics do not paint a complete picture of any individual or group, but knowing the demographics of your audience gives you a good place to start imagining their possible needs and interests. They help keep your audience foremost in your mind when deciding how to approach your topic.

> The ways in which populations can be divided into smaller groups according to key characteristics such as sex, ethnicity, age, and social class.

Gathering Demographic Data

Student speakers have an advantage over speakers in other settings. For speeches you give in class, some demographic categories—educational level, for instance—will be obvious. You can also note the ratio of women to men and get a good sense of audience members' age range. Additionally, you may have some idea of their ethnic backgrounds. Some demographic information is less observable, however. For example, you may not know the income level or socioeconomic class of audience members, although you can sometimes make reasonable assumptions by considering the type of school you attend and noting how your classmates dress and talk.

People who give presentations in their workplace or other familiar settings also often know a lot about their audience beforehand. For instance, you would probably have a good sense of the demographic composition of the audience for a report on a project at work or a speech to members of a club you belong to. Speakers in other settings often don't have personal access to their audience before the speaking event. In such situations, the best source of information is the person or organization that invited you to speak. Ask them for information about the audience—the size and purpose of the group, members' demographic characteristics, what they know about the topic, how they feel about it, what they might expect from the speaker, even how best to reach them with your message. Gathering this information will help you prepare and present your message effectively to that particular group. (Because you will have a better idea of what to expect, it will help reduce your nervousness too.)

Demographic information about an audience can best be obtained through personal observation, using a questionnaire, or consulting with people who are familiar with the group. However, sometimes those options aren't available. General demographic information about the American public—for example, current political affiliations of men and women, number of people of different races living in various states, or employment statistics among different age groups—can be found on the websites of national opinion polling organizations like the Pew Research Center, the Gallup Poll, the Zogby Poll, and the National Opinion Research Center at the University of Chicago.

Using Psychographic Information

Psychological data about an audience, such as standpoints, values, beliefs, and attitudes.

In contrast to audience demographics, **psychographics** focuses on psychological concepts such as standpoints, values, attitudes, and beliefs (**Figure 5.1**). Many marketers rely on psychographic data to develop strategies that might motivate consumers to buy a company's products or services. For example, healthy and unhealthy eaters differ not only in their eating behaviors but also in their values associated with overall health, exercise, and other lifestyle issues. Marketing to healthy and unhealthy eaters thus requires different strategies that address each group's psychological orientations. Likewise, understanding the psychographics of your audience will help you develop your speech effectively for that particular group

Audience Standpoints

The psychological location or place from which an individual views, interprets, and evaluates the world.

Standpoint refers to the location or place from which an individual views, interprets, and evaluates the world. An individual takes a "stand" about her or his "point" of view. Having a standpoint signals independence of mind, personal commitment, and a willingness to act on one's convictions.[16] A person's standpoint stems to some degree from her or his objective position in society, based on demographics such as socioeconomic status, sex, dis/ability, and age. The groups to which an individual belongs—for example, a Catholic Latina college student with a learning disability who comes from a working-class family or a 40-year-old African American gay man from an upper-middle-class family—influences her or his view of society.[17] Within any audience, members hold a variety of standpoints, which are linked to their values, attitudes, and beliefs.

Figure 5.1 Levels of Psychographic Data

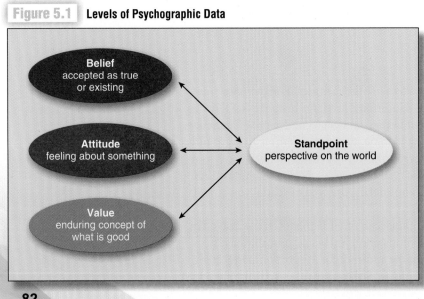

Considering standpoints moves audience analysis beyond simply categorizing individuals based on demographics. Standpoints recognize how audience members differ in ways that are more subjective. In the case of a classroom audience, for instance, everyone shares the experience of being a college student. However, individuals in the group always have different standpoints arising from their personal experiences in life. For example, first-generation college students likely view higher education differently than do second-, third-, and fourth-generation college students. Non–native-English-speaking students see the world differently from those who are native born. Suburban rockers and hip-hop fans may share demographic similarities but often manifest very different perspectives and lifestyles. As a speaker, assess the standpoints of your audience members and design a strategy to appeal to them.

In a speech on diversity given to middle- and high school students in Granite Falls, Washington, *Seattle Times* publisher Frank Blethen[18] recognized different standpoints in his audience and sought to bridge them in this way:

> The Reverend Dr. Martin Luther King, Jr. Holiday. What is it? What is it not? First, what it is not: It is not a black holiday. It is not a yellow holiday. It is not a brown holiday. It is not a white holiday. It is not a man's holiday. It is not a woman's holiday. It is not a baby boomer holiday. It is not a generation X or Y holiday. It is not a poor person's holiday. It is not a rich person's holiday. It is not a religious holiday. It is not a commercial shopping holiday. It is not a day off.
>
> So, what is it? It is America's celebration. It is every individual's day of celebration. It is a moment of rejoicing for all Americans. It is a moment of reflection for all Americans. It is a moment of renewal on our long diversity journey. It is a moment of challenge for each of us.

As Blethen's speech illustrates, identifying audience standpoints highlights similarities as well as differences among audience members.[19] Members of the same generation may share a common standpoint that transcends religion or class. Conversely, women in a particular society may share a common standpoint regardless of age—a standpoint that differs from that of men in that society.

Audience Values

A **value** is an enduring concept of what is good, right, worthy, and important. You've learned your values from the people you interact with, from the mass media, and from your society and culture. You express your values when you judge something as good or bad, excellent or poor, right or wrong, attractive or unattractive. Your values and your standpoints are closely linked. Your values often influence your point of view. For instance, if you value social justice deeply, you will likely take a strong stand against racist language when you hear it. Conversely, sometimes your standpoint influences your values. For example, research on environmentalism found that women view altruism as a more important value than men do, which in turn leads women to be more concerned about the environment.[20] If you were giving a speech on an environmental issue, knowing that women and men in your audience have differing value priorities would help you adapt your speech to both groups.

An enduring concept of what is good, right, worthy, and important.

Companies carefully analyze their audiences' values when developing an advertising campaign. Apple Inc., long known for its innovative advertisements, faced this issue with its Mac-versus-PC ads. Although the campaign was highly successful in the United States, audiences in Great Britain and Japan didn't find the ads as appealing or funny. The company even developed ads specifically for British and Japanese audiences. Yet after those ads aired, audiences' views of the company were even more negative, and sales dropped. Surveys found that what was viewed as hip and trendy in the United States was considered smug and overbearing in Britain. Moreover, the Japanese consider directly attacking a competitor—which Apple did—unseemly and obnoxious.[21]

Knowing the values your audience members think are important can help you choose a topic they're interested in, identify relevant supporting materials, and deliver your speech in a way they will find informative, persuasive, or entertaining.

Audience Attitudes

An **attitude** reflects how a person feels about something. Attitudes indicate approval or disapproval and liking or disliking of a person, place, object, event, or idea. You might like the bus driver, approve of the new student union building, dislike a concert you recently attended, and disapprove of your city's plan for redeveloping the downtown area. Your attitudes are related to your standpoint, values, and beliefs, but these psychographic variables are not always consistent. For example, from the standpoint of a person with a dis/ability, you might value universal access to public transit and believe that public transit is essential to your community, yet dislike your local public transit system. These conflicting psychological factors may stem from a negative experience or from a conflict between two competing beliefs.

How an individual feels about something.

Audience Beliefs

A **belief** is something a person accepts as true or existing. Beliefs can be changed by exposure to new evidence or a good argument. For instance, you may have believed that hypnosis is some kind of gimmick with no value until you learned from a credible source that it can help treat eating and sleep disorders, compulsive gambling, and depression. Still, some people seldom question their beliefs, even when new information seems to contradict them. For example, research indicates that consuming large quantities of antioxidants can have negative health consequences. Yet if you believe that antioxidants can improve your health, you might interpret the research with skepticism, thereby keeping your belief intact.

Something an individual accepts as true or existing.

Apply it

Byte-Sized Audience Expectations

Audiences today are accustomed to media snacking—consuming a variety of media in bite-sized chunks, skipping from one medium to the next, or paying attention to several media simultaneously.[22] You may text while flipping through a few blogs and listening to your iPod, or chat on your cell phone while watching a video on YouTube and downloading the podcast of a class lecture. In a world of 30-second video games, 2-minute versions of rock music classics, and 11-minute online TV episodes, audiences expect rapid information delivery. Does this mean that you should develop your speeches as a series of sound bites? No. Audiences may like to snack, but they also want substance.[23] Still, to keep their attention, you must consider their media-saturated environment and the tendency to move quickly through media choices—channel surfing, hyperlinking, scrolling—to find the information they want. You can appeal to snackers who also want substance by keeping your main points concise but informative, avoiding too much detail unless it's necessary, using a variety of sources as your supporting materials, and using presentation media that complement rather than repeat your points.

Gathering Psychographic Data

In your public speaking class, careful observation will help you gather psychographic data about your audience. It pays to be a good listener. What do your classmates talk about before and after class? What topics do they choose for their speeches? How do they respond to other students' speeches? The more you interact with and observe the other students in your class, the more familiar you'll become with who they are and how they think.

Most of the speeches you'll give in your life, however, will not be in front of students you get to know over the course of many class meetings. In some situations you may have little access to your audience beforehand and will need to make educated guesses about them based on general knowledge about the groups to which they belong (such as students at an urban high school or members of a community theatre troupe). Still, in many instances you'll be familiar with your audience through work or social interactions. In those cases, reflecting on what you know about your audience will give you important insights into their standpoints, values, attitudes, and beliefs. For example, consider the topics they talk about, the ideas they argue about, the emotions they express, and how they behave when they meet someone new. Observing audience members thoroughly before you present your speech will help you adapt to their particular characteristics.

Another way to gather both psychographic and demographic data about audience members is to have them complete an audience research questionnaire. The next section explains how to develop such a questionnaire.

Developing an Audience Research Questionnaire

Speakers can use **audience research questionnaires** to gather useful information about audience demographics and psychographics. Getting a sense of your audience's standpoints, values, attitudes, and beliefs—especially those related to your topic—will greatly influence the way you research, organize, and present your speech. Developing and distributing your questionnaire well in advance of speech day will help keep your audience at the forefront throughout the speechmaking process.[24]

> A questionnaire used by speakers to assess the knowledge and opinions of audience members; can take the form of email, web-based, or in-class surveys.

An effective audience research questionnaire features two basic types of questions—closed-ended and open-ended.

Asking Closed-Ended Questions

Closed-ended questions give the respondent a set of possible answers from which to choose. For instance, to gather demographic information you might ask questions such as

> A question that limits the possible responses, asking for very specific information.

- What is your sex?

  _____ Female _____ Male

- To which ethnic group do you belong?

  _____ African American _____ Asian American _____ European American

  _____ Latin/Hispanic American _____ Native American _____ Other

Similarly, you may want to learn basic facts about the audience that will help you develop an effective approach to your speech topic. If you want to persuade your audience to stop watching television, for instance, or to watch it more selectively, you might include closed-ended questions like these:

- On average, how many hours do you watch TV each week?

  _____ 0–9 _____ 10–19 _____ 20–39 _____ 40 or more

- Do you have a television in your bedroom? _____ Yes _____ No

- Why do you usually watch TV?

  _____ because I'm bored _____ to socialize with family or friends _____ to escape

  _____ as a reward _____ to learn things _____ for entertainment _____ other

You can also use the questionnaire to gather psychographic data related to your topic. If you are developing an informative speech about your school's 150th anniversary, for example, you might ask these questions:

- Our school has a long history of excellent education.

  _____ True _____ False

- It's important to me that people in the community have a positive view of our school.

  _____ Agree _____ Disagree

- I would enjoy participating in events to celebrate our school's 150th anniversary.

  _____ Yes _____ No _____ Maybe

You can find out about audience members' beliefs by using a different closed-ended question format that ascertains the strength of respondents' views. For example:

- Women make excellent bosses:

  _____ strongly agree _____ agree _____ neither agree nor disagree

  _____ disagree _____ strongly disagree

- Marijuana should be made legal for medical purposes:

  _____ strongly agree _____ agree _____ neither agree nor disagree

  _____ disagree _____ strongly disagree

Responses to these questions give you an idea of what respondents believe as well as how strongly they believe it. Your classmates probably already have experience with these kinds of questionnaires, so they should be able to give you informed responses.

Asking Open-Ended Questions

Closed-ended questions can provide important information about the basic characteristics and beliefs of your audience. However, speakers usually want more information. **Open-ended questions** are designed to elicit more in-depth information by asking respondents to answer in their own words. Additional insights can be gained by asking questions such as

A broad, general question, often specifying only the topic.

- What do you know about identity theft?

- Why do you think some people don't think climate change is real?

- What changes, if any, would you make to our school's basic course requirements?

- What does the word *freedom* mean to you?

Combining Question Types

Combining closed-ended and open-ended questions can clarify audience positions and elicit additional useful information. Here are some examples:

- Should the academic year for high school be extended to 12 months?

  _____ Yes _____ No

  Why did you answer that way? _____

- Have you ever thought about joining a fraternity or sorority?

  _____ Yes _____ No

  Why or why not? _____

- Do you think it's a good idea to keep a handgun at home? _____ Yes _____ No

  Why do you think this? _____

Leave enough room after each open-ended item for respondents to give useful answers, and keep your questionnaire short.

Distributing Your Questionnaire

You can distribute questionnaires to your audience in paper form or via an online distribution method. The easiest way to administer an audience research questionnaire online is through a free survey-building website. These websites offer much more than ease of use and anonymous responses; often they provide tools for organizing and tabulating survey data. Putting your audience research questionnaire on a survey-building website works well for audiences outside the classroom as well. You'll find links to some of these websites, as well as various polling sites, on your CourseMate for *Public Speaking: The Evolving Art*—look under the resources for this chapter. Once you've developed your survey, contact your audience, provide the link, and set a deadline for completion.

Keep the length of your questionnaire manageable. Five to ten questions usually will give you plenty of data and avoid burdening your audience. If your questionnaire is too long, respondents will tire of answering questions and may not respond as fully as you'd like (or at all). In addition, you'll end up with far more data than you need, causing you to waste time sifting through irrelevant information.

Questionnaires for Non-Classroom Audiences

Surveying your audience isn't always possible. Sometimes you'll have to make do with asking a few people key questions. For instance, if you don't know any members of the audience for a speech you've been invited to give to a local community group, you might contact the person who organized the event and ask for the names of some of the likely attendees. Then email or phone those individuals, asking them questions that will give you a sense of your audience's knowledge level, standpoints, values, attitudes, and beliefs. When you don't have direct access to your audience, pose your questions to people who are familiar with the group you'll be addressing.

Gathering relevant information about your audience as you prepare your speech will help you be audience-centered and credible when you deliver your speech.

Using Audience Research Data in Your Speech

Data gathered from a well-constructed audience research questionnaire can help you in two ways. First, you will learn more about who your audience members are, what they know about your topic, and how they feel about it. Second, the questionnaire gives you data and comments you can refer to in the speech itself.

Types of Audience Data

Just mentioning questionnaire data in your speech will catch your audience's attention. But how can you use the data to achieve the best possible effect? You will have two basic types of information to work with: summary statistics and direct quotes.

Summary Statistics **Summary statistics** reflect trends and comparisons. For instance, you may find that 75 percent of an audience of adult women you plan to speak to believe that annual screening for breast cancer is necessary despite recent research to the contrary. That is a statistic you obtained by asking the question, "Do you believe women over 40 should be screened every year for breast cancer?" Because you also asked respondents to state their age, you can make some useful comparisons. For instance, you may have found that older women in your audience are much more likely than younger women are to support the idea of annual screenings. Comparisons like this allow you to break down summary statistics into useful subcategories that help you identify individual audience members' standpoints.

Information in the responses to an audience research questionnaire that reflects trends and comparisons.

87

Direct quotes are comments written in response to open-ended questions. For example, after asking college students the closed-ended question "Should the U.S. military draft be reinstated?" you probably will get some passionate responses to the following open-ended question: "Why do you think that way?" In selecting quotes, choose ones that are short, well expressed, and clearly linked to the point you want to make, such as

> The draft should not be reinstated because a voluntary military is more motivated, professional, and dedicated.

> I don't want to die in a war I don't believe in!

Comments written in response to open-ended questions in an audience research questionnaire.

The quotes you use should accurately reflect the respondents' overall sentiments. Be sure to select comments that serve your speech purpose well and that will make sense to the audience. As a responsible speaker, avoid quotes that would obviously identify the person who made the comment or that would embarrass audience members or portray them in a negative way. Even if such quotes support your point, using them violates the ethical principles of public speaking, hurts your credibility, and makes the audience less inclined to listen.

Referring to Audience Data in Your Speeches

Summary statistics and direct quotes are valuable material you can use to get the audience's attention, support your main points, make transitions from one point to another, and conclude your speech. For example, you could begin a speech promoting public transportation in this way:

> More than 90 percent of the people sitting in this room say they support toughening environmental standards against air pollution, yet very few of you say you carpool or use public transportation. Today I'm going to show you how you can personally follow through on your interest in protecting the environment by making informed and responsible decisions about the forms of transportation you use every day.

Or you could use a quote as your attention getter:

> "It's the biggest scam out there!" That's what one of you said about all the weight-loss programs we see advertised on TV. Let's take a closer look at just what those magical weight loss programs are really all about.

Data from your audience research questionnaire also can be used to support your main points. For instance, you might integrate summary statistics into your speech in this way:

> According to the questionnaire you filled out last week, more than three-fourths of you say you expect to take at least five years to finish your college degree–exactly the national average. For most students in the United States, the four-year college degree is a thing of the past.

In addition, summary statistics and direct quotes can provide effective transitions from one point to the next. For example:

> That may seem impressive, but does it accomplish what someone in the audience calls "the single most important thing we have to do in America today—stop exporting good jobs to foreign countries"? Let's talk about how that might be done.

Statistics and quotes gleaned from the audience research questionnaire can prove effective in speech conclusions as well, because a key statistic or compelling quote will stay with the audience long after the speech is over. You can leave the source of your data implicit and try something like this:

> Finally, I encourage each of you to do the right thing and what the vast majority of you say must be done. Demand that the university adopt a strong hate speech policy and that administrators do it now!

When using a quote in a conclusion, you might say something like this:

> You've heard my appeal for reforming the way presidential debates are conducted in this country. As one of your classmates asked, "How can the most democratic country in the world fail to represent the full range of diverse voices in this vital exercise of democracy—the Presidential debates?" Think about it.

▶ Watch it

SPEECH BUDDY VIDEO 5.1
Analyzing and Using Audience Data

In this video, Evan reviews some key points about audience questionnaires and demonstrates how to use questionnaire data in a speech. As you watch the video, consider what you've learned about developing and using audience analysis questionnaires.

▶ Use it

Watch your Speech Buddy video ...

... and use what you've learned in your next speech.

ACTIVITY 5.1
According to Our Data

In this activity, you're asked to analyze three sample audiences and make decisions based on available data, and then consider how you might use audience data in your own speech.

Adapting to the Setting

The setting for your speech plays an important role in audience-entered public speaking. The location of the speech, the occasion, and the time when you give your speech are factors to consider during speech preparation and delivery.

The Location

Where you give your speech—a large auditorium, a small conference room, or outside on the steps of your school's student union—influences what you say and how you say it. Identify in advance the advantages and disadvantages of where you'll be speaking. For example, a small conference room can allow for a more informal presentation in which you can personalize your speech and easily make eye contact with each audience member. However, that informality may also lead listeners to whisper comments to each other, text friends, or check email. Even in a casual setting, you'll want to maintain a degree of formality so that audience members will focus on you.

Large auditoriums likewise come with both positive and negative features. These settings often have built-in systems for displaying digital slides, video, and audio. Using presentation media can prove crucial in maintaining the attention of a large audience.

However, listeners become more anonymous—especially if the room is dark and the spotlight is on you—and may be tempted to chat, arrive late, or leave early.

Analyze the room where you will be speaking. You may be accustomed to the setting, but probably from the vantage point of the audience, not of the speaker. Note the room's configuration and the availability of technical equipment. Identify possible sources of noise, such as open windows or doors. If you plan to use visual presentation media, be sure you can darken the room sufficiently so your images will show up clearly. If necessary, arrange ahead of time to have a screen put in place. Determine whether you'll use a podium, a desk, or nothing at all. Knowing the possibilities and constraints of the location in advance helps you adapt to the setting.

Also consider the geographic location of your speech. Referring to the place where you're speaking lets the audience know you've thought about them in advance. For example, Time Warner Inc. chairman and CEO Richard D. Parsons[25] made these references to location during a speech he gave in Chicago:

> This city also has a rich African American heritage, beginning with Jean Baptiste Point du Sable—a black man from Haiti—who built Chicago's first permanent settlement in 1779. And your president, Hermene Hartman, publisher of *Savoy* and *N'Digo*, is the latest in a long line of African American publishers from Chicago who have been role models for many of us who walk in their footsteps today—from Robert Abbott, who founded the *Chicago Defender* in 1905, to the late John H. Johnson, who founded the Johnson Publishing Company, home of *Ebony* and *Jet,* in 1942.

By integrating information about Chicago's origins and its role in the development of African American–owned media businesses, Parsons linked his speech to the setting in which it took place.

If you have an opportunity to make a presentation on a webcast or in a videoconference, your audience may be in several physical locations, even in other states or countries. Gathering information about the possibilities and constraints of these technologies and knowing where the audience members are located will help you adapt to the setting. Chapter 16 provides more detail about public speaking and new media.

The Occasion

The occasion often indicates the reason for the speech. Why have people gathered for this event? Is the audience voluntary or captive? **Voluntary audiences** choose to attend (or not attend) a speaking event, as when you attend a guest lecture on campus because you find the topic interesting or listen to a political candidate's campaign speech at a town hall. **Captive audiences**, in contrast, feel they *must* attend. Mandatory staff meetings at work and required college orientations are examples of occasions when audience attendance is involuntary. The audience for your public speaking class may be captive if the course is required. Generally, voluntary audiences are more motivated to listen. Speakers may have to work harder to engage captive audiences. Knowing in advance the type of audience you will face will help you adapt to the occasion. For example, Cathleen Black, president of Hearst Magazines, explicitly referred to the occasion when she began a speech[26] to a group of magazine publishers:

> Good morning. It's great to be back. The last time I was a speaker at one of these breakfast sessions was 2002. Even though that was a few short years ago, it was a very different world. I talked about our high hopes for *O, the Oprah Magazine*, which went on to make publishing history. I also talked about our high hopes for *Lifetime Magazine*, which didn't. I talked about a lot of aspects of the magazine business. But I mentioned the word "Web" only twice … and then only in passing. I didn't mention social networking, or Google, or blogging, or long-tail marketing, or interactive advertising, or high-speed

Individuals who can choose to attend or not attend a speaking event.

Individuals who feel they must attend an event.

connections, or tagging, or platforms, or any of the other things that are reshaping the world of publishing. It's not that I wasn't aware of these things. It's just with the ruins of the dot-com economy still smoldering … it didn't seem like they would be factors any time soon. Obviously, any time soon came a lot sooner than any of us could have predicted.

Black links her comments from the previous speech with her remarks at the current one for the same event. By adapting her speech to the occasion, she provides continuity for her listeners.

Knowing what an audience expects or hopes for can also help a speaker adapt nicely to the occasion. After thanking the school president for inviting him to speak at Lafayette College's graduation ceremony, historian Michael Beschloss[27] began his speech by dispelling a common fear in this setting:

What Dan didn't tell you is he took a real risk by inviting me here today, because he knows that one occupational hazard of presidential historians is sometimes they become a lot like the people they are writing about. One person I have been writing about is not a president, but he was a vice-president, Hubert Humphrey, known for giving speeches that were about three hours too long. Once Humphrey did this and even knew he was overdoing it. He yelled at the audience, "Anybody got a watch?" and someone yelled back, "How about a calendar?"

Have no fear. I know the lesson that commencement speeches should not be too long. I learned it at Williams College, where I graduated exactly 30 years ago this month. It was about 98 degrees, and we had a commencement speaker who droned on for at least 45 or 50 minutes. People were getting very hot; some people were about to faint; people were in danger of losing their airplane reservations because they were about to fly out that afternoon. Finally, he seemed to be coming to the end, and there was a collective sigh of relief, at which point the speaker said, "Now for the second half of my talk." There was a groan from the audience, and I guess if I learned nothing else from Williams, I learned one thing: Keep it brief if you ever speak at a commencement.

Many occasions for speaking arise from events that affect the speaker directly, like a university fee increase. How might you adapt your speech to your audience on the occasion depicted here, a protest outside a university board meeting?

Michael Beschloss encouraged the audience to listen to his speech by promising it wouldn't go on too long. Sensitively, he considered the occasion from the audience's perspective, not his own.

The Time

Adapting to time means taking into account the time of day you'll give your speech, when you'll speak during the event (for example, your position in the order of speakers on the day you speak in class), and current events that might impact your speech.

Time of day influences your audience's alertness, interests, and needs. An audience at 7:30 A.M. is very different from the same group at 7:30 P.M., with listeners likely to be more alert in the morning than in the evening. Speaking close to a mealtime can prove challenging, with audience members distracted by hunger before eating and drowsy afterward.

As you prepare your speech, also consider at what point you'll speak during the occasion. Even if you're the only speaker, your speech will take place within a larger flow of events, such as meetings, workshops, coffee breaks, and the like. As part of adapting to the setting, you acknowledge other events and speakers that occur before and after your speech. In your public speaking class, being alert to what other speakers have talked about earlier that day or previously in the term will help you integrate your topic with what others have covered. In addition, referring to other speakers personalizes the topic for your audience and helps gain and maintain their attention.

Showing how current events relate to your topic helps your speech come off as fresh and credible. Integrating current events into your speech places your topic within the larger flow of happenings at the local, regional, national, and global levels. This makes your presentation timely and relevant, especially if the news applies to the audience. For example, referring to a recent increase in unemployment might help audience members understand the importance of thorough preparation for a job search.

Developing Credibility with Your Audience

An audience's perception of a speaker's competence, trustworthiness, dynamism, and sociability.

Regardless of the demographics of your audience, appearing credible is critical to your success. Speaker **credibility**, or what the Greek philosopher Aristotle called *ethos*, arises from audience perceptions of a speaker's competence, trustworthiness, dynamism, and sociability. Four dimensions of credibility work together to give the audience an overall impression of the speaker, as shown in **Figure 5.2**. That impression greatly influences whether or not the audience will listen to and believe the speaker.

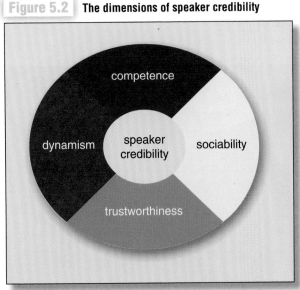

Figure 5.2 The dimensions of speaker credibility

Competence

Competence refers to the qualifications a speaker has to talk about a particular topic. Listeners view speakers as more credible when they appear knowledgeable and informed about their topic.[28] This expertise may stem from a speaker's specialized training and experience related to the topic or from careful research. Speakers demonstrate their competence when they present relevant supporting materials. Different audiences will have different expectations about what constitute effective and appropriate supporting materials.[29] Carefully analyzing your audience will give you insights into what they'll find interesting and convincing.

The qualifications a speaker has to talk about a particular topic.

Trustworthiness

The second dimension of speaker credibility is **trustworthiness**. Unlike competence, which relates to specific qualifications, information, and authority, trustworthiness is a much more general idea. Audiences regard you as trustworthy when they consider you to be honest, ethical, sincere, reliable, sensitive, and empathic. Aristotle argued that a trustworthy public speaker demonstrates **goodwill** by showing he has the audience's true needs, wants, and interests at heart.[30]

An audience's perception of a speaker as honest, ethical, sincere, reliable, sensitive, and empathic.

An audience's perception that a speaker shows she or he has the audience's true needs, wants, and interests at heart.

Dynamism

The third dimension of credibility, **dynamism**, refers to how the audience regards your activity level during your presentation.[31] Dynamic speakers appear lively, strong, confident, and fluent in what they say and how they present their ideas. Being dynamic makes a speaker more charismatic.[32] Audience members listen to, remember, enjoy, and are convinced by speakers who are dynamic.

An audience's perception of a speaker's activity level during a presentation.

92

Sociability

Sociability reflects the degree to which an audience connects with a speaker. Sociable speakers are those the audience considers to be friendly, accessible, and responsive.[33] Appearing sociable requires establishing rapport with the audience. An effective way to achieve rapport is to show how you and the audience share some common ground or similarities. Speaking before a group in California, Queen Noor of Jordan reached out to her audience in this way:

> California has played a seminal role in my journey to the Middle East. It is here that I first became aware of my connection to that remarkable region of the world. When I was growing up, my family lived for a time in Santa Monica. My parents had a bedroom overlooking the ocean, and one day there my mother told me the story of our family. Her ancestors had emigrated here from Sweden, my father's father and uncles had emigrated from the Arab world. I remember sitting there after our conversation, staring out the window at the Pacific Ocean, and feeling connected for the first time to a larger family and a wider world.[34]

Although born and educated in the United States, when she made this speech Queen Noor had not lived there for some time. Referring to an experience in California when she was a child allowed her to connect with her audience. An engaging delivery style always helps too. In addition to talking about living in California, Queen Noor used her voice to convey a warm and inviting tone.

The degree to which an audience feels a connection to a speaker.

Summary

Adapting to your audience requires thorough analysis. Only then can you design a speech that is likely to accomplish your objective. Especially today, audience members represent many different backgrounds, knowledge levels, and interests. Interacting with diverse groups of people presents many advantages, such as learning how to promote a more supportive communication climate and better articulate your own cultural identity. Being considerate of everyone in the audience is a key quality of a successful public speaker. Techniques for speaking to diverse audiences include finding commonalities, establishing credibility, incorporating relevant supporting materials, using language that all audience members understand, and being sensitive to all audience members throughout the speech.

When analyzing your audience, you gather two types of information: demographic and psychographic. Demographic information includes age, educational level, socioeconomic status, religious affiliation (if any), ethnic background, dis/ability, and sex. With this information, you can draw some general conclusions about your audience's interests and needs. The perspective of those who invite you to speak is particularly valuable for gathering demographic data. Online sources of demographics and public opinion can also help.

Psychographic information refers to psychological data about audience members, including their standpoints, values, attitudes, and beliefs. This information provides important insights into what might motivate them. In many cases, you can infer audience psychographics based on observable behaviors, such as what they talk about, what they read, and which activities they participate in.

One method for gathering demographic and psychographic data is the audience research questionnaire. Carefully designed closed- and open-ended questions can elicit valuable information about your audience's interests and needs as well as those of subgroups within the larger audience.

You can integrate information from the audience research questionnaire into your speech. Closed-ended questions provide trends and averages, and open-ended questions elicit audience members' feelings, expressed in their own words. Quoting clever or insightful remarks by audience members is a great way to capture their attention, support your main points, make transitions from one point to the next, or create an effective conclusion.

Adapting to your audience also means adapting to the setting in which you give a speech. The location is the physical place where you give your speech, such as an auditorium, a classroom, or the steps of the county courthouse. New communication technologies allow speakers and audiences to participate in events from different geographic locations. The occasion is the purpose of the event. Audiences may attend out of choice, or attendance may be involuntary. The time of the speech, including time of day, speaking order, and current events, also influences the setting for the speech.

Whatever your audience and setting, developing your credibility is crucial to your success as a speaker. Competence, trustworthiness, dynamism, and sociability work together to form a speaker's credibility.

Review it

Directory of Study and Review Resources

IN THE BOOK
- Summary
- Key Terms
- Critical Challenges

MORE STUDY RESOURCES
- Quizzes
- WebLinks
- Peer-reviewed videos

STUDENT WORKBOOK
- 5.1: Understanding Your Target Audience's Beliefs
- 5.2: Seeing Your Topic through Your Audience's Eyes
- 5.3: Designing a Questionnaire
- 5.4: Tracking Credibility
- 5.5: Sample Audience Member

SPEECH BUDDY VIDEOS
- **WATCH It Video 5.1**
- Analyzing and Using Audience Data
- **USE It Activity 5.1**
- According to Our Data

SAMPLE SPEECH VIDEOS
- Matthew, "Drinking," persuasive speech
- Courtney, "Light Pollution," persuasive speech

SPEECH BUILDER EXPRESS

- Goal/purpose
- Thesis statement

- Supporting material
- Introduction
- Conclusion
- Works cited
- Outline

INFOTRAC
- **Recommended search terms**
- Audience and public speaking
- Audience analysis
- Audience adaptation
- Audience centered
- Classroom audience
- Demographic information
- Psychographic information
- Personal values
- Personal beliefs
- Personal attitudes
- Survey questions
- Online survey services
- Research data and public speaking

AUDIO STUDY TOOLS
- "Drinking" by Matthew
- Critical thinking questions
- Learning objectives
- Chapter summary

CourseMate

SPEECH Studio

Guide to Your Online Resources

CourseMate Your Speech Communication CourseMate for *Public Speaking: The Evolving Art* gives you access to the Speech Buddy video and activity featured in this chapter, additional sample speech videos, Speech Studio, Speech Builder Express, InfoTrac College Edition, and study aids such as glossary flashcards, review quizzes, and the Critical Challenge questions for this chapter, which you can respond to via email if your instructor so requests. In addition, your CourseMate features live WebLinks relevant to this chapter, including sites regarding opinion polls, such as the Pew Research Center, the Gallup Poll, Zogby Poll, and the National Opinion Research Center at the University of Chicago. Links are regularly maintained, and new ones are added periodically.

Key Terms

attitude 84

audience 78

audience analysis 77

audience-centered 79

audience research questionnaires 85

belief 84

captive audiences 90

closed-ended questions 85

competence 92

credibility 92

demographics 81

direct quotes 88

dynamism 92

goodwill 92

open-ended questions 86

psychographics 82

sociability 93

standpoint 82

summary statistics 87

target audience 79

trustworthiness 92

value 83

voluntary audiences 90

Critical Challenges

Questions for Reflection and Discussion

1. Consider a controversial topic, such as abortion, stem cell research, or capital punishment. Are you comfortable with the way political and cultural issues tend to become so polarized? Who benefits from discussions when only extreme positions are put forward? Do you think the media are primarily responsible for this situation? How might your speeches give you an opportunity to explore alternatives to this black-or-white way of talking about issues—the middle ground?

2. Do you assume that men and women differ on sensitive issues like amnesty for illegal immigrants? On what information or impressions do you base your assumptions? How might age influence what women and men think and do? While speakers want to be alert and sensitive to differences between the sexes, they don't want to assume differences that might not exist. For example, assuming that the women in your audience are more concerned than the men are about issues associated with family and children may be completely wrong. What can you do as a speaker to be sure you don't fall into this trap?

3. In what ways would an audience composed of students likely differ from other audiences? How might the demographic profile and interests of a student audience differ from those of professionals in a work setting, for instance, or from those of members of a club, voluntary association, or activist organization? Would these audiences be equally familiar with a topic and feel the same way about it?

4. Check out Speech Studio to evaluate other students adapted their speeches to their audiences. Or record a speech you're working on, upload it to Speech Studio, and ask your peers for their feedback. What feedback could you use to fine-tune how audience centered your speech is before you give your speech in class?

6 Researching Your Topic

Read it

Cengage Learning

Watch it

Use it

Cengage Learning

Review it

CourseMate SPEECH Studio SPEECH BUILDER EXPRESS

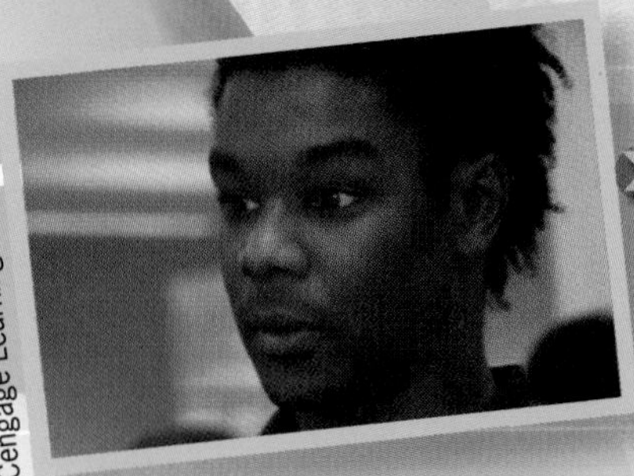

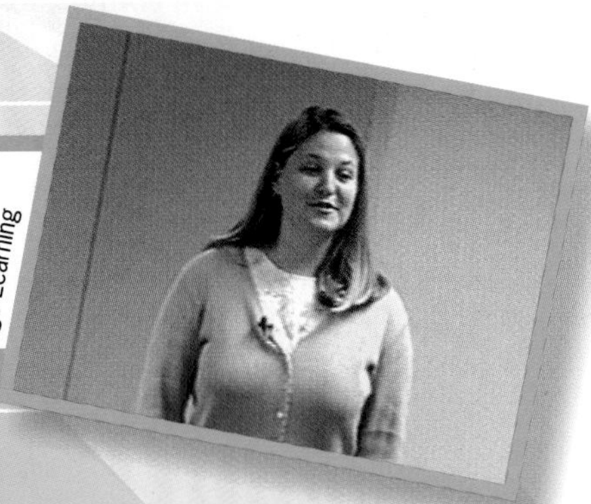

If you're like most college students, doing research for your classes often begins with Wikipedia. A recent survey of college students in the United States found that three-quarters of the respondents used Wikipedia at least some of the time for their classes.[1] Wikipedia provides general background information on a topic, but it's just a start. Learning how to do good research involves using the right navigation tools to search out information from the library, organizations, the internet, and interviews. Audience members depend on you to provide them with accurate, current, and balanced information—a key component of speaking ethically.

The research process consists of three phases: (1) preparing for the search, (2) gathering the information, and (3) evaluating the information found. **Table 6.1** on page 98 summarizes these phases.

Yellow Dog Productions/ Getty Images

Table 6.1 Phases in the Research Process

Prepare	Identify
	• What you know
	• How you learned it
	• Multiple perspectives and sources
Gather → Library	• Books
	• Academic journals, magazines, newspapers
	• Government publications
	• Reference materials
	• Nonprint resources
Gather → Internet	• Websites
	• Deep web
	• Blogs
Gather → Interviews	• Research interviews with experts
Evaluate	Assess information's
	• Reliability
	• Validity
	• Currency

Preparing to Research Your Topic

The first step in developing a clear research plan is determining what you already know about a topic, how you found out about it, and possible sources of information about your topic. This section suggests strategies you can use as you prepare to research your topic.

Examining Your Own Experience

To establish what you already know about your topic, jot down a list of words you associate with it. For example, if you were developing a speech on global climate change, you might be familiar with these aspects of the topic:

- Rainforest depletion

- Climate change

- Copenhagen Climate Treaty

- Carbon dioxide

- Greenhouse gases

Write out a few sentences for each phrase, explaining what you know about it.

Second, identify how you learned about the topic. Did you read about it in a newspaper, magazine, or blog? Discuss it in a class? Hear a story about it on a radio or TV program? You may have acquired information about your topic from multiple sources. In the example of global warming, you may have learned about the topic from

- A chemistry class

- A special report on your public radio station

- A pamphlet from an environmental organization

- An article in your local newspaper

- A guest speaker on your campus

- A documentary film

Each of these sources provides a starting point for gathering additional information. For example, you might dig out your notes from that chemistry class, listen to the podcast of a radio program you heard, visit the local chapter of an environmental organization, go to the library for a copy of a newspaper article or search for it using a periodicals database, contact the college's public relations office for a videotape of the speaker's talk or search its website for a webcast archive, or check out the DVD of a documentary film from a video store or your campus library.

In exploring how you learned about a topic, you go beyond your personal experience to identify additional sources. What you already know about your topic is important, but serves only as a starting point. You must become an expert on your topic, drawing information from many diverse sources. In addition to reducing any speech anxiety you may have, becoming an expert on your topic allows you to determine the reliability of what you know and the credibility of your original sources.

Identifying Multiple Perspectives and Sources

Learning about and respecting others' viewpoints are essential to a democratic society. The information sources you access when preparing a speech should reflect this diversity. As you conduct your research, seek multiple perspectives, regardless of your topic. Identifying a full range of perspectives works to your advantage because it helps you challenge your assumptions. It also gives you an idea of what kind of resistance you might face when you speak, and helps ensure that you will speak ethically.

Considering multiple perspectives on your topic also encourages you to explore multiple sources of information. People often develop habitual ways of accessing information that greatly narrow the possibilities for a search, such as relying exclusively on one search engine.[2] As discussed later in the chapter, some information may be available only in your local library. For example, if you were giving a speech on media coverage of presidential campaigns at the beginning of the nineteenth century, you might need to visit the library to view microfilm copies of newspapers from that time.

Experts provide an important source of information. As you conduct your research, note credible organizations and individuals associated with your topic. After reviewing this chapter's discussion of research interviews, contact those experts and try to schedule an interview to get firsthand information for your speech.

The latest communication technologies have not created a paperless society, but the internet has transformed libraries from shelves and paper to networks and electronic databases.[3] Although you may still go to the library from time to time as you research your speeches, you'll probably do most of your work online from your home or campus computer. Nearly all newspapers, journals, government publications, and other print resources are available online as well as in paper form. Even when sources of information are not online, they are often indexed online, such as in a library's catalog or other electronic database.

To find multiple points of view on your topic, ask the following questions to guide your search for information.

Who Might Be Knowledgeable about This Topic? Using a search engine to locate information about a topic may be as easy as typing in a person's name. For example, if you were to speak on the civil rights movement in the United States, you might search using the names "Rosa Parks" and "Malcolm X." Also consider people you know, such as professors, coworkers, family members, and friends, who may be experts on your topic.

What Organizations Address the Topic You Are Researching? Particularly if your topic touches on a local issue, such as how your city addresses traffic problems or the resurgence of the local art community, local organizations often can provide information that is not available from any other source. For example, suppose you're conducting research for a speech on hospice, which provides spiritual, emotional, and medical care to terminally ill people and their families. Although you can get general information from the National Hospice and Palliative Care Organization's website, your audience will appreciate information about hospice care in their community.

Not every organization has a website, but basic contact information likely is available online in websites such as Yellow Pages (yellowpages.com) or Superpages (superpages.com). If the organization you want to contact is not listed in an online directory, use keywords to search the business section of your local telephone book. In the case of hospice, once you find a local one, you can contact the staff, request pamphlets or other information, and possibly schedule an interview with the director.

What Events Are Happening Related to Your Topic? The answer to this question may lead you to information posted on a web page or in a newsgroup, or to an event such as a book reading or a public lecture. Campus websites often list diverse and interesting weekly events. Yahoo! Local (local.yahoo.com) allows you to identify traditional as well as online events for most cities in the United States. Check your local newspaper as well.

How Can I Find the Information I Need? Often there are many sources for the same information and many ways to get to those sources. For example, online databases available through your library will produce different articles and stories about the same topic. Different **keywords**, terms associated with a topic that are used to search for information related to it, will also lead you in multiple directions. In addition to determining the best keywords to use in searching online for information about your topic, identify the best physical places to search. For example, libraries often have special collections dealing with local topics, such as the Steinbeck Center, the Beethoven Center, and the California Room at San José State University. Public libraries often have extensive reference sections that include telephone books, college catalogs, and historical documents.

Speaking of . . .

Primary versus Secondary Sources

Primary sources express the authors' original ideas or findings from original research. For example, research reports produced by the Pew Internet & American Life Project present data that the Project's researchers collect. **Secondary sources** are others' interpretations or adaptations of primary sources. For example, when a newspaper reporter incorporates findings from a particular Pew Internet & American Life Project report into a story to make a point, she's interpreting and reusing that report's primary information. In researching your speeches, generally it's best to use primary sources so you're not depending on someone else's interpretations, which may not be accurate or complete.

Information that expresses an author's original ideas or findings from original research.

Others' interpretations or adaptations of a primary source.

A term associated with a topic and used to search for information related to that topic.

100

Gathering Research Materials

Now that you've identified what you already know about your topic, you're ready to launch into your outside research. But where should you start? This section discusses two primary sources of information: libraries and the internet.

Exploring Library Resources

Researching a speech topic often begins with the library. Your campus library's website will provide links to books, academic journals, magazines, newspapers, government publications, reference materials, and nonprint resources.

You may not be familiar with all the services, especially online ones, which your library offers.[4] Many college libraries offer online guided tours that explain the library's resources and how to access them. In addition, most libraries have an email reference service. A trip to the library to discuss your topic with a librarian may quickly and efficiently narrow your search for relevant information. Browsing through the library's on-site materials can lead to serendipitous findings—useful information you locate unexpectedly. A visit to your library also allows you to examine various resources available only at the library, including many books, complete periodicals such as journals, magazines and newspapers, government publications, reference works, and nonprint resources such as films and material on microform.

Books Books remain a key source of information, even in today's digital environment. Typically, books are credible information sources because they have gone through an intense editorial process, often including peer review. However, they are almost always somewhat dated because of the time it takes to write and publish a book. Books, therefore, are most useful for historical information or topics that are not especially time sensitive. For example, if you were developing a speech on trends in surfing culture, you might find valuable information and photographs in a book about the early days of surfing. But if you need information about the latest developments in surfing equipment and styles, you would be better off searching for information in periodicals such as magazines and journals.

For extremely current information, such as the most recent unemployment figures or college graduation rates, books are not the right choice. If you find a book that appears promising, however, always check its copyright page (usually following the page displaying its author, title, and publisher) to determine when it was published. Library catalog entries also note a book's year of publication if it's known, as do online booksellers.

Begin your search for books related to your topic by checking your campus library's online catalog. Unless you know the title of a book or author, use the keyword function to search for relevant books. When you identify a book you think will be useful, write down its **call number** so you can check it out from the library the next time you're on campus. Or, if it's an e-book, you can review it on screen.

> The number assigned to each book or bound publication in a library to identify that book in the library's classification system.

A library's online catalog entry for a book often includes links to related topics. For example, a search for books about immigration in the United States produced nearly 3000 titles, including *Immigration, Diversity, and Education*, edited by Elena L. Grigorenko and Ruby Takanishi, and published by Routledge in 2010. The subject list included links to related resources in three areas:

- Children of immigrants—Education
- Immigrants—Social conditions
- Cultural pluralism—United States

By clicking on the links to these areas, you could browse other library materials that might be useful for a speech on U.S. immigration.

Journals, Magazines, and Newspapers Published at regular intervals, or periods, periodicals include journals, magazines, and newspapers. Your library provides access to full-text databases of articles from periodicals. Follow the library's instructions for accessing those databases, such as LexisNexis Academic (newspapers, magazines, trade publications, and company information), ProQuest (extensive collection of U.S. and international news sources), and Social Science Full Text (journals in social science and interdisciplinary areas).

Newspapers have the most current print information about your topic. Although you could search the websites of individual newspapers, using a database such as ProQuest allows you to search multiple news sources simultaneously. ProQuest gives you many options for searching, such as selecting specific databases and limiting the date range. Advanced Search allows you to enter multiple words and choose where those words must be present, such as in citations and abstracts. Topic Guide helps you identify additional keywords and topics for your search.

Some periodicals charge a fee for web access, especially for archived materials, and others are not available online. Still, you can often identify relevant articles from online indexes such as Academic Search Premier, America's Historical Newspapers, Directory of Open Access Journals, and Global Market Information Database. Then you'll need to make a trip to the library to find articles in paper, microfilm, or microfiche sources.

Michael Doolittle/Alamy

Your brick-and-mortar library has much to offer, including special collections and unusual sources that are not always available online.

Government Publications Cybercrime, endangered species, housing, nursing, solar power, water—these are just a few of the topics addressed in U.S. government publications. The Catalog of United States Government Publications, available free online, indexes documents from the three branches of the U.S. government dating back to July 1976. New publications are added every day. Reports, monographs, handbooks, pamphlets, and audio files are among the types of resources you'll find in government publications. If you were conducting research for a speech on solar power, for instance, a keyword search would yield NASA documents, consumer guides, Senate testimony, and reports from the National Renewable Energy Laboratory related to solar power and other forms of alternative energy.

Reference Works Reference materials you typically use only in the library include paper versions of maps, atlases, encyclopedias, dictionaries, and various print indexes. If you were doing research for a speech on water conservation, you might consult maps that would help you (and your audience) pinpoint areas in which people have implemented innovative conservation strategies. *The African-American Almanac* could be a useful resource if you were planning a speech on the achievements of African Americans.

Sometimes it's helpful to define precisely the terms you use in your speeches. Although you can find dictionaries online, some specialized dictionaries are found only in print. *The Morris Dictionary of Word and Phrase Origins* traces the etymology of words as well as how their use developed over time. Such dictionaries not only provide definitions, but also cover a wide range of topics, from dance to women artists. For example, *Dow's Dictionary of Railway Quotations* includes excerpts from songs, films, novels, TV broadcasts, and other sources. Visual dictionaries can prove particularly helpful for informative speeches. They include photographs, drawings, diagrams, and illustrations that help readers understand the meanings of words. For example, the *Ultimate Visual*

Dictionary 2000 defines more than 30,000 terms with detailed color illustrations. *A Visual Dictionary of Chinese Architecture* includes detailed descriptions and line drawings.

Use your library's online catalog to locate reference materials. Note their locations and call numbers so you can review them when you go to the library.

Nonprint Resources If you've seen Martin Luther King, Jr.'s "I Have a Dream" speech on film, you understand the potential impact of visual or multimedia resources. Although the words alone move people, seeing and hearing Dr. King deliver this landmark speech influences the audience much more profoundly. His image—gesturing, nodding, scanning the crowd, the deep voice compelling listeners to fight for freedom—stays with us even if we forget his exact words.

Audio sources may also convey an image or set a tone that a simple verbal description cannot accomplish. For example, an exhibit at the Experience Music Project in Seattle includes interviews with local hip-hop artists. Hearing their stories in their own voices generates an emotional force that visitors can't experience just by reading printed statements.

Your campus library includes many nonprint resources you can explore via electronic databases. *Oxford Art Online* includes over 6000 searchable images ranging from a chart of the Arabic alphabet to a photograph of the Zigzag Bridge in the Jiangsu Province of China. *ARTstor* boasts over one million images associated with the arts, humanities, and social sciences that you can browse by topic, collection, geography, or classification. With *Naxos Music Library,* you can listen to streaming audio of classical, jazz, world, and other music genres and read artist biographies and opera synopses.

Table 6.2 on pages 104 and 105 summarizes examples of general and specialized library databases you'll find useful as you research topics for your speeches. Not all libraries will have all the databases listed. Your librarian will help you find the databases most relevant to your speech topics.

Accessing Internet Resources

Websites, the deep web, blogs, and the real-time web offer additional resources for researching your speeches. More than likely, you've already done a lot of internet searching. But can you find the information you need for a well-researched speech? That's what you'll learn to do in this section.

Websites On a typical day, about half of the internet users in the United States rely on a search engine to find information on the web.[5] This section explains how to use metasearch engines, search engines, and web directories to find relevant resources for your speeches. Different search tools have different ways of determining which websites are most relevant. Generally, however, **relevance** refers to how closely a web page's content is related to the keywords used in a search. The better your keywords represent the topic you're researching, the greater the likelihood you'll find relevant information.

> How closely a web page's content is related to the keywords used in an internet search.

To get you started, **Table 6.3** on page 106 presents an overview of internet search tools and their features. Each site is listed here, and you'll find live links to each URL in the book's online resources.

Metasearch engines rely on other search engines to find information on the web. Although metasearch engines like those listed in Table 6.3 may seem like the best strategy for online searching, they provide breadth rather than depth. For example, if you were giving an informative speech on the history of TV, you'd want more general information about the topic. In contrast, a speech focusing on a specific TV genre, such as reality shows, would require more in-depth information. In combining the results of several search engines, metasearch engines reveal the websites and web pages most frequently listed by the different search engines. Metasearch engines' results represent only a small portion of the websites you'd find if you used each search engine individually. The results listed may be the most popular websites each search engine has identified, but they may not be the best or most relevant sources of information.

> A search tool that compiles the results from other search engines.

Table 6.2 | Examples of General and Specialized Library Databases

Database	Description	Useful for searching...	Search hint
General			
Academic Search Premier	Full-text articles from nearly 4700 publications in multiple disciplines.	A wide variety of sources, including academic journals, newspapers, and magazines.	Search by document type, such as speech, short story, poem, book review, and case study.
Essay & General Literature Index	Indexes nearly 86,000 essays from 7000 anthologies and collections in the humanities and social sciences.	Literary works in multiple disciplines, including performance studies, psychology, art, film, economics, history, and political science.	Enter names of fictional characters in the basic or advanced search option to find works about them.
JSTOR	Full-text archive of over 1000 older issues of scholarly journals in the arts, sciences, humanities, and social sciences.	Historically important research and scholarly work.	Explore collections such as African Cultural Heritage Sites and Landscapes, and 19th-Century British Pamphlets.
LexisNexis Academic	Full-text articles and reviews from news, industry, medical, legal, and governmental sources.	Specific publication types, such as public records, reference materials, law directories, and government reports.	Use the LexisNexis wiki to maximize the search potential of this database.
MasterFILE Premier	Abstracts for over 2700 periodicals with full-text for nearly 1800.	Almanacs and reference publications as well as primary source documents.	Find images such as maps, flags, photographs, and illustrations.
OmniFile Full Text	Includes several databases in agriculture, art, biology, business, education, law, library and information science, science, technology, humanities, and social science.	A single topic across different types of sources such as newspapers, academic journals, and trade publications.	Narrow results by author, subject, peer-reviewed, and non–peer-reviewed.
Opposing Viewpoints Resource Center	Nearly five million full-text articles on current social issues.	Multiple viewpoints on contested topics such as capital punishment.	Choose the publication format to search, such as Facebook, encyclopedia, blog, or newswire.
Project MUSE	More than 160,000 full-text scholarly journal articles in the social sciences and humanities.	Peer-reviewed journal articles on the latest topics of interest in the social sciences and humanities.	Browse journals by disciplines, such as music, philosophy, and women's studies.
ProQuest	Full-text articles from U.S. and international business, education, and news sources.	Newspapers and business trade journals on a multitude of topics.	Select specific databases to search within the ProQuest menu, such as Dissertations & Theses and Ethnic NewsWatch.
Readers' Guide Retrospective	Indexes 375 U.S. magazines published from 1890 to 1982.	Articles, interviews, book reviews, and film reviews related to U.S. history and popular culture.	Examine subject headings that reflect how issues were framed in the past.
Web of Knowledge	A compilation of databases such as Web of Science, Global Health, Biological Abstracts, and Index Chemicus.	Multiple databases simultaneously, with a special focus on the sciences.	Get citation alerts, save searches, and create a list of frequently read journals when you set up a free account.
World News Collection	Current issues and events from nearly 100 print and broadcast media sources outside the U.S.	International perspectives on business, politics, science and technology, and social issues.	View the latest headlines from around the world by region.

Table 6.2 Continued

Database	Description	Useful for searching...	Search hint
Specialized			
Alt-Press Watch	Full-text articles from more than 220 independent and alternative presses.	Sources and perspectives not found in mainstream media outlets.	Locate biographical profiles of individuals active in social justice and free-press issues.
American Film Scripts Online	Film scripts and full texts of movies.	American cultural issues portrayed in films.	Review images of over 500 screenplays.
Audio Drama: The L.A. Theatre Works Collection	More than 300 dramatic works in streaming audio.	Audio clips on a range of topics in science, medicine, humanities, and law.	Use keywords to identify plays related to current events and social issues.
Black Thought and Culture	Essays, letters, song lyrics, interviews, and speeches by African Americans.	Historical and current information on the African American experience in the United States	Browse by authors, interview questions, sources, historical events, and personal events.
Communication & Mass Media Complete	Full-text articles from nearly 300 scholarly journals in communication and media studies.	Research related to all aspects of communication, including public speaking.	Use the communications thesaurus to identify additional key terms for your search.
Gilded Age	Full-text documents, photos, songs, letters, cartoons, interviews about and from the Gilded Age in the United States (1865–1900).	Primary sources related to key topics of this era, such as race, woman suffrage, and immigration.	Review the critical documentary essays that focus on central issues of the time.
GreenFile	Indexing, abstracts, and full-text articles for scholarly and general-interest publications related to the environment.	Topics associated with the environment, including global climate change, recycling, sustainable agriculture, and renewable energy.	Limit your search by document type, including bibliography, case study, or science experiment.
In the First Person	Index of nearly 4000 collections of personal narratives—diaries, letters, oral histories.	Individuals' experiences described in their own words.	Browse by repository, collection, historical event, geographic location, date, and subject.
Latino American Experience	Full-text database that includes primary sources, images, and vetted websites.	Resources on the history and culture of Latino/as living in the United States	Read the blog written by the database's advisory editor for highlights of key Latino/a current events.
Music Index Online	Surveys more than 875 music periodicals from over 40 countries.	News related to music, musicians, and the music industry.	Try browsing the geographic subject list for music news about a specific country or region.
Opera in Video	Nearly 150 searchable opera performances, interviews, and documentaries.	Video clips related to opera.	Scroll through the playlists created by database users or create your own.
Women and Social Movements in the United States 1600–2000	More than 3600 documents, 1000 images, and 900 links to related websites.	Primary documents related to the U.S. women's movement, as well as newspaper articles, pamphlets, books, and images.	Search or browse document projects that group together documents related to a specific question, such as "How did women participate in the Underground Railroad?"

Table 6.3   Metasearch Engines, Search Engines, Specialized Search Engines, and Web Directories

	Web address	Features
Metasearch engines		
Clusty	clusty.com	Groups together similar results.
CurryGuide	web.curryguide.com	Directory includes topics such as technology museums, flowers, and puzzle games.
Dogpile	dogpile.com	Sorts by relevance as well as search engine.
Jux2	jux2.com	Compares results from major search engines.
KartOO	kartoo.com	Visually displays search results in interactive maps.
Ixquick	ixquick.com	Rates each result by how many search engines choose it.
Mamma	mamma.com	Targets searches by categories, including jobs, videos, and travel.
Metacrawler	metacrawler.com	Lists popular searches you can click on and review results.
ZapMeta	zapmeta.com	Advanced search includes filters by region, domain, and host.
Search engines		
Ask	ask.com	Offers question-based searching and ideas for related topics.
Bing	bing.com	Keeps a list of your search history for easy backtracking.
Cuil	cuil.com	Maps results with image and page snapshots.
Exalead	exalead.com/search	Presents page thumbnails and charts of results by country and language.
Gigablast	gigablast.com	Includes Giga Bits that offer suggestions for refining your search.
Google	google.com	Offers specialized search engines, such as Google Scholar, Video, Wireless, News, and U.S. Government.
Yahoo!	search.yahoo.com	Allows you to use tabs to search images, news, local, video, and other specialized content.
Yebol	yebol.com	Displays results by categories, such as related topics, top sites, news, and Twitter.
Specialized search engines		
MedHunt	hon.ch/MedHunt	Searches medicine-related websites, news, conferences, and images.
Scirus	scirus.com	Focuses on science information.
SearchEdu	searchedu.com	Indexes education, military, government, dictionary, and encyclopedia sites.
Topix.net	topix.net	Aggregates news from global sources.
ZoomInfo	zoominfo.com	Finds information on people and companies.
Web directories		
InfoGrid	infogrid.com	Covers traditional topic areas plus listings by four grids: info, personal, lifestyle, and kids.
JoeAnt.com	joeant.com	Organizes information by subject, blog type, and region of the world.
Kosmix	kosmix.com	Highlights popular video, searches, topics, news, images, and celebrities.
ilp2	ilp2.org	Houses special collections on topics such as U.S. presidents, museums, the Iraq War, and Native American authors.
Open Directory Project	dmoz.org	An international network of volunteers gives this directory a global scope.
The WWW Virtual Library	vlib.org	The oldest web directory; experts review each site listed in the library.
Yahoo!	dir.yahoo.com	One of the originals; lists new additions to the directory.

Metasearch engines can be useful as a starting point—they give you a sampling of websites associated with your topic. Also, some metasearch engines tap into specialized search engines you may not find on your own. For instance, Harvester42 includes specialty search engines that allow you to search for information on people, jobs, universities and colleges, patents, Wikipedia entries, movies, science news, and shopping.

Search engines use sophisticated software programs that hunt through computer documents to locate those associated with particular keywords. Search engines search only files that they've indexed—and no search engine has indexed the entire web. Each search engine applies its own methods to scour the web. Thus, different search engines will produce different results, and the same search engine will produce different results on different days. So although your natural inclination may be to use just one or two search engines, trying several will give you a more comprehensive search. In addition, research shows that search engine users rarely go past the first page of results and will click on only a few links before giving up.[6] But if you keep digging and search with a variety of keywords, you're more likely to locate information relevant to your topic.

> A sophisticated software program that hunts through documents to find those associated with particular keywords.

With the total number of websites now nearly 235 million,[7] finding useful information quickly requires precise searching. Although you may want to initially use metasearch and search engines, web directories like those listed in Table 6.3 can help you refine your search strategies. **Web directories**, also called search indexes, organize web pages hierarchically by categories. For example, Yahoo!'s web directory includes subject areas such as business and economy, health, education, and social science, which in turn are broken down into subcategories. You can browse directories by category or search using keywords.

> An online list that organizes web pages and websites hierarchically by category; also called a search index.

The Deep Web Traditional metasearch engines and search engines index only a fraction of the content on the web. For example, medical research, financial information, and legal cases often are available only through direct queries to specialized databases.[8] Welcome to the **deep web**, sometimes called the invisible or hidden web, composed of all the databases and dynamically generated content that most regular search engines can't access.

How can you access the deep web? A few specialized metasearch engines, such as Pandia Powersearch and Turbo10, tap into database search engines. Some websites provide directories with links to thousands of databases. **Table 6.4** lists several key access points for the deep web.

> The portion of the web composed of specialty databases, such as those housed by the U.S. government, that are not accessible by traditional search engines; also called the invisible or hidden web.

Table 6.4 Accessing the Deep Web

Name	Web address	Features
Beaucoup!	beaucoup.com	Lists over 2500 search engines by category.
CompletePlanet	completeplanet.com	Includes thousands of databases you can browse and search.
GeniusFind	geniusfind.com	Provides access to thousands of search engines and databases organized by categories.
IncyWincy	incywincy.com	Allows you to refine your searches by category.
NewsVoyager	newsvoyager.com	Searches local U.S. newspapers.
Pandia Powersearch	pandia.com/powersearch	Lists social search, microblog search, and bookmark-based search tools.
Search Engine Colossus	searchenginecolossus.com	Provides access to an international directory of search engines.
USA.gov	usa.gov	Centralizes browsing and searching for all U.S. government websites.

Blogs and the Real-time Web **Blogs**, or web logs, are web pages individuals update regularly, often daily, with topical entries. You might have your own blog. Although early blogs were mostly text, blogs now often include audio and video files.

Short for web log, a web page that a blog writer, or blogger, updates regularly with topical entries.

Blogs come in a range of types and purposes. Journalists blog about news, students blog about their classes, economists blog about the latest economic trends, employees blog about their work, political insiders blog about politics, chefs blog about recipes—if you can think of a topic, someone is blogging about it. Individuals produce blogs to express themselves, network with others, engage new ideas, expose unethical practices, share their experiences, comment on current events—any number of motives might spur someone to create a blog.[9]

Without the usual gatekeepers watching over bloggers, can you trust any of the information available in the blogosphere? Yes. Millions of people read blogs every day, and those readers often quickly identify and correct false, slanted, and inaccurate information. A recent survey of over 1200 bloggers found that most reported engaging in ethical practices, including presenting accurate information and taking responsibility for what they posted. In addition, a small but growing number of blogs include a code of ethics that incorporates standards for accuracy and credibility.[10] As discussed later in the chapter, successful speakers critically examine all information they gather, including what they gather from blogs. **Table 6.5** lists some places to begin a blog search.

The real-time web refers to materials posted on the web within a few hours of your search. Videos, photos, blogs, microblogs—any content individuals share with others on the web—are collected by search engines devoted to hyper-current information. Because these materials are uploaded to the web within hours, minutes, or even seconds of your search, traditional search engines such as Google overlook these types of materials. Some real-time search engines, such as OneRiot, filter information based on what internet users are viewing the most—the most popular content. Others, such as Almost. at, prioritize information based on recency. Real-time web search engines, like the ones included in Table 6.5, allow you to find out the kinds of topics people are focusing on at the moment and gather information as an event is unfolding.

Table 6.5 Accessing Blogs and the Real-time Web

Name	Web address	Features
Blogdigger	blogdigger.com	Includes Blogdigger local to search for bloggers where you live.
BlogPulse	blogpulse.com	Identifies top news stories and sources, phrases, blogs, blog posts, and links.
Blog Search Engine	blogsearchengine.com	Spotlights featured blogs.
Collecta	collecta.com	Scans real-time news posted on blogs, Twitter, YouTube, Flickr, and similar sites.
Google Blog Search	blogsearch.google.com	Lists hot queries, recent posts, and top videos.
IceRocket	icerocket.com	Offers specialized real-time searches of blogs, the web, Twitter, MySpace, news, and images.
PubSub	pubsub.com	Tracks trending stories and terms.
Scoopler	scoopler.com	Lists current hot topics and browsing categories.
Surchur	surchur.com	Ranks real-time hot topics across multiple sources: blogs, Twitter, news, Yahoo Buzz, and Google Trends.
Technorati	technorati.com	Monitors blogs and links in real time.

Maximizing Your Search of Library and Internet Resources

Your campus library and the internet offer a wide array of sources to help you research your speech topics. The following search strategies will maximize your ability to get the most out of those resources in an efficient manner.

Use a Variety of Keywords

Search tools produce results based on the keywords you enter. Different libraries, databases, search engines, and web directories use different indexing and keyword systems.[11] Choose your keywords carefully and consider alternatives to your original choice. For example, for "computer literacy" also try "information literacy," "computer knowledge," and "computer learning." Each set of keywords produces different results. Most search engines and databases will give you suggestions for additional search terms.

Use the Advanced Search Option

Many search tools offer an advanced or guided search option that allows you to refine your search by keyword, date, type of media, and other specific parameters. In addition, nearly all search tools include a section on "tips for searching" that explains the best strategies for using that particular search tool.

Search a Variety of Sources

Getting multiple perspectives on a topic means going to multiple sources for information. Your library connects you with books, journals, newspapers, magazines, government publications, reference materials, and nonprint resources that will give you a range of viewpoints and perspectives. Organizations, websites, the deep web, blogs, newsgroups, and discussion lists provide additional angles on your topic. You don't need to search every source, but a good sampling increases your expertise on the topic.

Use a Variety of Search Tools

Each database, metasearch engine, search engine, and web directory uses its own search methods. No search tool accesses the entire web, and no database contains all the resources relevant to your topic.

Search for More than Text

As you're searching for information, consider more than text. Nearly all metasearch engines and search

U.S. government sites offer many reliable sources you can access on the internet. Browse and search these sites from USA.gov, the web portal for all U.S. government offices and departments.

109

engines allow you to search for image, MP3, video, and audio files. Read the **copyright information** carefully before using any files you download. Copyright information is a statement about the legal rights of others to use an original work. Use of website images and similar files in classroom speeches generally is allowed under fair use laws if you credit the author properly.

> **Watch** it

Cengage Learning

SPEECH BUDDY VIDEO 6.1
Managing the Research Process

In this video segment, Evan demonstrates some key strategies for researching a speech topic.

> **Use** it

Cengage Learning

ACTIVITY 6.1
The Research Detective

In this activity, you have an opportunity to try out various research strategies and then create a plan for researching your own speech topic.

Conducting Research Interviews

Research interviews with experts on your topic can help you obtain valuable information. Particularly in classroom speeches—where much of your credibility derives from accurate information—interviews must be carefully planned and implemented. The research interview process consists of six steps:

1. Determine the interview's purpose.
2. Select interviewees.
3. Develop questions.
4. Organize the interview.
5. Conduct the interview.
6. Integrate the information.

In this section, you'll learn how to meet these requirements and conduct an effective research interview.

Determine the Interview's Purpose

Identify your reason for interviewing a particular individual about your speech topic. If you can gather the same information from other sources, there's no need to conduct the interview. In addition, consider how you'll use the expert's information in your speech. Research for a speech on city government, for instance, might greatly benefit from an interview with the mayor to get an insider's view of how local leadership works. That's information you can't obtain in other ways.

Select Interviewee(s)

Choose interviewees based on your purpose and what you already know about the topic. Identify the additional information you need and who may have it. Select interviewees based on their expertise, availability, and willingness to answer your questions. Just because someone has the information you need doesn't mean she or he will reveal it to you.[12] If an interviewee views you as credible, you'll have a better chance of getting the information you want. To enhance your credibility, research the topic and the interviewee, carefully prepare for the interview, use active listening skills, and demonstrate sensitivity to the interviewee's cultural background.

Develop Questions

The questions you plan to ask form the basis of your **interview guide,** the list of all the questions and possible probes you will ask in the interview, as well as how you'll begin and end the interview. The interview guide serves as a road map for gathering the information you seek and developing a productive relationship with your interviewee.

> A list of all the questions and possible probes an interviewer asks in an interview, as well as notes about how the interviewer will begin and end the interview.

Questions can be categorized in three ways: primary versus secondary, open versus closed, and neutral versus leading.[13] **Primary questions** introduce a new topic or subtopic. They can stand alone, without the need for other statements or questions to provide context. "How did you choose your major?" and "What advice do you have for first-year college students?" are examples of primary questions. **Secondary questions** ask an interviewee to elaborate on a previous response. These follow-up questions may be as simple as "Go on," or more direct, as with, "Please tell me more about your experiences as a tour guide in Southeast Asia." Secondary questions depend on a previous statement or question to make sense.

> A question that introduces a new topic or subtopic in an interview.

> A question that asks the interviewee to elaborate on a response.

Open-ended questions are broadly worded, often only identifying a topic, such as, "What interesting things did you learn on your trip to Cambodia?" Closed-ended questions seek a specific piece of information. They limit the interviewee's response choices, as in, "On a scale of 1 to 5, with 5 being excellent and 1 being poor, how would you rate the quality of communication in your workplace?"

All the previous examples are **neutral questions** in that they're unbiased and impartial, simply seeking a direct answer. Most of the time, you'll ask neutral questions in research interviews. In contrast, **leading questions** suggest the answer you want. "Wouldn't you agree that soccer is a better sport for children than baseball?" and "Don't you think *The Office* is the best show on TV?" are examples of leading questions, whereas "Which sport do you think is better for children, soccer or baseball?" and "What do you think of the TV show *The Office*?" are neutral questions. Asking leading questions in a research interview usually produces little useful information, and the interviewee often feels harassed.

> An unbiased and impartial question seeking a forthright answer.

> A question that suggests the answer the interviewer seeks.

As a general rule, your questions should be neutral and open-ended. For every primary question, you'll need at least one secondary question. You may have a talkative interviewee who needs little prodding, but your interviewee could also be more reticent than you'd anticipated. If you have secondary questions ready, you'll be prepared for either situation. **Table 6.6** summarizes the types of interview questions and when to use them.

Organize Your Interview Guide

After you've developed your questions, you need to put them in order and decide how to begin and end the interview. How you open an interview sets the tone for

Table 6.6 | **When to Use Different Types of Questions**

Type of question	Example	Use when...
Primary	What college experiences had the greatest impact on your professional career?	Introducing a new topic or subtopic.
Secondary	Tell me more about the volunteer work you mentioned earlier.	Eliciting additional information from the interviewee.
Open-ended	How did you first become involved in local politics?	The interviewee feels free to talk and is knowledgeable about the topic.
Closed-ended	Where were you born?	Seeking a specific piece of information, or the interviewee seems reluctant to talk.
Neutral	When do you plan to complete the project?	Always, with rare exceptions.
Leading	Wouldn't you say that our campus is a friendly one?	The interviewee is uncooperative.

the entire conversation. Your two main tasks in the opening are to (1) establish rapport and (2) provide orientation. Accomplishing these early on provides a basis for effective communication throughout the interview.[14] If you are interviewing one of your instructors, for instance, you might talk a bit about a recent class meeting or something else related to the class. If you're interviewing the president of a company, you'll want to keep small talk to a minimum and get to the point of the interview quickly.

A clear orientation lets your interviewee know how you're going to proceed. For the research interview, identify the purpose of the interview, the topics you'll cover, your prior research on the topic, the expected length of the interview, and how the information will be used. For example, the interviewer might say

> I'm researching tax reform for a persuasive speech in my public speaking class. I've read about different ideas the county is considering, but would like your personal views on the topic. As we discussed on the phone, the interview should take about 30 minutes. I'll ask you questions about why you think our county needs tax reform, how you think your proposal will solve current problems, and the predicted effects of your proposed reforms on county residents.

Your prepared questions make up the body, or main portion, of the interview. They should follow a logical sequence. Begin with general questions so you get a sense of the interviewee's breadth of knowledge; then ask more specific questions. Group questions by subtopic. Within each subtopic, ask general questions and then move to more specific ones.

A student who conducted an interview on public transportation organized questions into four groups:

1. How the interviewee got started working in public transportation
2. Promoting public transportation
3. Responding to critics of public transportation
4. The interviewee's predictions regarding future innovations in public transportation

This grouping follows a logical order: asking fairly easy questions about how the interviewee got involved in public transportation, then asking how the interviewee promotes public transportation and responds to critics, and finally inviting the interviewee to speculate about possible innovations in public transportation.

The closing of an interview should leave the interviewee feeling positive and satisfied with the exchange. Generally, the closing progresses through three stages:

1. The *conclusion preview* signals that the interview is drawing to a close. To prepare the interviewee for the interview closing, you might say something like, "My final question is…" or "We have just a few minutes left…"

2. In the *closure statement,* summarize the main points you gleaned from the interview and thank the interviewee for participating. Ask if you may contact the interviewee should you have any questions while preparing your speech.

3. Finally, *post-interview conversation* occurs after the formal interview, once you've turned off your audio recorder or closed your notebook. This informal interaction may include small talk or general discussion of the topic. The interviewee may relax and reveal important information related to your topic. During the post-interview discussion, you'll say your final good-byes and once again express appreciation for the interviewee's cooperation.

In structuring your questions and determining the opening and closing, you'll complete your interview guide. Effective interviewers remain flexible, diverging from interview guide if the interviewee provides useful, but unexpected, information. **Figure 6.1** presents a sample interview guide.

Once you have prepared your interview guide, practice by reading it aloud several times. Does the opening sound warm and cordial? Have you stated the purpose of

Figure 6.1 **Sample Interview Guide**

Interviewee: Lauria Quijas, founder and CEO
Organization: Internet Ideas
Purpose: To gain a better understanding of what is involved in founding a company
Opening: My name is Barrett Yip, and I am a student at City College taking a class in public speaking. Thank you for taking the time to meet with me. I've browsed through your company's website and I'm so interested to learn more about it.

As I mentioned in my email when we scheduled this interview, I'm researching a speech on the steps involved in starting your own company. This interview should take about 45 minutes. The questions I have cover four main topics: your motivations for starting Internet Ideas, its current status, your view of the company's future, and your advice for anyone wanting to start their own business. As we discussed previously, I will record the interview so I have an accurate record of what you said. What questions do you have before we get started?

1. First, I'd like to ask you about the origins of Internet Ideas. What motivated you to start this company?
    1.1. Tell me more about your initial motivation.
    1.2. What else prompted your decision?
2. What made you hesitate to start your own company?
    2.1. How did you overcome that hesitation?
    2.2. Go on.
3. How did others influence your decision to form Internet Ideas?
    3.1. Please give me an example of what people said.
    3.2. How did you respond?
4. How did you choose the name *Internet Ideas*?
    4.1. What other names did you consider?
    4.2. How difficult was it to make the final choice?
5. Let's talk about Internet Ideas as it is today. How do you describe your organization to someone who is entirely unfamiliar with it?
    5.1. Why do you say that?
    5.2. I see.

(Continued)

Figure 6.1   **Continued**

6. On the Internet Ideas website, the mission statement emphasizes the "open exchange of ideas to revolutionize the internet." How do you go about achieving that mission?

   6.1. Is there anything that's kept you from achieving that goal?

   6.2. How do you encourage employees to exchange ideas openly?

7. What stories do "old-timers" tell new employees? *[skip this question if time is running short]*

   7.1. How does that story fit with your view of the company?

   7.2. What do you think of that story?

   7.3. A recent article in the local newspaper about Internet Ideas both praised and criticized you and the company. What was your response to the article?

   7.4. How did employees respond?

   7.5. What effect overall did the article have on the company?

8. Now let's look to the future. In what ways do you think Internet Ideas will be different in five years?

   8.1. What about in ten years?

   8.2. What other changes do you foresee?

9. Imagine Internet Ideas has made the headlines twenty-five years from now. What would that headline be? *[skip this question if time is running short]*

   9.1. Why do you say that?

10. What would be your role in making that headline happen?

11. As you know, I'd like to start my own company someday. What are the positive aspects of starting your own company?

   11.1. What other pluses have you experienced?

   11.2. Does that apply to any new company?

12. What are the pitfalls in starting your own company?

   12.1. Please give me an example.

   12.2. How can founders avoid that pitfall?

13. What advice do you have for entrepreneurs interested in starting their own company?

   13.1. What other suggestions do you have?

   13.2. Any other bits of wisdom?

14. Finally, is there anything else you think I should know about starting a company?

   14.1. Is there additional information related to the topic I should be sure to include in my speech?

   14.2. What else should I know that I haven't covered?

Closing:

Those are all the questions I have for you. Let me briefly summarize the main points you covered in your responses *[quickly review interviewee's responses here]*.

   If I need clarification on something we covered, may I email or phone you? You've given me a lot of firsthand information on starting a company that I'm sure my listeners will be eager to learn about. I know how busy you are, so I really appreciate your answering all my questions. Thank you again for your time.

the interview and previewed the questions you'll ask? Are the questions clear, neutral, straightforward, moderately open ended, and relevant to your purpose? Does the closing wrap up the interview and leave the interviewee with positive feelings? You might also conduct mock interviews with family members, friends, or classmates. Play the roles of interviewer and interviewee so you can get a sense of both perspectives.[15]

Conduct the Interview

You've done all your preparation; now it's time to conduct the interview. Reviewing your interview guide, recording the interview, choosing an appropriate setting, and monitoring your verbal and nonverbal behaviors will help assure a more productive interview.

Being familiar with your interview guide allows you to use it the way you use note cards in your speeches—to trigger your memory. With the interviewee's permission, record the interview electronically for later review. Also take notes, writing down main points and key ideas that will help you recall what the person said. In addition, record important nonverbal cues, your general impressions, and ideas that occur to you during the interview. For example, if the interviewee seems nervous or uncertain about a response, note that.

Choose an appropriate setting, ideally a quiet, private place free from interruptions, for in-person interviews. For other real-time interviews, such as web chat or telephone interviews, minimize distractions at your location and ask the interviewee to do the same.

Journalists depend on research interviews to gather information. Now that you know how to conduct an effective interview, observe journalists on TV and online. What kinds of questions do they ask? What verbal and nonverbal cues do they use?

Ask one question at a time. If you ask multiple questions, the interviewee will become confused and likely only answer one part of the question asked.[16] For example, instead of asking, "How and why did you begin your own business?" phrase the question as two separate ones. First ask, "What led you to start your own business?" and then, after the interviewee has responded, ask, "How did you go about opening your business?"

Monitor your verbal and nonverbal cues to avoid unintentionally biasing the interviewee's responses. To indicate that you're listening, say "I understand" or "I see." The interviewee should be doing most of the talking, not you. Put all your active listening skills to work. Use eye contact and other nonverbal cues to let the interviewee know you are paying attention.[17]

Apply it

Interviewing in Your Community

For thousands of years, humans relied on the spoken word to pass along stories, values, and beliefs from one generation to the next. Although most cultures now rely primarily on the written word for such information exchange, the oral tradition retains a key place in transmitting community knowledge. Practice your interviewing skills by identifying a member of your community—at school, at work, or at home—who can provide insight into the community's history. Arrange the interview, develop your interview guide, and conduct the interview. Reflect on what you learned about your community, your role in that community, and the interview process. How might you use the information you gathered in the interview to promote positive change in your community? How might you share the information with others?

Integrate the Information

Information from experts on your topic can personalize, enliven, and add credibility to each section of your speech. A catchy quote in the introduction can grab your audience's attention as well as establish your credibility. Here's an example:

> Ever think about the information websites gather when you're online? Jamie Anderson, professor of information science here at Southern University for ten years, has. Dr. Anderson told me in a recent interview, "If people knew how much information corporations gathered on each

visitor to their websites, they would be shocked—even embarrassed—and much more careful about their internet use."

The speaker underscores the importance of the topic, making it relevant to her audience by identifying the interviewee as a "professor of information science here at Southern University." She enhances her credibility by pointing out the interviewee's credibility with "for ten years."

Information from an interview can also be a source of personal, recent evidence in the body of your speech. When including quotes or summarized information from research interviews, clearly state your interviewee's full name and title and explain what makes that person an expert on the topic, as the speaker does in the following example:

> Mae Hawthorne, a local organic farmer for more than fifteen years, predicts three trends in organic farming innovations: incorporating effective farming methods from thousands of years ago, using the internet to link together farmers from around the world, and community-supported agriculture. Recent research suggests similar trends. For example…

Here, the speaker first presented a summary of the interviewee's predictions and then included supporting information from other sources.

Speakers use interview information in the conclusion of a speech in two ways: (1) to provide a sense of closure and (2) to leave listeners in an appropriate state of mind. For example, if you quote an interviewee in your introduction, you could quote the same person in your conclusion, as in the following example:

> When you go online, you focus on the information you *get*. But information scientists recognize the dangers in the information you *give* others in your internet travels. Professor Jamie Anderson believes, "The hallmark of the internet is the free exchange of information. However, individuals must know what information they're revealing when they visit websites, and corporations must restrict and safeguard the personal information they gather."

This quote ties in neatly with the one the speaker used in the introduction, reminding the audience of information presented early in the speech. In addition, a good quote in the conclusion can leave audience members with a lasting, personalized impression of the topic.

Evaluating Your Research Materials

As you locate information for your speech, apply three evaluation criteria: reliability, validity, and currency. **Reliability** refers to the consistency and credibility of the information. Information is reliable when it fits with what other experts have concluded and the source is an authority on the topic. An article in *Science* on how carbon monoxide contributes to global climate change, for instance, would be reliable because the findings are consistent with those of other researchers and the magazine is well respected in the scientific community.

Validity refers to the soundness of the logic underlying the information. To test the validity of your information, examine the author's logic, evidence, and conclusions. For example, when researching a speech about people's shopping preferences, suppose you interview the president of the local chamber of commerce. Your interviewee claims that all downtown parking should be free because having to pay for parking drives away shoppers. However, the only evidence provided to support this assertion is the interviewee's own experience that parking downtown can be expensive, whereas parking at a suburban mall is free. There are at least two reasons not to trust this evidence. First, you don't know that people are avoiding downtown shopping. Second, even if they are, they could be doing so for other reasons, such as the types of stores available and the

The consistency and credibility of information from a particular source.

The soundness of the logic underlying information presented by a source.

Table 6.7 Critical Questions for Evaluating Information

Critical question	Goal
Who is the author?	Determine who produced the information and if the author is an authority on the topic.
Who is the publisher?	Determine the organization that published the information and if the source is unbiased.
What are the author's purposes?	Determine the author's reasons for presenting the information.
What evidence has the author provided?	Determine if the author has used a variety of types of information from knowledgeable sources.
Has any information been omitted?	Determine if the author has left out any information that might lead to alternate conclusions.
What are the author's underlying assumptions?	Determine the assumptions the author is making and if different assumptions might produce different conclusions.
What inferences or conclusions has the author drawn?	Determine if the author's conclusions are valid and if other conclusions could be drawn from the same information.
How current is the information?	Determine if the author's information is as up to date as possible.

distance from their homes. In this case, the interviewee's conclusion *might* make sense, but there's no evidence to back it up.

Currency refers to the recency of the information. You want information that is as up to date as possible. Even when researching a topic considered ancient history, such as dinosaurs, what is known about the topic changes over time. For example, although the most popular explanation for why dinosaurs became extinct centers on the theory that an asteroid hit the earth at about that time, more recent explanations posit an exploding star or volcanic eruptions as the cause. Checking the date when printed material was published, a television or radio show was broadcast, or a web page was revised reveals the currency of your information.

How recent information is—the more recent it is, the more current it is.

Regardless of its source, critically examine the information you gather. Asking the questions summarized in **Table 6.7** will help you determine the reliability, validity, and currency of information.

Acknowledging Your Sources

Public speakers acknowledge their sources in two ways: orally in the speech and in written form in the bibliography. With **oral citations**, speakers mention, or *cite*, the sources of their information during the speech. Here are some examples that demonstrate both how to set up an oral citation and how to punctuate it:

A source of information that a speaker mentions, or cites, during a speech.

- In a December 2009 blog post on race and ethnicity in the use of social networking sites, researcher Danah Boyd stated, "2009 is the year in which Facebook went 'mainstream' among all measured racial/ethnic groups in the U.S."

- You've heard about blogs influencing politics. But you may not know about a 13-year-old from a Chicago suburb who has blogged her way to fame and fortune in the fashion world. *Chicago Tribune* reporter Megan Twohey writes in a December 2009 article that Tavi Gevinson's blog, Style Rookie, has become a must-read for top fashion designers and fashion-conscious celebrities.

- Jacqueline and Milton Mayfield, professors at Texas A&M International University, found in their research that a supervisor's language use affects employee absenteeism. Their 2009 article in the *Journal of Business Communication* reported that when organizational leaders use clear language, express empathy, and tell meaningful work-related stories, employees view attendance more positively and are less likely to miss work.

In these examples, the speaker tells the audience who authored or published a particular piece of information. If a speaker must also provide a written reference list, these sources would be cited like this:

Boyd, D. (2009, December 29). Race and social networking sites: Putting Facebook's data in context. Message posted to http://www.zephoria.org/thoughts.

Twohey, M. (2009, December 30). Tavi Gevinson earns acclaim with Style Rookie fashion blog. Retrieved December 30, 2009, from http://www.chicagotribune.com/features/style/chi-teen-fashion-sensationdec30,0,7899258.story.

Mayfield, J., & Mayfield, M. (2009). The role of leader motivating language in employee absenteeism. *Journal of Business Communication, 46,* 455–479.

A source's complete citation, including author, date of publication, title, place of publication, and publisher.

Table 6.8 shows how to format written citations, or **bibliographic information**, for a variety of types of information sources. The bibliographic information is a source's

Table 6.8 Documenting Source Information

APA Style	
Book	Baym, G. (2010). *From Cronkite to Colbert: The evolution of broadcast news.* Boulder, CO: Paradigm.
Essay in book	Beck, U., Levy, D., & Sznaider, N. (2009). Cosmopolitanization of memory: The politics of forgiveness and restitution. In M. Nowicka & M. Rovisco (Eds.), *Cosmopolitanism in practice* (pp.111–128). Burlington, VT: Ashgate.
Journal article	Mayfield, J., & Mayfield, M. (2009). The role of leader motivating language in employee absenteeism. *Journal of Business Communication, 46,* 455–479.
Newspaper article	Webby, S. (2009, December 30). Police use of Tasers faces new scrutiny after court ruling. *San Jose Mercury News,* pp. A1, A14.
Blog	Boyd, D. (2009, December 29). Race and social network sites: Putting Facebook's data in context [Web log message]. Retrieved from http://www.zephoria.org/thoughts
Web page	Kaiser Family Foundation (2009). *Views on the U.S. role in global health update.* Retrieved from http://www.kff.org/globalhealth/posr111209pkg.cfm
MLA Style	
Book	Weatherford, Dorris. *American Women During World War II: An Encyclopedia.* New York: Routledge, 2010. Print.
Essay in book	Reyes, Iliana, and Yuuko Uchikoshi "Emergent Literacy in Immigrant Children: Home and School Environment Interface." *Immigration, Diversity, and Education.* Ed. Elena L. Grigorenko and Ruby Takanishi. New York: Routledge, 2010, 259–275. Print.
Journal article	Bode, Graham D. "A Racing Heart, Rattling Knees, and Ruminative Thoughts: Defining, Explaining, and Treating Public Speaking Anxiety." *Communication Education* 59.1 (2010): 70–105. Print.
Newspaper article	Revkin, Andrew C. "Plateau in Temperatures Adds Difficulty to Task of Reaching a Solution." *The New York Times* 23 September 2009: A6. Print.
Blog	Hansen, Kathryn. "ICECAP Investigates East Antarctica." Operation Ice Bridge Blog. NASA. 30 December 2009. Web. 30 December 2009.
Web page	"What is Hospice and Palliative Care?" The National Hospice and Palliative Care Organization, n.d. Web. 30 Dec. 2009.

complete citation, including author, date of publication, title, place of publication, and publisher. You'll need this information to attribute your sources correctly in your speech and reference list. Most communication researchers use either Modern Language Association (MLA) or American Psychological Association (APA) style to record citations.[18] Ask your instructor which style you should use.

Research Guidelines

The guidelines summarized in this section will make researching your topic a positive and productive experience.

- **Start early.** How early to start developing your speech depends on the length of your class (semester, quarter, or condensed session); access to the resources you need; and your own approach to research. So get out the calendar, note when your speaking materials and speech are due, and work backward from there. Build in enough time to identify your supporting materials (Chapter 7), organize and outline your ideas (Chapter 8), integrate effective language (Chapter 10), develop relevant presentation materials (Chapter 11), and practice (Chapter 12).

- **Schedule research time.** Block out research time in your daily planner. Think of that time as an appointment and make a commitment to keep to it.

- **Ask questions.** Campus librarians and your instructor are key resources in your search for reliable, valid, and current information. When you encounter a sticking point in researching your topic, ask for help. If you wait until speech day, it will be too late.

- **Keep accurate records.** Carefully record the publication information for each source you find.

- **Take notes on each source.** When you record a source's bibliographic information, also write down the ideas that seem most relevant to your topic.

- **Revise as needed.** As you do your research, you may find yourself going off in a direction you hadn't planned on. Review your specific purpose and thesis. Decide whether they need to be revised or whether your research needs to be refocused.

- **Know when to move on.** You have a set amount of time to prepare your speech. If you spend too little time on research, your speech will lack substance; if you spend too much time, you'll neglect the other steps in the speechmaking process. When you feel comfortable talking about your topic with others and think you can answer your audience's questions, it's time to move on.

- **Know when to go back.** Later in the process of developing your speech, you may find gaps in your research or a question you want to answer. Do the additional research necessary to close those gaps and answer that question. Your audience and your confidence depend on your expertise.

Speech for Review and Analysis

The World's Tipping Point[18]

Bianca Jagger, Founder and Chair, Bianca Jagger Human Rights Foundation

Ms Jagger presented this speech on October 14, 2009, at Ecogram Week, Columbia University. The following is an excerpt from her speech. As you read it, notice how she cites her sources.

Jagger, B. (2009, October 14). The world's tipping point. Speech presented at Ecogram Week, Columbia University. Reprinted by permission of the author.

Today we stand at a crossroads in history. The warnings from our most respected scientists are loud and clear, yet government leaders continue to ignore the scale of the threat. According to many scientists, we have less than a decade left to address the issue of climate change before we reach the "tipping point," or the point of no return. The earth is perilously close to dramatic climate change that threatens to spiral way out of control. Scientists now generally accept that current pledges of 20 percent greenhouse gas emission reductions by 2020 are inadequate given the gravity of the current situation: We have already reached the stage of dangerous climate change. The task now is to prevent catastrophic climate chaos. Failure to act effectively is likely to precipitate cataclysmic changes that may obliterate life on earth.

In January 2009, the National Oceanic and Atmospheric Administration in the U. S. presented the results of a pioneering study: the study concluded that climate change was largely irreversible. The report states "if CO_2 is allowed to peak at 450–600 parts per million, the results would include persistent decreases in dry-season rainfall that are comparable to the 1930s North American Dust Bowl in zones including southern Europe, northern Africa, southwestern North America, southern Africa, and western Australia."

Four hundred and fifty ppm is not far off; we are close to fulfilling this prophecy. Global climate expert Professor James Hansen, head of the NASA Goddard Institute for Space Studies, and adjunct Professor of the Earth Institute here at Columbia University, observed in March this year that "eleven of the past twelve years rank among the twelve warmest years since records began." He is emphatic about the urgency of reducing CO_2 levels, stressing the fact that "the safe upper limit for atmospheric CO_2 is no more than 350 ppm." Professor Hansen suggested that the United Nations International Panel on Climate Change (UNIPCC) fourth assessment has been proved far too conservative and might even be "absurdly optimistic." As of today, the planet has concentrations of around 385 parts carbon dioxide molecules per million. This number is rising by around 2 parts per million every year. Professor Hansen is unequivocal that "If you leave us at 450 ppm for long enough, it will probably melt all the ice—that's a sea rise of 75 meters. What we have found is that the target we have all been aiming for is a disaster—a guaranteed disaster."

U.N. Secretary Ban Ki-moon sent a sobering message in his May 24, 2009, speech at the World Business Summit on Climate Change "Our excessive reliance on a fossil fuel–based economy is destroying our planet's resources. It is impoverishing the poor. It is weakening the security of nations. And it is choking global economic potential."

There is no doubt that the developing world would suffer first, and most, from the decreased rainfall and "dust-bowl" climate prophesied in the National Oceanic and Atmospheric Administration report. Water is already dangerously scarce in dry areas. A study released by the American Meteorological Society sees significant reduction in the flow of one-third of the world's rivers. The River Jordan is rapidly drying up, due to a combination of pollutants, massive irrigation withdrawals, and an ongoing drought." The river has suffered a catastrophic water flow reduction from 1,300 million cubic meters annually to about 70,000 cubic meters due to direct water loss through mineral extraction and irrigation. The surface area of the Dead Sea has shrunk by a third in the past 50 years and the level of the sea, the world's lowest point, is dropping by a meter a year. Climate change will have a devastating effect on lives and economies in these fragile environments. . . .

The Global Humanitarian Forum, an organization led by former U.N. Secretary General Kofi Annan, issued a report this year which estimates that climate change accounts for over 300,000 deaths throughout the world each year and that, by 2030, this death toll will have increased to half a million people a year. The report also highlights the serious impact of climate change on the lives of 325 million people at present and an estimated 660 million, 10 percent of the world's population, in 20 years' time. As to economic losses due to climate change, which today amount to over $125 billion per year, they are projected to almost treble by 2030, to $340 billion annually.

Climate change is not just an environmental threat, but a critical human rights issue which impacts every aspect of our lives: peace, security, poverty, hunger, health, mass migration, and economics. It is a global issue, and it calls for global action and solutions entrenched in an international legally binding framework.

The world situation is deteriorating faster than previously anticipated. In Professor Nicholas Stern's words: "Global eissions of greenhouse gases are growing more quickly than projected; the ability of the planet to absorb those gases now appears lower than was assumed, the potential increases in temperatures due to rising gas concentrations seem higher, and the physical impacts of a warming planet are appearing at a faster rate than expected."

Questions for Analysis and Discussion

1. How does Jagger's speech reflect multiple perspectives and sources?

2. What experts does Jagger rely on in this part of her speech? How effective are her choices?

3. What organizations does she use as sources of information? How appropriate are these organizations for the topic of her speech?

4. How does she orally cite her sources?

5. How would you evaluate her research materials? Are they reliable, valid, and current?

6. What have you learned from this speech excerpt about researching a speech topic?

Summary

Researching your speeches requires three activities: preparing to do your research, gathering information, and evaluating what you've found. Preparation begins with determining what you know and don't know about your topic. Use your own experiences as the basis for developing your research strategy. Preparation also requires identifying multiple perspectives and sources, particularly those that challenge your assumptions.

Its vast variety of sources makes your campus library the logical first stop in gathering information. A short email or in-person exchange with a librarian can save you hours of frustration. Library databases often contain hundreds of full-text articles, so you can download them onto your own computer.

Internet sources include websites, the deep web, blogs, and the real-time web. Metasearch engines, search engines, and web directories assist you in your quest for information. Specialty search engines provide windows into the deep web—databases that traditional search engines can't reach.

Interviews with experts can yield personal and current information about your topic. Planning and preparation form the basis of a successful interview. Developing a solid interview guide with thoughtfully phrased questions that are logically organized facilitates productive interaction during the interview. Flexibility and a genuine interest in knowing more about your topic will aid you tremendously when you conduct your interview.

As you gather information, evaluate it for reliability, validity, and currency. In evaluating information, ask critical questions such as, "What are the author's assumptions?" and, "What evidence is presented to support the conclusions drawn?"

Doing sound research means starting early, setting aside specific time to research your topic, asking questions when you run into problems, keeping accurate records, taking accurate notes on each source, revising and refocusing when necessary, knowing when you have enough information, and knowing when to continue your research.

IN THE BOOK

Summary

Key Terms

Critical Challenges

MORE STUDY RESOURCES

Quizzes

WebLinks

Peer-reviewed videos

STUDENT WORKBOOK

6.1: In-Class Interview

6.2: Myth Search

6.3: Discussing Your Sources

6.4: Evaluating Websites

6.5: How to Start a Hobby In ...

SPEECH BUDDY VIDEOS

WATCH It Video

6.1: Managing the Research Process

USE It Activity

6.1: The Research Detective

SAMPLE SPEECH VIDEOS

Dory, handed-down story, impromptu speech

Shaura, "Terrestrial Pulmonate Gastropods,"
    persuasive speech

SPEECH BUILDER EXPRESS

Goal/purpose

Thesis statement

Supporting material

Introduction

Conclusion

Works cited

Outline

INFOTRAC

Recommended search terms

Multiple perspectives and
    public speaking

Online librarians

Free online library

Evaluating online sources

Citing sources in public speaking

Oral citations

AUDIO STUDY TOOLS

Handed-down story speech by Dory

Critical thinking questions

Learning objectives

Chapter summary

CourseMate

Studio

Guide to Your Online Resources

CourseMate Your Speech Communication CourseMate for *Public Speaking: The Evolving Art* gives you access to the Speech Buddy video and activity featured in this chapter, additional sample speech videos, Speech Studio, Speech Builder Express, InfoTrac College Edition, and study aids such as glossary flashcards, review quizzes, and the Critical Challenge questions for this chapter, which you can respond to via email if your instructor so requests. In addition, your CourseMate features live WebLinks relevant to this chapter, including sites that can assist you in researching information for your speeches. Links are maintained regularly, and new ones are added periodically.

Key Terms

Critical Challenges

Questions for Reflection and Discussion

1. The first step in researching your topic is to determine what you already know. How might what you know get in the way of doing good research? How might you check the reliability, currency, and validity of what you already know about a topic?

2. If something is in a book, journal article, magazine, newspaper or other printed source, is it necessarily accurate? Gatekeepers such as editors can miss both intentional and unintentional errors, as *The New York Times* did in the case of journalist Jayson Blair, who fabricated or plagiarized hundreds of stories. Moreover, desktop publishing allows authors to bypass traditional gatekeepers. How can you apply your critical thinking skills to evaluate the accuracy of printed materials?

3. Blogs are criticized for their lack of a gatekeeper such as an editor or publisher. But who's blogging may be just as important. When searching blogs for information about your topic, consider the authors. Are you finding a diversity of perspectives? How might you find a variety of blogs that represent multiple points of view?

4. In using information gathered from interviews, you need to consider what information to include in your speech and what to leave out. For example, how you frame an interviewee's remarks or how you place a quote in your speech can greatly influence how others interpret that information and how they perceive the interviewee. As an ethical speaker, what steps should you take to ensure that you accurately represent what the interviewee said?

5. Check out Speech Studio to analyze the research other students cited in their speeches. Or record a speech you're working on, upload it to Speech Studio, and ask your peers for their feedback. What feedback could you use to fine-tune your research and source citations before you give your speech in class?

☑ SPEECH Studio

7

Supporting Your Ideas

Cengage Learning

Cengage Learning

CourseMate   **SPEECH Studio**   SPEECH BUILDER EXPRESS

Although you are certainly familiar with Dr. Martin Luther King, Jr.'s instrumental role in the civil rights movement in the United States, you may not realize how his speeches have inspired people in other countries to take action. Shen Tong, one of the students who led the Chinese pro-democracy movement in 1989, spoke at a conference in honor of Dr. King.[1] In the first part of his speech, Shen Tong said,

> To fight without fighting, that is the razor's edge of nonviolence. This is what I believe happened in the American civil rights movement. I am here to learn as well as to inform, so you must teach me. But I know that this definitely happened during the spring of 1989 in Beijing's Tiananmen Square.

He went on to say,

> China has suffered through more than four thousand years of violence and revolution. The Chinese people have suffered oppression and tyranny for over four thousand years. One dynasty after another was established and then violently destroyed.

Shen Tong then asked the audience to help him understand why some nonviolent protests work and others don't. He said,

> So many nonviolent struggles succeed, like the civil rights movement and Eastern Europe. But the question still remains for the Chinese youth: How? It is time for us to really learn and practice the principle, to learn from the examples of struggles like yours.

Near the end of his speech, Shen Tong related this story:

> And the most moving picture I have in my mind is that of one of my schoolmates: He got a rifle, he held it in his hand and above his head, but the soldiers didn't listen to him. They hold

Shen Tong, a student activist in China and currently president and founder of the Web 2.0 company VFinity, has applied his public speaking skills in many contexts, including guest lectures at universities around the world.

Evidence used to demonstrate the worth of an idea.

Appeals to emotion.

Appeals to logic.

Appeals to cultural beliefs and values.

billy club, begin to beat him. But my schoolmate, he kneeled on the ground, still holding the gun above his head till the death.

In his conclusion, Shen Tong argued that achieving democracy in China requires a global commitment:

> All our communities must learn peace from each other…. And together, as one movement for human rights and peace worldwide, we will be able to look at the tyrants and oppressors of history and say to them, in Dr. King's words, "We have matched your capacity to inflict suffering with our capacity to endure suffering. We have matched your physical force with soul force. We are free."

As a central participant in the Tiananmen Square demonstrations and a member of the student group that negotiated with the Chinese government during the protests, Shen Tong had a great deal of personal experience he could use in his speech. Yet he also relied on a variety of **supporting materials**—narratives, examples, definitions, testimony, facts, and statistics—to bolster his position.

Supporting materials provide the substance of your speeches—the "stuff" that holds together, illustrates, clarifies, and provides evidence for your ideas. When you're researching your topic, you're gathering the supporting materials that you'll use to inform, persuade, and entertain your audience.

Aristotle argued that when speakers present their ideas, they rely on **pathos**, or emotional appeals, and **logos**, or logical appeals.[2] More recent scholars argue that speakers also rely on **mythos**, or appeals to cultural values and beliefs.[3] Shen Tong's story about his schoolmate appeals to emotions such as grief, anger, and sadness. His examples of the civil rights movement and new democracies in Eastern Europe provide a logical reason to support his position. And quoting Dr. Martin Luther King, Jr. appeals to the deeply held belief in freedom that is so prevalent in American and other cultures.

Table 7.1 summarizes the types of supporting materials discussed in this chapter.

126

Table 7.1 Types of Supporting Materials

Type	Appeal	Useful for...	Strengths	Weaknesses
Narratives	Emotional, cultural	Engaging audience	Dramatize topic; help audience identify with topic	Single view on topic; distract from focus of speech
Examples	Emotional	Personalizing topic	Make topic concrete; simplify complex concepts	Not able to be generalized; lack representativeness
Definitions	Emotional, logical	Establishing common meaning	Clarify concepts; delineate topic boundaries	Inaccurate or inappropriate; ignore connotations associated with terms
Testimony	Emotional, cultural, logical	Enhancing speaker credibility	Provides specific voices on topic; demonstrates expertise	Biased information (depends on credibility of source)
Facts and statistics	Logical	Demonstrating the scope of a problem	Promote agreement; provide foundation for topic's importance	Overwhelming or difficult to comprehend; subject to manipulation

Narratives

Sometimes called **anecdotes**, **narratives** describe events in a dramatic way, appealing to audience members' emotions. Well-known cultural, societal, and group narratives appeal to deeply held beliefs and values. The structure of narratives generally includes a beginning, middle, and end. Compelling stories have coherence—audience members can follow the plot. Stories also have a ring of truth—the story seems plausible. Narratives dramatize a topic and help the audience identify with the speaker's ideas, making this form of evidence one of the most persuasive.[4]

A brief narrative.

A description of events in a dramatic fashion; also called a story.

Effective storytelling involves creating a sense of drama, developing compelling characters, and using evocative language to transport audience members' imaginations into the narrative.[5] In the lecture she gave upon accepting the Nobel Prize in Literature, author Toni Morrison began with, "Once upon a time there was an old woman. Blind but wise. Or was it an old man? A guru, perhaps. Or a griot soothing restless children." The words "Once upon a time" tell us that this is some sort of story, likely a fable or other traditional narrative. The initial ambiguity about the central character keeps the audience interested—a woman or a man? A guru or a griot? And what is a griot? Listeners are intrigued and want to know more.

When telling a story, you must choose what information to include and what to leave out, where to begin the story and where to end it, how much of the story's moral or main point you want your audience to figure out for themselves and how much you want to state outright. Too much rambling in telling your story can distract audience members from the main points of your speech. For example, Morrison used the word *griot* in her narrative. Although not all audience members likely knew the word's meaning (a West African storyteller), she didn't stop to define it. Why? Because this would slow down the narrative, and knowing the precise meaning of *griot* wasn't essential to the story. Storytelling requires that you pay special attention to the presentation part of public speaking, using your voice, gestures, facial expressions, and body movement to bring your audience into the narrative. To hear how Morrison used her voice—rhythm, tone, pitch, and timing—as she related her narrative, listen to her lecture on the Nobel Foundation's website (nobelprize.org).

Speakers rely on four types of narratives: their own stories, stories about others, institutional stories, and cultural stories.

Your Own Stories

Shen Tong told a story about his own experiences—an event he had observed. Such firsthand accounts can move audience members in powerful ways. Relating your own narrative personalizes the topic and helps listeners understand why you choose it.

Others' Stories

Stories about others relate events that the speaker didn't directly observe or participate in. During his commencement speech at the University of Pennsylvania, U2 lead singer Bono used this story to illustrate the role Ireland played in the development of American democracy:

> In 1771 your founder, Mr. Franklin, spent three months in Ireland and Scotland to look at the relationship they had with England to see if this could be a model for America, whether America should follow their example and remain a part of the British Empire. Franklin was deeply, deeply distressed by what he saw. In Ireland he saw how England had put a stranglehold on Irish trade, how absentee English landlords exploited Irish tenant farmers and how those farmers, in Franklin's words, "lived in wretched hovels of mud and straw, were clothed in rags and subsisted chiefly on potatoes." Not exactly the American dream. So instead of Ireland becoming a model for America, America became a model for Ireland in our own struggle for independence.[6]

Bono's story connects his audience's history with the history of his own country far more powerfully than if he had simply stated a fact: "You fought the British and won; we're still fighting." And because the story of the American Revolution holds mythic status in the United States, Bono tapped into audience members' strongly held beliefs in freedom and independence. In addition, mentioning Benjamin Franklin, someone with high credibility, enhanced Bono's credibility.

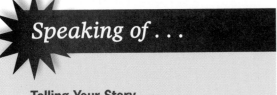

Speaking of . . .

Telling Your Story

Think about the topic for your next speech. What got you interested in the topic? How did you decide this would be a good topic for a speech? Why do you feel compelled to bring this topic to the attention of your audience? When you talk with friends, coworkers, and others about this topic, what do you say about it? Considering these questions will reveal your own stories associated with your topic. Using one or two of these personal narratives in your speech can help you relate your topic to your listeners and gain their attention.

Institutional Stories

Institutional stories center on specific organizations, such as a university, corporation, church, or social club. These stories tell us how individuals should act in the organization and the values it emphasizes. Randy Kelly, former mayor of Saint Paul, Minnesota, told this story about a transitional housing program for homeless teens in Saint Paul during a state-of-the-city address:

> Laura was seventeen when she moved into Rezek House after staying at Safe House. Her mother, an alcoholic and crack cocaine user, had abandoned her family long ago. Her father kicked her out of the house when she refused to turn over her paycheck to him to buy drugs. Laura stayed at Rezek for a year, during which she got back into school and found a better-paying job…. Laura has moved on and is doing well…. Let's not fool ourselves. Everyone in this audience is one tragedy, one health crisis, job loss, or cruel turn of fortune from being in need ourselves. And so I challenge all of us … all of Saint Paul… to see ourselves in those who are most in need. Reach out and build, strengthen and repair the links in this human chain that is our city.[7]

The narrative suggests how Saint Paul residents should behave: Work hard, get an education, and contribute to the well-being of others. Laura's success depended both on her willingness to juggle a job and school and on the city's provision of temporary shelter. You don't need to live in Saint Paul to understand the moral of the story: Helping others improves life for everyone.

Compelling stories help an audience relate to a speaker's topic, experience a sense of drama, or understand a complex idea.

Cultural Stories

You hear and read cultural stories from the time you're very young. You might even think of these stories as myths or fables. Cultural stories best represent mythos as they transmit basic values and ways of behaving. In her Nobel lecture, Toni Morrison[8] began her speech with a tale about communication between people and across generations:

> Once upon a time there was an old woman. Blind but wise. Or was it an old man? A guru, perhaps. Or a griot soothing restless children....
>
> In the version I know, the woman is the daughter of slaves, black, American, and lives alone in a small house outside of town. Her reputation for wisdom is without peer and without question. Among her people she is both the law and its transgression...
>
> One day the woman is visited by some young people who seem to be bent on disproving her clairvoyance and showing her up for the fraud they believe she is. Their plan is simple: they enter her house and ask the one question the answer to which rides solely on her difference from them, a difference they regard as a profound disability: her blindness. They stand before her, and one of them says, "Old woman, I hold in my hand a bird. Tell me whether it is living or dead."
>
> She does not answer, and the question is repeated. "Is the bird I am holding living or dead?"
>
> Still she doesn't answer. She is blind and cannot see her visitors, let alone what is in their hands. She does not know their color, gender, or homeland. She only knows their motive.
>
> The old woman's silence is so long, the young people have trouble holding their laughter.
>
> Finally she speaks and her voice is soft but stern. "I don't know," she says. "I don't know whether the bird you are holding is dead or alive, but what I do know is that it is in your hands. It is in your hands."

Morrison explained the cultural moral of the story: how individuals exercise power and the moral implications of their actions. She wove the narrative throughout the speech, the bird symbolizing language and the woman symbolizing a writer. Using a cultural narrative, Morrison helped the audience understand something unfamiliar—the experiences of an acclaimed author—with something familiar—a story they'd probably heard before in one form or another.

129

Gathering Community Stories

Humans are storytellers and story listeners. Much of what you've learned about yourself, your family, your neighborhood, your society, and your culture comes from stories you've heard and stories you've told. Because they're such a natural part of human interaction, you may not have examined the important role stories play in the life of your community. Begin by identifying a few key people and organizations in your community. Develop a list of questions you plan to ask, following the interview guidelines described in Chapter 6. Consider what you want to know about your community. For example, you might ask about memorable events or people. After you've conducted the interviews, determine which stories are the most compelling or provide the greatest insight into your community. How might you document and share these stories with others? How might these stories help those both in and outside of your community better understand it? In gathering community stories, what have you learned about narratives and public speaking?

Examples

An illustration or case that represents a larger group or class of things.

Examples are illustrations or cases that represent a larger group or class of things. Examples make ideas more concrete and personalize the topic, appealing to the audience's emotions. In his speech, Shen Tong stated, "So many nonviolent struggles succeed, like the civil rights movement and Eastern Europe." "Nonviolent struggles" may be somewhat vague in audience members' minds, but most people probably were familiar with the civil rights movement in the United States and the Solidarity movement in Poland.

Especially for complex ideas, an example can help audience members get a better grasp of key points and concepts related to the topic. Listening to a speech on the importance of community service, audience members might have a vague notion of what that entails. A few examples, such as volunteering at the local public library and tutoring elementary-school students in math, provide the audience with a clear picture of what community service involves.

Examples can prove particularly persuasive when they go against the norm or demonstrate some anomaly.[9] The survivor of an especially aggressive form of cancer, the winner of a $50 million state lottery, the gold medalist in an ultra-competitive Olympic sport—they've all beaten the statistical odds against them. When an example runs counter to what statistical evidence shows, audience members find the example more believable.

Yet examples may give misleading information if they fail to represent accurately the group to which they belong. For instance, Microsoft chairman and co-founder Bill Gates never completed his college degree at Harvard, yet has become one of the wealthiest people in the world. However, using Gates as an example of the earning power of college dropouts would be misleading because few people have Gates's computer programming abilities.

The next section discusses three types of examples you might use in your speech: general examples, specific examples, and hypothetical examples.

General Examples

General examples, such as those Shen Tong used, provide little detail; the speaker expects audience members to be familiar with the situation, person, object, or event cited. For instance, if you refer to Yosemite National Park or the Grand Canyon, most people in your audience will probably know about these places—you don't need to explain where they're located or that they're part of the U.S. national park system.

Specific Examples

Specific examples give listeners much more detail. In a recent speech, one of our students presented specific examples that demonstrated the impact of the Ford Motor Company on U.S. culture.

> Although the Ford Motor Company has influenced American cultures in many ways, three events stand out. First, Ford's production of the first Model T in 1908 paved the way for an automobile-centered society. Assembly line technology dramatically lowered production costs and greatly increased the affordability of a car for the general public.
>
> Second, in 1914 Ford offered wages of five dollars per day, over twice the previous pay rate. Paying workers more encouraged them to spend more, launching what has become known as a consumer culture.
>
> Third, and much more recently, the first Ford Explorer SUV rolled off the assembly line in 1990. The Explorer has come to represent what Americans love—and hate—about suburban life.

With each specific example, the student linked a company event with a trend in U.S. lifestyles. Providing concrete examples that are familiar to the audience clearly demonstrated to listeners the connection between each event and the long-term impact on American culture.

An Assembly Line of the Ford Motor Company

Archives Charmet/The Bridgeman Art Library

Providing specific examples in a speech helps the audience clearly understand the connections among your ideas. For example, in a speech about the impact of the Ford Motor Company on U.S. culture, one speaker illustrated how Henry Ford's innovations in automobile/assembly line technology contributed to today's car-oriented society.

Hypothetical Examples

In contrast to general and specific examples, which are based on actual events, hypothetical examples stem from conjecture or supposition. That is, with hypothetical examples, speakers ask the audience to imagine something. In a speech on exercise, the speaker might use a hypothetical example such as "Let's go through a typical day for the average person. Rather than getting out of bed and going immediately to the kitchen, our average person stretches and then warms up by jogging in place for a few minutes. Next, our average person…."

Effective hypothetical examples contain a high degree of plausibility—audience members must believe the situation could actually occur. To make his point about ways to solve current problems such as climate change, Amory Lovins, chair and chief scientist at Rocky Mountain Institute, asked the audience to

> imagine a world, a few short generations hence, where spacious, peppy, ultra-safe, 120- to 200-mpg cars whisper through revitalized cities and towns, convivial suburbs, and fertile, prosperous countryside, burning no oil and emitting pure drinking water—or nothing; where sprawl is no longer mandated or subsidized, so stronger families eat better food on front porches and more kids play in thriving neighborhoods; where new buildings and plugged-in parked cars produce enough surplus energy to power the now-efficient old buildings; and where buildings make people healthier, happier, and more productive, creating delight when entered, serenity when occupied, and regret when departed.[10]

Using hypothetical examples of what the future might hold, Lovins encouraged his audience to consider alternative ways of envisioning their lives. Hypothetical examples provide a good way to show audience members what might happen as well as what might not happen. In using hypothetical examples, you're asking your listeners to imagine something, so what you suggest can't be too far-fetched.

Definitions

A statement that describes the essence, precise meaning, or scope of a word or a phrase.

An agreed-upon definition of a word, found in a dictionary.

A unique meaning associated with a word based on a person's own experiences.

Definitions explain or describe what something is. Words have both denotative and connotative meanings. **Denotative meanings** are the definitions you find in dictionaries—what speakers and writers of a language generally agree a specific word represents. **Connotative meanings** are the personal associations individuals have with a particular word. Even a simple word like *chair* has multiple denotative meanings—the *Compact Oxford English Dictionary* lists six—and infinite connotative meanings. Speakers use definitions to clarify for audience members how they should interpret a term. In this way, definitions based on a dictionary provide a logical appeal for speakers. Peter K. Bhatia, executive editor of *The Oregonian*, used such a definition in his introduction of Edward Seaton, president of the American Society of Newspaper Editors, at the group's annual meeting:

> The dictionary defines dignity as the quality of being worthy of esteem and/or honor. I've seen Edward in action in many ways this year, living that definition. I saw him standing up before hostile audiences this past summer during debates over ASNE's commitment to diversity. He was ever calm, ever thoughtful, ever listening, and always kept his cool when others around him gave way to emotion.[11]

First, Bhatia defined the word *dignity* for the audience in order to establish a common meaning for the word. Second, he explained how Seaton's actions fit that definition, demonstrating that describing Seaton as dignified was appropriate.

Speakers commonly use two types of definitions: definitions by function and definitions by analogy.

Definition by Function

When speakers define something by its function, they explain what it does or how it works. One of our students presented an informative speech on the Hawai'ian lei.

Although class members already knew *what* a lei was, they didn't know its purpose or function. The student explained that leis serve a variety of purposes, such as welcoming, giving thanks, celebrating a special occasion, and expressing sorrow or grief. The dictionary definition simply describes a lei as a garland of flowers. But defining a lei by its functions opens up other avenues of discussion, such as the integral role leis play in many Hawai'ian ceremonies. Dictionary and functional definitions both appeal to audience members' logic by defining words in concrete, agreed-upon ways.

Definition by Analogy

An **analogy** describes something by comparing it to something else it resembles. Speakers often use analogies to help an audience understand something new to them. That is, they use an analogy referring to something familiar to define something unfamiliar to the audience. For example, in emphasizing the importance of learning first-aid techniques, a speaker might say, "It's like studying for an exam—you want to be prepared for any situation that might arise."

A type of comparison that describes something by comparing it to something else that it resembles.

Metaphors and **similes** are sometimes grouped with analogies. A metaphor relies on an implicit comparison, while a simile makes an explicit comparison. Shen Tong employed a metaphor in his speech when he stated, "To fight without fighting, that is the razor's edge of nonviolence." He referred to something that was concrete and familiar to audience members—the edge of a razor—to describe something quite abstract: the idea of fighting without engaging in physical conflict. Native American orators use metaphors extensively in their speeches.[12]

A figure of speech that makes an implicit comparison between two things.

A figure of speech that makes an explicit comparison between two things, using the words *like* or *as*.

As a literary device, metaphors bring an element of poetry to definitions, appealing to audience members' emotions. For example, a dictionary definition of grief, such as "intense sorrow, especially caused by someone's death,"[13] doesn't embody the deep feelings of a metaphor like the one used in this speech, presented during a memorial for a member of the Tlingit tribe:

> The river would swell, the river. In the river, in the lake, the rain would fall on the water. When the river had swollen, it would flow under the tree. The earth would crumble along the bank…. When it had broken, down the river it would drift, down the river…. From there the wind would blow over it. After the wind would blow over it, it would begin to roll with the waves to a fine sand. When it rolled on the waves to the sand, it would drift ashore. It would be pounded there by the waves, it would be pounded there…. In the morning, sun would begin to shine on it, in the morning. After the sun had been shining on it, it would begin to dry out. My hope is that you become like this from now on, my brothers-in-law, whoever is one.[14]

The metaphor of river, earth, wind, and sun moves us and gives us a more comprehensive understanding of what grieving feels like in ways that a dictionary definition cannot.

A figurative analogy compares two things that seem to have little in common yet share some similarity. Figurative analogies often juxtapose objects, processes, or ideas in unique and novel ways, heightening the audience's interest. For example, a speaker explaining how to find a job might compare it to preparing a dinner party for friends— you need to match your skills and interests to your target audience.

Literal analogies don't offer the poetic quality of figurative analogies, but instead appeal to audience members' sense of logic. For literal analogies to work, the things being compared must be sufficiently similar in ways that are relevant to the speaker's point. When they do not share important similarities, the analogy is false. For example, proponents of reinstating the football program at Santa Clara University offered the new one at the University of South Alabama as an example.[15] However, South Alabama is a public school with over 14,000 students located in Mobile—a city with no professional sports teams. In contrast, Santa Clara University is a private school with just over 5000 students, located in the San Francisco Bay Area—home to two professional football teams and several well-known college teams. South Alabama had a successful first season in its record (7–0) and attendance, but differences in student population and potential game attendees make it a poor literal analogy in support of a football program at Santa Clara.

Definitions of all types help audience members understand a topic's scope and increase the likelihood that the speaker and the audience think about the topic in similar ways. Definitions also tell your audience what you *won't* be talking about or how you *won't* use a word. In a speech on stress, for instance, the speaker might talk about the differences between situational stress, which arises in specific contexts, and chronic stress, which never goes away, and then say, "Today I'm going to focus on situational stress."

Although definitions may clarify your topic, they can also cause problems. No matter how clearly you define your terms, audience members always will have connotations associated with those words. For example, Chapter 1 defines the term *style* as the language used in a speech, but you might associate style with fashion or having a flair for doing something. Definitions also may be inappropriate. This often happens when speakers use a standard dictionary definition for a technical term. Chapter 1 defines the term *invention* as Cicero did, to refer to discovering what a speaker wants to say in a speech. However, using a dictionary definition of *invention*—creating something new—to describe Cicero's approach would be inadequate because it wouldn't offer the precision needed to apply the term to public speaking.

Testimony

An individual's opinions or experiences about a particular topic.

When speakers use **testimony**, they rely on an individual's opinions or experiences related to a particular topic. Using testimony to support your points works only if listeners believe in the source's credibility and feel a personal connection to the source or topic.[16] Speakers use testimony from experts, celebrities, and laypeople. For an expert, credibility means extensive knowledge based on research, activities, speeches, and writing about the topic. For a celebrity, audience members must perceive a logical link between the person and the topic. Finally, lay testimony requires that the individual has personal experience with the topic and clearly articulates her or his views.

Expert Testimony

The effectiveness of expert testimony rests on the individual or group's qualifications related to the topic. In quoting well-known civil rights leader Martin Luther King, Jr., Shen Tong used testimony to support his point that meeting oppression with nonviolent resistance works. Audience members consider King's words expert testimony because he was an authority on the topic—his long association with the U.S. civil rights movement gives him credibility.

Celebrity Testimony

The effectiveness of celebrity testimony stems from the person's stature or the audience's overall impression of the person. That is, audiences find celebrity testimony compelling because of the person's fame or star power, not the person's knowledge about the topic. For example, actor William Macy played a person with cerebral palsy in a film based on a true story. Macy later joined United Cerebral Palsy's (UCP's) board of trustees. Listeners consider what he has to say about this disability credible because of his celebrity status, role in the film, and participation in UCP. Actor and *Superman* star Christopher Reeve became a strong advocate for stem cell research after an accident in which he broke two vertebrae in his neck. Both his reputation as an actor and his experience as a person with a dis/ability gave credibility to his views.

Lay Testimony

Lay testimony involves individuals who have experience with a topic but aren't experts or well known. Journalists often use lay testimony when reporting on human-interest stories, For example, in a speech on keeping costs low for college students, the speaker might interview a few students to find out their strategies for saving money.

Facts and Statistics

Speakers typically rely on facts and statistics when making a logical appeal. Your senses serve as the basis for **facts**, observations you make based on your experiences. **Statistics** are numerical data or information, such as the average price of a home or how many students are enrolled at your university this year.

> An observation based on actual experience.

> Numerical data or information.

> Appeals that are linked to the speaker's credibility.

For the most part, speakers rely on others when gathering facts and statistics. As Chapter 5 explains, an author's credibility, or **ethos**, influences the degree to which audience members think information is accurate. Source credibility is especially important for facts and statistics. Even the credibility of highly respected sources can be hurt if those sources don't check their facts. During the 2004 presidential race, the CBS television magazine *60 Minutes* showed viewers memos related to President Bush's service with the National Guard. After questions arose about the documents' authenticity, CBS News revealed that reporters had not reviewed the information thoroughly. Although at the time of the broadcast CBS executives believed the documents were valid, two weeks later they admitted that they'd been tricked and the memos were fake.[17] By using sources that were not credible, CBS News tarnished its own credibility.

You may think of facts and statistics as objective, yet these supporting materials are still subject to interpretation—and manipulation. For example, if a speaker said, "The number of bicycles stolen on this campus has quadrupled in the past year," listeners would reasonably conclude that bicycle theft was a major problem. However, if only two bicycles had been stolen in the previous year, "quadrupled" would mean eight were stolen in the current year. In contrast, if 50 bikes were stolen the previous year and 200 in the current year, the speaker would have a stronger case for identifying bicycle theft as a serious problem.

Because they appeal to logic, audience members generally find statistics and facts convincing in persuasive situations.[18] But sometimes speakers overwhelm audience members with facts and statistics to such a degree that listeners simply tune out. When selecting facts and statistics as supporting materials for your speeches, always keep your audience in mind. How will they respond? What would you think if you were in the audience?

Facts

When you include facts in a speech, you're not limited to your own observations. You accept others' observations as well. For example, you weren't alive when George Washington became president, but you accept his presidency as a fact based on what others have reported. To support this, you can examine historical documents located in the Library of Congress collections (loc.gov), and read accounts of Washington's inauguration. When Shen Tong stated, "China has suffered through more than four thousand years of violence and revolution," he based his statement of fact on events in history that others had recorded, rather than on his own observations.

Facts generally foster agreement because they often can be verified as true or false. However, audiences do not always interpret facts the same way speakers do. For example, in testimony before Congress urging quick passage of the Specter-Harkin "Pro-Living" Stem Cell Research Bill, actor Michael J. Fox[19] began with two facts:

> The issue of stem cell research is one I know something about, both as a Parkinson's disease patient and as the head of a foundation that is now the largest nonprofit funder of Parkinson's disease research outside of the U.S. government.

Fox began by stating two facts about himself. Based on these facts, the audience could reasonably infer, or draw the conclusion, that stem cell research is something Fox knows about. Later in the speech he provided additional facts related to the bill:

> I also know that there's broad support from the American public. Just take a look at the polls, which show a majority of Americans are in favor, including those who consider themselves pro-life…. I just heard that sixty-eight religious leaders are supporting this bill. They have come to the same conclusion as a majority of Americans— loosening Federal restrictions through HR 810 is not only pro-life, it is pro-living.

These two facts—polls showing most Americans in favor of fewer restraints on stem cell research and numerous religious leaders supporting the bill—led Fox to infer that the proposed legislation was "pro-living." However, although the majority of Americans seem to embrace federal support for stem cell research, they may not have agreed with the wording of this particular bill. As a speaker, recognizing that your audience may not infer what you do about the facts you present will help you use facts that truly support your ideas.

Statistics

Statistics allow speakers to quantify the magnitude of a problem and make comparisons across groups and time periods. For example, a speaker might claim that increased reliance on computers has led to increased incidents of identity theft. How could you find out if this claim is true? By going to the Federal Trade Commission (FTC) website (ftc.gov), you can view the latest statistics on consumer fraud complaints: In 2007, the FTC reported that 32 percent of the complaints it received involved identity theft. That number becomes important when you learn that the FTC received nearly 814,000 consumer fraud complaints—so about 260,000 were related to identity theft. The FTC also compares the percentage of fraud complaints across categories. The top five were identity theft (32 percent), shop-at-home and catalog sales (8 percent), internet services

(5 percent), foreign money offers (4 percent), and prizes, sweepstakes, and lotteries (4 percent). If you were preparing for a speech on identity theft, these statistics would provide good support for a claim that this problem affects many Americans.

One of our students used statistics to demonstrate the importance of rice to people around the world.

> Do you eat rice every day? About 20 percent of Americans do. And you might need rice more than you think. In addition to serving as a basic food source, rice is used for making biofuels, feeding livestock, and producing organic fertilizer, as just a few examples.
>
> About 50 percent of the people in the world depend on at least one serving of rice every day for their diet. The global production of rice has more than tripled from 200 million tons in 1960 to nearly 700 million tons in 2010.
>
> Rice consumption worldwide has risen tremendously as well, from about 150 million tons in 1960 to about 440 million tons today. Although in the U.S. the average person relies on rice for only about 2 percent of their total daily calories, the global average is 20 percent, with people in some countries such as Vietnam, Cambodia, and Bangladesh relying on rice for about 70 percent of their calories each day.
>
> So when the price of rice spikes up to nearly double its cost 10 years ago, everyone is affected—you, me, and especially the people who need rice every day to survive.

By using statistics to support his inference that everyone is affected by the cost of rice, the speaker demonstrated that people around the world depend on rice for food and other aspects of daily living.

> Watch it

SPEECH BUDDY VIDEO 7.1
Selecting the Best Supporting Materials

Erin discusses different types of supporting materials and introduces examples of supporting materials she used in one of her persuasive speeches.

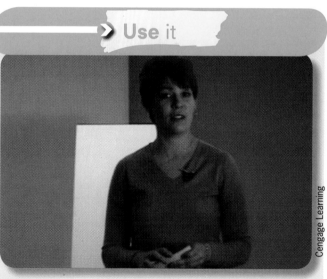

> Use it

ACTIVITY 7.1
Use Your Support System

In this activity, you're asked to watch for and evaluate the different types of supporting materials used in a student speech, and then assess your own speech project to determine how you'll find the appropriate types of supporting materials for it.

Popular Media as Sources of Information

The credibility of your supporting materials depends on the credibility of your sources. When using popular media, including social media such as Facebook and Twitter, as a source of support for your speech, you must apply the same standards of credibility that you apply to other sources. Audiences are more likely to trust popular media that don't seem to have a blatant bias or project an air of overwhelming self-interest. Keeping factual information separate from opinion and advertising is one way media organizations try to establish and maintain their credibility with their audiences. Still, even the most highly regarded media outlets, such as CNN, CBS, *The New York Times*, and *USA Today*, have been tarnished by recent scandals. As a result, over half the U.S. public does not trust news organizations. Nevertheless, Americans view the news media more favorably than they view political institutions and both major political parties, and they generally agree that the press plays an important watchdog role in American politics.[20]

The internet serves as an essential hub for traditional news sources, and earns high credibility ratings for doing so. For instance, it functions as a conduit for major news organizations in the United States, and operates the same way in many countries and in many languages. It's the place TV networks send you for additional information, for instance, and for updates on their stories twenty-four hours a day. People generally judge a news website as more credible when a familiar newspaper or TV network sponsors the site. CNN.com ranks as one of the most frequently visited of *all* websites.[21] Interestingly, many people view the website of a news source such as ABC News or *USA Today* more favorably than they view the television or print versions.[22] As the digital age continues to evolve, making technical distinctions among media less clear, more people will rely on the internet as a trusted source for news.

United Features Syndicate

Despite the growing popularity of the internet, television remains the most popular news source for Americans. Even those who've grown up with the internet continue to rely more on TV than on online sources for their news. Audiences trust TV in part simply because they are so used to it. But not all TV news sources rate equally on credibility. Research shows that CNN and CBS's *60 Minutes* are the most trusted TV news sources overall. Local newscasts are viewed more favorably than cable and commercial network news. Americans generally rank cable TV as more credible for news than the national commercial networks ABC, NBC, CBS, and Fox.[23]

Although some have predicted the demise of the print newspaper, people view their local daily newspaper more favorably than they view cable TV news, network TV news, and major national newspapers. Over 50 percent of Americans read the newspaper daily. Newspapers are viewed as providing more in-depth and wider coverage of issues than television. Readers feel they have more time to analyze the information presented and consider a story's implications. Similarly, because newspaper journalists and editors don't have to work with the severe time constraints of TV newscasts, they have more time and space to develop and present their stories. Some people prefer the interpretive accounts that appear in weekly news magazines like *Time, Newsweek,* and *U.S. News & World Report.* Generally, though, weekly print news magazines receive lower credibility ratings than most metropolitan newspapers.[24]

The first electronic mass medium, radio, still maintains an important role in disseminating information, especially through local news stations. Radio also shares with TV the ability to instantly report and update the news. Radio will always have a place as a news medium in America's car-oriented society, with national outlets such as National Public Radio (NPR) ranked higher in credibility than newspapers (but lower than local TV). Still, local radio remains a source of news for about 15 percent of Americans, well below local television (over 65 percent) and local and national newspapers (28 percent each), and just ahead of internet news outlets (11 percent).[25]

Not all audience members consider news media highly credible sources. Still, you shouldn't hesitate to cite news media and social media as sources when appropriate. Up-to-date references and comments from the media can help you establish the currency of your topic and supporting information. Use media references in a way that balances well with other sources of information, promotes your specific purpose, and supports your thesis. Use reputable and appropriate sources, clearly identifying them during your speech.

> Watch it

SPEECH BUDDY VIDEO 7.2
Evaluating Media Credibility

In this video, Evan discusses examples of popular media that can be used as supporting material in speeches and highlights credibility issues.

> Use it

Watch your Speech Buddy video . . .

. . . and use what you've learned in your next speech.

ACTIVITY 7.2
Press Pass

In this activity, you're asked to evaluate the media sources used in a student speech, and then apply what you have learned about selecting credible media sources to your own speech.

Summary

As you research your topic, you'll find information related to your points and ideas. These supporting materials form the substance of your speech. They bring your ideas to life, demonstrate the weight and seriousness of your topic, and help you build credibility. Supporting materials may appeal to your audience's emotions, logic, and cultural beliefs.

There are five basic types of supporting materials. Narratives dramatize a topic and help your audience identify with it. A speech might include your own stories, stories about others, organizational stories, or cultural stories. Telling a good story requires having a sense of timing and drama.

Examples make ideas less abstract and personalize a topic. General examples are broad and provide little detail. Specific examples provide greater detail. Hypothetical examples are based on supposition—the audience imagines the circumstances—and must seem plausible to be effective. Examples help listeners better understand the topic, yet an example can mislead if it doesn't accurately represent the larger class to which it belongs.

Definitions establish a common meaning between the speaker and the audience. Speakers use definitions to clarify concepts and identify the boundaries of a topic. Definitions may explain how something functions or offer analogies for a word or concept. Specialized dictionaries can provide more descriptive and technical meanings for a word than standard dictionaries can. In using definitions as supporting materials, speakers must recognize that the audience likely will associate connotations with words, no matter how those words are defined.

Experts, celebrities, and laypeople may provide testimony or their experiences about a topic. The effectiveness of testimony rests on the degree to which audience members perceive the person as a credible source of information about the topic.

Facts and statistics clearly appeal to an audience's logical thinking processes. These supporting materials show listeners the scope of a problem and can demonstrate a topic's importance. Including too many facts and statistics, especially without using presentation media to show all the numbers and figures, can overwhelm the audience. In addition, facts and statistics may be interpreted—and misinterpreted—in many ways.

The major communications media—internet, television, newspapers, news magazines, and radio—can also enhance the content and style of your presentations when used judiciously as references, illustrations, and examples. The media inspire different levels of confidence in terms of credibility. For example, local newspapers and television newscasts receive highly favorable ratings from most Americans, yet internet news outlets are increasingly viewed as a first stop for current information.

IN THE BOOK
Summary
Key Terms
Critical Challenges

MORE STUDY RESOURCES
Quizzes
WebLinks
Peer-reviewed videos

STUDENT WORKBOOK
7.1: Workshop on Supporting Materials
7.2: Source Credibility
7.3: Supporting Material Diversity
7.4: Mastering Your Materials
7.5: Adding a Narrative

SPEECH BUDDY VIDEOS
WATCH It Video
7.1: Selecting the Best Supporting Materials
7.2: Evaluating Media Credibility
USE It Activity
7.1: Use Your Support System
7.2: Press Pass

SAMPLE SPEECH VIDEOS
Chris, "Impressionistic Painting,"
   informative speech
Peter, "Drinking and Driving," persuasive speech

SPEECH BUILDER EXPRESS

Goal/purpose
Thesis statement
Supporting material
Introduction
Conclusion
Works cited
Outline

INFOTRAC
Recommended search terms
Supporting materials and public speaking
Credibility of supporting materials
Narratives and public speaking
Examples and public speaking
Definitions and public speaking
Testimony and public speaking
Facts and statistics and public speaking
Media credibility and public speaking
Using media in speeches

AUDIO STUDY TOOLS
"Impressionistic Painting" by Chris
Critical thinking questions
Learning objectives
Chapter summary

Guide to Your Online Resources

CourseMate Your Speech Communication CourseMate for *Public Speaking: The Evolving Art* gives you access to the Speech Buddy video and activity featured in this chapter, additional sample speech videos, Speech Studio, Speech Builder Express, InfoTrac College Edition, and study aids such as glossary flashcards, review quizzes, and the Critical Challenge questions for this chapter, which you can respond to via email if your instructor so requests. In addition, your CourseMate features live WebLinks relevant to this chapter, including sites that can assist you in finding credible information for your speeches. Links are regularly maintained, and new ones are added periodically.

Key Terms

analogy 133	facts 135	pathos 126
anecdotes 127	examples 130	similes 133
connotative meanings 132	logos 126	statistics 135
definitions 132	metaphors 133	supporting materials 126
denotative meanings 132	mythos 126	testimony 134
ethos 135	narratives 127	

Critical Challenges

Questions for Reflection and Discussion

1. Humans love to tell and listen to stories, so listeners find stories in speeches especially engaging. What are the negative aspects of using narratives in speeches? How can audience members enjoy a story yet listen critically at the same time?

2. Critical listeners closely examine how speakers define words. Definitions can be very powerful in a speech if audience members simply accept the definitions the speaker offers. Reflect on a recent public speaking situation in which you were in the audience. Did you question the speaker's definitions? In what other ways might the terms have been defined? How would those definitions change the nature of the speech and the speaker's conclusions?

3. When you're listening to a speaker, how convincing do you find expert, celebrity, and lay testimony? What makes you skeptical of testimony?

4. Which of the media—radio, television, newspapers, news magazines, internet—do you trust most for news? What are your reasons for trusting or not trusting the different media? If you took a poll of your classmates, what answers do you suppose you'd get? How do you and your classmates judge media credibility?

5. CourseMate On September 22, 2009, Professor Clay Shirky, adjunct professor in New York University's Interactive Telecommunications Program, gave a talk about newspapers and the internet. Go to the Chapter 7 resources at your CourseMate for *Public Speaking: The Evolving Art* to read an excerpt from his talk, "Internet Issues Facing Newspapers." As you read it, notice how he uses supporting material and cites his sources.

   a. How did Professor Shirky use narratives in his speech? Identify the type(s) of narratives he included.

   b. How did he use examples in his speech? Identify the type(s) of examples he included.

   c. How did he define "accountability journalism"? Are there any terms you think he should have defined? Give an example.

   d. What type(s) of testimony did he use in the speech? How effective was that type of supporting material?

   d. What facts did he state in his speech?

   e. What statistics did he include in his speech?

   f. Overall, how effective was Professor Shirky in providing supporting materials for his main points?

g. If you were advising him on how to improve his use of supporting materials, what would you say?

h. What have you learned about supporting materials that you'll apply in your own speeches?

5. Check out Speech Studio to analyze the supporting materials other students use in their speeches. Or record a speech you're working on, upload it to Speech Studio, and ask your peers for their feedback. What feedback could you use to fine tune how you use supporting materials before you give your speech in class?

8 Organizing and Outlining Your Speech

Read it

Cengage Learning

Watch it

Cengage Learning

Use it

Review it

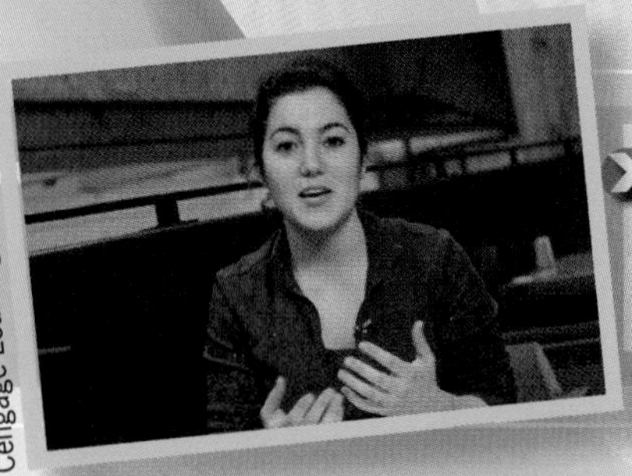

CourseMate Speech Studio Speech Builder Express

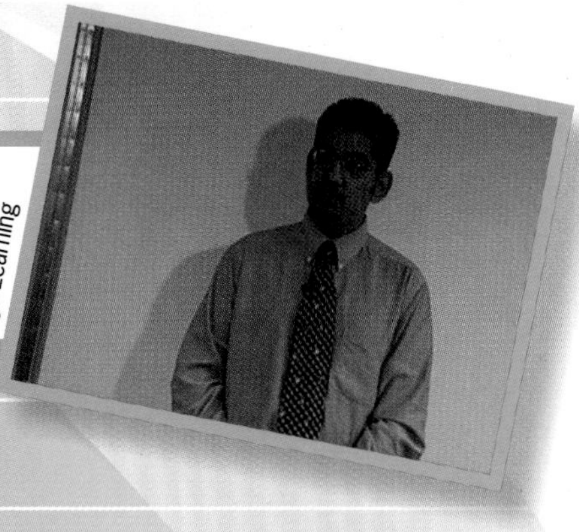

When you organize a speech well, audience members follow your ideas more easily and better understand what you have to say. In addition, good organization helps you stay on track, keeping your purpose and thesis in mind. With a thoughtful plan for the order in which you want to present your points, you'll feel more confident. Organizing your speech is like planning a trip: Reaching your destination is much less stressful when you know how to get there. In addition, when your speech is well organized, audience members don't need to worry about where you are in your speech, where you've been, or where you're going. Carefully organizing your speech increases the chances that you'll achieve your specific purpose and that your audience will respond as you'd planned.

Andersen Ross /Getty images

Figure 8.1   The parts of a speech

Introduction		Body		Conclusion
get audience's attention	transition from introduction to body and first main point	first main point subpoint subpoint	transition from body and last main point to conclusion	review main points
indicate purpose and thesis		transition to second main point		reinforce purpose
establish credibility		second main point subpoint subpoint		provide closure
preview main points		transition to third main point		
		third main point subpoint subpoint		

The Parts of a Speech

Every speech has four main parts: introduction, body, transitions, and conclusion (**Figure 8.1**). In the first part of the speech, the *introduction*, the speaker must get the audience's attention, indicate the purpose and thesis, establish credibility, and preview the speech's main points. The *body* of a speech includes all the speaker's main points and subordinate points. Speakers use *transitions*, words, phrases, sentences, or paragraphs to move from the introduction to the body, from one point to the next, and from the body to the conclusion. The *conclusion* ends the speech, with the speaker reviewing the main points, restating the thesis, and providing closure.

When you present a speech, you proceed from the introduction through the body to the conclusion. But when you put together a speech you typically develop the body and transitions first, the introduction second, and the conclusion last. **Figure 8.1** shows the logic underlying this seemingly illogical order. You need to know what you're going to say in the body before you develop the introduction and the conclusion. You may find, however, that as you work on the body of your speech you'll think of something you want to say in the introduction or get an idea for a great way to end your speech. Organizing your speech, like speechmaking in general, doesn't always follow a linear path.

This chapter focuses on developing the body of your speech and connecting your points together, as those are the starting points for most speakers. Chapter 9 discusses how to begin and end your speech.

Organizing the Body of Your Speech

The **body** is where the action of your speech takes place—where you inform, persuade, or entertain your audience. This section identifies and describes the main elements of this part of your speech (**Figure 8.2**).

The middle and main part of a speech; includes main and subordinate points.

Developing Your Main Points

Your working outline provides a useful guide for developing your main points (Chapter 4). The working outline includes your topic, general purpose, specific purpose, thesis, and keywords for the main ideas and subpoints. As you review your working outline, applying the principles of clarity, relevance, and balance will help you identify what points to include and what points to leave out of your speech.

Clarity Your main points should identify for your audience what your speech is about and the response you seek. They must also clearly support your specific purpose and be consistent with your thesis. In the following example, notice how the main points elaborate on the ideas expressed in the thesis, providing clarity on the topic of happiness. They also support the specific purpose, allowing the speaker to reach the goal of informing the audience.

Topic:	A Scientific Approach to Happiness
General purpose:	To inform
Specific purpose:	To inform my audience about the science of happiness.
Thesis:	According to scientists, people achieve happiness through involvement with daily activities and other people, contributing in meaningful ways to larger goals, and finding pleasure in everyday life.

Main points:

I. The first component of happiness is being engaged in activities and interacting with others.

II. The second component of happiness is feeling like what you do contributes in meaningful ways to some larger goal or objective.

III. The third component of happiness is simply finding pleasure in the everyday things you do.

Even slightly altering what you want to say about a topic changes the specific purpose and thesis. In turn, the main points must also change to clearly reflect different focus. For example:

Topic:	The Myths of Happiness
General purpose:	To inform
Specific purpose:	To make my audience aware of myths about happiness.
Thesis:	Scientists have dispelled three common myths about happiness: Money makes you happy, intelligence makes you happy, and being young makes you happy.

Main points:

I. "Wealth makes you happy" is one myth scientists have proven false.

II. "Greater intelligence makes you happier" is a second myth scientists have proven false.

III. "Youth as the key to happiness" is a third myth scientists have dispelled.

These examples of two approaches to the same topic, happiness, demonstrate the importance of the early steps you take in topic development: clearly refining your topic, phrasing your specific purpose, and writing your thesis statement (Chapter 4).

Relevance The main points of your speech must pertain directly to your topic. As you research your topic, you'll gather more information than you'll use in your speech. Continually review your specific purpose and thesis, and identify the points that are truly relevant to your specific purpose. You'll always know more about your topic than what you include in your speech—you're the expert—but avoid including information that would detract from your goal.

Main points must be relevant to one another as well as to the topic. Consider the main points for this informative speech about U.S. science fiction writer Octavia E. Butler:

Topic:	The Achievements of Octavia E. Butler
General purpose:	To inform

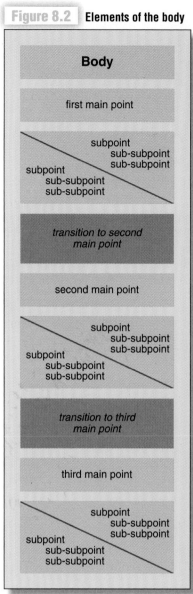

Figure 8.2 **Elements of the body**

Body

first main point

subpoint
  sub-subpoint
    sub-subpoint
subpoint
  sub-subpoint
    sub-subpoint

transition to second main point

second main point

subpoint
  sub-subpoint
    sub-subpoint
subpoint
  sub-subpoint
    sub-subpoint

transition to third main point

third main point

subpoint
  sub-subpoint
    sub-subpoint
subpoint
  sub-subpoint
    sub-subpoint

An informative speech about Octavia E. Butler might focus on the major writing awards she won rather than everything she accomplished in her entire career.

Specific purpose:	To increase my audience's awareness of some of Octavia E. Butler's important achievements.
Thesis:	Octavia E. Butler's many achievements include winning two Hugo and two Nebula awards, a MacArthur genius grant, and a lifetime achievement award from the PEN American Center.

Main points:

    I. Butler won two Hugo and two Nebula awards for her science fiction stories.

    II. In 1995, Butler became the first, and so far only, science fiction writer to win a "genius grant" from the MacArthur Foundation.

    III. Butler won the PEN American Center Lifetime Achievement Award in writing in 1999.

Each main point focuses on an important award that brought Butler recognition. She also achieved success in other ways, such as writing a science fiction movie at age 12 and selling 250,000 copies of her novel *Kindred*. Although these are important accomplishments, they're not directly relevant to a discussion of the awards she won.

Balance Also consider how balanced your main points are. Each point should be about equal in importance relative both to your topic and to the other points. All your points may not be *completely* equal in importance, but one point shouldn't be much more or much less important than the others. Let's consider an example for an informative speech about an event.

Topic:	The Ann Arbor Street Art Fair
General purpose:	To inform
Specific purpose:	To teach my audience about the many interesting facets of Ann Arbor's annual Street Art Fair.
Thesis:	The people, the place, and the art make the annual Ann Arbor Street Art Fair an exciting event to attend.

Main points:

    I. Performers, artists, volunteers, and fairgoers make the Ann Arbor Street Art Fair lively.

    II. Home to the University of Michigan, Ann Arbor is no stranger to making people feel welcomed.

    III. The nearly twenty different types of art—from pottery to fine jewelry—provide a feast for the senses.

In this example, the three aspects of the Ann Arbor Street Art Fair contribute about equally to the event. You'd likely plan to talk about each of them for about the same amount of time.

If the main points you want to discuss are of unequal importance, you can still achieve a rough balance by spending less time on less important points. Consider a speech about the people who come together for the Ann Arbor Street Art Fair:

Topic:	The People of the Ann Arbor Street Art Fair
General purpose:	To inform
Specific purpose:	To inform my audience about the people of Ann Arbor's annual Street Art Fair.
Thesis:	The people of the Ann Arbor Street Art Fair include the organizers, volunteers, artists, performers, and fairgoers.

Main points:

    I. The organizers work all year planning the event.

    II. Volunteers do everything from giving tours of the fair to reuniting lost parents and children.

III. The nearly 200 artists display their creative work.

IV. Performers keep everyone in good cheer.

  V. Thousands and thousands of fairgoers from around the world attend the event every year.

You'd probably spend more time talking about the artists and performers because they're the reason people attend the fair. Or you could emphasize the behind-the-scenes work of the organizers and volunteers. Whatever your emphasis, maintain balance by spending a similar amount of time on each point. For example, you could spend two minutes each on the artists and performers, and one minute each on the organizers, volunteers, and fairgoers.

Evaluating the balance of your main points also requires that you identify the appropriate number of points to include in your speech. To help you determine the right number of main points, consider (1) what information you must cover to achieve your specific purpose and (2) how much time you have to present your speech. Say you have five minutes to present the informative speech about the people of the Ann Arbor Street Art Fair. Can you adequately talk about each main point and give sufficient attention to the introduction and conclusion in that amount of time? No. You'd have less than one minute for each main point, giving you little time to provide the audience with any in-depth information. You need either more time or fewer points. If you can't change the amount of time allotted, you must reduce the number of main points. You could, for instance, focus just on the creative people associated with the fair—the artists and the performers. Or you could talk about the unnoticed people—the organizers and the volunteers. Or you could concentrate on the two groups that interact with each other— the artists and the fairgoers.

Patterns for Organizing Your Main Points

Once you've selected the main points for your speech, organize them in a clear and logical pattern. **Patterns of organization** are structures for ordering the main points of your speech that help audience members understand the relationships among your ideas. Choosing an effective pattern of organization requires careful consideration of your speech topic, general purpose, specific purpose, and thesis.

A structure for ordering the main points of a speech.

Speakers commonly rely on seven patterns of organization. **Table 8.1** provides an overview of the organizational patterns discussed in this chapter.

Table 8.1 Patterns of Organization

	Brief definition	Useful for . . .	Provides your audience with . . .	Examples from student speeches
Chronological	The way in which something develops or occurs in a time sequence	Recounting the history of a subject, a sequence of events, or a step-by-step procedure	A sense of how a topic unfolds over time	*Topic:* The Job Search *Thesis:* Finding a job requires four steps: self analysis, résumé development, application, and follow-up.
Spatial	The physical or geographical relationship between objects or places	Describing an object, a place, or how something is designed	A visual understanding of the relationship between the parts of the topic	*Topic:* Badlands National Park *Thesis:* The terrain in the Badlands National Park ranges from soaring pinnacles and spires to flatland prairies.

(Continued)

Table 8.1 Continued

	Brief definition	Useful for . . .	Provides your audience with . . .	Examples from student speeches
Topical	Arranged by subtopics of equal importance	Explaining the elements that make up a topic	An image of the subpoints within the topic	*Topic:* Local Public Transportation Can Work for You. *Thesis:* The primary modes of public transit in our area are light rail, trolley, and bus.
Narrative	Dramatic retelling of events as a story or a series of short stories	Encouraging audience involvement and participation	A basis for sharing the speaker's point of view	*Topic:* Kayaking Adventure *Thesis:* Kayaking the Menominee River on the Wisconsin–Michigan border was filled with whitewater, white knuckles, and fun.
Cause-and-effect	Shows how an action produces a particular outcome	Demonstrating a causal link between two or more events	A view of the relationships between conditions or events	*Topic:* Diabetes and Dieting *Thesis:* Eating too much sugar has caused the recent increase in the number of people with diabetes in the United States.
Problem–solution	Describes a problem and provides possible solutions	Convincing audience members to agree with a course of action	A rationale for considering a particular solution to a problem	*Topic:* Telecommuting *Thesis:* Because too many people commute long distances to work, more companies should promote telecommuting.
Monroe's Motivated Sequence	Each step designed to facilitate audience involvement and interest	Gaining audience interest or agreement	Reasons to listen and take action	*Topic:* Recycling Old Computers Thesis: Recycling old computers prevents landfills and groundwater from contamination caused by chemical toxins in computer components.

Chronological When you use a **chronological pattern** of organization, you arrange your ideas in a time sequence. For example, in a speech on how to build a birdhouse, you'd start with what listeners need to do first, then explain what they need to do second, and so on, covering each step in order of completion.

• A pattern that organizes a speech by how something develops or occurs in a time sequence.

You can also use the chronological pattern to trace the history of a topic. For example, a speech on the history of the Internet might focus on major events such as the development of ARPANET—the precursor to the Internet—in 1969 and Tim Berners-Lee's idea for the web twenty years later.[1] These events or turning points would provide main points for the speech:

Topic:	History of the Internet
General purpose:	To inform
Specific purpose:	To teach my audience about important events in the history of the Internet.
Thesis:	There are four key turning points in the history of the Internet: the Advanced Research Projects Agency (ARPANET) connects four major U.S. universities, emoticons are first used, Tim Berners-Lee develops the idea for hypertext, and Napster is launched.

Main points:

    I. In 1969 the Advanced Research Projects Agency (ARPANET) connects four major U.S. universities.

    II. In 1979 members of a science fiction email list use the first emoticons as a way to express emotions online.

    III. In 1989 Tim Berners-Lee develops the idea for hypertext, which becomes the basis for the World Wide Web.

    IV. In 1999 Shawn Fanning invents Napster, the peer-to-peer file-sharing program.

Spatial Speeches that rely on a **spatial pattern** of organization link points together based on their physical or geographical relationships, such as their locations. This pattern works particularly well for informative and entertaining speeches about places and objects. For example, when you describe a room you identify the objects in it and their place in terms of each other: "As you walk in the room, the bright orange couch is on the far wall, facing the television and the aquarium." An informative speech on the solar system might discuss each planet in order of increasing distance from the sun: Mercury, Venus, Earth, Mars, Jupiter, Saturn, Uranus, and Neptune. Similarly, a speech to entertain about intriguing places you've visited could start with the location farthest from where you're speaking and progress to the closest one:

Topic:	Intriguing Places I've Visited
General purpose:	To entertain
Specific purpose:	To amuse my audience with the features of some intriguing places I've visited.
Thesis:	Maine's haunted Hitchborn Inn, Tennessee's Salt and Pepper Shaker Museum, the Mice Graves of Montana's Boot Hill Cemetery, and Seattle's Underground City are four intriguing places I've visited.

A pattern that organizes a speech by the physical or directional relationship between objects or places.

Main points:

    I. Maine's haunted Hitchborn Inn, near Penobscot Bay, may be the greatest distance from us, but sometimes I still feel the ghosts are right here.

    II. As we travel west and south, we come to the Salt and Pepper Shaker Museum in Gatlinburg, Tennessee.

    III. Heading west and north, we reach Virginia City, Montana, and the graves of three rogue mice buried in Boot Hill Cemetery.

    IV. Finally, as we continue west, we reach the intriguing place closest to us, the Underground City of Seattle.

Topical A **topical pattern** of organization divides a topic into subtopics that address its components, elements, or aspects. For example, in a speech on what you learn about people when they play golf, one of our students discussed these three points:

A pattern that organizes a speech by arranging subtopics of equal importance.

Topic:	Learning about People on the Golf Course
General purpose:	To inform
Specific purpose:	To inform my audience about what they can learn about people when they're playing golf.
Thesis:	When people play golf, they reveal how they handle the unexpected, their level of patience, and their concern for others.

Time Machine

A chronological pattern of organization allows you to move backward as well as forward through time. Filmmakers sometimes use this strategy, essentially revealing the movie's end and then going back to the beginning, as with Steven Spielberg's film *Munich*, about the terrorist attacks on the Israeli Olympic team at the 1972 Games. Presenting events out of chronological sequence works only if your audience members don't know the first step, stage, or event. You need an element of suspense to hold your audience's attention so they'll listen with anticipation to find out what led up to the end—an ending they already know. For example, most people are familiar with today's Internet, but few know about yesterday's (or yesteryear's) Internet, so it's one topic that could fit this pattern.

Main points:

I. Observing people as they play golf gives you insight into how they handle unexpected events.

II. Observing people as they play golf gives you a good indication of how patient they are.

III. Observing people as they play golf lets you know how—or if—they show concern for other people.

These points are clearly relevant to the main topic, what you learn about people by observing them playing golf. However, points also related to golf, such as "Golf is a great game to play" or "You can play golf at any age," would not be appropriate for this speech because they are not subtopics of the topic the speaker is focusing on.

Narrative With a **narrative pattern** of organization, you structure your main points in story form. Speeches of tribute and introduction often follow a narrative format. Listeners find stories compelling and memorable, which makes the narrative pattern an engaging organizational option.[2]

A pattern that organizes a speech by a dramatic retelling of events as a story or a series of short stories.

Many stories follow this sequence: setting the scene, describing an initial conflict, increasing action, escalating conflict, taking conflict to its peak, and arriving at the final outcome.[3] Consider an informative speech on the history of the Fabergé eggs:

Topic:	The History of the Fabergé Eggs
General purpose:	To inform
Specific purpose:	To inform my audience about the history of Fabergé eggs.
Thesis:	The history of Fabergé eggs involves royalty, wealth, theft, legal battles, and a happy ending.

The history of the Fabergé eggs provides intriguing points that work well with a narrative pattern of organization for an informative speech.

Stan Honda/AFP/Getty Images

Main points:

I. The first Fabergé egg was produced for Russia's Czar Alexander III in 1885 as an Imperial Easter egg.[4] (*setting the scene*)

II. In 1918 Russia's imperial family was murdered. (*initial conflict*)

III. When their homes were ransacked, eight eggs were lost. (*increasing action*)

IV. Nearly 100 years later a Russian billionaire purchased the missing eggs. (*escalating conflict*)

V. A legal battle ensued. (*peak conflict*)

VI. Finally, just a few years ago, the eight once-missing eggs were returned to Russia. (*final outcome*)

Cause-and-Effect The **cause-and-effect pattern** of organization relies on the idea of one action leading to or bringing about another. When using this pattern you must clearly and carefully link the cause with the effect, providing appropriate and effective supporting materials. Although most often used for persuasive speeches, the cause-and-effect pattern can also be applied to informative speeches. For example, an informative speech on the positive effects of meditation works well with a cause-and-effect pattern of organization.

A pattern that organizes a speech by showing how an action produces a particular outcome.

Topic:	Positive Effects of Meditation
General purpose:	To inform
Specific purpose:	To inform my audience about the positive effects of meditation.
Thesis:	By using less oxygen, lowering your heart rate, and altering your brain waves, meditation helps you relax, feel more content, and think more creatively.

152

Main points:

    I. Meditation causes three changes in your body.

        A. When you meditate, you use less oxygen.

        B. When you meditate, you lower your heart rate.

        C. When you meditate, your theta brain waves—those associated with daydreaming—increase in frequency.

    II. These three changes in your body as you meditate have three main effects.

        A. You feel more relaxed.

        B. You feel more content.

        C. You think more creatively.

When you use the cause-and-effect pattern for a persuasive speech, your audience must come to agree with you about what causes a particular circumstance or event. Consider the topic of homelessness in the United States.

Topic:	Homelessness in the United States
General purpose:	To persuade
Specific purpose:	To convince my audience that lack of education and affordable health care cause homelessness.
Thesis:	People in the United States become homeless because they lack educational opportunities and do not have access to affordable health care.

Main points:

    I. There are two primary causes of homelessness in the United States.

        A. Serious inequities in the American educational system mean some people have limited educational opportunities.

        B. Many Americans are uninsured and cannot afford regular health care.

    II. These two conditions result in two effects that contribute to homelessness in the United States.

        A. Without a good education, individuals can't get the jobs they need to pay for a place to live.

        B. Without affordable health care, individuals often must choose between getting treatment and paying rent.

If your listeners agree with the initial causes—inequities in the U.S. educational system and lack of affordable health care—they will be more inclined to agree that the effects contribute to homelessness. In contrast, if listeners disagree with the causes you cite, or identify different causes, your speech will be less persuasive.

Problem–Solution When speakers use a **problem–solution pattern** of organization, they're attempting to convince audience members that a specific dilemma or problem requires a particular course of action or solution. Clearly establishing that a problem exists provides the foundation for persuading the audience that the solution should be implemented. Imagine that the football team at your school perpetually loses money, using more funds than it produces. A persuasive speech that proposes to terminate the football program would be appropriate. If listeners don't think there's a problem, however, they're unlikely to support your solution.

A pattern that organizes a speech by describing a problem and providing possible solutions.

Topic:	Ending the Football Program on Our Campus
General purpose:	To persuade
Specific purpose:	To convince my audience that we should no longer have a football program at our school.

| Thesis: | The football program at our school drains resources from our campus, so it should be eliminated. |

Main points:

    I. The football program at our school loses money each year.

   II. The football program drains money from the school's budget that could be used for other programs.

  III. Our school's football program should be eliminated.

In addition, speakers must demonstrate that the proposed solution will adequately address the issue described and can be reasonably implemented. For example, let's say you identify air pollution as a problem and suggest limiting every household in the United States to one vehicle as a remedy. Audience members, especially in the United States, likely would view your solution as too extreme and difficult to implement. So rather than ask audience members to give up their cars, you could ask them to take a smaller step: giving up driving one day each week. This solution provides a balanced response to the problem and also presents a behavioral change that listeners might consider reasonable.

Monroe's Motivated Sequence **Monroe's motivated sequence** encourages speakers to focus on audience outcomes when organizing ideas. Composed of five steps, this pattern of organization requires that speakers identify and respond to what will motivate the audience to pay attention:[5]

> A five-step pattern of organization that requires speakers to identify and respond to what will motivate an audience to pay attention.

- In the first step, gaining the audience's attention, the speaker relates the topic to listeners, linking it to their lives and providing them with a reason to listen.

- To complete the second step, establishing the need for something or the existence of a problem, the speaker shows listeners that they lack important information or that there's an issue requiring their attention.

- In the third step, satisfying the problem, the speaker provides audience members with the information they lack or the solution to the problem.

- In the fourth step, the speaker helps audience members visualize an outcome by describing for them what will happen if they apply or don't apply the solution.

- To complete the final step, moving an audience to action, the speaker details how audience members can implement the solution.

For the motivated sequence to work, each step must build on the previous one. If earlier steps don't elicit the desired audience response, then the later steps will fall short as well. The motivated sequence can be used for both informative and persuasive speeches (**Table 8.2**). The first three steps—attention, need, and satisfaction—give you the basic structure for an informative speech (Chapter 13). Adding the fourth step, visualization, provides an organizational pattern for a persuasive speech that focuses on changing listeners' beliefs, attitudes, or opinions. A persuasive speech that involves altering audience members' behaviors requires the addition of the last step, the call to action (Chapter 14).

The motivated sequence can prove especially effective with an informative speech topic that may not instantly resonate with your audience. By focusing on gaining the audience's attention at the start, the motivated sequence helps you encourage your audience to listen. Giving a speech on opera to an audience unfamiliar with it provides a good example. First, get your audience's attention by playing a very short audio clip from a contemporary opera. In the next step, show the audience why they need to know more about opera by highlighting its popularity around the world, the drama and mystery of each opera's storyline, and the timeless topics of courage, love, betrayal, and deceit. Finally, in the satisfaction step, explain one of the more popular operas, such as *La Bohème*, and demonstrate how its themes resonate with people today, giving your audience the information they need to appreciate opera.

Adding the visualization step to a speech represents a key move from an informative to a persuasive speech. In asking listeners to visualize the benefits or costs associated

Table 8.2   Monroe's Motivated Sequence for Informative and Persuasive Speeches

Step	Speaker's action	Audience's response	Speech purpose
Attention	Relate topic to audience to gain and attention.	I will listen because this is relevant to me.	Informative
Need	Show that there's information the audience needs to know (informative speech). *or* Establish the problem or current harm (persuasive speech).	There is important information I'm lacking (informative speech). *or* There's a problem that needs my attention (persuasive speech).	
Satisfaction	Present information that audience members lack (informative speech). *or* Describe the solution to the problem (persuasive speech).	Here is the information I need to know (informative speech). *or* Here's the solution to the problem (persuasive speech).	
Visualization	Show audience the benefits of the proposed solution and/or the costs of not implementing the solution.	I can visualize the benefits of this solution and/or the costs of not implementing this solution.	Persuasive (influence attitudes, beliefs, values)
Action	Explain how the audience can implement the proposed solution.	I will do this.	Persuasive (influence actions)

with a particular solution, the speaker seeks to modify how the audience thinks about something. Say you wanted to persuade your audience that video games should promote more cooperation and less competition. In the attention step, you might pique your audience's interest by countering video game stereotypes, providing information such as "Did you know that women account for over 40 percent of interactive game players and that the average age of a player is twenty-eight?" You could also provide a new view on the problem by telling your audience about the importance of learning to work with others and about the lack of games that foster cooperation rather than violent competition. The satisfaction step then becomes obvious—create and promote video games based on cooperation rather than competition. For the visualization step, you could suggest that facilitating the ability to cooperate with others contributes more to society. In this step, you could imagine for your audience situations in which individuals cooperate more to accomplish tasks, rather than competing in unproductive ways.

For a speech in which you want to influence the audience's action, you add the action step. This step may seem similar to the satisfaction step, but the action step includes much greater detail—you want your audience to implement your suggestions. Let's consider a speech about simplifying your life. You'd begin your speech with the attention step, possibly presenting statistics on how much Americans work and consume in relation to the rest of the world. In the need step, you might draw attention to the ways in which audience members needlessly complicate their lives, and the resulting harms. This leads to the satisfaction step, where you'd discuss in general the idea of simplifying our lives. The topic lends itself to visualizing both the benefits of simplification and the costs of a life grounded in consumerism. The action step then details exactly how audience members might simplify their lives, such as gardening, changing spending habits, reducing clutter, and consuming responsibly.

You've learned about seven patterns for organizing your speech: chronological, spatial, topical, narrative, cause-and-effect, problem–solution, and Monroe's motivated sequence. **Table 8.3** on page 156 demonstrates how the discussion of one topic, voting, changes based on which organizational pattern you apply.

Table 8.3 Applying Patterns of Organization to a Single Topic: Voting

Pattern	General purpose	Specific purpose	Thesis	Main points
Chronological	To inform	To teach my audience about key amendments to the U.S. Constitution in the history of voting in the United States	Three amendments to the Constitution changed voting in the United States: the 15th, 19th, and 24th amendments.	I. The 15th Amendment to the U. S. Constitution granted all U.S. citizens the right to vote regardless of race, color, or previous condition of servitude. II. The 19th Amendment gave women the right to vote. III. The 24th Amendment ended the practice of poll taxing, or forcing people to pay a tax to vote.
Spatial	To inform	To help my audience understand the layout of a typical ballot	The layout of a ballot includes four main sections: the election's title and description, the instructions, a list of individuals and items to vote on, and the space to record the vote.	I. The election's title and description are at the top of the ballot. II. How to complete the ballot is explained next. III. Candidates, proposals, propositions, and initiatives are listed in a specified order. IV. Space to record your vote is usually to the right of each item.
Topical	To inform	To make my audience aware of how voting occurs in other democratic countries	The Philippines, South Africa, and Australia provide examples of democratic countries whose voting systems differ from ours.	I. The Philippines' voting system II. South Africa's voting system III. Australia's voting system
Narrative	To entertain	To share with my audience the lighter side of getting out the vote for student elections on a college campus	My adventures in getting out the vote for student government elections on my campus nearly ended my college career but finished on an unexpected note.	I. My campus's student election day was more like doomsday for me. II. Getting out the vote almost got me expelled from school. III. My political science advisor suggested I change my major. IV. The ending of this story surprised even me.
Cause-and-effect	To persuade	To persuade my audience that the United States needs standardized federal voting regulations	The lack of consistency in voting rules and procedures across states in our country has led to voting problems on election day.	I. Local and state governments are in charge of voting procedures. II. Variation in voting standards has led to ballot counting problems at the national, state, and local levels.

Table 8.3 Continued

Pattern	General purpose	Specific purpose	Thesis	Main points
Problem–solution	To persuade	To encourage my audience to consider alternative voting procedures in the United States	Giving people greater flexibility in how they vote will solve the problem of not being able to reach a polling place on election day.	I. Many people don't vote because they have difficulty getting to their polling places on election day. II. Alternative voting methods, such as mailed ballots, will solve the problem of not being able to get to the polls.
Monroe's motivated sequence	To persuade	To persuade my audience to vote	One important part of exercising your voice in a democratic society is voting in every election.	I. Although voter participation in the last election was up, only about 50% of eligible voters cast a vote. (*attention*) II. A healthy democracy requires voter participation. (*need*) III. You must vote. (*satisfaction*) IV. There are benefits to voting and costs to not voting. (*visualization*) V. These are the steps you need to take to vote. (*action*)

> **Watch it**

SPEECH BUDDY VIDEO 8.1
Reviewing Patterns of Organization

Anthony helps you review the patterns of organization commonly used to organize the main points of a speech.

> **Use it**

Watch your Speech Buddy video . . .

. . . and use what you've learned in your next speech.

ACTIVITY 8.1
Everything in Its Place

This two-part activity gives you a chance to (1) correct an outline that is organized incorrectly and identify the patterns of organization used for the outline, and (2) determine patterns of organization used in a professional speech.

Organizing Speeches About Service Learning

One key component of service learning is reflecting on what you've learned from your community experience and telling others about it. Identify one aspect of your service learning work that you'd like to share with others. For example, you may have gained insight into how your city makes policies or into teaching strategies to get third-graders interested in environmental issues.

How might each pattern of organization discussed in this chapter lead to different ways to talk about your topic? Which pattern best fits with your topic, your specific purpose, and your audience? What have you learned about patterns of organization that will help you with your classroom speeches and other speaking contexts?

Connecting Your Ideas with Transitions

Effective speaking demands more than researching your topic well and developing a logical way to organize your material. Your speech must also have **coherence**, an obvious and plausible connection among your ideas. **Transitions** play an important role in creating coherence: They help direct your audience from one idea or part of your speech to the next.[6] Effective transitions allow you to

- Move smoothly and clearly from the introduction to the body of the speech.

- Move from one main point to the next main point within the body of the speech.

- Exit from the body of the speech to the conclusion.

Table 8.4 provides examples of transition words and phrases.

An obvious and plausible connection among ideas.

A word, phrase, sentence, or paragraph used throughout a speech to mark locations in the organization and clearly link the parts of a speech together

Table 8.4 Types of Transitions

Type of transition	Word or phrase	Example
Ordering	*first, second, third; next, then, finally*	First I'll review the history of the missions in California.
Reinforcing	*similarly, also, likewise, in addition, moreover, further*	Also, you could volunteer as a tutor in a local elementary school.
Contrasting	*however, yet, in contrast, whereas, unless, although, even though, instead*	However, your best strategy is to prepare well in advance.
Chronology/time	*when, while, now, before, after, currently, recently, then, during, later, meanwhile*	During this process you must keep a close watch on your time.
Causality	*therefore, so, consequently, since, because, for this reason, with this in mind*	Therefore, learning to manage your money now will help you avoid problems in the future.
Summarizing/ concluding	*in summary, let me summarize, finally, let's review, as I've discussed*	Finally, good study habits require evaluating what works and what doesn't.

Use brief, clear transitions to make it as effortless as possible for listeners to navigate through the content of your speech. This section more closely examines how you can use transitions in three key places: introducing the first main point, moving from one main point to the next, and finishing the last main point and going on to your conclusion.

Introducing the First Main Point

After you've given your speech introduction, you're ready to move on to the first main point in the body of your speech. To accomplish this task smoothly, include a brief transition to **signpost** the direction of your speech. Signposts, which include ordering transitions such as *first, next,* and *finally,* let audience members know where you are in a speech, where you're going, and how your points relate to one another. You might say,

> A transition that indicates a key move in the speech, making its organization clear to the audience.

- "Now, let me elaborate on that first point I referred to in the introduction, (*then refer to the first point*)...."

- "As I mentioned, we'll first consider (*first point*)...."

- "To begin, I'll describe (*first point*)...."

After voicing the transition, begin discussing your first main point.

Transitions between Main Points

When you shift from one main point to the next within the body of the speech, use internal transitions that clearly signpost the direction in which you're going. Here are some examples of what you might say as you move through the body of a speech on human biological cell cloning:

- "Now that I've described what human biological cell cloning is, let's turn to my second main point, the advantages human cloning offers to medical research...."

- "We've learned the basics of human biological cell cloning. Now let's consider what it offers to medical research...."

- "As you can tell, human biological cell cloning is a complex and intriguing subject. Equally intriguing is the potential for medical research, which I want to elaborate on...."

Internal summaries are longer transitions that also help listeners move from one main point to the next. These transitions remind listeners of previously presented information so that they have a solid grasp of those ideas before you move on to the next point. The following example, from an informative speech on the International Spy Museum in Washington, D.C., uses chronological transitions.

> A review of main points or subpoints, given before going on to the next point in a speech.

> So you'll start your tour of the museum by learning about the basics of espionage and choosing your own cover identity. Fully engaging in this first part of the museum provides the essential framework for enjoying the remainder of your tour. The spy gadgets, weapons, and bugs you'll find in the next exhibit are all the more fascinating when you think about them in terms of your spy identity. Then you'll view those tricks of the trade in action in the third part of the museum, which focuses on the history of spying. Some of the secret spies will surprise you. Now let's turn to more recent history presented in the International Spy Museum.

With eight main exhibits, as well as special exhibits, listeners may well lose track of the information presented earlier. Refreshing their memories about the first three exhibits discussed allows the speaker to move with confidence to the next main point, the fourth exhibit.

In the next example, the speaker uses reinforcing and contrasting transitions in an internal summary during a persuasive speech on the need for greater security in radio frequency identification tags.

> Before I move on, let's briefly review the basics of radio frequency identification tags, or RFIDs. These ID tags are becoming commonplace. We use them for our pets—the computer chips we implant that contain information in case our pets get lost. RFIDs are used in the new electronic passports issued by the U.S. government. These tiny chips contain personal information such as your name, birthplace, and date of birth. Additionally, the electronic passports include a digital photograph designed for use with face-recognition software. RFIDs can hold a great deal of information— your medical records, financial history, and other personal data. They're cheap to produce and easy to manufacture. However, as we'll see next, they're also easy to infect with computer viruses.

This internal summary provides an essential link between the explanation of what RFIDs are used for and the potential problems computer viruses could cause.

Internal summaries perform two functions for the speaker: (1) They remind the audience of the key points the speaker has talked about, and (2) they link previous points with the upcoming one. The more you reinforce your ideas by reminding your audience of what you said—without becoming repetitive and long winded—the greater the likelihood they'll remember your points.

Transitions to the Conclusion

Letting your audience know you're moving from the final main point to the end of your speech prepares them for the conclusion. The transition to the conclusion requires little more than a few words or a phrase. Link the transition from your last main point to the actual content of the conclusion as seamlessly as possible. Consider these examples that use summarizing, or concluding, phrases:

- "In summary, I've covered key points about (*transition and review main points*) ...."
- "Let's review the main issues to keep in mind (*transition and review main points*) ...."

When you use a transition to signal your audience that the end of your speech is near, they will expect you to finish shortly. For speeches of 10 minutes or less, that generally means no more than a minute for the conclusion.

Putting Your Ideas Together:
The Complete-Sentence Outline

Recall that as you're working on your speeches you'll create three different outlines: (1) the working outline, for initially identifying the main ideas you want to address (Chapter 4); (2) the complete-sentence outline, for elaborating on your points (covered in this chapter); and (3) the presentation outline, for giving your speech (Chapter 12). **Table 8.5** on page 162 reviews these outlines.

The Purpose of the Complete-Sentence Outline

A formal outline using full sentences for all points developed after researching the speech and identifying supporting materials; includes a speech's topic, general purpose, specific purpose, thesis, introduction, main points, subpoints, conclusion, transitions, and references.

While your working outline gives you general directions for researching and organizing your speeches and the presentation outline helps you practice and present your speech, the **complete-sentence outline** offers a highly detailed description of your ideas and how they're related to one another.

160

SPEECH BUDDY VIDEO 8.2
Linking Effectively: Transitions

In this video, Erin describes different types of transitions. As you watch the video, keep in mind what you've learned in this chapter about the role and types of transitions, as well as what makes each type effective.

ACTIVITY 8.2
Polite to Point

This activity gives you an opportunity to evaluate transitions in sample speeches and suggest ways in which they could be improved.

The complete-sentence outline provides much greater depth than the other two types of outlines. In the complete-sentence outline, also referred to as a *full-sentence* or *preparation outline*, you'll use complete sentences that clearly reflect your thinking and research on your topic.[7] Keep in mind, though, that the complete-sentence outline reflects a plan of your speech, not every word you'll say when you give your presentation.

Formatting the Complete-Sentence Outline

Using symbols and indentation, outlines provide a visual representation of how you've put your speech together. Outlines show the priority of your ideas, from first to last, and how they're related. Typically, upper-case Roman numerals (I, II, III) indicate the main points of the speech, and these points sit at the left margin of the page. For the first subpoints under a main point, indent one level and use a capital letter (A, B, C). For sub-subpoints, use Arabic numbers (1, 2, 3) and indent another level. For lengthy speeches, you might need to add sub-sub-subpoints, using lower-case letters (a, b, c) and indenting another level, and sub-sub-sub-subpoints, using lowercase Roman numerals (i, ii, iii,) and indenting once again. A period follows each number or letter, as shown in **Figure 8.3** on page 162.

Some basic rules provide the guidance you need for formatting your complete-sentence outline.

Preface the Outline with Identifying Information Listing your topic, general purpose, specific purpose, and thesis right at the top of your outline keeps you on track as you develop the outline. Clearly label each item, as in this example:

Topic:	Taking Good Photographs
General purpose:	To inform

Table 8.5 Types of Outlines

Type of outline	Functions	Key features	Chapter
Working	Assists in initial topic development; guides research	Includes main points and possible subpoints; revised during research process	Chapter 4: Developing Your Purpose and Topic
Complete-sentence	Clearly identifies all the pieces of information for the speech; puts ideas in order; forms the basis for developing the presentation outline	Uses complete sentences; lists all sections of speech and all references; revised during preparation process	Chapter 8: Organizing and Outlining Your Speech
Presentation	Assists you in practicing and giving your speech	Uses keywords; revised as you practice your speech; often transferred to note cards for use during practice and the final presentation	Chapter 12: Delivering Your Speech

You are here ▶

Figure 8.3 Basic Outline Format

```
I. First main point
   A. First subpoint
      1. First sub-subpoint
      2. Second sub-subpoint
         a. First sub-sub-subpoint
         b. Second sub-sub-subpoint
            i. First sub-sub-sub-subpoint
            ii. Second sub-sub-sub-subpoint
```

Specific purpose: To demonstrate to my audience how to take good photographs.

Thesis: Key guidelines for taking good photographs are to get close, avoid background clutter, go for the action, and check your light source.

State Points and Subpoints in Complete Sentences Writing out your points and subpoints as complete sentences helps you elaborate on your thoughts. Your working outline, which includes just keywords or phrases, represents the rudiments of your speech—your ideas before you fully developed them. In the complete-sentence outline, you articulate your thoughts more clearly by writing out your points and subpoints in complete sentences. In addition, each main point or subpoint expresses only one idea, so use just one sentence for each point.

Comparing the main points of the working and complete-sentence outlines for the speech on choosing a major, discussed in Chapter 4, demonstrates key differences between the two types of outlines (**Table 8.6**). The complete-sentence outline shows how each point is developed. For example, the sentence "Practical considerations in choosing a major include the department's reputation, the time it will take to graduate, the job market, possible salary, and requirements for the major" suggests five subpoints within that main point. In the working outline, the phrase "practical considerations" doesn't give enough information about how the speaker might elaborate on that point.

Table 8.6 Main Points for the Working and Complete-Sentence Outlines

Main points in the working outline	Main points in the complete-sentence outline
I. Practical considerations	I. Practical considerations in choosing a major include the department's reputation, the time it will take to graduate, the job market, possible salary, and requirements for the major.
II. Academic resources	II. Academic resources include openings in the program, the department's instructors, curriculum, and support for students.
III. Personal orientations	III. Personal orientations include career goals, personal goals, what you enjoy, what you don't like, and what you're good at.

List Your Main Points in Order List main points in the order you'll present them. You'll identify the main points of your speech like this:

I. First main point

II. Second main point

III. Third main point

Maintain Levels of Importance All items at the same level on the outline should have the same level of importance. That is, all main points must be equally important in relation to your topic, all subpoints must be equally important in relation to a main point, and so on. For example, in a speech on business etiquette, the main points might be:

I. Telephone etiquette is necessary for the four parts of a phone conversation.

II. Face-to-face etiquette is necessary for the three parts of an in-person conversation.

III. Online etiquette is necessary for the three parts of a message exchange.

All three items are of equal importance because they discuss ways to communicate. A fourth main point about "etiquette with the boss" wouldn't fit because it refers to a specific person you might communicate with at work, an idea that is subordinate to the main points about ways in which people communicate.

Subordinate Ideas That Support Your Main Points The term *subordinate* comes from the Latin *sub*, meaning "under," and *ordinare*, meaning "to order."[8] So subordinate points are those that are "under" your main points, providing evidence and information that support your main ideas. In the speech on business etiquette, the first main point and subpoints might look something like this:

I. Telephone etiquette is necessary for the four parts of a phone conversation.

   A. There are etiquette rules for answering the telephone.

   B. There are etiquette rules for placing a call.

C. There are etiquette rules for fulfilling your obligations during the phone conversation.

D. There are etiquette rules for ending a call.

In this example each subpoint provides a piece of information that supports the main idea that etiquette rules apply to different parts of a telephone conversation.

Check the Number of Subpoints If you can't identify at least two pieces of information to support a point or subpoint, reexamine how you're organizing your ideas, consider conducting additional research, or determine whether the point really requires additional explanation. An informative speech on media literacy might include the following main points and subpoints:

I. Media literacy requires that an individual be an effective consumer and producer of mediated communication.

    A. Media literacy differs from information literacy.

    B. Media literacy differs from digital literacy.

II. Media literacy has three components.

    A. The first component is analyzing mediated communication.

    B. The second component is evaluating mediated communication.

    C. The third component is creating mediated communication.

III. There are three ways to determine whether you're media literate.

    A. Analyze media messages such as television news.

    B. Evaluate media messages such as magazine advertisements.

    C. Create media messages such as web pages.

Notice that each main point has at least two subpoints. For example, if the third main point had been as follows, you'd have to question the strength of the main idea:

III. There's a test for media literacy.

    A. Take the test for media literacy.

Should you just drop it from the speech? Search for more information? Audience members probably would be curious about their media literacy, so stating the main point more clearly and then elaborating on it would be the best choice.

Include and Label Your Introduction, Conclusion, and Transitions Because the preparation outline includes every detail of your speech, incorporate your introduction, conclusion, and transitions into your outline. Some instructors may ask you to write out your introduction and conclusion word for word in paragraph form. Others may ask you to outline those parts of your speech, as shown in the sample complete-sentence outline at the end of this chapter. In addition, label your transitions as shown in the sample outline. This will help you remember to use them when you give your speech.

Use a Consistent System of Symbols and Indentation Generally, speakers use the following system of symbols and indentation:

I. First main point

    A. First subpoint

        1. First sub-subpoint

            a. First sub-sub-subpoint

            b. Second sub-sub-subpoint

        2. Second sub-subpoint

    B. Second subpoint

List References for Your Speech At the end of your outline, list the references for your speech—the sources of all the supporting material you included. In the sample preparation outline in the next section of this chapter, the references are listed using the formatting rules of the American Psychological Association. Some instructors require students to use the Modern Language Association reference formatting rules.[9] Check with your instructor to find out how you should format your references.

Sample Complete-Sentence Outline for Review and Analysis

The Colors of the Filipino Flag

Introduction

I. What's red, blue, white, and brown, has three stars, and has a bright shining sun? (*Pause.*)
  A. Well, it's me wearing this shirt with a Filipino flag.
  B. If you're familiar with what I'm wearing (a shirt called *barong Tagalog*), you can probably infer that I'll be talking about an artifact from the Philippines, my very own culture.

II. In the early stages when I was thinking about this speech, I kept asking myself three questions.
  A. What's something important in my culture?
  B. What do Filipinos value?
  C. What has a lot of meaning and history for Filipinos?

III. I was raised with the motto, "Know history, know self, because without history, there's no self."
  A. The Filipino flag helps me know my self—who I am.
  B. This flag tells a lot about Filipino history.
  C. The flag reflects the Filipino culture.

IV. Today I'll talk about the most significant parts of the flag for Filipino history and culture, its three major colors: red, blue, and white.

AP Photo/Aaron Favila

Transition: To begin, I'll explain the importance of the color red in the flag.

Body

I. Red is the first major color of the Filipino flag.
  A. The color red represents courage or, in the Tagalog language, *ma tapang*.
  B. Courage led the Filipinos toward freedom from Spanish tyranny.
    1. The Spaniards ruled the Filipinos for more than 300 years.
      a. The Spaniards were first attracted to the region by its gold and spices.
      b. King Philip II subsequently decided to expand his empire and took the land.
      c. Friars (Spanish priests) ruled the Filipinos.
    2. Courage helped the Filipinos win their freedom from the Spaniards.
      a. In 1892, Andres Bonifacio formed a secret revolutionary society called Katipunan.
      b. In 1898, the Filipinos, with the help of the United States, won their freedom from Spain.

Transition: As you can see, red has great meaning for Filipinos. Blue has important meaning as well.

II. Blue is the second major color of the Filipino flag.
  A. The color blue represents justice or, in the Tagalog language, *justicia*.
  B. Filipinos consider justice very important in their way of life and in their government.
    1. Filipinos value justice in their way of life.
    2. Filipinos value justice in their government.
      a. The Filipinos stepped into the realm of self-government.
      b. The commonwealth elected Manuel Luis Quezon as their first president.

Transition: Finally, I'll tell you about the last color in the flag.

III. White is the third major color of the Filipino flag.
  A. The color white represents equality or, in the Tagalog language, *pan-tay pan-tay*.
  B. Filipinos consider equality very important in their way of life.
    1. Ethnic and religious diversity in the Philippines makes equality especially important.
      a. There is much ethnic diversity, including indigenous ethnic groups such as Bicolano and Sambal, and those who have immigrated to the country, such as Chinese and Latinos.
      b. There are several major religious groups represented: Christians, Muslims, and Pagans.
    2. There is great equality in the household.
      a. Unlike men in many Asian countries, Filipino husbands treat their wives as equals.
      b. Filipino wives are usually in charge of the family's money.

Transition: Let's review those questions I was wondering about at the beginning of my speech.

Conclusion
  I. There were three questions I wanted to answer.
    A. What's something important in my culture?
    B. What do Filipinos value?
    C. What has a lot of meaning and history?
  II. The Filipino flag tells us a lot about the country's culture.
    A. We learned that Filipinos are individuals with great courage, represented as red on the Filipino flag.
    B. We learned that Filipinos are people of justice, represented as blue on the Filipino flag.
    C. And we learned that Filipinos value equality, represented as white on the Filipino flag.
  III. Well, with my motto, "Know history, know self, because without history, there's no self," I can honestly tell you right now that I do know more about myself and my identity than I ever did before from this very flag, and that as an individual I'm proud to be Filipino.

References
Hemley, R. (2003). *Invented Eden: The elusive, disputed history of the Tasaday.* New York, NY: Farrar, Straus and Giroux.
Kwiatowski, L. (2005). Introduction: Globalization, change, and diversity in the Philippines. *Urban Anthropology and Studies of Cultural Systems and World Economic Development, 34,* 305–316.
National Statistics Office, Republic of the Philippines. (2010). *Census facts and figures.* Retrieved from http://www.census.gov.ph
Perez, M. E. (2006). Life challenges and coping: The construction of meaning within Filipino cultural context. *Reflections, 12*(3), 48–53.

Pertierra, R. (2006). Culture, social science & the Philippine nation-state. *Asian Journal of Social Science, 34*, 86–102.

Woods, D. L. (2005). *The Philippines: A global studies handbook.* Santa Barbara, CA: ABC-CLIO.

Questions for Analysis and Discussion

1. Identify the speaker's general purpose, specific purpose, and thesis.

2. How clear is each main point? How relevant is each point to the speaker's general purpose, specific purpose, and thesis? How balanced are the main points?

3. Which pattern of organization did the speaker use? How effective was that pattern in helping him achieve his specific purpose? How might he have applied a different pattern of organization?

4. How effective were the speaker's transitions? Were there places in the speech that were missing transitions?

5. If you were advising the speaker on how to improve the way he organized his ideas, what would you say?

6. What have you learned about organizing your ideas and outlining that you'll apply in your own speeches?

Summary

Organizing your speech effectively helps you provide a clear message for your audience. Every speech includes four key parts: introduction, body, transitions, and conclusion.

The body of the speech comprises most of what you'll present: your main points and supporting materials. As you select and then develop your main points, apply the principles of clarity, relevance, and balance. Your main points must support your specific purpose and clearly indicate the response you want from your audience. In addition, main points must be relevant both to your topic and to one another, and they must be balanced in terms of their relative importance.

Seven patterns of organization are commonly used to organize a speech: chronological, spatial, topical, narrative, cause-and-effect, problem–solution, and Monroe's motivated sequence. An effective pattern of organization complements your topic, specific purpose, and audience.

Transitions link together the elements of your speech. Types of transitions include ordering, reinforcing, contrasting, chronology, causality, and summarizing or concluding. Key places to use transitions are between the introduction and the first main point, between main points, and between the last main point and the conclusion.

The complete-sentence outline is where you record all the parts of your speech. The most detailed outline you'll produce for your speech, the complete-sentence outline includes your topic, general purpose, specific purpose, thesis, introduction, main points, subpoints, conclusion, transitions, and references. You'll revise and rework this outline as you research your speech and identify appropriate supporting materials. Developing this comprehensive outline clearly identifies each bit of information you want to include in your speech and helps you visualize the order of your ideas.

IN THE BOOK
Summary
Key Terms
Critical Challenges

MORE STUDY RESOURCES
Quizzes
WebLinks
Peer-reviewed videos

STUDENT WORKBOOK
8.1: Subpoint Shuffle
8.2: State It; Explain It; Prove It; Conclude It
8.3: Balance Check
8.4: Organizational Change-Up
8.5: Listening for an Outline

SPEECH BUDDY VIDEOS
WATCH It Video
8.1: Reviewing Patterns of Organization
8.2: Linking Effectively: Transitions
USE It Activity
8.1: Everything in Its Place
8.2: Polite to Point

SAMPLE SPEECH VIDEOS
Ganiel, "Educational Requirements to Become a Pediatrician," informative speech
Cara, "Left on a Doorstep," self-introduction speech

SPEECH BUILDER EXPRESS
Goal/purpose
Thesis statement
Organization
Outline
Supporting material
Transitions
Introduction
Conclusion Works cited
Completing the speech outline

INFOTRAC
Recommended search terms
Organizing a speech
Outlining a speech
Main points of a speech
Subpoints of a speech
Patterns of organization for speeches
Transitions in a speech
Complete-sentence outline
Full-sentence outline
Preparation outline
Formatting a speech outline

AUDIO STUDY TOOLS
"Educational Requirements to Become a Pediatrician" by Ganiel
Critical thinking questions
Learning objectives
Chapter summary

Guide to Your Online Resources

CourseMate Your Speech Communication CourseMate for *Public Speaking: The Evolving Art* gives you access to the Speech Buddy video and activity featured in this chapter, additional sample speech videos, Speech Studio, Speech Builder Express, InfoTrac College Edition, and study aids such as glossary flashcards, review quizzes, and the Critical Challenge questions for this chapter, which you can respond to via email if your instructor so requests. In addition, your CourseMate features live WebLinks relevant to this chapter, including sites where you can watch public speeches and evaluate how they are organized, such as C-SPAN.org. Links are regularly maintained, and new ones are added periodically.

Key Terms

body 146

cause-and-effect pattern 152

chronological pattern 150

coherence 158

complete-sentence outline 160

internal summaries 159

Monroe's motivated
   sequence 154

narrative pattern 152

patterns of organization 149

problem–solution pattern 153

signpost 159

spatial pattern 151

topical pattern 151

transitions 158

Critical Challenges

Questions for Reflection and Discussion

1. Although you probably think of narratives as unfolding in a linear fashion, starting with the beginning, then the middle, and finally the end, stories can be told in a variety of ways. Consider a topic you might organize using the narrative pattern of organization. What are the different ways in which you might order the sequence of events? Which order do you think will work best for your audience?

2. The section on organizing the body of your speech includes an example of applying the six different patterns of organization to a single topic. Choose a topic and do the same, identifying the main points you'd cover for each pattern. How does the topic change as you apply each pattern of organization?

3. In everyday conversations, communicators often don't use transitions—they just skip from point to point and topic to topic. But in public speaking, audience members rely on speakers to use transitions to show how the different parts of the speech fit together. Choose a speech to view in person or online. How effective are the speaker's transitions? How does the speaker's use of transitions (or the absence of transitions) influence your evaluation of the speech?

4. Outlining helps you visualize all the elements of your speech and determine whether your ideas are organized in the most effective way. Critically examine one of your own outlines. For each section ask yourself, "Is this the best way to say this or present this idea? What are my alternatives?"

5. Return to the speech given by Ford Motor Company's executives in USE it Activity 8.1. As you consider each of the following questions, think about how you could apply your conclusions to your own speeches.
   a. Identify the main points in the speech. How clear is each point? How relevant is each point to the speaker's general purpose, specific purpose, and thesis? How balanced are the main points?
   b. Give examples of the transitions the speaker used. How effective were those transitions? Were there places in the speech that were missing transitions?
   c. Develop a complete-sentence outline of the speech.
   d. If you were advising the speaker on how to improve the way he organized his ideas, what would you say?

169

9 Beginning and Ending Your Speech

> Read it

> Watch it

Cengage Learning

> Use it

Cengage Learning

> Review it

CourseMate   SPEECH Studio   SPEECH BUILDER EXPRESS

At a Technology, Entertainment, and Design (TED) conference, Jacqueline Novogratz, CEO of the nonprofit Acumen Fund, began her talk[1] about a new approach to helping the poor in developing countries this way:

I want to start with a story from when I was twelve years old. My Uncle Ed gave me a beautiful blue sweater…It had fuzzy zebras walking across the stomach and Mount Kilimanjaro and Mount Meru right across the chest that were also fuzzy. And I wore it whenever I could, thinking it was the most fabulous thing I owned. Until one day in ninth grade when … a boy, who was undeniably my nemesis in high school, said in a booming voice that we no longer had to go far away on ski trips. We could all ski on Mount Novogratz. I was so humiliated and mortified that I immediately ran home to my mother and chastised her for ever letting me wear the hideous sweater. We drove to the Goodwill and we threw the sweater away somewhat ceremoniously, my idea being that I would never have to think about this sweater nor see it ever again.

Fast forward eleven years later. I'm a twenty-five-year-old kid working in Kigali, Rwanda, jogging through the steep slopes when I see ten feet in front of me a little boy, eleven years old, running toward me wearing my sweater. I'm thinking, "No, this is not possible," but so curious I run up to the child … grab him by the collar, turn it over, and there is my name written on the collar of this sweater.

I tell that story because it has served and continues to serve as a metaphor to me about the level of connectedness that we all have on this earth. We so often don't realize what our action—and our inaction—does to people we think we will never see and never know. I also tell it because it tells a larger contextual story of what aid is and can be. That this [sweater] traveled into the

TED/Mike Femia

Goodwill in Virginia and moved its way into the larger industry, which at that point was giving millions of tons of secondhand clothing to Africa and Asia—which was a very good thing, providing low-cost clothing. And at the same time, certainly in Rwanda, it destroyed the local retailing industry.

Although many audience members likely had little direct experience with her topic, Novogratz got their attention with a story they probably could relate to—a painful experience in high school that led to a positive action, contributing clothing to a charity organization. Then the speaker provided an update on the sweater's life: She met a boy in Rwanda who was wearing her sweater. But then what appeared to be a happy ending was not, as Novogratz recounted the damage that clothing contributions did to the Rwandan economy. This brief narrative with its unexpected twist got the audience's attention and prepared them to consider aid to the poor in developing countries in a new way.

In the conclusion to her speech, Novogratz reminded the audience of people's interconnectedness:

> There's enormous opportunity to make poverty history. To do it right, we have to build business models that matter, that are scalable, and that work with Africans, Indians, people all over the developing world who fit in this category to do it themselves. Because at the end of the day it's about engagement; it's about understanding that people really don't want handouts. They want to make their own decisions. They want to solve their own problems… So I urge all of you to think next time as to how to engage with this notion and this opportunity that we all have to make poverty history by really becoming part of the process and moving away from an us-and-them world and realizing that it's about all of us and the kind of world we together want to live in and share.

With her brief closing remarks, the speaker drew a clear link between the speech's beginning and end, neatly tying together the parts of the speech and reinforcing the purpose of her talk.

The beginning and ending of your speech are crucial moments for achieving your objectives. Chapter 8 focused on how to develop the central element of your speech—the body—and how to link together the parts of your speech with transitions. This chapter completes the discussion of the four parts of the speech, elaborating on the introduction and conclusion.

Novogratz, J. (2005, July). TEDTalks: Jacqueline Novogratz. Retrieved March 19, 2007, from ted.com/tedtalks.
Used by permission.

Developing Your Introduction

The beginning of a speech, including an attention getter, a statement of the thesis and purpose, a reference to the speaker's credibility, and a preview of the main points.

In the **introduction** to your speech you gain your audience's attention, explain what you want to accomplish in your speech, establish yourself as an expert on the topic, and tell your audience what you're going to talk about (**Figure 9.1**). The introduction gets your audience ready to listen to the main ideas you'll present in the body of your speech.

Get Your Audience's Attention

You never get a second chance to make a first impression. The influence of first impressions on later perceptions is known as the **primacy effect**. Audiences tend to recall what the speaker says right at the start of the speech because this is when they're most attentive. In addition, often an audience decides whether or not to pay attention to a speaker within the first moments of a speech.[2]

The introduction's first element is the **attention getter**, a device used to create interest in your speech. Effective attention getters are relevant to your topic and encourage the audience to listen to you.[3] Popular attention getters include asking a question, describing an especially poignant image, telling a brief story, or playing a brief clip from a song. To create an effective attention getter, consider your speech's purpose, the amount of time you have to present your introduction, creative strategies, common attention getters, and presentation media related to your topic.

Consider Your Purpose The nature of the attention getter depends on the general purpose of your speech, the topic you choose, and the specific purpose you have in mind. Any attention getter should make clear right away that your topic merits your listeners' time and energy. But more than that, an effective attention getter

- Focuses attention on the importance and relevance of the topic by showing how the topic relates to the audience.

- Entices the audience to want to hear more about the topic by piquing their interest.

- Connects you and your audience by demonstrating your competence in selecting an appropriate attention getter.

- Reduces your nervousness by giving you a well-designed, well-practiced entry to your speech.

- Introduces a theme that joins together the elements of your speech.

In the following example, Oprah Winfrey presented an effective attention getter when she accepted the first Bob Hope Humanitarian Award during the 2002 Emmy Awards:

> Thank you, everybody. Thank you, Tom [Hanks], and Bob and Dolores [Hope], who are home watching I hope, thank you so much, and to everyone who voted for me. There really is nothing more important to me than striving to be a good human being. So, to be here tonight and be acknowledged as the first to receive this honor is beyond expression in words for me. "I am a human being, nothing human is alien to me." Terence said that in 154 B.C. and when I first read it many years ago, I had no idea of the depth of that meaning.[4]

Winfrey's initial "thank you" acknowledged some members of her audience, such as Tom Hanks, the Hopes, and those who had voted for her. Then she established a bond with the larger audience—people who were present at the ceremony and watching on TV—and focused attention on the topic by saying, "There really is nothing more important to me than striving to be a good human being." Most people can relate to trying their best. Winfrey inserted some mystery for her audience when she said, "I had no idea of the depth of that meaning." The simple, timeless quote provided a natural transition to the body of her speech.

Creating a theme in the introduction helps join together the parts of your speech. As Winfrey continued her acceptance speech, she emphasized her theme of being human and sharing similar hopes and dreams. You can also use stories to provide a theme for your speech. For example, you might begin your speech with a short human-interest story that you purposefully leave unfinished. Then, as you conclude your speech several

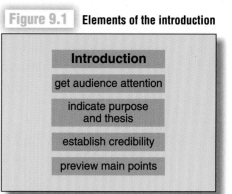

Figure 9.1 **Elements of the introduction**

Introduction

get audience attention

indicate purpose and thesis

establish credibility

preview main points

An audience is more likely to pay attention to and recall what speakers present at the beginning of a speech than what they present in the speech body.

The first element of an introduction, designed mainly to create interest in a speech.

minutes later, refer back to the story or characters you introduced in the attention getter. Starting with part of a story and finishing with the rest of it gives your speech coherence. As the audience understands how the elements of your speech tie together, they view you more positively because of your organizational skills.

In the attention-getter for a speech to persuade (Chapter 14), you also want to

- Establish the seriousness of your purpose.

- Dramatize the controversial nature of your topic.

- Initiate the process of persuasion by presenting a strong logical, cultural, or emotional appeal.

Bill Cosby fulfilled these objectives in the introduction of his "Pound Cake Speech," delivered at the NAACP's gala to commemorate the 50th anniversary of *Brown v. Board of Education*:

> Ladies and gentlemen, these people [the members of the U.S. Supreme Court] … opened the doors, they gave us the right, and today … in our cities and public schools we have 50 percent drop out. In our own neighborhoods, we have men in prison. No longer is a person embarrassed because they're pregnant without a husband. No longer is a boy considered an embarrassment if he tries to run away from being the father of the … child. Ladies and gentlemen, the lower economic and lower-middle economic people are not holding their end in this deal. In the neighborhood that most of us grew up in, parenting is not going on. In the old days, you couldn't hooky school because every drawn shade was an eye. And before your mother got off the bus and to the house, she knew exactly where you had gone, who had gone into the house, and where you got on whatever you had on and where you got it from. Parents don't know that today.[5]

Talk show host and businessperson Oprah Winfrey is well known as an engaging public speaker. She's adept at using attention getters to encourage her audience to listen to her.

Frank Micelotta/Getty Images Entertainment/Getty Images

Using facts and examples, Cosby stressed the seriousness of the topic. He referred to his audience's experiences in "the neighborhood that most of us grew up in" to dramatize differences between then and now. Finally, he appealed to the audience's emotions—parents don't know what their kids are up to—and grabbed their attention. Cosby's hard-hitting introduction caught his audience by surprise and made them sit up and take notice.

Consider Your Time Your attention getter shouldn't last long. It should draw attention to the topic but not cut into the time you need for the body of the speech. Some attention getters last only fifteen seconds. Others may take a minute, or even longer in some cases.

Here's how Fran Visco, president of the National Breast Cancer Coalition, began a speech at the organization's Advocacy Training Conference:

> This past year, we lost too many women to breast cancer, and we lost too many breast cancer advocates. In addition to the women for whom we have a moment of silence at this conference and to Elva Fletcher, to whom we dedicate this conference, we lost Ann Marcou, one of the founders of Y-Me. And we lost Jan Platner, who died of multiple myeloma but who was on the staff of the National Breast Cancer Coalition, on the board of NBCC, and an incredible activist on our behalf. It's been a very difficult year, but it's a reminder of how much more we need to do.[6]

Visco quickly got her audience's attention, personalizing the topic by naming breast cancer advocates who had recently died.

Use Your Creativity Creating and delivering an effective attention getter presents a special challenge for public speakers. It demands that you use your imagination well. Former Supreme Court Justice Sandra Day O'Connor demonstrated her creative side in a commencement address at Stanford University. In the introduction to her speech, she poked fun at lawyers and herself:

> A commencement speech is a particularly difficult assignment. The speaker is given no topic and is expected to be able to inspire all the graduates with a stirring speech about nothing at all. I suppose that's why so many lawyers are asked to be commencement speakers; they're in the habit of talking extensively even when they have nothing to say. And in this case President Hennessy asked not only a lawyer but an elderly judge to be the commencement speaker. I was born in Texas. In Texas they say an old judge is like an old shoe—everything is all worn out except the tongue. All in all, it seems we should have no trouble filling our time today.[7]

O'Connor's gentle humor worked well because it was unexpected—most people think of Supreme Court justices as staid and serious. So O'Connor's tactic charmed her audience and captured the audience's attention.

Try Using Common Attention Getters So far, you've learned about general approaches and ideas for gaining your audience's attention in the speech introduction. You have to decide what you think works best for your audience, your topic, and you. Here are some proven strategies you might want to try.

- *Cite a surprising fact or statistic to call attention to your topic.* Say, for instance, "Do you realize that more than three-fourths of all college graduates don't get jobs in the fields they prepare for?" Or, "According to the Centers for Disease Control, your chances of contracting anthrax are far less likely than your chances of being hit by lightning—twice!" Although this strategy suffers from overuse, if your fact or statistic really surprises or alarms your audience, you may quickly gain their attention.

- *Tell an emotionally arousing but brief human-interest story.* To begin persuading your audience about the perils of child abuse, for example, you could tell the story of a child who becomes ill and eventually dies as a result of health problems caused by parental neglect. You hope to appeal to the audience's sense of basic human rights by pointing out children's vulnerability to abuse. In relating the story, keep it brief and appropriate to the topic, setting, and occasion, as Jacqueline Novogratz did in the example at the beginning of the chapter.

Although she is best known for writing the Harry Potter series, J. K. Rowling's own rags-to-riches story intrigues audiences.

- *Tell a joke to introduce the topic and get the audience interested.* Laughing together helps audience members identify with you and with one another. An effective joke or humorous story related to your topic also puts your audience in a more positive frame of mind about your speech.[8] In her commencement address at Harvard University, author J. K. Rowling began her speech with, "The first thing I would like to say is 'thank you.' Not only has Harvard given me an extraordinary honor, but the weeks of fear and nausea I have endured at the thought of giving this commencement address have made me lose weight. A win–win situation!"[9] She smiled and her audience responded with laughter. However, offensive or demeaning jokes will alienate your audience, as discussed in this chapter's Speaking Of . . . box.[10]

■ *Use the information you have about your audience.* The audience research you conduct may produce data your listeners will find provocative or interesting. For instance, you could begin an informative speech about euthanasia of stray animals by saying, "According to the survey conducted in class, nearly three-fourths of you don't know the meaning of the term *euthanasia*." But getting their attention in and of itself isn't enough. The data must be sufficiently intriguing to motivate them to continue listening.

■ *Ask a question that you want your audience to answer or consider.* To get an idea of how important a topic is for an audience, you might begin with a question such as, "How many of you couldn't find a parking place on campus this morning?" or, "Have you thought about saving for retirement? If you have, raise your hand." Some speakers ask rhetorical questions—ones listeners aren't expected to answer—to gain attention. Examples of rhetorical questions are "How can we best prepare for the technology of the future?" and "Do we really know what's in our drinking water?" Rhetorical questions encourage listeners to think about the answer to the question, but they expect the speaker to provide the answer in the speech.

Integrate Presentation Media Starting your speech with a brief audio or visual clip, a photograph on a digital slide, or other presentation media offers another way to capture the audience's attention and inspire interest. For example, you might display a colorful and richly detailed image of muscle tissue to introduce a speech about MRI (magnetic resonance imaging) technology.

Presentation media can be effective attention getters if they are well designed, well practiced, and clearly relevant to the topic. As with any attention getter, brevity is key. Thirty seconds seems like a brief time, yet in a five-minute speech that's one-tenth of your speaking time. Also consider what you'll be doing as audience members listen to or watch the presentation media you've designed for your attention getter. Especially when you're trying to gain your audience's attention at the beginning of your speech, you don't want to find yourself staring off into space while your listeners watch thirty seconds of a film clip. Chapter 11 discusses designing and using presentation media in detail.

Apply it

Focusing Attention on Service Learning

Telling others about your service learning experiences promotes this important aspect of your college career and demonstrates how institutions of higher education serve their communities. You might give a formal speech in which you try to persuade classmates to get involved in service learning, or you might talk informally with friends and family members about your experiences. Whatever the context, you must first get your audience's attention. How might you do that? Do you know of some startling fact or statistic about service learning? Do you have a compelling story to tell based on your project? Did something humorous happen related to your service learning experience? What do you know about your audience in relationship to service learning? Is there a question about service learning you want your audience to consider? Generate a list of attention getters and the audiences they best match.

Indicate Your Purpose and Thesis

Now that you've gotten your audience's attention, shift smoothly to the next element of your introduction, a clear indication of your speech's purpose and thesis. Recall that the specific purpose succinctly expresses the response you want from your audience ("To help my audience learn the basic steps of jazz dance" or "To teach my audience about how Arabic numerals replaced Roman numerals in mathematics"). When you deliver your speech, you might not state your purpose exactly in those terms. But your audience should know what the purpose of your speech is and what you expect from them. Consider the introduction to a speech by Mary Fisher, a former assistant to President Gerald Ford. Fisher gave this speech, "A Whisper of AIDS," at the 1992 Republican Convention, at a time when many people believed only "bad" or reckless people could contract AIDS. In her introduction she said,

> In the context of an election year, I ask you, here in this great hall, or listening in the quiet of your home, to recognize that the AIDS virus is not a political creature. It does not care whether you are Democrat or Republican; it does not ask whether you are black or white, male or female, gay or straight, young or old. Tonight I represent an AIDS community whose members have been reluctantly drafted from every segment of American society. Though I am white and a mother, I am one with a black infant struggling with tubes in a Philadelphia hospital.[12]

How do you know the purpose of her speech? She doesn't declare outright "My purpose is to make you believe that anyone, including you, can get AIDS." She's more subtle, referring to how people often categorize, and sometimes demonize, others—black/white, female/male, gay/straight, young/old. So she establishes her purpose—her audience knows why she's there and what she wants them to believe. She then states her thesis that AIDS affects "every segment of American society" and that people don't choose to get AIDS.

Indicating the speech's purpose and thesis typically requires just a few sentences. As with the attention getter, you don't want to go on and on. But you do want your audience members to know the response you expect from them and the basic idea you're conveying.

Establish Your Credibility

Your introduction gives you the first opportunity to show you've thoroughly researched your topic. As with the other parts of the introduction, presenting yourself as a credible speaker takes only a few moments. But those moments play a key role in getting your audience to listen to you. For example, Nigel Atkin, speaking about Aboriginal communities at the University of Victoria in Canada, said in his speech introduction,

> I recently worked with the Victoria Foundation to help bridge communication between the foundation, four regional trust advisory committees, and many First Nations, independent Bands, Metis, and urban Aboriginal organizations to effect change towards what many Aboriginal leaders call for—the ability in law and capacity to administer services to their own children and families.[13]

Right away, the audience knew the speaker had some knowledge of the topic through his own experience. Similarly, if your speech topic is how to save people from drowning and you've worked as a lifeguard,

Chris Bernacchi/AFP/Getty Images

Audience members view professionals speaking about their industries as highly credible. For example, an airline safety expert talking about an assessment of a crash site is viewed as highly credible because of his direct experience.

177

you might say, "In my five years as a lifeguard, I've successfully applied three basic techniques to save someone who's drowning." That brief mention of your experience tells the audience you have some expertise on the topic.

You also let your audience know about your credibility when you refer to the research you've done on your topic. For a speech on staying safe and healthy at work, for instance, you might refer to information you've gathered on the topic, as with, "According to the U.S. Department of Labor, over 4 million people get hurt or become ill at work each year."

Preview Your Main Points

Successful speakers keep audiences focused throughout the speech by describing the speech's structure and repeating main points. Thus, the speaker

- Previews in the introduction what will be said in the body of the speech.

- Presents the main points and subpoints in the body.

- Reviews the main points in the conclusion.

A **preview of main points** concisely tells the audience what the main points of the speech will be, establishing an expectation of what the speech will address. The preview provides the first step in helping the audience follow your main ideas as you move from one main point to the next. Transitions help connect the various elements of the introduction together. For example, you might start an informative speech about herb gardens in this way:

> Growing a simple indoor herb garden is easy and enjoyable (*indicate thesis*). Today, you'll learn how to set up your own garden (*indicate purpose*). To begin (*transition*), I will explain the basic equipment you'll need that I've found in my many years of herb gardening (*establish credibility*). Next (*transition*), I will show you how to plant your indoor herb garden. Finally (*transition*), I'll give you some tips on keeping your herbs happy and healthy (*preview main points*).

Similarly, a persuasive speech about meditation could begin like this:

> Incorporating meditation into our daily lives reduces stress and can even increase our longevity (*indicate thesis*). I meditate regularly—and did so this morning as part of my preparation for this speech (*establish credibility*). As part of a balanced lifestyle, you should take the necessary steps to make meditation part of your daily routine (*indicate purpose*). There are different types of meditation that will improve the balance in your life and that you can easily incorporate into your day-to-day activities (*reinforce thesis*). To make clear how to start meditating, I will first (*transition*) explain the positive effects meditation can give you. I will then (*transition*) describe several different kinds of meditation. After (*transition*) describing the types, I will explain how you can begin meditating on a daily basis (*preview main points*).

Even entertaining speeches require a clear preview of main points, as in this example:

> Some people claim they learned everything they needed to know in kindergarten, but I learned everything I needed to know my first year of high school (*indicate thesis*). I think you'll appreciate all the lessons I learned in spite of what my teachers were trying to tell me (*indicate purpose*). I admit this may sound odd, but I was an unusual teenager, recording my first year of high school like I was writing a documentary (*establish credibility*). Before I regale you with my many brilliant insights (*transition*), I will give you some background on my high school. Second, (*transition*) I'll explain the three most important lessons I learned. Finally (*transition*), I'll tell you how I've applied those lessons recently, even for this class (*preview main points*).

The final element of the introduction, in which the main points to be presented in the body of the speech are mentioned.

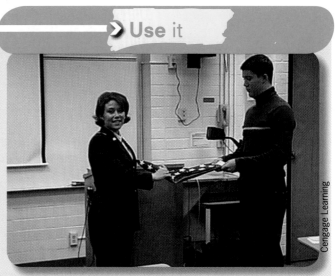

SPEECH BUDDY VIDEO 9.1
Beginning Effectively: Introductions

Evan presents sample speech introductions and highlights ways of evaluating each. As you watch the video, keep in mind what you've learned about the role of speech introductions, as well as the elements and characteristics of an effective introduction.

ACTIVITY 9.1
Here We Go

This activity provides an opportunity to evaluate the introductions of several sample speeches and suggest ways they could be improved.

Developing Your Conclusion

You've presented your main points, and now you're ready to wrap up your speech. But you're not quite finished. The flip side of the primacy effect—the critical influence of your speech introduction on the audience's attention and memory—is the recency effect. With the **recency effect,** audience members recall what the speaker presents last better than they recall the information contained in the body of the speech.[14] Of course, listeners will remember more than only the beginning and ending of your presentation. However, the primacy and recency effects underscore the key role the introduction and conclusion play in achieving your purpose. The introduction gets your audience ready to listen to your ideas; the conclusion reinforces what you talked about.

> An audience is more likely to remember what speakers present at the end of a speech than what they present in the speech body.

In the **conclusion** to your speech, you review the main points, reinforce the speech's general and specific purposes, and provide closure so your audience knows your speech is over (**Figure 9.2**). In addition, integrating visual and auditory imagery in the conclusion can make your topic more memorable and reinforce your purpose.[15] Judicious use of presentation media, such as a few video frames, a particularly poignant photograph, or a very short audio clip, can spark your audience's imagination. Use the conclusion to continue building rapport with your audience and emphasize your points, but do it efficiently. Audiences perk up when they know your speech is coming to an end.[16] They are ready for you to stop talking, but they are also willing to listen closely to your final remarks. Your words, facial expression, and body movement should all indicate that your presentation has purposefully concluded. By preparing, practicing, and presenting an effective conclusion, you will reinforce your key points, strengthen a call to action or a persuasive argument, and give your audience a lasting impression of your message.

> The end of a speech, in which the speaker reviews the main points, reinforces the purpose, and provides closure.

Figure 9.2 **Elements of the conclusion**

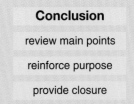

Conclusion

review main points

reinforce purpose

provide closure

179

Review Your Main Points

Use the conclusion to remind your audience of the main points presented in the body of your speech. The **review of main points** normally follows a transition word or phrase that indicates you're moving from the body to the conclusion. That is, once you've made the transition from the body of the speech to its conclusion, quickly summarize by restating your speech's main points. When you review your main points, you're helping listeners recall where they've been, but without the specific details. Here are some examples:

- *In a speech to inform:* In summary (*transition*), today you've learned how to get started windsurfing. I described the history of windsurfing, the equipment you'll need, and where you can try out this fun sport (*review main points*).

- *In a speech to persuade:* Let's review (*transition*) what I covered in my speech. I told you about how you can improve your study habits and get better grades almost immediately. I've described the most common problems students create for themselves, how those mistakes lead to poor results in the classroom, and what to do about it to improve your grades (*review main points*).

- *In a speech to entertain:* Now (*transition*) you know my secrets of backpacking in style: Treat your backpacking guide very, very well; bring the proper equipment; and make backup reservations at a nearby resort hotel (*review main points*).

Reinforce Your Purpose

The conclusion gives you a final opportunity to reinforce your specific purpose by highlighting the reason your information is important (for a speech to inform), crystallizing your argument and making a final appeal to the audience (for a speech to persuade), or getting that last laugh (for a speech to entertain).

In reinforcing your specific purpose, you provide a **memorable message** to capture the audience's attention in a way that makes the information or persuasive argument you've given impossible to ignore or refute. What you say must be brief, clear, strong, and striking, as in the following examples:

- "We've finally got the evidence that proves what scientists had long suspected: Humans are evolved apes." (*informative speech reporting new DNA evidence*)

- "The three aspects of matching you to the right profession are identifying what you ideally want in a job or profession, what you must have, and what you absolutely don't want." (*informative speech on how to choose a job or profession*)

- "Now's the time to decide: Are you going to give up or shape up?" (*persuasive speech promoting exercise program for college students*)

- "You will be the ones who will have to pay for that new football stadium!" (*persuasive speech against constructing a new stadium*)

Provide Closure

Sometimes speakers find the very end of the speech the most difficult part. You've probably heard speakers say, "That's about it," "Okay, well, that's all I have to say," or "I guess I'm done." The conclusion is the last chance you have to make an impression on your audience, and you want it to be a good one.

There are many strategies for providing closure. You must decide what will work best for your audience, your topic, and you. Here are some specific techniques you might want to try.

- *End with a quotation.* "As author Rita Mae Brown once said, 'The statistics on sanity are that one out of every four Americans is suffering from some form of mental illness. Think of your three best friends. If they're okay, then it's you.'"[17] (*entertaining speech on staying sane in today's world*)

- *Use presentation media*: In the sample speech conclusion at the beginning of this chapter, Jacqueline Novogratz showed a vivid digital slide of herself talking with a Rwandan man as she told the audience, "Because at the end of the day it's about engagement; it's about understanding that people really don't want handouts. They want to make their own decisions. They want to solve their own problems." The powerful visual image reinforced what she said, making audience members more likely to recall the action she wanted them to take. (*persuasive speech on new ways to help the poor in developing countries*)

- *Make a dramatic statement.* "And in the ten minutes I've been talking, twenty people in Africa have died of malaria." (*informative speech on the impact of malaria around the world*)

- *Refer to the introduction.* "Now I'll finish the story I started in the introduction. And this story has a happy ending. I found a great summer job that will pay for my two weeks in Mexico over winter break." (*informative speech on how to find a good summer job*)

- *Refer to subsequent events.* "Later, in coordination with the U.S. Department of Justice, AMBER Alert plans were passed in all fifty states." (*informative speech on Americans Missing: Broadcast Emergency Response program*)

- *Reinforce the speaker-audience connection.* "Like many of you, I thought the idea of freedom was a pretty basic thing. But now that I've learned how people in other cultures view freedom and shared that information with you, we all realize that there are many different ways to think of this common word." (*informative speech on defining freedom*)

- *Thank the audience.* "Thank you for considering my proposal to increase the number of elective courses and reduce the number of required courses for all students attending our school." (*persuasive speech on changing graduation requirements*)

> **Watch it**

Cengage Learning

SPEECH BUDDY VIDEO 9.2
Ending Effectively: Conclusions

Evan introduces sample speech conclusions and highlights different ways of evaluating them. As you watch the video, keep in mind what you've learned about the role of speech conclusions, as well as the elements and characteristics of an effective conclusion.

> **Use it**

Cengage Learning

ACTIVITY 9.2
It's a Wrap

This activity provides an opportunity to evaluate the conclusions of several sample speeches and suggest ways they could be improved.

U.S. Supreme Court Judge Sonia Sotomayor is the first Latina to serve on the court. What follows is her opening statement before the U.S. Senate Judiciary Committee during her confirmation hearing on July 13, 2009.[18]

AP Photo/Ron Edmonds

In recent weeks, I have had the privilege and pleasure of meeting eighty-nine senators, including all of the members of this committee. Each of you has been gracious to me, and I have so much enjoyed meeting you. Our meetings have given me an illuminating tour of the fifty states and invaluable insights into the American people.

There are countless family members and friends who have done so much over the years to make this day possible. I am deeply appreciative for their love and support. I want to make one special note of thanks to my mother. I am here, as many of you have noted, because of her aspirations and sacrifices for both my brother, Juan, and me. Mom, thank you. I am very grateful to the president and humbled to be here today as a nominee to the United States Supreme Court.

The progression of my life has been uniquely American. My parents left Puerto Rico during World War II. I grew up in modest circumstances in a Bronx housing project. My father, a factory worker with a third-grade education, passed away when I was nine years old.

On her own, my mother raised my brother and me. She taught us that the key to success in America is a good education. And she set the example, studying alongside my brother and me at our kitchen table so that she could become a registered nurse. We worked hard. I poured myself into my studies at Cardinal Spellman High School, earning scholarships to Princeton University and then Yale Law School, while my brother went on to medical school. Our achievements are due to the values that we learned as children, and they have continued to guide my life's endeavors. I try to pass on this legacy by serving as a mentor and friend to my many godchildren and to students of all backgrounds.

Over the past three decades, I have seen our judicial system from a number of different perspectives—as a big-city prosecutor, as a corporate litigator, as a trial judge, and as an appellate judge. My first job after law school was as an assistant district attorney in New York. There I saw children exploited and abused. I felt the pain and suffering of families torn apart by the needless death of loved ones. I saw and learned the tough job law enforcement has in protecting the public. In my next legal job, I focused on commercial instead of criminal matters. I litigated issues on behalf of national and international businesses and advised them on matters ranging from contracts to trademarks.

My career as an advocate ended, and my career as a judge began, when I was appointed by President George H. W. Bush to the United States District Court for the Southern District of New York. As a trial judge, I did decide over 450 cases and presided over dozens of trials, with perhaps my most famous case being the Major League Baseball strike in 1995.

After six extraordinary years on the district court, I was appointed by President Clinton to the United States Court of Appeals for the Second Circuit. On that court, I have enjoyed the benefit of sharing ideas and perspectives with wonderful colleagues as we have worked together to resolve the issues before us. I have now served as an appellate judge for over a decade, deciding a wide range of constitutional, statutory, and other legal questions.

Throughout my seventeen years on the bench, I have witnessed the human consequences of my decisions. Those decisions have not been made to serve the interests of any one litigant, but always to serve the larger interests of impartial justice. In the past month, many senators have asked me about my judicial philosophy.

Simple: fidelity to the law. The task of a judge is not to make law. It is to apply the law. And it is clear, I believe, that my record in two courts reflects my rigorous commitment to interpreting the Constitution according to its terms, interpreting statutes according to their terms and Congress's intent, and hewing faithfully to precedents established by the Supreme Court and by my circuit court. In each case I have heard, I have applied the law to the facts at hand.

The process of judging is enhanced when the arguments and concerns of the parties to the litigation are understood and acknowledged. That is why I generally structure my opinions by setting out what the law requires and then explaining why a contrary position, sympathetic or not, is accepted or rejected. That is how I seek to strengthen both the rule of law and faith in the impartiality of our judicial system. My personal and professional experiences helped me to listen and understand, with the law always commanding the result in every case.

Since President Obama announced my nomination in May, I have received letters from people all over this country. Many tell a unique story of hope in spite of struggle. Each letter has deeply touched me. Each reflects a dream—a belief in the dream that led my parents to come to New York all those years ago. It is our Constitution that makes that dream possible, and I now seek the honor of upholding the Constitution as a justice on the Supreme Court.

Senators, I look forward in the next few days to answering your questions, to having the American people learn more about me, and to being part of a process that reflects the greatness of our Constitution and of our nation. Thank you.

Questions for Analysis and Discussion

1. What was the purpose of Sotomayor's speech? How did she address it in the introduction?

2. How did she get her audience's attention?

3. What did she do to relate her topic to her audience?

4. How did Sotomayor establish her credibility in the beginning of her speech?

5. What was the thesis of her speech? How did she weave it into the introduction?

6. What did Sotomayor say to summarize her main points?

7. How did she reinforce the purpose of her speech?

8. How did she provide closure?

9. If you were advising this speaker on how to improve the way she began and ended her speech, what would you suggest?

10. What have you learned about speech introductions and conclusions that you'll apply in your own speeches?

Summary

In the speech introduction you get the audience's attention, indicate your purpose and thesis, establish your credibility, and preview your speech's main points. In creating the attention getter, consider your specific purpose and how much time you have to give the speech. Also, use your creativity and imagination to find a way to make your audience sit up, take notice, and want to listen to your speech. Present your thesis clearly, so the audience understands the response you expect. Let the audience know you're an expert on your topic. Complete the introduction by previewing your main points.

In your conclusion, review your main points, reinforce your specific purpose, and provide closure. Strategies for providing closure including ending with a quotation, making a dramatic statement, referring to the introduction, referring to subsequent events, reinforcing the speaker–audience connection, and thanking the audience. Increase the likelihood you'll achieve your specific purpose by leaving your audience with a lasting and positive impression.

Directory of Study and Review Resources

IN THE BOOK
Summary
Key Terms
Critical Challenges

MORE STUDY RESOURCES
Quizzes
WebLinks
Peer-reviewed videos

STUDENT WORKBOOK
9.1: Solid Previews
9.2: Introductions and Conclusions
9.3: Notable Quotables
9.4: Imitable Introductions
9.5: Sounding Like You're Done

SPEECH BUDDY VIDEOS
WATCH It Video
9.1: Beginning Effectively: Introductions
9.2: Ending Effectively: Conclusions
USE It Activity
9.1: Here We Go
9.2: It's a Wrap

SAMPLE SPEECH VIDEOS
Katy, "Why Pi?" informative speech
Mary Fisher, "A Whisper of AIDS," persuasive speech

SPEECH BUILDER EXPRESS
Introduction
Conclusion

INFOTRAC
Recommended search terms
Speech introduction
Attention getter
Humor in speeches
Establishing credibility in public speaking
Speech conclusion

AUDIO STUDY TOOLS
"Why Pi?" by Katy
Critical thinking questions
Learning objectives
Chapter summary

Guide to Your Online Resources

CourseMate Your Speech Communication CourseMate for *Public Speaking: The Evolving Art* gives you access to the Speech Buddy video and activity featured in this chapter, additional sample speech videos, Speech Studio, Speech Builder Express, InfoTrac College Edition, and study aids such as glossary flashcards, review quizzes, and the Critical Challenge questions for this chapter, which you can respond to via e-mail if your instructor so requests. In addition, your CourseMate features live WebLinks relevant to this chapter. Links are regularly maintained, and new ones are added periodically.

Key Terms

attention getter 173

conclusion 179

introduction 172

memorable message 180

preview of main points 178

primacy effect 173

recency effect 179

review of main points 180

Critical Challenges

Questions for Reflection and Discussion

1. Getting the audience's attention is a primary function of the introduction to your speech. What must ethical speakers consider when getting the attention of the audience? (You might want to refer to the section on ethical communication principles in Chapter 3.) For example, how might a statistic or fact be too startling? How might a story mislead the audience?

2. Speakers often neglect the conclusion of a speech and lose the opportunity to take advantage of the recency effect. What will you do to make sure you develop effective conclusions for your speeches?

3. Check out Speech Studio to analyze the introductions and conclusions of other students' speeches. Or record a speech you're working on, upload it to Speech Studio, and ask your peers for their feedback. What feedback could you use to fine-tune your introduction and conclusion before you give your speech in class?

10

Using Language Effectively

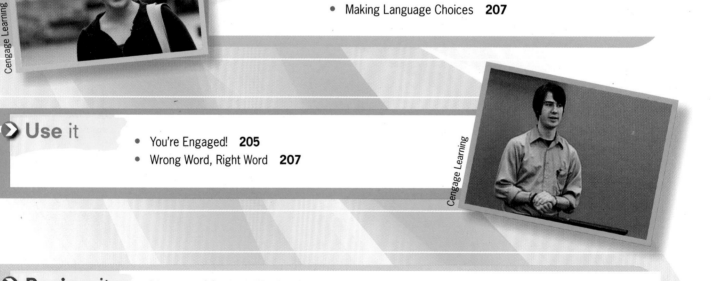

Cengage Learning

Cengage Learning

CourseMate   **SPEECH Studio**   BUILDER EXPRESS SPEECH

As keynote speaker at the 2004 Democratic National Convention in Boston, Barack Obama electrified his audience and launched himself into the national limelight. Without a single digital slide or video clip, Obama brought listeners to their feet and won accolades across the country through, as one newspaper noted, the "power of his words."[1] Effective language in public speaking invites audience members to listen, stirs their emotions, and touches their senses. Near the end of his speech, Obama said

> I'm talking about something more substantial. It's the hope of slaves sitting around a fire singing freedom songs. The hope of immigrants setting out for distant shores…. The hope of a skinny kid with a funny name who believes that America has a place for him, too. Hope in the face of difficulty. Hope in the face of uncertainty. The audacity of hope![2]

You could summarize that quote with something like, "Hope is important to achieving our goals." But those words wouldn't adequately describe what Obama was able to achieve. Why not? That's what you'll find out in this chapter.

STAN HONDA/AFP/Getty Images

Language refers to the system of words people use when communicating with others. The power of language rests in its ability to create images in the minds of listeners. Those images inform, persuade, and entertain audience members. When you speak in public, your words also encourage your audience to think, reason, contemplate, feel, evaluate, and otherwise respond to what you have to say.

> The system of words people use to communicate with others.

How do words work? Words are **symbols** that stand for something else—material things such as an object, person, place, or event. Symbols may also represent ideas that are more abstract, such as freedom, justice, and happiness. Words don't *transfer* information or ideas from your mind to others' minds. Instead, words *trigger* the meanings and thoughts people have for words in their minds. So when Barack Obama said, "It's the hope of slaves sitting around a fire singing freedom songs," his words brought up an image for each person in the audience, but not everyone had the same image. This example underscores the arbitrary, ambiguous, abstract, and active nature of language.

> Something, such as a word, that stands for something else, such as a person, place, thing, or idea.

Language Is Arbitrary

Researchers have identified more than 6,800 languages spoken by people around the world.[3] The vast number of languages suggests that the meanings of words are arbitrary. Because there's no direct connection between a word and what it represents, different groups of people have different words that stand for the same things. **Figure 10.1** demonstrates that when you have an idea or thought, there's a clear association between the object that led to your thought and the words you choose to express that thought. But there's no direct link between the object itself and the words you choose.

Consider the word *tree*. In Dutch, the word is *boom*. In Greek, it's *dentro*. In Japanese, *tree* is 木 . And in Spanish, you'd say *árbol*. Each language has a different way of representing what is called "tree" in English. That's why language is considered arbitrary.

Communicators use words to stand for their thoughts and ideas. The link between a word and what it stands for always goes through your mind.[4] As the example in **Figure 10.2** shows, the person views some palm trees, triggering the memory of a vacation in Florida, and then says, "Palm trees remind me of the Florida Keys."

> An individual's internal process of assigning meaning to words.

The meanings others assign to the words you use—their **interpretations**—may not be what you intend. Former Education Secretary Ron Paige found this out when he referred to the National Education Association (NEA) as a "terrorist organization" in a conversation about education reform with some of the nation's governors.[5] Paige argued that the teachers' union stood in the way of change and misrepresented its members' wishes. But even those who agreed with him noted that the negative feelings associated with the word *terrorist* obscured Paige's main point. After educators and politicians criticized his characterization of the NEA, he apologized for his word choice.

Language Is Ambiguous

Speakers usually assume that if they say "X," others will think "X." But that's not necessarily the case. Language is

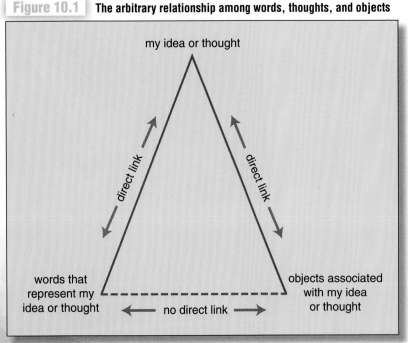

Figure 10.1 **The arbitrary relationship among words, thoughts, and objects**

my idea or thought

direct link

direct link

words that represent my idea or thought

← no direct link →

objects associated with my idea or thought

Source: Adapted from Ogden & Richards (1923).

ambiguous—words have multiple meanings and individuals have their own meanings, or associations, for words and the concepts those words stand for. **Denotative meanings** refer to formal, or literal, meanings—the definitions you find in dictionaries. **Connotative meanings** are the unique meanings you have for words based on your own experiences.

Even words you might think of as straightforward, such as the word *car*, can have multiple meanings. The *Compact Oxford English Dictionary* lists two definitions: "a powered road vehicle designed to carry a small number of people" and "a railway carriage or … wagon." But that's just the beginning. *Webster's Revised Unabridged Dictionary* lists seven definitions, including "a chariot of war or triumph," "the cage or lift of an elevator," and "a floating perforated box for living fish." Investorwords.com explains that in the financial world *car* means "The amount of a commodity underlying a commodity futures contract." According

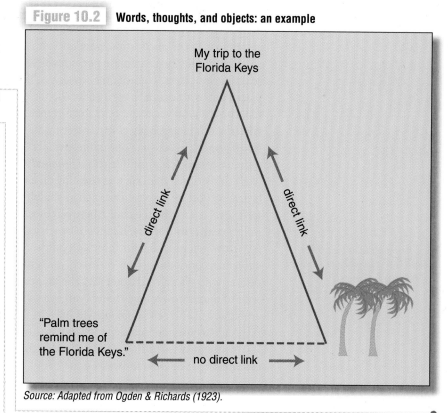

Figure 10.2 | **Words, thoughts, and objects: an example**

My trip to the Florida Keys

direct link

direct link

"Palm trees remind me of the Florida Keys."

no direct link

Source: Adapted from Ogden & Richards (1923).

An agreed-upon definition of a word found in a dictionary.

A unique meaning for a word based on an individual's own experiences.

"*And since when is loyalty a bad word?*"

to *Dorland's Illustrated Medical Dictionary*, CAR refers to the Canadian Association of Radiologists.[6] And those are just the denotative meanings. Think about all the meanings you associate with *car*, such as independence, financial burden, and traveling.

The ambiguity of language pervades all aspects of the speechmaking process. When selecting your topic, consider the words you'll choose to identify it. Would you refer to plagiarism as academic *integrity* or academic *dishonesty*? Would a speech on plans to repurpose a local vacant lot refer to *open space* or to *undeveloped land*? In a speech on the effects of our increasingly global society, would you use the term *antiglobalization* or the term *global justice*? To take just one of these examples, consider the differences between academic dishonesty and academic integrity. *Dishonesty* has negative connotations; listeners will likely think of activities such as cheating on a test or plagiarizing a speech outline. *Integrity* brings up positive associations such as studying for a test and carefully documenting sources for a speech. Making the choice between those two words—*dishonesty* and *integrity*—will influence the **tone** or general mood associated with the speech (Chapter 3).

Use of language to set the mood or atmosphere associated with a speaking situation

How you phrase your topic will guide you in framing the idea, analyzing your audience, conducting your research, and choosing your supporting materials. When you deliver your speech (Chapter 12), the language you use to frame and define your topic will influence how your listeners interpret your message. It's during delivery that the ambiguous nature of language will have its most obvious effects. The way your audience responds to your speech depends in part on the language you choose.

Ambiguity isn't necessarily bad, and can even work in your favor. In his speech, for example, Barack Obama stressed the commonalities Americans share:

> Tonight, we gather to affirm the greatness of our nation—not because of the height of our skyscrapers, or the power of our military, or the size of our economy. Our pride is based on a very simple premise, summed up in a declaration made over 200 years ago: "We hold these truths to be self-evident, that all men are created equal. That they are endowed by their Creator with certain inalienable rights. That among these are life, liberty and the pursuit of happiness." That is the true genius of America—a faith in simple dreams, an insistence on small miracles.

Simple dreams, small miracles, life, and *liberty*—these words mean many different things to Americans. Yet they're deeply embedded in American culture, so they call up positive connotations for listeners. Even so, the audience might view these words positively but still not agree on how to define them.

Language Is Abstract

You experience your world with all your senses—you smell bread baking, you see a friend smiling, you taste a square of chocolate, you touch the computer keyboard, you hear a coworker laughing. These things exist in the physical world. Although communicators say, hear, write, and read words, what those words represent is abstract. You can place your hand on this page and touch the printed words, but the meanings those words conjure up exist in your mind.

Although all words are abstract, they vary in their level of abstractness. Some words are fairly specific, such as "my friend Kyoung." Others are very abstract, such as "human being." **Figure 10.3** shows how words vary along a continuum from more to less abstract. In the example, "living thing" is the most abstract—the phrase could refer to plants or animals, humans or insects. The words become less abstract as you progress up the levels until you reach a particular living thing, 12-year-old Pink-White, a famous sea otter living in Monterey Bay, California.

U.S. Representative Tammy Baldwin used different levels of abstraction to her advantage in her speech at the Millennium March for Gay and Lesbian Rights in Washington, D.C. At each point in her speech, she contrasted language that is more abstract with specific examples:

Figure 10.3 Levels of abstraction in language

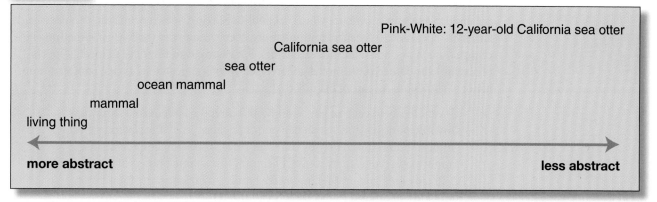

Pink-White: 12-year-old California sea otter
California sea otter
sea otter
ocean mammal
mammal
living thing

more abstract ⟵⟶ **less abstract**

Never doubt that there is a reason to be hopeful. Never doubt that Congress will pass legislation that expands the definition of hate crimes … But we must make it so—by daring to dream of a world in which we are free. So, if you dream of a world in which you can put your partner's picture on your desk, then put his picture on your desk—and you will live in such a world.[7]

By invoking abstract, yet powerful, words, Baldwin provided common ground for the audience to agree with her. Then, using less abstract terms, she told listeners how they could put those abstract ideas into action.

Language Is Active

Like time, language doesn't stand still. As people learn new things about the world and encounter new experiences, they develop new words. Before the internet, words such as *phishing, webisode,* and *blog* didn't exist. Each year, *Merriam-Webster's Collegiate Dictionary* adds about 100 words to its current edition.[8]

Similarly, specific events change the meanings of words. For example, after the 9/11 attacks, *jihad* developed negative connotations. In a Harvard University commencement address, Zayed Muhammed Yasin, a senior graduating with a degree in biomedical engineering, explained the original meaning of *jihad*:

> The word for *struggle* in Arabic, in the language of my faith, is *jihad*. It is a word that has been corrupted and misinterpreted, both by those who do and do not claim to be Muslims, and we saw last fall, to our great national and personal loss, the results of this corruption. Jihad, in its truest and purest form, the form to which all Muslims aspire, is the determination to do right, to do justice even against your own interests. It is an individual struggle for personal moral behavior.[9]

In his speech, Yasin acknowledged the impact of 9/11 on the meaning of *jihad* and sought to replace negative associations with more positive ones.

Communicators continually alter the meanings of words. The advent of the internet brought with it new meanings for *spam, zombie,* and *cookie.* You might think the term web*page* traces its origins from the pages of a printed book. Yet scrolling through a page on a website is more like unrolling and reading a papyrus document from ancient Egypt.[10] After the 2004 tsunami that devastated Asia, many businesses reconsidered their use of the word. For example, Toyota changed the name of its Celica Tsunami to Celica Sport Package and a water park in Ohio replaced Tsunami pool with Whitecap.

Speaking of . . .

Engaging in Lexpionage

New words enter the English language daily—the Global Language Monitor (languagemonitor.com) estimates English gains one new word every 98 minutes or nearly 15 new words each day. Want to find out more about them? Websites such as Word Spy (wordspy.com), the *Macmillan English Dictionary* (macmillandictionary.com), and Double-Tongued Dictionary (doubletongued.org), will clue you in on the latest additions. The American Dialect Society (ADS; americandialect.org), identifies the most influential words of the year. For example, ADS members voted *tweet* as the Word of the Year for 2009 and *google* as the word of the decade. Ten years earlier, *Y2K* was the top choice, *web* was the word of the decade, and *jazz* was the word of the century.

Language is dynamic in another way, too. You've probably heard sayings such as "All talk, no action" and "Actions speak louder than words." Yet language *is* action. You accomplish goals when you use words. In public speaking, speakers inform, persuade, and entertain. Speakers get listeners to think more deeply, laugh out loud, learn something new, change their views, and alter their behaviors. For example, in response to media reports of his infidelity, famed professional golfer Tiger Woods appeared in a press conference on national television. As part of his speech, he said,

> I want to say to each of you, simply, and directly, I am deeply sorry for my irresponsible and selfish behavior I engaged in…. I was wrong. I was foolish. I don't get to play by different rules. The same boundaries that apply to everyone apply to me. I brought this shame on myself. I hurt my wife, my kids, my mother, my wife's family, my friends, my foundation, and kids all around the world who admired me.[11]

The speech served as an apology for Tiger Woods' behavior. You take similar actions with words in your everyday conversations. You promise, calm down, cheer up, compliment, accuse, blame, support, criticize, affecting those around you with words.

Language and Culture

Language and culture are inseparable: how you use language reflects your culture, and your culture influences the language you use and how you interpret it. Consider how people in the United States refer to time. You probably say things like, "That's a waste of time," "I like spending time with you," and "Time is money." Most Americans view time as a commodity that can be given ("I can give you a few minutes of my time") and taken away ("I won't take much of your time"). You likely think of time as something you "own," referring to "my" time and "your" time. The words people use give strong clues about what's important in a culture and what's not.

Americans generally consider speech and speaking extremely important, in part because the U.S. Constitution guarantees free speech. *FreeThesaurus.net* lists almost three hundred synonyms for *speak*—words such as *articulate, chatter, gab, muse, take the floor,* and *vocalize*. Yet listening—a central aspect of democracy as well—doesn't get nearly the attention that speaking gets. *FreeThesaurus.net* includes just thirty-one synonyms for *listen,* about one-tenth the number for *speak*.[12] Even though communicators listen more than they speak, American culture puts a much greater emphasis on speaking than on listening.

Culture tells you what words mean and the associations you should have for them. For example, in the aftermath of Hurricane Katrina, controversy arose over what to call people in New Orleans and other areas who were forced to flee their homes. Were they victims? Survivors? Displaced persons? Refugees? Each word calls up a different image. Generally, *refugee* refers to an individual who crosses international borders to avoid political or religious persecution. So the word suggested that the now-homeless people in Louisiana and Mississippi were not U.S. citizens. Yet *displaced person* missed the enormity of the problem. Most media organizations settled on *evacuee* and *flood victim,* although these terms did not fully capture the dire circumstances many people faced.[13] And choosing to use one word over another can lead to different outcomes. For example, people are more likely to buy a "pre-owned" car than a "used" one—even when it's the exact same car.

In public speaking contexts, culture becomes especially evident when speakers use slang, jargon, idioms, euphemisms, and clichés. **Slang** refers to informal language typically used in an interpersonal setting, such as *whatever, all that,* and *word*. Because public speaking is more formal than conversations with your friends, you'll want to avoid using slang in speeches. Slang can hurt your credibility, giving your audience the impression that you're not taking the event seriously or are unprepared.

Jargon is technical language associated with a specific profession or subject. Since the beginning of the war in Iraq, some military jargon has become more

Informal, nonstandard language, often used within a particular group.

Technical language used by members of a profession or associated with a specific topic.

commonplace, such as MRE (meal, ready to eat), IED (improvised explosive device), and SOP (standard operating procedure). Both slang and jargon require an insider's knowledge to understand what the words mean. If you're part of the military culture, for example, you've internalized its jargon as part of your own vocabulary. Similarly, jargon associated with new communication technologies frequently finds its way into everyday conversations. People *text, blog,* and *chat.* Computer users are concerned about *spam, viruses,* and *malware,* and look for *hotspots* so they can go *wireless.*

Idioms are expressions whose practical meanings are very different from their literal meanings. Listeners must have a solid command of the language as people use it in everyday conversation to interpret an idiom correctly. Here are some examples of the literal meanings of idioms and their common interpretations:

> An expression that means something other than the literal meaning of the words.

- That test was a piece of cake.

  Literal meaning: That test was a confection made of flour, sugar, and eggs.
  Idiomatic meaning: That test was easy.

- You'd better hit the books if you're going to pass your classes.

  Literal meaning: You'd better strike your books with your hand or an object if you're going to pass your classes.

  Idiomatic meaning: You'd better study if you're going to pass your classes.

- Would you lend me your ear for a few minutes?

  Literal meaning: Would you remove your ear and give it to me for a few minutes?

  Idiomatic meaning: Would you listen to me for a few minutes?

You might laugh at the literal meanings if you've grown up speaking English, because you're so accustomed to hearing and using idioms—you don't even think about how you've learned to interpret them.

Speakers use **euphemisms** in place of words that are viewed as more disagreeable or offensive. For example, pornographic movies are called "adult films," and those who star in such movies become "adult entertainers." Euphemisms can prove useful if you're concerned you might offend your audience. For the most part, though, euphemistic language simply confuses listeners. For example, organizations typically refer to employee layoffs and firings as "downsizing" and "rightsizing," which may sound less harsh, but not to the people who have lost their jobs.

> A word used in place of another word that is viewed as more disagreeable or offensive.

Clichés are trite or obvious expressions—phrases used so often they lack any important meaning. At one point, the remark was original, but overuse has made it dull. Examples of clichés include "the big picture," "thinking outside the box," and "better late than never." Clichés cause problems for speakers in two ways. First, as with slang, jargon, idioms, and euphemisms, listeners must possess the cultural knowledge to interpret clichés. Second, because clichés are overused, listeners may think they've heard the speaker's message before and lose interest in the speech.

> An expression so overused it fails to have any important meaning.

Universal Press Syndicate.

If you've grown up in the United States and English is your first language, you probably wouldn't be fazed by someone saying, "My bad," "Let's Skype later," "We're on the same page," "I fell on my tush ice skating," and "Money doesn't grow on trees." But not all your audience members will have the cultural knowledge necessary to understand slang, jargon, idioms, euphemisms, and clichés. Unless they're an essential part of your speech, minimize your use of these types of language.

Language and Gender

Language and gender intersect with public speaking in two ways. First, how listeners interpret what speakers say can depend on the listeners' gender.[14] Let's take an example from research on powerful and powerless language. Powerful language conveys the speaker's certainty about the topic. "This proposal will win over our client!" and "Our team effort led to our success" make clear the speaker's confidence. Audience members view speakers who use powerful language as dynamic and competent. Powerless language such as "I guess," "sorta," and "right?" indicates uncertainty and hurts a speaker's credibility.[15] Even in everyday conversations, listeners are less likely to believe someone who sounds uncertain.

Researchers usually categorize **tag questions** as powerless language. Speakers tack on tag questions at the end of a sentence, as in "This proposal will win over our client, *don't you think*?" Men usually interpret "don't you think?" as uncertainty. But women generally view "don't you think?" as an invitation for others to state their opinions. Similarly, **hedges**—words that qualify what the speaker is saying—often function differently for men than for women. Women might interpret "Our team effort *likely* led to our success" as acknowledging that other factors may have contributed to the group's accomplishments. For men, "likely" could indicate a speaker's self-doubt.[16] In addition, listeners evaluate a woman as less competent when she uses tag questions and hedges, whereas such language has little impact on how listeners evaluate men.[17]

Powerful language can lead to similar misunderstandings. Statements such as "This research leaves no doubt that the program will fail" and "Employee morale has never been higher" convey certainty and conviction. But for women such language can also convey arrogance and disdain for other perspectives.

Second, using language that excludes or demeans some audience members will cause many of them to stop listening to you. To be sure, you're addressing all members of your audience equally, use **nonsexist language**, or words that are not associated with either sex. Consider the difference between *stewardess* and *flight attendant*. The first word suggests a woman; the second could be a woman or a man. **Table 10.1** provides some examples of nonsexist alternatives to sexist language. Using nonsexist language also refers to the order in which speakers refer to people. Generally, listeners think of the first item in a list as the most important and the last as the least important. Do you always say "men and women," "boys and girls," "husband and wife"? To avoid privileging one sex over the other, rotate the order of gendered terms.

Also, avoid language that demeans either women or men. For example, referring to a "female doctor" suggests that women aren't typically physicians. Yet a recent survey found that 25 percent of all U.S. physicians and 41 percent of physicians younger than 40 were women.[18] Use inclusive pronouns, as in "A bicyclist should always wear her or his helmet." Better yet, use the plural and avoid gendered language, such as "Bicyclists should always wear their helmets."

Using nonsexist or gender-neutral language in your speeches also means using similar language for women and men when describing them and their accomplishments. From sports to political campaigns, women and men are often portrayed in very different ways.[19] For example, sportscasters typically describe male athletes in terms of their physical abilities but describe female athletes in terms of their personalities, looks, appearance, and sexual attractiveness.[20] Consider the differences in these two statements: "His ability to make the key shots is amazing!" and "She looks fabulous in the team's new uniform!"

A question added onto the end of a declarative statement that lessens the impact of that statement.

A qualifier, such as *probably*, that makes a statement ambiguous.

Words that are not associated with either sex.

194

Table 10.1 Replacing Sexist Language with Nonsexist Language

Instead of saying this . . .	Say this . . .
mankind	humankind, humanity
man-hours	staff hours, hours
the common man	ordinary people, average person
chairman	chair, chairperson
freshman	first-year student
waitress/waiter	server
male nurse	nurse
lady lawyer	lawyer
career woman	professional

The bias works both ways. When talking about a man in the nursing profession, a speaker might say, "He's so sensitive and caring." Yet those are qualities you'd associated with any nurse. In the 2008 presidential election, you heard about "hockey moms" and "NASCAR dads." Yet women make up nearly 40 percent of NASCAR fans,[21] and plenty of dads go to their kids' hockey games.

So far, you've learned about the general characteristics and qualities of language. Although written and spoken language share these general traits, they differ in important ways. Since audience members listen to your words rather than reading them, use spoken language in your speeches. The remainder of the chapter focuses more specifically on spoken language.

Spoken versus Written Language

Because spoken and written language differ in important ways, audiences find memorized speeches or speeches read word for word ponderous and difficult to follow. Audiences usually prefer an extemporaneous delivery method (Chapter 12), in which speakers use conversational and engaging language. The specific differences between written and spoken language are explored in this section.

Dynamic versus Static

Public speaking occurs "in the moment" as the speaker and the audience come together to create a speaking event. As a result, speaking is dynamic. Unless participants record the event in some way, what they say is fleeting and impermanent. Listeners will recall some of what they hear, but they can't go back and rehear what you've said. Redundancy helps overcome the transient nature of spoken language, and audience members expect some redundancy to help them recall what the speaker said. Speakers therefore preview main points, provide internal summaries, and review key ideas in the conclusion. In contrast, written language is static. Readers can reread a passage of text over and over again, so they don't need the redundancy that listeners need.

Immediate versus Distant

The immediacy of spoken language affects public speaking in several ways. First, listeners receive the message right away, while the speaker

Xavi Arnau/iStockphoto

Audiences today prefer speakers who use engaging, conversational language.

is talking, and can provide nearly instantaneous feedback. In contrast, writers receive no immediate feedback from their audiences. Second, public speaking involves all the senses—audience members hear how the words are spoken and see how the speaker uses nonverbal communication. Gestures, movements, and vocal intonations provide a context for the words speakers use. Third, immediacy allows speakers to refer to the situation in which the speech is taking place. So speakers can make comments such as "I can see you've dressed for the warm weather we're supposed to get later today" and "How many of you have studied for your finals next week?" John Furlong, CEO for the Vancouver Organizing Committee, referred to the speaking situation as he began his remarks at the opening of the 2010 Winter Olympics:

> Excellencies, president and members of the International Olympic Committee, members of the Olympic family, athletes of the world, ladies and gentlemen: *bienvenue*—welcome to Vancouver. I commit that the men and women of Vancouver 2010—our partners and our friends—are ready to deliver the performance of a lifetime. As you, the best Winter Olympic athletes of all time, enter the arena prepared for you here in Canada to compete in the honor and glory of sport—seizing the moment to inspire the youth of the world through your heroic efforts—you carry with you the hopes and the dreams of so many.[22]

Furlong sprinkled in other references to the speaking event, such as "And tonight the longest domestic torch relay in Olympic history ends in this stadium…" and "On this, the proudest night of my life …." Even brief references to the speaking situation make audience members feel as if you're speaking with them personally.

Informal versus Formal

When you talk with friends, neighbors, coworkers, and others, your language is rather informal. You might say, "Hey, what's up?" and "How's your day?" You use slang and jargon. Your sentences are short and often incomplete. Ordinarily, in these interpersonal situations you're not concerned with choosing the perfect words to express your ideas. In contrast, the language you use when you give a speech is more formal than your everyday conversations, yet still conversational. However, you don't speak as casually in your speeches as you do with your friends, even if your friends are in the audience.

Irreversible versus Revisable

Once you've said something, it's out there. You can try to take it back, but listeners will still have heard what you said. You can immediately correct what you've said, as with, "Oh, sorry. I meant to say North Dakota, not South Dakota." In addition, you can reframe statements. For example, Fox News newscaster Greg Gutfeld made fun of Canadian soldiers in Afghanistan, saying they wanted to "do some yoga, paint landscapes, [and] run on the beach in gorgeous white capri pants."[23] He later explained that he intended his remarks to be humorous and lighthearted. Question-and-answer sessions also allow you to further clarify and elaborate on what you say in a speech. Shortly after her visit to Darfur, Sudan, Angelina Jolie spoke at the National Press Club in her role as goodwill ambassador for the United Nations High Commissioner for Refugees. After Jolie's formal remarks about the plight of refugee children, journalists asked her for specifics about several topics, such as the National Center for Refugee and Immigrant Children that she recently helped establish. These questions provided a venue for Jolie to elaborate on U.S. and UN plans for addressing the needs of young refugees.[24]

Unlike spoken language, written language allows for nearly infinite revisions—at least until the deadline for submitting a document. For example, this book underwent many, many revisions and multiple drafts as we worked to make the text right for you, our audience.

Narratives versus Facts

Although you often read stories, storytelling has its roots in oral communication. With its informality and immediacy, spoken language provides an ideal vehicle for telling a dramatic and engaging story. Oral language allows audience participation, sometimes including nonverbal feedback and additional information. The next time you're with friends or family, observe what happens when someone starts telling a story. Others likely will jump in with a bit of dialogue or description. When you're telling a story, it's often a group effort.

Written language handles facts, statistics, and other technical information more readily than spoken language because readers have time to review numbers and facts. Listeners don't have that luxury. Citing too many facts and statistics during a speech loses their attention—they can't comprehend all the information in one sitting.

Rhythm versus Image

Spoken language has a rhythm or a flow that helps listeners interpret words. For example, a speaker's vocal pitch goes up with a question and down at the end of a sentence. Speakers pause to give audience members time to contemplate an idea, and speak more loudly when emphasizing a point. Vocal qualities, including pitch, rate, tone, and volume, give additional meaning to a speaker's words.

In contrast, written language is rich in images. Writers and publishers choose specific fonts and layouts for organizing text to increase readability and interest. Arranging text in tables and charts clarifies the writer's ideas. This text, for example, includes tables and figures to visually summarize and highlight key ideas.

Keep the differences between spoken and written language in mind as you read the next section on using audience-centered language in your speeches.

Audience-centered Language

Language geared toward your audience helps you get your message across in a way that resonates with them. You vary the words you use based on the intended recipients and the situation. For example, you use different language when welcoming newcomers to a student organization than when welcoming friends to a get-together in your home.

Your success as a speaker depends in part on using words that appeal to your audience.[25] This section, summarized in **Table 10.2** on page 198 describes ways to develop audience-centered language in your speech: Put your language in context, personalize your language, use inclusive language, use visual language, and spark imagination with your language.

Put Your Language in Context

The in-the-moment qualities of public speaking work to your advantage. Integrating comments about the physical location, current events, and the speech situation brings spontaneity to your speech and keeps your listeners interested. For a report you're presenting at work, for instance, you might begin with, "The original idea for this project began in this very room, with many of you who are here today sitting around this conference table." Or maybe you're giving a speech of welcome to new students. You could say, "This campus—the people, buildings, and traditions—may seem strange to you now. But by the end of the semester what you see around you today will be familiar and comforting—almost like home." These direct references to the context in which

Table 10.2 Audience-Centered Language

Put your language in context by . . .	• mentioning the location • referring to current events • responding to what happens during the speech
Personalize your language by . . .	• integrating audience analysis information • remarking on what other speakers have said using "we," "us," "you," and "I"
Use inclusive language by . . .	• avoiding language that discriminates and stereotypes
Use visual language by incorporating . . .	• similes • metaphors • parallelism • rhyme • alliteration • antithesis
Spark imagination with your language by using . . .	• imaginative invitations • humor

you're speaking help you gain and maintain your listeners' attention and lets them know you've designed the speech for them.

At a concert in South Africa to raise funds for Nelson Mandela's HIV/AIDS awareness campaign, musician Annie Lennox brought the context into her speech in several ways:

> We have come here tonight to bring your attention to an unacceptable situation. What I have to say is going to alarm you …and you need to be alarmed in order to wake up to the fact that the AIDS crisis has reached unprecedented epidemic proportions. Among men, women, and children, here and in other parts of Africa, AIDS is effectively causing mass genocide. Let me give you some facts …In Africa, more people are wiped out by AIDS every year than in the entire Asian tsunami disaster. There are probably 25,000 people here in the stadium tonight …look around and take it in …now double that number …every day, more than two stadiums like this become infected with HIV. It's horrific …think about it. And for every ten that are infected… six are women.[26]

Lennox began by referring to the concert's purpose. Comparing the death toll from the tsunami disaster in Asia to AIDS deaths in Africa linked her topic to a cataclysmic event in recent memory. Then she asked her listeners to "look around" at the 25,000 people in the stadium and imagine twice that number becoming infected with HIV every day. Lennox could have said, "Fifty thousand people contract HIV every day," but visualizing two stadiums filled with concert attendees had a much greater impact.

Putting context in your language also means responding to events that happen during your speech. If many people were to applaud during a speech of tribute, for example, you could say, "I can tell you agree with me" or, "I share your enthusiasm." In your public speaking class, you might acknowledge audience feedback by saying, "I see a lot of heads nodding" or "Some of you look puzzled."

Personalize Your Language

In most public speaking situations, you and your audience share the same physical space. Even with video conferencing, speakers and listeners hear and see each other. When you are the speaker, this gives you an opportunity to personalize your speech, using language tailored to your audience that promotes dialogue and collaboration (Chapter 3).

In your public speaking class, you get to know your audience from the speeches they give and from your audience analysis (Chapter 5). Integrating information from audience questionnaires can help maintain your audience's attention. You might say something like "Based on your responses to my questionnaire, about half of you exercise once a week and a quarter of you exercise almost every day," or "Your responses to my questionnaire helped me narrow down my topic."

Musician and activist Annie Lennox effectively referred to the speech context when she spoke about HIV/AIDS awareness at a fundraising concert. She asked her listeners to look around at 25,000 people in the stadium and imagine twice that number in Africa getting infected with HIV every day.

You can make your speeches even more personal by referring to specific people in the class. You might even refer to a speech presented earlier in the term, as with "As Sondra mentioned in her speech a few weeks ago …," or to one given shortly before yours, as with "In his speech a few minutes ago, Trent said …." During your speech, you might also comment on a specific audience member's nonverbal communication: "Dana, you look skeptical. Let me tell you more about my idea…."

Audiences expect some informality in spoken language, such as using the pronouns *we, us, you,* and *I* in your speeches. Using these pronouns includes the audience in your speech and encourages them to listen. For example, if you're speaking at a meeting of a student organization, you might say, "We've raised awareness of three important issues on this campus" or, "I'm proud of the work you've accomplished in raising awareness on these three important campus issues."

Words like *we* and *us* let your audience know you share similar experiences, values, beliefs, and attitudes. In her "Consciousness Is Power" speech at the 1995 Asian American Convocation at Brown University, Yuri Kochiyama said,

> How do we measure Asians? We are not a monolithic entity. We are many different ethnic people. We are Asian immigrants, Asian American, part Asian, Amerasian, Asian national, Asian adoptee (mostly Korean), and a Korean category that calls itself "1.5." We are divided by class, religion, culture, language, and political affiliation. But because of racism and discrimination inherent in this society, despite our differences, we are not just thrust together as Asians, but considered as "outsiders," foreigners, and "not quite Americans."[27]

Kochiyama uses *we* in every sentence. She's telling her audience that she understands their perspective because it's the same as hers.

Audience members also take notice when speakers use *you.* Near the end of her speech, Kochiyama appealed directly to her audience:

> For you young Asian American students, or students in general of any background, who are searching, who have the idealism and enthusiasm, and a natural love for all peoples—fight against racism, chauvinism,

and imperialism.... Your role can be that [of] supporters. You can also support political prisoners—most of whom are black, Puerto Rican, and American Indian. The world you will help develop will surely be more understanding, harmonious, and just, with equal opportunities; where human dignity and human rights become accessible to all. Leave new footsteps for those following after you.[28]

The word *you* makes Kochiyama's speech more persuasive. Read the same selection below, this time with *students* and *they* replacing *you*:

For young Asian American students, or students in general of any background, who are searching, who have the idealism and enthusiasm, and a natural love for all peoples—fight against racism, chauvinism, and imperialism.... Students' role can be that [of] supporters. Students can also support political prisoners—most of whom are black, Puerto Rican, and American Indian. The world students will help develop will surely be more understanding, harmonious, and just, with equal opportunities; where human dignity and human rights become accessible to all. Students should leave new footsteps for those following after them.

The words *students* and *they* create distance between the audience and the topic. In contrast, *you* personalizes the speech and make listeners feel included. In this example, *you* suggests that audience members can take action and make a difference. Saying *students* and *they* removes the audience from the scene and suggests that someone else—they—will solve the problem.

When you use the pronoun *I,* you let audience members know you're the one who thinks or believes a certain way. "It's important for all college students to take a public speaking class" doesn't have the same meaning—or the same force—as "I think all college students should take a public speaking class." In the first example, the speaker remains distant from the topic; listeners don't know whether she agrees with the statement or not. In the second example, the speaker takes a stand, letting the audience know her position.

Use Inclusive Language

When you use **inclusive language** in your speeches, you choose words that don't privilege one group over another. Noninclusive language promotes discrimination and stereotyping, even if the speaker's word choices are unintentional. Language that needlessly emphasizes someone's race, class, gender, age, dis/ability, sexual orientation, and the like is noninclusive.

Sexist language, discussed earlier in the chapter, provides a clear example of noninclusive language, but speakers may exclude groups in other ways. Here are some examples:

- Jeannette and her *Latina friend* Maria volunteer at a local food bank.

   Problem: Why identify Maria as Latina? Should you assume Jeannette is white?

- The *disabled actor* put on a great performance.

   Problem: If the person did not have a disability, would it be okay to say, "The nondisabled actor put on a great performance"? Of course not. What, then, would be the best way to identify the actor being discussed? Something like "The actor who played the lead role put on a great performance" works fine.

- She's the *senior citizen* on her crew team.

   Problem: Words such as *aged, elderly,* and *senior citizen* suggest the person is frail or impaired in some way. If the person's age is significant to the accomplishment,

inclusive language
Words that don't privilege one group over another.

Using inclusive language invites all audience members to listen to your speech.

include it, as in "At 75, she's the oldest active member of her crew team." If age isn't important, don't mention it, as in "She belongs to a crew team."

- The *primitive people* of Africa relied on oral communication to pass along cultural stories.

  Problem: Primitive implies deficiency or incompetence. Because the reference is to a time period, *early* is a more accurate word.

These may seem like small distinctions, but all instances of noninclusive language affect everyone—the people left out and the people singled out.

Using inclusive language doesn't mean talking about people only in generic terms. Sometimes the point you're making requires you to identify people by the various groups to which they belong. When Linda Chavez-Thompson addressed a Hotel Employees and Restaurant Employees convention on immigration reform, she used her own and others' ethnic backgrounds as examples of immigrants in the United States:

> Immigration is the very core of who we are as a movement. Just look at the executive officers of the AFL-CIO. John Sweeney is the son of immigrants from County Antrim, Ireland … Rich Trumka is from a family of Polish and Italian miners …and I am the daughter of Mexican American sharecroppers. Immigrants are the history of the union movement …but too often in the past, our movement hasn't fully embraced new immigrants.[29]

In this case, identifying each person's ethnic background demonstrated listeners' common bond as immigrants and served as inclusive language. Chavez-Thompson also used inclusive language at other points in her speech, such as "undocumented workers" rather than "illegal aliens" and "workers with disabilities" rather than "disabled workers."

Use Visual Language

Similes and metaphors are *analogies*—a shorthand way of comparing two dissimilar things. Language devices such as simile, metaphor, parallelism, rhyme, alliteration, and antithesis give your speech force and help your audience visualize your ideas.

Similes suggest that two things share some similar qualities. Similes use *like* and *as* to make a comparison, as in "That story is like an old friend" and "The car rode as smoothly as a tin can on plastic wheels." **Metaphors** equate one thing with another. They often compare something more abstract with something more concrete, such as "Life is a rollercoaster" and "Ideas are wildflowers." Similes and metaphors make your speech memorable by comparing things that listeners might not ordinarily think of as going together. For example, in a speech at the Kimmel Center for the Performing Arts, Minnesota high school student Laura Roehl compared embarking on the process of forgiveness with playing baseball, saying, "Even when life throws us a curve, it's time for us to step up to the plate—and play ball.[30] The image Roehl evoked likely stayed in the minds of listeners much longer than if she'd said, "So we need to forgive people."

Similes and metaphors also help audience members understand something unfamiliar by comparing it with something familiar. For example, Vice Admiral Richard H. Carmona, Surgeon General of the United States, said this in a speech presented at a conference on early childhood:

> I'm almost ashamed to say that the medical profession has too often *sent people with disabilities to the back of the bus*. The reality is that for too long we have provided lesser care to developmentally and physically disabled people.[31]

Carmona's reference to "the back of the bus" compared something familiar—the now-illegal practice in the southern United States of forcing African Americans to sit in the back of a public bus—to something that most audience members likely found unfamiliar: the medical treatment of persons with disabilities.

When using **parallelism**, speakers use the same phrase, wording, or clause multiple times to add emphasis. In a speech delivered at the Women's Soccer Breakfast hosted by the National Soccer Coaches Association of America, professional soccer player Yael Averbuch used parallelism when talking about her views on the game:

> I will always smile when I think about the time at UNC [University of North Carolina] when we were about to start our first of ten cones (a dreaded fitness drill) and, as Anson yelled, "GO!" we all fell to the ground as a joke.
>
> I will always look forward to being home in New Jersey, where I can go kick the ball around at the local schoolyard with my sister.
>
> I will always feel sentimental when I think about playing pickup on Fetzer Field, our UNC game field, in Chapel Hill at midnight, under the single light that's left on.
>
> I will always laugh when I reminisce on the absurdity and turbulence of Sky Blue FC's first season, when, it seems, we had more coaches than are currently sitting in this room.
>
> And my eyes will always light up when I see a ragtag group of guys playing soccer in some random park on the side of the road.[32]

The last phrase, "and my eyes will always light," gets its impact from the multiple repetitions of "I will always." Through her use of parallelism, Averbuch builds up interest—listeners know she loves soccer, but not why—and she holds her audience's attention.

You've likely heard **rhymes** since you were a young child. Rhyming words have similar sounds, usually the last syllable. Advertisers use rhyme to embed their products more clearly in our memories. For example, travel company Thomas Cook uses the slogan "Don't just book it. Thomas Cook it," and Alka-Seltzer coined "Plop, plop, fizz, fizz, oh what a relief it is." During O.J. Simpson's 1995 trial for the murder of his ex-wife, Simpson's attorney, Johnnie Cochran, used the phrase "If it doesn't fit, you must acquit"

A language device that compares two things that are generally dissimilar but share some common properties, expressed using *like* or *as*.

A language device that demonstrates the commonalities between two dissimilar things.

Using the same phrase, wording, or clause multiple times to add emphasis.

Using words with similar sounds, usually at the end of the word, to emphasize a point.

to point out perceived flaws in the district attorney's case. That phrase alone didn't win the jury's not-guilty verdict, but the rhyme helped jurors visualize the defense attorney's contention that the prosecutor's arguments were not supported by the evidence presented.

Speakers use **alliteration** when they repeat a sound in a series of words, usually the first consonant. Classic tongue twisters provide examples of alliteration, such as "She sells sea shells by the sea shore" and "Fat frogs flying past fast." Alliteration can increase audience members' recall, but avoid alliterative phrases or sentences you find difficult to say. In his speech on integrity at Tuskegee University, Samuel P. Jenkins, a vice president of Boeing, described the organization's ethics website in this way: "We established a special portal so *anyone* could reach us *anytime* from *anywhere, anonymously* if necessary."[33]

Repetition of a sound in a series of words, usually the first consonant.

Antithesis refers to the juxtaposition of two apparently contradictory phrases that are organized in a parallel structure. With antithesis, the *meanings* of the phrases are in opposition, but the *arrangement* of the words within the phrases is in alignment. Antithesis gets listeners' attention because the speaker brings together words in an unexpected, yet balanced, way. For example, in his commencement address at the University of Portland, author Paul Hawken said, "Working for the earth is not a way to get rich. It is a way to be rich."[34] Hawken's use of antithesis underscored how practicing sustainability and caring for the environment creates wealth that cannot be measured in dollars.

Juxtaposition of two apparently contradictory phrases that are organized in a parallel structure.

Spark Imagination with Your Language

Two language techniques can spark your audience's imagination: *invitations to imagine* and *humor*. **Invitations to imagine** ask listeners to create a scene or situation in their minds. Visualizing a place or series of events makes the audience feel more involved in your topic. Use your imagination when developing invitations to imagine with phrases like these:

Asking listeners to create a scene or situation in their minds.

- "The miners were trapped 250 feet below ground and the water was rising. How do you suppose they felt, not knowing if anyone knew they were alive?"

- "Does a weekend of snowboarding at Stowe, Vermont sound like a good idea to you?"

- "What would you have done under the circumstances?"

Some of the best stories are the ones you refer to but don't tell entirely. By reminding your audience of events, circumstances, narratives, or jokes you are confident they already know you can ignite their imagination without repeating something that is already familiar. University of Chicago professor Martha C. Nussbaum used this strategy in a speech at Georgetown University. She began with "I want to ask you to pause for a minute, and to think of the ending of a tragic drama, Euripides's *The Trojan Women*," and then told the story in four sentences—just enough to help listeners recall the narrative's key turning points.[35]

Speakers sometimes use jokes to connect with their audiences, especially for particular kinds of public presentations, such as after-dinner speeches. Humorous stories and anecdotes can relax the speaker and create common ground with the audience. Appropriate use of humor can also help the speaker gain the audience's confidence, generate an emotional atmosphere consistent with the purpose of the speech, and provide a pleasant, memorable experience for listeners.[36]

Effectively told humorous stories and asides inherently provoke audiences to imagine and visualize, inviting listeners to actively engage with the speaker's topic. Use short humorous stories to get the audience's attention at the beginning of the speech or to conclude in a dynamic, unforgettable way. For example, Wabash College senior Dustin

Stephen Colbert, host of Comedy Central's *Colbert Report*, uses humor to draw attention to current political events.

DeNeal began his commencement speech, "Katabasis and Anabasis: A Four-Year Journey," this way:

> I know, I know. You're looking at the title and thinking: "What in the world is this supposed to mean?" Well, to be honest, I'm not completely sure. But out of the countless lessons I'll take away from Wabash, one of the most important is that half the game is looking like you know what you're talking about even if you really don't. Big thanks to campus BS artist Chris Morris for that one. No, seriously.[37]

DeNeal's familiarity with his audience allowed him to gently poke fun at the title of his speech and gain his audience's attention.

Incorporating brief stories, quips, and humorous observations throughout your speech can help illustrate a point in the body of the speech and connect the audience with the topic and speaker. DeNeal included humor at several points in his speech, such as "We took the road less traveled and committed four years to an all-male institution. What were we thinking?"

Incorporating jokes and anecdotes into a speech can produce positive results if they're well planned and practiced. Follow these guidelines for using humor in your speeches:

- Tell only jokes or anecdotes appropriate for you, the topic, the audience, and the situation.

- Use humor strategically to attract attention, make a point, illustrate an idea, or conclude in a witty way.

- Keep jokes and humorous stories brief and to the point.

- Avoid trite and unoriginal jokes.

If you're not comfortable telling jokes or making funny comments, don't include humor in your speech. Some research suggests that women face challenges using humor in speeches due to cultural and societal norms.[38] Self-disparaging humor, in which speakers make jokes about their own shortcomings, negatively affects speaker credibility.[39] Poor use of humor damages the dialogue you strive to establish with your audience. For example, when accepting an award for leadership, Miami Dolphins player Junior Seau told a derogatory joke about gays. Although he apologized the next day, his remarks offended members of the audience and hurt his credibility.

Apply *it*

Using Audience-centered Language in Service Learning

Whatever type of service learning or similar community project you're pursuing, finding the right words to talk with your audience provides an essential basis for effective communication. You may not give formal presentations to the people you're helping, but you're probably talking with them regularly. Identify ways you can put your language in context (such as referring to current events), personalize your language (integrating what you know about your audience), use inclusive language (avoiding words that stereotype or discriminate), use visual language (such as metaphors and parallelism), and spark imagination (such as telling a humorous story). Observe how others respond when you use audience-centered language. Which strategies work the best? Why do you think they're effective?

SPEECH BUDDY VIDEO 10.1
Engaging Your Audience with Language

Anthony discusses several strategies for using audience-centered language in your speeches.

Watch your Speech Buddy video . . .

. . . and use what you've learned in your next speech.

ACTIVITY 10.1
You're Engaged!

This activity asks you to identify language for your own speech that will engage your audience.

Guidelines for Using Language in Your Speech

The words you choose to convey your message to the audience play a key role in developing your credibility and achieving your purpose. Your language should fit the topic, occasion, and audience. Speaking ethically requires that you use language that is respectful of yourself and your audience. This section explores several specific guidelines for using language in your speeches: Use spoken language, choose meaningful words, balance clarity and ambiguity, be concise, avoid offensive and aggressive language, build in redundancy, and don't get too attached to your words.

Use Spoken Language

Audiences quickly lose interest when speakers read from a manuscript. Choose conversational, engaging, personal, and active language that speaks directly to your audience. Compare "It's important to investigate this topic in depth so students can gain more knowledge of their civil liberties on university campuses" with "I researched this topic so we could learn more about our civil liberties on campus."

Choose Meaningful Words

Avoid jargon, idioms, euphemisms, slang, and clichés that listeners won't understand or will find offensive. If you must use technical terms, define them clearly. Groups with specialized interests often use jargon or technical language that speakers can weave into their speeches. But even experts find listening to a speech filled with technical language difficult and tiresome.[40] Thoroughly analyzing your audience will help you strike a balance between precision and comprehension. Use words that are on your audience's level—not above or below it.

Balance Clarity and Ambiguity

Clear language promotes understanding. Compare "Many people believe in this proposal" with "351 individuals signed the proposal." By replacing "many" with an actual number, the speaker provides a concrete indication of the proposal's support. *Many* could mean thousands, tens of thousands, millions, or fewer than ten. At times, however, ambiguous language can bring people together. Nearly everyone would agree that "We need to give children the best education possible." Such statements motivate audience members to tackle tough projects. If you begin with specific ideas that not everyone supports, listeners will focus on areas of disagreement rather than agreement.

Be Concise

Concise language avoids unnecessary words. Compare "We must get the up-to-date version of our computer applications and software packages on a regular basis" (seventeen words) with "We must regularly update our computer software" (seven words). As you're practicing your speech, listen to the words you use and try out ways to present your points as concisely as possible.

Avoid Offensive and Aggressive Language

Connotative meanings often stir deep emotions. People link emotions with words and words with experience. As a speaker, you don't want to use language with negative connotations. You certainly would never use words that denigrate any group. Language that audience members consider aggressive—such as demanding that they take action or questioning their intelligence—puts up a barrier to listening and damages your credibility as a speaker.[41]

Build in Redundancy

Recall the fleeting nature of spoken language. Listeners can't stop, go back, and re-listen to your speech the way they might reread written material. Build in redundancy through previews, reviews, clear transitions, and internal summaries. A few words, such as "Now let's examine," "As I mentioned earlier," and "Last, I'll talk about," serve to remind your audience of what you've covered and where you're headed.

Don't Get Too Attached to Your Words

Sometimes speakers get caught up in finding the perfect words for their speeches and forget about the purpose—informing, persuading, or entertaining the audience. As you practice your speech, try out different phrasing and listen to how it sounds. If you focus on choosing the "right" words, you'll lose the flexibility you need to adapt to your audience.

SPEECH BUDDY VIDEO 10.2
Making Language Choices

Erin discusses several tips for making effective language choices for your speeches.

ACTIVITY 10.2
Wrong Word, Right Word

The activity gives you a chance to evaluate language choices speakers make and suggest improvements.

Speech for Review and Analysis

On January 15, 2010, Tamia Gaines, a fifth-grade student at John Neely Bryan Elementary School in Dallas, Texas, presented this first-place speech at the 18th Annual Gardere Martin Luther King, Jr. Oratory Competition in Dallas. The fourth- and fifth-grade speakers were to answer the question, "What will I be able to achieve in my life because of what Dr. King achieved in his?" If you'd like to watch her speech online, it's available on YouTube.

Reprinted by joint permission of Gardere Wynne Sewell LLP and Tamia Gaines and her parents.

I am Tamia Gaines. And I stand here today to answer the question, What can I achieve in my lifetime because of what Dr. Martin Luther King achieved in his?

Dr. King once said, "At the center of nonviolence stands the principle of love." That quote inspired me to believe that it does not matter what color or race we are, we're still brothers and sisters. And love is what we need in order to change things.

Do we ignore or do we care? Do we hate or do we relate?

Dr. King stressed that we must live together as brothers and sisters or perish together as fools. Well, my mother did not raise any fools. She always told me, God does not like ugly. You can look good on the outside, but the way you look on the inside matters more than just a pretty face.

You must learn to love your fellow man and help him any way you can. Dr. King struggled for African Americans to have the same advantages Caucasians have. His words, efforts, and passion showed me I can be anything I want to be as long as

207

I have good character. I want to become a lawyer, and Dr. King has inspired me to be determined to reach that goal. I will start by completing elementary, middle, and high school. Then I plan on going to college to get my bachelor's and master's degrees. I already know it's not going to be easy, but I believe I can do it. I won't let anything or anyone put me down.

Don't hate; appreciate. Don't judge me; get to know me. Don't kill my dream; get a dream of your own. God created this great big world, but it is up to me to decide what kind of world I want to live in. If I fight, the world will fight back. But if I love, the world will love me back.

We should do as Dr. King preached: Make this world a better place. And every day you look yourself in the eye, you should say, "I want a better world for myself, my children, my children's children, and their children." But we can't do that if we don't start to do something more than just stand on the corner with our pants hanging below our buttocks. We can't do that if every word that comes out of our mouths is a curse word. Or the only way we know how to solve a problem is to use our fists.

And I am not just talking to the kids, either. Wake up, grown-ups, and show us a better way. Wake up, grown-ups—you're poisoning young minds of the world.

Dr. King preached nonviolence. If you're fussing and fighting all the time, we fuss and fight. What can you do to help us? Remind yourself what Dr. King stood up for—a better way to live. Be the mammas and daddies. Raise your children to respect you, to respect themselves, and to respect others—blacks, whites, Hispanics, Asians, and Native Americans. Dr. King was convinced that we could all live as one race—the human race.

Are we supporting that dream? Are we helping mankind so our world will be a better place for now and in the future? The time to stand up for rights is right now. I imagine Dr. King looking down right now and shaking his head and wondering, Did I really make a difference? Yes, Dr. King, you did make a difference, but we still have a long way to go.

And today I can stand here and say, I support Dr. King's beliefs. The belief that segregated schools should be ended. The belief that violence against blacks should end. The hatred and prejudice should end. Dr. King gave his life for these beliefs. And I will not let his dreams die. I will not be lazy or uneducated. I will not hate my Hispanic neighbors just because they don't look like me.

I will achieve the dream of becoming an outstanding black female attorney. Dr. King believed that we could overcome. And today, January 15, 2010, I, Tamia Gaines, pledge to all who will hear me: I can, I must, I will achieve my dreams and my successes. Why? Because Dr. King kicked down the door so I can walk through. Thank you, Dr. King. And thank you, ladies and gentlemen.

Questions for Analysis and Discussion

1. How does Tamia's language reflect the qualities of spoken language? For example, how was her language immediate?

2. How was Tamia's language audience-centered? Give an example of how Tamia
   a. Put her language in context.
   b. Personalized her language.
   c. Used inclusive language.
   d. Used visual language.
   e. Sparked imagination with her language.

3. How well did Tamia follow the guidelines for using language in public speaking? Give examples for each area.
   a. Used spoken language.
   b. Chose meaningful words.
   c. Balanced clarity and ambiguity.
   d. Was concise.

e. Avoided offensive and aggressive language.

f. Built in redundancy.

g. Didn't get too attached to her words.

4. If you were giving Tamia suggestions for improvement, what would you say?

Summary

L anguage enlivens your ideas. The words you choose get your audience's attention, help them visualize your main points, and facilitate their ability to remember what you say. Language refers to the system of words you use to communicate with others. It is arbitrary, ambiguous, abstract, and active, characteristics that present speakers with both opportunities and challenges. Because language is arbitrary, audiences may interpret your words in ways you don't intend. Because language is ambiguous, consider both the connotative and denotative meanings of the words you use. Because language is abstract, consider when to discuss ideas and concepts rather than tangible objects and specific actions. Because language is active, the words you use and how you use them change over time.

Language and culture are interdependent. You learn about the meanings of words from your culture, and words help you interpret culture. Slang, jargon, idioms, euphemisms, and clichés highlight the link between language and culture. Because your audiences may not always share your cultural background, it's best to avoid these types of culture-specific words or phrases unless they're essential to the speech. You must also pay attention to gender and language when you give a speech, considering how the gender of your listeners will affect how they interpret your message. In addition, use nonsexist language to avoid alienating some members of your audience.

Spoken language differs from written language in that it is dynamic, immediate, informal, irreversible, based in narrative, and rhythmic, whereas written language is static, distant, formal, revisable, able to describe multiple facts, and rich in imagery. When you give a speech to an audience, use spoken language in an engaging, conversational manner and use audience-centered language. When you take an audience-centered approach, you put your language in context, personalize your language, use inclusive language, use visual language, and spark imagination with your language.

To use language successfully to engage your audience, use spoken language, choose meaningful words, balance clarity and ambiguity, strive for conciseness, avoid offensive or aggressive language, build in redundancy, and don't get too attached to your words.

Directory of Study and Review Resources

IN THE BOOK
- Summary
- Key Terms
- Critical Challenges

MORE STUDY RESOURCES
- Quizzes
- WebLinks
- Peer-reviewed videos

CourseMate

Speech Studio

STUDENT WORKBOOK
- 10.1: Written and Spoken Style
- 10.2: Working Up a Sentence
- 10.3: Creating Clusters
- 10.4: Analyzing Presidential Style
- 10.5: Stylistic Devices

SPEECH BUDDY VIDEOS
WATCH It Video
- 10.1: Engaging your Audience with Language
- 10.2: Making Language Choices

USE It Activity
- 10.1: You're Engaged!
- 10.2: Wrong Word, Right Word

SAMPLE SPEECH VIDEOS
Stacey, "Fallen Soldiers," commemorative speech

Brandi, "Feeding the Wildlife: Don't Do It!" persuasive speech

SPEECH BUILDER EXPRESS
- Goal/purpose
- Thesis statement
- Organization
- Outline
- Supporting materials
- Transitions
- Introduction
- Conclusion
- Title
- Works cited
- Completing the speech outline

INFOTRAC
Recommended search terms
- Language and public speaking
- Language and culture
- Language and gender
- Nonsexist language
- Spoken versus written language
- Inclusive language
- Figures of speech
- Imagery and language

AUDIO STUDY TOOLS
- "Feeding the Wildlife: Don't Do It!" by Brandi
- Critical thinking questions
- Learning objectives
- Chapter summary

Guide to Your Online Resources

CourseMate Your Speech Communication CourseMate for *Public Speaking: The Evolving Art* gives you access to the Speech Buddy video and activity featured in this chapter, additional sample speech videos, Speech Studio, Speech Builder Express, InfoTrac College Edition, and study aids such as glossary flashcards, review quizzes, and the Critical Challenge questions for this chapter, which you can respond to via e-mail if your instructor so requests. In addition, your CourseMate features live WebLinks relevant to this chapter. Links are regularly maintained, and new ones are added periodically.

Key Terms

alliteration 203

antithesis 203

clichés 193

connotative meanings 189

denotative meanings 189

euphemisms 193

hedges 194

idioms 193

inclusive language 200

interpretations 188

invitations to imagine 203

jargon 192

language 188

metaphors 202

nonsexist language 194

parallelism 202

rhymes 202

similes 202

slang 192

symbols 188

tag questions 194

tone 190

Critical Challenges

Questions for Reflection and Discussion

1. Although ambiguity can produce positive results, it can also obscure the speaker's true intentions. Consider your use of ambiguous language. Have you ever used vague language to mislead or deceive others? Or has someone ever misled or deceived you in this way? What was the outcome? How did you feel about what happened? What did you learn from your experience?

2. Similes and metaphors help audience members visualize your ideas. Brainstorm for similes and metaphors that describe your college. How do those analogies help you visualize your campus? How do different similes and metaphors reveal or hide different aspects of your college? What ethical responsibilities do speakers have when choosing similes and metaphors to compare things?

3. Swear words can get your audience's attention and give added impact to what you say. But is it the impact you want? Should you swear in your speech? Recall an instance in which you heard or read about a speaker cursing during a presentation. How did you react? Do you think that's the reaction the speaker intended? Is using such words ever appropriate in public speaking? Why or why not?

4. Go to Speech Studio to analyze the type and style of language other students use in their speeches. Alternatively, record a speech you're working on, upload it to Speech Studio, and ask your peers for their feedback. What feedback could you use to fine-tune your language use before you give your speech in class?

11

Integrating Presentation Media

Cengage Learning

Cengage Learning

Today's technology offers an array of visual and audio resources that can enhance your speech. **Presentation media** are technical and material resources, ranging from presentation software such as PowerPoint and Keynote to flip charts and handouts, that speakers use to highlight, clarify, and complement the information they present orally. Knowing how and when to use these resources is especially important for public speakers because presentation media are often misused. Resources such as PowerPoint can add a lot to your message, but the unimaginative use of presentation media will bore the audience.

When integrated effectively into a speech, even low-tech presentation media can greatly enhance the look and feel of your speeches, strengthen your message, and help ensure the speech fulfills its purpose. In this chapter, you'll learn about the most popular presentation media used today, the basics of good design, and guidelines for using presentation media effectively.

Technical and material resources ranging from presentation software and real-time web access (RWA) to flip charts and handouts that speakers use to highlight, clarify, and complement the information they present orally.

Audiences appreciate speakers who use technological and symbolic resources creatively. When used appropriately, presentation media can become a core feature of your speeches. Learning how to use presentation media well involves more than mastering a set of technical procedures. Your use of presentation media must also be properly motivated and well executed to clarify, support, dramatize, exemplify, or complement information you present orally.

You can use presentation media to attract and connect with audience members, spark their imagination, make sure they get the full meaning and impact of what you have to say, and demonstrate your creativity. Used properly, presentation media add something special to your speech by giving the audience additional sensory input about your topic or your argument. However, like everything else in your speech, you must have good reasons for incorporating media into your presentation. You can use presentation media to

- Draw attention to your topic.
- Illustrate an idea that can't be fully described by words alone.
- Stimulate an emotional reaction.
- Clarify a key point.
- Support your argument with a graphical display of facts and figures.
- Help your audience remember your main ideas.

Each type of presentation media has advantages and limitations, summarized in **Table 11.1**. The remainder of this chapter explores the most useful applications of the most popular presentation media and considers how you can best employ them in your speeches.

Table 11.1   Advantages and Limitations of Presentation Media

Type	Advantages	Limitations
Overhead transparency	Technical simplicity; ease of use	Transparency placement and order; speaker tends to talk to screen
Flip chart or poster	Documents audience feedback and ideas	Lacks a professional look; may be hard for all audience members to see
Whiteboard or chalkboard	Records spontaneous thoughts	Writing takes away from speaking time; speaker may appear unprepared, rude
Document camera	Projects images with great detail; can zoom in, capture images, display 3-D renderings	Expensive equipment; complex to use
Video	Evokes emotions in audience; portrays examples	Interferes with speaking pace and audience focus
Handout	Enhances audience recall after speech; reinforces key ideas	Disrupts continuity of presentation; wasteful
Model	Provides specific references; helps audiences visualize materials and concepts	Can be too small or detailed; not suitable for large audiences
Audio media	Set mood; trigger imagination	Decrease speaking time; distracting
Digital slide	Blends text, images, video, sound	Overused, boring, speech content neglected; speaker tends to talk to screen
Real-time web access	Fresh, current information	Slow connections and download times; available systems can be unreliable

Table 11.2 General Guidelines for Visual Design

Keep it simple.	Avoid including too much information in a graphic. The impact should be immediate and clear. By keeping visual material simple, you maintain maximum personal contact with your audience.
Emphasize only key ideas.	When you call attention to ideas with a graphic representation, make sure the graphic clearly illustrates your key points or most important supporting data.
Show what you can't say.	The best use of visual media is to reveal material you can't easily describe orally or with text. Photographs, drawings, simple charts, and graphs can all accomplish this objective.
Use close-up photographs and other images.	Select and present photographs, video, and other images that will create real impact. Close-ups can be very effective, especially to evoke emotional responses from your audience.
Keep the number of images you present manageable.	Too many images will tire your audience. Eight or ten relevant images should be the maximum number for most presentations (unless you're giving a speech about a highly visual topic).
Combine variety with coherence.	If you use several images, vary the design enough to make them interesting but keep them aesthetically consistent. For instance, use the same colors or type font, but vary the content. Or mix photographs with graphics that maintain the same style throughout.
Use large lettering.	Use large lettering so the audience can read the text easily. Avoid presenting lengthy blocks of text.

Understanding the Basics of Visual Design

The principles of good design apply to every visual medium.[1] To get the maximum impact from visual presentation media, follow the general guidelines for visual design outlined in **Table 11.2**. Strive to be clear and concise. For example, putting too much information on a single digital slide will overwhelm and distract audience members—they'll either dismiss the slide or try to read it instead of listening to you. Choose your visual materials carefully, using just enough to make your points and draw attention to the ideas you want the audience to remember. Visual material that is not obviously relevant to your topic is not appreciated by audiences and not likely to be remembered.[2] Use visual materials when images will say more than words. For example, close-up images often have a powerful impact because they're perceived as personal and intimate. To avoid boring your audience, balance variety with coherence by developing a consistent theme for your visual media while varying the content. Finally, large lettering makes it easier for the audience to see your visual media and grasp your points quickly.

Using Traditional Visual and Audio Media

Traditional visual and audio media used in public speaking include overhead transparencies, flip charts and posters, whiteboards and chalkboards, document cameras, video, handouts, models, and sound recordings.

Overhead Transparencies

Although most speakers in work-related speaking situations use digital slides and document cameras, overhead transparencies are still often used in classrooms. To use an overhead projector, you must first make transparencies of the material you want to show. **Transparencies** are clear acetate pages displayed by an overhead projector during a speech. You can create high-quality transparencies in color or black and white by using the presentation, word-processing, or graphics software on your computer, Color is more expensive, but the impact it creates for many applications often makes the extra investment worth it.

Many classrooms are equipped with an overhead projector for displaying transparencies. If yours is not, arrange to have one delivered to the room on the day of your speech. Check out the location of the overhead projector in the room. Is it mounted on a mobile stand, or will you have to place the projector on a table or a stand? Be sure you know this *before* the day of your speech.

To integrate overhead transparencies smoothly into your speech, apply the following guidelines:

■ *Display your transparencies only when you talk about them.* Place your first slide on the overhead projector, focus it before you begin your speech, and turn the machine off. When you reach the point in your speech where you want to show the image, turn the projector on. Generally, activate the projector only when you want to project an image. Similarly, if you will spend several minutes on material unrelated to the last image you've shown, turn the machine off. If you intend to show several images, especially in rapid succession, it's okay to keep the machine on between them. When you finish with the final image, turn the projector off for good. If the projector is mounted on a mobile stand, push the stand out of your way to give yourself center stage for the remainder of your speech.

■ *Number the sheets in the order you'll use them.* Use a small sticker or piece of adhesive paper, about the size of a quarter, for each transparency. Write a number plainly on each dot and place it in the upper right corner of the image. Place the dots consistently in such a way that the dots guide you toward placing the transparency on the projector properly, so that the image will appear correctly on the screen. Then make a pile of the transparencies in the order in which you will use them, each with the dot in the same position on the page.

■ *Practice with your transparencies before you give your speech.* Take a few minutes before the day of your speech to find out exactly how to position the projector, turn the machine on and off, place your images on the glass properly, and focus the image on the screen. Then practice facing your imaginary audience the way you'll speak to the real audience on the day of your speech.

Don Hammond/Design Pics/Corbis

Although most speakers in the workplace use digital slides in their presentations, it's a good idea to know how to use overhead transparencies. They are easy to prepare and use, and they're still often used in academic settings.

Flip Charts

Sometimes speakers want to document good ideas brought up during an interactive brainstorming session. An excellent medium for accomplishing this is a **flip chart,** a large pad of paper propped up on an easel placed near the speaker. Write on the flip chart with a big, bold marker so everyone in the room can see what you've written.

216

Even the biggest high-tech companies routinely use flip charts for their in-person brainstorming sessions. The audience stays lively during such interactive meetings, as long as the meeting is attended by a relatively small number of people. In large spaces with large audiences, flip charts won't hold the audience's attention or serve the purpose of facilitating interaction among audience members.

Whiteboards and Chalkboards

Using a **whiteboard** with colored pens, or even a chalkboard with white chalk, can help you achieve the same outcome as a flip chart or an easel. The board, however, should be used *only* when brainstorming with the audience about ideas, never for presenting materials. Although it may be tempting, don't even use it for posting telephone numbers, web addresses, mailing addresses, and the like. Turning your back to the audience while you scribble something on the board can make you look less prepared and professional than you are. You'll be more effective if you include this sort of information on a digital slide that you project during the speech or put in a handout for distribution after you conclude your speech.

A smooth whiteboard that can be written or drawn on with markers.

Document Cameras

Document cameras function somewhat like overhead projectors but provide features that are far more sophisticated and project images in a higher resolution. Unlike overhead projectors, which use light and mirrors to display the image on a transparency, document cameras use a video camera to capture and display the image. Document cameras allow you to zoom in on a specific part of an image, capture an image for later use, and show highly detailed images—abilities an overhead projector doesn't give you. As with all presentation media, prepare the images you want to display well in advance and practice using the document camera so you're comfortable with all its features.

A projection device that uses a video camera to capture and display images, including 3-D visual materials.

Video

To determine whether you should use a video clip, ask yourself whether it will contribute something truly important to your speech. Showing a video clip can elicit an emotional response from the audience and improve their recall of your speech.[3] But it also dramatically changes the mood of the speech and may disturb the relationship between speaker and audience.

With the availability of online video sites such as YouTube and Hulu, searching for and identifying a relevant video clip has become much easier than it used to be. If you use video clips well, audiences are increasingly prepared to appreciate them as part of your speech. More than 90 percent of internet users aged eighteen to twenty-nine watch content on video sharing sites, which is more than visit social networking sites, download podcasts, or use Twitter.[4]

If you decide to incorporate a video clip into your speech, consider these guidelines:

- *Keep the clip short.* With other visual media, speakers continue talking while showing the images or text. Unless you turn off the audio for a video clip, you can't speak while it's playing, so you lose valuable speaking time. In addition, a lengthy clip takes the audience's attention away from you. Choose a short clip for maximum impact.

- *Treat the video component as an integral part of your speech.* Determine how you will transition into and out of the video to provide a seamless experience for your audience.

- *If possible, embed the video within your digital slides.* Presentation software such as PowerPoint and Keynote allows you to insert video into a slide so you can avoid relying on a separate piece of equipment such as a DVD projector.

- *Make sure the video is not offensive.* Video clips can be used to stimulate a strong reaction. Just be sure the content won't offend audience members, which may cause them to stop listening to you or to dismiss your message.

- *Cite the source of the video clip.* As you introduce the video segment during your speech, say where it originated, not just where you got it. For example, many videos on YouTube and Hulu come from primary sources such as television networks or movie trailers.

- *Be sure the clip is legitimate.* Just as you have to make sure your written sources of information are credible, be certain your visual sources are too. Anyone can post almost anything on video sharing sites, including hoaxes. Be sure you know that the clip you're using is authentic and legitimate.

Be wary of incorporating an attention-getting video clip at the risk of neglecting the most important elements of your speech—the content and the delivery. In addition, keep in mind that relating a film clip to your speech in a way that truly advances your purpose can prove challenging. Audience members may enjoy watching a brief video clip, but it may not inform or persuade them in ways related to your topic.

Handouts

The paper **handout** can be very effective in some instances. For example, you might use a handout to provide a list of website addresses where audience members can make donations to a charity you've described in a persuasive speech. You might give your audience a diagram illustrating how to administer emergency cardiopulmonary resuscitation (CPR) treatment. You could hand out copies of a letter you've written to your state senator promoting tougher child pornography laws, and encourage your listeners to sign and mail them.

Sheets of paper containing relevant information that are distributed before, during, or after a speech.

Some speakers use a handout in conjunction with other presentation media.[5] For instance, you might use digital slides to provide photographic detail and graphic summaries of the effectiveness of a new cancer-treating drug, then pass out a handout that provides a list of websites where the audience can find additional information about the new treatment.

If you decide to use a handout, think carefully about when you'll distribute it. You have three options: Before you begin the speech, during the speech, or after you conclude. To help you decide which option to use, determine when the audience needs the information. Also think about how the physical act of distributing the handout will affect your speech performance. Passing paper around the room is noisy and may disrupt your audience's attention and concentration. In addition, the audience will read the handout and not pay attention to you. All things considered, it's almost always best to distribute handouts after you finish your formal remarks.[6]

Apply it

Extending the Speech

You can use various techniques to extend and enhance the audience's experience beyond your original presentation. For instance, at the end of your speech, pass out a handout that indicates how to contact you or the persons or institutions mentioned in the speech, where to locate relevant web resources, or how to review the digital slides you presented. Or collect the email addresses of audience members and send your slides to them after the speech. In some cases, speakers even dispense with showing digital slides in their speeches and just mail the slides to audience members afterward.

Models

For certain subjects, physical **models** that represent the topic being discussed can add a helpful, sometimes necessary, visual dimension to a speech. Models are especially useful for describing and explaining scientific topics that involve a physical structure. For instance, the molecular structure of an atom can be demonstrated with a model. A small-scale replica of fossil remains can help a speaker describe the physical characteristics of an extinct species. In fact, speeches about medical and biological topics such as the anatomy of the brain or the physiology of hearing would be difficult to present *without* the appropriate model.

Other types of speech topics also lend themselves to the use of models. Community planners and architects often use models to promote their ideas. For example, a model of a proposed new building for the community or campus helps audience members visualize what the structure would look like. An alternative to using a physical model is to use a software program that allows you to project animated three-dimensional models onto a screen. This option eliminates the two greatest disadvantages of using a physical model: its small size, which limits the audience's ability to see the model, and the difficulty of trying to handle or show the model during the speech.

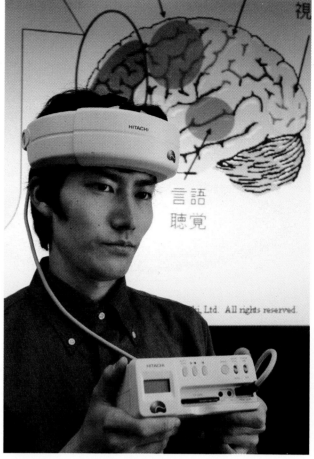

You don't have to limit yourself to just one type of presentation media during your speech. Sometimes a combination of media can help your audience better understand your ideas. For example, this speaker is demonstrating a model of a machine that measures brain activity. At the same time, he's showing a digital slide of the areas of the brain that the machine measures.

A copy of an object, usually built to scale, that represents the object in detail.

Sound Recordings

Sound, like visual images, can stimulate mental images, triggering the imagination and setting a mood.[7] Sound can provide examples of something that is difficult to explain with words. How might you convince your audience that a proposal for a new freeway through your city is a bad idea? Play a tape of traffic noise—loudly. How might you set the mood for a demonstration of massage therapy? Begin with a few seconds of calming ambient music, played softly. Of course, keep your audience in mind: Avoid music or other sounds that would offend or alienate audience members, such as songs containing profane or sexually explicit language.

Audio technology is usually relatively easy to manage. If the place where you'll be speaking doesn't provide audio equipment, bring your own portable CD or MP3 player and speakers. Better yet, embed the audio file in a digital slide so that you can transition into and out of your audio clip smoothly. Set the volume high enough so everyone can hear the sound clearly, but don't turn it up so loud that it annoys your audience. Some public speakers briefly sing or play an acoustic instrument as part of their speeches. That can be effective too; just don't confuse giving a speech with giving a concert.

Using Computer Technology

Depending on the speaking context, you may want to use a computer to enhance your presentation. The two computer technologies speakers use most commonly are digital slides and real-time web access.

219

Digital Slides: Do's and Don'ts

The name PowerPoint has become synonymous with presentation software, but Apple has presentation software too—Keynote, an easy-to-use program that is rapidly gaining in popularity. Other computer-generated slide software is available from Corel Presentations, Lotus Freelance Graphics, and MagicPoint. **Presentation software** allows computer users to display information in multimedia slide shows.

Without question, presentation software is the most versatile and dynamic multimedia tool for most public speaking purposes. When it is used effectively, audiences pay increased attention to speakers, understand main ideas better, and retain information well.[8] But not every speech or occasion calls for the use of digital slides.[9] Many audiences have tired of overblown PowerPoint-driven speeches. Some classrooms and boardrooms have even banned the use of PowerPoint.[10] Still, when used appropriately, presentation software can greatly enhance your speech.

You may already feel comfortable and confident using PowerPoint or Keynote. If you're just getting started, consult the online help and documentation that come with the software. Your school may provide tutorials for learning how to use presentation software. You can also find free tutorials online. When used in moderation, presentation software can help you produce a more conversational and engaging presentation.[11] But remember: *Presentation software will not give your speech for you.* Nor should it be more prominent than you, the speaker.[12] You give a "speech," not a "PowerPoint presentation." You and your message must remain the primary focal points.

To use digital slides effectively, follow these guidelines:

- *Carefully develop your speech and then consider how you'll support your oral materials with digital slides.* Avoid taking the reverse approach, overpreparing your digital slides and underpreparing the rest of your presentation. The success of your speech depends primarily on the quality of what you have to say.[13]

- *Use digital slides sparingly.* Audiences tire of too much visual information and will tune you out if they feel visually overwhelmed.[14] When used inappropriately, digital slides take the emotion and personality out of the speech and diminish the vital connection between speaker and audience.[15] Use digital slides in a way that keeps your audience connected to you and your topic. Keep in mind that some types of information are better suited to digital slides than others. For example, integrating highly technical material into a speech is one of the most effective uses of presentation software.[16]

- *Balance creativity with clarity and predictability with spontaneity.* Avoid depending on the standard templates, clip art, and animation techniques that presentation software programs provide. Because PowerPoint is so widely used today, everyone immediately recognizes those predictable visual forms. Although audiences generally prefer digital slides to overhead transparencies, they usually don't like the software's animations and sound effects.[17] Keep your slides clear and easy for the audience to understand.

© 2009 Ted Goff

"I would have learned how to use my presentation software if I actually cared what any of you thought."

©Ted Goff

The next section provides specific strategies for designing slides and managing the computer hardware used to present them.

Digital Slide Design Tips

With presentation software, you have more elements to consider than with other visual media. For example, you can make visual transitions from one slide to the next and select special effects that animate your graphical material. These features represent real advantages over other presentation media, but only when you use them strategically and sparingly.

The general guidelines for visual design presented in Table 11.2 outline most of what you need to know about designing digital slides. If you use presentation software, keep the following additional guidelines in mind when designing the slides for your speech:

- *Avoid relying on text or numbers.* The most effective use of presentation software is for visual, not textual or numerical, representation. The visuals may be still or moving images. (See **Figure 11.1**.)

- *Limit the number of bullet points for each slide.* If you decide to use text, don't bore your audience with lengthy, wordy slides. Use a maximum of four to six bullet points per slide. (See **Figure 11.2**.)

- *Limit the number of words for each bullet point.* Use just a few words or a brief phrase for each bullet point. (See **Figure 11.3**.)

- *Make the type font large and clean.* Keep the font size large (40-point and above for titles; 20-point and above for text), and stay away from script or overly abstract lettering styles. Use sans-serif fonts, such as Arial, Verdana, and Geneva, for maximum readability. (See **Figure 11.4**.)

Figure 11.1   Too much text

Definitions of Patriotism

Merriam Webster Dictionary: love for or devotion to one's country

Wiktionary: Love of country; devotion to the welfare of one's country; the virtues and actions of a patriot; the passion which inspires one to serve one's country.

Ultralingua Online Dictionary: Love of country and willingness to sacrifice for it.

Cambridge International Dictionary of English: when you love your country and are proud of it

Infoplease Dictionary: devoted love, support, and defense of one's country; national loyalty

The Wordsmyth English Dictionary: love for, and devotion and loyalty to, one's nation

Figure 11.2   Too many bullet points

TYPES OF PERFORMING ARTS

- *Juggling*
- *Dance*
- *Circuses*
- *Magic*
- *Opera*
- *Musicals*
- *Storytelling*
- *Art Festivals*
- *Fire Arts*
- *Variety Entertainment*
- *Comedy*

Figure 11.3   Wordy bullet points

Components of Education

- *Knowledge - what you are confident you understand or know about a subject*
- *Learning - how you go about acquiring knowledge and wisdom through studying a subject*
- *Pedagogy - considered both an art and a science, refers to the methods teachers use in the process of instruction*

Figure 11.4   Large, clean type font

International Independence Days

- Afghanistan - August 19
- Guatemala - September 15
- Poland - November 11
- Zambia - October 24

- *Choose transitions that fit the tone of your topic and visual material.* Presentation software gives you many ways to move from one slide to the next. Good choices include "fade through black" and "dissolve." Keynote also includes three-dimensional transitions, such as "page flip" and "revolving door." Within a speech, use the same type of transition for all your slides to give the audience a sense of consistency.

- *Avoid special effects.* Special effects allow you to manipulate the visual field of a digital slide in order to put portions of the field in motion. For instance, you can have an image "fly" in from top or bottom, left or right. Audiences usually find these effects annoying and distracting. Any special effect you use should serve a purpose directly related to your speech's purpose.

- *Use color well.* To make your slides easy to read, choose colors that produce a high contrast between the background and the font. Most speakers prefer a clean white background with dark lettering. Sometimes it makes sense to match the color scheme of the slide set with the speech event or organization, like using your school's colors for a presentation about a campus issue.

> **Apply** it

Digital Literacy and Creativity

Knowing how to use digital slides offers you advantages that extend far beyond the public speaking classroom. In a competitive job market, being able to use digital slides well gives you a communication skill that is highly valued by professional employers. You can also incorporate digital slides into presentations for civic organizations, nonprofit groups, public events, clubs, and even family gatherings. But don't think of digital literacy strictly as a technical skill. Like all forms of human expression, composing and presenting digital images gives you a great opportunity to exercise your imagination and creativity. Digital media is not just a tool—it's also an art form. Enjoy!

VALERY HACHE/AFP/Getty Images

Hardware Setup Tips

The hardware you use for your presentation software depends mainly on the equipment your school and instructor can make available. Fortunately, most schools and businesses are well equipped to handle PowerPoint, Keynote, and similar software. Your institution may provide a computer and an LCD projector in the room where you'll present your speech. In that case, you'll probably only have to save your digital slides on a flash drive and bring it with you. Familiarize yourself with the equipment in the room well before the day of your speech.

When equipment is not readily available, you may decide to use your own laptop and connect it to a projector supplied by your school. Many speakers find this to be a good solution because they feel most comfortable using their own computers. Any setup you use requires careful planning. Even if you bring your own equipment, know

In the award-winning film *An Inconvenient Truth,* former U.S. Vice President Al Gore used digital slide imagery creatively to dramatize his argument about the dangers of global climate change.

how to make it function properly in the room where you'll be speaking.

If you'd like greater freedom to move around the room during your speech, use a remote control device when you present your digital slides. With a remote, you can advance the slides whenever you want from any place in the room.

Real-time Web Access

Today more and more classrooms and meeting rooms have internet access, which gives you the option of displaying a website during your speech. This is a dynamic resource that can be very useful for certain kinds of presentations. When applied to speechmaking, this functionality is termed **real-time web access** (RWA). With RWA, you navigate in real time through web pages associated with your topic. You can use RWA to demonstrate how to do something specific on the web, such as researching an idea, checking the current status of any topic, or displaying articles found on websites that support your purpose or argument. This web evidence, or **webidence**, gives your presentation an in-the-moment feeling not possible with static digital slides.[19] Because the audience understands that you are speaking in real time, you can also encourage audience participation in your navigations or searches.

The spontaneous nature of RWA and webidence can be used to the speaker's advantage. Still, if you plan to display a web page in real time during your speech, check immediately beforehand to make sure access is possible and that the site you intend to show is available.

Employing a live internet feed as a visual media or information resource during a public speech.

Web sources displayed as evidence during a speech, found by using real-time web access or webpage capture software.

> **Watch** it

SPEECH BUDDY VIDEO 11.1
Using Digital Slides

Erin introduces sample digital slides and highlights design successes and failures.

> **Use** it

Watch your Speech Buddy video . . .

. . . and use what you've learned in your next speech.

ACTIVITY 11.1
PowerPoint Makeover

This activity gives you a chance to evaluate several digital slides and suggest ways to improve them.

Presentation media can enhance your effectiveness as a speaker but can also detract from your message if they are not used correctly. The following tips will help you integrate presentation media into your speech successfully.

Consider Your Room and the Audience

To get the maximum effect from your presentation media, be sure you have unobstructed access to the equipment while you speak. This will boost your confidence and make you appear more comfortable to your audience. Project your images at a height and distance that will make them easy to see for everyone in the audience. This may require moving a table or a stand to a better position.

When using digital slides or other media that require a screen, avoid turning toward the screen where the images are projected. Remain facing your audience while they look at the screen. One advantage of digital slides and real-time web access is that the same images your audience sees appear on your computer screen. You will always know exactly what's on the big screen simply by observing what's on your computer screen.

Practice with Your Media

When you practice your speech, incorporate your digital slides, document camera images, and other presentation media so you learn to integrate them smoothly into your speech. Sometimes speakers forget about their media as they give their speeches, so include reminders on your note cards or outline indicating when to use your presentation media. It's a good idea to write these reminders in a different color from the rest of your cards or outline so they'll catch your attention during your speech.

Arriving early and checking on the technical equipment for your speech will help you manage nervousness and avoid technology mishaps. If possible, check the sharpness and placement of projected images before audience members enter the room. Put your transparencies in order. Set the volume levels of your audio system.

Although presentation media greatly enhance the public speaking experience, you must be prepared for those technologies to fail. Sometimes quick repairs are possible; at other times, you just have to continue your speech without the technology you'd planned to use. In these cases, you must improvise. Use the chalkboard or whiteboard. Ask for volunteers from the audience to demonstrate a point. Bring backup visual materials, such as overhead transparencies with key images or graphics. In short, always be prepared to give your speech without your presentation media in case something goes wrong—the audience will understand!

Effectively managing your technology requires planning and practice. Design digital slides, overhead transparencies, audio clips, and other technological components of your presentation prior to the day you must give your speech. Practice using the technology so it becomes a natural part of your presentation.

corbis rf/First Light

There's no need to look at your digital slides while presenting. It's even less effective to read the content of your slides to audience members. Let them view your slides on their own while you engage them directly with your words.

Speak to Your Audience, Not Your Media

Whatever presentation media you use, always keep your focus on the audience. You may be tempted to look at the screen when projecting an image. But when you look at the screen, you turn your back on the audience. Listeners will feel ignored, and their attention will wane. Instead, glance at the actual image on the media equipment, such as the computer screen. Most importantly, never read the content of your presentation media to your audience. As you practice with your presentation media, make a conscious effort to face your practice audience or face where the audience would be sitting.

> **Watch** it

Cengage Learning

SPEECH BUDDY VIDEO 11.2
Integrating Presentation Media

Anthony introduces examples of speakers who have integrated presentation media into their speeches effectively.

> **Use** it

Cengage Learning

ACTIVITY 11.2
Exhibit A

This activity gives you practice in evaluating the effectiveness of different kinds of presentation media.

Summary

Speakers use presentation media to draw attention to their topic, illustrate an idea, evoke an emotional reaction, clarify points, support an argument, and assist with audience recall. General guidelines for designing effective visual media include keeping it simple, emphasizing only key ideas, showing what you can't say, using close-ups of photographs and other images, combining variety with coherence, and using large, readable lettering.

Traditional visual and audio media such as overhead transparencies, flip charts and posters, whiteboards and chalkboards, document cameras, video, handouts, models, and sound recordings allow you to enrich your speech. Digital slides have become a frequently used form of presentation media. Although some speakers rely too much on computer-generated slides, the versatility of software programs such as PowerPoint and Keynote offers tremendous flexibility in creating dynamic visual and audio materials.

By treating your presentation media as essential components of your speech that require careful preparation and delivery, you can maximize their impact and avoid

225

common problems associated with their use. The key to success in using presentation media is balance: Give media the proper supporting role in your speech. With all the resources available to you, remember that *you* will always be the best delivery system for communicating ideas to your audience.

Review it

Directory of Study and Review Resources

IN THE BOOK
- Summary
- Key Terms
- Critical Challenges

MORE STUDY RESOURCES
- Quizzes
- WebLinks
- Peer-reviewed videos

STUDENT WORKBOOK
- 11.1: Brainstorming Images
- 11.2: Presentation Media Effects
- 11.3: Slides or a Handout?
- 11.4: Is It Worth It?
- 11.5: Ignite Speeches

SPEECH BUDDY VIDEOS
- **WATCH It Video**
- 11.1: Using Digital Slides
- 11.2: Integrating Presentation Media
- **USE It Activity**
- 11.1: PowerPoint Makeover
- 11.2: Exhibit A

SAMPLE SPEECH VIDEOS
- Amanda, "Domestic Violence," problem-cause-solution speech
- Cindy, "U.S. Flag Etiquette," informative speech

SPEECH BUILDER EXPRESS
- Visual aids

INFOTRAC
- **Recommended search terms**
- Presentation tips
- Visual aids and public speaking
- Visual aid design tips

AUDIO STUDY TOOLS
- "Domestic Violence" by Amanda
- Critical thinking questions
- Learning objectives
- Chapter summary

Guide to Your Online Resources

CourseMate — Your Speech Communication CourseMate for *Public Speaking: The Evolving Art* gives you access to the Speech Buddy video and activity featured in this chapter, additional sample speech videos, Speech Studio, Speech Builder Express, InfoTrac College Edition, and study aids such as glossary flashcards, review quizzes, and the Critical Challenge questions for this chapter, which you can respond to via e-mail if your instructor so requests. In addition, your CourseMate features live WebLinks relevant to this chapter, including the Gettysburg PowerPoint Presentation, which includes background on how the presentation's slides were developed and statistics on its viewership. Links are regularly maintained, and new ones are added periodically.

Key Terms

document cameras 217

flip chart 216

handout 218

model 219

presentation media 213

presentation software 220

real-time web access 223

transparency 216

webidence 223

whiteboard 217

Critical Challenges

Questions for Reflection and Discussion

1. Although this chapter focuses on how to use presentation media, when should you *not* use them? Why might you not want to use presentation media?

2. Reflect on a public speaking event you've attended recently, or one that you recall particularly well, in which the speaker used presentation media. How effective was the speaker's use of presentation media? How did the media add to the speech? Were there ways in which the presentation media detracted from the speech? How might the speaker have improved his or her use of presentation media?

3. With digital visual and audio files, it's easy to alter an original photograph, video, song, or taped conversation. What are a speaker's ethical responsibilities when developing presentation media for a speech?

4. Check out Speech Studio to analyze the presentation media that other students use in their speeches. Or record a speech you're working on (being sure to tape so that your presentation media can be seen), upload it to Speech Studio, and ask your peers for their feedback. What feedback could you use to fine-tune your presentation media before you give your speech in class?

✓ SPEECH Studio

12

Delivering Your Speech

Cengage Learning

Cengage Learning

CourseMate **SPEECH Studio** SPEECH BUILDER EXPRESS

Maya Angelou, Susan B. Anthony, Erin Brockovich, Cesar Chavez, John F. Kennedy, Martin Luther King, Jr., Marlee Matlin, Barack Obama—all are known for their skills in the fifth canon of rhetoric: delivery (Chapter 1). **Delivery** refers to presenting a speech in public. When you deliver a speech, you merge its verbal and visual components into a presentation before an audience. Scholars have long recognized the importance of delivery for the effective public speaker.[1] Effective delivery brings together all the planning, researching, and organizing you've done for your speech. The volume of your voice, your posture, how you manage your time during a speech—all of these and more are aspects of delivery.

Your audience will not expect perfection from your speech, as there is always room for improvement. However, you want to make the best impression you can and achieve your goals for the speech. This chapter discusses several aspects of effective delivery: selecting an appropriate delivery method; understanding factors that influence a speaker's delivery; managing your voice, body, and audience during your speech; preparing your presentation outline; and practicing your speech.

The public presentation of a speech.

Theo Wargo/WireImage/Getty Images

There are four types of delivery methods: impromptu, extemporaneous, manuscript, and memorized. **Table 12.1** provides an overview of these four methods and the best situations in which to use them. When deciding on a delivery style, choose one that enhances the content of your speech and doesn't distract your audience.

Impromptu Speaking

In public speaking, delivery with little or no preparation is called **impromptu speaking**. You engage in impromptu speaking every day as you communicate thoughts and ideas that spring up in the moment with no preparation or practice whatsoever. For example, when you answer a question in class or speak up during a meeting of a campus organization, you're using impromptu speaking. In this respect, impromptu speaking is simply another way to use the basic communication skills you already have and use regularly. Learning how to express yourself on the spot without relying on research, extensive preparation, or notes will help you do well in your public speaking class and in less-structured speaking situations beyond the classroom.

An impromptu speaker is given a topic on the spot and often has a minute or two to think about what to say. **Figure 12.1** provides questions you can ask yourself to quickly develop and organize your thoughts when you're faced with an impromptu speaking situation. As you present your speech, do your best to speak coherently. Keep your general purpose in mind—are you informing, persuading, or entertaining your audience about your topic? Don't worry about making mistakes—no one expects an impromptu speech to be perfect.

> A type of public speaking in which the speaker has little or no time to prepare a speech.

Table 12.1 Delivery Methods

Method	Brief definition	Advantages	Disadvantages	Typical situations
Impromptu	Speaking without preparation	Flexibility; complete spontaneity	Not researched; can be disorganized; speaker has little, if any, time to practice	Responding to audience questions
Extemporaneous	Giving a speech that has been planned, researched, organized, and practiced	Allows speaker to develop expertise on a topic; allows structured spontaneity; allows speaker to adjust to audience feedback	Researching, organizing, and practicing a speech is time-consuming	Most classroom, professional, and community presentations
Manuscript	Giving a speech that has been written out word for word	Allows speaker to choose each word precisely and time the speech exactly	Speaker uses written rather than spoken language; difficult to modify based on audience feedback	Political speeches
Memorized	Giving a speech that has been committed to memory	Allows speaker to present speech without notes; same speech can be presented many times	Can seem artificial; requires intensive practicing	Short ceremonial speeches

Extemporaneous Speaking

For **extemporaneous speaking**, you carefully research, organize, and rehearse your speech before you deliver it. This approach to speaking balances adapting to the audience in the moment with thorough planning and practicing. Because extemporaneous speaking requires both flexibility and forethought, it is sometimes called "structured spontaneity." When you appear spontaneous, your speech comes across as natural and authentic. Speaking extemporaneously helps you deliver an audience-centered and engaging message, greatly maximizing your chances of connecting with your listeners and having your speech achieve its purpose. For most of the public speaking situations you'll encounter, the extemporaneous method is the most desirable because its structured spontaneity usually makes it the most effective.

A type of public speaking in which the speaker researches, organizes, rehearses, and delivers a speech in a way that combines structure and spontaneity.

Manuscript Speaking

When politicians and world leaders give speeches, they usually appear to be speaking from just a few notes as they look directly at the audience and the camera. However, they're often reading from a teleprompter that displays a manuscript speech—a speech written out word for word. One advantage of **manuscript speaking** is that you can compose the exact language you want to use for your speech. In situations in which a misspoken word might lead to a tragic misunderstanding—such as when negotiating a peace treaty—manuscript speaking is necessary to maintain absolute precision. However, most public speakers will never have to speak in such sensitive situations.

A type of public speaking in which the speaker reads a written script word for word.

Manuscript speaking may seem easy—you just write your speech out and read it to your audience. But reading from a manuscript greatly reduces your ability to make eye contact with your listeners and adapt to their feedback. Audience members may also feel ignored. In addition, when speakers write out their entire speech word for word, they tend to use written rather than spoken language. Because written language is more complex and less personal than spoken language, audience members may struggle to understand a speaker who is using language that's meant for reading rather than listening. Audiences tend to favor an extemporaneous style, so avoid reading a speech from a manuscript unless the situation calls for it.

Memorized Speaking

When delivering a memorized speech, the speaker commits the entire speech to memory and then presents it to an audience. **Memorized speaking** can be useful and appropriate in certain situations. For short speeches, such as a wedding toast or acceptance of an award, knowing exactly what you're going to say reduces the chances that you'll sound unprepared or make comments you'll regret later. And memorizing small sections of your speech, such as your introduction, key transitions, and conclusion, helps reduce anxiety and can increase your self-confidence (Chapter 2). However, memorizing an entire lengthy speech can cause several problems. First, if you forget a line or a word, you may find it difficult to recover and continue your speech. Second, you can't adapt to audience responses during your speech. Third, memorized speeches often seem artificial and lack spontaneity.

A type of public speaking in which the speaker commits a speech to memory.

Understanding Factors That Influence Delivery

The speaking situation and speech type are external factors that help determine how you will deliver your speech. This section addresses four important factors unique to each speaker that influence delivery: culture, gender, language fluency and dialect, and physical dis/abilities.

231

Culture and Delivery

Cultural factors influence how a speaker behaves in front of an audience and how the audience perceives the speaker. For example, people from China, Japan, Korea, Vietnam, and other East Asian countries often consider it rude to highlight their own accomplishments. This unwillingness to draw attention to themselves may explain the finding that college students in Thailand perceive themselves as less competent in public speaking than their American counterparts. Similarly, the greater emphasis on public speaking in American schools likely contributes to college students in the United States. reporting higher levels of communication competence and willingness to communicate than students in Sweden.[2] In contrast, public speaking forms a central part of Kenyan culture, with people of all ages expected to give speeches at ceremonies and other occasions.[3]

Culture also influences how audiences perceive speakers. For example, what American audiences perceive as nervousness in a speaker, Asian audiences may view as modesty or less-direct communication.[4] If, based on your cultural, social, or family background, you're used to asserting yourself in more subtle ways, you might have to develop new skills to adapt to the expectations of American audiences.

Gender and Delivery

In the past, audiences evaluated female and male speakers differently. For example, men were granted higher status and greater credibility, while women were typically judged based on their clothing and physical attractiveness.[5] Much has changed over the years, and some of the most powerful and eloquent speakers today, such as Maureen Dowd, Michelle Obama, Gloria Estefan, and Oprah Winfrey, are well-respected women. Yet research shows that audiences still tend to evaluate speakers based on their gender.

Studies of college public speaking classrooms reveal that a speaker's gender has little impact on overall evaluations of competence: Male and female speakers are viewed as equally capable. However, male speakers are often viewed as more influential and persuasive, even when female and male speakers display similar behaviors. In addition, audiences seem to judge men's and women's credibility differently. Female speakers' credibility tends to rest primarily on their use of trustworthy information sources. In contrast, male speakers' credibility enjoys a broader base, including believable sources, eye contact, organization of ideas, and vocal variety.[6] Of course, many factors contribute to a speaker's credibility, regardless of gender. A woman who avoids making eye contact, speaks in a monotone, and organizes her points poorly risks making a negative impression on the audience. Similarly, a man who relies only on his voice, eye contact, and speech structure to win over listeners likely will earn low marks as a speaker.

One challenging delivery issue women face is making themselves heard. Women generally speak at a higher pitch and a lower volume than men, making women's voices more difficult to hear. (**Pitch** is the highness or lowness of the speaker's voice, and **volume** is the loudness of the speaker's voice.) This difference stems partly from biology—women have shorter vocal cords than men do—and partly from culture—girls are expected to talk more quietly than boys.[7] Whatever the reason, female speakers usually must work harder than male speakers to project their voice. Speaking more loudly and at a slightly lower pitch while delivering a speech may feel odd at first, because you're used to hearing your voice sound a certain way. But good vocal volume is essential to public speaking, because you want your audience to hear your message.

The use of vocal pitch also affects how audiences judge a woman's confidence as a speaker. One way you indicate you're asking a *question* is to raise the pitch of your voice.

> The highness or lowness of a speaker's voice.

> The loudness of a speaker's voice.

Because women's voices are often harder to hear than men's voices, women speakers must use strategies to make sure their audiences hear them. Even when women use a microphone, speaking at a higher volume and with a slightly lower pitch will help their audiences understand them.

AP Images/Tiffany Michalka

When a speaker's voice goes up at the end of a *statement*, audience members view the speaker as less confident and less sure of the information presented. Research suggests that women tend to do this more than men,[8] so women speakers should watch for this problem, and correct it if necessary, as they practice their speeches.

Fluency, Dialect, and Delivery

Stuttering is one of the more common speech impairments that affect public speakers. Researchers estimate that more than 3 million Americans stutter, although most children who stutter cease to do so as they grow older.[9] People who stutter are often characterized as nervous, shy, quiet, withdrawn, and fearful. Although studies show these attributes are unfounded, fluent speakers continue to view people who stutter negatively.[10] However, people who stutter can employ three strategies to change those negative perceptions: acknowledgment, goal attainment, and eye contact. First, research has found that simply acknowledging you stutter reduces the pressure you may feel to speak perfectly, improves your fluency, and causes the audience to view you more favorably. Second, concentrating on the goal for your speech—presenting your ideas to the audience—keeps you focused on your role as a speaker and builds your confidence. Third, making eye contact with your audience may not reduce your stuttering, but it will help others view you more positively and respond in more supportive ways. When you look at your audience, you're better able to monitor their feedback and respond to it appropriately.[11]

Dialect is another factor that influences delivery. A **dialect** is the vocabulary, grammar, and pronunciation used by a group of people. Everyone speaks in some dialect, even if they don't recognize it. Although dialects are often associated with specific regions of the United States, such as the South and New England, dialects can also be ethnically based, as with African American English and Cajun or Creole English.[12] Dialects also reflect migration patterns, as in the case of 2008 vice-presidential nominee and former Alaska governor Sarah Palin. A detailed analysis of her speech found that her dialect, such as saying *goin'* rather than *going* and using terms such as *gosh darn* and *you betcha*, reflected features of Upper Midwest speakers, a region of the United States from which many Alaskans can trace their roots.[13]

> The vocabulary, grammar, and pronunciation used by a specific group of people, such as an ethnic or regional group.

Dialects can reveal rich cultural traditions and help bind a group together. No dialect is inferior to any other way of speaking, although historically public speaking students have been encouraged to speak in the mainstream American English dialect that most newscasters use.[14] The importance of examining dialect rests in how well your audience can understand you. When you're talking with others in your own dialect group, you don't notice how you use language. But when you speak in front of an audience, you must be more aware of how you use language so that you can ensure your audience understands your message. If you articulate your words clearly, pronounce them correctly, and define terms that might be unfamiliar to your audience, you will be able to bridge most of the differences between your dialect and your audience's.

Physical Impairments and Delivery

If you are a speaker with a physical impairment, it may affect how you deliver your speech. The following sections offer strategies for speakers using mobility aids and speakers with visual or hearing impairments.

Speakers Using Mobility Aids Speakers who use crutches or a walker must consider several issues before presenting a speech. First, identify your plan for

© Bob Daemmrich/The Image Works

If you use a mobility aid, reduce stress when you give a speech by planning ahead. For example, consider how you'll approach and leave the speaker's area.

approaching and leaving the speaker's area to make the minutes before and after your speech as stress free as possible. Check that your path to and from the area is unobstructed and easy to reach. Second, decide if standing for your entire presentation will work for you. As you practice your speech, you may find that you become uncomfortable or needlessly tired if you stand up. If that's the case, consider sitting when you give your speech. Third, find the best way to manage your note cards and presentation media so you easily integrate them into your speech delivery.

Speakers who use a wheelchair or need to sit for their presentations must pay special attention to visibility and voice projection. You can increase your visibility by not having a large object, such as a table, between you and your audience. This allows you to get physically closer to your listeners and keeps the focus on you.

Practice speaking aloud to attain the best possible voice projection. Sit up as straight as possible, take a deep breath, and breathe out as you speak. To check your volume, practice with a friend in a room that is similar in size to the one where you'll be speaking. Have your friend sit at the back of the room and tell you when your voice can be heard easily. If voice projection is still a problem, use a microphone.

Speakers with Visual Impairments About 14 million Americans are visually impaired.[15] For public speakers with visual impairments, the key issue is how to recall everything you want to say. Memorization is a safe strategy for short speeches, but committing long speeches to memory is a challenge. Notes in braille are a good solution. If you don't read braille but are able to read large print, try using big note cards with clearly written keywords.

If your visual impairment is such that written notes are not feasible, you might consider three alternatives. First, develop your speech by capturing your ideas on an MP3 player (such as an iPod) or other digital audio recording device, revising until you are satisfied with the speech. Using an earbud, present the speech as you listen to it on an MP3 player. Second, if you write in braille, write out your speech, have a sighted person record it in a digital format, and use the MP3 player as in the first strategy. Keep in mind that listening to and saying your speech at the same time is quite difficult to do and takes considerable practice. The third alternative is to write out your speech and have a sighted person present it for you. You should then be prepared to answer questions after the speech.

Speakers with Hearing Impairments The Gallaudet Research Institute estimates that nearly 20.3 million people in the United States are deaf or hard of hearing.[16] As a public speaker with a hearing impairment, consider your ability to hear and your comfort with using your voice. If you usually communicate using American Sign Language (ASL), signing and using a sign-to-voice interpreter is a logical choice. If you're confident about your vocal abilities, present your speech aloud. During the question-and-answer session, ask listeners to state questions loudly and clearly, or request a microphone for audience members to use.

People with impairments should adapt the preceding techniques to suit their own physical, cognitive, and sensory requirements. There's no need to tell your audience why you are doing things your way.[17] If you have an impairment that affects your speech delivery, you may want to discuss the matter with your instructor so you'll get the most out of your public speaking class and your audience will get the most out of your speeches.

Managing Your Voice During Your Speech

Your voice is a key tool for getting your audience's attention, emphasizing points, stirring emotions, and conveying the content of your message. Good voice volume, variations in vocal qualities, minimal pauses, and clear articulation and pronunciation are essential for effective public speaking.

Speak Loudly Enough

Right from the beginning of your speech, speak so that everyone in your audience can hear you. This may take some practice if you feel uncomfortable raising your voice

234

volume above an everyday speaking level. However, sufficient volume is crucial; audience members shouldn't have to strain to hear you. If you're not sure what "loud enough" sounds like, practice with a friend in the room where you'll present the speech, or in a similar space. Have your friend sit in the farthest corner of the room, and raise your voice volume until she or he can easily hear you.

Vary Your Rate, Pitch, and Volume

Differences stand out to listeners; sameness does not. Not every point or statement included in a speech carries the same weight or tone. Some parts of your speech may be on the lighter side; others may be more serious. A faster rate (the speed at which a speaker speaks), higher pitch, and louder volume suggest energy and excitement. A slower **rate**, lower pitch, and softer volume indicate a more solemn and contemplative tone. Speaking in a **monotone**, or with little alteration in pitch, signals nervousness and boredom to your audience.[18] Use **vocal variety** to fit your topic and evoke emotion in the audience.

Avoid Vocalized Pauses

Some speakers talk more rapidly in front of an audience; others speak more slowly. As you're giving your speech, observe how much time it takes to present the introduction. If you used less time than you did when you practiced, assess your speaking rate. You may be running your words together or not pausing between sentences and phrases. In contrast, if you used more time for your introduction than you did when you practiced, perhaps you're speaking too slowly. You may be using **vocalized pauses** such as "ah," "umm," and "you know." These verbal fillers use up time without providing any information, and they hurt your credibility because they make you sound unsure of yourself.[19]

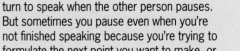

Speaking of . . .

Banishing Vocalized Pauses

In everyday conversations, you know it's your turn to speak when the other person pauses. But sometimes you pause even when you're not finished speaking because you're trying to formulate the next point you want to make, or you can't quite think of the word you want. You don't want the other person to jump in and start talking, so you say "ah" or "um" to tell the other person, "I'm not done talking yet." This habit carries over to public speaking, even though you know listeners will not start talking if you pause. When you hear yourself using a vocalized pause, concentrate on just pausing—your audience will wait for you. Also, as you practice your speech you'll become more certain of what you want to say, reducing those "ahs" and "ums."

The speed at which a speaker speaks.

A way of speaking in which the speaker does not alter his or her pitch.

Changes in the volume, rate, and pitch of a speaker's voice that affect the meaning of the words delivered.

"Ah," "um," "you know," and other verbal fillers that speakers use when they're trying to think of what they want to say.

Articulate Your Words Clearly and Pronounce Them Correctly

In everyday speech, speakers often articulate poorly, leaving off the endings of words ("I'm leavin' soon"), skipping sounds entirely ("I'm gonna leave in twenny minutes"), and running words together ("Waddaya think?"). Poor **articulation** isn't necessarily a problem in casual conversation, but during a speech it may cause your audience to strain to understand you and may hurt your credibility. Incorrect **pronunciation** can also damage your credibility. Some common mispronunciations are "git" for *get*, "excape" for *escape*, "pitcher" for *picture*, and "reckanize" for *recognize*. If you're unsure of a word's correct pronunciation, check a dictionary—many online dictionaries include audio files so you can listen to how a word is pronounced. And when you practice your speech in front of a small audience, ask them to point out words you pronounce incorrectly, then practice saying the words aloud correctly until you're comfortable saying them.

The physical process of producing specific speech sounds to make language intelligible.

The act of saying words correctly according to the accepted standards of the speaker's language.

235

SPEECH BUDDY VIDEO 12.1
Reviewing Vocal Delivery

In this video, Janine and Anthony demonstrate effective and ineffective vocal delivery.

ACTIVITY 12.1
Speak Up

This activity asks you first to evaluate various speakers' vocal delivery and then to apply what you're learning about vocal delivery by considering what your own vocal challenges might be.

Managing Your Body During Your Speech

Everything about how you present yourself should tell your audience that you're poised, confident, and enthusiastic. In addition, knowing what to do with your body can significantly reduce speech anxiety. This section outlines specific ways to use attire, facial expressions, and body movement effectively when giving your speech. If you live with a dis/ability, you may need to modify some of these guidelines to suit your situation.

Dress for the Occasion

Appearances count, especially in public speaking. Your clothing should enhance your speech and contribute to listeners' perceptions of your dynamism and overall credibility. Dressing appropriately for your speeches demonstrates respect for your audience—you care enough about them and your speech to look your best. Some instructors require that students dress in corporate business attire for their speeches in order to emphasize the differences between social conversation and public speaking. Your instructor's dress code may not be that formal, but you should dress at least one step up from what you usually wear to class. This advice also applies to audiences outside of school, so try to dress about a step up from what you think your audience will be wearing. If you look the part, it will be easier to play the part and manage your nervousness.[20]

Face Your Audience and Make Eye Contact with Them

Your listeners want to know you're talking to them—not the floor, your notes, a tree outside the window, or a spot on the wall at the back of the room. Look at all your listeners, from those in the front row to those in the back corners. Avoid scanning the room from one side to the other, looking only at audience members who happen to be sitting in the middle of the room, or concentrating your attention on the instructor. When you don't look at audience members, they become invisible to you and you become invisible to them.[21] Avoid addressing your audience from a sideways angle or from one side of the room, and never speak with your back to the audience. Even when you write something on a chalkboard or white board, turn around and speak to your audience after you've finished writing. Talk to your audience—not to the screen—when using digital slides or an overhead projector. Glance quickly and infrequently at your notes, using them simply to trigger your memory. Good eye contact signals that you are competent, trustworthy, dynamic, and sociable.

Display Appropriate Facial Expressions

You communicate much of how you feel through your face. A smile, frown, or puzzled look can underscore a point. Adjust your facial expression according to the content of your speech and the message you're trying to send. For example, smiling nervously when talking about a serious topic, such as whether the United States should intervene in the conflict in Darfur, sends a mixed message, and may cause your audience to misunderstand your intent. However, smiling as you greet your audience before you start your speech lets them know you're pleased to be there.

Maintain Good Posture

Your **posture** is the way you position and carry your body. When you have your shoulders back, head up, hands loosely at your sides, knees slightly bent, feet shoulder width apart and flat on the floor, and weight evenly distributed, you can easily move and gesture. Standing up straight demonstrates your self-assurance; keeping your feet flat on the floor prevents you from shifting your weight from foot to foot or crossing and uncrossing your feet.

The way a speaker positions and carries her or his body.

Move with Purpose and Spontaneity

When planning your speech, consider what body movements can help you communicate your message in a dynamic way. As you practice, experiment with movement that helps you underscore a point, demonstrates your confidence, and captures your audience's attention. For example, you might step closer to your listeners to make them feel included, especially when discussing how a point affects them personally. Or you might take a few steps to the left or right to signal a transition from one main point to the next.

Have a reason or purpose for movements you make while you speak. For instance, you might want to walk toward one side of the room as you begin a narrative and move to the other side for the dramatic ending. However, you don't want to walk around aimlessly—your audience will wonder why you're pacing and may miss what you're saying. In addition, avoid movements that appear staged or overly dramatic. You sometimes see speakers in classic speeches using stock gestures that clearly were meant to signal specific information, such as holding up three fingers with the statement, "I'll cover three main points in this speech." Today, audiences prefer a more natural, conversational style.

Avoid Physical Barriers

Although a few public speaking contexts require a using a podium due to convention and formality, in most cases you won't need one. A podium constrains your ability to use your entire body to convey your message and puts a physical barrier between you and your audience. If you need to use a podium or table to support your visual materials or laptop, stand to the side, not behind the furniture.

Applying the delivery strategies outlined in these discussions of voice and body will help you give dynamic, engaging, extemporaneous presentations. **Figure 12.2**

Figure 12.2 Strategies for effective delivery

- Speak loudly enough.
- Vary your voice's rate, pitch, and volume.
- Avoid vocalized pauses.
- Articulate your words clearly and pronounce them correctly.
- Dress for the occasion.
- Face your audience and make eye contact with everyone.
- Display appropriate facial expressions.
- Maintain good posture.
- Move with purpose and spontaneity.
- Avoid physical barriers.

provides a quick summary of these strategies. After a while, most of this will come quite naturally. You'll develop your own style as you become more confident about your public speaking abilities.

Managing Your Audience During Your Speech

Managing your audience begins with researching your listeners and designing your message to achieve their goals as well as your own (Chapter 5). If you have developed a speech that your audience finds useful and interesting, and if you present the speech in an enthusiastic, engaging manner, listeners will more likely respond the way you expect them to. You can also help influence an audience's response to you by adjusting your speaking space, involving your audience, respecting your audience's time, accommodating audience members with impairments, responding calmly to rude or hostile audiences, and being prepared for question-and-answer sessions.

Adjust Your Speaking Space as Needed

Set up the speaking space in a way that's comfortable for you and your audience. Even small modifications can influence how the audience listens to you. For example, if you're in a small conference room with a large table, suggest that audience members turn their chairs so it's easier for them to see you and your digital slides or other presentation materials. This also reduces the likelihood that audience members will talk among themselves. If lighting is harsh or glaring, dim or turn off a few lights so audience members will feel more relaxed. Close doors to hallways and other rooms so you're not interrupted. In a large auditorium, don't be afraid to get out from behind the podium. Audience members will view you as more confident and personable and will pay more attention to your speech.

Involve Your Audience

Involving your audience requires careful attention to your listeners' feedback (Chapter 3). Make the audience part of your speech by

- Referring to what others have said in their speeches ("As Tasha mentioned in her speech last week . . . ").

- Calling on specific audience members ("Hector, what's your reaction to the video clip we just saw?").

- Asking for volunteers ("I need two people to help me demonstrate this process").

As you're speaking, observe the audience, noting if they seem interested, bored, confused, supportive, hostile, uncertain, or the like. **Nonverbal messages**, such as facial expressions and tone of voice, can be ambiguous. So you may want to check your interpretations of audience behaviors. If someone seems confused about a point, you could say, "Anya, you look puzzled. Are you? Other people might be as well, so I can explain that last point in more detail." Some nonverbal behaviors are fairly clear, such as listeners shaking their heads in disagreement or nodding in agreement. Commenting on the behaviors you observe lets your audience know you are interested in their feedback. When you notice those shaking heads, you might say, "Some of you seem to disagree with me. Let me tell you something that might change your mind." If listeners are nodding, you might say, "I can tell by your reactions that some of you have had the same experience." These strategies allow you to integrate audience members into your speech.

> Information that is not communicated with words, but rather, through movement, gesture, facial expression, vocal quality, use of time, use of space, and touch.

Respect the Audience's Time

You may be familiar with time-oriented phrases such as "Don't waste my time," "I like to spend my time wisely," and "Time is money." Your listeners will expect you to manage your time effectively. Remember, it's *their* time as well. Make the most of your speaking time so you achieve your goals and your listeners feel satisfied with the information you've provided.

When you practice your speech, record your time so you stay within your time limit. Have a general idea of how much time you spend on each part of your speech. This information will help you pace yourself when presenting your speech to your audience.

As you progress through your speech, monitor your time so that each part of your speech receives adequate attention. For instance, if you have three main points and spend half of your speaking time on the first point, you won't be able to develop the other two points fully. In addition, as you adjust to your audience's feedback, you may find it necessary to devote more time to a particular point and leave out other parts of your speech. For example, you might omit an example or shorten a story in your conclusion. That's part of extemporaneous speaking—adapting your speech to your audience and the context during the presentation.

How can you monitor your time when so many other aspects of delivery demand your attention? Many public speaking instructors use time cards for student speeches. For example, if you have five minutes for your speech, the instructor or a designated student will show you cards that tell you how many minutes you have left. If your instructor doesn't use a timing method, use a watch or stopwatch to keep track of your speaking time.

John Oates/Alamy

Asking an audience member to volunteer for a demonstration is a great way to involve your audience in your speech.

Accommodate Audience Members with Impairments

When presenting a speech to audience members with cognitive, sensory, or physical impairments, accommodate their needs so they can participate fully in the speaking event. Your goal as a speaker is to include everyone and ensure that no one is left out. First, check that audience members who require accommodations have them. For example, an audience member with a hearing impairment may need an interpreter. Second, face the audience so everyone can easily see and hear you. Make sure nothing interferes with your voice projection. Third, speak loudly, clearly, and not too rapidly. This is especially important for interpreters, who need a moment or two to translate what you're saying. Fourth, describe the content of any visual materials you use, such as digital slides or overhead transparencies, explaining images as well as text. Finally, if you're not sure what you need to do to accommodate audience members, privately ask them before you start your speech.

Respond Calmly to Rude or Hostile Audience Members

Sometimes audience members express hostility during or after the speech, although this seldom happens in public speaking classes. Some topics can trigger deep emotions. If you're speaking on a controversial topic such as capital punishment or gun control laws, be prepared for negative reactions from audience members who disagree with you. In handling these responses, remain calm. Engaging in a shouting match with audience members will damage your credibility and increase your anxiety level.[22] Let hostile audience members know you understand that they disagree with you. If they don't calm down, suggest that you continue the discussion after you've finished your speech.

Be Prepared for a Question-and-Answer Period

In many cases, once you've finished your speech, audience members will have an opportunity to ask you questions. Researching your audience helps you anticipate those questions; researching your topic helps you answer them. Apply the following guidelines in the question-and-answer session:

- Listen carefully to the question, giving the audience member time to complete it.

- Repeat the question if other audience members couldn't hear it.

- Answer questions as completely as possible.

- If you don't know the answer to a question, admit it and offer to look up the necessary information.

When audience members ask questions, they're most often seeking clarification or more information—they're not evaluating you. Think of the question-and-answer session as a friendly conversation and answer questions as best you can.

Apply it

Helping Others Deliver Their Speeches

One of the best ways to find out if you've really learned something is to teach others about it. In your service learning location or other place where you volunteer your time, identify a few people who are interested in learning more about speech delivery. Develop a short workshop or module about how to deliver a speech, such as how to use your voice and body to enhance your message.

Then follow up in a few weeks by having attendees meet again to present brief speeches. Evaluate the effectiveness of their delivery and your effectiveness as a teacher. What did you learn about speech delivery from teaching others about it? How will you apply what you've learned in your own presentations?

Preparing Your Presentation Outline

In the beginning stages of speech development, you use a working outline (Chapter 4). The complete-sentence outline (Chapter 8) elaborates on the working outline by including full sentences detailing all the parts of your speech. The **presentation outline** distills your complete-sentence outline into a list of words and phrases to guide you through the main parts of your speech and the transitions between them. Like the working outline, the presentation outline is brief. Although you may initially create it on your computer or on paper, you'll transfer your presentation outline to note cards to practice and deliver your speech. **Table 12.2** summarizes the three types of outlines.

An outline that distills a complete-sentence outline, listing only the words and phrases that will guide the speaker through the main parts of the speech and the transitions between them.

Knowing how to create and use a presentation outline is a fundamental skill for extemporaneous public speaking. The presentation outline allows you to

- Refer comfortably and precisely to the information you have gathered.

- Present that information in a clear and organized way.

- Engage your audience personally and professionally during the speech.

As you practice your speech, you'll develop the confidence to rely on brief notes while speaking in front of an audience. A presentation outline makes it possible for a well-prepared speaker to deliver an abundance of ideas effectively.

Identify Keywords

The **keywords** in a presentation outline are very similar to the keywords or search terms you use online: They identify subjects or points of primary interest or concern. Keywords represent the most important points you want to talk about in your speech.

A word that identifies a subject or a point of primary interest or concern.

Table 12.2   Types of Outlines

Type of outline	Functions	Key features	Chapter	
Working	Assists in initial topic development; guides research	Includes main points and possible subpoints; revised during research process	4: Developing Your Purpose and Topic	◀ **You are here**
Complete-sentence	Clearly identifies all pieces of information for the speech; puts ideas in order; forms basis for developing the presentation outline	Uses complete sentences; lists all sections of speech and all references; revised during preparation process	8: Organizing and Outlining Your Speech	
Presentation	Assists in practicing and giving your speech	Uses keywords; revised as you practice your speech; often transferred to note cards for use during practice and the final presentation	12: Delivering Your Speech	

Because they're listed in the same order as the sentences in your complete-sentence outline, they indicate the order in which you want to present those points.

Although presentation outlines are usually quite short, they can be created only after you've fully researched and developed your speech. As you use your presentation outline or note cards to practice your speech, you'll find that you need to move back and forth between your complete-sentence outline and your presentation outline, revising the former and then the latter several times. Each time, you'll be challenged to condense your ideas and information into keywords for your presentation outline that will trigger your memory as you present your speech. **Figure 12.3** shows an example of a presentation outline.

Transfer Your Presentation Outline to Note Cards

Once you've completed your presentation outline, you're ready to transfer the information from your outline to the note cards you'll use during your speech. Write your keywords on the note cards to remind you of the points you want to cover in your speech. Organize and number the cards in the order in which you want to present those points. Stick to your keywords and don't write out sentences, quotations, or other lengthy bits of information. And make sure the print is large enough for you to read easily as you're giving your speech.

During your presentation, hold your note cards in one hand. The only time you should have both hands on your note cards is when you move from one card to the next. The audience expects you to consult your notes during the speech—it shows you planned your speech but didn't memorize it. Maintain eye contact with your audience, glancing at your notes briefly and infrequently. It's better to lose your place for a moment than to hide your face for most of the speech.

The presentation outline and note cards are your dependable assistants. When developed and used effectively, the presentation outline helps you give an extemporaneous speech that centers your attention on the audience. Using note cards demonstrates your planning and preparation, keeps you organized, and allows you to create a good rapport with your listeners.

Practicing the Delivery of Your Speech

Too little practice and you won't be ready the day of your speech. Too much practice and your speech loses spontaneity. Moreover, rehearsing your speech over and over will not ensure a successful presentation on speech day.[23] Practicing your speech effectively requires devoting quality time to rehearsing your presentation.

Rather than practicing it just once, you will practice your speech in different ways and at different stages until you are completely ready. But being fully prepared does not mean that the speech you give to your audience will be exactly the same as the speech you practice. You want to present an engaging and dynamic speech, not one that is programmed and predictable.

Give a Version of Your Speech

Think of each speech you give as just one of many possible speeches you could have given with exactly the same information and preparation. You don't have to give a "perfect" speech—you must simply give an excellent version of your speech. If you were to give the same speech tomorrow, and again the next day, you would not deliver those speeches in exactly the same way. The speechmaking method you are learning prepares you to give excellent versions of your speeches adapted to your audience and the speaking context.

Figure 12.3 Sample presentation outline

Title: The History and Etiquette of Chopsticks

Attention-getter: [hold chopsticks and click together twice] Why are these called chopsticks? Because [click, click] they help you eat fast!

Thesis: Chopsticks have a central place in the eating etiquette of several Asian cultures.

Preview: First, I'll tell you about the history of chopsticks in the four "chopstick" countries: China, Vietnam, Japan, and Korea. Then I'll talk about how each culture has developed its own chopsticks etiquette.

I. History
  A. China: origin—5000 years ago
    1. Confucius influence
    2. Cook over fire
    3. 12 inches
    4. Bamboo/wood
  B. Vietnam: 2000 years ago
    1. Like China
    2. Old: wood; now: plastic
  C. Korea: 2000 years ago
    1. 8–9 inches
    2. Old: silver; now: wood/stainless
  D. Japan: 1500 years ago
    1. Shorter and sharper
    2. 10 inches
    3. Lacquered wood
II. Etiquette
  A. China
    1. Hold up bowl
    2. Don't tap
    3. Don't spear
  B. Vietnam
    1. Eat from own bowl
    2. Don't hold in mouth
    3. Always use two
  C. Korea
    1. Use spoon for rice
    2. Spoon and chopsticks
    3. Dishes on table
  D. Japan
    1. Use chopstick rest
    2. Don't cross
    3. Don't rub together

Review: I explained the history of chopsticks in four Asian countries and the differences in chopsticks etiquette in those four cultures.

Reinforce purpose: Chopsticks have a long history, but what they look like and how they're used varies based on cultural practices.

Closure: Learning about chopsticks history and etiquette gave me an appreciation for something I've used all my life. Now I know why I eat so quickly [click, click]. Thank you.

With extemporaneous speaking, you should not commit your whole speech or even large sections of it to memory. With thorough preparation and sufficient practice, you'll know what you want to say well enough to say it effectively when you deliver your speech. For example, you will recall certain words and phrases that sounded good when you practiced. You may not say things exactly the same way as you did when you practiced, but you'll feel confident that you know how to make your ideas clear.

Practice Your Speech in Stages

Practicing permeates the entire speech preparation process. As you research your topic (Chapter 6), organize your ideas (Chapter 8), identify the language you'll use in your speech (Chapter 10), and incorporate presentation media (Chapter 11), you'll practice various parts of the presentation, rethinking and revising what you plan to say. Review your complete-sentence outline as you go along, trying out the introduction, main points, transitions, and conclusion to find out how they work or don't work. Practice in stages, section by section. Don't wait until you think you have a finished product.

Practicing Parts of Your Speech During this stage of practice, your goals are to check that your speech makes sense, identify keywords that will best trigger your memory, and try out your presentation materials. When you practice, say the words of your speech out loud to determine if your ideas are clear and if your language and delivery techniques work together to achieve your purpose. By speaking out loud when you practice, you hear your main points and supporting materials and can consider how you might say something more clearly, precisely, humorously, seriously, or persuasively. Practicing out loud allows you to become your own audience, ready to give instant, productive feedback. Try saying small portions of your speech as if you were facing an audience. Listen for how you've organized and supported your ideas, make adjustments, and keep adjusting with the individual segments of your speech.

Practicing your speech during this stage includes practicing with your presentation materials. No matter how briefly you'll be using presentation materials, include them in your practice sessions to find out if they accomplish what you want them to and if you can integrate them into your speech easily.

Practicing Your Whole Speech Now that you've practiced the various parts of your speech, you're ready to practice the entire speech. You'll want to practice just like you're giving your speech to the audience: standing up (or sitting, depending on ability), holding your note cards, and integrating all your presentation materials. Practicing the whole speech with any presentation media you plan to use allows you to observe how your main points flow. You'll also be able to perfect your introduction and conclusion (Chapter 9).

In this stage of practicing, invite friends, family members, coworkers, and others to provide constructive feedback. If you want them to focus on a particular aspect of your presentation, such as transitions or gestures, tell them before you begin your speech. Then be ready to listen to their comments without becoming defensive, knowing they want you to do your best. Research shows that practicing your speech in front of four or more people improves your presentation on speech day.[24] Videotaping yourself a few times as you practice can also prove helpful because you'll get an idea of how you look and sound.

Time Your Speech

Your speech should fit within the time allotted and should not go under or over the time limit. When you give your speech, you want to use your time well, presenting the introduction, main points, and conclusion at a comfortable pace that is neither slow nor rushed. During practice sessions, note the time you need for the sections of your speech so you have a rough idea of how long it takes you to get through each part. Then when you deliver your speech, you'll be better able to monitor how you're using your time. Knowing how long your speech will last also gives you confidence and control during the presentation.

> **Watch** it

SPEECH BUDDY VIDEO 12.3
Practicing Your Speech

In this video, all the Speech Buddies describe and demonstrate how they practice their speeches.

> **Use** it

Watch your Speech Buddy video ...

... and use what you've learned in your next speech.

ACTIVITY 12.3
Take It from the Top

This activity first asks you to evaluate different speech scenarios to determine effective plans to guide the speakers when they practice their speeches, and then gives you a chance to develop a plan for practicing your own speech.

Summary

Delivering your speech brings together all your planning and preparation. Speakers use four delivery methods: impromptu, extemporaneous, manuscript, and memorized. For most speeches, you'll want to speak extemporaneously, balancing careful planning with flexibility.

Several factors influence a public speaker's delivery, including culture and gender. Cultural norms that differ from those of the United States might require a public speaking student to develop new and adaptive skills. Similarly, women speakers often have to adapt to the fact that audiences evaluate women and men differently in some aspects of speech delivery. In addition, women often have trouble being heard because they tend to speak in a lower volume and at a higher pitch. A well-prepared speaker can overcome negative audience perceptions, regardless of gender.

Other factors that influence delivery are language fluency, dialect, and physical impairments. Regarding fluency, stuttering and dialect are common issues. Research has found that speakers who stutter may best manage the problem through acknowledgement and eye contact with the audience. And all speakers should examine their dialect and make any adjustments necessary for audience comprehension. Speakers with physical impairments may need to adjust their delivery in ways that work best for them and the audience.

Delivering your speech well means effectively managing your voice, your body, and your audience. In managing your voice and body, apply strategies such as using good vocal variety, clearly articulating your words, dressing for the occasion, and making eye contact with your entire audience. To manage your audience effectively, adjust your

245

Chapter 12 : Delivering Your Speech

speaking space as needed, involve the audience in your speech, respect the audience's time, accommodate audience members with impairments, handle hostile or rude audience members calmly, and be prepared for questions.

Careful research, planning, organizing, and preparation provide a solid base for presenting your speech. The presentation outline helps you achieve an organized, engaging, and professional presentation. Practice your speech in stages, distilling your complete-sentence outline into a brief presentation outline. Incorporate any presentation materials into the speech as you practice, making modifications as necessary. Put in quality practice time so that when speech day arrives you're prepared to give an excellent version of your speech. Closely manage your time, adjusting your speech as needed.

Review it

Directory of Study and Review Resources

IN THE BOOK
Summary
Key Terms
Critical Challenges

MORE STUDY RESOURCES
Quizzes
WebLinks
Peer-reviewed videos

STUDENT WORKBOOK
12.1: Model Speakers
12.2: Deliver a Full Thought to One Person
12.3: Rotating Audiences
12.4: Movement for Clarity
12.5: Filling the Space with Sound

SPEECH BUDDY VIDEOS
WATCH It Video
12.1: Reviewing Vocal Delivery
12.2: Reviewing Physical Delivery
12.3: Practicing Your Speech
USE It Activity
12.1: Speak Up
12.2: Move with Purpose
12.3: Take It from the Top

SAMPLE SPEECH VIDEOS
Katherine, "Is That Kosher?"
   informative speech
Tiffany, self-introduction speech

SPEECH BUILDER EXPRESS
Goal/purpose
Thesis statement
Organization
Outline
Supporting material
Transitions
Introduction
Conclusion
Title
Works cited
Completing the speech outline

INFOTRAC
Recommended search terms
Speech delivery
Physical speech delivery
Vocal speech delivery
Speech practice
Anxiety and speech delivery

AUDIO STUDY TOOLS
"Turn Off Your TV" by Lisa
Critical thinking questions
Learning objectives
Chapter summary

246

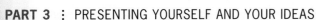

Guide to Your Online Resources

Your Speech Communication CourseMate for *Public Speaking: The Evolving Art* gives you access to the Speech Buddy video and activity featured in this chapter, additional sample speech videos, Speech Studio, Speech Builder Express, InfoTrac College Edition, and study aids such as glossary flashcards, review quizzes, and the Critical Challenge questions for this chapter, which you can respond to via email if your instructor so requests. In addition, your CourseMate features live WebLinks relevant to this chapter, including the American Rhetoric website, classic speeches on the History Channel site, and a site about taming speech anxiety hosted by the University of Hawai'i Maui Community College Speech Department. Links are regularly maintained, and new ones are added periodically.

Key Terms

articulation 235

delivery 229

dialect 233

extemporaneous speaking 231

impromptu speaking 230

keywords 241

manuscript speaking 231

memorized speaking 231

monotone 235

nonverbal messages 239

pitch 232

posture 237

presentation outline 241

pronunciation 235

rate 235

vocalized pauses 235

vocal variety 235

volume 232

Critical Challenges

Questions for Reflection and Discussion

1. Public speaking classes usually focus on extemporaneous speaking. What are some situations in which you'll likely give extemporaneous speeches in the future? You encounter impromptu speaking situations almost daily, especially in a college classroom. Give an example of a recent experience you had with impromptu speaking. While you're in school, you usually don't do much manuscript or memorized speaking. When might you use these methods in the future?

2. How have you practiced for speaking situations in the past? How effective were those practice strategies? How do you plan to practice for speeches in the future?

3. One aspect of adapting to your audience is accommodating individuals with disabilities. How might you do this in classroom speeches? In speeches outside the classroom?

4. During and after your speech, you may find that audience members challenge your ideas and conclusions. How might you avoid becoming defensive—a natural reaction—and encourage reasoned discussion?

5. Check out Speech Studio to analyze how other students deliver their speeches. Or record a speech you're working on, upload it to Speech Studio, and ask your peers for their feedback. What feedback could you use to fine-tune your delivery before you give your speech in class

13

Informative Speaking

Cengage Learning

Cengage Learning

CourseMate   SPEECH Studio   SPEECH BUILDER EXPRESS

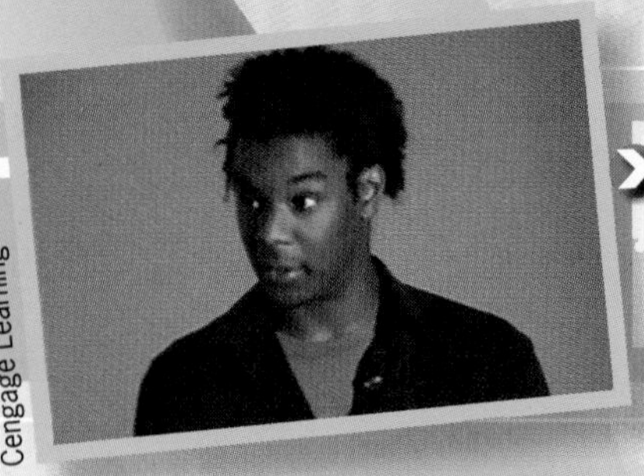

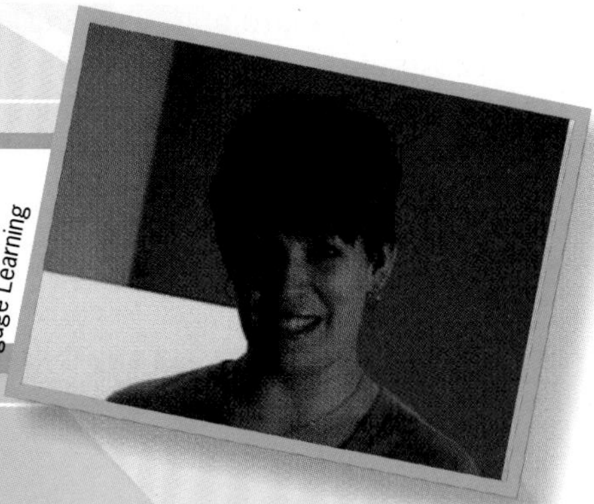

Their unique ability to exchange thoughts and instructions eventually allowed early humans to become the dominant species in the animal kingdom. Our ancestors' sheer survival depended on communication skill. By using speech and language effectively, they were able to coordinate their efforts to hunt wild animals, teach each other how to make simple tools, and take care of their children.[1] In terms of basic communication, not much has changed since then. To survive and thrive, people still need to pass information on to others clearly and convincingly. Being able to describe or explain something in a way that enables others to benefit from what you have to say—like what the fireman is doing in the image that opens this chapter—forms a solid foundation for becoming an excellent public speaker.

Today, public speakers have an advantage that speakers in every earlier period in human history lacked: Information from all over the world is easily available from a seemingly unlimited number of sources. What's more, the information age has morphed into the communication age. From the convenience of gathering information and images to the incredible ease with which you can send information to people almost anywhere on the planet, digital communication technologies give you new ways to retrieve and share information.[2] You can find jobs, take classes, research health issues, learn about other cultures, sell products and services, and conduct a host of other information exchanges online.[3] As a public speaker, you can rely on today's vastly expanded information environment to research your speech topics, find support for your main points, locate images for presentation media, and refer audiences to additional information and insights about your ideas.

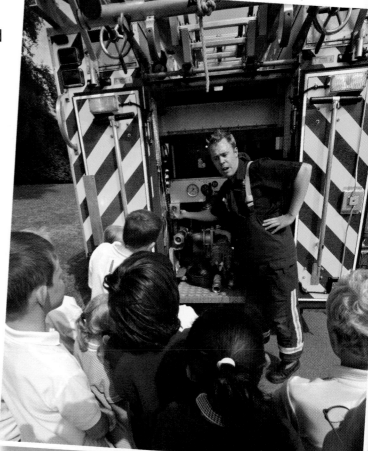

© SHOUT/Alamy

In **informative speaking** situations, the speaker seeks to deepen understanding, raise awareness, or increase knowledge about a topic. When you speak to inform, you want audience members to learn something from your speech. To do this, you share information with them. Your skill as a speaker is the mechanism that allows you to transfer information and knowledge accurately to others.[4]

Presenting a speech in which the speaker seeks to deepen understanding, raise awareness, or increase knowledge about a topic.

At the root of all human communication is the connection people make when they share information.[5] When you speak informatively, you make this important connection with your listeners. For this to happen, your listeners must find the speech meaningful, the information accurate, and the message clear. These three qualities, shown in **Figure 13.1**, form the basis of your competence as an informative speaker.

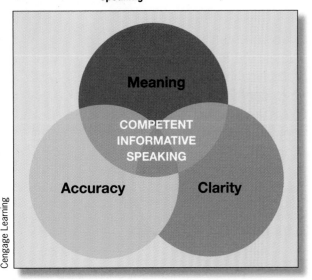

Figure 13.1 Characteristics of competent informative speaking

Cengage Learning

An Informative Speech Is Personally Meaningful

By effectively relating the topic to the audience, speakers can make their presentations come alive and be personally meaningful. Personalizing your speech begins with the topic you choose, which should be relevant to your audience. You can also personalize your message by using a narrative approach to organize the informative speech topic. Presentation media can help personalize your information too. Even the creators of today's digital media try to make the experience of long-distance interaction as personal as possible for users. For example, emoticons (smiley-face icons) were invented to warm up online communication. Many of the emotional techniques you use to personalize instant messages, text messages, photos, and files can also be used to personalize the information you share with others in your speeches.

An Informative Speech Is Accurate

Today's robust information environment has heightened the expectations people have about the accuracy and legitimacy of facts that are now so easy to access. Information sources have to satisfy today's audience's demand for accuracy.[6] For example, the traditional news media have always sought to gain the public's trust by hiring internal fact checkers to investigate the truthfulness of their stories. But now, online independent news outlets, bloggers, newsgroups, and other gatewatchers also evaluate the information generated by traditional media. **Gatewatching** involves monitoring news sources to analyze and assess the information those sources produce.[7] This increased vigilance has led news organizations to check their work even more carefully. The principle of gatewatching also applies to informative speaking. Informing your audience effectively requires that you present accurate information. Your listeners act as gatewatchers, expecting accuracy in every aspect of your speech: topic choice, supporting materials, organization, language, delivery, and presentation media.

Monitoring news sources to analyze and assess the information they produce.

An Informative Speech Is Clear

Your audience should not have to work hard to figure out what you're trying to say. When they do, your message could be lost. Audiences understand and recall information best when it is clearly presented and easy to follow. Clarity unravels confusing and complex ideas, making them unambiguous and coherent. Still, clarity often presents the greatest challenge to informative speakers.[8] What seems clear to you might not be clear to your listeners—another good reason to remain audience centered as you prepare your speech. Analyzing your audience, selecting appropriate supporting materials, avoiding technical jargon, and organizing your speech so that it flows logically from one idea to the next will help make your informative speech clear. And when you give your speech and sense that your audience understands you well, your nervousness will decrease—another benefit of clarity!

Types of Informative Speeches

There are five common types of informative speeches:

1. Speeches about objects and places
2. Speeches about people and other living creatures
3. Speeches about processes
4. Speeches about events
5. Speeches about ideas and concepts

These categories represent general topic areas and you should not consider them mutually exclusive. For instance, a speech about a famous person, such as an inventor, would probably include information about the person's best-known ideas. A speech about a place might also be about an event that occurs there, which you would probably want to describe briefly. Still, an informative speech generally has one primary focus you'll highlight in your speech.

Speeches about Objects and Places

An **object** is any nonliving, material thing that the human senses can perceive. **Places** are geographic locations. Here are several speech topics and titles addressing objects and places:

Any nonliving, material thing that can be perceived by the human senses.

Geographic locations.

Topic	Sample Speech Titles
3-D movies	"Beyond the Flat Screen: How 3-D Movies Work"
	"Revisiting Classic 3-D Movies"
Tijuana	"Tijuana: The Challenges of a Mexican Border Town"
	"The Delights of Tijuana"
toys for special needs kids	"Choosing Toys for Kids with Special Needs"
	"How Toys Improve Special Needs Kids' Skills"
silver mines	"The Great Silver Mines of Colorado"
	"How Silver Is Mined Today"
extraterrestrials	"Ancient Beliefs in Extraterrestrials"
	"Humorous Films about Extraterrestrials"
laser medical technology	"The Latest Advances in Laser Medical Technology"
	"Common Types of Medical Lasers"
Thai food	"The Secret Spices of Thai Food"
	"Thai Food and Drink as Healthy Alternatives"
blogs	"What Makes a Successful Blog?"
	"The Daily Read: My Favorite Blogs"
active volcanoes	"The Active Volcanoes of Latin America"
	"The Causes of Volcanic Eruptions"
folk art	"Folk Art in Our Community"
	"How Does Folk Art Differ from Commercial Art?"

What speech topics could you generate about the nation of Kenya in Africa? For example, have you ever visited there? How do some of the cultures in Kenya differ from those in other African nations? What are some interesting facts about Kenya's history? What is significant about Kenya in the area of sports?

Ami Vitale/Getty Images

Your own interests and knowledge can often generate excellent speech topics. Sometimes students believe that the things they know about would not interest an audience. However, with skillful research and delivery, almost anything that is important or interesting to you can be made important or interesting to an audience. Think of the town or area where you grew up. What would visitors consider its main attractions? Could you show presentation media that would make those attractions come alive for listeners? If the place doesn't have a lot of attractions that might interest tourists, what interesting people live there? What interesting or enlightening experiences occurred there? Don't discount a topic just because you think it wouldn't interest anyone other than you. Consider how you could *make* it interesting.

Speeches about People and Other Living Creatures

When choosing a topic for an informative speech about people or other living creatures, reflect on the people who fascinate you or the creatures you think your audience would like to learn more about. Who or what would your audience find meaningful? A well-known celebrity or a lesser-known individual? An international figure or someone much closer to home? Would they be interested in an exotic creature, such as the flying squirrel or the banded bamboo shark? Or something more common that they know little about, such as the bald eagle or the bottlenose dolphin? Here are some sample topics and titles for this type of speech:

Topic	Sample Speech Titles
Michelle Wie	"The Asian Wave in Women's Golf"
	"Michelle Wie: Professional Golf's New Superstar"
Koko, the "talking gorilla"	"When Gorillas Talk, What Do They Say?"
	"Learning about Human Speech from Koko, the Talking Gorilla"
Stephen Colbert	"The Real World of Comedian Stephen Colbert"
	"The Many Roles of Stephen Colbert"
dinosaurs	"When Dinosaurs Ruled the World"
	"Dinosaurs and the Great Extinction Debate"

Gloria L. Velásquez	"The Poetry of Gloria L. Velásquez"
	"How Gloria L. Velásquez Became Superwoman Chicana"
The Dalai Lama	"A Brief Biography of the Dalai Lama"
	"Pathways to Peace According to the Dalai Lama"
Shaun White	"Shaun White: The Heart of a Snowboarding Champion"
	"Shaun White's Snowboarding Techniques"
a local artist	"Insight into the Art of Rolando Diaz"
	"The Struggles and Successes of Local Artist Rolando Diaz"
tarantulas	"The Truth about Tarantulas"
	"Tarantulas: Evolution of the World's Scariest Spider"
Kathryn D. Sullivan	"Kathryn D. Sullivan: The First American Woman to Walk in Space"
	"How to Become an Astronaut Like Kathryn D. Sullivan"

For the most part, audiences are highly interested in other people and living creatures—that's why the Biography Channel, History Channel, National Geographic Channel, and Discovery Channel attract lots of viewers. With careful audience analysis, solid research, and presentation media that include that include images of interesting people and animals, informative speeches about these topics can captivate your audience.

Managing Information for Life

Apply *it*

Gathering and organizing information in a smart way helps you prepare your speeches and succeed as a public speaker. But these skills can also pay off for you beyond the classroom. Taking control of information that is relevant to your life allows you to manage your finances, get the health services you need, apply for a job or graduate school, give briefings at work, or even set up a business or charity. In today's data-driven world, it's to your great advantage to be really good at finding and managing the information you need.

Speeches about Processes

A speech about a **process**—how something is done, how it works, or how it has developed—facilitates an audience's understanding of the process or explains how audience members can engage in the process themselves. Here are some examples of topics and titles for informative speeches about processes:

How something is done, how it works, or how it has developed.

Topic	*Sample Speech Titles*
matching DNA samples	"How DNA Affects Criminal Prosecutions"
	"DNA and Genetics: Our Genes Tell Our Stories"
selling an item on eBay	"How to Sell Your Stuff on eBay"
	"The Do's and Don'ts of Selling on eBay"
testing new cars for safety	"Standards for Testing New Cars for Safety"
	"Test Results on the Safety of New Cars"
dancing the Brazilian samba	"Dancing the Brazilian Samba with Ease"
	"Fusing Culture with Movement in the Samba"
removing computer spyware	"Basic Steps for Removing Computer Spyware"
	"Avoiding Common Mistakes in Removing Computer Spyware"
fighting wildfires	"Tactics and Techniques Used for Fighting Wildfires"
	"What I Learned Fighting Wildfires"

buying camping equipment	"Buying Good Camping Equipment at a Low Price"
	"Choosing the Right Camping Equipment for Your Needs"
studying abroad	"Real Opportunities for Studying Abroad"
	"Priorities for Choosing an International Studies Program"
tracking global climate change	"The Main Indicators of Global Climate Change"
	"Tracking Global Climate Change over the Centuries"
podcasting	"Basic Steps in Making Your First Podcast"
	"Getting People to Listen to Your Podcasts"

Analyze your audience thoroughly before deciding whether you simply want them to understand a process or to enact it themselves. For example, a newscaster speaking to broadcasting students could expect them to participate in producing a TV newscast. In contrast, the listeners in your public speaking class aren't likely to go out and produce a TV newscast, so simply learning more about the process would be sufficient for them. Further, if your listeners already know how to perform a process, they likely won't be very interested in your speech. For instance, many students have iPods or other MP3 players. A speech on how to use an iPod probably isn't appropriate for a group of college students. Many of those students, however, probably don't know how to produce a podcast. Therefore, a speech explaining how to go through that process may be of great interest to them.

Brad Barket/Getty Images

There are a lot of great examples of speaking about processes on do-it-yourself TV shows like *Kitchen Impossible*, *Divine Design*, and *30-Minute Meals*.

Speeches about Events

A significant occurrence that an individual personally experiences or otherwise knows about.

An **event** is a significant occurrence you experience personally or otherwise know about. An event can take place in the past, present, or future. An event does not necessarily have to occur in public—important personal activities and occurrences can be events too. Some events, such as concert tours, holiday rituals, fairs, and athletic contests, take place repeatedly. To call something an event gives it a special status and makes this category of informative speeches appealing to public speakers and their audiences. Here are some suggested topics and titles for informative speeches about events:

Topic	*Sample Speech Titles*
college graduation day	"Graduation Day: A Great American Ritual"
	"The Changing Nature of Graduation Day"
birthday parties	"Ten Essential Ingredients for a Perfect Birthday Party"
	"Birthday Celebrations in Different Cultures"
Chinese New Year	"The Ancient Tradition of Chinese New Year"
	"The Best Chinese New Year's Parades in America"

254

assassination of President Kennedy	"Why We Remain Fascinated by the Assassination of President John F. Kennedy"
	"How the Assassination of President Kennedy Changed Presidential Security Forever"
World Cup football	"World Cup Football: Who Gets to Play?"
	"The Cultural Significance of World Cup Football"
Career Day on campus	"Successfully Meeting Employers on Career Day"
	"The Basics of Career Day at Our School"
the Grammy Awards	"The Grammy Awards as a Pop Culture Ceremony"
	"The Grammy Awards Yesterday and Today"
the AIDS Walk	"The AIDS Walk: A Response to a Global Crisis"
	"The AIDS Walk in Our Community"
the birth of a baby	"Giving Birth: What to Expect Before and During Delivery"
	"The Role of Midwives in Childbirth through the Ages"
Ramadan	"Ramadan: The History of Islam's Holy Ninth Month"
	"The Importance of Fasting during Ramadan"

What would you want to say about an event in your speech? Consider a celebratory event for the recipient of a Habitat for Humanity house. You can talk about what it takes to plan and promote the event, who attends the event and why, or the social significance of the event. When developing an informative speech about an event, consider its many different aspects and choose the ones you think will most interest your audience.

Speeches about Ideas and Concepts

Mental activity produces **ideas and concepts**, which include thoughts, understandings, beliefs, notions, or principles. Ideas and concepts tend to be abstract rather than concrete. However, over time, an idea or concept may be actualized in the physical world and thus become more concrete. For example, a fundraising event usually starts with someone thinking, "We should raise some money so the community center can buy a new computer." In another case, a concept car displayed at an auto show begins its life as an automobile designer's idea and may develop into a marketable product later. Initially, however, all ideas and concepts start out as abstractions, and many remain abstract.

> Mental activity, including thoughts, understandings, beliefs, notions, and principles.

When delivering an informative speech about an idea or a concept, the speaker usually explains the origin and main elements of the idea or concept. These aspects of a topic can prove quite extensive and complex, so select a topic that is manageable within your time frame. Here are some sample topics and titles for informative speeches about ideas and concepts.

Events naturally appeal to audiences because they suggest an unfolding action, such as the actions that led to this celebratory event for the recipient of a Habitat for Humanity house.

Topic	*Sample Speech Titles*
liberty	"Looking Back on Liberty in 1776"
	"Defining Liberty after 9/11"
religious fundamentalism	"The Roots of Religious Fundamentalism"
	"What Does It Mean to Be a Religious Fundamentalist?"

255

the electoral college	"The American Electoral College: How Does It Function?"
	"Tracing the History of the Electoral College"
marriage	"Views of Marriage across Cultures"
	"How Marriage Has Changed with the Times"
binge drinking	"Binge Drinking: What are the Risks?"
	"The Binge Drinking Epidemic on Our Campus"
individual human rights	"What Are Your Individual Human Rights?"
	"Individual Human Rights: A Guarantee from the United Nations"
dance therapy	"Dance Therapy as a Psychological Technique"
	"Effective Dance Therapy Techniques"
cyber bullying	"When Does Online Behavior Become Cyberbullying?"
	"Legal Steps You Can Take against Cyberbullies"
niche marketing	"How Niche Marketing Developed"
	"Niche Marketing in a Multicultural Society"
distance learning	"The Beginning of Distance Learning"
	"Future Directions in Distance Learning"

This list reveals that subjects for speeches about ideas and concepts can be complex and controversial. That's no reason to avoid such a topic. To the contrary, audiences generally like to learn more about intriguing and provocative topics, especially if you come across as knowledgeable and enthusiastic about the topic.

Specific Purposes and Thesis Statements for Informative Speeches

The specific purpose you develop for an informative speech should reflect your general purpose: to deepen understanding, raise awareness, or increase knowledge about a topic. For informative speaking, your general purpose is *to inform*, so your specific purpose should begin with a phrase such as "to help my audience learn" or "to make my audience understand."

As you phrase your specific purpose, ask yourself, "What do I want my audience to learn?" Then, as you phrase your thesis, ask yourself, "What does my audience need to know?" Keep in mind that your specific purpose and thesis should clarify your topic for your audience, make it meaningful, express the main ideas accurately, and pique the audience's interest. **Table 13.1** on page 257 presents several examples of specific purposes and thesis statements for different types of informative speeches.

Organizational Patterns for Informative Speeches

Nearly all the patterns of organization discussed in Chapter 8 work well for informative speeches, including the chronological, spatial, topical, narrative, and cause-and-effect patterns. When choosing a pattern for your informative speech, pick one that complements your topic and promotes your specific purpose.

The Chronological Pattern

The chronological pattern allows you to explain how someone or something has developed over a period of time. With this pattern, you highlight the importance of

Table 13.1 Specific Purposes and Thesis Statements for Informative Speeches

Informative speech about …	Topic	Specific purpose	Thesis statement
Objects and places	The Secret Spices of Thai Food	To help my audience learn about the secret spices of Thai food	Three secret spices give Thai food its unique flavor: lemongrass, galangal, and coriander.
	Beyond the Flat Screen: How 3-D Movies Work	To make my audience understand how the technology of 3-D movies differs from that of conventional cinema	A 3-D movie differs from a traditional film in its technical makeup and viewing requirements.
People and other living creatures	How Gloria L. Velásquez Became Superwoman Chicana	To help my audience learn about how Gloria L. Velásquez became Superwoman Chicana	Gloria L. Velásquez became Superwoman Chicana through her poetry, fiction, and music.
	The Truth about Tarantulas	To make my audience understand the truth about tarantulas	True tarantulas are not deadly to humans, usually live a long life, and make great pets.
Processes	How a Dog Show Is Run	To educate my audience about how a professional dog show is run	A professional dog show involves grouping dogs into categories, judging the dogs according to standard criteria, and choosing winners by breed and for the overall show.
	Create Your Own Podcast	To help my audience understand how to create their own podcasts	Creating your own podcast requires creating the content, recording the content, and publishing the podcast.
Events	Career Day	To help my audience understand the features of Career Day on our campus	Career Day on our campus involves meeting with prospective employers, finding out about internships, and enrolling in career-building workshops.
	The Grammy Awards	To make my audience aware of major milestones in the history of the Grammy Awards Ceremony	The major milestones in the history of the Grammy Awards ceremony include the first ceremony in 1959, the first live TV broadcast of the ceremony in 1971, Michael Jackson's sweep of eight Grammy awards in 1984, and the canceled ceremony in 2008.
Ideas and concepts	Binge Drinking	To help my audience understand the risks of binge drinking	Binge drinking is a form of alcohol abuse that poses serious short-term and long-term health risks to the individual.
	Individual Human Rights	To educate my audience about the individual human rights guaranteed by the United Nations	Adopted in 1948, the United Nations' Universal Declaration of Human Rights promotes equal rights, worth, and dignity for all individuals.

Chapter 13 : Informative Speaking

each step in that development. This pattern works well with informative speeches about objects and places, people and other living creatures, and processes. In the following example, the chronological pattern is used to describe the stages in the life cycle of a living creature.

Topic:	The Life Cycle of Butterflies
General purpose:	To inform
Specific purpose:	To help my audience understand the life cycle of butterflies
Thesis:	Butterflies go through four stages in their life cycle: egg, larva, pupa, and metamorphosis.

Main points:

    I. The first stage in the life cycle is the butterfly egg.

    II. The second stage is the larva, known as the caterpillar.

    III. The third state is the pupa, also referred to as the chrysalis.

    IV. In the fourth stage, the organism becomes an adult butterfly through metamorphosis.

For informative speeches that demonstrate how to do something, the best approach is a chronological pattern that leads the audience through the process step by step.

Topic:	Packing for a trip by air
General purpose:	To inform
Specific purpose:	To help my audience learn how to pack a carry-on suitcase for a trip by air
Thesis:	Packing a carry-on for an airplane trip involves making a list, checking for banned items, taking only what you need, using the "roll up" technique, and putting breakables in plastic containers.

Main points:

    I. First, make a list of everything you think you'll need for the trip.

    II. Second, check the Transportation Security Administration's website for a list of banned items.

    III. Third, check the banned item list against your packing list and cross off any disallowed items.

    IV. Fourth, reduce your list by bringing only what you absolutely need.

    V. Fifth, pack using the "roll up" technique to conserve space and prevent wrinkling.

    VI. Sixth, place breakable items in airtight plastic containers.

    VII. Last, double-check your list of items to be sure you didn't forget anything.

The Spatial Pattern

The spatial pattern allows you to describe the physical or directional relationship between objects or places. This pattern works well with informative speeches about objects, places, people, or other living creatures. For example, if your specific purpose is to highlight certain locations, areas, or spaces in a particular place, use a spatial pattern of organization, as in the following example.

Topic:	Zuni Indian Reservation
General purpose:	To inform
Specific purpose:	To familiarize my audience with where Zuni Indians live

| *Thesis:* | The Zuni Indians live on the Zuni Indian Reservation in western New Mexico and on surrounding lands in New Mexico and Arizona. |

Main points:

I. The tribal government is based on the Zuni reservation in McKinley County and Cibola County, New Mexico

II. Some members of the Zuni tribe also live in Catron County, New Mexico, south of the main reservation in the western part of the state.

III. The Zuni tribe has land holdings and residences in Apache County, Arizona, in the eastern part of the state, where it shares territory with Navajo tribes.

The spatial pattern also can be appropriate for informative speeches about people and other living creatures, as in this speech about a person.

Topic:	Gudridur Thorbjarnardottir: World Traveler in the Middle Ages
General purpose:	To inform
Specific purpose:	To educate my audience about the travels of Gudridur Thorbjarnardottir, who lived during the Middle Ages

Main points:

I. Gudridur Thorbjarnardottir was a native of Iceland.

II. She also lived in Greenland.

III. She explored Vinland, or what is now America.

IV. She went to Rome to tell the Pope about her travels.

The Topical Pattern

When using the topical pattern, you divide your topic into subtopics that address the components, elements, or aspects of the topic. Almost any informative speech topic can be organized using this pattern, in which the subtopics become the main points of the

Barry Winiker/PhotoLibrary

How would you use the spatial pattern to organize a speech about the city of Nashville, Tennessee?

speech. For example, when you simply want your audience to understand a process, use the topical pattern to describe the main features of the process.

Topic:	Dog shows
General purpose:	To inform
Specific purpose:	To make my audience aware of how a professional dog show is run
Thesis:	A professional dog show involves grouping dogs into categories, judging the dogs according to standard criteria, and choosing winners by breed, group, and best in show.

Main points:

I. In professional dog shows, dogs are divided into breeds, and breeds are classified into groups such as sporting or working dogs.

II. Dogs are judged according to conformity with the breed standard, as well as personality, age, and sex within breeds.

III. The winner of each breed then competes within the appropriate group.

IV. The winners of the groups then compete for best in show.

In speeches about concepts and ideas, when you want to explain rather than simply describe important elements of the topic, the topical pattern can help make your explanation clear.

Topic:	Globalization
General purpose:	To inform
Specific purpose:	To help my audience understand the main differences among the major forms of globalization
Thesis:	The five forms of globalization are economic, religious, political, cultural, and media globalization.

Main points:

I. Trade and commerce between cultural groups represents economic globalization.

II. The spread of religious ideas and conversions represents religious globalization.

III. The flow of international political influence represents political globalization.

IV. The movement of cultural goods from one part of the world to another represents cultural globalization.

V. Connecting the world with new communication technologies represents media globalization.

The Narrative Pattern

The narrative pattern allows you to retell events as a story or a series of short stories. This pattern works best with informative speeches about objects, places, people, or other living creatures. The narrative pattern has much in common with the chronological pattern, but more strongly emphasizes the dramatic unfolding of events, as in this speech about an object.

Topic:	Pluto, a Dwarf Planet
Specific purpose:	To help my audience understand why Pluto is a dwarf planet
Thesis:	The story of Pluto began with the discovery of Neptune, reached its peak with Pluto's naming as a planet in the early 1900s, and ended recently with Pluto's demotion to dwarf planet.

Main points:

I. The story of Pluto began with the discovery of Neptune in the 1840s.

II. By the late nineteenth century, scientists believed a mysterious planet was affecting Neptune's orbital plane.

III. In the early twentieth century, the planet Pluto was discovered and named.

IV. Beginning in 2000, scientists began to doubt that Pluto should have the same status as the other celestial bodies circling the sun.

V. In 2006, the International Astronomical Union reduced Pluto to a secondary status: dwarf planet.

The narrative pattern works well for turning the chronology of a person's life events into an absorbing story, adding suspense and dramatic flair to the topic.

Topic:	Oprah Winfrey
General purpose:	To inform
Specific purpose:	To make my audience aware of major turning points in Oprah Winfrey's life
Thesis:	Oprah Winfrey was born to poor parents, was a motivated elementary-school student, went on to high school and college, became a highly successful TV talk show host, and came full circle when she opened a school for disadvantaged girls in South Africa.

Main points:

I. Oprah was born in 1954 in Mississippi to poor, unwed teenage parents.

II. She moved to Milwaukee, where she became a highly motivated and successful student in elementary and middle school.

III. Oprah's love of education became the central part of her life as she advanced through high school and college.

IV. She developed a highly successful career as a television talk show host.

V. Oprah opened a school for black girls from disadvantaged families in South Africa, saying that doing so was her true calling in life—she had come full circle.

The Cause-and-Effect Pattern

The cause-and-effect pattern shows how an action produces a particular outcome. This pattern works well with informative speeches about events—after all, events happen for a reason. This example explains how an alternative holiday now celebrated by the Maoris, the indigenous people of New Zealand, came into being when the country declared independence from Great Britain.

travelstock44/Alamy

What other organizational patterns could you use to give an informative speech about the Matariki celebration? How would changing the pattern change the focus of your speech?

Topic:	Matariki: The Maori New Year
General purpose:	To inform
Specific purpose:	To raise my audience's awareness of the Maori New Year celebration
Thesis:	Matariki, the Maori New Year, is now an official celebration in New Zealand, part of an effort to reclaim and celebrate the Maoris' cultural heritage.

Main points:

    I. The Maoris inhabited New Zealand when it was conquered by the English in the eighteenth century.

    II. Maoris lost much of their cultural heritage in the transition to British rule.

    III. In 2004, the Maori New Year became an official day of celebration, resulting in the Maoris reclaiming some of their cultural heritage.

    IV. The Maori New Year, Matariki, refers to the appearance of a star cluster that traditionally signals the beginning of the new year.

    V. Matariki is now widely celebrated among the Maoris of New Zealand.

Guidelines for Effective Informative Speeches

The success of your speech depends greatly on your planning and preparation. The following guidelines will help you prepare an excellent informative speech and add to your repertoire of public speaking skills.

Keep Your Speech Informative

Whenever you speak about any topic, you may be tempted to evaluate the subject matter, give opinions, or make a suggestion, particularly if you hold strong feelings about the subject. In an informative speech, however, you should avoid expressing your personal views. Keep your speech at the level of information sharing. Describe, explain, or demonstrate something, but don't tell the audience what to think or do about it.

Choose a topic that interests you. At the same time, determine what you might realistically expect your audience to get out of your speech. Let's say, for instance, you want to speak on the subject of rainforests. What would be an appropriate specific purpose and thesis for an informative speech about rainforests? What do you want your audience to think or do after listening to you? Given the complexities of the topic and the limited time you have to give your speech, you might reasonably expect only to raise the audience's level of awareness about rainforests generally, focusing on their characteristics.

Topic:	Rain Forests
General purpose:	To inform
Specific purpose:	To educate my audience about the characteristics of a rain forest
Thesis:	Rain forests are characterized by high levels of rainfall, specific types of trees, and four forest layers.

Main points:

    I. Rain forests receive high levels of rain.

    II. Only certain types of trees live in rain forests.

    III. Four layers of vegetation exist in a rain forest.

Notice that the main points focus on informing the audience and avoid taking a position on the topic. In this case, the difference between informing and persuading lies in explaining what rainforests are without advocating an environmental policy.

If you believe you can focus on your informative purpose, and not stray into a persuasive purpose, you will be able to give an acceptable informative speech.

Make Your Speech Topic Come Alive

Informative speeches come alive when speakers demonstrate a positive attitude and connect the topic to the audience in meaningful ways. You can accomplish this by establishing a context for your topic that excites the audience's imagination and using vivid language to describe the main points. For example, Queen Rania of Jordan opened an exhibit on the ancient Middle Eastern city of Petra at the New York Museum of Natural History with an informative speech on the city's history.[9] Here is part of what she said:

> The magical rose-red city of Petra—whose wonders will enchant you tonight—is like nothing else on earth. It is a remarkable testimony to the human spirit, etched for all time in sandstone and shale....
>
> But Petra is more than just an archeological treasure. Petra, I believe, offers an enduring message to all mankind. In Petra, human beings—ordinary mortals like you and me—saw potential beauty and grandeur in walls of sheer stone. They imagined the possibility of elegance and splendor where others would see only a barren and desolate wilderness.
>
> Most importantly, they had the vision and courage to attempt the impossible.... Petra teaches us that nothing is impossible and that even the bleakest and most barren situation contains the promise of hope.
>
> It takes a dream, a plan and a supreme effort—but anything is possible. This is the true wonder of Petra, magical and constant through the centuries. In Jordan, we are proud to be the trustees of this heritage of hope.... and bear with pride our responsibility to share it with our region and to the entire world.

Notice how, in just a few words, Queen Rania makes the "Lost City of Stone" come alive and provides a context for appreciating the exhibit's art and artifacts. She links the story of Petra to recent world events and then suggests that her nation, Jordan, serves as a bridge between the Islamic Middle East and the more diverse West. The exhibit that accompanied her speech further enhanced the appeal of her message.

Connect Your Topic to Your Audience

By using techniques that reduce the distance between themselves and their audiences, good speakers encourage audience members to pay attention and focus more intently on the topic. For audiences unfamiliar with your topic, you'll have to connect it to their general life experiences.[10] For audiences familiar with your topic, you can attract and maintain attention by reinforcing commonalities between you and your listeners. Help the audience understand how learning about your topic benefits them, and how they can perhaps even incorporate the short lesson into their own lives. Raph Koster, chief creative officer of Sony Online Entertainment, connected his speech topic, "Theory of Fun for Games," to his audience at a Game Developers Conference with language, examples, and humor.[11]

> Hi, my name is Raph, and I am a gamer. [Audience laughs.] Why do we recognize that reference? Why are we ashamed about "Hi, my name is Raph, and I am a gamer"? Why do we see that connection? Why do we have to defend gaming to people? Why do we have to explain to someone or justify why we do what we do?
>
> A Theory of Fun came out of this: a "back to the basics" process of why and how games work....
>
> People are *really good* at pattern matching. I'm going to offer the vast oversimplification that what we think of as "thinking" or consciousness is really just a big memory game. Matching things into sets. Moving things into the right place, and then moving on.... A really good example of this is faces. The amount of data in a face is enormous. Just enormous. We've only just started to figure things about it in the

past few decades; when a bird-watcher spots a bird, the face recognition part of the brain goes off. We see faces everywhere....

So when we see a pattern that we get, we do it over and over again. We build neural connections. Now this is what I call *fun*.

Building those patterns is necessary for our survival.... *Fun is the feedback the brain gives while successfully absorbing a pattern.* We need to absorb patterns, otherwise we die. So the brain *HAS* to give positive feedback to you for learning stuff. We tend to think of fun as being frivolous. The stuff that doesn't matter. And this is the serious games cheer line: I'm here to tell you that fun is not only *not* frivolous but *fundamental to human nature and required for survival.* Therefore what we do is saving the human race from extinction. [laughs]

Right from the beginning, Koster emphasized the powerful natural relationship he has with his listeners. "Hi, my name is Raph, and I'm a gamer." The audience laughed at this clever introduction because, first, they all knew who he was. Raph Koster is a legendary figure in the world of online gaming, and the audience was there specifically to hear what he had to say. Second, he echoed the way people introduce themselves in twelve-step addiction recovery programs. Because gaming is considered an addiction by some, his opening words offered a sly joke. Third, by stating the obvious, "I'm a gamer," he made fun of his own superstar status by suggesting that the audience might not know he plays online games. And, because most audience members were online gamers, he was able to establish and reinforce a sense of community with them.

A tireless advocate for protecting chimpanzees, gorillas, and other primates in the wild, Jane Goodall describes her experiences as a field researcher in Africa. Personal stories helped her connect the topic to her college audiences. How could you make your next speech come alive for your listeners?

Throughout the presentation, the speaker used language that reaffirms the experiences online gamers share. He used the informal language common in gaming culture and constantly referred to online game players as "we." His tone was upbeat and fresh. He hit on a key word—*fun*—as a featured idea. Then he tied gamers' shared appreciation of fun to his thesis: "Fun is the feedback the brain gives while successfully absorbing a pattern."

Inform to Educate

Informative speaking involves more than simply imparting information. A successful informative speaker informs the audience in a way that educates them. After hearing the speech, audience members should understand the nature and importance of the topic.

Educating your audiences requires demonstrating the relevance of the speech topic to their lives or values. By nature, people respond better to information that promises to enhance their lives in some way. As an informative speaker, you must give your audience a reason to listen. In the following example, Jean-Michel Cousteau addressed a congressional committee in late 2001 about progress in researching and preserving the world's oceans. Notice how he skillfully connects his topic to the tragedy of 9/11 and uses audience-centered language to educate this audience.[12]

Particularly in light of recent events, many of you may wonder why we've chosen to go ahead with Oceans Day. In times of tragedy and trial, the human spirit seeks constancy. What does constancy mean? On a personal level, it might be the constancy of our families, and the love we have for each other. On a professional level, it might be the constancy of our work and the sense of purpose we derive from it. I'd like to suggest even another level of constancy—one we take for granted every day. It's the constancy of the physical environment that surrounds us—the earth, the sky, and of course the water….

We are, in fact, a water planet. Two-thirds of the earth is covered in water, the vast majority being the salt water of the ocean. As you know so well, the ocean is vital to life on earth … whether it be as a driver of the climate that provides life-giving rains, as a source of protein, or as a source of life-saving medicines. Yet, we take this precious resource for granted, polluting it, extracting from it—without regard to its now very noticeable limits to handle such activities. Last year alone, 92 stocks in the United States were determined to be over-fished. Coastal wetlands are disappearing at an alarming rate. And polluted waters result in everything from coral reef die-offs to beach closures. As an example of how pollution is affecting the St. Lawrence waterway—beluga whales in that area have shown such high levels of contaminants that they would qualify as toxic waste!

Cousteau's challenge was to educate his audience about the importance of preserving the world's water resources, especially the endangered oceans. To connect his message to the audience, he appealed to their sense of "constancy." People want stability and reliability in their family and professional lives, he said. They need predictability in their physical environments too—in this case, their water supplies. Cousteau encouraged his listeners to become educated about the subject by tying his message to their most basic personal interest—the instinct for survival.

He also employed a variety of relevant supporting materials to illustrate the seriousness of the threat to the world's water supply without trying to overwhelm the audience with too much technical information. Cousteau believes that the way to assure a more favorable water environment in the future is to educate people about the perilous state of the oceans. In his speech, he helped his audience develop knowledge and understanding about the subject, not just receive information.

> **Watch** it

Cengage Learning

SPEECH BUDDY VIDEO 13.1
Speaking to Inform

In this video, Janine and Evan present complete informative speeches. Janine's speech is about the first Kodak camera, and Evan's speech is about techno music.

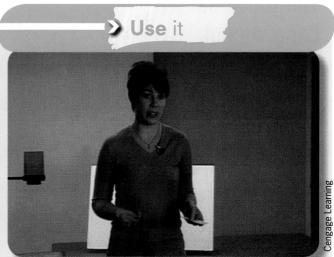

> **Use** it

Cengage Learning

ACTIVITY 13.1
Pleased to Inform You

This activity gives you a chance to analyze an informative speech and then identify ways to apply what you've learned in your own speech.

Use Presentation Media to Inform

Informative speeches frequently include some form of presentation media. However, because you often have only a few minutes to give an informative speech, you have to keep your presentation media limited and basic. A few well-placed images to introduce your topic or audio or visual references in support of your main points can prove effective. When you limit and carefully select your presentation media, you direct more attention to the images and increase their potential impact.

Developing an engaging delivery rhythm that moves smoothly and confidently between you as the speaker and your presentation media is crucial to becoming an excellent speaker. For example, change your slides at just the right time to illustrate and reinforce the specific points you want to make. When used well, presentation media can help make your informative speech a positive experience for you and your audience.

Speech for Review and Analysis

Tudor Matei gave this informative speech in an introductory public speaking class at San José State University. The assignment was to give a four- to six-minute informative speech that incorporated presentation media and at least three sources. Students were also asked to annotate their references section, explaining why they chose the sources listed. As you read the outline of Tudor's speech, consider how audience-centered, clear, and accurate the speech is. Is the speech structured in a way that helps Tudor deepen the audience's understanding of the topic? You can use your CourseMate for Public Speaking: The Evolving Art *to watch and listen to Speech Buddy Evan deliver this speech in video 13.1, "Speaking to Inform."*

CourseMate

The Universal Language of Techno Music

Cengage Learning

by Tudor Matei[13]

Specific purpose: To have the audience understand how techno music has brought different nations together.

Thesis statement: Techno music comes from computers, and just as computers are common ground for people all around the world, techno is like a universal language that enables people from diverse cultures to communicate and enjoy technology in a creative way.

Introduction

I. You probably hear the word *techno* just about every day, but what exactly is *techno music*?
   A. Up until recently, people just responded to it, but nobody knew what it really was.
   B. The real question most of you may have is, "Why is techno music so popular?"
   C. In his article "A Brief History of Techno," Jacob Arnold says that its "recent popularity is due to the growing number of people who are accepting computer technology as an integral part of their lives. Because techno is created almost entirely with electronics, much of it has become an expression of the interface between humans and machines."
II. Before I talk to you about when and where techno was invented, I want to cover some basics about this type of music.

Body

I. What are the basics of techno music?
   A. Techno falls under the broader category of electronic dance music.
   B. The name "techno" is derived from the word *technology* because techno music is made on a computer using digital sound.
   C. Techno has electronic sounds, little melody, high energy, and rhythmic beats.

Transition: Since we now have some techno basics down, I can talk about where techno music was invented.

II. Where was techno invented?
   A. Techno was created in the 1980s in Detroit, Michigan.
   B. You may be surprised that this genre was developed in Detroit, also the birthplace of Motown.
   C. Three pioneers—called the "Belleville Three"—are credited with creating techno.
      1. Their names are Derrick May, Juan Atkins, and Kevin Saunderson.
      2. The music they created is classified as Detroit techno.

Transition: Yes, there are subcategories of techno. I'll tell you a bit about each.

III. Techno can currently be divided into three subcategories.
   A. The first subcategory is the original form, Detroit techno.
      1. This form is distinguished by simple rhythms and a small number of electronic sounds.
      2. It only has a small number of sounds because technology back in the day was limited
      3. Detroit techno is not very interesting compared to today's other forms.
   B. Trance techno is probably the type of techno you were already familiar with.
      1. Trance is one of the most popular styles of techno at large parties and in clubs.
      2. Trance started in the early 1990s in Germany at a party.
         a. The party was called "Age of Love."
         b. DJ Sakin played a song called "Protect Your Mind."
      3. Trance techno is louder than most genres of music.
         a. It features bass fluctuating between high and low points.
         b. Trance techno also contains many drum climaxes and wavy sounds.
   C. Hardcore techno is, at least for now, the last subcategory of techno.
      1. This form basically features a bunch of sounds played together to create a chaotic feeling.
      2. The sounds may include anything from happy vocals to pianos to drums and even airplanes crashing.
      3. Frankly, it is enjoyed often by people who take Ecstasy—not something I recommend.

Transition: All of the subcategories of techno music are essentially made the same way.

IV. The musicology (history and science) of techno is unique.
   A. Techno music generally has around 130 to 140 beats per minute or higher.
   B. The music is usually created with separate keyboards and synthesizers, but it can also be created with one single computer.
   C. Most producers try to push the limits of how many sounds they can cram into a song, but they also try to achieve a listenable dance mix.

Transition: If you're getting interested in this kind of music, you might be especially curious about where it stands today.

V. Techno is still popular and developing.
   A. Techno has been very popular in the recent years.
      1. It retains its popularity despite its association with the controversial rave scene.
      2. A lot of clubs have a special "techno dance floor" or dedicated "techno nights."
   C. Techno's influence has spread throughout the world and throughout entertainment.
   D. Probably the biggest group of techno listeners is in Australia.
   E. Techno influences other music genres, such as hip-hop.
   F. Tons of new movies use techno songs, especially action movies.

Transition: That techno can be enjoyed by people from all different cultures is one of the things I like best about it.

Conclusion

I. Like computers, techno music provides a universal language for people around the world and brings together people from diverse backgrounds.
II. Although there are a lot of electronic genres in music, techno is by far the most popular.
   A. Trance techno in particular is really popular.
   B. People can easily dance to trance—even without doing drugs.
III. In the end, I feel that techno is not just another music genre, but also a way for people to communicate and enjoy technology in a very creative way.
IV. Any requests to hear one of those samples again?

References

Flavell, K. (Producer), & Mittmann, J. D. (Director). (2003). *Sounds Like Techno* [Video file]. Retrieved from http://www2.abc.net.au/arts/soundsliketechno/swf/default.asp (*This website is probably my most important source of information. The Australian Broadcasting Corporation did a documentary on techno music.*)

i:Vibes crew. (2009). i:Vibes: Your guide to electronic music [Website]. Retrieved from http://www.ivibes.nu/ (*This website had free samples of techno music. It helped me more easily understand the type of music I am dealing with.*)

Jacob, A. (2008, November). A brief history of techno. Gridface. Retrieved from http://www.gridface.com/features/a_brief_history_of_techno.html (*This website helped me with the history of techno. I even quoted a line in my speech about it.*)

Savage, J. (Summer 1993). Machine soul: A history of techno. [Rock & Roll Quarterly insert] The Village Voice. Retrieved from http://music.hyperreal.org/library/machine_soul.html (*This website also helped me with history of techno. It helped me understand the way producers worked.*)

Technomusic.com (2010).[Audio podcast]. Retrieved from http://www.technomusic.com/ (*A good site for listening to samples of techno music.*)

Thigpen. (n.d.) Thigpen's techno music page. Retrieved from http://www.ccs.neu.edu/home/thigpen/html/music (*This website is very old, but it has interesting early techno songs. I found some old playlists.*)

Wikipedia. (2010, June). Techno. In Wikipedia. Retrieved from http://en.wikipedia.org/wiki/Techno (*This website has a tremendous amount of information. However because it is Wikipedia, I did not trust everything the site said. I used the information as a starting point, and found a lot of original sources in the Bibliography, Filmography, and References sections.*)

Questions for Analysis and Discussion

1. Was Tudor's speech likely to be considered personally meaningful by her audience? What did she do or fail to do to connect her topic to the audience?

2. The specific purpose of Tudor's speech was to have the audience understand how techno music has brought different nations together. Did she accomplish her purpose?

3. How familiar are you with techno music? Did you learn anything new from Tudor's speech about techno music? If yes, what?

4. What organizational pattern did she use? Given the specific purpose of her speech, was that the best choice? What organizational pattern would you have chosen?

5. Can audio or video samples be used effectively in a four- to six-minute speech to inform? If yes, how would you use presentation media in this speech? If no, why wouldn't you use presentation media?

6. Did you find anything in Tudor's speech to be inaccurate or unclear?

7. Does the conclusion of Tudor's speech advance her purpose for giving the speech? How might she have concluded more effectively?

Summary

When you give an informative speech, you seek to deepen understanding, raise awareness, or increase knowledge about a topic. To connect effectively with an audience in order to share information, you must ensure that your speech is meaningful, accurate, and clear.

Most informative speeches are about objects and places, people and other living creatures, processes, events, or ideas and concepts. The general and specific purposes you develop for an informative speech should reflect your overall goal—to foster understanding about a subject or to explain to your audience how to perform a process. Several patterns of organization work well for informative speeches, including the chronological, spatial, topical, narrative, and cause-and-effect patterns. The pattern you choose for an informative speech should complement your general and specific purposes for that speech.

Five strategies for delivering an effective informative speech are to keep your speech informative rather than persuasive, make your speech come alive with colorful language and a topic that sparks your audience's imagination, connect your topic to your audience in meaningful ways, inform to educate, and use presentation media to inform.

IN THE BOOK
Summary
Key Terms
Critical Challenges

MORE STUDY RESOURCES
Quizzes
WebLinks
Peer-reviewed videos

CourseMate
Speech Studio

STUDENT WORKBOOK
13.1: Short Informative Speeches
13.2: Audience Outcomes
13.3: Grading a Teacher
13.4: Audience Attention
13.5: Document a Documentary

SPEECH BUDDY VIDEOS
WATCH It Video
13.1: Speaking to Inform
USE It Activity
13.1: Pleased to Inform You

SAMPLE SPEECH VIDEOS
Curt, "The Illongot Headhunters," informative
speech
Jeff, "History of Fort Collins, Colorado,"
informative speech

SPEECH BUILDER EXPRESS
Goal/purpose
Thesis statement
Organization
Outline
Supporting material
Transitions
Introduction
Conclusion
Title
Works cited
Visual aids
Completing the speech outline

INFOTRAC

Recommended search terms
Informative speaking
Informative speech topics
Biography
How things work
Community events
Organizational patterns for speeches

AUDIO STUDY TOOLS
"The Illongot Headhunters" by Curt
Critical thinking questions
Learning objectives
Chapter summary

Guide to Your Online Resources

CourseMate Your Speech Communication CourseMate for *Public Speaking: The Evolving Art* gives you access to the Speech Buddy video and activity featured in this chapter, additional sample speech videos, Speech Studio, Speech Builder Express, InfoTrac College Edition, and study aids such as glossary flashcards, review quizzes, and the Critical Challenge questions for this chapter, which you can respond to via email if your instructor so requests. In addition, your CourseMate features live WebLinks relevant to this chapter, including sites that provide examples of excellent informative speeches. Links are regularly maintained, and new ones are added periodically.

Key Terms

event 254

gatewatching 250

informative speaking 250

ideas and concepts 255

object 251

places 251

process 253

Critical Challenges

Questions for Reflection and Discussion

1. Does clarity or lack of clarity raise ethical questions? How does clarity relate to transparency—the visibility or accessibility of information disclosed by government, big business, and other organizations? Why might professional public speakers, especially some politicians and business leaders, purposefully avoid being clear about their messages?

2. The difference between an informative speech and a persuasive one can sometimes be difficult for speakers to grasp. Consider the topics you might choose for an informative speech. How would you keep those topics safely inside the boundaries of speaking to inform?

3. We are bombarded with lots of information every day. Is there such a thing as too much information? Does "information overload" really exist? (*Information overload* is a term coined by U.S. writer Alvin Toffler to describe the difficulty individuals can have understanding an issue and making decisions when they take in more information than they can process.) Under what circumstances would you personally choose *not* to learn something new?

4. Check out Speech Studio to watch and listen to other students' informative speeches. Or record a speech you're working on, upload it to Speech Studio, and ask your peers for their feedback. What feedback could you use to fine-tune your informative speech before you give it in class?

☑ SPEECH Studio

14 Persuasive Speaking

Read it

Cengage Learning

Watch it

Cengage Learning

Use it

Review it

CourseMate Speech Studio Speech Builder Express

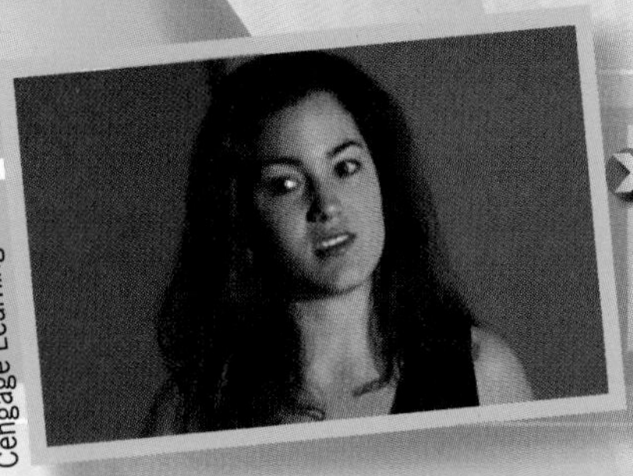

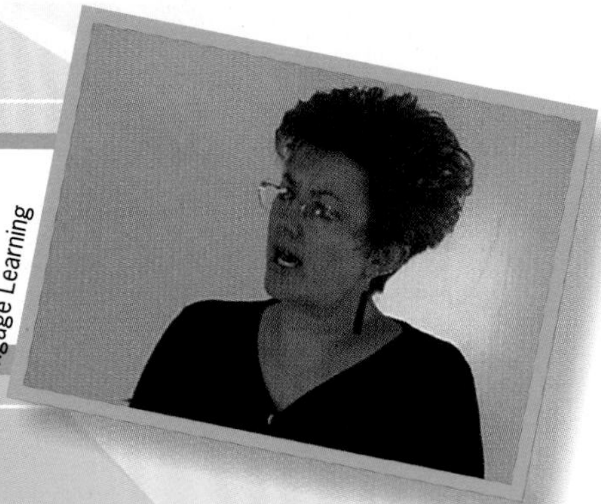

When Antonio Villaraigosa was elected mayor of Los Angeles, he represented great hope for millions of Mexican Americans who live in the City of Angels. Villaraigosa grew up in East L.A., a poor Latino part of the city. Before he turned seventeen, Villaraigosa had dropped out of high school—twice. But soon he straightened himself out, started working hard, and learned to appreciate education. In addition, Villaraigosa developed outstanding persuasive speaking skills. In a **persuasive speech,** the speaker attempts to reinforce, modify, or change audience members' beliefs, attitudes, opinions, values, and behaviors. Through many inspirational public speeches, Los Angeles's first elected Latino mayor in modern history convinced many of the city's residents to envision a brighter future, even in times of declining budgets and economic instability. In his first state of the city address, Villaraigosa said

> This day isn't about addressing the state of things as they are. It's about the state of our city as it should be. Over nine months ago, I stood before you on the south steps of City Hall, and I asked you to dream with me about a different kind of future for Los Angeles. A future where LA is taking the lead as the great global city of the twenty-first century. A future where people in communities around our city are drawn closer together by a world-class transit system. A future where we are growing greener as we grow. Where children can walk to school in safety. And where no kid in any neighborhood in any part of Los Angeles is ever robbed of his or her childhood.
>
> And I asked you to imagine a future where it doesn't matter who you are or where you come from…. Whether you're African American, Latino, Caucasian, or Asian…. Whether you're gay or straight, rich or poor…. Where every Angeleno has a chance to show their talent.[1]

A speech in which the speaker attempts to reinforce, modify, or change audience members' beliefs, attitudes, opinions, values, and behaviors.

Getty Images

Antonio Villaraigosa has become a major figure in American politics because he understands how to connect with people, stir their hopes and dreams, and move them to act. In short, he speaks persuasively.

This chapter covers the basics of persuasive public speaking, and Chapter 15 explains how you can apply the elements of argument in persuasive situations. The two chapters work together to provide specific strategies for giving an effective and ethical persuasive speech.

Defining Persuasion

Persuasion relies on language, images, and other means of communication to influence people's beliefs, attitudes, values, or actions.[2] Every day you encounter and manage a constant flow of persuasive messages. Friends want to make plans with you for the weekend. A coworker texts you for advice on a project. Television constantly tries to sell you more products. Family members need help. Instructors explain why what they're teaching you is useful. Pop-up ads interrupt your online searches. Charitable organizations solicit donations. Demands like these for your attention and cooperation never stop.

In addition to being influenced, you also must influence others so you can fulfill your personal needs and be an effective member of society. Since ancient times—when philosophers emphasized the positive role of persuasion in public discourse—democratic societies have depended on the ability of ordinary citizens to make their voices and opinions heard. Businesses, organizations, media, groups of friends, sporting teams, and even families reward people who can express their views convincingly and motivate others to act.

Whether persuasive attempts deal with relatively minor personal matters or serious issues that involve entire groups, people subjected to social influence must always have the freedom to say no. Persuasion implies choice. **Coercion**, however, does not. When a person is forced to think a certain way or feels compelled to act under pressure or threat, they are *not* being persuaded. They are being coerced. Brainwashing or intimidating people to get a desired effect is not persuasion. Neither is physically restraining or bullying someone. Free societies are founded on the right of individuals to choose courses of action willfully.

Informative and persuasive speaking differ in an important way. Informative speakers fulfill the role of *expert* on a topic and seek to facilitate audience understanding about it. In contrast, persuasive speakers take on the role of *promoter* or *proponent*, advocating a particular view on a topic they want the audience to adopt. As a persuasive speaker, you'll become an expert on your topic, but you'll go beyond your expertise to argue for a specific viewpoint that you want the audience to accept. Persuasive speakers voice a clear position on a topic, whereas informative speakers remain neutral. For example, for an informative speech on the digital camera, the speaker would make the audience more aware of the topic, say, by describing the camera's history. In contrast, a persuasive speaker would advocate a particular view of the topic, perhaps arguing that traditional cameras are superior to digital ones.

Using language, images, and other means of communication to influence people's attitudes, beliefs, values, or actions.

Forcing someone to think a certain way or making someone feel compelled to act under pressure or threat.

George Jartos/CartoonStock

Persuasive speeches address three types of questions: fact, value, and policy. While each of these types of speeches has the general purpose of persuading an audience, they differ in the kind of outcome the speaker seeks. The type of persuasive speech you give influences how you develop your specific purpose and thesis, select main points, and organize your ideas.

Speeches on Questions of Fact

A **question of fact** asks whether something is true or false. In speeches addressing questions of fact, the speaker tries to persuade an audience that something did or did not occur, or that one event caused another. For example, in a criminal court the prosecution attempts to persuade the jury the defendant did engage in illegal activity, while the defense argues the defendant did not.

A questions that asks whether something is true or false.

Chapter 7 defined *facts* as observations you make from your own and others' experiences, and *inferences* as conclusions you draw based on facts. In speeches addressing questions of fact, speakers and listeners must carefully distinguish between facts and inferences. An infamous example of a speech that blurred the line between facts and inferences is former Secretary of State Colin Powell's address to the United Nations on February 5, 2003.[3] In his speech, Powell argued that Iraq's leader, Saddam Hussein, possessed weapons of mass destruction and would use them against other countries, including the United States. Employing satellite images, artists' drawings, intelligence findings, audiotapes, and other information, Powell argued that an attack was imminent. But much of what Powell presented as fact turned out to be invalid inferences based on contestable information.[4] The satellite photos, for instance, did show some trucks, but they were water or fire trucks, not decontamination units for people working with biochemicals as Powell implied. Several years later, after weapons of mass destruction had not been found in Iraq, Powell admitted he regretted giving the speech and presenting as facts information he later found out was unreliable.[5]

Speeches on questions of fact typically address three issues: what is observed or known, how the observations were made, and whether new observations have changed what people once thought of as fact. Generally, individuals agree on facts because they're verifiable—they can be proven true or false. But sometimes people disagree about what they observe or how the observations were made. For example, a recent study found that on average Americans talk regularly about their personal troubles with two people, down from three in 1985. However, the questions asked implied face-to-face communication only, leaving out other ways to interact, such as phone calls, emails, text messages, and online chats. You might agree with the study's results but disagree with how the questions were worded. Because facts can be contested, the speaker must persuade the audience that the version of the facts presented is correct.

The persuasiveness of a speech addressing a question of fact rests on the speaker's ability to present sound, credible evidence. Facts and statistics typically provide the foundational evidence for speeches on questions of fact. But speakers may also use examples, testimony, definitions, or narratives as supporting evidence. For example, in a persuasive speech arguing that mandatory seat belt laws save lives, the speaker might include quotes from an interview with a highway patrol officer or a personal narrative about how wearing a seat belt saved the speaker's life in a car crash.

Specific Purposes, Thesis Statements, and Main Points for Speeches on Questions of Fact

For persuasive speaking, your general purpose is *to persuade,* so your specific purpose should begin with something like "To persuade my audience to [take some sort of action]" or "To convince my audience to [think a certain way]."

When you give a speech on a question of fact, you want the audience to believe or agree with you that something is true or false. You focus on reinforcing or changing how people think, not on how they behave, as the following example shows.

Topic:	The Peak in Worldwide Oil Production
General purpose:	To persuade
Specific purpose:	To convince my audience that oil production in the world has peaked
Thesis:	Historical evidence shows that worldwide oil production has peaked and can no longer increase.

This example demonstrates how the topic, general purpose, specific purpose, and thesis work together to answer a question of fact. In this speech, you're asking, "Has oil production in the world reached its peak?" Your specific purpose and thesis provide the answer you want your audience to agree with: Yes, "historical evidence shows that worldwide oil production has peaked and can no longer increase."

When creating your main points for a speech on a question of fact, ask yourself, "What would make someone think this claim is true (or false)?" For example, in a speech about the causes of autism, the thesis suggests that the speaker will address theories associated with autism's causes.

Topic:	Causes of Autism
General purpose:	To persuade
Specific purpose:	To convince my audience that the causes of autism are unknown
Thesis:	Current theories about autism have not identified its cause.

Main points:

    I. Genetic theories of autism suggest the disease is caused by an anomaly in the ways certain genes interact with each other, but the research is inconclusive.

    II. Viral theories suggest that autism is caused by a virus or infection, although research findings are inconsistent.

    III. Some theories, such as the notions that childhood vaccines and poor parenting cause autism, have not been supported.

Organizational Patterns for Speeches on Questions of Fact

As with an informative speech, choose a pattern of organization for a persuasive speech consistent with your specific purpose and thesis. All the organizational patterns discussed in Chapter 8 can be used for persuasive speeches. For speeches that address questions of fact, speakers usually arrange their main points in a chronological, spatial, topical, or cause-and-effect pattern. The thesis often provides guidance about how best to organize a speech. For example, the thesis for the oil production speech, shown again below, suggests a chronological pattern, which allows the speaker to trace production trends from the past to the present.

Organizational pattern:	Chronological
Topic:	Worldwide Oil Production
General purpose:	To persuade
Specific purpose:	To convince my audience that oil production in the world has peaked
Thesis:	Historical evidence shows that worldwide oil production has peaked and can no longer increase.

Main points:

    I. The rate of new oil discoveries worldwide has declined since the 1960s.

    II. In 1970, U.S. oil production peaked.

    III. In 1976, the last major oil reserve was found in the Middle East.

    IV. Oil production has not increased in the past ten years.

    V. Demand for oil has quadrupled in the past five years.

The next two examples show how speeches on questions of fact can be organized according to the spatial and topical patterns. Notice how the thesis statements suggest the appropriate pattern to use.

Organizational pattern:	Spatial
Topic:	Health Risks in International Travel
General purpose:	To persuade
Specific purpose:	To convince my audience they will encounter health risks when visiting foreign countries
Thesis:	Visiting foreign countries brings various health risks.

Main points:

    I. When visiting South America, you must consider certain health concerns.

    II. When visiting East Asia, you should be aware of other health risks.

    III. U.S. visitors to South Asia encounter important health risks as well.

    IV. U.S. visitors traveling to Africa face several health risks.

Organizational pattern:	Topical
Topic:	The Effectiveness of Vitamin Pills
General purpose:	To persuade
Specific purpose:	To convince my audience that vitamin pills don't improve health
Thesis:	Although vitamin intake through the foods we eat is necessary for good health, vitamin pills are unnecessary and risky to good health.

Main points:

    I. Vitamin intake is necessary for good health.

    II. Sufficient vitamin intake occurs through proper eating habits.

    III. Vitamin pills add nothing to natural vitamin intake.

    IV. Vitamin pills can create health risks.

Speakers use the cause-and-effect pattern of organization for speeches on questions of fact when attempting to prove or disprove that one behavior or event causes another. Consider this example about bans on handheld cell phone use while driving.

Topic:	Handheld Cell Phone Use While Driving
General purpose:	To persuade
Specific purpose:	To convince my audience that banning handheld cell phone use while driving reduces accidents and saves lives
Thesis:	Statistics show that banning the use of handheld cell phones while driving reduces accidents and saves lives.

Main points:

    I. Many states have banned the use of handheld cell phones for drivers.

    II. As indicated by traffic accident statistics, banning handheld phone use while driving reduces accidents and saves lives.

In applying the cause-and-effect pattern of organization to speeches on questions of fact, the speaker must clearly demonstrate causation—that action A led to action B. The handheld cell phone ban example appears to do that, with statistics showing reduced accidents and fewer lives lost after the ban was enacted. Still, the speaker must not confuse *correlation* with *causation*. Two actions may appear linked, but that does not mean they are causally connected. For example, while it's true that banning handheld phones may save lives, decreases in the number of accidents and deaths on the road may be influenced by other factors too. For example, at the time the cell phone ban went into effect, the economy was slowing down. People were driving less and were therefore less likely to get into an accident. In addition, in recent years improved safety technology in cars, more sophisticated road engineering, and crackdowns on drunk driving have also contributed to lowering the number of accidents and deaths on U.S. highways.[6]

Speeches on Questions of Value

A **question of value** asks for a subjective evaluation of something's worth, significance, quality, or condition. Questions of value ask if something is good or bad, right or wrong, beautiful or ugly, boring or engaging, funny or serious—all qualitative judgments about something's significance. A question of value, therefore, addresses individual opinions and cultural beliefs rather than proving something true or false.

> A question that asks for a subjective evaluation of something's worth, significance, quality, or condition.

Sarah Palin shot to political and cultural stardom on the basis of a "values" speech she gave when accepting the nomination for vice president at the Republican National Convention in 2008. She became famous for associating herself with what she calls "the real America"—conservative small towns in the country's heartland, where she says love of country and "family values" dominate. Early in her acceptance speech, she brought up the notion of patriotism, telling an enthusiastic audience that her son Track was headed to Iraq to serve the United States as an Army infantryman. She continued to emphasize the value of patriotism by pointing out that he would depart for combat on September 11. Palin then attempted to establish more strongly her credibility as a conservative by portraying herself as a politician who puts traditional family values first:

> A writer observed: "We grow good people in our small towns, with honesty, sincerity, and dignity." I know just the kind of people that writer had in mind. . . I grew up with those people. They are the ones who do some of the hardest work in America, who grow our food, run our factories, and fight our wars. They love their country, in good times and bad, and they're always proud of America. I had the privilege of living most of my life in a small town.

Palin went on to tell the enthusiastic crowd and huge television audience that she was "just your average hockey mom who signed up for the PTA." She said she married her high school sweetheart, loves her kids, drives to work, dismissed the governor's personal chef, sold Alaska's luxury jet on eBay, and at the end of her speech, like all politicians in the United States, she asked God to bless America.[7]

Sarah Palin had a clear behavioral objective in mind. She tried to link "small-town values" to voters' values in order to drum up support for the McCain–Palin ticket in the general election. But not all speeches on questions of value include a well-defined call to action like Palin's did. Similar to speeches on questions of fact, most speeches on questions of value focus on persuading the audience to believe a certain way. They don't necessarily ask the audience to take action or change their behavior.

AFP/Getty Images

Addressing the Republican National Convention in her vice-presidential nomination speech, Sarah Palin spoke of patriotism and family values to connect with voters.

278

Speeches on questions of value address timeless issues such as the morality of war or concerns like the ethical uses of social networking websites like Facebook or Twitter. Topics may be serious, as with the best way to address terrorism, or more lighthearted, as with a critique of a city's worst architecture. Still, any discussion based on applying subjective standards will result in some level of disagreement. Because questions of value can prove contentious, they often make for stimulating persuasive speeches, especially if you and your audience view the topic differently.

Specific Purposes, Thesis Statements, and Main Points for Speeches on Questions of Value

In a speech on a question of value, your specific purpose reveals your evaluation of the topic's quality. Do you think something is good or bad, right or wrong, moral or immoral, the best or the worst? Make your position clear so your audience will know exactly what you think after listening to your speech. Then develop a thesis that supports your position.

Topic:	Public Art
General purpose:	To persuade
Specific purpose:	To convince my audience that public art is good for everyone
Thesis:	Public art is good for everyone because it rejuvenates commercial areas, gives residents a better quality of life, encourages tourism, and energizes local artist communities.

Speaking of . . .

Learning about What Americans Value at America.gov

What do Americans value? Because the U.S. population is diverse in so many ways, there's no easy answer to that question. The U.S. Department of State's Bureau of International Information Programs includes on its website (America.gov) two collections of information related to American values. One, American Life, discusses topics such as education, the arts, diversity, and education. The other, Democracy, focuses on U.S. efforts to support democracy and human rights worldwide. The site targets an international audience, especially foreign media organizations, government officials, and leaders, as well as the general public. Go to America.gov and explore the site. What values is the site attempting to communicate to the international community? To what extent do you think all Americans share those values? How can knowing about these values help you in public speaking?

The main points for a speech on a question of value must clearly present and strongly support your position. Some speeches addressing questions of value focus on fairly noncontroversial topics, such as "recycling is good" or "littering is bad." But because questions of value reflect individual judgments, speeches on questions of value more often touch on controversial and sensitive topics such as capital punishment, abortion, the right to die, and animal rights. Your challenge is to make your position on the topic seem reasonable to an audience, especially a negative audience.

As you prepare your main points, ask yourself questions such as "What kinds of supporting materials will best convince my audience to accept my position or change their views? What ideas support my position and how should I organize them? What can I reasonably expect my audience to think after listening to my speech about this topic?" The value of school vouchers provides a useful example. This topic has caused much debate among parents, teachers, administrators, church groups, and others concerned with public education. One way to address this controversy is to examine how well school vouchers perform here and in other countries.

Topic:	School Vouchers
General purpose:	To persuade
Specific purpose:	To convince my audience that school vouchers are the best way to solve education problems in K–12 schools
Thesis:	School reform movements in the United States and other countries show that school vouchers are the best way to solve current problems in K–12 schools.

Main points:

   I. School reform movements in Australia provide support for the superiority of a school voucher program over other choices.

II. Education reform movements in Japan also provide support for school vouchers.

III. Recent changes in Canada's public school system indicate a school voucher program would work in the United States.

IV. Trial programs in U.S. schools show that school vouchers solve current problems.

Organizational Patterns for Speeches on Questions of Value

For speeches that address questions of value, speakers usually arrange their main points in a chronological, spatial, or topical pattern. As with all persuasive speeches, choosing the appropriate organizational pattern for a speech on a question of value influences your ability to convince the audience. For example, in a speech about the use of computer-generated imagery (CGI) in films, a chronological pattern allows you to begin by discussing highly acclaimed movies made before CGI, strengthening your argument that CGI-based movies are inferior.

Organizational pattern:	Chronological
Topic:	Computer-generated Imagery (CGI) in Movies
General purpose:	To persuade
Specific purpose:	To convince my audience that movies using CGI are inferior to movies that don't use CGI
Thesis:	Movies using CGI are inferior to movies without CGI because movies with CGI focus more on the CGI technology than on telling a good story.

Main points:

I. Before computer-generated imagery (CGI), Hollywood produced rich narratives such as *Citizen Kane, Sunset Boulevard,* and *One Flew Over the Cuckoo's Nest.*

II. CGI was introduced in the early 1970s with the movie *Westworld,* and attention then turned to CGI and away from writing good stories.

III. Today, the emphasis is on CGI, and telling a good story is forgotten, as with *Jumper* and *Pirates of the Caribbean: At World's End.*

A topical pattern of organization works well for a question of value speech when the main points are of about equal importance. In the following example, all three points contribute in different but equally important ways to the thesis.

Organizational pattern:	Topical
Topic:	Skin-lightening Products
General purpose:	To persuade
Specific purpose:	To convince my audience that skin-lightening products are unethical
Thesis:	Skin-lightening products are unethical because they can cause physical and psychological harm to users and imply that light skin is better than dark skin.

Main points:

I. Cosmetic products used to lighten the skin can cause physical harm to the users.

II. Cosmetic products used to lighten the skin can cause psychological harm to the users.

III. Cosmetic products used to lighten the skin create a racist impression that light skin is preferable to dark skin.

For an example of a speech on a question of value organized using the spatial pattern, review the speech on school vouchers earlier in the section.

Speeches on Questions of Policy

A **question of policy** asks what course of action should be taken or how a problem should be solved. Note the word *should*—that's your clue that a speech addresses a question of policy rather than a question of fact or value.

A question that asks what course of action should be taken or how a problem should be solved.

Questions of policy may reflect current controversies, such as U.S. immigration policies, or less contentious topics, such as getting more exercise. These questions also range from the general, such as promoting democracy around the world, to the specific, such as academic integrity policies on your campus. Examples of questions of policy include the following:

- Should consumers buy products made in the United States?

- Should we eliminate remedial courses in U.S. higher education?

- How should people protect themselves from identity theft?

Speeches on questions of policy ask the audience to personally take (or not take) a particular action or support (or not support) a particular position.[8] Speakers might request immediate involvement, general support for a social or political movement of some kind, disapproval of an idea, or a change in behavior. For example, a speaker might propose that

- College students should circulate a petition to ban junk food on campuses.

- People should support the animal rights movement.

- Local residents should not approve of changes in the zoning law.

- Everyone should exercise more.

In a general sense, policies are formal doctrines used by institutions like governments, organizations, schools, teams, and clubs. These policies often take the form of rules, laws, plans, or codes of behavior that institutions create and enforce. A speech that calls for making noisy leaf blowers illegal, for instance, or a proposal for constructing more affordable housing units in your community, falls into this category. But as the above examples demonstrate, questions of policy address a wide range of issues at the personal, group, institutional, societal, and cultural levels. Moreover, many questions of policy call for individualized responses, such as recommending that consumers carefully monitor their food and clothing purchases or protect themselves against identity theft.

When choosing a topic for a speech about a question of policy, you need not stick with traditional public policy controversies like gun control, capital punishment, and the right to die. Indeed, unless there's a current discussion surrounding the issue you may want to avoid these topics. Original, thought-provoking topics or unique positions on well-known subjects are more likely to interest your audience than material they've heard many times before. Most important, choose something you truly care about that will resonate with your audience. You might consider, for instance, policy questions involving universal human rights, social justice, or the environment. Do schools have the right to strip-search students? Should a tax be imposed on cosmetic surgery? Should online sports gambling be legalized and regulated? Is the new generation of clean nuclear power plants key to solving America's energy crisis? Are parents who deny their children medical care for religious reasons guilty of murder if the child dies? You may want to present your views on one of the many controversies springing from interpretations of the U.S. Constitution or government policy, such as flag burning, separation of church and state, or limits on the president's discretion to start a preventive war. Developing regional public transportation, raising teachers' salaries, or banning negative political campaign ads are other debatable issues that spring from government policy. Or you may want to choose a more specific, local issue arising from your campus, your workplace, or your community. Are new regulations needed to control the local police department's use of excessive force? Are the visiting rules in your school's dormitories too restrictive? Should smoking be completely banned on your campus?

Be an Advocate!

Why not put your skills as a persuasive speaker to work outside school by advocating for causes you think deserve support? To advocate means to speak in favor of or recommend something. An advocate is a person who argues for, supports, or defends a cause. Many advocates try to influence decisions about government and institutional policies or the use of resources that affect people's lives.[9] Lawyers advocate for their clients. Advocacy groups try to influence policies or sway public opinion on a particular issue. There is also plenty of room in a democratic society for individuals to advocate for causes they care about. Advocates often speak up on behalf of citizens whose interests are not well represented in the legal system—homeless people, for example, or consumers, special needs children, indigenous groups, or an individual who is unfairly accused of a crime. Your public speaking skills help prepare you for getting personally involved in this important form of social activism.

Speeches on questions of policy often ask an audience to take a course of action addressing a need or solving a problem in their community. What problem in your community do you think would make a good topic for a persuasive speech?

Specific Purposes, Thesis Statements, and Main Points for Speeches on Questions of Policy

Unlike speeches on questions of fact and value, speeches on questions of policy often include a call to action, urging the audience to engage in a specific behavior. You may ask your audience to take immediate action, such as signing a petition, or do something in the future, like carefully reading the fine print when they sign an employment contract. Sometimes you ask your listeners simply to lend passive support, as with favoring a campus regulation on skateboards or opposing new zoning laws.

Phrase your specific purpose to indicate clearly what you want your audience to do or agree with. Then develop your thesis so it outlines how you'll support your position. When you create your main points, choose ones that clearly show why a change to an existing policy or situation is necessary, what the benefits of a change are, and what you want the audience to take away from your message. As you're preparing your speech, ask yourself these questions:

- What support can I show for my position?
- How close is my audience to my position—positive, negative, divided, uninformed, or apathetic?
- How does what I suggest solve the problem or move the cause forward in some way?

The following examples, one calling on audience members to take action and the other asking for their support of a position, demonstrate how the main points flow from the thesis.

Topic:	Personal Emergency Preparedness
General purpose:	To persuade
Specific purpose:	To persuade my audience to better prepare themselves for natural disasters that may occur in our area
Thesis:	Individuals increase their chances of surviving a natural disaster by practicing personal emergency preparedness.

Main points:

I. Recent natural disasters demonstrate what happens when we fail to prepare for such calamities.

II. Responses to recent natural disasters in our area show that most people are not prepared for them.

III. Personal emergency preparedness is essential to responding appropriately to natural disasters.

IV. Personal emergency preparedness increases your likelihood of surviving a natural disaster.

V. Personal emergency preparedness involves developing an emergency plan, assembling a disaster supply kit, and identifying local disaster shelters.

Topic:	Year-round Education in K–12
General purpose:	To persuade
Specific purpose:	To persuade my audience to support the institution of year-round education nationwide
Thesis:	Year-round K–12 education should be instituted nationwide because of its educational, social, and economic benefits.

Main points:

I. The current nine-month school calendar shortchanges students, taxpayers, and society.

II. Having K–12 students attend school year-round provides educational, economic, and societal benefits.

In the first example, the speaker indicates why a change is necessary, explains what change should occur, and then tells listeners the specific actions they need to take. In this way, the main points support the response the speaker seeks from the audience: to prepare for natural disasters. In the second example, the speaker simply asks the audience to support the position, first demonstrating why a change is necessary and then describing the benefits of the change.

Organizational Patterns for Speeches on Questions of Policy

Because speeches on questions of policy ask for some sort of change, speakers must clearly articulate why the change must occur and what should be done. Although the organizational patterns previously described can be applied to this type of speech, three other patterns generally are more effective: problem–solution, problem–cause–solution, and Monroe's motivated sequence.

The Problem–Solution Pattern of Organization The problem–solution pattern presents a need or problem and then shows how to solve it, as the following example demonstrates:

Topic:	Corporal Punishment by Parents
General purpose:	To persuade
Specific purpose:	To persuade my audience that parents never should physically strike their children
Thesis:	Because it's harmful, parents should not strike their children.

Main points:

I. Children suffer serious physical and psychological consequences as a result of corporal punishment.

II. Parents should never physically strike their children.

Using this pattern successfully requires clearly establishing the problem's existence. If listeners aren't convinced the problem exists, the solution becomes irrelevant. Once they think there's a problem, the solution must seem reasonable. In the corporal punishment speech, the solution flows naturally from the problem—hitting children harms them, so parents shouldn't do it. However, if you called for long prison sentences to be given to parents who spank their children, most members of the audience likely would consider your solution too extreme.

The Problem–Cause–Solution Pattern of Organization The problem–cause–solution pattern of organization extends the problem–solution pattern by adding an additional step: the cause of the problem. Consider this example of a speech about junk food on campuses.

© 2010 Ted Goff www.tedgoff.com

"All we need to do is rename 'the problem' to 'the solution' and I think we're done here."

Ted Goff

Topic:	Junk Food on Our Campus
General purpose:	To persuade
Specific purpose:	To encourage my audience to sign a petition banning the sale of junk food on our campus
Thesis:	Junk food should be banned on campus because it contributes to obesity, poor nutrition, and immune system problems.

Main points:

I. Many college students are overweight, eat poorly, and have weak immune systems.

II. Junk food is a major contributing factor to these problems.

III. We must work to ban the sale of junk food on our campus.

The first main point explains the problem: Many college students are overweight, eat poorly, and have weak immune systems. The second point identifies the cause of this problem—junk food. The third point provides a solution: Get rid of junk food, at least on campus. Here's another example of a speech about a question of policy that applies the problem–cause–solution pattern.

Topic:	Border Security
General purpose:	To persuade
Specific purpose:	To convince my audience to support increased border patrols between the United States and Canada
Thesis:	We must have better security to prevent illegal immigrants from crossing the U.S.–Canada border.

Main points:

   I. Every year, thousands of people cross into the United States illegally from our neighbor to the north, Canada.

  II. Security on the U.S.–Canada border is lax, making it easy for people to enter our country illegally.

 III. We must increase border patrols between the United States and Canada.

In a persuasive speech on reducing credit card use by college students, you could use the problem–cause–solution pattern to argue that students often spend more money than their budget allows (problem); easy credit causes students to spend money they don't have on purchases they don't need (cause); and refraining from using credit cards is the only way to get spending under control (solution). How would the focus of this speech change if you organized it using another pattern?

As with the problem–solution pattern of organization, getting the audience to believe a problem exists provides the foundation for the remainder of a speech using the problem–cause–solution pattern. The speaker must then link the problem with the cause and show that the solution represents a reasonable answer to the problem.

Monroe's Motivated Sequence Your primary challenge in persuasive speaking is to motivate your audience to respond to your speech the way you want them to. With Monroe's motivated sequence, you organize your speech in such a way that you lead your audience through a five-step thought process that encourages them to agree with you and take action (Chapter 8). You ask your listeners to grasp the relevance and importance of your topic, understand the problem you describe, become satisfied that the solution you offer is a good one, imagine how the solution could be enacted, and feel motivated to do their part in solving the problem.

The motivated sequence allows you to take an audience-centered approach to public speaking. When you use this organizational pattern, you focus clearly on what you want the audience to think and do every step of the way throughout your speech.[10] **Table 14.1** provides a reminder of what you need to do to get the desired response from your audience at every step of the sequence.

Table 14.1   Monroe's Motivated Sequence

Step	Speaker's Action	Audience's Response
Attention	Relate topic to audience to gain attention.	I will listen because this is relevant to me.
Need	Establish the problem/current harm.	There's a problem that needs my attention.
Satisfaction	Describe the solution to the problem.	Here's the solution to the problem.
Visualization	Show benefits of proposed solution and/or costs of not implementing it.	I can visualize the benefits of this solution and/or the costs of not implementing it.
Action	Explain how audience can implement proposed solution.	I will do this.

If you're giving a persuasive speech in which you ask your audience to take some sort of action, all five steps of the motivated sequence apply, as in the following example:

Topic:	Simplify Your Life
General purpose:	To persuade
Specific purpose:	To persuade my audience to take steps to simplify their lives
Thesis:	Our consumer culture makes our lives needlessly complex, so we should take concrete steps to simplify our lives.

Attention:

I. We work more hours, spend more time commuting, take fewer vacations, and wade through more email and voicemail than at any time in the past.

Need:

II. We buy things we don't need, waste time watching television and surfing the web, and drive miles out of our way to save a few pennies on gasoline.

Satisfaction:

III. Simplifying your life means figuring out what you value most and focusing on activities that help you fulfill those values.

Visualization:

IV. Think about all the time you'd have to do what you like if you cut out all the things you do that aren't really necessary.

Action:

V. There are specific steps you can take to simplify your life, such as concentrating on a few goals and doing them well, setting aside time for yourself, and getting rid of clutter by donating to charity or throwing away the things you don't really use.

If you simply want the audience's agreement or support, you can drop the fifth step of the motivated sequence, the action step, as with the following example:

Topic:	Cooperation in Video Games
General purpose:	To persuade
Specific purpose:	To persuade my audience to support video games that contribute to society by promoting more cooperation and less competition
Thesis:	Video games that encourage players to cooperate with each other rather than compete against each other would benefit our society.

Attention:

I. The stereotypical video game player is a teenage male, but did you know that women account for over 40 percent of interactive game players and the average age of a player is twenty-eight?

Need:

II. Violent video games make the headlines, but the real problem is the lack of games that help players develop the teamwork skills that are so essential in today's world.

Satisfaction:

III. Video games based on cooperation rather than on competition provide a logical way to facilitate the development of teamwork skills.

Visualization:

IV. Even if you don't play video games, facilitating people's ability to cooperate with others contributes more generally to society, as you've probably experienced yourself when working with a team.

In this example, you're not asking the audience to play or develop cooperation-based video games. Instead, you're asking them to agree with you that such games contribute positively to society. You want your audience to understand your argument and then agree with your point of view. The logical progression of the steps in the sequence helps you meet this goal. Compared with other organizational patterns, the motivated sequence is particularly good at helping audience members understand main points, which helps you persuade them to change their attitudes.[11]

Developed in the last century by Alan Monroe, a well-known professor of speech, the motivated sequence draws its core ideas from the philosophy that John Dewey expressed in his classic book, *How We Think*.[12] The motivated sequence works well because it mirrors the way we naturally process information and make decisions in our everyday lives. This organizational pattern can also be used for practical purposes other than public speaking, including how to compose a convincing business letter[13] or write clear and compelling technical documents.[14]

Persuading Different Types of Audiences

Just as advertisers must know their audiences well and understand how to reach them effectively, you should know where your audience stands on your topic so you can design a message that will encourage them to listen and consider your views. Chapter 5 explains how to analyze an audience for any type of speech. This section provides specific strategies persuasive speakers use to address the attitudes, values, and beliefs of five common audience positions: negative or hostile, positive or sympathetic, divided, uninformed, and apathetic.[15] These audience positions and strategies are summarized in **Table 14.2**.

The Negative Audience

A **negative audience,** also called a **hostile audience,** is informed about your topic and holds an unfavorable view of it. A negative audience may seem intimidating, but simple exposure to differing points of view is where effective persuasion starts for many audience members. Suppose, for instance, you want your audience to support an initiative on your campus to abolish all general education requirements. That goal may be immediately unattainable, so you might want to argue for a more moderate step, such as reducing the required number of general education units.

When you know you'll likely encounter a high degree of resistance to your position on a topic, several strategies will help you achieve your goal.[16]

- *Establish your credibility with the audience.* Developing a positive relationship with the audience, showing an interest in them, and demonstrating your expertise on the topic all contribute to making a good impression.

- *Take a common-ground approach to the topic.* Identify areas of agreement with the audience, then move to areas of disagreement. If listeners perceive they share similar viewpoints with you, they'll be more open to your message.[17] In a speech on same-sex marriage, you might draw parallels between the right of gays and lesbians to marry and other struggles over civil rights—abolishing slavery, passing laws against child labor, or giving women the right to vote, for instance. You could demonstrate how much resistance there was to each of these changes and then point out that these rights are now considered ordinary.

- *Help your audience visualize your topic in positive ways.* Often just helping the audience get used to a new idea is the first step in effective persuasion. In a speech advocating increased funding for space exploration, you might

An audience that is informed about a speaker's topic and holds an unfavorable view of the speaker's position.

Table 14.2 | **Types of Audiences**

Type of Audience and View of Topic	Persuasive Strategies
Negative (informed → unfavorable or highly unfavorable)	• Establish credibility • Take common-ground approach • Visualize topic in positive ways • Anticipate and address objections • Keep persuasive objectives within reason
Positive (informed → favorable or highly favorable)	• Rely on engaging evidence to reinforce commitment • Use vivid language and images • Incorporate narratives when possible • Suggest action
Divided (informed → split: half favorable, half unfavorable)	• Acknowledge reasonableness of both sides • Establish credibility • Take common-ground approach • Integrate strategies for negative and positive audiences
Uninformed (uninformed → no opinion)	• Show relevance of topic to audience • Demonstrate expertise and fairness • Use repetition and redundancy • Keep persuasion subtle
Apathetic (informed → not important)	• Gain attention and interest • Show how topic affects audience • Display energy and dynamism • Take a one-sided approach • Use presentation media

show a few compelling digital slides of Mars or distant galaxies to spark the audience's imagination and give them a more favorable impression of the topic.

■ *Prepare for your audience's negative reaction to your position.* Consider all the reasons your audience may not agree with you. Then determine how you will confront and overcome those objections in your speech. For example, in a speech on raising the minimum wage in the United States, you could address your listeners' concerns about job loss by pointing to research that shows no such effect. When you acknowledge the audience's concerns in your speech, you demonstrate an understanding of their perspective, which increases your likelihood of winning them over.

■ *Finally, keep your persuasive objectives within reason.* You are not very likely to move your audience to act in a way that conflicts with strong feelings they already hold about your topic. In this case, make it your objective to get the audience to start thinking about the topic in a different way. For instance, an audience that is strongly opposed to allowing the U.S. government to collect DNA samples from all citizens is not going to sign a petition in favor of doing that right after listening to your speech advocating the idea. But you might be able to reduce their resistance and start them thinking about the advantages you think a national DNA archive provides.

The Positive Audience

A **positive audience,** also called a **sympathetic audience,** is informed about your topic and has a favorable view of your position. These audience members want to have their views confirmed and reinforced, learn more about the topic, and in some cases, join a community of like-minded people or find out what they can do personally to advance the cause. Political campaign speeches and religious rallies commonly attract positive audiences. Several strategies will help you focus on reinforcing thoughts and behaviors.[18]

An audience that is informed about a speaker's topic and has a favorable view of the speaker's position.

- *Incorporate engaging evidence that reinforces the audience's commitment to the topic.* Use testimony and examples your audience will find captivating; stay away from long lists of facts, endless statistics, and dull definitions. For instance, you might explain how various successful political initiatives—saving forests, rivers, wetlands, and lakes from pollution and urban sprawl, for example—have preserved valuable natural resources and improved the quality of life for all the planet's inhabitants.

- *Use vivid language and images to heighten your audience's enthusiasm for the topic.* Refer to "flourishing, green forests; icy cold, raging rivers; wetlands teeming with wildlife; and cool, inviting lakes" rather than "forests, rivers, wetlands, and lakes." Incorporating a short series of colorful slides displaying the beauty of land and water saved from destruction through political action can also deepen your audience's appreciation for the topic. They're already on your side, so give them something tangible to take away from the speech that confirms their opinion and extends their knowledge on the topic.

- *Rely on narratives to elaborate your points.* Stories work especially well to reinforce the position audience members already hold. For example, if you know that your audience believes in the value of environmental responsibility, a speech promoting environmental activism might begin with a story about the personal experience that got you involved in the topic.

- *When audience members already agree with your view, rally them to take action.* For example, you might encourage your audience to join an environmental group in the community or on campus, participate actively in Earth Day this year, support impending environmental legislation, purchase reusable cloth shopping bags, stop junk mail, or boycott products that degrade the environment.

Christopher Ena/AP Photo

Forced to be a boy soldier in his native Sierra Leone, Africa, Ishmael Beah, now in his twenties, advocates for the rights of children exploited in war-torn countries. His personal experiences, friendly speaking style, and well-supported arguments lead audiences to view him and his cause sympathetically.

The Divided Audience

A **divided audience** is informed about your topic but split in its views: half have a favorable view and half have an unfavorable one. Speakers are often faced with divided audiences, especially when addressing diverse audiences or speaking about controversial issues. With a divided audience, the main challenge is persuading those audience members who disagree with you. Therefore, you can employ the same basic approach used for a negative audience. This means that you'll want to establish your credibility and connection with the audience clearly, take a common-ground approach, visualize the topic in positive ways for

An audience that is informed about a speaker's topic but equally split between those who favor the speaker's position and those who oppose it.

289

the audience, and confront possible objections. Still, you want to acknowledge those who agree with you as well. Relevant narratives, appealing testimony and examples, and engaging images will help you target sympathetic audience members and may appeal to hostile listeners as well.

Suppose you're speaking to a community group in an urban neighborhood that has experienced a high rate of street crime in recent years. The specific purpose of your speech is to convince your audience that video surveillance cameras should be installed throughout the area. Some members of your audience favor the idea as a practical way to reduce crime. Other members oppose the idea, viewing it as an intrusion on their right to privacy. Here are a few strategies that will help you address the entire audience effectively:

- *Demonstrate that you recognize the legitimacy of the arguments for and against the issue.* Street crime is a problem that must be solved, yet the right to privacy is a fundamental principle of democracy and should be upheld.

- *Establish your credibility* by citing statistics showing that video surveillance does reduce street crime significantly.

- *Establish common ground among all audience members* by saying you are certain everyone in the room agrees with the right to privacy.

- *Integrate strategies for negative and positive audiences.* In this case, you could address the objection that surveillance cameras intrude on the community's right to privacy by saying that the point is not to take away anyone's rights but rather to restore privacy rights that have been taken away. You can also reinforce the position of those who agree with you with testimony and examples from places where surveillance cameras are used.

In the end, you encourage the resisters to rethink their position not only by the strength of your argument and supporting evidence but also because you, the speaker, understand what's at stake in terms of privacy.

The Uninformed Audience

Uninformed audiences are unfamiliar with your topic and have no opinion about it. Audience members potentially could be interested in a topic you care about, but they simply lack exposure to it. For example, people who are not serving in the military often know very little about military benefits. Yet you can argue that members of the armed forces put their lives on the line to protect all of us and deserve to receive decent salaries and benefits. Several strategies will help you provide the information listeners need to facilitate their agreement with you.[19]

An audience that is unfamiliar with a speaker's topic and has no opinion about it.

- *Show the relevance of your topic to the audience.* By linking the audience with the topic you can help them realize, "I don't know much about this, but I should." For example, you'd show how not only military families but audience members too would be affected by changing benefits for veterans. Changing benefits may not seem at first to affect nonveterans, but increased benefits might mean higher costs for all taxpayers. It's worth it, though, because decreased benefits might result in a greater financial burden on local social services. Benefits influence troop morale too, and that can affect everyone's security.

- *Demonstrate your expertise on the topic and fairness in addressing all perspectives.* As a persuasive speaker, you will argue one side of the issue or the other. What changes in benefits for military families do you support? Without turning your persuasive speech into an informative one, you must describe the issue. Show you've done your research on the topic and can provide listeners with what they need to know to formulate an opinion. Audience members will be much more likely to agree with your position if they believe you have given them a fair and comprehensive sense of the issue.

- *Use repetition and redundancy to reinforce your points.* Your audience is new to this topic, so provide them with basic information about the topic in several forms. In our example about veterans' benefits, you could define the purpose of the benefits, present facts about the services the government currently offers veterans, show statistics comparing those services with the proposed services, offer testimony from a scholar who studies veterans' benefits, and tell a story about a veteran who used those benefits to achieve an important goal, such as completing college. These different types of supporting materials all focus on the veterans' benefits, building redundancy into the speech.

- *Keep your persuasion subtle.* Let the audience know your position, but avoid emphatic, inflammatory, or overly-passionate statements. Instead, take a matter-of-fact approach. In our example, you might say, "I support the changes to veterans' benefits currently under consideration. Let me tell you about it." If you wait too long to let audience members know your position on the topic, they'll feel deceived and might devalue the information you've presented. But if you've motivated your listeners to learn more about the topic and have established yourself as an expert, they'll be more likely to trust you to treat the topic fairly, whatever position you take.

The Apathetic Audience

Apathetic audiences are informed about your topic but not interested in it. They may be apathetic because think it doesn't apply to them. Why bother to pay attention? This type of audience challenges a speaker to forge a positive link between topic and audience, which can be achieved in the following ways:

An audience that is informed about a speaker's topic but not interested in it.

- *Gain their attention and pique their interest.* Even more than with an uninformed audience, you have to show apathetic audience members *why* they should care about the topic. For instance, let's say that you want to argue that the United States should provide economic support to developing countries. To do this, you propose that America should provide start-up loans for small businesses in those countries. But your audience analysis, or at least your hunch, indicates that your listeners believe the topic has no relevance to their lives. They may have heard about it, but it hasn't interested them enough to get them to think about it very much. However, you know they tend to give to charity and support strengthening local communities overall. This convinces you that with the right appeal you'll be able to connect your topic to their sense of social responsibility. Using strong supporting evidence, you might demonstrate the positive impact that economic aid can have on the lives of people who live in the developing world while providing more stability and security for us here at home.

- *Show how the topic affects them specifically.* When listeners identify with a topic and feel it's relevant to them, they're more likely to be persuaded.[20] You might be able to convince your audience to care about this seemingly distant topic by explaining how the health of the U.S. economy depends on the presence of a stable global economic system. You tell them that so long as developing countries struggle economically, the stability of the global economic system is threatened. That precarious condition negatively affects the American economy, the value of the dollar overseas, and even national security. So the question of supporting developing countries directly affects the audience's pocketbook and its safety—primary human motivations.

- *Show your audience how much you care about the topic through your energy and dynamism.* In promoting U.S. economic support for developing countries, you must demonstrate your deep commitment to and interest in the topic. So you speak rapidly but clearly, raise your vocal volume a bit, take only short pauses, and gesture and move with energy and purpose. These types of nonverbal behaviors signal your passion for the subject.[21]

■ *Take a one-sided approach to the topic.* Although you must make a balanced presentation of information, you need not address all perspectives on it, as you would when facing a negative audience. When audience members are generally apathetic, taking a one-sided approach to the topic is both reasonable and ethical. In persuading the audience, you will want to advocate a viewpoint that corresponds with the reasons they should care about the topic.

■ *Use presentation media.* Incorporating appropriate presentation media helps the audience visualize your topic, stirs their emotions, and is often more persuasive than words alone.[22] In the case of encouraging people to support U.S. economic aid to developing countries, several photographs demonstrating the positive effects of such aid or a fifteen-second clip from a documentary on life in the developing world could interest an apathetic audiences from the start.

In our visual society, using interesting or dramatic presentation media can help engage an apathetic audience. This can be particularly true when you're discussing a topic that seems "boring" or when audience members have heard many other speeches about the same topic.

The Ethics of Persuasive Speaking

Ethical public speakers must meet the National Communication Association's standards of ethical communication (Chapter 3). Persuasive speakers must adhere to this principle in particular: "We condemn communication that degrades individuals and humanity through distortion, intimidation, coercion, and violence, and through the expression of intolerance and hatred." Ethical speakers do not attempt to deceive or manipulate the audience. Instead, they present their information and arguments truthfully, accurately, and honestly. In addition, they "endorse freedom of expression, diversity of perspective, and tolerance of dissent."[23]

To demonstrate differences between a persuasive speech that meets ethical standards and one that doesn't, consider the subject of DNA testing to determine a person's genetic ancestry. DNA testing has become an indispensable tool for criminologists—in many cases it is the key to helping them accurately identify who did or did not commit a crime. And DNA makes it possible for scientists to determine the age of fossil remains. But the science of DNA has also become available for another purpose: to trace personal genetic history.[24]

Encouraging an audience to subscribe to one of the services that analyzes personal DNA certainly could be developed into an interesting persuasive speech. But what ethical considerations are associated with this topic? An ethical speaker would carefully research how DNA tests are done and properly used to show the audience how they can benefit from the testing process, as well as the risks involved. For example, the speaker might discuss how DNA tests can help diagnose a genetic disorder like Huntington's disease, warn of predispositions to addictions, or estimate the risk of passing on a genetic disease to a child. The speaker might try to motivate

292

the audience by explaining how DNA tests can help people find unknown parents, siblings, or other relatives. In addition, the speaker could mention that DNA tests can reveal where every audience member's ancestors come from.

Two categories of ethical violations can be identified on this *Topic:* (1) suggesting that DNA tests can deliver something they cannot and (2) failing to mention the drawbacks of DNA testing, which can be serious. For instance, although the tests can indicate a person's genetic makeup (European, African, Asian, Native American), they cannot reveal a person's race.[25] Race is an unreliable way of categorizing people by appearance; it is not a scientific category based on genetics. An ethical speaker would not try to convince an audience that DNA testing could help people identify their race.

Perhaps most important, the speaker must warn the audience about the biggest danger associated with DNA testing: the shock many people receive when their DNA results don't match up with their long-held sense of ethnic identity—who they imagined themselves to be. For example, the head of Harvard's African-American Studies Department, Henry Louis Gates, Jr., discovered that his genetic ancestry is as much European as African, completely altering the way he imagined how he descended from his ancestors.[26] Companies that conduct DNA tests warn clients about these risks, especially the possible threat to their ethnic identity. Thus, when persuading others, ethical speakers must consider and address the possible harms their audiences may encounter.

Speaking of . . .

Persuasion or Manipulation?

Persuasion involves using language, images, and other means of communication to influence people's attitudes, beliefs, values, or actions. How does this differ from manipulation? What is the line someone must cross to go from persuader to manipulator? There are two key differences between the two. First, manipulation involves using dishonest means to influence others. Omitting crucial evidence, presenting inaccurate or false information, or intentionally misrepresenting research to influence others to your advantage are examples of manipulation. Second, manipulation often involves abuse of social power by those in a dominant group.[27] For example, a boss who threatens to fire or punish an employee who doesn't agree with the boss's position or a physician who overstates dire health consequences for an uncooperative patient are examples of abusing power to manipulate others. As an ethical speaker, persuade rather than manipulate your audience.

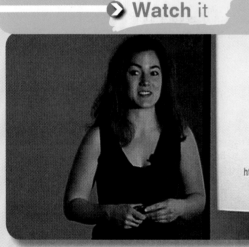

> **Watch it**

SPEECH BUDDY VIDEO 14.1
Speaking to Persuade

In this video, Erin presents a complete persuasive speech about the dangers of driving while using a cell phone.

> **Use it**

ACTIVITY 14.1
Persuasion Equation

This activity gives you a chance to analyze a persuasive speech and then to identify ways you can apply what you've learned about persuasive speaking in your own speech.

Lisa Taylor gave this persuasive speech in an introductory public speaking class at San José State University. Her assignment was to give a six- to eight-minute persuasive speech that incorporated presentation media and at least three sources. As you read the outline of Lisa's speech, consider how effective she is at remaining audience-centered, how well she supports her ideas, and how reasonable her proposed solution is. You can use your CourseMate for Public Speaking: The Evolving Art *to watch and listen to Lisa deliver this speech. Look for it in the Chapter 14 resources.*

Outline of student Lisa Taylor Tulee's speech, "Turn Off Your TV." Used with permission.

Turn Off Your TV

by Lisa Taylor[28]

Specific purpose: To persuade my audience to spend their leisure time doing more productive and fulfilling things than watching TV.

Thesis: We Americans waste much of our valuable leisure time watching TV, when we should be spending that time on more productive and fulfilling activities.

Introduction

I. "Dost thou love life? Then do not squander time, for that's the stuff life is made of." (Benjamin Franklin)

II. If you're like me, you don't have enough hours in the day.
    A. You attend classes.
    B. You work part time or full time.
    C. You have family commitments, personal business, and homework.
        1. You have family errands such as grocery shopping, dry cleaning, and doctor's appointments.
        2. You have personal business such as car repair and banking.
        3. You have school commitments such as homework and research for papers.

Body

I. Every day I have a long list of tasks, and often I must add more before I can even complete the tasks already on the list.
    A. There are only twenty-four hours in the day.
    B. If you subtract time for necessities such as sleep and personal care, you probably have fewer than ten hours a day of leisure time.

Transition: There simply aren't enough hours in the day, are there?

II. What if I told you that you could find more time in the day?
    A. Since 1985, Americans have gained four to eight hours a week of leisure time. (Bureau of Labor Statistics, American Time Use Survey, 2006 results)
        1. We've doubled the amount of time we spend in sports and exercise activities.
        2. We spend fewer hours in paid employment than we did previously.
        3. We spend 20 percent less time on our grooming than we did twenty years ago.
        4. We sleep an hour a night more than we did forty years ago.
        5. We spend three hours a day, more than twenty hours a week, watching television.

Cengage Learning

Transition: So, what does this mean to you?

    B.   Almost half of our leisure time is spent watching television.
        1.   My goal here is not to talk about the ills of television.
            a.   I'm not going to talk about whether the media has too much control over our lives.
            b.   I'm not going to talk about whether sex and violence on television is good or bad for society.
            c.   And I'm not going to talk about the fact that Americans are overweight because we watch too much television and are too sedentary.
        2.   My goal is to talk about how much time we waste in front of the television.

Transition: Some suggest that computers, electronic toys, and the internet waste even more time than watching television.

    C.   Outside of paid work, we spend only about twenty minutes a day on our computers (ATUS, 2006 results).
        1.   The experience of using our computers is much different from the experience of watching TV.
            a.   The interaction with electronics is less passive; we make choices and decisions, and we tell the equipment what to do. (Winn, *The Plug-In Drug*, 2002)
            b.   "You watch television to turn your brain off, and you work on your computer when you want to turn your brain on." (Steve Jobs, co-founder of Apple Computer)
        2.   Much of the time we spend using computers is multitasking.
        3.   In addition, computers can save us time.
            a.   For example, online search engines enable us to do research in much less time than it takes to do research at the library.
            b.   The internet also allows us to spend less time on tasks such as errands and shopping.

Transition: So why am I standing here telling you this? What does this mean to you?

III. Outside of work and sleep, we spend more hours a day watching television than any other activity.
    A.   The time we spend watching television is time wasted.
        1.   Watching television is passive and doesn't stimulate our minds.
        2.   It's time we could be using to do something more productive and fulfilling.
    B.   If you think there aren't enough hours in the day, try turning off your TV.
        1.   What could you do with three more hours a day?
            a.   Spend time with friends, hang out at the quad or the coffee shop, or have a beer.
            b.   Read a book, study, learn a new sport or a new hobby, or have more time for your friends.
            c.   Spend time with your family.

Transition: As Benjamin Franklin suggested, if you love time, don't waste it.

        2.   If you're game, turn off your television for one week.
            a.   Depending on your TV habits, you could have twenty to thirty more hours of free time.
            b.   To motivate you, make a list of things you'd like to do with that time.

Conclusion

I. Consider turning off your TV for a week as a social experiment or a class assignment.
   A. Do whatever it takes to motivate you.
   B. Try it and see what happens.
II. If you're like me, you'll never turn on the TV again.

References

BrainyQuote.com. Benjamin Franklin Quotes. http://www.brainyquote.com/quotes/authors/b/benjamin_franklin.html (accessed September 6, 2010).

Kaiser Family Foundation. "The Media Family: Electronic Media in the Lives of Infants, Toddlers, Preschoolers and their Parents." May 2006. http://www.kff.org/entmedia/upload/7500.pdf (accessed September 13, 2010).

Snell, Jason. "Steve Jobs on the Mac's 20th Anniversary." *Macworld*, February 2004.

U.S. Census Bureau. "American Time Use Survey, 2006 results." Sponsored by the Bureau of Labor Statistics. June 28, 2007. http://www.bls.gov/news.release/pdf/atus.pdf

Winn, Marie. *The Plug-In Drug: Television, Computers, and Family Life.* New York: Penguin Group, 2002.

Questions for Analysis and Discussion

1. How does Lisa gain her audience's attention at the beginning of the speech? How effective is her attention-getter?

2. Identify the types of supporting materials Lisa uses to persuade her audience. How do they work together to help her achieve her specific purpose? How convinced are you after reading through her outline?

3. Does this speech address a question of fact, value, or policy? How closely does Lisa follow the guidelines for the type of persuasive speech she gave?

Summary

When you persuade others, you use language, images, and other means of communication to influence their attitudes, beliefs, values, or actions. Persuasive speeches may address questions of fact, value, or policy. Speeches on questions of fact ask whether something is true or not true. Speeches on questions of value take a position on the worth of something. Speeches on questions of policy are concerned with what should or should not be done. Speeches on questions of fact or value are typically organized using topical, chronological, spatial, or cause-and-effect patterns. Because speeches on questions of policy ask for action or passive agreement on the part of the audience, the problem–solution, problem–cause–solution, or motivated sequence are the best patterns of organization for such speeches.

In general, persuasive speakers face five types of audiences: negative, positive, divided, uninformed, and apathetic. Each type calls for different persuasive strategies. For example, negative audiences require persuasive speakers to thoroughly demonstrate their credibility, take a common-ground approach, visualize the topic in positive ways, and address audience objections. And for apathetic audiences, speakers must gain and maintain audience attention, relate the topic to the audience, display dynamism, and take a one-sided approach to the topic.

Ethical public speakers must meet the National Communication Association's standards of ethical communication. Ethical persuasive speakers present their information and arguments truthfully, accurately, and honestly, and never deceive or manipulate the audience.

296

Directory of Study and Review Resources

IN THE BOOK
- Summary
- Key Terms
- Critical Challenges

MORE STUDY RESOURCES
- Quizzes
- WebLinks
- Peer-reviewed videos

CourseMate

Speech Studio

STUDENT WORKBOOK
- 14.1: Debate
- 14.2: Learn about Your Target Audience
- 14.3: RFK in Indy
- 14.4: Fact, Value, and Policy in Supporting Materials
- 14.5: Watch Commercials for Ethics

SPEECH BUDDY VIDEOS
- **WATCH It Video**
- 14.1: Speaking to Persuade
- **USE It Activity**
- 14.1: Persuasion Equation

SAMPLE SPEECH VIDEOS
- Katherine, "Is That Kosher?" informative speech
- Tiffany, self-introduction speech

SPEECH BUILDER EXPRESS
- Goal/purpose
- Thesis statement
- Organization
- Outline
- Supporting material
- Transitions
- Introduction
- Conclusion
- Title
- Works cited
- Visual aids
- Completing the speech outline

INFOTRAC
- **Recommended search terms**
- Persuasive speech
- Question of fact
- Question of value
- Question of policy
- Ethical communication
- Ethical speaking
- Audience adaptation
- Hostile audience
- Sympathetic audience

AUDIO STUDY TOOLS
- "Breast Cancer Awareness" by Lisa
- Critical thinking questions
- Learning objectives
- Chapter summary

Guide to Your Online Resources

CourseMate Your Speech Communication CourseMate for *Public Speaking: The Evolving Art* gives you access to the Speech Buddy video and activity featured in this chapter, additional sample speech videos, Speech Studio, Speech Builder Express, InfoTrac College Edition, and study aids such as glossary flashcards, review quizzes, and the Critical Challenge questions for this chapter, which you can respond to via email if your instructor so requests. In addition, your CourseMate features live WebLinks relevant to this chapter, including sites where you can find topics for interesting and timely persuasive speeches. Links are regularly maintained, and new ones are added periodically.

Key Terms

apathetic audience 291

coercion 274

divided audience 289

negative (hostile) audience 287

persuasion 274

persuasive speech 273

positive (sympathetic) audience 289

question of fact 275

question of policy 281

question of value 279

uninformed audience 290

Critical Challenges

Questions for Reflection and Discussion

1. How are you immersed in a sea of persuasion? Give some examples of persuasive messages you've received in interpersonal, public speaking, and mass media contexts. What can you do to become a more critical consumer of persuasive messages?

2. As a persuasive speaker, what steps must you take to avoid manipulating your audience? As an audience member, how can you make sure speakers don't manipulate you?

3. Adapting to the audience is especially important for the persuasive speaker. Consider the other side of the podium—when you're in the audience. What are your responsibilities as a listener in a persuasive speaking situation? What can you do to contribute to the productive communication climate discussed in Chapter 3? For example, how can you disagree with the speaker yet still maintain a climate that encourages dialogue?

4. What unique ethical considerations face persuasive speakers when they're addressing questions of fact? What are the ethical considerations associated with questions of value? What ethical issues must a persuasive speaker addressing a question of policy confront?

5. Check out Speech Studio to watch and listen to other students' persuasive speeches. Or record a speech you're working on, upload it to Speech Studio, and ask your peers for their feedback. What feedback could you use to fine-tune your persuasive speech before you give it in class?

15 Understanding Argument

Read it

Cengage Learning

Watch it

Use it

Cengage Learning

Review it

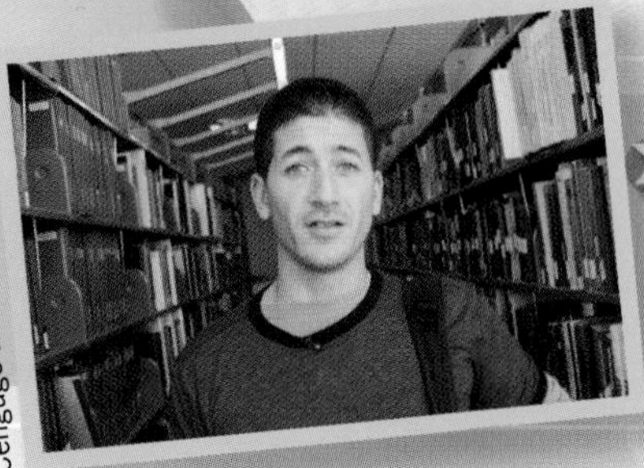

CourseMate SPEECH Studio SPEECH BUILDER EXPRESS

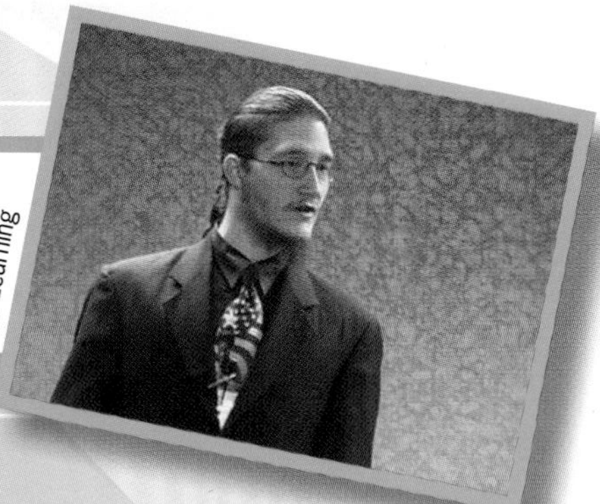

At four o'clock in the morning on Thursday, March 28, 1979, the reactor in Unit 2 of the Three Mile Island Nuclear Generating Station near Harrisburg, Pennsylvania, suffered a partial meltdown. Radioactive gasses were released into the air, causing panic throughout North America. Seven years later, Reactor 4 in the Chernobyl Nuclear Power Plant in the former Soviet Union exploded, sending a plume of radioactive smoke over Europe. Thirty-one people died and many more suffered acute radiation sickness.

It was against this unsettling history that President Barack Obama called for construction of "a new generation of safe, clean nuclear power plants" in his 2010 State of the Union address.[1] It was a highly controversial proposal because the American public is understandably wary of nuclear power. Knowing this, before the President and Congress were even able to consider proposing construction of new power plants, they themselves had to be convinced it was a good idea. Experts would have to demonstrate that the benefits of nuclear power outweigh the risks.

A specialist on the subject—Eileen Claussen, president of the Pew Center on Global Climate Change—gave a particularly important speech that helped influence the politicians to go ahead with legislation to construct new nuclear power plants.[2] As her job title suggests, Claussen even argued that modern sources of nuclear power could begin to reverse the ravages of global climate change.

Jim Arbogast/Digital Vision/Jupiter Images

What Is an Argument?

Presenting claims and supporting them with evidence and reasoning.

A position or assertion that a speaker wants an audience to accept.

Supporting materials—narratives, examples, definitions, testimony, facts, and statistics—that a speaker presents to reinforce a claim.

The method or process used to link claims to evidence.

In common usage, the term *argument* refers to a disagreement or a conflict. But in public speaking, *argument* does not have negative connotations. To the contrary, arguments are constructive. They support persuasive speakers' positions on questions of fact, value, or policy (Chapter 14). Argument forms the foundation of persuasion. Successful speakers formulate arguments effectively and present them well.

An **argument** makes a claim and backs it up it with evidence and reasoning.[3] In public speaking, a **claim** is the position or assertion a speaker wants the audience to accept, and **evidence** refers to the supporting materials—narratives, examples, definitions, testimony, facts, and statistics—the speaker presents to reinforce the claim. **Reasoning** is the method or process used to represent the claim and arrive at the argument's conclusion.[4] **Figure 15.1** illustrates the elements of an argument.

Who contributes arguments to contemporary public discourse is changing in today's expanding media landscape.[5] For instance, we're used to the idea of the news media presenting speeches delivered by important people. Media commentators respond to the speeches, often adding their own views to the ideas discussed in the speech. Given spontaneously just after the speech, their remarks generally are not well organized or argued. But in recent years MSNBC news anchor Keith Olbermann began to give a series of "Special Comments" on his program. Olbermann's comments are, in essence, persuasive speeches.[6] Topics range from his views of the Middle East wars to Supreme Court decisions and the plight of people without health care. Together with Rachel Maddow and Chris Matthews, Olbermann argues the progressive side of American politics. The conservative side is represented by Bill O'Reilly, Glen Beck, Sean Hannity, and others on Fox News.

This chapter discusses the elements of argument in detail and how they work together to create the foundation of a persuasive speech. You'll also learn how speakers use argument and avoid fallacies in persuasive speaking.

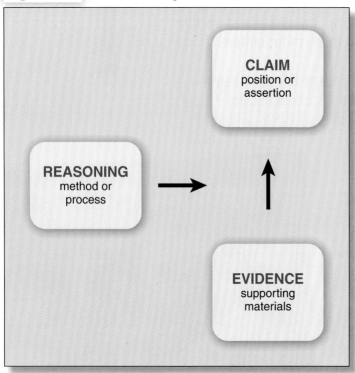

Figure 15.1 Elements of an argument

CLAIM
position or assertion

REASONING
method or process

EVIDENCE
supporting materials

Source: Adapted from Toulmin (2003).

Using Claims Effectively

Claims go beyond facts and other supporting materials to propose conclusions based on the evidence presented. For example, a speaker might say, "Video games are addictive." That is a claim, or a position the speaker is taking. The speaker might then present scientific studies to support that claim. But the claim "Video games are addictive" is still an inference based on the results of those studies. So claims require that listeners make a leap from what is known—the evidence—to some conclusion.[7]

Claims lay the groundwork for your thesis. They respond to basic questions about your topic and the position you take. Claims answer the question, "What is the speaker asserting?" As you develop your speech, consider the questions your topic raises and how you might respond to them. How you answer those questions will help you

Table 15.1 Questions and Claims for Speech on Banning Handguns

Topic Question	Claim
Why ban handguns and not other types of weapons?	Handguns pose a specific problem that can be addressed by legislation.
To what extent are handguns responsible for violent crime?	Handguns contribute more than other weapons to violent crime.
Wouldn't banning handguns violate the Second Amendment of the Constitution, which guarantees Americans the right to bear arms?	The Second Amendment needs to be reconsidered in today's context.
How can we be sure that banning handguns will have a positive effect?	Violent crime decreases in places where handguns are illegal.

identify the claims you'll make in your speech and reveal your position on the topic. **Table 15.1** provides an example of the questions a speaker might ask about a speech on banning handguns in the United States and the claims that correspond with those questions.

Types of Claims

Arguments include two types of claims: premises and conclusions. The **conclusion** is the primary claim or assertion a speaker makes. A **premise** gives a reason to support a conclusion. Both conclusions and premises are claims, but premises are smaller claims that lead up to a conclusion—the central claim or position the speaker promotes.[8] For example, in Eileen Claussen's speech supporting nuclear power plant construction, she offered one conclusion and three premises as support:

> *A primary claim or assertion.*
>
> *A claim that provides reasons to support a conclusion.*

Premise 1:   Climate change is real.

Premise 2:   Protecting the global climate is necessary.

Premise 3:   All forms of energy have problems.

Conclusion: Nuclear power should be part of the solution to climate change.

For audience members to agree with the conclusion, they must agree with all the premises leading up to it. If they find fault with one premise, they're highly unlikely to support the conclusion.

Specific words, either implied or stated, often identify premises and conclusions. Words indicating a premise include *because, whereas, since, on account of,* and *due to.* Words indicating a conclusion include *therefore, consequently, and so, thus,* and *accordingly.* Think of the relationship between premises and conclusions in this way:

Because *(premise 1),* because *(premise 2),* and because *(premise 3),* therefore *(conclusion).*

Claussen asserted that *because* climate change is real, *because* protecting the environment is necessary, and *because* all forms of energy have problems, it is *therefore* right to create a role for nuclear energy in the national energy policy. Although *because* and *therefore* were unstated, Claussen made the relationship between her premises and conclusion clear. **Table 15.2** on page 304 presents additional examples of premises and conclusions.

Sometimes an argument's premises or conclusion are implied rather than stated. Such arguments, called **enthymemes**, assume the audience will figure out the premise or conclusion on their own. Enthymemes depend on the audience's social information or

> *An argument in which a premise or conclusion is unstated.*

Table 15.2 Examples of Premises and Conclusions

	Visual Ergonomics	Globalization and Labor	Online Dating Services
Premises	1. Poor visual ergonomics when using a computer causes eyestrain. 2. Poor visual ergonomics when using a computer leads to neck and shoulder problems.	1. Globalization allows for the free movement of goods between countries. 2. Globalization allows for the free movement of services between countries. 3. Globalization allows organizations to locate freely to other countries.	1. In today's world, single people are too busy to join clubs and organizations to meet other singles. 2. Today, people have fewer friends to introduce them to potential romantic partners.
Conclusion	Improving visual ergonomics is essential for the health and safety of computer users.	Globalization should also allow for the free movement of individual workers between countries.	Online dating services are a practical way to meet romantic partners in today's world.

knowledge to complete the argument.[9] For example, in a speech on a question of policy about making copies of DVD movies, the speaker might argue:

> *Premise:*   Burning DVDs of copyrighted movies is against the law.
>
> *Conclusion:*   Don't burn DVDs of copyrighted movies.

This basic argument leaves out one premise: If you're caught burning DVD copies of movies, you could go to jail, pay a fine, or both. But there's no need for the speaker to say that because the audience already knows it.

Speeches on questions of fact or value often leave the conclusion unstated. In a speech on traffic congestion, for example, the speaker might include these premises:

> *Premise 1:*   Traffic congestion in our city wastes time.
>
> *Premise 2:*   Traffic congestion in our city wastes resources.
>
> *Premise 3:*   Traffic congestion in our city increases pollution.

Advertisers often rely on visual enthymemes, especially when the product's appeal is highly subjective—like taste. This ad is trying to persuade you to buy Coke, claiming that if you drink Coke you'll be the super-cool person that the women in the ad are excited to see. The ad assumes your social conditioning will persuade you to come to the conclusion that, yes, you would be cool if you drank Coke.

The unstated conclusion is that something should be done about traffic congestion. But as this is a speech addressing a question of fact, the speaker is concerned only with whether or not something is true (or false), not with taking some kind of action.

An enthymeme invites audience participation as listeners mentally fill in the missing parts of the argument, facilitating a dialogue between the speaker and the audience.[10] Encouraging these kinds of thought processes can give the audience a better understanding and a more favorable view of the speaker's argument.[11] Dr. Martin Luther King, Jr., was well known for his persuasive oratory. In a speech at the Dexter Avenue Baptist Church in Montgomery, Alabama, during the early days of the Civil Rights Movement[12] he made these claims:

> *Premise 1:*   Love is the best way to respond to enemies.
>
> *Premise 2:*   Mass nonviolent resistance to oppression is based on the principle of loving one's enemies.

But King left one premise and the conclusion unstated. First, he omitted the premise that audience members were oppressed. Although he did refer to people of color around the world as oppressed, he did not say, "We are oppressed" or "You are oppressed." He didn't need to—his audience knew it. Second, he left out the conclusion that audience members should join in mass nonviolent demonstrations. This gave his audience something to consider: Should they join in the protests or not? Leaving out part of his argument was one of many strategies King used to engage his audience more deeply in the speech and his position on the topic.

Advertisers often pile on claims in their commercials but leave out the conclusion, although there's rarely any doubt about what they want the audience to conclude. The claims must be relevant to the conclusion, but they need not be stated explicitly. For instance, in a television commercial for the insurance company Liberty Mutual, a fast-paced series of individual acts of kindness is shown for nearly a minute. A woman picks up and returns a toy to a baby in a stroller, a man holds open an elevator door for someone rushing to get in, a woman keeps a man from falling over backward in his chair, a man helps a driver get out of a parking place safely, and so on. No narration accompanies the visuals; we hear only music. At the very end, a female voiceover says, "When people do the right thing, they call it responsible. When it's an insurance company, they call it Liberty Mutual." Even when an argument is made in an abstract and creative way like this, the premises and the conclusion must be clear:

Premise 1:   Acting responsibly is a highly desirable human quality.

Premise 2:   Liberty Mutual is a responsible insurance company.

The conclusion desired by the sponsor is that the audience will put together the two premises and decide they should consider Liberty Mutual next time they buy car, home, or life insurance.

Guidelines for Phrasing Claims

To accept a claim, an audience must view it as reasonable. Because claims are assertions, they can always be challenged. Some claims, such as "smoking causes cancer" and "a college education leads to a better job," are easily supported. But others, such as "U.S. employers don't give employees enough vacation time" and "Hunting whales does not impact their survival rates," are not so widely accepted. Even topics that seem completely uncontroversial are not without question. By the seventeenth century, science had proved the Earth revolves around the sun, but 20 percent of the American public today still believes the sun revolves around the Earth.[14]

Qualifiers provide a way to make your claims more reasonable to an audience. A **qualifier** indicates the scope of the claim with words such as *probably, likely, often,* and *usually.* These words help you stay away from indefensible assertions or claims that must hold up in every case. Qualifiers answer the question "How strong is the claim?" For example, instead of claiming "Major airline outsourcing of plane maintenance increases the number of plane accidents," you might say, "Major airline outsourcing of plane maintenance *likely* increases the number of plane accidents." Here you acknowledge that outsourcing probably increases accidents, but you're not definitely sure. There may be other factors leading to an increase in accidents, or it may be that accidents haven't increased at all. **Figure 15.2** on page 306 shows how a qualifier fits in with the elements of argument.

As a persuasive speaker, you want to anticipate alternative assertions or claims related to your topic by acknowledging, and carefully refuting, objections or different

A word or phrase that clarifies, modifies, or limits the meaning of another word or phrase.

Figure 15.2 **Elements of an argument with qualifier**

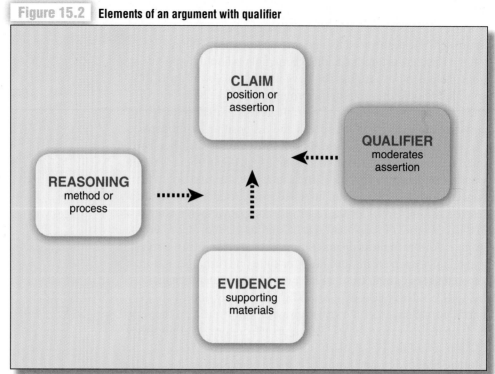

Source: Adapted from Toulmin (2003).

points of view in your speech. Considering other claims lets audience members know you are not just single-minded about the topic. Acknowledging positions held by audience members that differ from your view shows you understand their perspective, even if you don't agree with it. This helps you establish a respectful and productive connection with your listeners.[15] Eileen Claussen used this strategy in her speech advocating construction of new nuclear power plants. Claussen is well aware that many people, including some environmental groups, oppose further development of nuclear power. After claiming that "nuclear power could make a substantial contribution to our efforts to reduce greenhouse gasses," she said,

> However, there are other things we can't ignore. And these are the potential problems associated with the expanded use of nuclear power in this country and around the world … The brutal facts for nuclear power include the fact that we still have not resolved a number of threshold issues that are essential to this industry's future…

She pointed out that the main objections to nuclear power today are the safety of the power plants and the storage of nuclear waste.

To put those problems into perspective, she briefly discussed the obstacles posed by wind and solar power—public opposition to huge wind farms and solar power's relatively low and intermittent power production. But her primary concern about the future of nuclear energy was America's lack of a comprehensive climate policy at the time of her speech:

> The federal government needs to be involved in solving some of the most urgent problems facing key energy alternatives,… I want to wrap up by making the point again that nuclear power can be an important part of the solution to global climate change. But first we need to … take a more discerning look at the world around us—what's possible, where the problems are, and how to overcome them in ways that don't create still more problems for humanity and for the world.

Eileen Claussen strongly advocated making nuclear power part of a comprehensive energy plan because she believes it offers a partial solution to climate change. The strength of her argument lies not only in the evidence she presents and the reasoning she uses to weave her ideas together, but in the way she deftly raises objections to her position and then gently and smartly refutes possible counterarguments.

Similarly, a speech designed to convince an audience that globalization helps poor countries raise their standard of living will be stronger if the speaker acknowledges that globalization has also widened the gap between rich and poor in many countries. By voicing alternative claims, the speaker gains the trust of the audience for being fair. When speakers ignore or hide information they disagree with, or try to mislead the audience about differing viewpoints, they behave unethically and undercut their own position on the topic.

Using Evidence Effectively

Evidence provides the foundation for your claims. Recall that a claim answers the question "What is the speaker asserting?" Evidence answers the question "What is the speaker's support for the assertion?" In presenting evidence to support a claim, the persuasive speaker relies on the four types of appeals introduced in Chapter 1: logos, ethos, pathos, and mythos. These appeals are summarized in **Table 15.3** and discussed in depth in this section.

Logos: Appeals to Logic

Logical appeals, or logos, can be the most persuasive type of appeal when presented well. In addition, audiences expect experts on a topic to use logical appeals in their speeches.[16] Although logical appeals typically are associated with facts and statistics, definitions and testimony may also fit this category of evidence. **Logical appeals** rely on appearing reasonable and rational to influence an audience. Generally, logical evidence is verifiable. For example, listeners can research the facts a speaker presents or look up a definition the speaker offers.

> Use of rational appeals based on logic, facts, and analysis to influence an audience.

When using logical appeals, effective speakers gather current statistical data, facts, definitions, or expert opinions. For example, a just-released poll of Americans' attitudes toward congressional reform would add considerable weight to an argument favoring changes in political lobbying laws. By demonstrating the currency of your research, you'll earn your audience's respect and keep them listening to you.

In addition, your audience must comprehend the logical evidence you present. Long lists of facts and statistics can overwhelm your listeners and cause them to lose interest. However, logical appeals need not be dry and boring. Successful persuasive speakers make evidence clear through their use of language and presentation media.

Dr. Nora D. Volkow, director of the National Institute on Drug Abuse, included logical appeals in her speech "Drug Addiction: Free Will, Brain Disease, or Both?"[17]

Table 15.3 Types of Appeals

Appeal	Brief Definition	Example
logos	logical proof	facts and statistics
ethos	speaker's credibility	references to own expertise on topic
pathos	emotional proof	a humorous quote or story
mythos	cultural beliefs and values	a well-known fable

Presenting verifiable evidence in a thought-provoking and easily understandable way increases the power of your logical appeals.

She presented her speech to Town Hall Los Angeles, an audience of city residents. In this part of her speech, she focused on her claim that drug addiction is a brain disease:

> Drug addiction is a developmental disease. What do we mean by that? What we've learned from many years of epidemiological studies is drug addiction develops during these periods of our lives, during adolescence and early adulthood. This is a graph [on a digital slide] that actually describes at what age individuals develop, at first, a dependence on marijuana. Similar graphs occur for cocaine, nicotine, and alcohol. You can see the peak at this case is around age eighteen. By age twenty-five, if you have not become addicted to marijuana the likelihood that you will do so is very minimal. It's not zero but it's very minimal.[18]

Volkow presented data from a large number of studies to support her claim. She used a digital slide to show the statistics, and then explained what the graph meant to the audience.

Ethos: Appeals to Speaker Credibility

The effectiveness of **appeals to speaker credibility**, or **ethos**, rests in the degree to which the audience perceives the speaker as competent, trustworthy, dynamic, and likeable—the speaker's ethos. Competence or expertise in particular has a direct positive impact on a speaker's persuasiveness. If your audience believes you're an expert on your topic, you're more likely to convince them.

Speaker credibility also depends on the degree to which listeners feel connected to you. Research shows that if you haven't established a good relationship with your audience, expertise alone will not convince them.[19] Your credibility as a speaker, then, relies on more than just doing your research. The audience must also perceive you as likeable or sociable. Open gestures, a slightly faster rate of speech, a somewhat raised voice volume, eye contact, smiling, and other nonverbal behaviors that suggest friendliness, energy, and enthusiasm all contribute to listeners' perceptions of a speaker's sociability.[20]

The degree to which an audience finds a topic personally relevant also influences the effects of speaker credibility.[21] When audience members view the source of a message as highly credible but find the subject uninteresting, they judge the speaker as not very persuasive. Similarly, if audience members don't think the topic applies to them, they don't pay much attention to it.

Dr. Carl J. Schramm's speech on entrepreneurship at a European Union Finance Ministers meeting provides a useful example of appeals to speaker credibility.[22] As president and chief executive officer of the Ewing Marion Kauffman Foundation and a member of the business school faculty at the University of Virginia, Schramm brought much training and experience (fixed qualifications) to the event. Yet he began his speech by establishing a connection with his listeners, gaining their interest with a bold statement, and indicating the topic's relevance to them:

> I am deeply honored to have been asked by Minister Crasser to speak with you about the new economy that awaits us. Simply, we are in the midst of a transformation of capitalism. What is emerging might be called Entrepreneurial Capitalism. This evolution continues to evade description for various reasons, not the least being that economists and officials charged with the management of economic affairs have understandably deep loyalties to our inherited wisdom. We are comfortable with a

Use of the audience's perception of the speaker as competent, trustworthy, dynamic, and likeable to influence an audience.

changing economic landscape that presents a steady stream of challenges requiring different policy approaches. We are not at ease, however, with changing economic theory. Nonetheless, the new economic order overtaking the U.S., Ireland, the U.K., and, to a remarkable degree, transforming China and India, must be recognized for what it is.[23]

Beginning with a humble statement directed to the audience provided a way for Schramm to appear more likeable and friendly. He then got their attention with the statement, "We are in the midst of a transformation of capitalism." He showed the topic's relevance to the audience, referring to "economists and officials charged with the management of economic affairs" and using the pronoun *we*. In these ways, Schramm laid a foundation for his primary appeal to speaker credibility, which he included at a later point in his speech:

> Elsewhere I have proposed part of a conceptual framework for entrepreneurial capitalism and here offer only a précis. The economic model that prevailed through the last century envisioned economic activity as dependent on three central players. Big labor, business, and government coexisted and engaged in a balance of power as a means of achieving two predominant goals—equilibrium and predictability. John Kenneth Galbraith described the balanced duopolies amongst any two players as "countervailing" power relationships.[24]

Schramm went on to explain his conceptual framework, using technical language appropriate to the audience. Note how he referred to his own work, yet also cited the work of others. He used both his research on the topic and an authoritative reference in his appeal to speaker credibility. And by including several charts and figures to help the audience visualize his points, he further demonstrated his competence and produced a more dynamic presentation, enhancing his credibility as a speaker.

Pathos: Appeals to Emotion

Emotional appeals, or **pathos**, rely on emotional evidence and stimulation of feelings to influence an audience. Speakers typically use stories, examples, definitions, and testimony when appealing to our emotions. Appeals to emotion work well when they tap into the audience's beliefs and needs, call up personal associations with the topic, and help listeners recall the speaker's message.[25] Emotion can reinforce or change an audience's position on a topic or stir people to action. Emotional appeals alone seldom work to convince an audience, yet in conjunction with other types of appeals they can win over even skeptical listeners.[26]

According to social psychologist Abraham Maslow, humans are motivated by five types of needs: physiological, safety, love/belonging, esteem, and self-actualization.[27]

- *Physiological needs* are those necessary for our body to function, including food, water, and sleep.

- *Safety needs* are associated with the desire to feel free from harm.

- *Love/belonging needs* include wanting to feel part of a group and loved by others.

- *Esteem needs* focus on our status and having others recognize our accomplishments.

- *Self-actualization needs* are concerned with personal growth and self-fulfillment.

You're motivated to fulfill your needs in a hierarchical order, satisfying more basic needs before progressing to higher-order ones (**Figure 15.3** on page 310). You interact emotionally and connect with others to satisfy your needs. For example, you depend on

Use of emotional evidence and stimulation of feelings to influence an audience.

309

Figure 15.3 **Maslow's hierarchy of needs**[29]

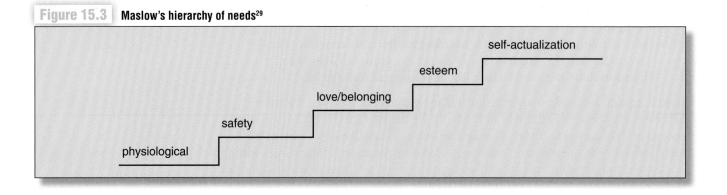

others to help you feel safe and loved. Obtaining even basic needs such as food and water requires the help of others.[28]

Understanding these needs can help you develop appropriate emotional appeals for your audience. Appealing to a positive emotion such as happiness usually proves more persuasive than appealing to a negative emotion such as fear. Yet persuaders commonly use fear appeals to scare audiences into doing or not doing something based on the horrible consequences that might result. These appeals often target the most basic needs—physiological and safety needs. Fear appeals can work, but they don't work very well if the appeal is so threatening that people feel overwhelmed by fear. When that happens, audience members resist the persuasive attempt, deny that the appeal applies to them, and reject any proposed change in thought or behavior. However, if the fear appeal produces a milder emotional response and leads the audience to believe they can do something to control the danger, they're much more likely to be persuaded.[30] In her speech at the first meeting of the President's Identity Theft Task Force, Deborah Platt Majoras, chair of the Federal Trade Commission, said:

> Personal information is the currency of our new information economy. It permits the global marketplace to be brought digitally to our doorsteps, indeed our fingertips. But like cash currency, it also attracts thieves. These identity thieves are cheats and cowards. Unlike their victims, identity thieves do not work to earn their resources and to establish good names and good credit. Instead, they steal from others in a most insidious manner—by taking their identities.[31]

In defining identity thieves and their victims, Majoras highlighted a fear many people share: that someone will steal their personal information and use it to run up bills that the thief never intends to pay. Here she appealed to the audience's safety needs—safety from the theft of private personal information rather than the more traditional sense of safety from physical harm. She went on to list the actions the new task force would take to address this fast-growing problem. When audience members believe they can take action to counteract a threat, a fear appeal is more successful.

Personal narratives are probably the most common way persuasive speakers appeal to audiences' emotions. In a speech given at the University of Richmond, author Lois Lowry recounted several narratives to support her claim that people often avoid or turn away from things that may seem too painful, difficult, or challenging.[32] Near the end of the speech, she told this story:

> In 1994, when *The Giver* was awarded the Newbery Medal, a picture book called *Grandfather's Journey* was awarded the Caldecott. Its author/ illustrator was Allen Say. Allen is Japanese, though he has lived in the USA since he was a young man.
>
> He gave me a copy of *Grandfather's Journey* and inscribed it to me. In return, I signed *The Giver* to him, writing my name in Japanese

below my usual signature. He chuckled, looking at it, and asked me how I happened to be able to do that.

You can picture the ensuing conversation.

"I lived in Japan when I was eleven, twelve, thirteen," I explain.

"What years?" asks Allen Say.

"1948, 49, 50. I was born in 1937."

"Me too. We're the same age. Where did you live?"

"Tokyo," I tell him.

"Me too," he says. "What part?"

"Shibuya."

"So did I! Where do you go to school?" Allen asks me.

"Meguro. I went by bus each day."

"I went to school in Shibuya."

"I remember a school there," I tell him. "I used to ride my bike past it."

Silence. Then: "*Were you the girl on the green bike?*"

Allen and I are close friends now. But we had lost fifty-seven years of friendship because we had both turned away. To do otherwise—in that place and that time—would have been *too hard*.[33]

Lowry's story evokes both happiness and sadness—she won a prestigious award and met a new friend, yet also missed out on that friendship for nearly sixty years. She appealed to listeners' esteem and belonging needs, suggesting that satisfying these needs means that individuals must bear some pain along the way.

Persuasive speakers also use presentation media as evidence to elicit emotion. For example, to support the claim that your community needs a new theater, you might show a short clip of an especially powerful performance by the local theater group, presented in its current dilapidated venue. Digital slides of unwanted pets waiting for adoption at the Humane Society can stir feelings of sympathy and buttress the claim that all pets should be spayed or neutered.

Emotional appeals must do more than stimulate an emotional response. Such appeals must serve as evidence—direct support for your claim. When you tell a story, define a term, recite a quote, or show a photograph, you appeal to your audience's emotions in ways that advance your claim. As with any evidence you include in your persuasive speech, an emotional appeal must be relevant to your topic and appropriate to your audience.

Mythos: Appeals to Cultural Beliefs

Appeals to cultural beliefs, or **mythos**, rely on the values and beliefs embedded in cultural narratives or stories to influence an audience. Speakers use traditional songs, tall tales, rhymes, proverbs, familiar stories, and the like to suggest a common bond with the audience. For example, the myth of the American hero, who does good deeds, works hard, and triumphs over misfortune, is deeply engrained in our culture.[34] Stories related to this mythic figure tap into our cultural beliefs in helping others, industriousness, and persevering in the face of adversity. Dr. J. Edward Hill, president of the American Medical Association (AMA), said this during a speech at the association's annual meeting:

Use of values and beliefs embedded in cultural narratives or stories to influence an audience.

As many of you know and have heard before, I spent twenty-seven years in Hollandale, Mississippi, a little town in the Delta that is home, not just to the blues, but to some of the poorest patients in America…. Worst of all— at least in the eyes of my partner, Dr. John Estes, and myself—shamefully high rates of maternal and fetal mortality. It all came home to me one day, when I drove off to care for a woman who had just given birth, unassisted, at home. She had lost so much blood, she couldn't raise her head without losing consciousness. I can still remember driving her to the town clinic after giving her an emergency transfusion. The woman recovered from her ordeal. But I did not. That night, on television, I watched Neil Armstrong take his famous walk on the moon's surface. I asked myself how a nation as great as ours could put a man on the moon but still couldn't provide basic obstetrical care to a poor, rural woman in the Mississippi Delta.[35]

Hill's reference to Armstrong's historic feat calls up the image of the American hero, in this case conquering space to set foot on the moon. When faced with a stubborn societal problem, it's common to hear the statement "We can put someone on the moon, but we can't [solve this problem]." Hill's appeal to cultural beliefs frames his story within a significant American event and forecasts that he and his partner do overcome the odds to provide better health care for their patients. The heroic image of Neil Armstrong also serves to support Hill's claim that physicians must be the leaders in changing America's health care system.

Presenting a cultural icon in a novel way provides another strategy that uses mythos. Author Michael Crichton did this in a speech titled "Fear, Complexity, and Environmental Management in the Twenty-First Century" by beginning with an upside-down map of the United States—Texas at the top, North Dakota at the bottom. Crichton used the map to advance his claim that individuals hold "assumptions so deeply embedded in our consciousness that we don't even realize they are there."[36] Showing a well-recognized cultural image from a unique perspective helps the audience examine beliefs they take for granted.

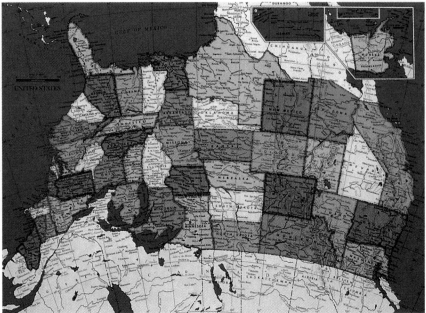

Michael Crichton's use of a recognized cultural image presented from a unique perspective, an inverted map of the United States, prepared the audience for an unconventional view of environmental management.

Apply it

Arguing for Alternative Policies

Because they enjoy a very high standard of living, Americans have a special responsibility to contribute to the global good. Nongovernmental organizations (NGOs) offer real opportunities to campaign for social responsibility on a range of issues. Spokespersons for NGOs argue for instituting or changing public policy in ways that often go against mainstream interests. For example, Michael Marx, an environmentalist and communications graduate from Gonzaga University, created Corporate Ethics International. His mission is to "transform the role of corporations so that they are once again in service to and under the control of civil society."[37] Among other issues, Marx's organization argues against extracting dirty oil from the Canadian wilderness, encourages big-box stores to "go green," and proposes sustainable environmental policies to government leaders in the United States and Canada.

Guidelines for Using Evidence in Argument

Follow these guidelines for using evidence effectively in your persuasive speech:

- *Keep your evidence relevant to your topic.* Your audience must be able to grasp quickly and clearly how the evidence you present supports your claim. For example, if you wanted your audience to support returning cultural artifacts

312

to their countries of origin, you would cite statistics concerning the scope of the problem. You might also provide examples of artifacts that have been returned. But you would not mention current artwork and other artifacts not involved in the controversy. Every piece of evidence you include must directly support your argument.

- *Draw your evidence from highly credible sources.* Credible evidence comes from identifiable, respected sources. If you want to demonstrate the unfairness of teachers' salaries, for example, provide data about what they earn from the government agencies that pay them. When conducting interviews, choose individuals who are truly experts on your topic.

- *Select evidence from diverse sources.* Integrating evidence from a variety of sources provides a stronger foundation for your claims, shows you've done your research, and enhances your credibility. For example, in a speech advocating a ban on personal fireworks, you could cite state and local statistics on fireworks-related injuries and property damage, interview the fire chief, and present facts from areas where such a ban is in place.

- *Incorporate evidence addressing all types of appeals.* Effective speakers rely on logos, ethos, pathos, and mythos to advance their claims. Speeches that include only one type of evidence seldom succeed in persuading the audience. Employing logical appeals, appeals to the speaker's credibility, emotional appeals, and appeals to cultural beliefs provides a broad foundation of evidence to support your claims.

Using Reasoning Effectively

Reasoning is the method or process speakers use to link their evidence and claims. Claims answer the question "What is the speaker asserting?" and evidence answers the question "What is the speaker's support for the assertion?" Reasoning answers the question "How are the support and assertion connected?" Reasoning provides the bridge between the claim and the evidence, indicating to the audience why the evidence presented should be accepted as support for the claim. Although there are many types of reasoning, this section discusses only those most relevant to persuasive speaking: deductive, inductive, causal, and analogical. **Table 15.4** summarizes those types of reasoning.

Deductive Reasoning

In **deductive reasoning**, the speaker argues from a general principle to a specific instance or case. Persuasive speakers apply deductive reasoning to categories of people, objects, processes, and events, claiming that what applies to the group also applies to the

Reasoning from a general condition to a specific case.

Table 15.4 Types of Reasoning

Type	Brief Definition	Strengths	Weaknesses
Deductive	From general principle to specific case	Relies on established formal logic	Invalid premises leading to false conclusions
Inductive	From specific examples to general principle	Visualizes and personalizes argument	Lack of representation, sufficiency, relevance
Causal	One event causes another	Useful for explanation and prediction	Incorrect cause–effect link
Analogical	Draw similarities between two distinct cases	Links the unfamiliar with the familiar	Ignoring of key differences

individual: "Compact fluorescent light bulbs save energy and last longer. The light bulb I bought is compact fluorescent, so it will save energy and last longer."

With deductive reasoning, if the general principle is true, the specific instance must be true as well. You use deductive reasoning in everyday life. You might read a favorable report on job prospects for college students in your major and reach the conclusion that your own job prospects will be good as well. Here you're reasoning from the general—all college students in your major—to the specific—yourself.

Deductive reasoning relies on formal logic and most commonly follows this pattern: major premise (general condition), minor premise (specific instance), and conclusion. With this form of reasoning, also called a **syllogism**, both premises must hold true for the conclusion to be true. Here are some examples:

A form of deductive reasoning consisting of a major premise, minor premise, and conclusion.

Major premise:	All triathletes are in excellent physical condition.
Minor premise:	Taylor is a triathlete.
Conclusion:	Taylor is in excellent physical condition.

Major premise:	All accredited colleges and universities must go through a rigorous assessment process for certification.
Minor premise:	My college is accredited.
Conclusion:	My college went through a rigorous assessment process.

Major premise:	No one in our family missed the reunion.
Minor premise:	Afarin is part of our family.
Conclusion:	Afarin did not miss the reunion.

Major premise:	Citizens may rightfully overthrow a tyrannical government.
Minor premise:	The king of Great Britain's rule in the American colonies is a tyrannical government.
Conclusion:	The citizens of the American colonies may rightfully overthrow the king of Great Britain's government in the colonies.

This last syllogism may sound familiar, as it outlines the essential argument set forth in the U.S. Declaration of Independence.[38] Reviewing the words used in each claim—the major premise, the minor premise, and the conclusion—helps you visualize the connections among the three parts of a syllogism. **Figure 15.4** outlines the syllogism underlying the Declaration of Independence.

Figure 15.4 Syllogism underlying the Declaration of Independence

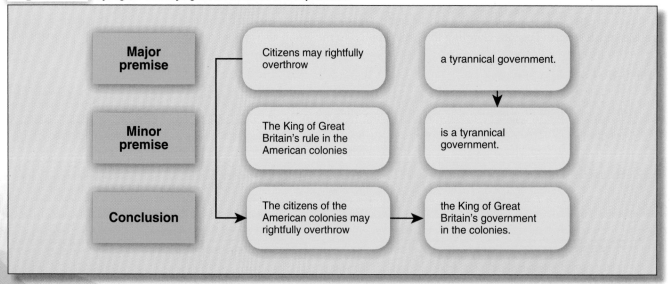

PART 4 : SPEAKING SITUATIONS

The major premise makes clear the general condition on which the Declaration of Independence is based: *Overthrowing a tyrannical government is right and moral.* The minor premise establishes the current system governing the American colonies as a tyrannical one. So the obvious conclusion is that the colonies are justified in ending their ties with Great Britain's rule. That's the power of deductive reasoning: the conclusion cannot be questioned, because it is determined by the major and minor premises.[39]

To successfully employ an argument based on deductive reasoning, persuasive speakers must demonstrate the validity of their major and minor premises with supporting evidence, then work their way toward the conclusion. If speakers do this well, listeners cannot easily refute the argument. Consider the following example from a student speech advocating a ban on smoking in public places:

Topic:	Smoking Ban in Public Places
General purpose:	To persuade
Specific purpose:	To convince my audience that smoking should be banned in all public areas in our state
Thesis:	Smoking should be banned in all public areas throughout our state because secondhand smoke harms nonsmokers.
Major premise:	One obligation of the state is to keep individuals safe from harm in public places.
Minor premise:	Smoking in public causes harm to nearby nonsmokers.
Conclusion:	Smoking should be banned in all public places in our state.

For the audience to accept the conclusion that smoking should be banned in public places, the speaker musts first show that (1) the state is responsible for protecting people from harm when they're out in public and (2) secondhand smoke harms nonsmokers. Supporting the major premise may pose a challenge, because the state government cannot protect individuals from all forms of harm. For example, driving, cycling, or walking on a road can be dangerous. Should the state ban all roads? That's not practical. Instead, states develop laws and regulations to make roads safer, though not completely safe. For the minor premise, the speaker must demonstrate the magnitude of the harm. Research does suggest a link between secondhand smoke and several diseases.[40] Still, the speaker's evidence must convince the audience that the minor premise is true. Once the audience accepts both premises, the conclusion becomes logically apparent.

Deductive reasoning may be *valid* or *invalid*. For deductive reasoning to be valid, the premises and conclusion must be true, as in the previous examples. Sometimes, however, premises do not guarantee a true conclusion. In those cases, the argument is invalid.[41] Consider the following syllogism:

Major premise:	Reducing stress helps students get good grades.
Minor premise:	Playing video games reduces stress.
Conclusion:	Playing video games helps students get good grades.

The speaker may be able to find evidence supporting the major and minor premises. And for some audience members the conclusion may hold true. But for others, playing video games wastes time that could be spent preparing for tests, writing papers, or doing other things that help assure good grades. Therefore, the conclusion that playing video games will help students get good grades is not proven. It may be true for some people, but other factors limit the conclusion's more general truth. In this case, the conclusion does not necessarily follow from the premises, so the argument is invalid.

In persuasive speaking, there are two keys to applying deductive reasoning when linking claims to evidence. First, the speaker must have sufficient supporting evidence to convince the audience that the general condition (major premise) and specific instance (minor premise) are true or correct. Second, the speaker must have sufficient supporting evidence to show that the conclusion is the correct one based on the premises.

Inductive Reasoning

Supporting a claim with specific cases or instances; also called *reasoning by example*.

Speakers use **inductive reasoning** when they support a claim with specific instances or examples. Also called *reasoning by example*, inductive reasoning asks the audience to accept a general claim based on a few cases or even just one case. People naturally think inductively, using their own experiences to draw conclusions about the world.[42] Suppose you practice a speech for your public speaking class in front of friends and do much better than when you only practiced by yourself. Based on that single experience, you decide that practicing with an audience is always better than practicing alone. In this case, you're applying inductive reasoning.

When speakers use inductive reasoning to make their arguments, they rely on the principle of probability—that the evidence they present in their argument leads to a conclusion that is *probably* correct. Inductive reasoning depends on the quality of the evidence presented and the way speakers make sense of it. Princell Hair, a journalist and former general manager of CNN/U.S., used inductive reasoning in a portion of his speech to the Radio–Television News Directors Association & Foundation:

> Journalism, be it CNN/U.S. television, CNN.com or any of the other hundreds of news outlets available in this country, provides a sort of "national campfire" around which people gather…. Our role as journalists in helping to frame a larger dialogue—to tend that national campfire I just mentioned—has never been more important, or more complicated. The good news for me, and for anyone in this room who wants to be a journalist or who already is a journalist, is that Americans seem to want to listen to—and even join—in the conversation. Simply put, news brands are reaching more people than ever before.
>
> For example, my network CNN alone reaches almost 107 million people in the United States each month. And this 107 million includes only the viewers in homes and using the Web—this doesn't include restaurants, gyms, airports and all those many other places where CNN is available. Worldwide, in a single day, CNN has the power to aggregate 1.7 billion audience impressions.[43]

Speaking of . . .

How Many Examples Are Enough?

How do you know when you have enough evidence when reasoning inductively? You can never know for sure. Unlike deductive reasoning or formal logic, where you're certain of your conclusion, inductive reasoning relies on probability—the idea that the conclusion is likely true. So that's your task as a persuasive speaker: to present enough evidence to show that your position has a high probability of being correct. But it's more than a numbers game. Three diverse and representative examples make a much stronger case than fifty similar examples. If you were arguing, for instance, that all students on your campus support building a new student center and you interviewed only students you knew, you wouldn't have an appropriate sample. But if you chose and interviewed a cross-section of students based on demographics such as age, major, class standing, and where they lived, you would have greater confidence in reasoning from those specific cases to the general student population.

Hair begins with his conclusion that news outlets produce a "national campfire" where people gather to talk with each other. He then presents the premise that large numbers of people watch or listen to the news. To support his claims, he uses CNN's viewership as an example. His reasoning follows an inductive pattern—from the specific (CNN) to the general (all news outlets are experiencing increased audience numbers).

Inductive reasoning can be persuasive because it provides specific, concrete evidence that makes the claim more real or understandable. In addition, humans naturally think inductively, so using such reasoning to connect claims and evidence fits well with the audience's thought processes. One example alone, however, seldom convinces an audience of a claim's legitimacy. Inductive reasoning works best when speakers use multiple, diverse, and relevant examples.[44] Later in his speech Hair referred to statistics on website news traffic, broadening the range of his supporting evidence. In addition, examples must clearly represent the general conclusion they support. As a network dedicated to broadcasting news, CNN provides a reasonable example for the claim that more people are watching the news.

Causal Reasoning

Persuasive speakers use causal reasoning in four ways: to *explain* why something happened, to identify who's *responsible* for something, to determine whether people can *control* an event, and to *predict* what might occur in the future. In each of these cases, the speaker wants to show the cause of something. In **causal reasoning**, the speaker argues that one action or event resulted in another.[45] People frequently use causal reasoning to make sense of their everyday experiences. You take on an extra project at work, for instance, and after you complete it you get a raise. To explain the increase in salary, you point to your efforts on the project as the cause. Causal reasoning also plays an important role in your attempts to predict the future. If you can determine a causal relationship between two events that occurs consistently, you can expect the relationship will continue to occur. You might observe, for instance, that if you take a brief nap during the day you feel more alert in the evening than on the days you skip a nap. You'd predict, then, that in the future taking a nap will help you feel refreshed later in the day.

> **causal reasoning**
> Linking two events or actions to claim that one resulted in the other.

U.S. Department of Education Deputy Secretary Raymond Simon used causal reasoning in his testimony about the No Child Left Behind Act before the House Committee on Education and the Workforce. As you probably know, No Child Left Behind is a federal law designed to improve elementary- and secondary-school education. The legislation has both supporters and detractors. Deputy Secretary Simon testified in support of the law:

> You deserve to know whether the No Child Left Behind Act is working as intended. I am here to report that it is. Across the country, test scores in reading and math in the early grades are rising, and the "achievement gap" is finally beginning to close. Students once left behind, I am pleased to say, are now leading the way, making some of the fastest progress.
>
> We know this because No Child Left Behind measures the academic performance of all students through testing. And we know it because the law breaks down these results by student subgroup—African American, Hispanic, students with disabilities, the economically disadvantaged, limited English proficient, and more.
>
> This disaggregation of data, as it's known, is at the heart of the law. It shines a bright light of accountability on our schools for all parents and taxpayers to see. And it allows teachers to catch students before they fall behind.[46]

In his remarks, Simon elaborated on the effects—better test scores, reduced achievement gap, and identifying students before they fall behind—and attributed them to the No Child Left Behind Act. Later in his comments, he provided more technical information to support his reasoning and described education problems the new law solved. His causal reasoning answered two questions: (1) What is responsible for improvements in K-12 education? (2) How does the No Child Left Behind Act improve K-12 education?

Causal reasoning can prove quite persuasive because humans are naturally inquisitive—they like to know why and how things happen. People also like a sense of stability and prediction, which causal reasoning can provide. As a persuasive speaker, however, you must be sure that the two events are indeed related and that one truly

Summit Entertainment/Everett Collection

When you use causal reasoning, think carefully about what the true causes of an event or action are. For example, does violence in movies cause people to commit violence? If so, should violent movies be censored? Or do other factors—broken homes, substance abuse, high unemployment, or mental illness, for instance—contribute more to violent behavior? Considering an event or action's true causes—and using supporting evidence to back up your claim—will help you present a stronger argument.

causes the other. You must consider, for example, other factors that might lead to a particular result. Deputy Secretary Simon credited No Child Left Behind with many academic improvements. But additional variables may be at work as well, such as changes in local and state education practices completely unrelated to No Child Left Behind.

Analogical Reasoning

An *analogy* is a comparison between two things. Analogies work well when the two things compared share clear points of relevance. For example, most people would probably understand the analogy "The internet is an information highway" because both the internet and highways involve speed, networks, points of access, and long-distance travel. But the analogy "The internet is an information country road" likely wouldn't resonate with an audience because the two objects don't have obvious points of comparison.

When persuasive speakers use **analogical reasoning**, they compare two similar objects, processes, concepts, or events and suggest that what holds true for one also holds true for the other. The similarities between the two provide the rationale for the conclusion the speaker offers. In a speech on diversity, McGill University professor Fahri Karakas[47] used analogical reasoning to compare North America and a sweet dessert called Noah's pudding:

• Comparing two similar objects, processes, concepts, or events and suggesting that what holds true for one also holds true for the other.

> We have today with us a very special, unique, authentic dessert. Let me introduce to you this marvelous dessert, called "Ashura" or "Noah's pudding." Noah's pudding is a sweet dessert prepared of mixed nuts and fruits in a pudding texture in the Middle East in remembrance of the event of Noah's ark, and the pudding is distributed to friends, family, and neighbors….
>
> Ashura symbolizes diversity and tolerance. Each of the forty ingredients is cooked and prepared in a different fashion. This

318

symbolizes a genuine respect for the differences. Ashura is essentially a celebration of diversity.... .

North America is like a cup of Noah's pudding as it embodies and contains the diversity and richness of almost all human civilizations. Canada and the United States have become post-national and multicultural societies, containing the globe within their borders, and we know that our diversity is a comparative advantage and a source of continuing creativity and innovation. We grow socially, economically, culturally, and spiritually by valuing our diversity and contributing to the world.[48]

Karakas went on to detail more explicitly the ways in which Ashura and diversity in North America are similar. He used this line of analogical reasoning as a platform to argue that diversity lies at the center of effectively solving global problems such as hunger, illiteracy, and war. The analogy works well—in large part because Karakas provides rich detail in describing the dessert and clearly linking different aspects of it to diversity.

For an analogy to be an argument and not simply a comparison, the speaker must state or imply a premise and a conclusion. Let's examine Karakas's speech:

Premise: Ashura shows that different ingredients can work together harmoniously to produce something extraordinary.

Premise: The people of North American are like a cup of Ashura.

Conclusion: North Americans can work together to produce something extraordinary.

> **Watch it**

SPEECH BUDDY VIDEO 15.1
Identifying the Elements of Argument

Anthony reviews the elements of a sound argument.

> **Use it**

ACTIVITY 15.1
Convince Me

This activity gives you a chance to analyze arguments in persuasive speeches and suggest ways in which each argument might be improved. Finally, it gives you a chance to identify the ways you can apply what you've learned about the elements of argument in your own persuasive speeches.

319

Chapter 15 : Understanding Argument

As with all arguments, analogical reasoning must include some conclusion.[49] In this case, Karakas applied the analogy to make the assertion that diverse people can jointly address global issues. But just saying, "North Americans are like Ashura" would not have been sufficient—it's only a comparison.

When speakers reason by analogy, the two things they compare must have enough similarities to make the comparison believable. For example, a persuasive speaker might argue that alcohol and marijuana are similar, so the latter should be legalized. But the audience must be convinced that the two are truly similar. In addition, the speaker must recognize differences between the things compared. If the differences are larger or more important than the similarities, the analogy won't work. For example, solutions to environmental problems in one city may not translate to another city due to differences in climate and geography, even if the two locations share similar environmental problems.

Avoiding Fallacies in Argument

A **fallacy** is an error in making an argument. The error may be in the claims offered, the evidence presented, or the reasoning process. Whatever the mistake, a fallacy results in an erroneous argument.[50] The challenge for speakers and listeners rests in identifying fallacies. Fallacies often appear valid and reasonable, but upon closer inspection they do not hold up. Fallacies may even persuade the uncritical listener.[51] Yet including fallacies in a persuasive speech—even if unintentionally—reflects poorly on the speaker and ultimately constitutes unethical behavior.

Fallacies fall into four main categories:

1. Faulty assertions
2. Flawed evidence
3. Defective reasoning
4. Erroneous responses

Effective speakers recognize fallacies in their arguments and eliminate them before they make their presentations. **Table 15.5** summarizes common fallacies in public speaking, which are discussed in more detail in this section.

Fallacies in Claims

Fallacies stemming from the claims a speaker makes refer to errors in basic assumptions or assertions. The **false dilemma fallacy**, also called *either–or thinking*, occurs when a speaker tries to reduce the choices an audience can make to two even though other alternatives exist. For instance, to say that "We must completely fund this program or it is doomed" fails to acknowledge other options, such as supporting parts of the program and eliminating other parts.

Begging the question, or *circular reasoning*, is another fallacy rooted in a speaker's claims. When speakers beg the question, they imply the truth of the conclusion in the premise or simply assert that the validity of the conclusion is self-evident. In attempting to persuade an audience to support closing some elementary schools to reduce costs, a speaker states, "Closing these schools will save the district money. We will only close schools whose closure will financially benefit the district." But the speaker has provided no support for the premise that closing these schools really will reduce costs. The premise implies the conclusion, which essentially restates the premise.

When a speaker says that one event will necessarily lead to another without showing any logical connection between the two, the speaker has used the **slippery-slope fallacy**. Although the conclusion might possibly follow from the premise, the speaker skips the steps between them. The speaker argues, for example, "If the

Table 15.5 Common Fallacies in Public Speaking

Fallacy	Brief Definition	Example
Fallacies in Claims		
False dilemma	Choices are reduced to just two.	We either raise student tuition or lay off teachers.
Begging the question	Something is true because it is.	Our program is the best one because we rate it highly.
Slippery slope	One event leads to another without a logical connection	If we improve this highway, it will lead to a decrease in traffic deaths.
Ad ignorantiam	A thing is true because it hasn't been disproved.	Angels must exist because we have no proof that they don't.
Fallacies in Evidence		
Red herring	Distract with irrelevant point or example	Spend less time online. Our community is losing its unity, so people should get more involved in it.
Ad populum	Appeal to popular attitude or emotion	If you're a true patriot, you'll support our petition for a new city hall.
Appeal to tradition	Support the status quo	In-person college classes are better than online classes because City College has always taught classes face to face.
Comparative evidence	Inappropriate use of statistics	Violent crime in our city doubled from last year. [Speaker omits previous year's number, which was very low.]
Fallacies in Reasoning		
Division	Parts of a whole share the same properties	The red states voted Republican. Pat lives in a red state and therefore must have voted Republican.
Hasty generalization	Insufficient examples or inadequate sample	Two local restaurants have seen an increase in business since the stadium was built, so all restaurants have benefited.
Post hoc	Misrepresent causal relationship	The year after the department hired a new manager, sales increased.
Weak analogy	Key dissimilarities make the comparison misleading	Buying stocks is like gambling because both involve money and risk.
Fallacies in Responding		
Ad hominem	Personal attack	That administrator is an idiot, and of course came to a wrong conclusion.
Guilt by association	Claim linked to objectionable person	Osama bin Laden would support this idea.
Straw man	Misrepresentation of a claim	My opponent's position is that the police force should be abolished. [In reality, the speaker's opponent is calling for minor budget cuts.]
Loaded words	Emotionally laden, misleading language	Hunting is the senseless murder of innocent creatures.

government passes a law requiring all citizens to carry a national identification card, it will be a lot easier for politicians to invade our private lives in other ways, too." So a national identity card will lead to the dismantling of all privacy rights. This type of argument is fallacious because one event will not necessarily lead to a much larger and more significant event.

The *ad ignorantiam* **fallacy**, or *appeal to ignorance*, suggests that because a claim hasn't been shown to be false, it must be true. It is also called the burden-of-proof fallacy. Senator Joseph R. McCarthy used this tactic in the 1950s to accuse people of being communists. He argued that if people couldn't disprove his allegations, they must be communists. Claims of UFOs, alien abductions, and paranormal activities usually rely on the *ad ignorantiam* fallacy: Scientists have no proof that UFOs don't exist. Therefore, there are UFOs.[52]

> Argument in which a speaker suggests that because a claim hasn't been shown to be false, it must be true; also called an *appeal to ignorance*.

Fallacies in Evidence

Even if a speaker presents valid claims, the evidence used to support those assertions may be irrelevant, inaccurate, or insufficient. Sometimes speakers present evidence that has nothing to do with the claim. In these cases, the speaker creates a **red herring**, distracting the audience with irrelevant evidence. To urge the audience to support abolishing all competitive sports on campus, a speaker might argue, "We need to end competitive sports here at our college. The state is in a budget crisis, and tuition is going up." The state's budget crisis and rising tuition are not necessarily related to the idea of abolishing competitive sports, but mentioning those points does sensationalize the topic—and take the audience's mind off the real issue.

> Argument that introduces irrelevant evidence to distract an audience from the real issue.

The **comparative evidence fallacy** occurs when speakers use statistics or compare numbers in ways that mislead the audience and misrepresent the evidence included to support the argument. This may happen unintentionally when a speaker simply misinterprets statistical data. In other cases, the speaker may manipulate the numbers or omit some information and purposefully deceive the audience. For example, some urban universities highlight their low rates of crime by reporting only crimes that occur on the campus itself, leaving out any that are reported even within a block or two of the campus's borders. While the statistics may be accurate, omitting nearby crime incidents may give students, faculty, and staff a false sense of security.

> Argument in which a speaker uses statistics or compares numbers in ways that misrepresent the evidence and mislead the audience.

In addition, speakers may favor statistical evidence too heavily, privileging numbers over other forms of evidence such as testimony, narrative, and examples. Although statistics can provide powerful evidence, they are not always the best choice. Statistics often shed little light on how things work, for instance. A speaker may present statistics showing that students who learn math using a new method score higher on tests than do students using an old method. But the reason for the higher scores may be the increased attention that students using the new method received, rather than the method itself. Without additional evidence, the audience can't be sure of the process that led to the results.[53]

The *ad populum* **fallacy** is commonly found in advertising. Although effective speakers do employ narratives, examples, and other evidence in appealing to an audience's emotions, the *ad populum* fallacy plays on popular attitudes without offering any supporting materials. Speakers may appeal to audience members' prejudices or their desire to be part of the group. If you want to be considered cool, for instance, you should drive a certain car or use a particular brand of computer. Diet fads fall into this category, too. Trying to persuade an audience to go on a reduced-carbohydrate diet because everyone's doing it is an example of the *ad populum* fallacy.

> Argument in which a speaker appeals to popular attitudes and emotions without offering evidence to support claims.

When speakers use the **appeal to tradition fallacy**, they argue that the status quo or current state of things is better than any new idea or approach. Audience members often find this fallacy persuasive because it argues against change and for the familiar and known. Although the appeal to tradition fallacy seems like an appropriate use of mythos,

> Argument in which a speaker asserts that the status quo is better than any new idea or approach.

or an appeal to cultural beliefs, this fallacy asserts the superiority of the status quo simply based on what's always been done. The appeal to tradition fallacy has been used to argue against allowing women in all-male colleges and in favor of forcing African American children to attend segregated schools. Sometimes traditional ways of doing things are indeed the best course of action. But the speaker must present sufficient evidence to support that stance.

Fallacies in Reasoning

Fallacies in reasoning involve errors in how the speaker links the evidence and the claims. One error in deductive reasoning is the **division fallacy**, in which speakers assume that what's true of the whole is also true of the parts making up the whole. A survey might find, for instance, that students at your college hold a favorable view of current general-education policies. Does this mean all students feel that way? Possibly, but you can't be sure that's the case.

When speakers draw a conclusion based on too few examples or from an unrepresentative sample, they've made a hasty generalization, a flaw in inductive reasoning. The **hasty generalization fallacy** occurs when the speaker makes a claim after offering only one or two examples, or when the examples offered don't represent the larger group. For example, a speaker who argues for improving the quality of national teacher training by using data drawn only from a few schools would not be able to establish convincingly the need for reform at the national level.

The ***post hoc* fallacy**, or *false cause fallacy,* involves concluding that a causal relationship exists simply because one event follows another in time. Say, for instance, that the police chief in your city was fired and shortly thereafter the crime rate increased. Did the firing necessarily lead to the higher crime rate? Maybe, but many other factors could be involved as well, such as the time of year, decreased patrols in an area, better reporting of crimes, or a sudden downturn in the economy. When a speaker argues that one event necessarily caused another, always consider additional possible explanations for why something occurred.

The **weak analogy fallacy** results when two things have important dissimilarities that make the comparison inaccurate and the analogy faulty. Although it's possible to identify similarities between almost any two things you might want to compare, the similarities must contribute to the argument and the dissimilarities must not detract from it. A speaker argues, for example, "Graffiti is like any other form of public art and should be supported." But the process for displaying public art is quite different from that for displaying graffiti. With public art, members of the community decide on the type of art and where it should be placed. With graffiti, the person applying the paint is making those choices.

Fallacies in Responding

Listeners may make errors in argument when critiquing a speaker's arguments. Probably the most common fallacy in responding is the ***ad hominem* fallacy**, or the *against the person fallacy*. This fallacy occurs when a claim is rejected based on perceptions of the speaker's character rather than the evidence. The *ad hominem* fallacy typically follows this pattern: "You think we should adopt the group's plan. Everyone knows you're an inconsiderate person. Your position is wrong." The person's character is irrelevant to the initial claim. Although you can certainly examine a speaker's credibility, you must critique an argument based on the evidence presented rather than something about the person that has nothing to do with the topic. Personally attacking the speaker or the source of the evidence takes attention away from the true merits of a claim.

Argument in which a speaker assumes that what is true of the whole is also true of the parts that make up the whole.

Argument in which a speaker draws a conclusion based on too few or inadequate examples.

Argument in which a speaker concludes a causal relationship exists simply because one event follows another in time; also called the *false cause fallacy.*

Argument in which a speaker compares two things that are dissimilar, making the comparison inaccurate.

Argument in which a speaker rejects another speaker's claim based on that speaker's character rather than the evidence the speaker presents; also called the *against the person* fallacy.

Speakers who use the straw man fallacy misrepresent an argument to the extent that it seems the argument is as easy to topple as the *Wizard of Oz*'s Scarecrow.

Argument in which a speaker suggests that something is wrong with another speaker's claims by associating those claims with someone the audience finds objectionable; also called the *bad company fallacy*.

Argument in which a speaker misrepresents another speaker's argument so that only a shell of the opponent's argument remains.

Argument in which a speaker uses emotionally laden words to evaluate claims based on a misleading emotional response rather than the evidence presented.

Like the *ad hominem* fallacy, the **guilt by association fallacy** suggests something wrong with the speaker's character—in this case, others who support the speaker's claim. Also known as the *bad company fallacy*, this fallacy links the speaker with someone the audience finds objectionable, deplorable, repulsive, or even evil. Responding to a speaker arguing for national health care, an audience member says, "Fidel Castro set up a national health care system in Cuba. I certainly wouldn't want something in the United States that was designed by a dictator." Of course, other democratic countries, such as Canada and Great Britain, have national health care, but by associating the speaker's claim with someone the audience probably dislikes, the person responding employs the guilt by association fallacy.

The **straw man fallacy** misrepresents a speaker's argument so that just a shell of the original claim remains. Then the argument is easily refuted because it appears so implausible or simplistic,[54] much like the ease of pushing over the straw Scarecrow in *The Wizard of Oz*. These fallacies often occur in political campaigns when candidates present distorted and exaggerated views of their opponents' positions. A candidate for mayor who favors education reform may be accused of seeking to abolish the public school system. A candidate for president of the student government who advocates revising the grading system used to assess student performance might be denounced as calling for an end to grades. In both cases, the original claim is misrepresented so that the argument against it becomes obvious.

The **loaded word fallacy** uses emotionally laden words to distract from the speaker's argument and evaluate claims based on a misleading emotional response rather than the evidence presented.[55] The intent in using such language is to refute a speaker's claims without offering any substantial evidence. Responding to a speaker's claim that online gambling should be legalized by saying, "Condoning the corrupt operations of the rapacious online gaming interests will only serve to allow more innocent victims to fall prey to this deplorable vice" may play on emotions but does nothing to refute the original argument.

Speech for Review and Analysis

Home Schooling: Not the Best Choice[56]

Robert gave this speech in an introductory speech class. His assignment was, with a partner, Dixie, to give one of two persuasive speeches that presented the pros and cons about a controversial topic. Robert chose to give a speech that presented the cons about home schooling. Go to the Chapter 15 resources in your CourseMate for Public Speaking: The Evolving Art *to watch and listen to Robert and Dixie's speeches and read their speech transcripts, outlines, and note cards.*

CourseMate

Specific purpose: To persuade my audience that educating our children in public schools is better than educating them through home schooling.

Thesis statement: Educating our children in public schools in preferable to educating them through home schooling because parents do not make effective teachers, the home is an ineffective schooling environment, and parental involvement provides the link to success for students who attend public schools.

We tell our children that they can do whatever they want to do if they only try. We tell our children that they should do the best that they can so that they can live up to their potential. How our children are educated plays a big role as to what their potential will be and what they will do the rest of their lives.

All of us have come from different educational backgrounds: from public and private schools to religious schools and even home schools. After having been exposed to what I consider to have been a positive learning environment, I will show that the home school is not the most beneficial to our children. To prove this I will address the issues of parents as teachers, the home as a schooling environment, and, last, parental-involvement link to student success.

So who is most qualified to teach our children? A key issue to home schooling rests with the fact that the parent is also the teacher of the student. Could any of us seriously imagine giving up our jobs and maybe our careers to staying home and teaching our children? Many obvious arguments arise without even putting any amount of thought into this issue. Is it really possible that parents could be just as effective, if not more effective, than classroom teachers? The answer is a clear no.

The September 1, 2000, edition of *Maclean's* stated that "the parents' greatest challenge is educating themselves on how and what to teach." The book by Ballmann, *How and Why of Home Schooling*, stated that many parents just don't take the time to make lesson plans each and every day. These facts should not be surprising, as parents can only do what they know how to do. They just simply aren't teachers. Let's think about this again: Even if some of our parents are teachers, can we seriously imagine them teaching us everything that we need to know, on every level, to be successful?

So far, I've addressed the issue of parents as teachers in the home. However, can the home itself be an effective environment for learning? The home cannot be a substitute for our school systems. For example, let's just take our homes right now. Do we have the equipment available to offer a complete educational environment? I know that in my home, we do not, and I'm pretty sure that in the majority of our homes we do not have the tools necessary to provide an adequate education. In the book by Colfax entitled *Homeschooling for Excellence* it was found that many home school students work on their studies for a short period of time, but find something else more interesting to do as a result of not having the same attention that they should when they're in a typical school environment.

The February 22, 1996 *U.S. News* online report stated that 76 percent of home-schooling parents surveyed from the states of Utah, Nevada, and Oregon found that they want to enroll their students at least part time in private or public school courses. Schools just have so many resources to offer students. They have the interest of many diverse teachers as well as access to numerous scholastic materials. There is no sufficient substitute for our school systems out there.

Up to this point, we have addressed the pitfalls to home schooling. So let's turn to what we know will create student success, that being parental involvement. The biggest factor that will determine this is parental involvement. Regardless of whether any of us have children, the benefits to parental involvement are very obvious. When we use this term, we are not necessarily saying that parents should teach their children. Rather, they should support them.

The journal article in *The World and I,* June 2000, interviewed Kathleen Lyons, a communications director for the National Education Association. In this article,

Kathleen contends, "It takes more than a good heart to be a good teacher." She went on to conclude that the quote-unquote "common denominator" to student achievement implies parental involvement. And this acknowledgement makes perfect sense, as parents have the responsibility to empower their children to succeed and be successful. They do not have to be classroom teachers to make this work. What they need to do, though, is support their children by talking to them and listening to what they have to say. Success for children rests with parental involvement.

Today I've shown clearly why parental involvement will help children and why home schooling is not as beneficial as our typical schooling environment. Keep in mind the issues I addressed involving parents as teachers, the home environment for learning, and the one thing that will create student success if used, that being parental involvement. We need to put our children in the most effective schooling environment. If we truly want our children in the most effective classrooms for learning, with the most effective teachers for teaching, then home schooling is not the answer.

Questions for Analysis and Discussion

1. What claim did Robert make? Did he sufficiently support his claim? Explain.

2. How could he have strengthened his argument?

3. The sources in this speech are old at this point, but Robert delivered it in 2000. Were his sources timely and appropriate when he gave the speech? If he wanted to update it to give to an audience today, how would you suggest he do it?

4. Overall, how effective do you think this persuasive speech was? Explain your answer.

Summary

The well-constructed argument forms the foundation of persuasive speaking. An argument consists of three elements: claims, evidence, and reasoning. Claims lay the groundwork for the thesis of your speech, answering the question "What am I asserting?" Every claim includes at least one premise and a conclusion. When speakers use an enthymeme, they omit part of the claim, leaving the audience to complete the claim. Qualifiers moderate a claim, indicating where there might be exceptions to the speaker's position.

Evidence refers to the supporting materials presented to back up the claim, answering the question "What is the support for my assertion?" Speakers may use logical appeals (logos), appeals to the speaker's credibility (ethos), emotional appeals (pathos), or appeals to cultural beliefs and values (mythos). Generally the strongest arguments are those that effectively integrate all four types of appeals. In addition, evidence should be relevant to the topic, come from highly credible sources, and represent a diversity of sources.

Reasoning is how speakers connect their evidence with their claims. Reasoning answers the question "How are my supporting materials and assertions linked together?" and shows the audience how the evidence you've chosen provides justification for your position on the topic. Persuasive speakers rely on four types of reasoning: deductive, inductive, causal, and analogical. Deductive reasoning refers to arguing from a general principle to a specific case. Inductive reasoning involves giving examples in support of a claim. In causal reasoning, the speaker argues that something caused something else. Speakers use analogical reasoning to compare two things that share similarities.

A fallacy occurs when an error is made in constructing an argument. Although fallacies may be persuasive, they are nonetheless a deceptive and unethical approach to convincing an audience. Fallacies may stem from errors in claims, evidence, reasoning, or responding. Common fallacies in claims are false dilemma, begging the question, slippery slope, and *ad ignorantiam*. Fallacies in evidence include red herring, *ad populum*, appeal to tradition, and comparative evidence. Division, hasty generalization, *post hoc*, and weak analogy are fallacies in reasoning. Audience members responding to persuasive arguments may also fall victim to fallacies, including *ad hominem*, guilt by association, caricature, and loaded words.

Directory of Study and Review Resources

IN THE BOOK
Summary
Key Terms
Critical Challenges

MORE STUDY RESOURCES
Quizzes
WebLinks
Peer-reviewed videos

CourseMate
SPEECH Studio

STUDENT WORKBOOK
15.1: Variations on a Claim
15.2: Presidential Premises
15.3: Faulty Letter to the Editor
15.4: We Hold These Truths to Be Self-Evident
15.5: I Need That

SPEECH BUDDY VIDEOS
WATCH It Video
15.1: Identifying the Elements of Argument
USE It Activity
15.1: Convince Me

SAMPLE SPEECH VIDEOS
Dixie, "Home Schooling: Superiority and Success," persuasive speech
Robert, "Home Schooling: Not the Best Choice," persuasive speech

SPEECH BUILDER EXPRESS
Goal/purpose
Thesis statement
Organization
Outline
Supporting material
Transitions
Introduction
Conclusion
Title
Works cited
Visual aids
Completing the speech outline

INFOTRAC
Recommended search terms
Public speaking and argument
Argument and claim
Argument and evidence
Reasoning
Argument and appeals
Enthymemes
Syllogisms
Reasoning fallacies

AUDIO STUDY TOOLS
"Home Schooling: Not the Best Choice" by Robert
Critical thinking questions
Learning objectives
Chapter summary

Guide to Your Online Resources

CourseMate Your Speech Communication CourseMate for *Public Speaking: The Evolving Art* gives you access to the Speech Buddy video and activity featured in this chapter, additional sample speech videos, Speech Studio, Speech Builder Express, InfoTrac College Edition, and study aids such as glossary flashcards, review quizzes, and the Critical Challenge questions for this chapter, which you can respond to via email if your instructor so requests. In addition, your CourseMate features live WebLinks relevant to this chapter, including sites where you can find interesting folklore and myths to use in appeals to cultural beliefs. Links are regularly maintained, and new ones are added periodically.

Key Terms

ad hominem fallacy 323

ad ignorantiam fallacy 322

ad populum fallacy 322

analogical reasoning 318

appeals to cultural beliefs (mythos) 311

appeals to speaker credibility (ethos) 308

appeal to tradition fallacy 322

argument 302

begging the question 320

causal reasoning 317

claim 302

comparative evidence fallacy 322

conclusion 303

deductive reasoning 313

division fallacy 323

emotional appeals (pathos) 309

enthymemes 303

evidence 302

inductive reasoning 316

fallacy 320

false dilemma fallacy 320

guilt by association fallacy 324

hasty generalization fallacy 323

loaded word fallacy 324

logical appeals (logos) 307

post hoc fallacy 323

premise 303

qualifier 305

reasoning 302

red herring 322

slippery-slope fallacy 320

straw man fallacy 324

syllogism 314

weak analogy fallacy 323

Critical Challenges

Questions for Reflection and Discussion

1. Choose a controversial topic you're interested in and identify the claims each side presents. What are the premises and the conclusions each side is asking the audience to accept?

2. Review three or four advertisements in magazines or newspapers, on TV, or online. What appeals do the advertisers use? Give specific examples. How effective are those appeals?

3. Reflect on a recent discussion you've had in which you tried to persuade others to accept your point of view. What type or types of reasoning did you use? How well did your reasoning work?

4. Research on instruction in argumentation and persuasion has found that students who learn about the fundamentals of argument are better at detecting fallacies than are students without training in argument. How has what you've learned in this chapter made you more alert to fallacious arguments? How has it influenced the way you respond to persuasive messages?

5. Check out Speech Studio to analyze how other students used reasoning and arguments in their speeches. As you watch their speeches, pay attention to whether they rely on logical fallacies. Or record a speech you're working on, upload it to Speech Studio, and ask your peers for their feedback. What feedback could you use to fine-tune your arguments before you give your persuasive speech in class?

16 Special Occasion and Group Speaking

Read it

Cengage Learning

Watch it

Use it

Cengage Learning

Review it

CourseMate **SPEECH Studio** SPEECH BUILDER EXPRESS

All college students look forward to graduation day. Commencement speeches are a central part of the ceremony. During these speeches, speakers often try to inspire the graduates or reflect on their own life experiences. For example, in his recent commencement speech at Bates College, Fareed Zakaria, author and host of CNN's *GPS: Global Public Square*, challenged graduating seniors to "recognize that *you* are the change you seek. *You* are the great change agents of the world."[1] Addressing the graduating class at the College of William & Mary, Jon Stewart, host and executive producer of Comedy Central's *The Daily Show*, reminisced about his undergraduate experiences there. Judy Woodruff's speech to graduates of American University focused on her work in journalism, from college reporting to hosting a news program on national public television. Kermit the Frog, giving a commencement address at Southampton College, reflected back on his time as a tadpole!

Many of the presentations you'll give outside the classroom will take place on special occasions or in a mediated setting, or involve working in a group. This chapter addresses speeches for special occasions, such as introducing a main speaker or accepting an award. In addition, the chapter provides basic guidelines for presenting in the media and describes how to participate effectively in various types of small-group presentations, including videoconferences.

Image provided by Bates College

Special occasion speeches extend the nature of what you do all the time—talk to others about what's going on in your lives. When you introduce a friend to someone else, for example, you might say something about your friend as part of the introduction—this is also a common aspect of special occasion speeches. Special occasion speeches include speeches of introduction, acceptance speeches, after-dinner speeches, tributes and eulogies, nomination speeches, public testimony, and roasts and toasts.

Speeches of Introduction

Whenever you attend a public speech given by a well-known person, you'll probably first hear a short speech that introduces that person to the audience. That's a **speech of introduction**. The speech of introduction should prepare the audience for who and what they came to hear: the main speaker and the main speech. A few basic principles apply to speeches of introduction: prepare the audience for the speaker and the occasion, give accurate information, and connect with the audience and the event.

> A short speech that introduces someone to an audience.

Prepare the Audience In introducing the main speaker, keep your remarks brief yet at the same time prepare the audience for the speaker and the occasion. The audience has gathered to hear the main speaker, not the introducer. While it may be tempting to go on and on about the speaker, especially if the person has impressive credentials, there is no need to spend more than a few minutes on an introduction. Most audience members already know quite a bit about the speaker—that's why they're attending the speech. Even if you and the main speaker are very friendly with each other, keep the attention focused on the speaker rather than on your relationship.

The audience expects the introductory speaker to quickly orient them to the main speaker, the topic, and the occasion. For example, when Jonas Gahr Støre, Norway's minister of foreign affairs, introduced Dr. Mohamed ElBaradei, former director general of the International Atomic Energy Agency (IAEA), at a luncheon in ElBaradei's honor, he began with

> At the outset let me congratulate you, Dr. ElBaradei and the IAEA, on receiving the Nobel Peace Prize. It is a prize well deserved. The IAEA is crucial to international peace and security. But people make a difference.
>
> It is thanks to the untiring efforts of Dr. ElBaradei and his collaborators that the agency continues to be an effective and efficient instrument of nuclear disarmament and nonproliferation. May the Prize inspire you to keep up this crucial work. And may the Prize serve as an inspiration to us all in our endeavours to strengthen the nonproliferation regime.
>
> As a citizen of Norway, I look forward to welcoming you to Oslo on 10 December for the Peace Prize ceremony. Norwegians love Nobel Peace Laureates, and I know this will be no exception.[2]

The speaker indicated the reason for the occasion—ElBaradei's recent receipt of the Nobel Peace Prize for his work in the IAEA—and offered a brief explanation of the Prize's importance.

Be Accurate and Up to Date When preparing a speech of introduction, research the speaker as you would any topic. If you're introducing someone you don't know personally, check online for any information the person may have posted, such as a website or social networking site such as Facebook or LinkedIn. Search for stories in the popular press and consult encyclopedic sources such as *Who's Who in America*. If possible, interview the speaker by email or phone or in person to get the most accurate and up-to-date information.

Justin Sullivan/Getty Images

A speech of introduction helps an audience get to know the featured speaker and establishes the speaker's credibility.

Connect with the Audience Even a speaker the audience knows well needs an introduction in order to create a positive response and generate maximum enthusiasm among the listeners. When the speaker is less well known, the introducer's role in connecting the speaker with the audience becomes all the more important. Making a strong connection between the main speaker and the audience requires that you know enough about the speaker and what the person intends to say so you can skillfully gain the audience's interest.

At a recent meeting of the International Women's Media Foundation, famed television journalist Christiane Amanpour introduced Amira Hass, an Israeli newspaper columnist and author, to the audience. Hass was being honored with the organization's Lifetime Achievement Award for her reporting on Israeli-Palestinian relations. Amanpour told the audience:

> She writes what the Palestinian journalists think about their country's leadership but dare not say themselves. She writes what she thinks citizens of Israel should know about their leadership but do not want to hear. Some call her a traitor. It is uncomfortable to hear the truth; it's very uncomfortable to tell the truth. Some say she is the only voice of truth in a polarized conflict. For twenty years she's paid no attention to either of these camps, choosing instead to follow her own path. Amira knows that dictators do not like journalists, but more than that, democracies don't like journalists either.[3]

Speaking to journalists, Amanpour emphasized how Amira Hass's investigative reporting has exposed the grim realities of the conflict between Israel and Palestine. Highlighting the essential principle of good journalism—objectivity—she praised Hass for her fearless reporting and commentary. Amanpour kept herself out of the introduction, shining a bright light instead on the recipient of the award.

Acceptance Speeches

Audiences expect individuals who are recognized, honored, or awarded to give an **acceptance speech** after they step up to the podium or move to the front of the room. If you were to find yourself in the position of being publicly recognized, what should you say? Most individuals who receive honors or awards know in advance that they have won, so you'll have plenty of time to prepare.

Speech given by an individual who is being recognized, honored, or given an award.

When accepting an award, some general rules apply. Most important, award recipients should thank the presenter, organization, and audience; demonstrate humility; and keep their remarks succinct. In addition, some acceptance speakers may contextualize the award by discussing the work or activity that won them the award or providing a personal narrative that is relevant to the occasion.

Be Thankful and Humble You've seen enough award ceremonies to know the audience expects certain responses from award winners. Everyone thanks the people who helped them succeed. For example, when Powderburn won Best Metal Band at the 2007 Austin Music Awards, the group thanked "everyone who has ever helped us or made it easier in this town for us to do what we love and appreciate us for being good songwriters and not just for our genre. Thank you, everyone." The group members went on to thank "our fans on YouTube and MySpace … and everyone who voted."[4]

On the occasion of his induction into the New Jersey Hall of Fame, Bruce Springsteen spoke of the love and gratitude he has for people in his home state. In his unassuming way, "The Boss" made good fun of the state he adores by reciting a "Garden State benediction":

> EST Rise up my fellow New Jerseyans, for we are all members of a confused but noble race. We, of the state that never gets any respect. We, who bear the coolness of the forever uncool. The chip on our shoulders of those with forever something to prove. And even with this wonderful Hall of Fame, we know that there's another bad Jersey joke coming just around the corner."[5]

Award winners also tend to minimize their accomplishments, demonstrating a sense of perspective, even humility. Accepting an award for her children's nonfiction book, *Gorilla Doctors: Saving Endangered Great Apes*, author Pamela S. Turner ended her speech by saying:

> I am so very grateful that the Bank Street College of Education has found *Gorilla Doctors* worthy of an award given for inspiring young readers. I certainly can't take credit for making children interested in animals; they already are interested. I can't take credit for making children empathize with animals, either; children already have empathy. I do hope I've encouraged children to combine scientific knowledge with their interest and empathy. I hope the result will be children better equipped to share this world respectfully, humbly, and lovingly with the rest of the animal kingdom. Thank you.[6]

Closing her speech in this way shifted the audience's focus to the more general goal of raising children's awareness of treating animals ethically. In this way, Turner acknowledged the impact her book might have on children's attitudes toward animals, but noted that many other factors are involved as well.

Be Succinct "Brevity is the soul of wit," quipped Polonius in Shakespeare's *Hamlet*. Listeners expect comments made when accepting an award to be brief and to the point. The Webby Awards likely hold the record for shortest and funniest acceptance speeches—recipients are allowed only five words. Recent speeches include "Had we lost, we'd sue" by the American Bar Association (Law category); "Even better than rocket science," by the National Science Foundation website (Government category); "Creativity is a renewable resource," Twitter co-founder Biz Stone (Breakout of the Year category); and "Me, me, me, me, me," by Stephen Colbert (Person of the Year category).[7] Few award ceremonies call for speakers to say only five words, but you still want to keep your remarks brief when accepting an award.

Accepting a nomination by President Barack Obama to be a U.S. Supreme Court judge, Sonia Sotomayor first thanked the "many friends and family who have guided and supported me throughout my life, and who have been instrumental in helping me realize

Frederick M. Brown/Getty Images

Showing enthusiasm for an award demonstrates for your audience how thankful you are. Be sure your level of enthusiasm is appropriate for the occasion—some awards presentations are more formal than others.

my dreams." She briefly recounted her professional record as a lawyer and lower court judge and stated how her background would guide her service on the Supreme Court if confirmed by the Senate:

> This wealth of experiences, personal and professional, has helped me appreciate the variety of perspectives that present themselves in every case that I hear. It has helped me to understand, respect, and respond to the concerns and arguments of all litigants who appear before me as well as to the view of my colleagues on the bench. I strive to never forget the real-world consequences of my decisions on individuals, business, and government.[8]

Sotomayor finished her short speech by thanking the President for the honor of the nomination. She said she wanted the American public to know she is just "an ordinary person who has been blessed with extraordinary opportunities and experiences" and "looked forward to working with the Senate in the confirmation process."

Contextualize the Award Speakers may provide a context for an award by describing activities they participated in that led to the award or telling a story related to the occasion. These comments, often emotionally touching and inspiring, personalize the award and help the audience feel more connected with the recipient. When Michael Giacchino won an Oscar for the music he wrote for the movie *Up*, he encouraged kids to unleash their creativity:

> Thank you, guys. When I was nine I asked my dad, "Can I have your movie camera? That old, wind-up 8 millimeter that was in your drawer?" And he goes, "Sure, take it." And I took it and I started making movies with it and I started being as creative as I could, and never once in my life did my parents ever say, "What you're doing is a waste of time." Never. And I grew up—I had teachers, I had colleagues, I had people that I worked with all through my life who always told me, what you're doing is not a waste of time. So it was normal to me that it was okay to do that. I know there are kids out there that don't have that support system, so if you're out there and you're listening, listen to me: If you want to be creative, get out there and do it. It's not a waste of time. Do it, okay? Thank you.[9]

In accepting the International Gandhi Award for his work on leprosy, Yohei Sasakawa traced his social activism to his father:

335

For more than thirty years, I have worked to eliminate leprosy from the world. My father, Ryoichi Sasakawa, was the main reason I became involved in this mission.

He died in 1995 at the age of ninety-six. As a young man, he had seen the misery and anguish that leprosy caused individuals and families, and his life's ambition was to alleviate their suffering. But more than just offering comfort and encouragement, he wanted to ensure that every single person who required treatment had access to it.

As his son, I am carrying on his work, and doing my utmost to finish what he began.[10]

Explaining the motivation for his work gave the audience a better understanding of Sasakawa's interests in eradicating both the physical disease and social stigma of leprosy. In addition, he provided a context for his work with which many people likely could identify.

After-Dinner Speeches

After-dinner speeches usually serve as a featured part of an organized event. These kinds of events were originally scheduled as dinner gatherings, but today they are just as likely to be scheduled for breakfast or lunch. Whatever the time of day, the goal of an after-dinner speech is to contribute something pleasurable to the occasion. After-dinner speeches amplify and extend the good feelings the sponsors of the event want to create for everyone in attendance. The topic for the speech can be serious for some occasions, but most after-dinner presentations are upbeat and often humorous. Some after-dinner speeches take place on special personal occasions like weddings, anniversaries, retirements, or graduation parties. As with any other speech, the after-dinner speech must fit the makeup and interests of the group that is gathered for the event.

Be Entertaining and Lighthearted Humor is a cornerstone of after-dinner speeches, but it isn't the only way to entertain and enlighten an audience. Although after-dinner speeches often include jokes or funny anecdotes, don't force yourself to be funny if you don't feel comfortable in that role. Above all else, after-dinner speakers should try to develop good rapport with their audiences and leave them feeling good about the time they've spent together. Sharing thoughtful reflections, telling a relevant story, making insightful comments about an issue of interest to the group, and using language creatively can please your listeners just as much as a good joke.

Focus on a Theme Although most after-dinner speeches have an upbeat, enjoyable quality, they should also develop a thesis and have a point. The audience should feel not only entertained but also enriched in some way. However, this doesn't mean you should drone on and on. Your job is to provide an enjoyable final touch to the event, not to lecture your audience.

Imagine, for example, that you've been asked to give an after-dinner speech to your former classmates at a high school reunion. You might good-naturedly tell a few stories about some of your old friends and teachers, but you'd also want to develop a theme. For instance, you might want to speak about how important those high school days were for everyone and how much you've all benefited from knowing each other. For an after-dinner speech at an annual sales convention, you might make fun of how difficult it was to introduce a new product line during the year. But ultimately you'd want to say something about how successful the product and company have become during the past year.

Avoid Presentation Media Audiences for after-dinner speeches don't want to be lectured to, be challenged too seriously, feel offended, or think they should be taking notes. Except for very special and limited purposes, speakers in these situations should avoid using presentation media. An audio or video segment might be appropriate for a speech that focuses on sports, media, music, or fashion, for instance, but even then, speakers must be careful. All the rules that apply to the use of presentation media in general pertain to the after-dinner speech in even greater measure, especially concerning the technical aspects. Unless the room is equipped precisely for the use of presentation media, speakers should avoid using them.

Tributes and Eulogies

Sometimes people are honored for something they've done, for who they are, for where they've been in life, or for where they're headed. **Speeches of tribute** give credit, respect, admiration, gratitude, or inspiration to a person or group who has accomplished something significant, lives in a way that deserves to be praised, or is about to embark on an adventure. **Eulogies** are a special kind of speech of tribute presented as retrospectives about individuals who have died.

> Speech that gives credit, respect, admiration, gratitude, or inspiration to someone who has accomplished something significant, lives in a way that deserves to be praised, or is about to embark on an adventure.

> Speech of tribute presented as a retrospective about an individual who has died.

You may very well have occasion to give one or more of these speeches. Perhaps you've already done so. Weddings, anniversaries, retirements, school reunions, even family birthday parties or welcome-home gatherings frequently call for speeches of tribute. The best man or maid of honor, or both, may be asked to give a brief tribute to a newly married couple. A returning veteran from a war zone might be praised by his best friend at a party in his honor. A successful classmate from high school might be recognized at a school reunion. The daughter of a couple celebrating their golden anniversary might toast her parents' marriage.

You sometimes see and hear impassioned praise of famous people—past presidents, civil rights leaders, sports heroes, or entertainers, for instance—in eulogies that are shown on television and the web. But most eulogies take place much closer to home. Family members and friends often find it appropriate to eulogize deceased loved ones at

JFB /Getty images

Speaking at a wedding is one of the most common forms of public speaking for many people. Some tips for giving an after-dinner speech at a wedding are to use humor that's appropriate to the occasion, tell a light-hearted story about people that many of the guests will know (such as the bride and groom), and practice several times before the wedding so you can deliver the speech extemporaneously.

337

funeral ceremonies. Eulogies not only praise or shed light on the person who has passed away, but also help surviving family members and friends cope with the loss.

Emphasize Emotion Appropriately   Tributes and eulogies often are quite emotional. The mood of the tribute depends on the occasion, but speeches of tribute are generally warm, friendly, and positive. For example, in a speech of tribute for the state's law librarians, Connecticut Chief Justice Chase T. Rogers said in part:

> We honor our law librarians with this year's Law Day Award. . . . Our law librarians … have one finger on the pulse of a keyboard and another on the pulse of how human beings assist, encourage, and educate others to learn and push ahead. An editorial in the *Denver Post* several years ago put it this way: "Librarians are very special people. They are the caregivers of the world of the mind, the nurturers of dreams and the defenders of truth. Perhaps no other profession is so marked by the singular generosity of its practitioners."
>
> On behalf of the entire Judicial Branch, I couldn't agree more. We are indeed fortunate that you have chosen to devote yourselves to the law libraries of the Judicial Branch, and most important, to the members of the public they serve. Thank you and congratulations.[11]

The chief justice identified the qualities of law librarians that led to the decision to honor them on the state's Law Day. She praised their work and contributions not only to the law but also to society in general.

At the memorial service for the late Tim Russert, a television journalist and long-time host of NBC's *Meet the Press*, Maria Shriver, who had been a colleague of Russert, remembered his personal qualities. She spoke of how he "loved helping people. He loved helping people who worked for him. He loved helping strangers. He loved anybody who he thought he could help. And with that Russert radar, he just knew who among us needed help." Reflecting on the moment she first met him, Shriver said:

> You see, I lost my heart to Timmy Russert the day I met him. And the entire time I knew him, he took care of it. He protected my heart when it needed protection. He nurtured it when it needed care. He helped it grow. And he never, ever, broke it.[12]

Provide Inspiration   Speeches of tribute often inspire the audience as well as praise the person being honored. In this eulogy for her father, "Crocodile Hunter" Steve Irwin, eight-year-old Bindi Irwin stressed the importance of continuing his work:

> My daddy was my hero. He was always there for me when I needed him. He listened to me and taught me so many things. But most of all he was fun.
>
> I know that Daddy had an important job. He was working to change the world so everyone would love wildlife like he did. He built a hospital to help animals and he bought lots of land to give animals a safe place to live. He took me and my brother and my mum with him all the time. We filmed together, caught crocodiles together, and loved being in the bush together.
>
> I don't want Daddy's passion to ever end. I want to help endangered wildlife just like he did. I had the best daddy in the whole world. And I will miss him every day. When I see a crocodile I will always think of him, and I know that Daddy made this zoo so everyone could come and learn to love all the animals. Daddy made this place his whole life. Now it's our turn to help Daddy. Thank you.[13]

Speaking to thousands of people gathered at Australia Zoo for the memorial service, Bindi Irwin revealed her personal feelings about her father and at the same time encouraged others to carry on his mission of wildlife conservation.

Mexican American labor leader Cesar Chavez co-founded the United Farmworkers Union in California in the 1970s. He struggled all his life to improve the plight of immigrant farm workers who were dying from cancer caused by pesticides sprayed onto the fields where the immigrants pick the crops. Chavez's tribute to Dr. Martin Luther King helped draw attention to the problem faced by immigrant farm workers and brought about a boycott of grapes:

> The time for action is upon us. The enemies of justice want you to think of Dr. King as only a civil rights leader, but he had a much broader agency. He was a tireless crusader for … the rights of workers everywhere. My friends, the suffering must end. So many children are dying, so many babies are born without limbs and vital organs, so many workers are dying in the fields. We have no choice; we must stop the plague of pesticides.[14]

The rules for giving an effective speech of tribute are flexible. Some speeches are written in manuscript form and read to the audience, while others are presented extemporaneously. In either case, the speaker must be exceptionally well prepared. Responsibly accepting and executing the challenge of giving a speech of tribute or eulogy is often greatly appreciated by the audience and particularly rewarding for the speaker.

Speeches of Nomination

Speeches of nomination focus on the qualifications or accomplishments of a particular person. **Nomination speeches** demonstrate why a particular individual would be successful at something if given the chance.

> Speech that demonstrates why a particular individual would be successful at something if given the chance.

For nomination speeches, a few simple guidelines apply. First, deciding on who does the nominating can be just as important as what is said about the nominee. For example, the person who nominates someone for an elected office, position, citation, prize, or award should be well respected and liked by the people who will select a winner from a field of candidates.

Often a person who seeks to be nominated for a position or prize asks a trusted individual to make the nomination speech on his or her behalf. At other times an individual or group approaches a person with the idea of nominating him or her. In any scenario, the speech of nomination can play a determining role in who gets elected or selected. Especially when the stakes are high, nomination speeches should be arranged well in advance.

The nominator must have accurate, concise, and compelling information about the nominee. Audience members want to know why they should consider a particular candidate favorably. What are the strongest reasons for choosing this person to serve in some capacity or be given recognition for something the nominee has accomplished? The speaker should justify the nomination in a way that creates confidence in the individual as deserving of the job or of formal appreciation.

Most nomination speeches are brief. When making a nomination, accurately identify the nominee, cite the best reasons for selecting the individual, personalize the candidate without being too informal, express confidence in how the nominee will perform, ask for the group's support, and thank the group. For instance, if you were nominating someone for treasurer of a school organization, you might say, "I nominate Rhea Salazar for treasurer of our club. Rhea is an excellent person for the position because she has earned top grades in all her accounting classes and has worked part-time as a bookkeeper for a local bakery. I've known Rhea for several years, and I've observed her dedication to the tasks she sets out to do. She's organized, detail-oriented, and a problem-solver. I know she'll serve our organization well. So please give her your support. Thank you."

Public Testimony

The U.S. system of government and way of life depend on the willingness and ability of individuals to share their knowledge and voice their opinions in public meetings.

Through **public testimony** you have many opportunities to participate in discussions that shape the policies that directly affect your world.

Government bodies are required to consider public opinion during their deliberations. For instance, the mayor of San José, California, recently notified citizens of their right to express their views about the construction of a new soccer stadium in the city. Two factions showed up at City Council chambers to comment on the proposal: fans of the team, who strongly supported the idea, and families from the neighborhood where the stadium would be constructed, who were generally opposed to construction. Dozens spoke up. Each individual was given one minute to speak. Don't think one minute is much time? By applying the principles of good speechmaking, you can say a lot in one minute.

■ Narrow your comments down to the basics. Introduce yourself by name and state any relevant fact or affiliation you may have (for example, "I live on a street that will be directly affected by the stadium" or "I'm a coach in the Youth Soccer League").

■ Then contribute something original and useful to the discussion, not only "I am in favor. It seems like a really good idea" or "I don't care about soccer." If you have relevant information, provide it (for example, "The freeway in our neighborhood is already loud, and noise is cumulative" or "Construction workers desperately need work in this economy").

■ Organize your thoughts into keywords and phrases you want your audience to remember. For instance, one supporter of the stadium proposal said, "San José is a big city. Let's make it a big-*league* city. Build the stadium now!" An opponent said, "The stadium will be nothing more than a bright and noisy eyesore in the neighborhood we love!"

Grammy award–winning singer Shakira (at left) joins students seeking support for legislation to establish basic education programs for children in poor nations.

Paul Morigi/WireImage

Roasts and Toasts

Comedians are paid to be entertaining and funny, but the rest of us rarely have an opportunity to make a humorous presentation in public. A roast may be your only chance, so make the most of it! While you may not immediately think of a roast as a public speech, it is a spoken-word performance before an audience. When you roast a piece of meat, you expose it to heat, usually in an oven. That's the idea behind a roast speech, too. The **roast** exposes a guest of honor to ironic and sometimes scathing (but never mean-spirited) ridicule in front of others. The idea is to amuse an audience at the guest of honor's expense, but in a good-natured way.

Speakers for roasts have two audiences—the person being roasted and everyone else in the room. You need to know the "roastee" well enough to come up with good material. Don't take that job lightly, even if you know the person well. Brainstorm. Jot down things you think the audience would also find funny or telling about the roastee. Select particular habits, personality quirks, or behaviors the audience would recognize and appreciate. At the same time, remember that although you want to poke fun at the roastee, you don't want to offend the audience or humiliate the roastee. Use good judgment when deciding what to include in your comments—and what to leave out. People attend roasts because they like or appreciate the person being roasted. And because the object of ridicule is a real person, you have to know where to draw the line.

While you don't have to go through all the steps for outlining a speech when preparing to give a roast, you still want to organize your ideas into a flow that makes sense. After brainstorming and coming up with a sequence of ideas, use a keyword outline written on an index card to prompt you from one comment or brief story to the next. Concise stories that call attention to unique characteristics of the roastee often work well. Be sure to practice telling the stories before the event, and keep them short. Don't write the stories down. The appeal of storytelling rests largely on its spontaneous nature, so practice beforehand and trust yourself to tell the story well.

Whereas a roast makes good fun of the guest of honor, a **toast** unabashedly celebrates the person or persons being toasted. While a funny anecdote or comment might be appropriate as part of the toast, consider the seriousness of the occasion. For example, although wedding receptions are often fun and can include lots of humorous moments, weddings are also important rituals. These sorts of occasion demand an extra level of sensitivity and preparation on the part of the people making the toasts. When giving a toast, keep your remarks short and upbeat. The person giving the toast should stand, while the person being toasted should remain seated. Refer to the person being toasted by name, briefly say something about your relationship to that person, mention the occasion for which the person is being toasted, and then finish up with something encouraging or inspiring like, "We are all very proud of you, Charles, and wish you great success in the future. Cheers!"

Roasts and toasts are among the most common public presentations people are asked to make. Welcome the chance to roast or toast your friends or colleagues. While it's certainly an honor to be the person or persons recognized on these special occasions, it's also a privilege to speak about them—a privilege that comes with responsibility.

> Humorous and good-natured ridicule directed toward the guest of honor at an event.

> Brief remarks celebrating the accomplishments of a guest of honor at an event.

Mediated Speaking

Access to the mass media opens up new ways to extend your ventures into public speaking. But traditional media make up only a part of the field of public speaking possibilities. Information and communication technologies offer a constantly expanding world of opportunities. For instance, you might want to set up a website for yourself or for an organization, where you deliver an introduction or other message by video streaming. Or you could prepare, deliver, and record a talk about any topic that interests you and post it on YouTube or another video-sharing website.

When presenting a speech in front of a camera, keep the following general guidelines in mind:

- If you'll be speaking at a media event, such as an interview at a local TV station, try to learn as much as possible about the structure and format of the event *before* your appearance. Ask about the event's format, how long your part will last, and whether an audience will be present.

- Dress appropriately. With the exception of black, dark colors generally work better than light colors, and solid colors should be worn rather than prints or

341

patterns. Pay the greatest attention to your shirt, jacket, blouse, or tie because in most situations you won't be shown below the waist.

- Write a brief presentation outline with keywords and phrases that you can quickly review shortly before the camera rolls. This will prompt you to stress the most important points you want to make.

- Limit your physical movement but try not to look stiff or uncomfortable.

- Be assertive, confident, and to the point, but present yourself as thoughtful, reasonable, comfortable, and friendly.

- Speak clearly, with good volume, and not too fast.

- Avoid jargon or acronyms that only specialists or others who are knowledgeable about your topic would understand.

- If you're speaking to an in-person audience, focus on them and not the camera.

There is no standard media appearance. Some appearances are initiated by a group or media spokesperson; others take the form of responses to inquiries from the media. Some appearances are planned well in advance; others occur without much notice at all. Media appearances can last an hour or more, or they can last a minute or less. You might talk one-to-one with an interviewer or be part of a group or panel. Media appearances may occur in a studio or at another location. However, the guidelines listed above apply to all of these situations.

Presenting in Small Groups

With the popularity of teams and groups in organizations on the rise, you'll encounter many situations that require you to work with others and then present information to an audience.[15] Group presentations usually involve both interacting within the group and speaking to those outside the group. A **small group** is a collection of individuals who interact and depend on one another to solve a problem, make a decision, or achieve another common goal. In your public speaking class, you may have worked in groups to develop various skills associated with public speaking, such as brainstorming for topics or analyzing your audience. Your instructor might also assign a group presentation. Working in groups in a classroom setting and giving group presentations prepare you for participating in team-based organizations and other professional contexts.[16] This section explains how to give and evaluate five types of group presentations: oral reports, panel discussions, round table discussions, symposiums, and forums.

A collection of individuals who interact and depend on one another to solve a problem, make a decision, or achieve a common goal or objective.

Oral Report

When a group presents an **oral report**, one representative from the group gives the entire report. This often happens with work teams in organizations. Various members of the organization develop the report, and then one of the group members is selected to present the findings to management or upper administration. Effective oral reports clearly recognize the contributions of all group members. The speaker should use pronouns such as *we* and *us* to indicate that the group, rather than the individual, produced the report. In addition, specific references to group members or units in the organization that wrote the report acknowledge everyone's contributions. The speaker must be fully versed in all aspects of the report, asking group members for clarification where needed. The oral report format provides consistency and smooth transitions between the sections of a presentation. Oral reports avoid the inherent disruptions associated with each team member taking her or his speaking turn. Audience members need only adjust to one person's speaking style.

A report in which one member of a group presents the group's findings.

Panel Discussion

You've likely viewed **panel discussions** on weekend TV talk shows. A moderator or facilitator asks questions to direct the group's interaction, which occurs in front of an audience. Group members are experts on the subject and know beforehand what will be covered. The moderator usually provides an introduction, giving an overview of the topic and stating the purpose of the discussion. The moderator may then briefly recite each person's credentials or ask panelists to introduce themselves.

Although panel discussions are not rehearsed, they are not entirely impromptu either. Participants often refer to notes during the discussion. Some questions may be unexpected and the responses spontaneous. Still, participants prepare carefully and don't simply "wing it" during the discussion. One example of a panel discussion occurs during the Career Day sponsored each semester by the Communication Studies Department at San José State University. To give students firsthand information about what they can do with a degree in communication, the department invites several alumni to talk about their careers in communication-related professions. A faculty member facilitates the flow of talk. After the formal presentations, audience members ask the panelists questions.

Although only one group member delivers an oral report, it's a good idea for members to work together to prepare the report. This ensures that the entire group contributes to the speech and can help answer questions after the formal presentation.

> A discussion in which a moderator asks questions of experts on a topic in front of an audience.

Round Table Discussion

Unlike panel discussions, **round table discussions** do not have audiences—only the group members are present. All group members participate in a round table discussion, which may or may not have a leader or facilitator. Because speakers are experts on the topic under discussion, responses are impromptu. Nevertheless, speakers arrive prepared, knowing the topic and often the other participants, too.

> A discussion in which expert participants discuss a topic in an impromptu format without an audience present.

The setting for a round table discussion is generally informal, with speakers sitting in a circle to facilitate dialogue and engaged participation. The facilitator or host first describes the purpose of the discussion, outlines procedures for conducting the round table, and sets a time limit. At the conclusion of the event, the facilitator or host summarizes the main themes that emerged from the discussion and indicates what will be done with the information. In addition, the discussion is recorded or someone is assigned to take notes so the information participants generate can be used at a later date.

Round table discussions provide a means for individuals to exchange information and ideas about a topic of common interest. All discussants are encouraged to participate, maximizing the opportunity to consider different points of view on the subject. Often roundtable discussions are convened to generate new ideas and innovative approaches to a problem. For example, in an effort to develop strategies for stimulating the local economy, the *Akron Beacon Journal* brought together local experts to discuss promoting entrepreneurship, small-business growth, and start-up businesses in northeastern Ohio. The product of that discussion was a list of recommendations distributed to community leaders.[17]

Speaking of . . .

Exchanging Ideas Around the Table

Participating in a round table discussion may seem intimidating at first because you don't have a rehearsed speech to present. But this format provides an excellent way to exchange ideas with others and learn about perspectives and topics you may not know much about. Consider organizing round table discussions on your campus that focus on local, regional, national, and global topics of interest to you and other students. Getting people together for discussions helps improve speaking skills and allows for the free flow of new ideas and information.

Symposium

If you're giving a group presentation in your public speaking class, you're probably using a symposium format. In a **symposium**, the group chooses a topic and divides it into

> A presentation format in which each member of a group presents a speech about a part of a larger topic.

343

different areas. Each group member then presents a speech on her or his subtopic. For example, your group might choose popular music and identify hip-hop, country, metal, and rock as the subtopics. Speakers usually follow the same organizational pattern in order to provide continuity among the speeches. In the music example, each speaker might discuss the music genre's history, identify two or three key artists or groups, and provide a few examples.

Most group interaction occurs in the early stages of the symposium's development. Thoroughly planning the format in advance is essential. For example, group members must discuss whether or not to use a podium, the formality of their attire, the presentation media they will use, how they will structure their speeches, and how they will transition from one speaker to the next.

Once the groundwork for the symposium is complete, group members work independently to prepare their individual speeches. In the later stages of speech preparation, group members come together to practice and make any necessary adjustments.

Forum

After listening to an oral report, panel discussion, or symposium, audience members often want to ask questions. The question-and-answer session following the formal group presentation is a **forum**. Group members must listen attentively and be ready to answer audience members' questions as thoroughly and honestly as possible, just as they would after individual speeches.

Coordinating group members' responses can prove challenging in forums because you don't want to appear disorganized or unsure of your answers. Before the presentation, decide which group members will handle which question areas. Choose someone to facilitate the forum. After a panel discussion, that person would probably be the moderator. For oral reports, the group may choose the presenter or ask another group member to coordinate the responses. In symposiums, anyone who participated may lead the question-and-answer session. Here are some tips that will help you and others in your group establish rapport with the audience:

- Maintain good eye contact with the questioner. A head nod or smile makes the questioner feel appreciated and listened to.

- When listening to a question, quickly make a note that reflects the questioner's concern or is something you or another person in the group wants to say in response.

- Thank the questioner and don't become defensive, even when responding to hostile questions. (And as an audience member asking a question, be sure not to disrespect the speaker or the position taken.)

The question-and-answer session following a group's formal presentation.

Videoconferencing

With webcams now standard on new computers, web chat and other forms of online video communication are becoming more commonplace for group presentations. In **videoconferencing**, people at multiple physical locations use video to communicate orally and visually in real time. Videoconferencing can be done using a personal computer, webcam, and interactive software, and hence has become inexpensive and more commonplace.[18] Nevertheless, videoconferencing still requires careful planning and preparation.

A small group presentation in which individuals at multiple physical locations interact in real time orally and visually, using video and high-speed computer technology.

Preparation and Practice

Good presenters in any situation prepare note cards based on a presentation outline. Before the videoconference, they practice what they're going to say when they display the visuals. Not surprisingly, research shows that individuals who are better prepared for their videoconference session have a more positive and productive experience.[19]

Videoconference presenters prepare their digital slides well in advance. In addition, before the presentation they check that all equipment in all locations functions properly. For example, microphones are tested for audibility and cameras for visibility.

During the Presentation On the day of the conference, arrive or set up early and complete a final check of the equipment. Dress appropriately—don't wear bright or white clothing or jewelry that will glare in the camera's eye. Have all your notes and your visual and audio materials ready.

Once the presentation begins, be mindful of what you are doing and saying at all times. Video is unforgiving, picking up sounds and movements not ordinarily noticed. Avoid extraneous noises such as tapping a pencil or unzipping a backpack. When you are not speaking, devote all your attention to whoever is speaking and appear genuinely interested in that person. For a videoconference, use the mute button on your microphone to keep background noises to a minimum, particularly when the videoconference involves many people or several sites.

When it's your turn to talk, speak clearly and crisply. Although you might think audience members focus most on the video aspect of videoconferencing, research shows that audio—your voice—receives the most attention.[20] Balance a dynamic delivery with the constraints of video. Excessive movement clutters the screen and distracts from your ideas. Too much moving about can also detract from the picture's technical quality. Monitoring your body movement is especially important when using a webcam because the camera doesn't follow you around. In addition, slow connection speeds often cause video problems. If necessary, switching to audio-only mode will at least allow you to continue speaking and complete your presentation.

Watch your time limit and stick to it so that everyone has a chance to speak. If the presentation includes a question-and-answer session, assign a facilitator beforehand. Explain the session's format as you begin, and announce how much time the group will allot to questions.

After the Presentation Once the presentation has ended, thank the speakers and audience members for their participation. Note what went well and what you would do differently the next time you speak in videoconference.

Dan Krauss/Getty Images

As videoconferencing becomes more common, it's important to understand how speaking on camera differs from speaking in person.

When evaluating your group's presentation, focus on your "groupness," or the way you fit together into a cohesive whole. Effective group presentations emphasize group rather than individual effort. So in addition to the qualities usually expected in an excellent oral presentation—that it be well researched and audience centered, employ engaging language and appropriate presentation media, and the like—evaluation focuses on signs that the presentation truly reflects a group endeavor.[21] Assess the coherence of your group's presentation in terms of how well prepared you were as a group, how well you coordinated the presentation, how effectively you listened to each other and to the audience, how many clear references you made to the group, and the degree to which you believe you achieved your group's goal.

Preparation as a Group

Preparation as a group provides the foundation for a coherent group presentation. Even in a panel discussion, for which presenters do not practice together, group members keep the others in mind as they prepare for the presentation. Similarly, participants in a round table discussion typically develop notes for their presentations within the context of what other presenters will say.

Symposiums require the most preparation as a group. Although group members talk about their own subtopics, those subtopics must come together and form a coherent whole in the presentation. For example, suppose a group chooses the topic of unusual team sports, with kabaddi, badminton, canoe polo, curling, and korfball as the subtopics. Before beginning in-depth research, group members must agree on the main points they'll cover in their speeches. Each one might, for instance, talk about his or her sport's general description, history, and what makes it especially unique or interesting. The group would want to avoid having one person discussing only history, another covering only how the game is played, and a third focusing on why the audience should learn how to the play the game. This advance preparation as a group becomes evident in the group's presentation, with speakers following a similar format, smooth transitions between speakers, and no repetition of identical material.

Coordinated Presentations

How well group members coordinate their presentations is a second area of assessment. For example, in a forum, group members should decide in advance who is responsible for questions in specific topic areas. This avoids two problems: several group members responding to a question at the same time, or all group members having blank looks and no one responding. With panel discussions, the moderator or facilitator assumes primary responsibility for the smooth flow of discussion. Still, listeners expect group members to avoid interrupting or talking over each other. Symposiums provide multiple points for evaluating how well the group members coordinate the presentation. For example, each speaker should provide a smooth transition to the next. And although presentation media need not be identical, some standardization gives the audience an impression of continuity and prior planning.[22] Finally, regardless of the type of group presentation, an effective opening overview and closing summary give the presentation a sense of cohesion.[23]

Effective Listening

Effective listening plays a key role in the success of any group presentation. No matter what the setting, group members should display active listening skills, such as giving the speaker their complete attention, nodding, looking at the speaker, taking brief notes, and showing interest in what the speaker has to say. Group members should not work on their own presentations, talk or whisper with each other, or engage in any other activities that detract from the group's presentation.

Careful listening is especially important in round table and panel discussions because participants likely do not know exactly what others will say. Appropriately responding to other speakers requires close attention to the discussion. In addition, round table and panel discussions typically include speakers with different—and opposing—viewpoints, making critical listening essential. In these types of group presentations, audience members expect participants to carefully examine other speakers' ideas and supporting evidence.

Clear References to the Group

Listening to group members as they present helps speakers refer to what their co-presenters have said. These clear references to the group are a fourth important area for evaluation and provide another mechanism for linking together the parts of a group presentation. In a symposium, a speaker might say, "As Sheila remarked in her presentation…" or, "Similar to what Drew found…" These comments help demonstrate how the different pieces of the presentation fit together. In an oral report, the speaker might refer to specific aspects of the project that individual group members worked on. These brief acknowledgments personalize the report and indicate how different members of the group contributed to the project. Using the pronouns *we, our,* and *us* also reflects a sense of groupness. Responding to a question during a forum, the speaker might say, "In our research, we found …" or, "It surprised us when …" In making clear references to the group, audiences should learn about both individual contributions and group efforts in the presentation.

> **Watch it**

SPEECH BUDDY VIDEO 16.1
Reviewing Group Presentations

In this video, Janine suggests key points to focus on when evaluating group speeches and shows a sample group presentation.

> **Use it**

ACTIVITY 16.1
As a Group

In this activity, you'll evaluate how your own group worked together and completed its presentation.

Goal Achievement

The final area for evaluating group presentations concerns the degree to which the group achieved its goal. For an oral report, the speaker must give a balanced view of all the members' perspectives and adequately cover the report's sections. All participants in a panel discussion should have an equal opportunity to speak and respond appropriately to the moderator's questions. Round table discussions rely on a free flow of information among speakers that produces possible solutions to problems. Symposiums are designed to either inform or persuade audience members. Forums should allow for full audience participation. Evaluation of the group's goal attainment determines the group's ultimate success: Did the group achieve what it set out to do?

Speech for Review and Analysis

Tara Flanagan gave this speech of tribute in an introductory public speaking class at Colorado State University. Her assignment was to give a three- to five-minute commemorative speech about a person she admired. As you read Tara's speech, consider how effective her use of language is and how well she commemorates her grandfather. You can use your CourseMate for Public Speaking: The Evolving Art *to watch and listen to Tara deliver this speech. Look for it in the Chapter 16 resources.*

Used by permission.

My Grandfather, John Flanagan Sr.

by Tara Flanagan[24]

Specific purpose: To commemorate my grandfather and his compassion, humor, and courage

Thesis statement: Although the day of my grandfather's funeral was the saddest day of my life, I was uplifted by my memories of him and by the stories that confirmed his compassion, humor, and courage.

Cengage Learning

As I wiped the streams that flooded down my face, I saw out of the corner of my eye a group of homeless men enter the room. My sadness turned to anger as I watched these uninvited guests interrupt *my grandfather's* funeral. They were like unwanted ants invading a family picnic. After our pastor concluded his eulogy, I went to the back of the room to ask them to leave. "Excuse me," I said, "but this is my grandfather's funeral, and only invited guests are allowed inside." And one of the men looked at me, and he said, "You must be Tara. Your grandfather carried a picture of you in his wallet." Much to my surprise, these homeless men were friends of my grandfather. My grandfather was never a good judge of people. He was just better at not judging them at all.

As I walked around the room, I saw many people that neither my family nor I recognized, but each one of them had a story on how my grandfather had touched them with his love and kindness. My grandfather was a loving, brave man with an amazing sense of humor, and these virtues never shone brighter for me than they did on the day of his funeral.

From the funeral home, our entourage headed to the cemetery to place my grandfather in his final resting place. It was a hot July day, and the sun was just pounding down on our car. We were following the white hearse when all of the sudden it stopped, and this terrible, white smoke began billowing out of the hood. It laid there like a huge, immovable beached whale. My father began laughing as the cars piled up behind us, and he said, "I bet your grandfather had something to do with this." My grandfather had an amazing sense of humor. This incident reminded us of the many jokes he told and pulled on our family. Making his own hearse break down on the day of his funeral to give us all a good laugh wasn't beyond him.

I remembered a time when my grandfather cheered me up when I was younger. I was visiting my father for the summer, and I was incredibly homesick. I missed my mom and my sister very badly. He spent the entire afternoon telling me silly knock-knock jokes and doing random things just to make me laugh. And I remember feeling so much better. My homesickness melted away. My grandfather always had a way of making our family laugh and feel better, and the day of his funeral was no exception.

When we finally got the white whale back on the road, we drove into the lush cemetery. There were flowers blossoming and a gentle stream that ran through the middle. It was like a scene out of the Garden of Eden. There to greet us were several gentlemen dressed in their Marine best. They carried with them large guns and gave my grandfather his twenty-one–gun salute. After the service I spoke with them, and they told me of my grandfather's bravery while he served in World War II. One of the men had actually served with my grandfather. He told me a story about how my grandfather had saved his life, and they ended up being the only two men out of the entire platoon to survive. At the end of the war they even saw the famous raising of the flag at Iwo Jima.

Living, laughing, loving life: My grandfather was an amazing man who taught me so much about humor, courage, and compassion. Even though his funeral was the saddest day of my life, I was uplifted by all the lives that he had touched. I hope that someday I can learn to love people more than I judge them, just like he did.

Questions for Analysis and Discussion

1. Tributes should shed light on the individual being praised. After reading Tara Flanagan's speech about her grandfather, do you feel you learned important things about him? What things stand out in your mind?

2. How did Tara use emotion to enhance the quality of her speech? Were the emotional elements she used appropriate for this speech? How did they help you appreciate her grandfather?

3. Tributes can inspire the audience to think about something in a different way. Her introductory story about the presence of uninvited guests at her grandfather's funeral was an attempt to do this. What was she trying to accomplish by telling that story?

4. Tara said she wanted to impart a sense of her grandfather's compassion, humor, and courage in her tribute to him. Did she provide enough material in the speech to accomplish this three-part objective?

Summary

Many special occasions call for some type of speech. Speeches of introduction prepare the audience to listen to the main speaker. Speakers accepting awards should be thankful and humble in their brief comments. After-dinner speeches are meant to entertain. Tributes and eulogies typically provide inspiration. Speeches of nomination focus on the qualities that make the nominee the best person for the position or award. Public testimony allows speakers to participate in discussions that shape the policies that directly affect their world. Roasts amuse an audience at the guest of honor's expense in a good-natured way, and toasts unabashedly celebrate another person. Some occasions call for mediated speaking.

Groups may give several types of presentations, including oral report, panel discussion, roundtable discussion, symposium, and forum. For an oral report, one member of the group presents the entire report. Panel discussions involve a moderator asking questions of experts on a topic in front of an audience. Round table discussions also include expert speakers, but the focus is on the exchange of ideas among participants, so an audience is not present. Symposiums are the most common form of classroom group presentations. Speakers each choose a subtopic of the group's topic and present individual speeches to an audience. Forums are question-and-answer sessions. They may stand alone, but more often they occur directly after an oral report, panel discussion, or symposium. Groups often use videoconferencing to connect people in geographically dispersed locations.

In addition to all the qualities that go into effective public speaking, group presentations must form a unified whole. The cohesiveness of a group's presentation depends on good preparation as a group, coordination of the presentation, active listening, clear references to the group, and achievement of the group's goal.

Review it

Directory of Study and Review Resources

IN THE BOOK
Summary
Key Terms
Critical Challenges

MORE STUDY RESOURCES
CourseMate
Studio
Quizzes
WebLinks
Peer-reviewed videos

STUDENT WORKBOOK
16.1: Introducing…
16.2: Elevator Speech
16.3: Watch and Critique an Award Show
16.4: Group Experiences
16.5: Failed Media Appearances

SPEECH BUDDY VIDEOS
WATCH It Video
16.1: Evaluating Group Presentations
USE It Activity
16.1: As a Group

SAMPLE SPEECH VIDEOS
Jennifer, Megan, Stephanie, and Daniel, "The Dirty Truth about Antibacterial Products," persuasive group presentation
Lawrence Small, Dedication address at the opening of National Museum of the American Indian, special occasion speech

SPEECH BUILDER EXPRESS

Goal/purpose
Thesis statement
Organization
Outline
Supporting material
Transitions
Introduction
Conclusion
Works cited
Visual aids

INFOTRAC

Recommended search terms
Speech of introduction
Nomination speech
Roasts
Toasts
Eulogy
Small group presentation
Effective small groups
Videoconferencing

AUDIO STUDY TOOLS
"The Dirty Truth about Antibacterial Products" by Jennifer, Megan, Stephanie, and Daniel
Critical thinking questions
Learning objectives
Chapter summary

Guide to Your Online Resources

CourseMate Your Speech Communication CourseMate for *Public Speaking: The Evolving Art* gives you access to the Speech Buddy video and activity featured in this chapter, additional sample speech videos, Speech Studio, Speech Builder Express, InfoTrac College Edition, and study aids such as glossary flashcards, review quizzes, and the Critical Challenge questions for this chapter, which you can respond to via email if your instructor so requests. In addition, your CourseMate features live WebLinks relevant to this chapter. Links are regularly maintained, and new ones are added periodically.

Key Terms

acceptance speech 333

eulogy 337

forum 344

nomination speech 339

oral report 342

panel discussion 343

public testimony 340

roast 341

round table discussion 343

small group 342

speech of introduction 332

speech of tribute 337

symposium 343

toast 341

videoconferencing 344

Critical Challenges

Questions for Reflection and Discussion

1. Which types of speeches for special occasions can you imagine yourself giving? Why?

2. *Forum* in Latin means "marketplace" and "a place of public discussion." As a speaker, how can you encourage audience members to offer differing views during your group's question-and-answer session? What do you need to avoid that might deter the audience from speaking out?

3. Check out Speech Studio to analyze other students' special occasion or group speeches. Or record a speech you're working on, upload it to Speech Studio, and ask your peers for their feedback. What feedback could you use to fine-tune your special occasion or group speech before you give it in class?

Glossary

acceptance speech Speech given by an individual who is being recognized, honored, or given an award.

ad hominem fallacy Argument in which a speaker rejects another speaker's claim based on that speaker's character rather than the evidence the speaker presents; also called the *against the person fallacy*.

ad ignorantiam fallacy Argument in which a speaker appeals to popular attitudes and emotions without offering evidence to support claims.

ad populum fallacy Argument in which a speaker suggests that because a claim hasn't been shown to be false, it must be true; also called an *appeal to ignorance*.

alliteration Repetition of a sound in a series of words, usually the first consonant.

analogical reasoning Comparing two similar objects, processes, concepts, or events and suggesting that what holds true for one also holds true for the other.

analogy A type of comparison that describes something by comparing it to something else that it resembles.

anecdotes A brief narrative.

antithesis Juxtaposition of two apparently contradictory phrases that are organized in a parallel structure.

apathetic audience An audience that is informed about a speaker's topic but not interested in it.

appeals to cultural belief (**mythos**) Use of values and beliefs embedded in cultural narratives or stories to influence an audience.

appeals to speaker credibility (**ethos**) Use of the audience's perception of the speaker as competent, trustworthy, dynamic, and likeable to influence an audience.

appeal to tradition fallacy Argument in which a speaker asserts that the status quo is better than any new idea or approach.

argument Presenting claims and supporting them with evidence and reasoning.

arrangement The way the ideas in a speech are organized.

articulation The physical process of producing specific speech sounds to make language intelligible.

attention getter The first element of an introduction, designed mainly to create interest in a speech.

attitude How an individual feels about something.

audience The intended recipients of a speaker's message.

audience analysis Obtaining and evaluating information about an audience in order to anticipate their needs and interests and design a strategy to respond to them.

audience centered Describes a speaker who acknowledges the audience by considering and listening to the unique, diverse, and common perspectives of its members before, during, and after the speech.

audience-centered communication Adapting a speech to a specific situation and audience.

audience research questionnaires A questionnaire used by speakers to assess the knowledge and opinions of audience members; can take the form of an email, web-based, or in-class survey.

award presentation Speech that recognizes individuals to celebrate something they have done well.

begging the question Argument in which a speaker uses a premise to imply the truth of the conclusion

or asserts that the validity of the conclusion is self-evident; also called *circular reasoning*.

behavior An observable action.

belief Something an individual accepts as true or existing.

bibliographic information A source's complete citation, including author, date of publication, title, place of publication, and publisher.

blogs Short for web log; a web page that a blog writer, or *blogger*, updates regularly with topical entries.

body The middle (main) part of a speech; includes main and subordinate points.

brainstorming The free-form generation of ideas in which individuals think of and record ideas without evaluating them.

call number The number assigned to each book or bound publication in a library to identify that book in the library's classification system.

captive audiences Individuals who feel they must attend an event.

caricature fallacy Argument in which a speaker misrepresents another speaker's argument so that only a weak shell of the original argument remains; also called the *straw man fallacy*.

causal reasoning Linking two events or actions to claim that one resulted in the other.

cause-and-effect pattern A pattern that organizes a speech by showing how an action produces a particular outcome.

channel A mode or medium of communication.

chronological pattern A pattern that organizes a speech by how something develops or occurs in a time sequence.

claim A position or assertion that a speaker wants an audience to accept.

clichés An expression so overused that it fails to have any important meaning.

closed-ended questions A question that limits the possible responses, asking for very specific information.

coercion Forcing someone to think a certain way or making someone feel compelled to act under pressure or threat.

coherence An obvious and plausible connection among ideas.

communication climate The psychological and emotional tone that develops as communicators interact with one another.

comparative evidence fallacy Argument in which a speaker uses statistics or compares numbers in ways that misrepresent the evidence and mislead the audience.

competence The qualifications a speaker has to talk about a particular topic.

complete-sentence outline A formal outline using full sentences for all points; developed after researching the speech and identifying supporting materials; includes a speech's topic, general purpose, specific purpose, thesis, introduction, main points, subpoints, conclusion, transitions, and references.

conclusion The end of a speech, in which the speaker reviews the main points, reinforces the purpose, and provides closure. In reasoning, a primary claim or assertion.

connotative meanings A unique meaning for a word based on an individual's own experiences.

context The situation within which a speech is given.

copyright A type of intellectual property law that protects an author's original work (such as a play, book, song, or movie) from being used by others.

copyright information A statement about the legal rights of others to use an original work, such as a song (lyrics and melody), story, poem, photograph, or image.

credibility An audience's perception of a speaker's competence, trustworthiness, dynamism, and sociability.

cultural diversity Differences in cultural backgrounds and practices around the globe.

cultural norms Prescriptions for how people should interact and what messages should mean in a particular setting.

culture Values, beliefs, and activities shared by a group.

currency How recent information is—the more recent it is, the more current it is.

deductive reasoning Reasoning from a general condition to a specific case.

deep web The portion of the web composed of specialty databases, such as those housed by the U.S. government, that are not accessible by traditional search engines; also called the invisible or hidden web.

definitions A statement that describes the essence, precise meaning, or scope of a word or a phrase.

delivery The public presentation of a speech.

demographics The ways in which populations can be divided into smaller groups according to key characteristics such as sex, ethnicity, age, and social class.

denotative meanings An agreed-upon definition of a word, found in a dictionary.

dialect The vocabulary, grammar, and pronunciation used by a specific group of people, such as an ethnic or regional group.

dialogue Occurs when speakers are sensitive to audience needs and listen to audience members' responses, and listeners pay careful attention to speakers' messages so they can respond appropriately and effectively.

direct quote Comments written in response to an open-ended question in an audience research questionnaire.

discussion list An email-based distribution list that allows members to email everyone who belongs to the list using just one email address; also called a listserv.

divided audience An audience that is informed about a speaker's topic but equally split between those who favor the speaker's position and those who oppose it.

division fallacy Argument in which a speaker assumes that what is true of the whole is also true of the parts that make up the whole.

document cameras A projection device that uses a video camera to capture and display images, including 3-D visual materials.

dynamism An audience's perception of a speaker's activity level during a presentation.

emotional appeals (pathos) Use of emotional evidence and stimulation of feelings to influence an audience.

enthymemes An argument in which a premise or conclusion is unstated.

environment The external surroundings that influence a public speaking event.

ethical communication The moral aspects of our interactions with others, including truthfulness, fairness, responsibility, integrity, and respect.

ethnocentrism The belief that one's own worldview, based on one's own cultural background, is correct and best.

ethos Appeal that is linked to the speaker's credibility.

eulogies Speeches of tribute presented as retrospectives about individuals who have died.

euphemisms A word used in place of another word that is viewed as more disagreeable or offensive.

event A significant occurrence that an individual personally experiences or otherwise knows about.

evidence Supporting materials—narratives, examples, definitions, testimony, facts, and statistics—that a speaker presents to reinforce a claim.

examples An illustration or case that represents a larger group or class of things.

extemporaneous speaking A type of public speaking in which the speaker researches, organizes, rehearses, and delivers a speech in a way that combines structure and spontaneity.

external noise Conditions in the environment that interfere with listening.

facts An observation based on actual experience.

fair use Using someone else's original work in a way that does not infringe on the owner's rights, generally for educational purposes, literary criticism, and news reporting.

fallacy An error in making an argument.

false dilemma fallacy Argument in which a speaker reduces available choices to only two even though other alternatives exist; also called the *either-or fallacy.*

feedback Audience members' responses to a speech.

flip chart A large pad of paper that rests on an easel, allowing a speaker to record text or drawings with markers during a speech.

forum The question-and-answer session following a group's formal presentation.

gatewatching Monitoring news sources to analyze and assess the information they produce.

general purpose The speaker's overall objective: to inform, to persuade, or to entertain.

goodwill An audience's perception that a speaker shows she or he has the audience's true needs, wants, and interests at heart.

guilt by association fallacy Argument in which a speaker suggests that something is wrong with another speaker's claims by associating those claims with someone the audience finds objectionable; also called the *bad company fallacy.*

handout Sheets of paper containing relevant information that are distributed before, during, or after a speech.

hasty generalization fallacy Argument in which a speaker draws a conclusion based on too few or inadequate examples.

hate speech Words that attack groups such as racial, ethnic, religious, and sexual minorities.

hearing The physical response to sounds.

hedges A qualifier, such as *probably,* that makes a statement ambiguous.

ideas and concepts Mental activity, including thoughts, understandings, beliefs, notions, and principles.

idioms An expression that means something other than the literal meaning of the words.

illusion of transparency The tendency of individuals to believe that how they feel is much more apparent to others than is really the case.

impromptu speaking A type of public speaking in which the speaker has little or no time to prepare a speech.

inclusive language Words that don't privilege one group over another.

inductive reasoning Supporting a claim with specific cases or instances; also called *reasoning by example.*

information overload Occurs when individuals receive too much information and are unable to interpret it in a meaningful way.

informative speaking Presenting a speech in which the speaker seeks to deepen understanding, raise awareness, or increase knowledge about a topic.

internal consistency A logical relationship among the ideas that make up any main heading or subheading in a speech.

internal noise Thoughts, emotions, and physical sensations that interfere with listening.

internal summary A review of main points or subpoints, given before going on to the next point in a speech.

interpretations An individual's internal process of assigning meaning to words.

interview guide A list of all the questions and possible probes an interviewer asks in an interview, as well as notes about how the interviewer will begin and end the interview.

introduction The beginning of a speech, including an attention getter, a statement of the thesis and purpose, a reference to the speaker's credibility, and a preview of the main points.

invention Discovering what you want to say in a speech, such as choosing a topic and developing good arguments.

invitations to imagine Asking listeners to create a scene or situation in their minds.

jargon Technical language used by members of a profession or associated with a specific topic.

keywords During research for supporting materials, a term associated with a topic and used to search for information related to that topic. In a presentation outline, a word that identifies a subject or a point of primary interest or -concern.

language The system of words people use to communicate with others.

leading questions A question that suggests the answer the interviewer seeks.

listening Involves hearing, interpreting, responding to, and recalling verbal and nonverbal messages.

listening anxiety Anxiety produced by the fear of misunderstanding, not fully comprehending, or not being mentally prepared for information you may hear.

loaded word fallacy Argument in which a speaker uses emotionally laden words to evaluate claims based on a misleading emotional response rather than the evidence presented.

logical appeals (logos) Use of rational appeals based on logic, facts, and analysis to influence an audience.

logos Appeal to logic.

manuscript speaking A type of public speaking in which the speaker reads a written script word for word.

media credibility Perceptions of believability or trust that audience members hold toward communications media, including TV, the internet, newspapers, radio, and news magazines.

memorable message A sentence or group of sentences included in the conclusion of a speech, designed to make the speaker's thesis unforgettable.

memorized speaking A type of public speaking in which the speaker commits a speech to memory.

memory Using the ability to recall information to give an effective speech.

message The words and nonverbal cues a speaker uses to convey ideas, feelings, and thoughts.

metaphors A language device that demonstrates the commonalities between two dissimilar things.

metasearch engines A search tool that compiles the results from other search engines.

model A copy of an object, usually built to scale, that represents the object in detail.

monologue Occurs when communication is one way and communicators are only concerned with their own individual goals.

monotone A way of speaking in which the speaker does not alter his or her pitch.

Monroe's motivated sequence A five-step pattern of organization that requires speakers to identify and respond to what will motivate an audience to pay attention.

mythos Appeal to cultural beliefs and values.

narratives A description of events in a dramatic fashion; also called a story.

narrative pattern A pattern that organizes a speech by a dramatic retelling of events as a story or a series of short stories.

negative (hostile) audience An audience that is informed about a speaker's topic and holds an unfavorable view of the speaker's position.

neutral questions An unbiased and impartial question seeking a forthright answer.

noise Anything that interferes with the understanding of a message.

nomination speechs Speech that demonstrates why a particular individual would be successful at something if given the chance.

nonsexist language Words that are not associated with either sex.

nonverbal messages Information that is communicated without words, but rather, through movement, gesture, facial expression, vocal quality, use of time, use of space, and touch.

object Any nonliving, material thing that can be perceived by the senses.

open-ended questions A broad, general question, often specifying only the topic.

oral citations A source of information that a speaker mentions, or cites, during a speech.

oral report A report in which one member of a group presents the group's findings.

panel discussions A discussion in which a moderator asks questions of experts on a topic in front of an audience.

parallelism Using the same phrase, wording, or clause multiple times to add emphasis.

pathos Appeal to emotion.

pattern of organization A structure for ordering the main points of a speech.

persuasion Using language, images, and other means of communication to influence people's attitudes, beliefs, values, or actions.

persuasive speech A speech in which the speaker attempts to reinforce, modify, or change audience members' beliefs, attitudes, opinions, values, and behaviors.

pervasive communication environment The ability to access and share information in multiple forms from multiple locations in ways that transcend time and space.

pitch The highness or lowness of a speaker's voice.

places Geographic locations.

plagiarism Presenting someone else's ideas and work, such as speeches, papers, and images, as your own.

positive (sympathetic) audience An audience that is informed about a speaker's topic and has a favorable view of the speaker's position.

post hoc fallacy Argument in which a speaker concludes a causal relationship exists simply because one event follows another in time; also called the *false cause fallacy*.

posture The way a speaker positions and carries her or his body.

premise A claim that provides reasons to support a conclusion.

presentation media Technical and material resources, ranging from presentation software and real-time web access (RWA) to flip charts and handouts, that speakers use to highlight, clarify, and complement the information they present orally.

presentation outline An outline that distills a complete-sentence outline, listing only the words and phrases that will guide the speaker through the main parts of the speech and the transitions between them.

presentation software Computer software that allows users to display information in multimedia slide shows.

preview of main points The final element of the introduction, in which the main points to be presented in the body of the speech are mentioned.

primacy effect An audience is more likely to pay attention to and recall what speakers present at the beginning of a speech than what they present in the speech body.

primary questions A question that introduces a new topic or subtopic in an interview.

primary sources Information that expresses an author's original ideas or findings from original research.

problem-solution pattern A pattern that organizes a speech by describing a problem and providing possible solutions.

process How something is done, how it works, or how it has developed.

pronunciation The act of saying words correctly according to the accepted standards of the speaker's language.

psychographics Psychological data about an audience, such as standpoints, values, beliefs, and attitudes.

public speaking A situation in which an individual speaks to a group of people, assuming responsibility for speaking for a defined length of time.

public testimony Factual information and opinions about policy issues presented to government bodies or other public institutions.

qualifier A word or phrase that clarifies, modifies, or limits the meaning of another word or phrase.

question of fact A question that asks whether something is true or false.

question of policy A question that asks what course of action should be taken or how a problem should be solved.

question of value A question that asks for a subjective evaluation of something's worth, significance, quality, or condition.

rate The speed at which a speaker speaks.

real-time web access Employing a live internet feed as a visual medium or information resource during a public speech.

reasoning The method or process used to link claims to evidence.

recency effect An audience is more likely to remember what speakers present at the end of a speech than what they present in the speech body.

red herring Argument that introduces irrelevant evidence to distract an audience from the real issue.

relabeling Assigning more positive words or phrases to the physical reactions and feelings associated with speech anxiety.

relevance How closely a web page's content is related to the keywords used in an internet search.

reliability The consistency and credibility of information from a particular source.

review of main points The portion of the conclusion of a speech in which the main points presented in the body of the speech are briefly mentioned again.

rhetoric Aristotle's term for public speaking.

rhymes Using words with similar sounds, usually at the end of the word, to emphasize a point.

roast Humorous and good-natured ridicule directed toward the guest of honor at an event.

round table discussions A discussion in which expert participants discuss a topic in an impromptu format without an audience present.

search engines A sophisticated software program that hunts through documents to find those associated with particular keywords.

secondary questions A question that asks the interviewee to elaborate on a response.

secondary sources Others' interpretations or adaptations of a primary source.

signpost A transition that indicates a key move in the speech, making its organization clear to the audience.

similes A language device that compares two things that are generally dissimilar but share some common properties, expressed using *like* or *as*.

slang Informal, nonstandard language, often used within a particular group.

slippery-slope fallacy Argument in which a speaker asserts that one event will necessarily lead to another without showing any logical connection between the two events.

small group A collection of individuals who interact and depend on one another to solve a problem, make a decision, or achieve a common goal or objective.

sociability The degree to which an audience feels a connection to a speaker.

spatial pattern A pattern that organizes a speech by the physical or directional relationship between objects or places.

speaker The person who assumes the primary responsibility for conveying a message in a public communication context.

specific purpose A concise statement articulating what the speaker will achieve in giving a speech.

speech anxiety Fear of speaking in front of an audience.

speech of introduction A short speech that introduces someone to an audience.

speeches of tribute Speeches that give credit, respect, admiration, gratitude, or inspiration to someone who has accomplished something significant, lives in a way that deserves to be praised, or is about to embark on an adventure.

sponsored link A link whose owner has paid a search engine company such as Google to place the link in the results list of a search.

spotlight effect A phenomenon that leads us to think other people observe us much more carefully than they actually do.

standpoint The psychological location or place from which an individual views, interprets, and evaluates the world.

statistics Numerical data or information.

style The language or words used in a speech.

summary statistics Information in the responses to an audience research questionnaire that reflects trends and comparisons.

supporting materials Evidence used to demonstrate the worth of an idea.

syllogism A form of deductive reasoning consisting of a major premise, minor premise, and conclusion.

symbols Something, such as a word, that stands for something else, such as a person, place, thing, or idea.

symposium A presentation format in which each member of a group presents a speech about a part of a larger topic.

tag questions A question added onto the end of a declarative statement that lessens the impact of that statement.

target audience The particular group or subgroup a speaker most wants to inform, persuade, or entertain.

technophobia Fear that others will react negatively if one appears inept at using technological aids.

testimony An individual's opinions or experiences about a particular topic.

thesis A single declarative sentence that captures the essence or central idea of a speech.

toast Brief remarks celebrating the accomplishments of a guest of honor at an event.

tone Use of language to set the mood or atmosphere associated with a speaking situation.

topic The main subject, idea, or theme of a speech.

topical pattern A pattern that organizes a speech by arranging subtopics of equal importance.

transition A word, phrase, sentence, or paragraph used throughout a speech to mark locations in the organization and clearly link the parts of a speech together.

transparency A clear acetate page displayed by means of an overhead projector.

trustworthiness An audience's perception of a speaker as honest, ethical, sincere, reliable, sensitive, and empathetic.

uninformed audience An audience that is unfamiliar with a speaker's topic and has no opinion about it.

validity The soundness of the logic underlying information presented by a source.

value An ideal that serves as a standard of behavior.

videoconferencing A small group presentation in which individuals at multiple physical locations interact in real time orally and visually, using video and high-speed computer technology.

visualization Imagining a successful communication event by thinking through a sequence of events in a positive, concrete, step-by-step way.

vocalized pauses "Ah," "um," "you know," and other verbal fillers that speakers use when they're trying to think of what they want to say.

vocal variety Changes in the volume, rate, and pitch of a speaker's voice that affect the meaning of the words delivered.

volume The loudness of a speaker's voice.

voluntary audiences Individuals who can choose to attend or not attend a speaking event.

weak analogy fallacy Argument in which a speaker compares two things that are dissimilar, making the comparison inaccurate.

web directories An online list that organizes web pages and websites hierarchically by category; also called a search index.

webidence Web sources displayed as evidence during a speech, found by using real-time web access or web page capture software.

whiteboard A smooth white board that can be written or drawn on with markers.

working outline An outline that guides you during the initial stages of topic development, helping to keep you focused on your general purpose and clarify your specific purpose.

References

CHAPTER 1

1 Naomi (2008). Eight classes I should have taken in college (Web log message). Retrieved from http://www.eduinreview.com/blog.

2 Frobish, T. (2000). Jamieson meets Lucas: Eloquence and pedagogical model(s) in *The Art of Public Speaking. Communication Education, 49,* 239–252.

3 Lull, J. & Neiva, E. (in press). *The great chain of communication: Human evolution's driving force.* Cambridge, England: Cambridge University Press.

4 Johanson, D. & Edgar, B. (2006). *From Lucy to language.* New York, NY: Simon & Schuster.

5 Stringer, C. & Andrews, P. (2005). *The complete world of human evolution.* New York, NY: Thames & Hudson.

6 Fritz, C. A. (1922). A brief review of the chief periods in the history of oratory. *Quarterly Journal of Speech Education, 8*(1), 26–48.

7 Pew Internet & American Life Project (2009). *The internet's role in campaign 2008.* Retrieved from http://www.pewinternet.org

8 Kaiser Family Foundation (2010). *Generation M2: Media in the lives of 8- to 18-year-olds.* Retrieved from http://www.kkf.org

9 Internet World Stats (2010) *Usage and population statistics.* Retrieved from http://www.internetworldstats.com

10 Pew Internet and American Life Project (2010). *Internet, broadband, and cell phone statistics.* Retrieved from http://www.pewinternet.org.

11 Fox, S. (2005). *Digital divisions: There are clear differences among those with broadband connections, dial-up connections, and no connections at all to the internet.* Pew Internet & American Life Project. Retrieved from http://www.pewinternet.org

12 Smith, C. R. (2003). *Rhetoric and human consciousness: A history* (2nd ed.). Prospect Heights, IL: Waveland.

13 Smith (2003).

14 Habinek, T. (2005). *Ancient rhetoric and oratory.* Oxford, England: Blackwell; Jasinski, J. (2001). *Sourcebook on rhetoric: Key concepts in contemporary rhetorical studies.* Thousand Oaks, CA: Sage; Smith (2003); Yagcioclu, S., & Cem-Deger, A. (2001). Logos or mythos: (De)legitimation strategies in confrontational discourses of sociocultural ethos. *Discourse & Society, 12,* 817–852.

15 Jasinski (2001).

16 Gross, A. G., & Dascal, M. (2001). The conceptual unity of Aristotle's rhetoric. *Philosophy and Rhetoric, 34,* 275–291.

17 Hoogestraat, W. E. (1960). Memory: The lost canon? *Quarterly Journal of Speech, 46,* 141–147.

18 Ishii, S. (1992). Buddhist preaching: the persistent main undercurrent of Japanese traditional rhetorical communication. *Communication Quarterly, 40,* 391–397.

19 Fisher, W. R. (1987). *Human communication as narration: Toward a philosophy of reason, value, and action.* Columbia, SC: University of South Carolina Press; Sprague, A. (2004). *The wisdom of storytelling in an information age.* Lanham, MD: Scarecrow Press.

20 Ford, W. S. Z., & Wolvin, A. D. (1993). The differential impact of a basic communication course on perceived communication competencies in class, work, and social contexts. *Communication Education, 42,* 215–223.

21 Ford & Wolvin (1993).

22 Fox, S. (2006). *Online health search 2006.* Retrieved 2007, from http://www.pewinternet.org

23 Seibold, D. R., Kudsi, S., & Rude, M. (1993). Does communication training make a difference? Evidence for the effectiveness of a presentation skills program. *Journal of Applied Communication Research, 21,* 111–131.

24 Langer, E. (1998). *The power of mindful learning.* New York: Perseus.

25 Fleury, A. (2005). Liberal education and communication against the disciplines. *Communication Education, 54,* 72–79.

26 Addley, E. (2005, June 5). Office hours: Stand up and be counted: Although we may hate public speaking, it's a vital skill, says Esther Addley. *The Guardian,* p. 2; Krapels, R. H., & Davis, B. D. (2003). Designation of "communication skills" in position listings. *Business Communication Quarterly, 66*(2), 90–96; Maes, J. D., Weldy, T. G., & Icenogle, M. J. (1997). A managerial perspective: Oral communication competency is most important for business students in the workplace. *Journal of Business Communication, 34,* 67–80.

27 Ford & Wolvin (1993).

28 Wirtz, C. (2003, April–May). Public speaking: An accounting marketing tool. *The National Public Accountant.* 14–15.

29 Gittlen, S. (2004, July 26). The public side of you: Be it for budget negotiations, project updates or industry conference panels, great public skills speaking will get you noticed—and promoted. *Network World,* p. 1; Green, M. C., & Brock, T. C. (2005). Organizational membership versus informal interaction: Contributions to skills and perceptions that build social capital. *Political Psychology, 26,* 1–25; Lublin, J. S. (2004, October 5). To win advancement, you need to clean up any bad speech habits. *Wall Street Journal,* p. B1.

30 Hassam, J. (2002). Learning the lesson—Speaking up for communication as an academic discipline too important to be sidelined. *Journal of Communication Management, 7*(1), 14–20; Murphy, T. A. (2005). Deliberative civic education and civil society: A consideration of ideals and actualities in democracy and communication education. *Communication Education, 53,* 74–91.

31 McMillian, J. J., & Harriger, K. J. (2002). College students and deliberation: A benchmark study. *Communication Education, 51,* 237–253; West, M., & Gastil, J. (2004). Deliberation at the margins: Participant accounts of face-to-face public deliberation at the 1999–2000 World Trade protests in Seattle and Prague. *Qualitative Research Reports in Communication, 5,* 1–7.

32 Hufstetter, P. J. (2005, November 13). Teen wins mayor race by 2 votes. Retrieved from http://www.post-gazette.com

33 Laswell, H. (1948). The structure and function of communication in society. In L. Bryson (ed.), *The communication of ideas.* New York, NY: Harper and Row.

34 Schramm. W. (1954). *The processes and effects of communication.* Urbana, IL: University of Illinois Press; Berlo, D. (1960). *The process of communication.* New York, NY: Holt, Rinehart, and Winston; Barnlund, D. (1970). A transactional model of communication. In K.Sereno & C.D. Mortensen (eds.), *Foundations of communication theory.* New York, NY: Harper and Row, 83–102.

35 Beck, U. & Beck-Gernsheim, E. (2002). *Individualization.* Newbury Park, CA: Sage; Lull, J. (2002). Superculture for the communication age. In J. Lull (ed.), *Culture in the communication age.* London, England: Routledge.

36 Coopman, T.M. (2009). Toward a pervasive communication environment perspective. *First Monday 14.* Retrieved from http://www.firstmonday.org

37 Johannesen, R. L. (2002). *Ethics in human communication* (5th ed.). Prospect Heights, IL: Waveland; Rosenstand, N. (2006). *The moral of the story: An introduction to ethics* (5th ed.). New York, NY: McGraw-Hill.

38 Baron, L. (2001). Why information literacy? *Advocate, 18*(8), 5–7.

39 Elwood, J. (2005). Presence or PowerPoint: Why PowerPoint has become a cliché. Development and Learning Organizations, 19(3), 12–14.

CHAPTER 2

1 Freeman, H. (2009, July 1). Prison inmates find their voice, build confidence through Toastmasters club. Retrieved from http://www.from herald-review.com

2 Ellis, M. (2003, April 30). Too scared for words: Fear of public speaking can be overcome, experts insist. *The Columbus*

Dispatch, p. G1; Zimmerman, J. (2003, May 19). Fear not: Alleviating your anxiety over public speaking takes practice, humor and knowing the audience. *The Press Enterprise*, p. D1.

3 Addison, P., Ayala, J., Hunter, M., Behnke, R., & Sawyer, C. (2004). Body sensations of higher and lower anxiety sensitive speakers anticipating a public presentation. *Communication Research Reports, 21*, 284–290; Phillips, G. C., Jones, G. E., Rieger, E. J., & Snell, J. B. (1997). Normative data for the personal report of confidence as a speaker. *Journal of Anxiety Disorders, 11*, 215–220.

4 Duff, D. C., Levine, T. R., Beatty, M. J., Woolbright, J., & Sun Park, H. (2007). Testing public anxiety treatments against a credible placebo control. *Communication Education, 56*, 72–88; Kelly, L., & Keaten, J. A. (2000). Treating communication anxiety: Implications of the communibiological paradigm. *Communication Education, 49*, 45–57.

5 Addison et al. (2004); Beatty, M. J., McCroskey, J. C., & Heisel, A. D. (1998). Communication apprehension as temperamental expression: A communibiological paradigm. *Communication Monographs, 65*, 197–219; Behnke, R. R., & Sawyer, C. R. (2001). Patterns of psychological state anxiety in public speaking as a function of anxiety sensitivity. *Communication Quarterly, 49*, 84–94; Dwyer, K. K. (2000). The multidimensional model: Teaching students to self-manage high communication apprehension by self-selecting treatments. *Communication Education, 49*, 72–81; Harris, K. B., Sawyer, C. R., & Behnke, R. R. (2006). Predicting speech state anxiety from trait anxiety, reactivity, and situational influences. *Communication Quarterly, 54*, 213–226; Witt, P. L., Brown, K. C., Roberts, J. B., Weisel, J., Sawyer, C. R., & Behnke, R. R. (2006). Somatic anxiety patterns before, during, and after giving a public speech. *Southern Communication Journal, 71*, 87–100.

6 Pearson, J. C., DeWitt, L., Child, J. T., Kahl, Jr., D. H., & Dandamudi, V. (2007). Facing the fear: An analysis of speech-anxiety content in public-speaking textbooks. *Communication Research Reports, 24*, 159–168.

7 Clarkson, M. (2003). *Intelligent fear: How to make fear work for you*. New York, NY: Marlowe.

8 Witt, P. L., & Behnke, R. R. (2006). Anticipatory speech anxiety as a function of public speaking assignment type. *Communication Education, 55*, 167–177.

9 Beatty, M. C., & McCroskey, J. C. (1998). Interpersonal communication as temperamental expression: A communibiological paradigm. In J. C. McCroskey, J. A. Daly, M. M. Martin, & M. J. Beatty (Eds.), *Communication and personality: Trait perspectives* (pp. 41–67). Cresskill, NJ: Hampton Press.

10 Kelly, L., & Keaten, J. A. (2000).

11 Witt, P. L., & Behnke, R. R. (2006). Anticipatory speech anxiety as a function of public speaking assignment type. *Communication Education, 55*, 167–177.

12 McCroskey, J. C. (1970). Measures of communication-bound anxiety. *Speech Monographs, 37*, 269–277.

13 Feldman, P. J., Cohen, S., Hamrick, N., & Lepore, S. J. Psychological stress, appraisal, emotion and cardiovascular response in a public speaking task. *Psychology and Health, 19*, 353–368.

14 Honour, D. (2007). Speech performance anxiety for non-native speakers. *Florida Communication Journal, 36*(2), 57–66.

15 Hsu, C. (2004). Sources of differences in communication apprehension between Chinese in Taiwan and Americans. *Communication Quarterly, 52*, 370–389; Sawyer, C. R., & Behnke, R. R. (1999). State anxiety patterns for public speaking and the behavior inhibition system. *Communication Reports, 12*, 33–41.

16 Field, A. P., Hamilton, S. J., Knowles, K. A., & Plews, E. L. (2003). Fear information and social phobic beliefs in children; A prospective paradigm and preliminary results. *Behaviour Research and Therapy, 41*, 113–123.

17 Kelly, L., & Keaten, J. A. (2000). Treating communication anxiety: Implications of the communibiological paradigm. *Communication Education, 49*, 45–57; Sawyer, C. R., & Behnke, R. R. (2002). Reduction in public speaking anxiety during performance as a function of sensitization processes. *Communication Quarterly, 50*, 110–121.

18 Hsu, C. (2009). The relationships of trait anxiety, audience nonverbal feedback, and attributions to public speaking state anxiety. *Communication Research Reports, 26*, 237–246.

19 Edwards, C. C., Myers, S. A., Hensley-Edwards, A., & Wahl, S. (2003). The relationship between student pre-performance concerns and evaluation apprehension. *Communication Research Reports, 20*, 54–61.

20 Cornwell, B. R., Johnson, L., Berardi, L., & Grillon, C. (2006). Anticipation of public speaking in virtual reality reveals a relationship between trait social anxiety and startle reactivity. *Biological Psychiatry, 59*, 664–666; Edwards et al. (2003); Horvath, N. R., Moss, M. N., Xie, S., Sawyer, C. R., & Behnke, R. R. (2004). Evaluation sensitivity and physical sensations of stress as components of public speaking state anxiety. *Southern Communication Journal, 69*, 173–181; Keaten, J. A., & Kelly, L. (2004). Disposition versus situation: Neurocommunicology and the influence of trait apprehension versus situational factors on state public speaking anxiety. *Communication Research Reports, 21*, 273–283; Kozasa, E. H., & Leite, J. R. (1998). A brief protocol of cognitive modification and gradual exposure of reduction of fear symptoms of public speaking. *Journal of Behavior Therapy and Experimental Psychiatry, 29*, 317–326.

21 Gilovich, T., Kruger, J., & Medvec, V. H. (2002). The spotlight effect revisited: Overestimating the manifest variability of our actions and appearance. *Journal of Experimental Social Psychology, 38*, 93–99; Gilovich, T., Medvec, V. H., & Savisky, K. (2000). The spotlight effect in social judgment: An egocentric bias in estimates of the salience of one's own actions and appearance. *Journal of Personality and Social Psychology, 78*, 211–222.

22 Ayres, J., & Sonandré, D. M. A. (2003). Performance visualization: Does the nature of the speech model matter? *Communication Research Reports, 20*, 260–268; Beatty, M. J., & Valencic, K. (2000). Context-based apprehension versus planning demands: A communibiological analysis of anticipatory public speaking anxiety. *Communication Education, 24*, 58–71; Honeycutt, J. M., Choi, C. W., & DeBerry, J. R. (2009). Communication apprehension and imagined interactions. *Communication Research Reports, 26*, 228–236; Vassilopoulos, S. P. (2005). Anticipatory processing plays a role in maintaining social anxiety. *Anxiety, Stress & Coping, 18*, 321–332.

23 Ayres, J. (2005). Performance visualization and behavioral disruption: A clarification. *Communication Reports, 18*, 55–63; Ayres, J., & Ayres, T. A. (2003). Using images to enhance the impact of visualization. *Communication Reports, 16*, 47–55; Ayres, J., Hsu, C., & Hopf, T. (2000). Does exposure to visualization alter speech preparation processes? *Communication Research Reports, 17*, 366–374.

24 Patient handout: Relaxation techniques. (2003). *Alternative Medicine Alert, 6*(7), 81–82; Cosnett, G. (2003). Just breathe: Taking in a bit of fresh air isn't as easy as you think. *Training & Development Journal, 56*(9), 17–18.

25 Donnet, N. (1989) Letting nervousness work for you. *Training & Development Journal, 43*(4), 21–23.

26 Behnke, R. R., & Sawyer, C. R. (1999). Public speaking procrastination as a correlate of public speaking communication apprehension and self-perceived public speaking competence. *Communication Research Reports, 16*, 40–47.

27 Ellis (2003).

28 Ayres, J. (1996). Speech preparation processes and speech apprehension. *Communication Education, 45*, 228–235.

29 MacIntyre, P. D., & Thivierge, K. A., (1995). The effects of audience pleasantness, audience familiarity, and speaking contexts on public speaking anxiety and willingness to speak. *Communication Quarterly, 43*, 456–466.

30 Smith, T. E., & Frymier, A. B. (2006). Get "real": Does practicing speeches before an audience improve performance? *Communication Quarterly, 54*, 111–125.

31 Smith & Frymier (2006).

32 Finn, A. N., Sawyer, C. R., & Schrodt, P. (2009). Examining the effect of exposure therapy on public speaking state anxiety. *Communication Education, 58*, 92–109.

33 Addison, P. (2003). Worry as a function of public speaking state anxiety tips. *Communication Reports, 16*, 125–131.

34 Clarkson (2003).

35 Gray, J. A. (1995). A model of the limbic system and basal ganglia: Applications to anxiety and schizophrenia. M. S. Gazzaniga (Ed.), *The cognitive neurosciences* (pp. 1165–1176). Cambridge, MA: Bradford.

36 Gilovich, T., Savitsky, K., & Medvec, V. H. (1998). The illusion of transparency: Biased assessments of others' ability to read one's emotional states. *Journal of Personality & Social Psychology, 75*, 332–346; Savitsky, K., & Gilovich, T. (2003). The illusion of

359

transparency and the alleviation of speech anxiety. *Journal of Experimental Social Psychology*, 39, 618–625.

37 MacIntyre, P. D., & MacDonald, J. R. (1998). Public speaking anxiety: Perceived competence and audience congeniality. Communication Education, 47, 359–365.

CHAPTER 3

1 Jenco, M. (2008, May 30). Lifted speech may cost principal: Reassignment called likely after plagiarism. *Daily Herald* (Arlington Heights, IL), p. 1.

2 Conway, M., & Groshek, J. (2009). Forgive me now, fire me later: Mass communication students' ethics gap concerning school and journalism. *Communication Education, 58*, 461–482; Rosenstand, N. (2009). *The moral of the story: An introduction to ethics* (6th ed.). New York, NY: McGraw-Hill; Ruggiero, V. R. (2008). *Thinking critically about ethical issues* (7th ed.). New York, NY: McGraw-Hill.

3 International Association of Business Communicators (2009). *IABC code of ethics for professional communicators.* Retrieved from http://www.iabc.com; National Communication Association (1999); National Speakers Association (2003). *Code of professional ethics.* Retrieved from http://www.nsaspeaker.org

4 Johannsen, R. L. (2010). *Ethics in human communication* (6th ed.). Prospects Heights, IL: Waveland.

5 National Communication Association (1999). *NCA credo for ethical communication.* Retrieved from http://www.natcom.org

6 Rosenfeld, L. B. (1983). Communication climates and coping mechanisms in the classroom. *Communication Education, 32*, 167–174.

7 Hammond, S. C., Anderson, R., & Cissna, K. N. (2003). The problematics of dialogue and power. In P. J. Kalbfleisch (Ed.), *Communication yearbook 27* (pp. 125–157). Mahwah, NJ: Erlbaum; Johannesen, R. L. (2000). Nel Noddings's uses of Martin Buber's philosophy of dialogue. *Southern Communication Journal, 2 & 3*, 151–160; Levine, L. (1994). Listening with spirit and the art of team dialogue. *Journal of Organizational Change Management, 7*(1), 61–73; Stewart, J., & Zediker, K. (2000). Dialogue as tensional, ethical practice. *Southern Communication Journal, 2 & 3*, 224–242.

8 Arnett, R. C., Arneson, P., & Bell, L. M. (2007). Communication ethics: The dialogic turn. In P. Arneson (Ed.), *Exploring communication ethics: Interviews with influential scholars in the field* (pp. 143–184). New York: Peter Lang; Pearce, W. B., & Pearce, K. A. (2000). Combining passions and abilities: Toward dialogic virtuosity. *Southern Communication Journal, 2 & 3*, 161–175.

9 Leets, L. (2001). Explaining perceptions of racist speech. *Communication Research, 28*, 676–706.

10 Chong, D. (2006). Free speech and multiculturalism in and out of the academy. *Political Psychology, 27*(1), 29–54; Demaske, C. (2004). Modern power and the first amendment: Reassessing hate speech. *Communication Law and Policy, 9*(3), 273–316.

11 Arneson, P. (2008). A dialogic ethic in the public rhetoric of Angelina Grimké. In K. G. Roberts & R. C. Arnett (Eds.), *Communication ethics: Between cosmopolitanism and provinciality* (pp. 139–154). New York, NY: Lang.

12 Jenco (2008).

13 Gayle, B. M. (2004). Transformations in a civil discourse public speaking class: Speakers' and listeners' attitude change. *Communication Education, 53*, 174–184.

14 Gates, Jr., H. L. (2004, January). *America behind the color line.* Speech presented at the Commonwealth Club. Retrieved from http://www.common wealthclub.org/archive/04/04-01gates-speech.html

15 Johannesen (2010).

16 Olson, S. (2005). Schools face prevalence of online plagiarism: Educators try to thwart growing cheating problem as Web sites make it easy for students to purchase papers. *Indianapolis Business Journal, 26*(13), 17; Tillman, L. (2009, August 9). Students nationwide say they cheat. *The Brownsville Herald.* Retrieved from http://www.brownsvilleherald.com

17 Belter, R., & du Pré, A. (2009). A strategy to reduce plagiarism in an undergraduate course. *Teaching of Psychology, 36*, 257–261.

18 Lipson, C. (2004). *Doing honest work in college: How to prepare citations, avoid plagiarism, and achieve real academic success.* Chicago, IL: University of Chicago Press.

19 Ludwig, M. (2008, March 31). UTSA honor code not original: Copied parts are an oversight, student says. *Houston Chronicle.* Retrieved from http://www.houstonchronicle.com

20 Lipson (2004).

21 Nienhaus, B. (2004). Helping students improve citation performance. *Business Communication Quarterly, 67*, 337–348.

22 Johannesen, R. L. (2001). Communication ethics: Centrality, trends, and controversies. In W. B. Gudykunst (Ed.), *Communication yearbook 25* (pp. 201–235). Mahwah, NJ: Erlbaum.

23 Agar, M. (1994). *Language shock: Understanding the culture of conversation.* New York, NY: Morrow.

24 Wise, J. M. (2008). *Cultural globalization: A user's guide.* Malden, MA: Blackwell.

25 Neuliep, J. W., Hintz, S. M., & McCroskey, J. C. (2005). The influence of ethnocentrism in organizational contexts: Perceptions of interviewee and managerial attractiveness, credibility, and effectiveness. *Communication Quarterly, 53*, 41–56.

26 Kang, O., & Rubin, D. (2009). Reverse linguistic stereotyping: Measuring the effect of listener expectations on speech evaluation. *Journal of Language & Social Psychology, 28*, 441–456.

27 Lund, D. (2006). Rocking the racism boat: School-based activists speak out on denial and avoidance. *Race, Ethnicity & Education, 9*, 203–221.

28 Habinek.

29 Oliver, R. T. (1965). *History of public speaking in America.* Boston, MA: Allyn and Bacon.

30 Sellnow, D. D., & Treinen, K. P. (2004). The role of gender in perceived speaker competence: An analysis of student peer critiques. *Communication Education, 53*, 286–296.

31 Brownell, J. (2010). *Listening: Attitudes, principles, and skills*, 4th ed. New York, NY: Pearson.

32 Halone, K. K., & Pecchioni, L. L. (2001). Relational listening: A grounded theoretical model. *Communication Reports, 14*, 59–71; Krauss, R. M. (1987). The role of the listener: Addressee influences on message formulation. *Journal of Language and Social Psychology, 6*(2), 81–98.

33 Reisberg, D. (1978). Looking where you listen: Visual cues and auditory attention. *Acta Psychologica, 42*, 331–341.

34 Coopman, S. (1997). Personal constructs and communication in interpersonal and organizational contexts. In G. Neimeyer & R. Neimeyer (Eds.), *Advances in personal construct psychology,* Vol. 4 (pp. 101–147). Greenwich, CT: JAI Press.

35 Clark, A. J. (1989). Communication confidence and listening competence: An investigation of the relationships of willingness to communicate, communication apprehension and receiver apprehension to comprehension of content and emotional meaning in spoken messages. *Communication Education, 38*, 237–248.

36 Bavelas, J. B., Coates, L., & Johnson, T. (2002). Listener responses as a collaborative process: The role of gaze. *Journal of Communication, 52*, 566–580; Thomas, L. T., & Levine. T. R. (1994). Disentangling listening and verbal recall: Related but separate constructs? *Human Communication Research, 21*, 103–127; White, G. (1998). *Listening.* Oxford, England: Oxford University Press.

37 Nichols, R., & Stevens, L. M. (1957). Listening to people. *Harvard Business Review, 35*, 85–92.

38 Brownell, J. (2010).

39 King, P. E., & Behnke, R. R. (2004). Patterns of state anxiety in listening performance. *Southern Communication Journal, 70*, 72–80.

40 Underwood, J. D. M., & Underwood, G. (2005). The selective nature of memory: Some effects of taking a verbal record: A response to A. Plaut. *Journal of Analytical Psychology, 50*, 59–67.

41 Gibb, J. R. (1961). Defensive communication. *Journal of Communication, 11*, 141–148.

CHAPTER 4

1 Cronkhite, G. (1986). On the focus, scope, and coherence of the study of human symbolic activity. *Quarterly Journal of Speech, 72*, 231–246; Kellermann, K. (1992). Communication: Inherently strategic and primarily automatic. *Communication Monographs, 59*, 288–300; Motley, M. T. (1990). On whether one can(not) not communicate: An examination via traditional communication postulates. *Western Journal of Speech Communication, 54*, 1–20.

2 Keith, W. (2004). Planning a no-sweat presentation. *Government Finance Review, 20*(4), 55–56.

3 Williams, G. (2002). Looks like rain: If you've thought and thought and still haven't come up with any great ideas, don't sweat. *Entrepreneur, 30*(9), 104–110.

4 Osborn, A. F. (1957). *Applied imagination.* New York, NY: Scribner; Prendergast, K. (2003, September 29). The ideal setting for ideas. Brainstorming sessions can be productive if done the correct way. *The Press Enterprise,* p. A7; Wellner, A. S. (2003). A perfect brainstorm. *Inc., 25*(10), 31–35.

5 Kupperman, M. A (2003). Perfect brainstorm. *Inc., 25*(10), 31–2, 35.

6 Snyder, A., Mitchell, J., Ellwood, S., Yates, A., & Pallier, G. (2004). Nonconscious idea generation. *Psychological Reports, 94,* 1325–1330.

7 Sutton, R. I., & Hargadon, A. (1996). Brainstorming groups in context. *Administrative Science Quarterly, 41*(4), 685–718.

8 Licuanan, B. F., Dailey, L. R., & Mumford, M. D. (2007). Idea evaluation. Error in evaluating highly original ideas. *The Journal of Creative Behavior, 41*(1), 1–27.

9 Guerrero, L. K, & Afifi, W. A. (1995). Some things are better left unsaid. Topic avoidance in family relationships. *Communication Quarterly 43(3),* 276–296; Caughlin, J. & Golish, T. (2002). An analysis of the association between topic avoidance and dissatisfaction: Comparing perceptual and interpersonal explanations. *Communication Monographs, 69*(4), 275–295.

10 Kollins, T. K. (1996). Tips for speakers. *Association Management, 48*(8), 175–179.

11 Ogden, H. V. S. (1948). On teaching the sentence outline. *College English, 10*(3), 152–158.

12 Higbee, R. W. (1964). A speaking approach to composition. *The English Journal 53*(1), 50–51.

13 House, J. (1993). The first shall be last: Writing the essay backwards. *The English Journal, 82*(6), 26–28.

14 Watkins, K. J. (2005) Will they throw eggs? *Journal of Accountancy, 199*(4), 57–61.

15 Sutton, R.I. & Hargadon, A. (1996). Brainstorming groups in context. *Administrative Science Quarterly, 41,* 685–718.

Chapter 5

1 Gates, B. (2005, October). Remarks by Bill Gates, Founder and Chief Software Architect, Microsoft Corporation, University of Michigan, Ann Arbor, MI. Retrieved, from http://www.microsoft.com/billgates/speeches.asp; Gates, B. (2005, October 13). Remarks by Bill Gates, Founder and Chief Software Architect, Microsoft Corporation, University of Waterloo, Waterloo, Ontario, Canada. Retrieved from http://www.microsoft.com/billgates/speeches.asp

2 Morgan, N. (2003). *Working the room.* Cambridge, MA: Harvard Business School Press.

3 Haynes, W. L. (1990). Public speaking pedagogy in the media age. *Communication Education, 38,* 89–102.

4 Welch, J. M. (2005). The electronic welcome mat: The academic library web site as a marketing and public relations tool. *The Journal of Academic Librarianship, 31,* 225–228.

5 Agrawal, A., Basak, J., Jain, V., Kothari, R., Kumar, M., Mittal, P. A., ... Sureka, R. (2004). Online marketing research. *IBM Journal of Research & Development, 48,* 671–676.

6 Park-Fuller, L. M. (2003). Audiencing the audience: Playback Theatre, performative writing, and social activism. *Text and Performance Quarterly, 23,* 288–310.

7 Weissman, J. (2003). *Presenting to win: The art of telling your story.* Harlow, Essex, England: Financial Times Prentice Hall.

8 Michael Jordan 2009 Hall of Fame Induction speech [Video file]. Retrieved from http://www.youtube.com/watch?v=z2jMzudeX1E

9 Bennett, S. (1998). *Theatre audiences.* London: Routledge; Jamieson, K. H., & Campbell, K. K. (2000). *The interplay of influence.* Belmont, CA: Wadsworth; McQuail, D. (1997). *Audience analysis.* London, England: Sage; Traudt, P. (2004). *Media, audience, effects: An introduction to the study of media content and audience analysis.* Boston: Allyn & Bacon; Yopp, J. J., & McAdams, K. C. (2002). *Researching audiences.* Boston, MA: Allyn & Bacon.

10 McCarty, H. (1998). *Motivating your audience.* Boston, MA: Allyn & Bacon.

11 Myers, F. (1999). Argumentation and the composite audience: A case study. *Quarterly Journal of Speech, 85,* 55–71.

12 National Center for Education Statistics. (2004). *Digest of education statistics, 2004: Chapter 3, postsecondary education.* Retrieved from http://www.nces.ed.gov

13 Carnevale, E.P., & Fry, R.A. (2000). *Crossing the great divide: Can we achieve equity when Generation Y goes to college?* Princeton, NJ: Educational Testing Service.

14 Brown, L. I. (2004). Diversity: The challenge for higher education. *Race Ethnicity and Education, 7,* 21–34; Bylander, J., & Rose, S. (2007). Border crossings: Engaging students in diversity work and intergroup relations. *Innovative Higher Education, 31,* 251–264; Engberg, M. E. (2007). Educating the workforce for the 21st century: A cross-disciplinary analysis of the impact of the undergraduate experience on students' development of a pluralistic orientation. *Research in Higher Education, 48*(3), 283–317; Mor Barak, M. (2005). *Managing diversity: Towards a globally inclusive workplace.* Thousand Oaks, CA: Sage; van Knippenberg, D., & Schippers, M. D. (2007). Work group diversity. *Annual Review of Psychology, 58,* 515–541.

15 Myers, F. (1999). Political argumentation and the composite audience: A case study. *Quarterly Journal of Speech, 85,* 55–71.

16 DeFrancisco, V.P. (2007). *Communicating Gender Diversity.* Thousand Oaks. CA: Sage; Harding, S. (2003). *The Feminist Standpoint Reader.* New York, NY: Routledge; Orbe, M.P. (1998). From the standpoint(s) of traditionally muted groups: Explicating a co-cultural communication theoretical model. *Communication Theory, 8,* 1–26; Wood, J.T. (2008) *Gendered Lives: Communication, Gender and Culture.* Boston, MA: Wadsworth.

17 Atkinson, J. (2005). Conceptualizing global justice audiences of alternative media: The need for power and ideology in performance paradigms of audience research. *The Communication Review, 8,* 137–157; Harding, S. (1991). *Whose science? Whose knowledge? Thinking from women's lives.* Ithaca, NY: Cornell University Press.

18 Blethen, F. (2003, January). *Diversity: The American journey.* Keynote address presented at the third annual Martin Luther King Jr. Holiday Assemblies of the Granite Falls, WA High School and Middle School. Retrieved from http://www.seattletimescompany.com

19 Orbe, M. P., & Warren, K. T. (2000). Different standpoints, different realities: Race, gender, and perceptions of intercultural conflict. *Qualitative Research Reports in Communication, 1*(3), 51–57.

20 Dietz, T., Kalof, L., & Stern P. C. (2002). Gender, values, and environmentalism. *Social Science Quarterly, 83,* 353–364.

21 Fowler, G. A., Steinberg, B., & Patrick, A. O. (2007, March 1). Mac and PC's overseas adventures: Globalizing Apple's ads meant tweaking characters, clothing and body language. *The Wall Street Journal,* p. B1.

22 Miller, N. (2007). Snack attack: Minifesto for a new age. *Wired, 15.03,* 124–135

23 Johnson, S. (2007). Snacklash. *Wired, 15.03,* 178.

24 Yook, E. L. (2004). Any questions? Knowing the audience through question types. *Communication Teacher, 18,* 91–93.

25 Parsons, R. D. (2007). A challenge to minority business owners. *Vital Speeches of the Day, 73*(1), 32–33.

26 Black, C. (2007, January). *Putting the pieces together.* Remarks given at the Magazine Publishers of American Breakfast with a Leader. Retrieved from http://www.hearstcorp.com/speeches/speechesarchive2007.html

27 *Michael Beschloss Speaks at 172*nd *Commencement.* Retrieved from http://www.lafayette.edu/news.php/viewnc/10374

28 Myers, S. A. (2004). The relationship between perceived instructor credibility and college student in-class and out-of-class communication. *Communication Reports, 17,* 129–137; Myers, S. A., & Bryant, L. E. (2004). College students' perceptions of how instructors convey credibility. *Qualitative Research Reports in Communication, 5,* 22–27.

29 Miller, A. (2002). An exploration of Kenyan public speaking patterns with implications for the American introductory public speaking course. *Communication Education, 51,* 168–182.

30 Smith, C. R. (2003). *Rhetoric and human consciousness: A history.* Prospect Heights, IL: Waveland.

31 Haskins, W. (2000). Ethos and pedagogical communication. *Current Issues in Education, 3,* 1–9.

32 Rosenberg, A., & Hirschberg, J. (2005). Acoustic prosodic and lexical correlates of charismatic speech. *Proceedings of Interspeech 2005,* 513–516.

33 Aune, R. K., & Kikuchi, T. (1993). Effects of language intensity similarity on perceptions of credibility, relational attributions, and persuasion. *Journal of Language and Social Psychology, 12,* 224–237; Myers & Bryant; Pfau, M., & Kang, J. G. (1991). The impact of relational messages on candidate influence in televised political debates. *Communication Studies, 42,* 114–128.

34 Queen Noor (2005, April). *Medallion speaker address.* Presented to the Commonwealth of California. Retrieved from http://www.commonwealthclub.org

361

Chapter 6

1 Head, A. J., & Eisenberg, M. B. (2010). How today's college students use Wikipedia for course-related research. *First Monday, 15*(3). Retrieved from firstmonday.org

2 Tsai, M. (2009). Online information searching strategy inventory (OISSI): A quick version and a complete version. *Computers & Education, 53,* 473–483.

3 Ivey, R. (2009). Perceptions of the future of cataloging: Is the sky really falling? *Cataloging & Classification Quarterly, 47,* 464–482.

4 Fry, L. (2009). Information behavior of community college students: A survey of literature. *Community & Junior College Libraries, 15*(1), 39–50; Higntte, M., Margavio, T., & Margavio, G. (2009). Information literacy assessment: Moving beyond computer literacy. *College Student Journal, 43*(3), 812–821.

5 Fallows, D. (2008). *Search engine use.* Retrieved from pewinternet.org

6 Anagnostopoulos, I. (2010). A capture–recapture sampling standardization for improving Internet meta-search. *Computer Standards & Interfaces, 32,* 61–70.

7 Netcraft (2009). *December 2009 web server survey.* Retrieved from news.netcraft.com

8 Bergman, M. K. (2007, February 21). Re: *The murky depths of the 'deep web'* [Weblog post]. Retrieved from mkbergman.com; Wright, A. (2009, February 23). Exploring a "deep web" that Google can't grasp. *The New York Times,* East Coast Late Edition, p. B4.

9 Bruns, A., & Jacobs, J. (2006). Introduction. In A. Bruns & J. Jacobs (Eds.), *The uses of blogs* (pp. 1–8). New York, NY: Lang.

10 Cenite, M., Detenber, B., Koh, A., Lim, A., & Soon, N. (2009). Doing the right thing online: a survey of bloggers' ethical beliefs and practices. *New Media & Society, 11,* 575–597; Perlmutter, D., & Schoen, M. (2007). "If I break a rule, what do I do, fire myself?" Ethics codes of independent blogs. *Journal of Mass Media Ethics, 22*(1), 37–48.

11 Redfern, V. (2004). Natural language thesaurus: A survey of student research skills and research tool preferences. *Australian Academic Research Libraries, 35*(2), 137–150.

12 Bangerter, A. (2000). Self-representation: Conversational implementation of self-presentation goals in research interviews. *Journal of Language and Social Psychology, 19,* 436–462; Johnson, J. C., & Weller, S. C. (2002). Elicitation techniques for interviewing. In J. F. Gubrium & J. A. Holstein (Eds.), *Handbook of interview research: Context & method* (pp. 491–514). Thousand Oaks, CA: Sage.

13 Stewart, C. J., & Cash, W. B. (2008). *Interviewing: Principles and practices* (12th ed.). New York: McGraw-Hill.

14 Johnson, J. M. (2002). In-depth interviewing. In J. F. Gubrium & J. A. Holstein (Eds.), *Handbook of interview research: Context & method* (pp. 103–119). Thousand Oaks, CA: Sage.

15 Spano, S., & Zimmermann, S. J. (1995). Interpersonal communication competence in context: Assessing performance in the selection interview. *Communication Reports, 8,* 18–26.

16 Stax, H. P. (2004). Paths to precision: Probing turn format and turn-taking problems in standardized interviews. *Discourse Studies, 6*(1), 77–94.

17 Stein, M. L., & Paterno, S. F. (2001). *Talk straight, listen carefully: The art of interviewing.* Ames, IA: Iowa State University Press.

18 American Psychological Association (2009). *Publication manual of the American Psychological Association* (6th ed.). Washington, DC: American Psychological Association; Gibaldi, J. (2009). *MLA handbook for writers of research papers* (7th ed.). New York, NY: Modern Language Association of America.

19 Jagger, B. (2009, October). *The world's tipping point.* Speech presented at Ecogram Week, Columbia University. Retrieved from http://greenbuilders.ning.com/profiles/blog/show?id=3914770%3ABlogPost%3A509

Chapter 7

1 Student dissident Shen Tong offers a firsthand account of the violent crackdown in Tiananmen Square, China. (1999). In R. Torricelli & A. Carroll (Eds.), *In our own words: Extraordinary speeches of the American century* (pp. 385–388). New York, NY: Kodansha International.

2 Smith, C. R. (2009). *Rhetoric and human consciousness: A history* (3rd ed.). Prospect Heights, IL: Waveland.

3 Clasen, P., & Lee, R. (2006). Teaching in a sanitized world: An exploration of the suburban scene in public communication pedagogy. *Communication Education, 55,* 438–463; Ivie, R., & Giner, O. (2009). American exceptionalism in a democratic idiom: Transacting the mythos of change in the 2008 presidential campaign. *Communication Studies, 60*(4), 359–375.

4 Fisher, W. R. (1987). *Human communication as narration: Toward a philosophy of reason, value, and action.* Columbia, SC: University of South Carolina; Limon, M. S., & Kazoleas, D. C. (2004). A comparison of exemplar and statistical evidence in reducing counter-arguments and responses to a message. *Communication Research Reports, 21,* 291–298; Moyer-Gusé, E., & Nabi, R. (2010). Explaining the effects of narrative in an entertainment television program: Overcoming resistance to persuasion. *Human Communication Research, 36,* 26–52.

5 Green, M. C., & Brock, T. C. (2000). The role of transportation in the persuasiveness of public narratives. *Journal of Personality and Social Psychology, 79,* 701–721.

6 Bono. (2004, May). *Because we can, we must.* Commencement speech, University of Pennsylvania, Philadelphia, PA. Retrieved from http://www.upenn.edu/almanac/between/2004/commence-b.html

7 Kelly, R. (2005, April. *Through our eyes: A shared community vision for Saint Paul.* State of the City Address, 2005, presented at the Dorothy Day Center, St. Paul, MN. Retrieved from http://www.stpaul.gov/mayor/speeches

8 Morrison, T. (2004, December). Nobel Lecture. Speech presented at the Nobel Foundation, Retrieved from http://www.nobelprize.org

9 Allen, M., Preiss, R., & Gayle, B. (2006). Meta-analytic examination of the base-rate fallacy. *Communication Research Reports, 23*(1), 45–51.

10 Amory, L. (2007, August). *Imagine a world … Speech presented at the Rocky Mountain Institute RMI25 Gala.* Retrieved from http://www.rmi.org

11 Bhatia, P. K. (2002) Introduction to presidential speech by Edward Seaton. Retrieved from http://www.asne.org

12 Clements, W. M. (2002). *Oratory in Native North America.* Tucson, AZ: University of Arizona Press; Dauenhauer, N. M., & R. Dauenhauer, R. (Eds.) (1990). *Haa tuwunáagu yís, for healing our spirit: Tlingit oratory* (Vol. 2). Seattle, WA: University of Washington Press/Juneau, AK: Sealaska Heritage Foundation.

13 *Compact Oxford English Dictionary* (2004). Grief. Retrieved from askoxford.com/concise_oed.

14 David Kadashan (1990). Hoohah, 1968. In N. M. Dauenhauer, & R. Dauenhauer (Eds), *Haa tuwunáagu yís, for healing our spirit: Tlingit oratory* (Vol. 2, pp. 235–239). Seattle, WA: University of Washington Press/Juneau, AK: Sealaska Heritage Foundation.

15 The case for Santa Clara football: Added and discontinued programs. (2007). Retrieved from http://www.letthemplay.com

16 Braverman, J. (2008). Testimonials versus informational persuasive messages: The moderating effect of delivery mode and personal involvement. *Communication Research, 35*(5), 666–694.

17 Freemantle, T. (2004, September 21). Eye on CBS; Rather apologizes for Guard story; After the mea culpa, what's left for Rather? Veteran anchor the latest face in the debate over media credibility. *The Houston Chronicle,* p. 1.

18 Hoeken, H. (2001). Anecdotal, statistical, and causal evidence: Their perceived and actual persuasiveness. *Argumentation, 15,* 425–437.

19 Fox, M. J. (2005, July). *Senate rally for HR 810.* Retrieved from http://www.michaeljfox.org/news

20 Pew Research Center for the People and the Press (2007, August). *Internet news audience highly critical of news organizations: Views of press values and performance: 1985–2007.* Retrieved from http://www.people-press.org.

21 Loory, S. H. (2005). CNN today: A young giant stumbles. *Critical Studies in Media Communication, 22,* 340–343.

22 Pew Research Center for the People and the Press (2007, August). *Internet news audience highly critical of news organizations.*

23 Fahmy, S., & Wanta, W. (2005). Testing priming effects: Differences between print and broadcast messages. *Simile, 5*(2); Lanie, L. (2001). *How Americans used the internet after the terror attack.* Pew Internet & American Life Project. Retrieved from http://www.pewinternet.org; Pew Research Center for the People and the Press (2004). *News audiences.* Pew Research Center for the People and the Press (2007). *Internet news audience highly critical of news organizations*; Project for Excellence in Journalism. (2007). *The state of the news media 2007.* Retrieved from http://www.stateofthemedia.org/2007

24 Fallows, D. (2007, February). *Election newshounds speak up: Newspaper, TV, and internet fans tell how and why they differ.*

REFERENCES

Retrieved from http://www.pewinternet.org; Pew Research Center for the People and the Press (2007). *Internet news audience highly critical of news organizations*; Project for Excellence in Journalism (2007).

25 Project for Excellence in Journalism (2007).

Chapter 8

1 Adams, T., & Scollard, S. (2005). *Internet effectively: A beginner's guide to the World Wide Web*. Boston, MA: Pearson.

2 Lynch, C. (1995). Reaffirmation of God's anointed prophet: The use of chiasm in Martin Luther King's "mountaintop" speech. *Howard Journal of Communications, 6*(1/2), 12–31; Schank, R., & Berman, T. (2006). Living stories: Designing story-based education experiences. *Narrative Inquiry, 16*, 220–228.

3 Campbell, K. K., & Huxman, S. S. (2009). *The rhetorical act: Thinking, speaking, and writing critically* (4th ed.). Belmont, CA: Wadsworth.

4 Awosika, M. (2003, March 18). Legendary Fabergé eggs still popular. *Sarasota Herald-Tribune*, p. E1.

5 McKerrow, R. E., Gronbeck, B. E., Ehninger, D., & Monroe, A. H. (2003). *Principles and types of public speaking* (15th ed.). Boston, MA: Allyn & Bacon.

6 Leech, T. (2004). *How to prepare, stage, and deliver winning presentations*. New York, NY: American Management Association.

7 Leech (2004).

8 Subordinate (2010). In *Merriam-Webster's online dictionary* (11th ed.fc). Retrieved from http://www.merriam-webster.com/dictionary/subordinate

9 American Psychological Association. (2009). *Publication manual of the American Psychological Association* (6th ed.). Washington, DC: American Psychological Association; Gibaldi, J. (2003). *MLA handbook for writers of research papers* (7th ed.). New York, NY: Modern Language Association of America.

Chapter 9

1 Novogratz, J. (2005). TEDTalks: Jacqueline Novogratz. [Video file.] Retrieved from http://www.ted.com/tedtalks.

2 Dennis, M. J., & Ahn, W.-K. (2001). Primacy in causal strength judgments: The effect of initial evidence for generative versus inhibitory relationships. *Memory & Cognition, 29*, 152–164; Kraljic, T., Samuel, A., & Brennan, S. (2008). First impressions and last resorts: How listeners adjust to speaker variability. *Psychological Science, 19*, 332–338; Miller, J. K., Westerman, D. L., & Lloyd, M. E. (2004). Are first impressions lasting impressions? An exploration of the generality of the primacy effect in memory for repetitions. *Memory & Cognition, 32*, 1305–1315;

3 Van De Mieroop, D., de Jong, J., & Andeweg, B. (2008). I want to talk about … A rhetorical analysis of the introductions of 40 speeches about engineering. *Journal of Business & Technical Communication, 22*(2), 186–210.

4 Winfrey, O. (2002). Acceptance speech. Retrieved from http://www oprah.com

5 Cosby, B. (2004, May). *Pound cake speech*. Speech at the NAACP's Gala to Commemorate the 50th Anniversary of *Brown v. Board of Education*, Washington DC. Retrieved from http://www.americanrhetoric.com

6 Visco, F. (2005, May). Speech presented at the 13th Annual Advocacy Training Conference, Washington DC. Retrieved from http://www.natlbcc.org

7 O'Connor, S. D. (2004, June). Full text of remarks by Supreme Court Justice Sandra Day O'Connor at the 113th Commencement Ceremony. Retrieved from http://www.news-service.stanford.edu

8 Greatbatch, D., & Clark, T. (2003). Displaying group cohesiveness: Humour and laughter in the public lectures of management gurus. *Human Relations, 56*, 1515–1544; McRoberts, D. A., & Larson-Casselton, C. (2006). Humor in public address, health care and the workplace: Summarizing humor's use using meta-analysis. *North Dakota Speech and Theatre Journal, 19*, 26–33.

9 Rowling, J. K. (2008, June). *The fringe benefits of failure, and the importance of imagination*. Commencement address at the Annual Meeting of the Harvard Alumni Association, Cambridge, MA. Retrieved from http://www.harvardmagazine.com/commencement/the-fringe-benefits-failure-the-importance-imagination

10 Frymier, A., Wanzer, M., & Wojtaszczyk, A. (2008). Assessing students' perceptions of inappropriate and appropriate teacher humor. *Communication Education, 57*, 266–288.

11 Hackman, M. Z. (1988). Reactions to the use of self-disparaging humor by informative public speakers. *Southern Speech Communication Journal, 53*, 175–183.

12 Fisher, M. (1992). *A whisper of AIDS*. 1992 Republication National Convention address. Retrieved from http://www.americanrhetoric.com

13 Atkin, N. (2005). Building capacity in Aboriginal communities and non-Aboriginal institutions. *Vital Speeches of the Day, 72*(1), 19–22.

14 Costabile, K. A., & Klein, S. B. (2005). Finishing strong: Recency effects in juror judgments. *Basic & Applied Social Psychology, 27*, 47–58; Sederberg, P., Howard, M., & Kahana, M. (2008). A context-based theory of recency and contiguity in free recall. *Psychological Review, 115*, 893–912; Unsworth, N. (2008). Exploring the retrieval dynamics of delayed and final free recall: Further evidence for temporal–contextual search. *Journal of Memory & Language, 59*, 223–236.

15 Eardley, A. F., & Pring, L. (2006). Remembering the past and imagining the future: A role for nonvisual imagery in the everyday cognition of blind and sighted people. *Memory, 14*, 925–936; Page, M. P. A., Cumming, N., Norris, D., Hitch, G. J., & McNeil, A. M. (2006). Repetition learning in the immediate serial recall of visual and auditory materials. *Journal of Experimental Psychology Learning, Memory & Cognition, 32*, 716–733; Tremblay, S., Parmentier, F. B. R., Guérard, K., Nicholls, A. P., & Jones, D. M. (2006). A spatial modality effect in serial memory. *Journal of Experimental Psychology/Learning, Memory & Cognition, 32*, 1208–1215.

16 Crano, W. D. (1977). Primacy versus recency in retention of information and opinion change. *Journal of Social Psychology, 101*(1), 87–96; Igou, E. R., & Bless, H. (2003). Inferring the importance of arguments: Order effects and conversational rules. *Journal of Experimental Social Psychology, 39*, 91–99.

17 Brown, R. M. (nd). Retrieved from http://www.quotationspage.com

18 Sotomayor, S. (2009, July 13). Opening statement before the U.S. Senate Judiciary Committee, Washington, DC. Retrieved from http://www.judiciary.senate.gov/hearings/testimony.cfm?id=3959&wit_id=8102

Chapter 10

1 Words of wisdom from a young orator (2004, July 29). *The Virginian Pilot*, p. B10.

2 Obama, B. (2004, July). Speech presented at the Democratic National Convention, Boston, MA. Retrieved from http://www.presidentialrhetoric.com

3 SIL International. (2005). A brief history of SIL International. Retrieved from http://www.sil.org

4 Ogden, C. K., & Richards, I. A. (1923). *The meaning of meaning: A study of the influence of language upon thought and of the science of symbolism*. New York, NY: Harcourt, Brace.

5 Pear, R. (2004, February 24). Education chief calls union "terrorist," then recants. *The New York Times*. Retrieved from http://www.nytimes.com

6 *Compact Oxford English Dictionary* (2010). Car. Retrieved from http://www.askoxford.com; Investorwords.com (2010). *Car*. Retrieved from http://www.investorwords.com; *Webster's Revised Unabridged Dictionary* (1913). Retrieved from http://machaut.uchicago.edu/websters, p. 216; *Dorland's Illustrated Medical Dictionary* (2002). *CAR*. Retrieved from http://www.mercksource.com

7 Baldwin, T. (2004). Keep the flame alive for rights. In Ridinger, R. B. (Ed.). *Speaking for our lives: Historic speeches and rhetoric for gay and lesbian rights (1892–2000)* (pp. 804–806). Binghamton, NY: Harrington Park Press.

8 Planning a staycation this year? Look it up now in the 2009 update of *Merriam-Webster's Collegiate® Dictionary, Eleventh Edition. (2010). Retrieved from http://www.merriam-webster.com/info/newwords09.htm*

9 Logue, C. M., & Messina, L. M. (Eds.) (2003). *Representative American speeches 2002–2003*. New York, NY: H. W. Wilson, p. 58.

10 Manovich, L. (2001). *The language of new media*. Cambridge, MA: MIT Press.

11 Woods, T. (2010, February). Apology: Full transcript. Retrieved from http://www.cnn.com/2010/US/02/19/tiger.woods.transcript/index.html

12 *FreeThesaurus.net* (2010). *Speak*; *Listen*. Retrieved from http://www.freethesaurus.net

13 Noveck, J. (2005, September 7). The use of the word "refugee" touches a nerve. *The Seattle Times*, p. A16.

14 Eckert, P., & McConnell-Ginet, S. (2003). *Language and gender*. Cambridge, England: Cambridge University Press; Mulac, A., Bradac, J. J., & Gibbons, P. (2001). Empirical support for the gender-as-culture

hypothesis: An intercultural analysis of male/female language differences. *Human Communication Research, 27,* 121–152.

15 Areni, C., & Sparks, J. (2005). Language power and persuasion. *Psychology & Marketing, 22,* 507–525; Blankenship, K., & Craig, T. (2007). Powerless language markers and the correspondence bias: Attitude confidence mediates the effects of tag questions on attitude attributions. *Journal of Language & Social Psychology, 26,* 28–47; Hosman, L., & Siltanen, S. (2006). Powerful and powerless language forms: Their consequences for impression formation, attributions of control of self and control of others, cognitive responses, and message memory. *Journal of Language & Social Psychology, 25,* 33–46.; Ruva, C. L., & Bryant, J. B. (2004). The impact of age, speech style, and question form on perceptions of witness credibility and trial outcome. *Journal of Applied Social Psychology, 34,* 1919–1944.

16 Timmerman, L. M. (2002). Comparing the production of power in language on the basis of sex. In M. Allen, R. W. Preiss, B. M. Gayle, & N. A. Burrell (Eds.), *Interpersonal communication research: Advances through meta-analysis* (pp. 73–88). Mahwah, NJ: Erlbaum.

17 Natalle, E. J., & Bodenheimer, F. R. (2004). *The woman's public speaking handbook.* Belmont, CA: Wadsworth; Palomares, N. (2009). Women are sort of more tentative than men, aren't they? How men and women use tentative language differently, similarly, and counterstereotypically as a function of gender salience. *Communication Research, 36,* 538–560

18 The Center for Studying Health System Change. (2009, September). *A snapshot of U.S. physicians: Key findings from the 2008 health tracking physician survey.* Retrieved from http://www.hschange.org/CONTENT/1079/

19 Billings, A. (2007). From diving boards to pole vaults: Gendered athlete portrayals in the "Big Four" sports at the 2004 Athens Summer Olympics. *Southern Communication Journal, 72,* 329–344; Carlin, D., & Winfrey, K. (2009). Have you come a long way, baby? Hillary Clinton, Sarah Palin, and sexism in 2008 campaign coverage. *Communication Studies, 60,* 326–343; Major, L., & Coleman, R. (2008). The intersection of race and gender in election coverage: What happens when the candidates don't fit the stereotypes? *Howard Journal of Communications, 19,* 315–333; Shugart, H. A. (2003). She shoots, she scores: Mediated constructions of contemporary female athletes in coverage of the 1999 U.S. women's soccer team. *Western Journal of Communication, 67,* 1–31.

20 Billings (2007); Shugart (2003).

21 Scarborough research examines NASCAR fan demographics. (2009, February 16). *Street & Smith's SportsBusiness Daily.* Retrieved from http://www.sportsbusinessdaily.com/article/127802

22 Furlong, J. (2010, February). Speech given at opening ceremonies: Vancouver 2010 Winter Olympics, Vancouver, Canada. Retrieved from http://www.vancouver2010.com

23 Harris, K. (2009, March 23). Fox News show host says he was 'misunderstood'. Retrieved from http://www.torontosun.com

24 Jolie, A. (2005, March). Speech at the National Press Club, Washington, DC. Retrieved from http://www.npr.org

25 McCormick, S. (2003). Earning one's inheritance: Rhetorical criticism, everyday talk, and the analysis of public discourse. *Quarterly Journal of Speech, 89,* 109–131.

26 Lennox. A. (2005, March). Speech. Retrieved from http://www.thedevelopmentline.co.uk/46664minisite.

27 Gottheimer, J. (Ed.) (2003). *Ripples of hope: Great American civil rights speeches.* New York, NY: Basic Books, p. 459.

28 Gottheimer (2003), p. 462.

29 In Logue, C. M., & Messina, L. M. (Eds.) (2002). *Representative American speeches 2001–2002.* New York, NY: H. W. Wilson, p. 87.

30 Roehl, L. (2005, June). *Bill Buckner would approve.* Forgiveness speech. Retrieved from http://www.americanrhetoric.com

31 Carmona, R. H. (2005, February). *The value and promise of every child.* Keynote speech presented at the 2005 National Early Childhood Conference hosted by U.S. Department of Education, Office of Special Education Programs, Washington, DC. Retrieved from http://www.surgeongeneral.gov/news/speeches/02072005.html. Emphasis added.

32 Averbuch, Y. (2010). Love the process. *Vital Speeches of the Day, 76*(3), 126–130.

33 Jenkins, S. P. (2005, March). Raising the bar on integrity. Retrieved from http://www.boeing.com

34 Hawken, P. (2009, May). Commencement address at the University of Portland, Portland, OR. Retrieved from http://www.paulhawken.com

35 Nussbaum, M. C. (2003, May). *Compassion and global responsibility.* Commencement address at Georgetown University, Washington, DC. Retrieved from http://www.humanity.org/commencements

36 Llewellyn, N. (2008). Identifying with the audience: A study of community police work. *International Journal of Public Administration, 31,* 971–987; McRoberts, D., & Larson-Casselton, C. (2006). Humor in public address, health care and the workplace: Summarizing humor's use using meta-analysis. *North Dakota Journal of Speech & Theatre, 19,* 26–33.

37 DeNeal, D. (2004, October 12). Katabasis and Anabasis: A four-year journey. *Wabash Magazine,* summer/fall. Retrieved from http://www.wabash.edu/magazine

38 Natalle & Bodenheimer (2004).

39 Hackman, M. Z. (1988). Reactions to the use of self-disparaging humor by informative public speakers. *Southern Speech Communication Journal, 53,* 175–183.

40 Hirst, R. (2003). Scientific jargon, good and bad. *Journal of Technical Writing and Communication, 33,* 201–229.

41 Edwards, C., & Myers, S. (2007). Perceived instructor credibility as a function of instructor aggressive communication. *Communication Research Reports, 24,* 47–53; Schrodt, P. (2003). Students' appraisals of instructors as a function of students' perceptions of instructors' aggressive communication. *Communication Education, 52,* 106.

CHAPTER 11

1 Kress, G. (2006). *Reading Images: The Grammar of Visual Design.* New York, NY: Routledge.

2 Bartsch, R.A. & Cobern, K.M. (2003). Effectiveness of PowerPoint presentations in lectures. *Computers and Education, 41,* 77–86.

3 White, C., Easton, P., & Anderson, C. (2000). Students' perceived value of video in a multimedia language course. *Educational Media International, 37,* 167–175.

4 Pew Internet and American Life Project (2009). *The audience for online video-sharing sites shoots up.* Retrieved from http://www.pewinternet.org/Reports/2009/13

5 Galbreath, S. C., & Booker, J. (2000). Making multimedia presentations easy. *Public Management, 82*(5), 10–17.

6 Wormald, K. E. (2004). Pump up your presentations. *OfficeSolutions, 21*(2), 48–49.

7 Lull, J. (1985). On the communicative properties of music. *Communication Research, 12,* 363–372; Lull, J. (ed.) (1992). *Popular Music and Communication.* Newbury Park, CA: Sage.

8 James, K.E., Burke, L., & Hutchins, H.M. (2006). Powerful or pointless? Faculty v. student perception of PowerPoint effectiveness in business education. *Business Communication Quarterly, 69,* 374–396.

9 Szabo, A. & Hastings, N. (2000). Using IT in the undergraduate classroom. *Computers and Education, 35,* 175–187.

10 Cyphert, D. (2004). The problem of PowerPoint. Visual aid or visual rhetoric? *Business Communication Quarterly, 27,* 80–84.

11 Mahin, L. (2004). PowerPoint pedagogy. *Business Communication Quarterly, 27,* 219–222.

12 DuFrene, D. D., & Lehman, C. M. (2004). Concept, content, construction, and contingencies: Getting the horse before the PowerPoint cart. *Business Communication Quarterly, 27,* 64–88.

13 Mahin (2004).

14 DuFrene & Lehman (2004).

15 Jones, J. H. (2004). Message first: Using films to power the point. *Business Communication Quarterly, 27,* 88–91.

16 Stark, D. & Paravel, V. (2008). PowerPoint in public. *Theory, Culture and Society, 25,* 30–55.

17 Blokzijl, W., & Naeff, R. (2004). The instructor as stagehand. Dutch student responses to PowerPoint. *Business Communication Quarterly, 27,* 70–77.

18 Stark & Paravel (2008).

19 Bell, S. (2004). End PowerPoint dependency now! *American Libraries, 35*(6), 56–59.

CHAPTER 12

1 Johnstone, C. L. (2001). Communicating in classical contexts: The centrality of delivery. *Quarterly Journal of Speech, 87,* 121–143.

2 Dilbeck, K., McCroskey, J., Richmond, V., & McCroskey, L. (2009). Self-perceived communication competence in the Thai culture. *Journal of Intercultural Communication Research, 38*(1), 1–7

3 Miller, A. (2002). An exploration of Kenyan public speaking patterns with implications

for the American introductory public speaking course. *Communication Education, 51,* 168–182.

4 Martini, M., Behnke, R. R., & King, P. E. (1992). The communication of public speaking anxiety: Perceptions of Asian and American speakers. *Communication Quarterly, 40,* 279–288; Merkin, R. (2009). Cross-cultural communication patterns—Korean and American communication. *Journal of Intercultural Communication, 20.* Retrieved from http://www.immi.se/intercultural

5 Natalle, E. J., & Bodenheimer, F. R. (2004). *The woman's public speaking handbook.* Belmont, CA: Wadsworth.

6 Sellnow, D. D., & Treinen, K. P. (2004). The role of gender in perceived speaker competence: An analysis of student peer critiques. *Communication Education, 53,* 286–296.

7 Natalle & Bodenheimer (2004).

8 Natalle & Bodenheimer (2004).

9 National Institute on Deafness and Other Communication Disorders (2006, January). *Quick stats for voice, speech, and language.* Retrieved from http://www.nidcd.nih.gov

10 Hughes, S., Gabel, R., Irani, F., & Schlagheck, A. (2010). University students' perceptions of the life effects of stuttering. *Journal of Communication Disorders, 43,* 45–60.

11 Iverach, L., O'Brian, S., Jones, M., Block, S., Lincoln, M., Harrison, E., et al. (2010). The Five Factor Model of personality applied to adults who stutter. *Journal of Communication Disorders, 43,* 120–132; Plexico, L., Manning, W., & Levitt, H. (2009). Coping responses by adults who stutter: Part II. Approaching the problem and achieving agency. *Journal of Fluency Disorders, 34,* 108–126; Plexico, L., Manning, W., & Levitt, H. (2009). Coping responses by adults who stutter: Part I. Protecting the self and others. *Journal of Fluency Disorders, 34*(2), 87–107; Whaley, B. B., & Golden, M. A. (2000). Communicating with persons who stutter: Perceptions and strategies. In D. O. Braithwaite & T. L. Thompson (Eds.), *Handbook of communication and people with disabilities: Research and application* (pp. 423–438). Mahwah, NJ: Erlbaum.

12 Connor, C. M., & Craig, H. K. (2006). African American preschoolers' language, emergent literacy skills, and use of African American English: A complex relation. *Journal of Speech, Language & Hearing Research, 49,* 771–792; Oetting, J. B., & Garrity, A. W. (2006). Variation within dialects: A case of Cajun/Creole influence within child SAAE and SWE. *Journal of Speech, Language & Hearing Research, 49,* 16–26.

13 Purnell, T., Raimy, E., & Salmons, J. (2009). Defining dialect, perceiving dialect, and new dialect formation: Sarah Palin's speech. *Journal of English Linguistics, 37,* 331–355.

14 Greene, D. M., & Walker, F. R. (2004). Recommendations to public speaking instructors for the negotiation of code-switching practices among black English-speaking African American students. *Journal of Negro Education, 73,* 435–442.

15 Vitale, S., Cotch, M. F., & Sperduto, R. D. (2006). Prevalence of visual impairment in the United States. *Journal of the American Medical Association, 295,* 2158–2163.

16 Harrington, T. (2004, July). Statistics: Deaf population of the United States. Retrieved from http://www.library.gallaudet.edu.

17 Omansky, B. (2006, August 2). Personal communication.

18 Laukka, P., Linnman, C., Åhs, F., Pissiota, A., Frans, Ö., Faria, V., et al. (2008). In a nervous voice: Acoustic analysis and perception of anxiety in social phobics' speech. *Journal of Nonverbal Behavior, 32*(4), 195–214.

19 Christenfeld, N. (1995). Does it hurt to say um? *Journal of Nonverbal Behavior, 19*(3), 171–186; Engstrom, E. (1994). Effects of nonfluencies on speakers' credibility in newscast settings. *Perceptual and Motor Skills, 78,* 739–749.

20 Geonetta, S. C. (1981). Increasing the oral communication competencies of the technological student: The professional speaking method. *Journal of Technical Writing and Communication, 11*(3), pp. 233–244.

21 Croft, A. C. (1992). Ten ways to ruin a good new business presentation. *Public Relations Quarterly, 37*(3), 25–29.

22 Fodor, E. M., & Wick, D. P. (2009). Need for power and affective response to negative audience reaction to an extemporaneous speech. *Journal of Research in Personality, 43,* 721–726.

23 Smith, T. E., & Frymier, A. B. (2006). Get "real": Does practicing speeches before an audience improve performance? *Communication Quarterly, 54,* 111–125.

24 Smith & Frymier (2006).

Chapter 13

1 Johanson, D. &Edgar, B. (2006). *From Lucy to language.* New York, NY: Simon & Schuster; Hrdy, S. (2010). *Mothers and others.* Cambridge, MA: Harvard University Press.

2 Castells, M. (2009). *Communication power.* Oxford, England: Oxford University Press.

3 U.S. Department of Commerce (2004). *Entering the broadband age: A nation online.* Retrieved from ntia.doc.gov

4 Reddy, W. & McCarthy, S. (2006). Sharing best practices. *International Journal of Health Care Quality Assurance 19,* 594–598.

5 Lull, J. & Neiva, E. (2011). *The great chain of communication.* Cambridge, England: Cambridge University Press.

6 Gillmor, D. (2004). *We the media: Grassroots journalism by the people, for the people.* Sebastopol, CA: O'Reilly.

7 Bruns. A. (2005). *Gatewatching: Collaborative online news production.* New York, NY: Lang.

8 Rowan, K. E. (1995). A new pedagogy for explanatory public speaking: Why arrangement should not substitute for invention. *Communication Education, 44,* 236–250.

9 Al-Abdullah, Rania, Queen of Jordan (2003, October). *Petra: Lost city of stone—excerpts.* Speech presented at the New York Museum of Natural History, New York, NY. Retrieved from http://www.queenrania.jo

10 Kalfadellis, P. (2005). Integrating experiential learning in the teaching of cross-cultural communication. *Journal of New Business Ideas and Trends 3,* 37–5.

11 Koster, R. (2005, March). *Keynote: A theory of fun for games.* Retrieved from http://www.crystaltips.typepad.com/wonderland/2005/03/raphs_keynote.html

12 Cousteau, J. (2001, September). *Congressional Oceans Day Keynote Address.* Retrieved from http://www.oceanfutures.org

13 Adapted from an informative speech by student Tudor Matei, San José State University. Used with permission.

Chapter 14

1 Villaraigosa, A. R. (2006, April). *Accelerating our ambitions.* State of the City address, Los Angeles, CA. Retrieved from http://www.lacity.org/mayor/

2 Borchers, T. A. (2005). *Persuasion in the media age* (2nd ed.). New York, NY: McGraw-Hill.

3 Powell, C. (2003, February). *Iraq: Denial and deception.* Speech presented to the United Nations Security Council, New York, NY. Retrieved from http://www.whitehouse.gov/news/releases/2003/02/20030205-1.html

4 Hanley, C. J. (2003, August 10). U.S. justification for war: How it stacks up now. *Seattle Times,* p. A4.

5 Weisman, S. R. (2005, September 9). Powell calls his U.S. speech a lasting blot on his record. *The New York Times,* p. A10.

6 National Safety Council, http://www.nsc.org; Utility Consumers' Action Network, http://www.ucan.org

7 Palin, S. (2008, September). Speech before 2008 Republican National Convention, St. Paul, MN. Retrieved from http://www.huffingtonpost.com/2008/09/03

8 Simons, H. W. (2001). *Persuasion in society.* Thousand Oaks, CA: Sage; Tracy, L. (2005). Taming hostile audiences. *Vital Speeches of the Day, 71*(10), 306–312.

9 Cohen, D., de la Vega, R., & Watson, G. (2000). *Advocacy for social justice.* Bloomfield, CT: Kumarian Press.

10 McKerrow, R. E., Gronbeck, B. E., Ehninger, D., & Monroe, A. H. (2003). *Principles and types of public speaking,* 15th ed. Boston, MA: Allyn & Bacon.

11 Micciche, T., Pryor, & Butler, J. (2000). A test of Monroe's motivated sequence for its effects on ratings of message comprehension and attitude change. *Psychological Reports, 86,* 1135–1138.

12 Dewey, J. (1997/1910) *How we think.* Belmont, CA: Wadsworth.

13 Plung, D.L. (1980). Writing the persuasive business letter. *Journal of Business Communication , 17, 3,* 45–49

14 Broadhead, G.J. & Wright, R.R. (1987). Problem/solution cases in technical writing. *Journal of Advanced Composition, 6,* 79-88.

15 The expanded approach to audience analysis for persuasive speaking presented here is based on Lull, J. & Cappella, J. (1981) Slicing the attitude pie: A new approach to attitude measurement. *Communication Quarterly, 7,* 67–80.

16 Simons (2001).

17 Neuman, Y., Bekerman, Z., & Kaplan, A. (2002). Rhetoric as the contextual manipulation of self and nonself. *Research on Language and Social Interaction, 35,* 93–112.

18 Simons (2001).

19 Simons (2001).

20 Claypool, H. M., Mackie, D. M., Garcia-Marques, T., McIntosh, A., & Udall, A. (2004). The effects of personal relevance and repetition on persuasive processing. *Social Cognition, 22*, 310–335.

21 Lewis, T. V. (1988). Charisma and media evangelists: An explication and model of communication influence. *Southern Communication Journal, 54*, 93–111.

22 Goossens, C. (2003). Visual persuasion: Mental imagery processing and emotional experience. In Scott, L. M., & Batra, R. (Eds.), *Persuasive imagery: A consumer response perspective* (pp. 129–138). Mahwah, NJ: Lawrence Erlbaum.

23 National Communication Association (1999). NCA credo for ethical communication. Retrieved from http://www.natcom.org

24 Brown, K. (2002, March 1). Tangled roots? Genetics meets genealogy. *Science*, 1634–1635; Jasanoff, S. (2006). Just evidence: The limits of science in the legal process (DNA fingerprinting and civil liberties). *Journal of Law, Medicine & Ethics, 34*, 328–241; Mulligan, C. J. (2006). Anthropological applications of ancient DNA: Problems and prospects. American Antiquity, 71(22), 365–380.

25 Ossorio, P N. (2006). About face: Forensic genetic testing for race and visible traits. *Journal of Law, Medicine & Ethics, 34*, 277–292.

26 Kalb, C. (2006, February 6). In our blood; DNA testing: It is connecting lost cousins and giving families surprising glimpses into their pasts. Now scientists are using it to answer the oldest question of all: Where did we come from? *Newsweek*, p. 46.

27 O'Brien, A. J., & Golding, C. G. (2003). Coercion in mental healthcare: The principle of least coercive care. *Journal of Psychiatric & Mental Health Nursing, 10*(2), 167–173; Van Dijk, T. A. (2006). Discourse and manipulation. *Discourse & Society, 17*, 359–383.

28 Adapted from an informative speech by student Lisa Taylor, San José State University. Used with permission.

CHAPTER 15

1 Obama, B. (2010, January). State of the Union address, Washington, DC.

2 Claussen, E. (2007, November). *Reality before the renaissance: Making nuclear power part of the climate solution*. Address given at the American Nuclear Society/European Nuclear Society international meeting, Washington, DC.

3 Munson, R., & Conway, D. A. (2001). *Basics of reasoning*. Belmont, CA: Wadsworth.

4 Toulmin, S. E. (2003). *The uses of argument* (updated ed.). Cambridge, UK: Cambridge University Press.

5 Coleman, S. & Ross, K. (2010). *The media and the public: "Them" and "us" in media discourse*. Boston, MA: Wiley-Blackwell.

6 Keith Olbermann's "Special Comments" can all be found at http://www.youtube.

7 Campbell, K. K., & Huxman, S. S. (2003). *The rhetorical act* (2nd ed.). Belmont, CA: Wadsworth.

8 Munson & Conway (2001).

9 Brugidou, M. (2003). Argumentation and values: An analysis of ordinary political competence via an open-ended question. *International Journal of Public Opinion Research, 15*, 413–430; Dickinson, G.; Anderson, K. V. (2004). Fallen: O. J. Simpson, Hillary Rodham Clinton, and the re-centering of White patriarchy. *Communication and Critical/Cultural Studies, 1*, 271–296; Smith, C A. (2005). President Bush's enthymeme of evil: The amalgamation of 9/11, Iraq, and moral values. *American Behavioral Scientist, 49*, 32–47.

10 Bitzer, L. F. (1959). Aristotle's enthymeme revisited. *Quarterly Journal of Speech, 45*, 399–408.

11 Walker (2006); Williams, M. A. E. (2003). Arguing with style: How persuasion and the enthymeme work together in *On Invention*, Book 3. *Southern Communication Journal, 68*, 136–151.

12 King, Jr., M. L. (1957, November). *Loving your enemies*. Speech delivered at the Dexter Avenue Baptist Church in Montgomery, AL. Retrieved from http://www.stanford.edu/group/King/popular_requests/voice_of_king.htm

13 Finnegan, C. A. (2001). The naturalistic enthymeme and visual argument: Photographic representation in the "Skull Controversy." *Argumentation and Advocacy, 37*, 133–149.

14 Moore, J.W. (2006). Science literacy and science standards. *Journal of Chemistry Education 83*(3), 343.

15 Simons, H. W. (2001). *Persuasion in society*. Thousand Oaks, CA: Sage; Tracy, L. (2005). Taming hostile audiences. *Vital Speeches of the Day, 71*(10), 306–312.

16 Artz, N., & Tybout, A. M. (1999). The moderating impact of quantitative information on the relationship between source credibility and persuasion: A persuasion knowledge model interpretation. *Marketing Letters, 10*(1), 51–62; Lindsey, L. L. M., & Ah Yun, K. (2003). Examining the persuasive effect of statistical messages: A test of mediating relationships. *Communication Studies, 54*, 306–321.

17 Volkow, N. D. (2006). Drug addiction: Free will, brain disease, or both? *Vital Speeches of the Day, 72*(16/17), 505–508.

18 Volkow (2006), p. 506.

19 Pornpitakpan, C. (2004). The persuasiveness of source credibility: A critical review of five decades' evidence. *Journal of Applied Social Psychology, 34*, 243–281.

20 Buller, D. B. (1992). Social perceptions as mediators of the effect of speech rate similarity on compliance. *Human Communication Research, 19*, 286–311.

21 Bordia, P., DiFonzo, N., Haines, R., & Chaseling, E. (2005). Rumors denials as persuasive messages: Effects of personal relevance, source, and message characteristics. *Journal of Applied Social Psychology, 35*, 1301–1331; Eckstein, J. J. (2005). Conversion conundrums: Listener perceptions of affective influence attempts as mediated by personality and individual differences. *Communication Quarterly, 53*, 401–419.

22 Schramm, C. R. (2006). Making the turn: Entrepreneurial capitalism and its European promise. *Vital Speeches of the Day, 72*(16/17), 480–488.

23 Schramm (2006), p. 480.

24 Schramm (2006), p. 481.

25 Braun-Latour, K. A., & Zaltman, G. (2006). Memory change: An intimate measure of persuasion. *Journal of Advertising Research, 46*(1), 57–72; Page, T. J., Thorson, E., & Heide, M. P. (1990). The memory impact of commercials varying in emotional appeal and product involvement. In Agres, S. J., Edell, J. H., & Dubitsky, T. M. (Eds.), *Emotion in advertising: Theoretical and practical explorations* (pp. 255–268). Westport, CT: Quorum Books

26 Perse, E. M., Nathanson, A. I., & McLeod, D. M. (1996). Effects of spokesperson sex, public service announcement appeal and involvement on evaluations of safe-sex PSAs. *Health Communication, 8*, 171–189.

27 Maslow, A. H. (1954). *Motivation and personality*. New York, NY: Harper; Maslow, A. H. (2000). *The Maslow business reader*. New York, NY: Wiley; Maslow, A. H., with Stephens, D. C., & Heil, G. (1971). *Maslow on management*. New York, NY: Wiley; Maslow, A. H. (1999). *Toward a psychology of being* (3rd ed.). New York, NY: Wiley; Rowan, J. (1998). Maslow amended. *Journal of Humanistic Psychology, 38*(1), 81–92.

28 Hanley, S. J., & Abell, S. C. (2002). Maslow and relatedness: Creating an interpersonal model of self-actualization. *Journal of Humanistic Psychology, 42*(4), 37–57.

29 Adapted from Maslow (1999).

30 Moore, D. J., & Harris, W. D. (1996). Affect intensity and the consumer's attitude toward high impact emotional advertising appeals. *Journal of Advertising, 25*(2), 39–50; Roskos-Ewoldsen, D. R., Yu, H. J., & Rhodes, N. (2004). Fear appeal messages affect accessibility of attitudes toward threat and adaptive behaviors. *Communication Monographs, 71*, 49–69; Witte, K. (1992). Putting the fear back into fear appeals: The extended parallel process model. *Communication Monographs, 59*, 329–349; Witte, K. (1994). Fear control and danger control: A test of the extended parallel process model (EPPM). *Communication Monographs, 61*, 113–134.

31 Majoras, D. P. (2006, May). Remarks by FTC chair Deborah Platt Majoras at the initial meeting of the President's Identity Theft Task Force, Washington, DC. Retrieved from http://www.ftc.gov/speeches/06speech.htm

32 Lowry, L. (2005, March). *How everything turns away*. Speech presented at the University of Richmond "Quest" series. Retrieved from http://www.loislowry.com

33 Lowry (2005), pp. 23–24.

34 Dorsey, L. G. (1997). Sailing into the "wondrous now": The myth of the American navy's world cruise. *Quarterly Journal of Speech, 83*, 447–465; Winfield, B. H., & Hume, J. (1998). The American hero and the evolution of the human interest story. *American Journalism, 15*(2), 79–99.

35 Hill, J. E. (2006, June). *The coming revolution will not be viewed on television: Physicians turning trust into action*. Speech at the annual meeting of the American Medical Association House of Delegates, Chicago, IL. Retrieved from http://www.ama-assn.org

36 Crichton, M. (2005, November). *Fear, complexity, and environmental management in the 21st century*. Speech presented at the Washington Center for Complexity and Public Policy, Washington, D.C. Retrieved from http://www.crichton-official.com.

37 Corporate Ethics International. (2011). www.corpethics.org

38 Howell, W. S. (1976). The Declaration of Independence: Some adventures with America's political masterpiece. *Quarterly Journal of Speech, 62,* 221–233.

39 Trent, J. D. (1968). Toulmin's model of an argument: An examination and extension. *Quarterly Journal of Speech, 54,* 252–259.

40 Centers for Disease Control and Prevention. (2004). *Surgeon General's 2004 report: The health consequences of smoking on the human body.* Retrieved from http://www.cdc.gov/Tobacco/sgr/sgr_2004/sgranimation/flash/

41 Munson, R. & Conway, D. A. (2001). *Basics of reasoning.* Belmont, CA: Wadsworth.

42 Lin, T., & McNab, P. (2006). Cognitive trait modeling: The case of inductive reasoning ability. *Innovations in Education & Teaching International, 43*(2), 151–161.

43 Hair, P. (2004, April). Remarks presented at the Radio-Television News Directors Association & Foundation luncheon, Las Vegas, NV. Retrieved from http://www.rtndf.org

44 Heit, E., & Feeney, A. (2005). Relations between premise similarity and inductive strength. *Psychonomic Bulletin & Review, 12,* 340–344.

45 Epstein, R. L. (2006). *Critical thinking* (3rd ed.). Belmont, CA: Wadsworth; Munson & Conway (2001).

46 Simon, R. (2006, June). Testimony before the House Committee on Education and the Workforce, Washington, DC. Retrieved from http://www.ed.gov/news

47 Karakas, F. (2006). Noah's pudding: Reflection on diversity, richness, living in harmony and peace through Ashura. *Vital Speeches of the Day, 72*(12), 369–373.

48 Karakas (2006), pp. 369–370.

49 Epstein (2006).

50 Ikuenobe, P. (2004). On the theoretical unification and nature of fallacies. *Argumentation, 18,* 189–211.

51 Hansen, H. V. (2002). The straw thing of fallacy theory: The standard definition of "fallacy." *Argumentation, 16,* 133–155; Neuman, Y., Glassner, A., & Weinstock, M. (2004). The effect of a reason's truth-value on the judgment of a fallacious argument. *Acta Psychologica, 116*(2), 173–184.

52 Walton, D. The appeal to ignorance, or *argumentum ad ignorantiam. Argumentation, 13,* 367–377.

53 Broadfoot, P. (2004). "Lies, damned lies, and statistics!": Three fallacies of comparative methodology. *Comparative Education, 40,* 3–6.

54 Munson & Conway (2001), p. 82.

55 Munson & Conway (2001), p. 83.

56 Used with permission.

CHAPTER 16

1 Zakaria, F. (2010). Commencement address at Bates College. Retrieved from bates.edu/x170838.xml

2 Støre, J. G. (2005, October 31). Remarks at luncheon in the honour of Dr. ElBaradei, New York. Retrieved from http://www.norway-geneva.org

3 Amanpour, C. (2009). Introduction of Amira Hass, Lifetime Achievement Award, International Women's Media Foundation. Retrieved from http://www.democracynow.org/2009/10/21/israeli_journalist_amira_hass

4 Powderburn (2007). Powderburn acceptance speech [Video file]. Retrieved from http://www.youtube.com

5 Springsteen, B. (2009). Acceptance speech for induction into New Jersey Hall of Fame. Retrieved from http://www.forum.aboutnewjersey.com

6 Turner, P. S. (2006). Acceptance speech for the 2005 Flora Stieglitz Straus Award. Retrieved from http://www.bankstreet.edu

7 Webby Awards (2006). Archived winner speeches. Retrieved from http://www.webbyawards.com/press/archived-speeches.php; cnet News (2008). The Meta Webbys: The awards for the best Webby acceptance speeches. Retrieved from http://www.news.cnet.com/8301-13577_3-9965724-36.html; Webby Awards (2009). Webby winners. Retrieved from http://www.webbyawards.com/press/speeches.php

8 Sotomayor, S. (2009). Full text: Judge Sonia Sotomayor's speech. Retrieved from http://www.time.com/time/printout/0,8816,1900940,00.html

9 Giacchino, M. (2010). Acceptance speech. Retrieved from http://www.Oscars.org

10 Sasakawa, Y. (2007). International Gandhi Award 2007 acceptance speech. Retrieved from http://www.nippon-foundation.or.jp/eng/

11 Rogers, C. T. (2007, May 1). *Chief Justice Rogers Law Day Ceremony Honoring Law Librarians.* Retrieved from http://www.jud.ct.gov/external/news/Speech/rogers_050107.html

12 Shriver, M. (2009). Eulogy for Tim Russert. Retrieved from http://www.huffingtonpost.com/2008/06/18/maria-shriver-at-tim-russ_n_107933.html?view=print

13 Irwin, B. (2006, September 19). Eulogy for Steve Irwin. Retrieved from youtube.com

14 Chavez, C. (1990). Lessons of Dr. Martin Luther King, Jr. Retrieved from http://www.wccusd.k12.ca.us/stc/waysofthinking/append/ChavezSpeech1.htm

15 LaFasto, F., & Larson, C. E. (2001). *When teams work best: 6,000 team members and leaders tell what it takes to succeed.* Thousand Oaks, CA: Sage; Pettigrew, A. M., & Fenton, E. M. (2000). *The innovating organization.* London, England: Sage.

16 Chen, G., Donahue, L. M., & Klimoski, R. J. (2004). Training undergraduates to work in organizational teams. *Academy of Management Learning & Education, 3*(1), 27–40; Greenberg, L. W. (1994). The group case presentation: Learning communication and writing skills in a collaborative effort. *Medical Teacher, 16,* 363–367.

17 Business roundtable discussion transcript (2006, February 5). *Akron Beacon Journal.* Retrieved from http://www.ohio.com/mld/ohio/business/ 13729361.htm

18 "Videoconferencing sees record growth" (2007). *Business Communications Review, 37*(8), 6.

19 Anderson, A. H. (2006). Achieving understanding in face-to-face and video-mediated multiparty interactions. *Discourse Processes, 41,* 251–287.

20 Adams, T., & Scollard, S. (2006). *Internet effectively: A beginner's guide to the World Wide Web.* Boston, MA: Pearson.

21 Light, W. H. (2007). Reframing presentation skills development for knowledge teams. *Organization Development Journal, 25,* 99–110.

22 Hanke, J. (1998). Presenting as a team. *Presentations, 12*(1), 74–78.

23 Bayless, M. L. (2004). Change the placement, the pace, and the preparation for the oral presentation. *Business Communication Quarterly, 67,* 222–225.

24 Used with permission.

Index

Page numbers followed by an **f** indicate figures; followed by a **t** indicate tables

Audience-centered communication, 7, 11, 20, 87
Audience-centered language, 197–205
Audiences' expectations, for public speakers, 84
Audience-speaker connection, 181, 333
Audio, 215–216, 218
Audio clips, 19, 105t, 154, 179, 219, 224
Audio materials, 50, 225
Audio media, 34
Audio study tools
　arguments, 327
　building confidence and, 37
　ethical speaking, 58
　group presentations, 350
　informative speeches, 270
　introductions, 184
　presentation media, 226
　public speaking, 21, 37
　research, 122
　special occasion, 350
　supporting ideas, 141
Author, 45, 49, 101, 118, 110
Averbuch, Yael, 202
Award presentations, 335–336

B

Bad company fallacy, 324
Balance, 148–149
Baldwin, Tammy, 190–191
Baross, John, 61
Basketball Hall of Fame, 78
Beah, Ishmael, 289
Beck, Glen, 302
Begging the question, 320
Beliefs, defined, 84
Belonging needs. (See Love/belonging needs)
Berners-Lee, Tim, 150–151
Beschloss, Michale, 91
Bhatia, Peter K., 132
Bibliographic information, 118
Billboards, 17
Biographies, 14, 103
Black, Cathleen, 90, 91
Blethen, Frank, 83
Blogdigger, 108
Blogging/blogs, 108
Board of Education, Brown v., 174
Body, 146–157
　in arrangement, 8
　defined, 146
　delivery and, 8
　elements of, 147f
　managing, 236–238
　as part of speech, 146
　body movement, 8, 31, 34, 54, 127, 179
Bono, 128
Books, 101
Brainstorming, 62– 63, 71, 73
　defined, 62
　images and, 63f
　rules for, 63
Breathing, 29–30
Brigham Young University, honor code, 48
Brokow, Tom, 61
Brown, Rita Mae, 180
Brown v. Board of Education, 174
Bryan, John Neely, 207–208
Buddhist preaching, and the five arts, 8

Bullet points, for digital slides, 221
Bush, George, 135
Butler, Octavia E., 147–148

C

Cable television, 6
Call number, 101
Calming techniques, 33
Camera(s), 217
Canadian Associaton of Radiologists (See CAR (Canadian Associaton of Radiologists))
Captive audiences, 90
CAR (Canadian Associaton of Radiologists), 190
Carmona, Richard H., 202
Castro, Fidel, 324
Catalog of United States Government Publications, 102
Causal reasoning, 9, 150t, 158t, 167, 317–318
Cause-and-effect pattern, 10, 150t, 152–153, 156t
CBS, 135, 138
Celebrity testimony, 135
Cell phones, 6, 9f, 17, 28, 44, 84
Central idea, 68
CGI. (See Computer generated imagery (CGI))
Chalkboards, 217
Challenges, ethical, 18, 20
Channel, 15, 17
Character
　public speakers and, 8, 18
　evoking in speeches, 127, 174
Chatting/chat, 6f, 12, 16f, 34, 45, 115, 193
Chavez, Cesar, 339
Chavez-Thompson, Linda, 201
Children
　as public speakers, 27
　speech anxiety and, 27
Chronological pattern, 149t, 150, 151, 156t, 256, 258
Cicero, 5f, 8–9
Circular reasoning, 320. (See also Begging the question)
Citing sources, 49–51
Civil rights movement, 99, 125–126, 130, 134–135
Claim(s), 302–307
　accuracy of, 136
　defined, 302
　fallacies in, 320–323
　guidelines for, 305–307
　overview, 302–303
　phrasing, 305–307
　premises and conclusions and, 303, 304t
　reasoning and, 323
　speech on banning handguns and, 303t
　types of, 303–305 (See also Evidence)
Clarity, 147, 250–251
Class, 199, 200
Classes, speaking in, 42
Classical era, 5, 20
Classroom, 18, 79
Classroom audiences, 79
Claussen, Eileen, 301
Clichés, 193
Clinton, Bill, 182
Closed-ended questions, 85–86

Closure, 180–181
Closure statement, 113
Clusty, 106t
CNN, 138, 316–317, 351
Cochran, Johnnie, 202
Coercion, 274
Coherence, 158
Coke, 304f
Colbert, Stephen, 204f, 334
Color, for digital slides, 222
Comedy Central, 204
Commonalities, audience and, 51–52, 80–81, 190, 202
Commonwealth Club, 46
Communibiology paradfigm, 26
Communication
　audience-centered, 79, 87
　degrading, 44
　digital, 7
　dishonest, 55, 190. (See also Plagiarism)
　electronic, 6
　ethical, 18
　honest, 44
　human, 14–15
　in-person, 115, 163
　interactional model of, 16
　internet, 103–108, 136, 150, 151
　interpersonal, 14
　mass, 15
　new model of, 15
　nonverbal, 16, 239
　online, 14
　organizational, 14
　public, 15
　public speaking as, 14–18
　small-group, 14
　spheres, 15–16f
　transactional model of, 16
　transmission model of, 15, 20
　unethical, 41
　verbal, 16–17, 20
Communication across the curriculum (CXC), 12
Communication anxiety. (See Speech/communication anxiety)
Communication climate, 42, 44
Communication contexts, 12–14, 14–15
Communication skills, 13f, 20
Community, 32, 42, 130
Community stories, 130
Compact Oxford English Dictionary, 132, 189
Comparative evidence fallacy, 321t, 322, 327
Competence, 92
CompletePlanet, 107t
Complete-sentence outline, 160–165
　formatting, 161–165
　labels, 164
　levels, 163
　main points, 162–163, 164
　outline preface, 161
　overview, 160, 167
　purpose of, 160–161
　reference list for, 165
　review and analysis sample, 165–167
　subordinate ideas, 163–164
　subpoints, 162–163, 164
　symbols and indentations, 164
　types of outlines, 161t

Computer-generated imagery (CGI), 280
Computers, 219–223
   creativity and, 222
   design tips, 221–222
   digital slides, 220–221, 223
   hardware setup tips, 222–223
   literacy and, 222
   real-time Web access, 223
Concepts, speeches about, 82, 255–256, 257t
Concise language, 84
Conclusion
   argument and, 303, 304t
   complete-sentence outline and, 70
   defined, 179
   developing, 179–181
   elements, 179f
   formatting, 164
   of interviews, 113
   organizing, 160–161
   as part of speech, 146
   presentating, 32
   speech anxiety and, 9–10
   transitions to, 160
Conclusion preview, 113
Confidence, 8–9, 28–30, 31–32. (See also
   Speech/communication anxiety)
   after the speech, 35
   before presentations, 33–34
   during the speech, 34–35
   overview of, 36
   planning and preparing and, 31–32
   relabeling, 29, 30f
   relaxation, 29–30
   strategies for, 36t
   visualization, 29, 30f, 154–155
Conflict, 46
Connor, Bull, 46
Connotative meanings, 132, 189
Content, 54
Context, 12–14, 14–15, 18
Contextualization of the award, in speeches,
   335–336
Coordinated presentations, 346
Copyright, 47
Copyright information, 47, 110
Copyright laws, 47
Corel Presentations, 220
Cosby, Bill, 174
Cousteau, Jean-Michel, 264–265
Crasser, Minister, 308
Creativity, 175
Creatures, speeches about, 252–253, 257t
Credibility, 92–93. (See also Ethos)
   appeals to speaker, 10, 308–309
   audience and, 10, 92–93
   audience-centered approach and, 79, 87
   Bono and, 128
   building, 10
   competence, 92
   current events and, 92
   defined, 92
   dynamism, 92
   ethnocentrism and, 52
   ethos and, 8, 92, 308–309
   gender and, 53
   in interview, 116
   introduction and, 177–178
   media, 138–139

Reeve and, 135
   sexism and, 52–53, 195t
   sociability, 93
   speaker, 92
   source, 18
   Tong and, 125–126, 136
   Trustworthiness, 92
Crichton, Michael, 312
Critical listening, 54
Critical thinking, 18
C-SPAN, 168
Cueing system, 16, 54, 56, 77
Cultural awareness, 19
Cultural context, 80
Cultural diversity, 52, 232
Cultural identity, 6, 80, 93
Cultural norms, 52
Cultural stories, 129
Culture(s), 51
Currency, 117
Current events, 65, 92
CurryGuide, 106t
CXC. (See Communication across the
   curriculum (CXC))

D

Data/databases, 81–82, 82–85, 102–103,
   104t–105t, 135
Decatur Correctional Center in Illinois, 25
Declaration of Independence, 314–315
Deductive reasoning, 313–316
Deep web, 107
Defective reasoning, 320
Definitions, 131–134
   by analogy, 133–134
   by function, 132–133
   defined, 132
Degrading communication, 44
Delivery, 228–247
   audience and, 238–240
   content and, 218
   defined, 8, 229
   dialect, 233
   effective, 12–14, 19
   example of, 8
   factors influencing, 231–234
   fluency, 233
   gender and, 232–233
   information, speed of, 84
   language and, 190
   managing body during, 236–237
   managing voice in, 234–236
   overview of, 229, 245–246
   physical disabilities/impairments, 233–234
   practicing, 31–32, 242–245
   presentation outline and, 240–242
   presentation software and, 19, 220
   question-and-answer period and, 240
   strategies for, 237
Delivery method, 195, 230t
Delivery options, 20
Democratic National Convention, 187
Demographic data, 81–82
Demographic information, 81–82
Demographics, 81
Demographic stereotyping, 82
Deneal, Dustin, 203–204
Denotative meanings, 132, 189

Department of Education, 317
Design, visual, 215–219
   basics of, 215
   audio, 215, 219
   document cameras, 217
   flip charts, 216–217
   handouts, 218
   models, 219
   overhead transparencies, 215–216
   traditional, 215–219
   use of design, 215
   video, 217–218
   whiteboards and chalkboards, 217
Desktop computers, 17f
Detroit Free Press, 49
Dialect, 191, 233
Dialogue, 44, 57
Diaphragmatic breathing, 29
Dictionaries, 102–103, 132–133, 134, 189–190
Digital age. (See Information/digital age)
Digital cameras, 6, 16
Digital communication, 7
Digital divide, internet and, 7
Digital slide software/digital slides, 220–222
Digital technology, 18, 41
Direct questions, 56
Direct quotes, 88
Directory of Open Access Journals, 102
Dis/ability, 55, 81, 82, 84, 135, 200
Discussion lists, 109
Dishonest communication, 55
Distance speaking, 14
Distant language, 195–196, 209
Distractions, 17, 55, 115
Diverse audience, 52–53, 79–81
Diversity, 52–53. (See also Cultural diversity;
   Ethical speaking/listening)
   culture and, 231
   ethnocentrism, 52
   sexism, 52–53
Diversity of perspective, 46f
Divided audience, 199, 289–290
Divine Design, 254
Division fallacy, 323
Document cameras, 217
Documentary films, 99, 178, 223
Dogpile, 106t
*Doing Honest Work in College: How to
   Prepare Citations, Avoid Plagiarism, and
   Achieve Real Academic Success*, 47
Dorland's Illustrated Medical Dictonary, 190
Dow's Dictionary of Railway Quotations, 102
Dramatic statement, 181
Dress, 33
   anxiety and, 33
   du Sable, Jean Baptiste Point, 90
   proper attire, 236
DVDs, 16f, 99, 217
Dynamic language, 195
Dynamism, 92

E

Educate, inform to, 264–265
Education level/education, 7, 80
Either-or thinking, 320. (See also False
   dilemma fallacy)
ElBaradei, Mohamed, 332
Electronic communication, 6, 41